The Ancient Stone Implements, Weapons and of Great Britain

John Evans

Alpha Editions

This edition published in 2024

ISBN : 9789366384627

Design and Setting By
Alpha Editions
www.alphaedis.com
Email - info@alphaedis.com

As per information held with us this book is in Public Domain.
This book is a reproduction of an important historical work. Alpha Editions uses the best technology to reproduce historical work in the same manner it was first published to preserve its original nature. Any marks or number seen are left intentionally to preserve its true form.

PREFACE TO THE FIRST EDITION.

In presenting this work to the public I need say but little by way of preface. It is the result of the occupation of what leisure hours I could spare, during the last few years, from various and important business, and my object in undertaking it is explained in the Introduction.

What now remains for me to do is to express my thanks to those numerous friends who have so kindly aided me during the progress of my work, both by placing specimens in their collections at my disposal, and by examination of my proofs. Foremost among these must be ranked the Rev. William Greenwell, F.S.A., from whose unrivalled collection of British antiquities I have largely drawn, and from whose experience and knowledge I have received much assistance in other ways.

To Mr. A. W. Franks, F.S.A.; Mr. J. W. Flower, F.G.S.; Mr. W. Pengelly, F.R.S.; Colonel A. Lane Fox, F.S.A.; Mr. E. T. Stevens, of Salisbury; Messrs. Mortimer, of Fimber; Mr. Joseph Anderson, the Curator of the Antiquarian Museum at Edinburgh; and to numerous others whose names are mentioned in the following pages, my thanks must also be expressed.

The work itself will, I believe, be found to contain most of the information at present available with regard to the class of antiquities of which it treats. The subject is one which does not readily lend itself to lively description, and an accumulation of facts, such as is here presented, is of necessity dull. I have, however, relegated to smaller type the bulk of the descriptive details of little interest to the ordinary reader, who will probably find more than enough of dry matter to content him if he confines himself to the larger type and an examination of the illustrations.

Whatever may be the merits or defects of the book, there are two points on which I feel that some credit may be claimed. The one is that the woodcuts—the great majority of which have been specially engraved for this work by Mr. Swain, of Bouverie Street—give accurate representations of the objects; the other is, that all the references have been carefully checked.

The Index is divided into two parts; the first showing the subjects discussed in the work, the second the localities where the various antiquities have been found.

Now that so much more attention than formerly is being bestowed on this class of antiquities, there will, no doubt, be numerous discoveries made, not only of forms with which we are at present unacquainted, but also of circumstances calculated to throw light on the uses to which stone implements and weapons were applied, and the degree of antiquity to be assigned to the various forms.

I will only add that I shall gladly receive any communications relative to such discoveries.

JOHN EVANS.

Nash Mills, Hemel Hempstead, May, 1872.

PREFACE TO THE SECOND EDITION.

The undiminished interest taken by many archæologists in the subject to which this book relates seems to justify me in again placing it before the public, though in an extended and revised form. I am further warranted in so doing by the fact that the former edition, which appeared in 1872, has now been long out of print.

In revising the work it appeared desirable to retain as much of the original text and arrangement as possible, but having regard to the large amount of new matter that had to be incorporated in it and to the necessity of keeping the bulk of the volume within moderate bounds, some condensation seemed absolutely compulsory. This I have effected, partly by omitting some of the detailed measurements of the specimens, and partly by printing a larger proportion of the text in small type. I have also omitted several passages relating to discoveries in the caverns of the South of France.

I have throughout preserved the original numbering of the Figures, so that references that have already been made to them in other works will still hold good. The new cuts, upwards of sixty in number, that have been added in this edition are distinguished by letters affixed to the No. of the Figure immediately preceding them.

The additions to the text, especially in the portion relating to the Palæolithic Period, are very extensive, and I hope that all the more important discoveries of stone antiquities made in this country during the last quarter of a century are here duly recorded, and references given to the works in which fuller details concerning them may be found. In some cases, owing to the character of the objects discovered being insufficiently described, I have not thought it necessary to cite them.

I am indebted to numerous collectors throughout the country for having called my attention to specimens that they acquired, and for having, in many cases, sent them to me for examination. I may take this opportunity of mentioning that while the whole of the objects found by Canon Greenwell during his examination of British Barrows has been most liberally presented to the nation, the remainder of his fine collection of stone antiquities, so frequently referred to in these pages, has passed into the hands of Dr. W. Allen Sturge, of Nice.

The two Indices have been carefully compiled by my sister, Mrs. Hubbard, and are fuller than those in the former edition. They will afford valuable assistance to any one who desires to consult the book.

For the new woodcuts that I have had engraved I have been so fortunate as to secure the services of Messrs. Swain, who so skilfully cut the blocks for the original work. I am indebted for the loan of numerous other blocks to several learned Societies, and especially to the Society of Antiquaries of Scotland and to the Geological Society of London. Mr. Worthington Smith has also most liberally placed a number of blocks at my disposal.

It remains for me to express my thanks to those who have greatly aided me in the preparation of this edition, the whole of the proofs of which have been kindly read by Mr. C. H. Read, F.S.A., of the British Museum, as well as by some members of my own family. Dr. Joseph Anderson, of the National Museum at Edinburgh, has been good enough to read the parts relating to Scotland, while Professor Boyd Dawkins has gone over the chapter on Cave Implements, and Mr. William Whitaker has corrected the account of the discoveries in the River-drift. To each and all I am grateful, and as the result of their assistance I trust that, though not immaculate, the book may prove to be fairly free from glaring errors and inconsistencies.

JOHN EVANS.

Nash Mills, Hemel Hempstead, May, 1897.

CHAPTER I.
INTRODUCTORY.

In the following pages I purpose to give an account of the various forms of stone implements, weapons, and ornaments of remote antiquity discovered in Great Britain, their probable uses and method of manufacture, and also, in some instances, the circumstances of their discovery. While reducing the whole series into some sort of classification, as has been done for the stone antiquities of Scandinavia by Worsaae, Montelius, and Sophus Müller, for those of France by Messrs. Gabriel and Adrien de Mortillet, and for those of Ireland by Sir William Wilde, I hope to add something to our knowledge of this branch of Archæology by instituting comparisons, where possible, between the antiquities of England and Scotland and those of other parts of the world. Nor in considering the purposes to which the various forms were applied, and the method of their manufacture, must I neglect to avail myself of the illustrations afforded by the practice of modern savages, of which Sir John Lubbock and others have already made such profitable use.

But before commencing any examination of special forms, there are some few general considerations on which it seems advisable to enter, if only in a cursory manner; and this is the more necessary, since notwithstanding the attention which has now for many years been devoted to Prehistoric Antiquities, there is seemingly still some misapprehension remaining as to the nature and value of the conclusions based upon recent archæological and geological investigations.

At the risk therefore of being tedious, I shall have to notice once more many things already well known to archæologists, but which, it would appear from the misconceptions so often evinced, even by those who speak and write on such matters, can hardly be too often repeated.

Not the least misunderstood of these subjects has been the classification of the antiquities of Western Europe, first practically adopted by the Danish antiquaries, under periods known as the Iron, Bronze, and Stone Ages; the Iron Age, so far as Denmark is concerned, being supposed to go back to about the Christian era, the Bronze Age to embrace a period of one or two thousand years previous to that date, and the Stone Age all previous time of man's occupation of that part of the world. These different periods have been, and in some cases may be safely, subdivided; but into this question I need not now enter, as it does not affect the general sequence. The idea of the succession is this:—

- 1. That there was a period in each given part of Western Europe, say, for example, Denmark, when the use of metals for cutting-instruments of any kind was unknown, and man had to depend for his implements and weapons on stone, bone, wood, and other readily accessible natural products.

- 2. That this period was succeeded by one in which the use of copper, or of copper alloyed with tin—bronze—became known, and gradually superseded the use of stone for certain purposes, though it continued to be employed for others; and

- 3. That a time arrived when bronze, in its turn, gave way to iron or steel, as being a superior metal for all cutting purposes; which, as such, has remained in use up to the present day.

Such a classification into different ages in no way implies any exact chronology, far less one that would be applicable to all the countries of Europe alike, but is rather to be regarded as significant only of a succession of different stages of civilization; for it is evident that at the time when, for instance, in a country such as Italy, the Iron Age may have commenced, some of the more northern countries of Europe may possibly have been in their Bronze Age, and others again still in their Stone Age.

Neither does this classification imply that in the Bronze Age of any country stone implements had entirely ceased to be in use, nor even that in the Iron Age both bronze and stone had been completely superseded for all cutting purposes. Like the three principal colours of the rainbow, these three stages of civilization overlap, intermingle, and shade off the one into the other; and yet their succession, so far as Western Europe is concerned, appears to be equally well defined with that of the prismatic colours, though the proportions of the spectrum may vary in different countries. [1]

The late Mr. James Fergusson, in his Rude Stone Monuments, [2] has analyzed the discoveries made by Bateman in his exploration of Derbyshire barrows, and on the analysis has founded an argument against the division of time into the Stone, Bronze, and Iron Ages. He has, however, omitted to take into account the fact that in many of the barrows there were secondary interments of a date long subsequent to the primary.

I have spoken of this division into Periods as having been first practically adopted by the Danish school of antiquaries, but in fact this classification is by no means so recent as has been commonly supposed. Take, for instance, the communication of Mahudel to the *Académie des Inscriptions* of Paris [3] in 1734, in which he points out that man existed a long time in different countries using implements of stone and without any knowledge of metals; or again, the following passage from Bishop Lyttelton's [4] "Observations on Stone Hatchets," written in 1766:—"There is not the least doubt of these stone instruments having been fabricated in the earliest times, and by barbarous people, before the use of iron or other metals was known, and from the same cause spears and arrows were headed with flint and other hard stones." A century earlier, Sir William Dugdale, in his "History of Warwickshire," [5] also speaks of stone celts as "weapons used by the Britons before the art of making arms of brass or iron was known." We find, in fact, that the same views were entertained, not only by various writers [6] within the last two centuries, but also by many of the early poets and historians. There are even biblical grounds for argument in favour of such a view of a gradual development of material civilization. For all, including those who invest Adam with high moral attributes, must confess that whatever may have been his mental condition, his personal equipment in the way of tools or weapons could have been but inefficient if no artificer was instructed in brass and iron until the days of Tubal Cain, the sixth in descent from Adam's outcast son, and that too at a time when a generation was reckoned at a hundred years, instead of at thirty, as now.

Turning, however, to Greek and Roman authors, we find Hesiod, [7] about B.C. 850, mentioning a time when bronze had not been superseded by iron:—

Τοῖς δ' ἦν χάλκεα μὲν τεύχεα, χάλκεοι δέ τε οἶκοι

Χαλκῷ δ' εἰργάζοντο, μέλας δ' οὐκ ἔσχε σίδηρος.

Lucretius [8] is even more distinct in his views as to the successive Periods:—

"Arma antiqua manus, ungues, dentesque fuerunt

Et lapides, et item sylvarum fragmina rami—

Posterius ferri vis est ærisque reperta;

Sed prior æris erat quam ferri cognitus usus—

Ære solum terræ tractabant, æreque belli

Miscebant fluctus et vulnera vasta ferebant."

So early as the days of Augustus it would appear that bronze arms were regarded as antiquities, and that emperor seems to have commenced the first archæological and geological collection on record, having adorned one of his country residences "rebus vetustate ac raritate notabilibus, qualia sunt Capreis immanium belluarum ferarumque membra prægrandia quæ dicuntur gigantum ossa et arma heroum." [9]

We learn from Pausanias [10] what these arms of the heroes were, for he explains how in the heroic times all weapons were of bronze, and quotes Homer's description of the axe of Pisander and the arrow of Meriones. He also cites the spear of Achilles in the temple of Pallas, at Phaselis, the point and ferrule of which only were of bronze; and the sword of Memnon in the temple of Æsculapius, at Nicomedia, which was wholly of bronze. In the same manner Plutarch [11] relates that when Cimon disinterred the remains of Theseus in Scyros he found with them a bronze spear-head and sword.

There is, indeed, in Homer constant mention of arms, axes, and adzes of bronze, and though iron is also named, it is of far less frequent occurrence. According to the Arundelian marbles, [12] it was discovered only 188 years before the Trojan war, though of course such a date must be purely conjectural. Even Virgil preserves the unities, and often gives bronze arms to the heroes of the Æneid, as well as to some of the people of Italy—

"Ærataeque micant peltæ, micat æreus ensis." [13]

The fact that in the Greek [14] language the words χαλκεύς and χαλκεύειν remained in use as significant of working in iron affords a very strong, if not an irrefragable argument as to bronze having been the earlier metal known to that people. In the same way the continuance in use of bronze cutting implements in certain religious rites—as was also the case with some stone implements which I shall subsequently mention—affords evidence of their comparative antiquity. The Tuscans [15] at the foundation of a city ploughed the pomærium with a bronze plough-share, the priests of the Sabines cut their hair with bronze knives, and the Chief Priest of Jupiter at Rome used shears of the same metal for that purpose. In the same manner Medea has attributed to her both by Sophocles and Ovid [16] a bronze sickle when gathering her magic herbs, and Elissa is represented by Virgil as using a similar instrument for the same purpose. Altogether, if history is to count for anything, there can be no doubt that in Greece and Italy, the earliest civilized countries of

Europe, the use of bronze preceded that of iron, and therefore that there was in each case a Bronze Age of greater or less duration preceding the Iron Age.

It seems probable that the first iron used was meteoric, and such may have been that "self-fused" mass which formed one of the prizes at the funeral games of Patroclus, [17] and was so large that it would suffice its possessor for all purposes during five years. Even the Greek word for iron (σίδηρος) may not improbably be connected with the meteoric origin of the first known form of the metal. Its affinity with ἀστήρ, often used for a shooting star or meteor, with the Latin "*sidera*" and our own "star" is evident.

Professor Lauth, [18] moreover, interprets the Coptic word for iron, **BENIΠE**, as "the stone of heaven" (Stein des Himmels) which implies that in Egypt also its meteoric origin was acknowledged.

Among the Eskimos [19] of modern times meteoric iron has been employed for making knives. Where an excess of nickel is present, the meteoric iron cannot well be forged, [20] but Dana seems to be right in saying, as a general rule it is perfectly malleable.

Some, however, are of opinion that during the time that bronze was employed for cutting instruments, iron was also in use for other purposes. [21] At the first introduction of iron the two metals were, no doubt, in use together, but we can hardly suppose them to have been introduced simultaneously; and if they had been, the questions arise, whence did they come? and how are we to account for the one not having sooner superseded the other for cutting purposes?

Another argument that has been employed in favour of iron having been the first metal used, is that bronze is a mixed metal requiring a knowledge of the art of smelting both copper and tin, the latter being only produced in few districts, and generally having to be brought from far, while certain of the ores of iron are of easy access and readily reducible, [22] and meteoric iron is also found in the metallic state and often adapted for immediate use. The answer to this is, first, that all historical evidence is against the use of iron previously to copper or bronze; and, secondly, that even in Eastern Africa, where, above all other places, the conditions for the development of the manufacture of iron seem most favourable, we have no evidence of the knowledge of that metal having preceded that of bronze; but, on the contrary, we find in Egypt, a country often brought in contact with these iron-producing districts, little if any trace of iron before the twelfth dynasty, [23] and of its use even then the evidence is only pictorial, whereas the copper mines at Maghara are said to date back to the second dynasty, some eight hundred years earlier. Agatharchides, [24] moreover, relates that in his time, *circa* B.C. 100, there were found buried in the ancient gold mines of Egypt the bronze chisels (λατομίδες χαλκαῖ) of the old miners, and he accounts for their being of that metal by the fact that at the period when the mines were originally worked the use of iron was entirely unknown. Much of the early working in granite may have been effected by flint tools. Admiral Tremlett has found that flakes of jasper readily cut the granite of Brittany. [25]

To return, however, to Greece and Italy, there can, as I have already said, be little question that even on historical grounds we must accept the fact that in those countries, at all events, the use of bronze preceded that of iron. We may therefore infer theoretically that the same sequence held good with the neighbouring and more barbarous nations of Western Europe. Even in the time of Pausanias [26] (after A.D. 174) the Sarmatians are mentioned as being unacquainted with the use of iron; and practically we have good corroborative archæological evidence of such a sequence in the extensive discoveries that have been made of antiquities belonging to the transitional period, when the use of iron or steel was gradually superseding that of bronze for tools or weapons, and when the forms given to the new metal were copied from those of the old. The most notable relics of this transitional period are those of the ancient cemetery at Hallstatt, in the Salzkammergut, Austria, where upwards of a thousand graves were opened by Ramsauer, of the contents of which a detailed account has been given by the Baron von Sacken. [27] The evidence afforded by the discoveries in the Swiss lakes is almost equally satisfactory; but I need not now enter further into the question of the existence and succession of the Bronze and Iron Ages, on which I have dwelt more fully in my book on Ancient Bronze Implements. [28]

I am at present concerned with the Stone Age, and if, as all agree, there was a time when the use of iron or of bronze, or of both together, first became known to the barbarous nations of the West of Europe, then it is evident that before that time they were unacquainted with the use of those metals, and were therefore in that stage of civilization which has been characterized as the Stone Age.

It is not, of course, to be expected that we should discover direct contemporary historical testimony amongst any people of their being in this condition, for in no case do we find a knowledge of writing developed in this stage of culture; and yet, apart from the material relics of this phase of progress which are found from time to time in the soil, there is to be obtained in most civilized countries indirect circumstantial evidence of the former use of stone implements, even where those of metal had been employed for centuries before authentic history commences. It is in religious customs and ceremonies—in rites which have been handed down from generation to generation, and in which the minute and careful repetition of ancient observances is indeed often the essential religious element—that such evidence is to be sought. As has already been observed by others, the transition from ancient to venerable, from venerable to holy, is as natural as it is universal; and in the same manner as some of the festivals and customs of Christian countries are directly traceable to heathen times, so no doubt many of the religious observances of ancient times were relics of what was even then a dim past.

Whatever we may think of the etymology of the word as given by Cicero, [29] Lactantius, [30] or Lucretius, [31] there is much to be said in favour of Dr. E. B. Tylor's [32] view of superstition being "the standing over of old habits into the midst of a new and changed state of things—of the retention of ancient practices for ceremonial purposes, long after they had been superseded for the commonplace uses of ordinary life."

Such a standing over of old customs we seem to discover among most of the civilized peoples of antiquity. Turning to Egypt and Western Asia, the early home of European civilization, we find from Herodotus [33] and from Diodorus Siculus, [34] that in the rite of embalming, though the brain was removed by a crooked iron, yet the body was cut open by a sharp Ethiopian stone.

EGYPT.—Fig. 1.

In several European museums are preserved thin, flat, leaf-shaped knives of cherty flint found in Egypt, some of which will be mentioned in subsequent pages. In character of workmanship their correspondence with the flint knives or daggers of Scandinavia is most striking. Many, however, are provided with a tang at one end at the back of the blade, and in this respect resemble metallic blades intended to be mounted by means of a tang driven into the haft.

In the British Museum is an Egyptian dagger-like instrument of flint, from the Hay collection, still mounted in its original wooden handle, apparently by a central tang, and with remains of its skin sheath. It is shown on the scale of one-fourth in Fig. 1. There is also a polished stone knife broken at the handle, which bears upon it in hieroglyphical characters the name of PTAHMES, an officer.

Curiously enough the bodies of the chiefs or Menceys of the Guanches in Teneriffe [35] were also cut open by particular persons set apart for the office with knives made of sharp pieces of obsidian.

The rite of circumcision was among those practised by the Egyptians, but whether it was performed with a stone knife, as was the case with the Jews when they came out of Egypt, is not certain. Among the latter people, not to lay stress on the case of Zipporah, [36] it is recorded of Joshua, [37] that in circumcising the children of Israel he made use of knives of stone. It is true that, in our version, the words חַרְבוֹת צוּרִים are translated sharp knives, which by analogy with a passage in Psalm lxxxix. 44 (43 E.V.), is not otherwise than correct; but the Syriac, Arabic, Vulgate, and Septuagint translations all give knives of stone; [38] and the latter version, in the account of the burial of Joshua, adds that they laid with him the stone knives (τὰς μαχαίρας τὰς πετρίνας) with which he circumcised the children of Israel—"and there they are unto this day." Gesenius (*s. v.* צוּר) observes upon the passage, "This is a circumstance worthy of remark; and goes to show at least, that knives of stone were found in the sepulchres of Palestine, as well as in those of north-western Europe." [39] In recent times the Abbé Richard, in examining what is known as the tomb of Joshua at some distance to the east of Jericho, found a number of sharp flakes of flint as well as flint instruments of other forms. [40]

Under certain circumstances modern Jews make use of a fragment of flint or glass for this rite. The occurrence of flint knives in ancient Jewish sepulchres may, however, be connected with a far earlier occupation of Palestine than that of the Jews. It was a constant custom with them to bury in caves, and recent discoveries have shown that, like the caves of Western Europe, many of these were at a remote period occupied by those unacquainted with the use of metals, whose stone implements are found mixed up with the bones of the animals which had served them for food. [41]

Of analogous uses of stone we find some few traces among classical writers. Ovid, speaking of Atys, makes the instrument with which he maimed himself to be a sharp stone,

>"Ille etiam saxo corpus laniavit acuto."

The solemn treaties among the Romans were ratified by the Fetialis [42] sacrificing a pig with a flint stone, which, however, does not appear to have been sharpened. "Ubi dixit, porcum saxo silice percussit." The "religiosa silex" [43] of Claudian seems rather to have been a block of stone like that under the form of which Jupiter, Cybele, Diana, and even Venus were worshipped. Pausanias informs us that it was the custom among the Greeks to bestow divine honours on certain unshaped stones, and ΖΕΥΣ ΚΑΣΙΟΣ is thus represented on coins of Seleucia in Syria, while the Paphian Venus appears in the form of a conical stone on coins struck in Cyprus. The Syrian god from whom Elagabalus, the Roman emperor, took his name seems also to have been an unhewn stone, possibly a meteorite.

The traces, however, of the Stone Age in the religious rites of Greece and Rome are extremely slight, and this is by no means remarkable when we consider how long the use of bronze, and even of iron, had been known in those parts of Europe at the time when authentic history commences. We shall subsequently see at how early a period different implements of stone had a mysterious if not a superstitious virtue assigned to them. I need only mention as an instance that, in several beautiful gold necklaces [44] of Greek or Etruscan workmanship, the central pendant consists of a delicate flint arrow-head, elegantly set in gold, and probably worn as a charm. Nor is the religious use of stone confined to Europe. [45] In Western Africa, when the god Gimawong makes his annual visit to his temple at Labode, his worshippers kill the ox which they offer, with a stone.

To come nearer home, it is not to be expected that in this country, the earliest written history of which (if we except the slight account derived from merchants trading hither), comes from the pen of foreign conquerors, we should have any records of the Stone Age. In Cæsar's time, the tribes with which he came in contact were already acquainted with the use of iron, and were, indeed, for the most part immigrants from Gaul, a country whose inhabitants had, by war and commerce, been long brought into close relation with the more civilized inhabitants of Italy and Greece. I have elsewhere shown [46] that the degree of civilization which must be conceded to those maritime tribes far exceeds what is accorded by popular belief. The older occupants of Britain, who had retreated before the Belgic invaders, and occupied the western and northern parts of the island, were no doubt in a more barbarous condition; but in no case in which they came in contact with their Roman invaders do they seem to have been unacquainted with the use of iron. Even the Caledonians, [47] in the time of Severus, who tattooed themselves with the figures of animals, and went nearly naked, carried a shield, a spear, and a sword, and wore iron collars and girdles; they however deemed these latter ornamental and an evidence of wealth, in the same way as other barbarians esteemed gold.

But though immediately before and after the Christian era the knowledge of the use of iron may have been general throughout Britain, and though probably an acquaintance with bronze, at all events in the southern part of the island, may probably date many centuries farther back, it by no means follows, as I cannot too often repeat, that the use of stone for various purposes to which it had previously been applied should suddenly have ceased on a superior material, in the shape of metal, becoming known. On the contrary, we know that the use of certain stone weapons was contemporary with the use of bronze daggers, and the probability is that in the poorer and more inaccessible parts of the country, stone continued in use for many ordinary purposes long after bronze, and possibly even iron, was known in the richer and more civilized districts.

Sir William Wilde informs us that in Ireland [48] "stone hammers, and not unfrequently stone anvils, have been employed by country smiths and tinkers in some of the remote country districts until a comparatively recent period." The same use of stone hammers and anvils for forging iron prevails among the Kaffirs [49] of the present day. In Iceland [50] also, perforated stone hammers are still in use for pounding dried fish, driving in stakes, for forging and other purposes; "knockin'-stones" [51] for making pot-barley, have till recently been in use in Scotland, if not still employed; and I have seen fruit-hawkers in the streets of London cracking Brazil nuts between two stones.

With some exceptions it is, therefore, nearly impossible to say whether an ancient object made of stone can be assigned with absolute certainty to the Stone Period or no. Much will depend upon the circumstances of the discovery, and in some instances the form may be a guide.

The remarks I have just made apply most particularly to the weapons, tools, and implements belonging to the period more immediately antecedent to the Bronze Age, and extending backwards in time through an unknown number of centuries. For besides the objects belonging to what was originally known by the Danish antiquaries as the Stone Period, which are usually found upon or near the surface of the soil, in encampments, on the site of ancient habitations, and in tumuli, there are others which occur in caverns beneath thick layers of stalagmite, and in ancient alluvia, in both cases usually associated with the remains of animals either locally or entirely extinct. In no case do we find any trace of metallic tools or weapons in true association with the stone implements of the old ossiferous caverns, or with those of the beds of gravel, sand, and clay deposited by the ancient rivers; and, unlike the implements found upon the surface and in graves, which in many instances are ground or polished, those from the caves, and from what are termed by geologists the Quaternary gravels, are, so far as at present known, invariably chipped only, and not ground, besides as a rule differing in form.

This difference [52] in the character of the implements of the two periods, and the vast interval of time between the two, I pointed out in 1859, at the time when the discoveries of M. Boucher de Perthes, in the Valley of the Somme, first attracted the attention of English geologists and antiquaries. Since then, the necessity of subdividing what had until then been regarded as the Stone Age into two distinct stages, an earlier and a later, has been universally recognized; and Sir John Lubbock [53] has proposed to call them the Palæolithic and the Neolithic Periods respectively, terms which have met with almost general acceptance, and of which I shall avail myself in the course of this work. In speaking of the polished and other implements belonging to the time when the general surface of the country had already received its present configuration, I may, however, also occasionally make use of the synonymous term Surface Period for the Neolithic, and shall also find it convenient to treat of the Palæolithic Period under two subdivisions—those of the River-gravels and of the Caves, the fauna and implements of which are not in all cases identical.

In passing the different kinds of implements, weapons, and ornaments formed of stone under review, I propose to commence with an examination of the antiquities of the Neolithic Period, then to proceed to the stone implements of human manufacture discovered imbedded with ancient mammalian remains in Caverns, and to conclude with an account of the discoveries of flint implements in the Drift or River-gravels in various parts of England. But before describing their forms and characters, it will be well to consider the method of manufacture by which the various forms were produced.

CHAPTER II.
ON THE MANUFACTURE OF STONE IMPLEMENTS IN PREHISTORIC TIMES. [54]

In seeking to ascertain the method by which the stone implements and weapons of antiquity were fabricated, we cannot, in all probability, follow a better guide than that which is afforded us by the manner in which instruments of similar character are produced at the present day. As in accounting for the vast geological changes which we find to have taken place in the crust of the earth, the safest method of argument is by referring to ascertained physical laws, and to the existing operations of nature, so, in order to elucidate the manufacture of stone implements by the ancient inhabitants of this and other countries, we may refer to the methods employed by existing savages in what we must judge to be a somewhat similar state of culture, and to the recognized characteristics of the materials employed. We may even go further, and call in aid the experience of some of our own countrymen, who still work upon similar materials, although for the purpose of producing different objects from those which were in use in ancient times.

So far as relates to the method of production of implements formed of silicious materials, there can be no doubt that the manufacture of gun-flints, which, notwithstanding the introduction of percussion-caps, is still carried on to some extent both in this and in neighbouring countries, is that best calculated to afford instruction. The principal place in England where the gun-flint manufacture is now carried on, is Brandon, on the borders of Norfolk and Suffolk, where I have witnessed the process. I have also seen the manufacture at Icklingham, in Suffolk, where thirty years ago, gun-flint factories existed, which have now I believe been closed. They were also formerly manufactured in small numbers at Catton, near Norwich. At Brandon, in 1868, I was informed that upwards of twenty workmen were employed, who were capable of producing among them from 200,000 to 250,000 gun-flints per week. These were destined almost entirely for exportation, principally to Africa. On July 18th, 1890, the *Daily News* [55] gave the number of workmen at Brandon as thirty-five.

Some other sites of the gun-flint manufacture in former times are mentioned by Mr. Skertchly, as for instance, Clarendon near Salisbury; Gray's Thurrock, Essex; Beer Head, Devon; and Glasgow; besides several places in Norfolk and Suffolk.

In France the manufacture of gun-flints is still carried on in the Department of Loir et Cher, [56] and various other localities are recorded by Mr. Skertchly. [57]

In proof of the antiquity of the use of flint as a means of producing fire, I need hardly quote the ingenious derivation of the word Silex as given by Vincent of Beauvais:—"Silex est lapis durus, sic dictus eò quod ex eo ignis exiliat." [58] But before iron was known as a metal, it would appear that flint was in use as a fire-producing agent in combination with blocks of iron pyrites (sulphide of iron) instead of steel. Nodules of this substance have been found in both French and Belgian bone-caves belonging to an extremely remote period; while, as belonging to Neolithic times, to say nothing of discoveries in this country, which will subsequently be mentioned, part of a nodule of pyrites may be cited which was found in the Lake settlement of Robenhausen, and had apparently been thus used. [59] In our own days, this method of obtaining fire has been observed among savages in Tierra del Fuego, and among the Eskimos of Smith's Sound. [60] The Fuegian tinder, like the modern German and ancient Roman, consists of dried fungus, which when lighted is wrapped in a ball of dried grass and whirled round the head till it bursts into flames. Achates, as will shortly be seen, is described by Virgil as following the same method.

The name of pyrites (from πῦρ) is itself sufficient evidence of the purpose to which this mineral was applied in early times, and the same stone was used as the fire-giving agent in the guns with the form of lock known as the wheel-lock. Pliny [61] speaks of a certain sort of pyrites, "plurimum habens ignis, quos vivos appellamus, et ponderosissimi sunt." These, as his translator, Holland, says, "bee most necessary for the espialls belonging unto a campe, for if they strike them either with an yron spike or another stone they will cast forth sparks of fire, which lighting upon matches dipt in brimstone (*sulphuratis*) drie puff's (*fungis*) or leaves, will cause them to catch fire sooner than a man can say the word."

Pliny also [62] informs us that it was Pyrodes, the son of Cilix, who first devised the way to strike fire out of flint—a myth which seems to point to the use of silex and pyrites rather than of steel. The Jews on their return to Jerusalem, under Judas Maccabæus, "made another altar and striking stones they took fire out of them and offered a sacrifice." [63] How soon pyrites was, to a great extent, superseded by steel or iron, there seems to be no good evidence to prove; it is probable, however, that the use of flint and steel was well known to the Romans of the Augustan age, and that Virgil [64] pictured the Trojan voyager as using steel, when—

"silici scintillam excudit Achates,

Suscepitque ignem foliis atque arida circum

Nutrimenta dedit, rapuitque in fomite flammam."

And again, where—

"quærit pars semina flammæ

Abstrusa in venis silicis." [65]

In Claudian [66] we find the distinct mention of flint and steel—

"Flagrat anhela silex et amicam saucia sentit

Materiem, placidosque chalybs agnoscit amores."

At Unter Uhldingen [67] a Swiss lake station where Roman pottery was present, was found what appears to be a steel for striking a light. However the case may have been as to the means of procuring fire, it was not until some centuries after the invention of gunpowder that flints were applied to the purpose of discharging fire-arms. Beckmann, [68] in his "History of Inventions," mentions that it was not until the year 1687 that the soldiers of Brunswick obtained guns with flint-locks, instead of match-locks, though, no doubt, the use of the wheel-lock with pyrites had in some other places been superseded before that time.

I am not aware of there being any record of flints, such as were in use for tinder-boxes, [69] having been in ancient times an article of commerce: this, however, must have been the case, as there are so many districts in which flint does not naturally occur, and into which, therefore, it would have by some means to be introduced. Even at the present day, when so many chemical matches are in use, flints are still to be purchased at the shops in country places in the United Kingdom; and artificially prepared flints continue to be common articles of sale both in France and Germany, and are in constant use, in conjunction with German tinder, or prepared cotton, by tobacco-smokers. At Brandon [70] a certain number of "strike-a-light" flints are still manufactured for exportation, principally to the East and to Brazil—they are usually circular discs, about two inches in diameter. These flints are wrought into shape in precisely the same manner as gun-flints, and it seems possible that the trade of chipping flint into forms adapted to be used with steel for striking a light may be of considerable antiquity, and that the manufacture of gun-flints ought consequently to be regarded as only a modification and extension of a pre-existing art, closely allied with the facing and squaring of flints for architectural purposes, which reached great perfection at an early period. However this may be, it would seem that when gun-flints were an indispensable munition of war, a great mystery was made as to the manner in which they were prepared. Beckmann [71] says that, considering the great use made of them, it will hardly be believed how much trouble he had to obtain information on the subject. It would be ludicrous to repeat the various answers he obtained to his inquiries. Many thought that the stones were cut down by grinding them; some conceived that they were formed by means of red-hot pincers, and many asserted that they were made in mills. The best account of the manufacture with which he was acquainted, was that collected by his brother, and published in the *Hanoverian Magazine* for the year 1772. At a later date the well-known mineralogist Dolomieu [72] gave an account of the process in the *Mémoires de l'Institut National des Sciences,* and M. Hacquet, [73] of Leopol, in Galicia, published a pamphlet on the same subject. The accounts given by both these authors correspond most closely with each other, and also with the practice of the present day, though the French process differs in some respects from the English. [74] This has been well described by Dr. Lottin. [75] The flints best adapted for the purpose of the manufacture are those from the chalk. They must, however, be of fair size, free from flaws and included organisms, and very homogeneous in structure. They are usually procured by sinking small shafts into the ground until a band of flints of the right quality is reached, along which low horizontal galleries, or "burrows," as they are called, are worked. For success in the manufacture a great deal is said to depend upon the condition of the flint as regards the moisture it contains, those which have been too long exposed upon the surface becoming intractable, and there being also a difficulty in working those that are too moist. A few blows with the hammer enable a practised flint-knapper to judge whether the material on which he is at work is in the proper condition or no. Some of the Brandon workmen, however, maintain that though a flint which has been some time exposed to the air is harder than one recently dug, yet that it works equally well, and they say further, that the object in keeping the flints moist is to preserve the black colour from fading, black gun-flints being most saleable.

A detailed account, by Mr. Skertchly, of the manufacture of gun-flints, with an essay on the connection between Neolithic art and the gun-flint trade, forms an expensive memoir of the geological survey, published in 1879; but it seems well to retain the following short account of the process.

The tools required are few and simple:—

- 1. A flat-faced blocking, or quartering hammer, from one to two pounds in weight, made either of iron or of iron faced with steel.

- 2. A well-hardened steel flaking hammer, bluntly pointed at each end, and weighing about a pound, or more; or in its place a light oval hammer, known as an "English" hammer, the pointed flaking hammer having been introduced from France.

- 3. A square-edged trimming or knapping hammer, which may either be in the form of a disc, or oblong and flat at the end, made of steel not hardened. In England, this hammer is usually made from a portion of an old flat file perforated to receive the helve, and drawn out at each end into a thin blade, about 1/16 of an inch in thickness; the total length being about 7 or 8 inches.

- 4. A chisel-shaped "stake" or small anvil set vertically in a block of wood, which at the same time forms a bench for the workman. In England, the upper surface of this stake is about 1/4 inch thick, and inclined at a slight angle to the bench.

The method of manufacture [76] is as follows:—A block of flint is broken by means of the quartering hammer in such a manner as to detach masses, the newly-fractured surfaces of which are as nearly as possible plane and even. One of these blocks is then held in the left hand, so that the edge rests on a leathern pad tied on the thigh of the seated workman, the surface to be struck inclining at an angle of about 45°. A splinter is then detached from the margin by means of the flaking hammer. If the flint is of good quality, this splinter may be three or four inches in length, the line of fracture being approximately parallel to the exterior of the flint. There is, of course, the usual bulb of percussion, or rounded protuberance at the end, [77] where the blow is given, and a corresponding depression is left in the mass of flint. Another splinter is next detached, by a blow given at a distance of about an inch on one side of the spot where the first blow fell, and then others at similar distances, until some portion of the block assumes a more or less regular polygonal outline. As the splinters which are first detached usually show a portion of the natural crust of the flint upon them, they are commonly thrown away as useless. The second and succeeding rows of flakes are those adapted for gun-flints. To obtain these, the blows of the flaking hammer are administered midway between two of the projecting angles of the polygon, and almost immediately behind the spots where the blows dislodging the previous row of flakes or splinters were administered, though a little to one side. They fall at such a distance from the outer surface as is necessary for the thickness of a gun-flint. By this means a succession of flakes is produced, the section of which is that of an obtuse triangle with the apex removed, inasmuch as for gun-flints, flakes are required with the face and back parallel, and not with a projecting ridge running along the back.

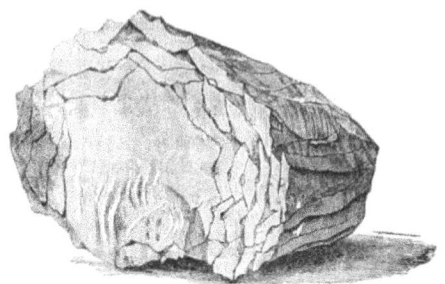

Fig. 2.—Flint-core with flakes replaced upon it.

Fig. 2, representing a block from which a number of flakes adapted for gun-flints have been detached and subsequently returned to their original positions around the central core or nucleus, will give a good idea of the manner in which flake after flake is struck off. Mr. Spurrell and Mr. Worthington Smith have succeeded in building up flakes of Palæolithic date into the original blocks from which they were struck. The former has also replaced ancient Egyptian flakes, [78] the one upon the other. Mr. F. Archer has likewise restored a block of flint from Neolithic flakes [79] found near Dundrum Bay, county Down.

To complete the manufacture of gun-flints, each flake is taken in the left hand, and cut off into lengths of the width required, by means of the knapping hammer and the stake fixed in the bench. The flake is placed over the stake at the spot where it is to be cut, and a skilful workman cuts the flake in two at a single stroke. The sections of flakes thus produced have a cutting edge at each end; but the finished gun-flint is formed by chipping off the edge at the butt-end and slightly rounding it by means of the fixed chisel and knapping hammer, the blows from which are made to fall just within the chisel, so that the two together cut much in the same manner as a pair of shears. Considerable skill is required in the manufacture, more especially in the production of the flakes; but Hacquet [80] says that a fortnight's practice is sufficient to enable an ordinary workman to fashion from five hundred to eight hundred gun-flints in a day. According to him, an experienced workman will produce from a thousand to fifteen hundred per diem. Dolomieu estimates three days as the time required by a *"caillouteur"* to produce a thousand gun-flints; but as the highest price quoted for French gun-flints by Hacquet is only six francs the thousand, it seems probable that his calculation as to the time required for their manufacture is not far wrong. Some of the Brandon flint-knappers are, however, said to be capable of producing sixteen thousand to eighteen thousand gun-flints in a week. Taking the lowest estimate, it appears that a practised hand is capable of making at least three hundred flint implements of a given definite form, and of some degree of finish, in the course of a single day. If our primitive forefathers could produce their worked flints with equal ease, the wonder is, not that so many of them are found, but that they do not occur in far greater numbers.

An elegant form of gun-flint, showing great skill in surface flaking, is still produced in Albania. A specimen, purchased at Avlona [81] by my son, is shown in Fig. 2A. Some gun-flints and strike-a-lights are formed of chalcedony or agate, and cut and polished.

Fig. 2A.—Gun-flint, Avlona, Albania. 1/1

The ancient flint-workers had not, however, the advantages of steel and iron tools and other modern appliances at their command; and, at first sight, it would appear that the production of flakes of flint, without having a pointed metallic hammer for the purpose, was a matter of great difficulty, I have, however, made some experiments upon the subject, and have also employed a Suffolk flint-knapper to do so, and I find that blows from a rounded pebble, judiciously administered, are capable of producing well-formed flakes, such as, in shape, cannot be distinguished from those made with a metallic hammer. The main difficulties consist—first, in making the blow fall exactly in the proper place; and, secondly, in so proportioning its intensity that it shall simply dislodge a flake, and not shatter it. The pebble employed as a hammer need not be attached to a shaft, but can be used, without any preparation, in the hand. Professor Nilsson tried the same method long ago, and has left on record an interesting account of his experience. [82]

In the neighbourhood of the Pfahl-bauten of Moosseedorf, in Switzerland, have been found numerous spots where flint has been worked up into implements, and vast numbers of flakes and splinters left as refuse. Dr. Keller [83] says, that "the tools used for making these flint implements do not seem to have been of the same material, but of gabbro, a bluish-green and very hard and tough kind of stone. Several of these implements have been met with; their form is very simple, and varies between a cube and an oval. The oval specimens were ground down in one or two places, and the most pointed part was used for hammering." There were nearly similar workshops at Wauwyl [84] and Bodmann, not to mention places where flint was dug for the purposes of manufacture.

Closely analogous sites of ancient flint-workshops have been discovered both in France [85] and Germany [86] as well as in Great Britain; such, for instance, as that at the confluence [87] of the Leochel and the Don, in Aberdeenshire, where, moreover, flint is not native in the neighbourhood; but proper attention has not, in all cases, been paid to the hammer-stones, which, in all probability, occur with the chippings of flint.

The blow from the hammer could not, of course, be always administered at the right spot; and I have noticed on some ancient flakes, a groove at the butt-end, the bottom of which is crushed, as if by blows from a round pebble, which, from having fallen too near the edge of the block, had at first merely bruised the flint, instead of detaching the flake.

There are, moreover, a certain number of small cores, or nuclei, both English and foreign, from which such minute and regular flakes have been detached, that it is difficult to believe that a mere stone hammer could have been directed with sufficient skill and precision to produce such extreme regularity of form. I may cite as instances some of the small nuclei which are found on the Yorkshire wolds, and some of those from the banks of the Mahanuddy, [88] in India, which, but for the slight dissimilarity in the material (the latter being usually chalcedony and the former flint), could hardly be distinguished from each other. Possibly in striking off the flakes some form of punch was used which was struck with the hammer as subsequently described. There are also some large nuclei, such as those from the neighbourhood of the Indus, [89] in Upper Scinde, and one which I possess from Ghlin, in Belgium, which are suggestive of the same difficulty. In form they much resemble the obsidian cores of Mexico, and it seems not improbable that they are the result of some similar process of making flakes or knives to that which was in use among the Aztecs.

Torquemada [90] thus describes the process he found in use:—"One of these Indian workmen sits down upon the ground, and takes a piece of this black stone" (obsidian) "about eight inches long or rather more, and as thick as one's leg or rather less, and cylindrical; they have a stick as large as the shaft of a lance, and three cubits or rather more in length; and at the end of it they fasten firmly another piece of wood, eight inches long, to give more weight to this part; then, pressing their naked feet together, they hold the stone as with a pair of pincers or the vice of a carpenter's bench. They take the stick (which is cut off smooth at the end) with both hands, and set it well home against the edge of the front of the stone (*y ponenlo avesar con el canto de la frente de la piedra*), which also is cut smooth in that part; and then they press it against their breast, and with the force of the pressure there flies off a knife, with its point, and edge on each side, as neatly as if one were to make them of a turnip with a sharp knife, or of iron in the fire." Hernandez [91] gives a similar account of the process, but compares the wooden instrument used to a cross-bow, so that it would appear to have had a crutch-shaped end to rest against the breast. So skilful were the Mexicans in the manufacture of obsidian knives, that, according to Clavigero, a single workman could produce a hundred per hour.

The short piece of heavy wood was probably cut from some of the very hard trees of tropical growth. I much doubt whether any of our indigenous trees produce wood sufficiently hard to be used for splintering obsidian; and flint is, I believe, tougher and still more difficult of fracture. We have, however, in this Mexican case, an instance of the manufacture of flakes by sudden pressure, and of the employment of a flaking tool, which could be carefully adjusted into position before the pressure or blow was given to produce the flake.

Mr. G. E. Sellers, in the Smithsonian Report for 1885, [92] has published some interesting "observations on stone chipping," and from the report of Mr. Catlin, who sojourned long among the Indians of North America, gives sketches of crutch-like flaking tools tipped with walrus tooth or bone which he had seen in use. He also describes a method of making flint flakes by the pressure of a lever. The whole memoir is worthy of study.

The subject of the manufacture of stone implements is also discussed by [93] Sir Daniel Wilson in an essay on the Trade and Commerce of the Stone Age.

There appears to have been another process in use in Central America, for Mr. Tylor [94] heard on good authority that somewhere in Peru the Indians still have a way of working obsidian by laying a bone wedge on the surface of a piece and tapping it till the stone cracks. Catlin [95] also describes the method of making flint arrow-heads among the Apaches in Mexico as being of the same character. After breaking a boulder of flint by means of a hammer formed of a rounded pebble of horn-stone set in a handle made of a twisted withe, flakes are struck off, and these are wrought into shape while held on the palm of the left hand, by means of a punch made of the tooth of the sperm whale, held in the right hand, and struck with a hard wooden mallet by an assistant. Both holder and striker sing, and the strokes of the mallet are given in time with the music, the blow being sharp and *rebounding*, in which the Indians say is the great medicine or principal knack of the operation.

The Cloud River [96] Indians at the present day use a punch made of deer's-horn for striking off obsidian flakes from which to make arrow-heads.

Such a process as this may well have been adopted in this country in the manufacture of flint flakes; either bone or stag's-horn sets or punches, or else small and hard pebbles, may have been applied at the proper spots upon the surface of the flints, and then been struck by a stone or wooden mallet. I have tried some experiments with such stone sets, and have succeeded in producing flakes in this manner, having been first led to suppose that some such system was in use by discovering, in the year 1864, some small quartz pebbles battered at the ends, and associated with flint flakes and cores in an ancient encampment at Little Solsbury Hill, near Bath, of which I have already given an account elsewhere. [97] I am, however, inclined to think that the use of such a punch or set was in any case the exception rather than the rule; for with practice, and by making the blows only from the elbow kept fixed against the body, and not with the whole arm, it is extraordinary what precision of blow may be attained with merely a pebble held in the hand as a hammer.

The flakes of chert from which the Eskimos manufacture their arrow-heads are produced, according to Sir Edward Belcher, [98] who saw the process, by slight taps with a hammer formed of a very stubborn kind of jade or nephrite. He has kindly shown me one of these hammers, which is oval in section, about 3 inches long and 2 inches broad, and secured by a cord of sinew to a bone handle, against which it abuts. The ends are nearly flat. This hammer is now in the Christy Collection at the British Museum and is figured by Ratzel. [99] Another from Alaska, [100] and several such hammers made of basalt from the Queen Charlotte Islands, [101] have also been figured. It seems doubtful whether the proper use of these hammers was not for crushing bones. [102]

Among the natives of North Australia a totally different method appears to have been adopted, the flakes being struck off the stone which is used as a hammer, and not off the block which is struck. In the exploring expedition, under Mr. A. G. Gregory, in 1855–6, the party came on an open space between the cliffs along one of the tributary streams of the Victoria River, where the ground was thickly strewn with fragments of various stones and imperfectly-formed weapons. The method of formation of the weapons, according to Mr. Baines, [103] was this, "The native having chosen a pebble of agate, flint, or other suitable stone, perhaps as large as an ostrich egg, sits down before a larger block, on which he strikes it so as to detach from the end a piece, leaving a flattened base for his subsequent operations. Then, holding the pebble with its base downwards, he again strikes so as to split off a piece as thin and broad as possible, tapering upward in an oval or leaf-like form, and sharp and thin at the edges. His next object is to strike off another piece nearly similar, so close as to leave a projecting angle on the stone, as sharp, straight, and perpendicular as possible. Then, again taking the pebble carefully in his hand, he aims the decisive blow, which, if he is successful, splits off another piece with the angle running straight up its centre as a midrib, and the two edges sharp, clear, and equal, spreading slightly from the base, and again narrowing till they meet the midrib in a keen and taper point. If he has done this well, he possesses a perfect weapon, but at least three chips must have been formed in making it, and it seemed highly probable, from the number of imperfect heads that lay about, that the failures far outnumbered the successful results. In the making of tomahawks or axes, in which a darker green stone is generally used, great numbers of failures must ensue; and in these another operation seemed necessary, for we saw upon the rocks several places were they had been ground, with a great expenditure of labour, to a smooth round edge."

In the manufacture of flint flakes, whether they were to serve as knives or lance-heads without any more preparation, or whether they were to be subjected to further manipulation, so as eventually to become arrow-heads, scrapers, or any other of the more finished implements, the form of the nucleus from which they were struck was usually a matter of no great importance, the chips or flakes being the object of the operator and not the resulting core, which was in most cases thrown away as worthless. But where very long flakes were desired, it became a matter of importance to produce nuclei of a particular form, specially adapted for the purpose. I have never met with any such nuclei in England, but the well-known *livres-de-beurre* chiefly found in the neighbourhood of Pressigny-le-grand (Indre et Loire), France, are typical instances of the kind. I have precisely similar specimens, though on a rather smaller scale, and of a somewhat different kind of flint, from Spiennes, near Mons, in Belgium; and a few nuclei of the same form have also been found in Denmark. The occurrence of flints wrought into the same shape, at places so far apart, might at first appear to countenance the view of this peculiar form being that of an implement intended for some special purpose, and not merely a refuse block. This, however, is not the case. I have treated of this question elsewhere, [104] but it will be well here to repeat a portion, at least, of what I have before written on this point.

These large nuclei or *livres-de-beurre* are blocks of flint, usually 10 or 12 inches long and 3 to 4 inches wide in the broadest part, the thickness being in most cases less than the width. In general outline they may be described as boat-shaped, being square at one end and brought to a point—more or less finished—at the other. The outline has been given by striking a succession of flakes from the sides of a mass of flint, until the boat-like contour has been obtained, with the sides slightly converging towards the keel, and then the upper surface corresponding to the deck of the boat has been chipped into form by a succession of blows administered at right angles to the first, and in such a manner that the deck, as originally formed, was convex instead of flat. After this convex surface was formed, one, two, or even more long flakes were dislodged along its whole length, or nearly so, by blows administered at the part represented by the stern of the boat, thus leaving one or more channels along what corresponds to the deck. In rare instances, these long flakes have not been removed, in others of more frequent occurrence, one of the flakes has broken off short before attaining its full length.

Strange as this boat-shaped form may at the outset appear, yet on a little consideration it will be seen that the chipping into such a form is in fact one of the necessities of the case for the production of long blades of flint. Where flakes only 3 or 4 inches long are required, the operator may readily, with his hammer, strike off from the outside of his block of flint a succession of chips, so as to give it a polygonal outline, the projections of which will serve for the central ridges or back-bones of the first series of regular flakes that he strikes off. The removal of this first series of flakes leaves a number of projecting ridges, which serve as guides for the formation of a second series of flakes, and so on until the block is used up.

Fig. 3.—Nucleus—Pressigny. 1/2

But where a flake 10 or 12 inches in length is required, a different process becomes necessary. For it is nearly impossible with a rough mass of flint, to produce by single blows plane surfaces 10 or 12 inches in length, and arranged at such an angle as to produce a straight ridge, such as would serve to form the back-bone, as it were, of a long flake; and without such a back-bone, the production of a long flake is impossible. It is indeed this ridge (which need not, of course, be angular, but may be more or less rounded or polygonal) that regulates the course of the fissure by which the flake is dislodged from the matrix or parent flint; there being a slight degree of elasticity in the stone, which enables a fissure once properly commenced in a homogeneous flint to proceed at right angles to the line of least resistance in the dislodged flake, while at the same time exerting a nearly uniform strain, so that the inner surface of the flake becomes nearly parallel to the outer ridge. It was to obtain this outer ridge that the Pressigny cores were chipped into the form in which we find them; and it appears as if the workmen who fashioned them adopted the readiest means of obtaining the desired result of producing along the block of flint a central ridge whenever it became necessary, until the block was so much reduced in size as to be no longer serviceable. For, the process of chipping the block into the boat-like form could be repeated from time to time, until it became too small for further use. The same process of cross-chipping was practised in Scandinavia in early times, and the obsidian cores from the Greek island of Melos, Crete, and other ancient Greek sites prove that it was also known there. The blocks are found in various stages, rarely with the central ridge still left on, as Fig. 3, and more commonly with one or more long flakes removed from them, like Figs. 4 and 5. The sections of each block are shown beneath them. Two of the flakes are represented in Figs. 6 and 7. All the figures are on the scale of one-half linear measure.

The causes why the nuclei were rejected as useless are still susceptible of being traced. In some cases they had become so thin that they would not bear re-shaping; in others a want of uniformity in the texture of the flint, probably caused by some included organism, had made its appearance, and caused the flakes to break off short of their proper length, or had even made it useless to attempt to strike them off. In some rare instances, when the striking off long flakes had proved unsuccessful on the one face, the attempt has been made to procure them from the other. The abundance of large masses of flint near Pressigny—some as much as two or three feet across—has, however, rendered the workmen rather prodigal of their materials. The skill which has been brought to bear in the manufacture of these long flakes is marvellous, as the utmost precision is required in giving the blow by which they are produced. Generally speaking, the projecting ridge left at the butt-end of the nucleus between the depressions, whence two of the short flakes have been struck off in chipping it square, has been selected as the point of impact. They appear to me to have been struck off by a free blow, and not by the intervention of a set or punch. No doubt the face of the flint at the time of the blow being struck was supported on some elastic body.

A few flints which bear marks of having been used as hammerstones are found at Pressigny.

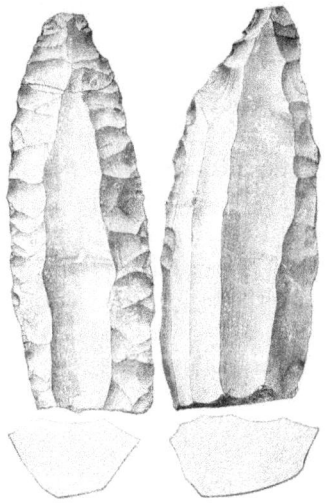

Fig. 4,

Fig. 5;

Nuclei—Pressigny. 1/2

An interesting lecture on the Flint Industry of Touraine was given on the occasion of the annual meeting of the Société Archéologique de Touraine, in 1891, by M. J. de Saint-Venant.

1/2 Fig. 6.—Flake—Pressigny.

Fig. 7.—Flake—Pressigny. 1/2

I have hitherto been treating of the production of flint flakes for various purposes. In such cases the flakes are everything, and the resulting core, or nucleus, mere refuse. In the manufacture of celts, or hatchets, the reverse is the case, the flakes are the refuse (though, of course, they might occasionally be utilized) and the resulting block is the main object sought. To produce this, however, much the same process appears to have been adopted, at all events where flint was the material employed. The hatchets seem to have been rough-hewn by detaching a succession of flakes, chips, or splinters, from a block of flint, by means of a hammer-stone, and these rough-hewn implements were subsequently worked into a more finished form by detaching smaller splinters, also probably by means of a hammer, previously to their being ground or polished, if they were destined to be finished in such a manner. In most cases, one face of the hatchet was first roughed out, and then by a series of blows, given at proper intervals, along the margin of that face the general shape was given and the other face chipped out. This is proved by the fact that in most of the roughly-chipped hatchets found in Britain, the depressions of the bulbs of percussion of the flakes struck off occur in a perfect state only on one face, having been partly removed on the other face by the subsequent chipping. There are, however, exceptions to this rule, and more especially among the implements found in our ancient river gravels. In some cases (see *postea*, Fig. 12) the cutting edge has been formed by the intersection of two convex lines of fracture giving a curved and sharp outline, and the body of the hatchet has been subsequently made to suit the edge. The same is the case with the hatchets from the Danish kjökken-möddings and coast-finds, though the intersecting facets are at a higher angle, and the resulting edge straighter, than in the specimens which I have mentioned. The edge is also, like that of a mortising chisel, at the extremity of a flat face, and not in the centre of the blade. The cutting edge has, however, in most of the so-called celts of the ordinary form, been fashioned by chipping subsequent to the roughing out of the hatchet; and even in the case of polished hatchets, the edge when damaged was frequently re-chipped into form before being ground afresh.

There hardly appears to be sufficient cause for believing that any of the stone hatchets found in this country were chipped out by any other means than by direct blows of a hammer; but in the case of the Danish axes with square sides, and with their corners as neatly crimped or puckered as if they had been made of pieces of leather sewn together, it is probable that this neat finish was produced by the use of some kind of punch or set. The hammer-stones used in the manufacture of flint hatchets appear to have been usually quartzite pebbles, where such are readily to be obtained, but also frequently to have been themselves mere blocks of flint. Many such hammer-stones of flint occurred in the Cissbury pits [105]—of which more hereafter—and I have found similar hammer-stones on the Sussex Downs, near Eastbourne, where also flint implements of various kinds appear to have been manufactured in quantities. Not improbably, these hammers were made of flints which had been for some time exposed on the surface, and which were in consequence harder than the flints recently dug from the pits. We have already seen that the gun-flint knappers of the present day are said to work most successfully on blocks of flint recently extracted, and those, too, from a particular layer in the chalk; and it seems probable that the ancient flint-workers were also acquainted with the advantages of using the flints fresh from the quarry, and worked them into shape at the pits from which they were dug, not only on account of the saving in transport of the partly-manufactured articles, but on account of the greater facility of working the freshly-extracted flints. This working the flints upon the spot is conclusively shown by the examination of the old flint-quarry at Cissbury, Sussex, by General Pitt Rivers (then Colonel A. Lane-Fox) and others. A very large number of hatchets, more or less perfectly chipped out, were there found, as will subsequently be mentioned. That they were in some cases at great pains to procure flint of the proper quality for being chipped into form, and were not content with blocks and nodules, such as might be found on the surface, is proved by the interesting explorations at Grime's Graves, near Brandon, carried on by Canon Greenwell, F.R.S. [106]

In a wood at this spot, the whole surface of the ground is studded with shallow bowl-shaped depressions from 20 to 60 feet in diameter, sometimes running into each other so as to form irregularly shaped hollows. They are over 250 in number, and one selected for exploration was about 28 feet in diameter at the mouth, gradually narrowing to 12 feet at the bottom, which proved to be 39 feet below the surface. Through the first 13 feet it had been cut through sand, below which the chalk was reached, and after passing through one layer of flint of inferior quality, which was not quarried beyond the limits of the shaft, the layer known as the "floor-stone," from which gun-flints are manufactured at the present day, was met with at the bottom of the shaft. To procure this, various horizontal galleries about 3 feet 6 inches in height were driven into the chalk. The excavations had been made by means of picks formed from the antlers of the red-deer, of which about 80 were found. The points are worn by use, and the thick bases of the horns battered by having been used as hammers, for breaking off portions of the chalk and also of the nodules of flint. Where they had been grasped by the hand the surface is polished by use, and on some there was a coating of chalky matter adhering, on which was still distinctly visible the impression of the cuticle of the old flint-workers. The marks of the picks and hammers were as fresh on the walls of the galleries as if made but yesterday. It is to be observed that such picks as these formed of stag's horn have been found in various other places, but have not had proper attention called to their character. I have seen one from the neighbourhood of Ipswich, [107] Suffolk. Canon Greenwell mentions somewhat similar discoveries having been made at Eaton and Buckenham, Norfolk. One was also found by him in a grave under a barrow he examined at Rudstone, near Bridlington, [108] and others occurred near Weaverthorpe and Sherburn. A polished hatchet of basalt had also been used at Grime's Graves as one of the tools for excavation, and the marks of its cutting edge were plentiful in the gallery in which it was discovered. There were also found some rudely-made cups of chalk apparently intended for lamps; a bone pin or awl; and, what is very remarkable, a rounded piece of bone 4 1/2 inches long and 1 inch in circumference, rubbed smooth, and showing signs of use at the ends, which, as Canon Greenwell suggests, may have been a punch or instrument for taking off the lesser flakes of flint in making arrow-heads and other small articles. It somewhat resembles the pin of reindeer horn in the Eskimo arrow-flaker, shortly to be mentioned. The shaft had been filled in with rubble, apparently from neighbouring pits, and in it were numerous chippings and cores of flint, and several quartzite and other pebbles battered at the ends by having been used as hammers for chipping the flints. Some large rounded cores of flint exhibited similar signs of use. On the surface of the fields around, numerous chippings of flint, and more or less perfect implements, such as celts, scrapers, and borers were found.

At Spiennes (near Mons, in Belgium), where a very similar manufacture but on a larger scale than that of Cissbury or even of Grime's Graves, appears to have been carried on, flints seem to have been dug in the same manner. Since I visited the spot, now many years ago, a railway cutting has traversed a portion of the district where the manufacture existed, and exposed a series of excavations evidently intended for the extraction of flint. Mons. A. Houzeau de Lehaie, of Hyon, near Mons, has most obligingly furnished me with some particulars of these subterranean works, a detailed account of which has also been published. [109] From this account it appears that shafts from 3 feet to 3 feet 6 inches in diameter were sunk through the loam and sand above the chalk to a depth of 30 or even 40 feet; and from the bottom of the shafts lateral galleries were worked, from 5 to 6 feet in height and about the same in width. Stag's horns which had been used as hammers, were found in the galleries, but it is doubtful whether they had been used as pick-axes like those in Grime's Graves. Among the rubble in the galleries, as well as on the surface of the ground above, were found roughly-chipped flints and splinters, and more or less rudely-shaped hatchets by thousands. There is one peculiar feature among these hatchets which I have not noticed to the same extent elsewhere, viz., that many of them are made from the nuclei or cores which, in the first instance, had subserved to the manufacture of long flint flakes, the furrows left by which appear on one of the faces of the hatchets. Sometimes, though rarely, the Pressigny nuclei have been utilized in a similar manner.

In France, pits for the extraction of flint have been discovered at Champignolles, Sérifontaine (Oise) [110] and at Mur de Barrez (Aveyron). [111]

Professor J. Buckman [112] has recorded a manufactory of celts and other flint instruments near Lyme Regis.

In these instances, especially at Cissbury and Grime's Graves in England, and at Pressigny and Spiennes on the Continent, and, indeed, at other places also, [113] there appears to have been an organized manufactory of flint instruments by settled occupants of the different spots; and it seems probable that the products were bartered away to those who were less favoured in their supply of the raw material, flint. At Old Deer, [114] Aberdeenshire, thirty-four leaf-shaped flints, roughly blocked out, were found together.

The chipping out of celts and some other tools formed, not of flint, but of other hard rocks, must have been effected in the same manner. The stone employed is almost always of a more or less silicious nature, and such as breaks with a conchoidal fracture.

Dr. F. A. Forel [115] chipped out a hatchet of euphotide or gabbro with a hammer formed of a fragment of saussurite. The process occupied an hour and ten minutes, and the subsequent grinding three hours more. He made and ground to an edge a rude hatchet of serpentine in thirty-five minutes.

To return, however, to the manufacture of the flint implements of this country, and more especially to those which are merely flakes submitted to a secondary process of chipping. We have seen that in the gun-flint manufacture the flakes are finally shaped by means of a knapping or trimming hammer and a fixed chisel, which act one against the other, somewhat like the two blades of a pair of shears, and the process adopted by the ancient flint-workers for many purposes must have been to some extent analogous, though it can hardly have been precisely similar. One of the most common forms of flint implements is that to which the name of "scraper" or "thumb-flint" has been given, and which is found in abundance on the Yorkshire Wolds, on the Downs of Sussex, and in many other parts of England and Scotland. The normal form is that of a broad flake chipped to a semicircular edge, usually at the end farthest from the bulb of percussion, the edge being bevelled away from the flat face of the flake, like that of a round-nosed turning-chisel. The name of "scraper" or "*grattoir*," has been given to these worked flints from their similarity to an instrument in use among the Eskimos [116] for scraping the insides of hides in the course of their preparation; but I need not here enter upon the question of the purpose for which these ancient instruments were used, as we are at present concerned only with the method of their manufacture. I am not aware of any evidence existing as to the method pursued by the Eskimos in the chipping out of their scraping tools: but I think that if, at the present time, we are able to produce flint tools precisely similar to the ancient "scrapers" by the most simple means possible, and without the aid of any metallic appliances, there is every probability that identically the same means were employed of old. Now, I have found by experiment that, taking a flake of flint (made, I may remark, with a stone hammer, consisting of a flint or quartzite pebble held in the hand), and placing it, with the flat face upwards, on a smooth block of stone, I can, by successive blows of the pebble, chip the end of the flake without any difficulty into the desired form. The face of the stone hammer is brought to bear a slight distance only within the margin of the flake, and, however sharp the blow administered, the smooth block of stone on which the flake is placed, and which of course projects beyond it, acts as a stop to prevent the hammer being carried forward so as to injure the form, and brings it up sharply, directly it has done its work of striking off a splinter from the end of the flake. The upper face of the flake remains quite uninjured, and, strange as it may appear, there is no difficulty in producing the evenly circular edge of the scraper by successive blows of the convex pebble.

Some of the other ancient tools and weapons, having one flat face, seem to have been fashioned in much the same manner. In the case of arrow-heads and lance-heads, however, another process would appear to have been adopted. It is true that we know not exactly how

> "the ancient arrow-maker
>
> Made his arrow-heads of sandstone,
>
> Arrow-heads of chalcedony,
>
> Arrow-heads of flint and jasper,
>
> Smooth and sharpened at the edges,
>
> Hard and polished, keen and costly."

And yet the process of making such arrow-heads is carried on at the present day by various half-civilized peoples, and has been witnessed by many Europeans, though but few have accurately recorded their observations. Sir Edward Belcher [117] who had seen obsidian arrow-heads made by the Indians of California, and those of chert or flint by the Eskimos of Cape Lisburne, states that the mode pursued in each case was exactly similar. The instrument employed among the Eskimos, which may be termed an "arrow-flaker," usually consists of a handle formed of fossil ivory, curved at one end for the purpose of being firmly held, and having at the other end a slit, like that for the lead in our pencils, in which is placed a slip of the point of the horn of a reindeer, which is found to be harder and more stubborn than ivory. This is secured in its place by a strong thong of leather or plaited sinew, put on wet, which on drying becomes very rigid. A representation of one of these instruments, in the Blackmore Museum at Salisbury, is given in Fig. 8. Another in the Christy Collection [118] is shown in Fig. 9. Another form of instrument of this kind, but in which the piece of horn is mounted in a wooden handle, is shown in Fig. 10, from an original in the same collection from Kotzebue Gulf. The bench on which the arrow-heads are made is said to consist of a log of wood, in which a spoon-shaped cavity is cut; over this the flake of chert is placed, and then, by pressing the "arrow-flaker" gently along the margin vertically, first on one side and then on the other, as one would set a saw, alternate fragments are splintered off until the object thus properly outlined presents the spear or arrow-head form, with two cutting serrated sides.

Fig. 8.—Eskimo Arrow-flaker. 1/2

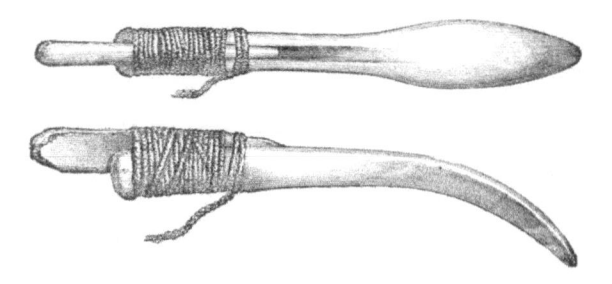

Fig. 9.—Eskimo Arrow-flaker. 1/2

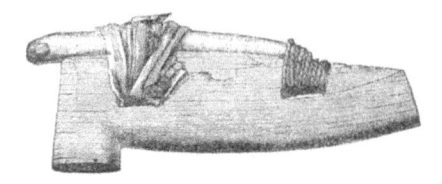

Fig. 10.—Eskimo Arrow-flaker. 1/2

Sir Edward Belcher some years ago kindly explained the process to me, and showed me both the implements used, and the objects manufactured. It appears that the flake from which the arrow-head is to be made is sometimes fixed by means of a cord in a split piece of wood so as to hold it firmly, and that all the large surface flaking is produced either by blows direct from the hammer, or through an intermediate punch or set formed of reindeer horn. The arrow-or harpoon-head thus roughly chipped out is afterwards finished by means of the "arrow-flaker."

The process in use at the present day among the Indians of Mexico in making their arrows is described in a somewhat different manner by Signor Craveri, who lived sixteen years in Mexico, and who gave the account to Mr. C. H. Chambers. [119] He relates that when the Indians wish to make an arrow-head or other instrument of a piece of obsidian, they take the piece in the left hand, and hold grasped in the other a small goat's horn; they set the piece of stone upon the horn, and dexterously pressing it against the point of it, while they give the horn a gentle movement from right to left, and up and down, they disengage from it frequent chips, and in this way obtain the desired form. M. F. de Pourtalès [120] speaks of a small notch in the end of the bone into which the edge of the flake is inserted, and a chip broken off from it by a sideways blow. Mr. T. R. Peale [121] describes the manufacture of arrow-heads among the Shasta and North California Indians, as being effected by means of a notched horn, as a glazier chips glass. This has also been fully described and illustrated by Mr. Paul Schumacher [122] of San Francisco. Major Powell confirms this account.

The Cloud River Indians [123] and the Fuegians, [124] also fashion their arrow-heads by pressure. Mr. Cushing [125] has described the process and claims to be the first civilized man who flaked an arrow-head with horn tools. This was in 1875. I had already done so and had described the method at the Norwich Congress in 1868.

The late Mr. Christy, [126] in a paper on the Cave-dwellers of Southern France, gave an account, furnished to him by Sir Charles Lyell, of the process of making stone arrow-heads by the Shasta Indians of California who still commonly use them, which slightly differs from that of Mr. Peale. This account by Mr. Caleb Lyon runs as follows:—"The Indian seated himself upon the floor, and, laying the stone anvil upon his knee, with one blow of his agate chisel he separated the obsidian pebble into two parts, then giving a blow to the fractured side he split off a slab a quarter of an inch in thickness. Holding the piece against his anvil with the thumb and finger of his left hand, he commenced a series of continuous blows, every one of which chipped off fragments of the brittle substance. It gradually seemed to acquire shape. After finishing the base of the arrow-head (the whole being little over an inch in length), he began striking gentle blows, every one of which I expected would break it in pieces. Yet such was his adroit application, his skill and dexterity, that in little over an hour he produced a perfect obsidian arrow-head. .... No sculptor ever handled a chisel with greater precision, or more carefully measured the weight and effect of every blow than did this ingenious Indian; for even among them, arrow-making is a distinct profession, in which few attain excellence." Dr. Rau [127] has, however, pointed out that this account of the manufacture requires confirmation; but Mr. Wyeth [128] states that the Indians on the Snake River form their arrow-heads of obsidian by laying one edge of the flake on a hard stone, and striking the other edge with another hard stone; and that many are broken when nearly finished and are thrown away.

Captain John Smith, [129] writing in 1606 of the Indians of Virginia, says, "His arrow-head he maketh quickly with a little bone, which he ever weareth at his bracert, [130] of any splint of stone or glasse in the form of a heart, and these they glew to the end of their arrowes. With the sinewes of deer and the tops of deers' horns boiled to a jelly, they make a glue which will not dissolve in cold water."

Beyond the pin of bone already mentioned, as having been found in one of the pits at Grime's Graves, I am not aware of any bone or horn implements of precisely this character, having been as yet discovered in Europe; but hammers of stag's horn and detached tines have frequently been found in connection with worked flints, and may have served in their manufacture. I have, moreover, remarked among the worked flints discovered in this country, and especially in Yorkshire, a number of small tools, the ends of which present a blunted, worn, and rounded appearance, as if from attrition against a hard substance. These tools are usually from 2 to 4 inches long, and made from large thick flakes, with the cutting edges removed by chipping; but occasionally, they are carefully finished implements of a pointed oval or a subtriangular section, and sometimes slightly curved longitudinally. Of these, illustrations will be given at a subsequent page. They are usually well adapted for being held in the hand, and I cannot but think that we have in them some of the tools which were used in the preparation of flint arrow-heads and other small instruments. I have tried the experiment with a large flake of flint used as the arrow-flaker, both unmounted and mounted in a wooden handle, and have succeeded in producing with it very passable imitations of ancient arrow-heads, both leaf-shaped and barbed. The flake of flint on which I have operated has been placed against a stop on a flat piece of wood, and when necessary to raise the edge of the flake I have placed a small blocking piece, also of wood, underneath it, and then by pressure of the arrow-flaker upon the edge of the flake, have detached successive splinters until I have reduced it into form. If the tool consists of a rather square-ended flake, one corner may rest upon the table of wood, and the pressure be given by a rocking action, bringing the other corner down upon the flake. In cutting the notches in barbed arrow-heads, this was probably the plan adopted, as I was surprised to find how easily this seemingly difficult part of the process was effected. Serration of the edges may be produced by the same means.

The edges of the arrow-heads made entirely with these flint arrow-flakers are, however, more obtuse and rounded than those of ancient specimens, so that probably these flint tools were used rather for removing slight irregularities in the form than for the main chipping out. This latter process, I find experimentally, can be best performed by means of a piece of stag's horn, used much in the same way as practised by the Eskimos. By supporting the flake of flint which is to be converted into an arrow-head against a wooden stop, and pressing the horn against the edge of the flake, the flint enters slightly into the body of the horn; then bringing the pressure to bear sideways, minute splinters can be detached, and the arrow-head formed by degrees in this manner without much risk of breaking. Not only can the leaf-shaped forms be produced, but the barbed arrow-heads, both with and without the central stem. The leaf-shaped arrow-heads are, however, the most easy to manufacture, and this simple form was probably that earliest in use. The counterfeit arrow-heads made by the notorious Flint Jack are of rude work, and were probably made with a light hammer of iron. Of late years (1895) a far more skilful workman at Mildenhall has produced imitations which can hardly be distinguished from genuine arrow-heads. He keeps his process of manufacture secret.

Among many tribes [131] of America, arrow-making is said to have been a trade confined to a certain class, who possessed the traditional knowledge of the process of manufacture; and it can hardly be expected that a mere novice like myself should be able at once to attain the art. I may, therefore, freely confess that, though by the use of stag's horn the ordinary surface-chipping characteristic of ancient implements may be obtained, yet the method of producing the even fluting, like ripple-marks, by detaching parallel splinters uniform in size, and extending almost across the surface of a lance- or arrow-head is at present a mystery to me; as is also the method by which the delicate ornamentation on the handles of Danish flint daggers was produced. It seems, however, possible that by pressing the flint to be operated upon on some close-fitting elastic body at the time of removing the minute flakes, the line of fracture may be carried along a considerable distance over the surface of the flint, before coming to an end by reason of the dislodged flake breaking off or terminating. It is also possible that the minute and elegant ornaments may have been produced by the use of a pointed tooth of some animal as a punch. Mr. F. C. J. Spurrell, [132] in an interesting article, has suggested that the final flaking was effected after the blades had been ground to a smooth surface, in the same manner as the flaking on some of the most symmetrical Egyptian blades. His view appears to be correct, at all events so far as certain parts of some Danish blades are concerned. It seems, however, very doubtful whether any such general practice prevailed. I have seen a delicate lance-head 6 inches long, of triangular section, with the broad face polished and the two other faces exquisitely fluted. In this case also the faces may have been ground before fluting. This blade was found in a cavern at Sourdes, in the Landes, and was in the collection of M. Chaplain-Duparc.

With regard to the process of grinding or polishing flint and other stone implements not much need be said. I may, however, refer the reader to Wilde's Catalogue [133] of the Museum of the Royal Irish Academy, for an account of the different processes. In all cases the grindstone on which they were polished was fixed and not rotatory, and in nearly all cases the striæ running along the stone hatchets are longitudinal, thus proving that they were rubbed lengthways and not crossways on the grinding-bed. This is a criterion of some service in detecting modern forgeries. The grinding-stones met with in Denmark and Scandinavia are generally of compact sandstone or quartzite, and are usually of two forms—flat slabs, often worn hollow by use, and polygonal prisms smallest in the middle, these latter having frequently hollow facets in which gouges or the more convex-faced hatchets might be ground, and sometimes rounded ridges such as would grind the hollow part of gouges. From the coarse striation on the body of most flint hatchets, especially the large ones, it would appear that they were not ground immediately on such fine-grained stones, but that some coarse and hard grit must have been used to assist the action of the grindstone. M. Morlot [134] thought that some mechanical pressure was also used to aid in the operation, and that the hatchet to be ground was weighted in some manner, possibly by means of a lever. In grinding and polishing the hollowed faces of different forms of stone axes, it would appear that certain rubbers formed of stone were used, probably in conjunction with sand. These will be more particularly described in a subsequent page. The surface of hard rocks or of large boulders fixed in the ground was often used for the purpose of grinding stone implements. Instances will be given hereafter.

Closely allied to the process of grinding is that of sawing stone. It is however rarely, if ever, that in this country any of the stone implements show signs of having been reduced into shape by this process. Among the small hatchets in fibrolite, so common in the Auvergne and in the south of France, and among the greenstone, and especially the nephrite celts found in the Swiss Pfahlbauten, [135] many show evident traces of having been partially fashioned by means of sawing. I have also remarked it on a specimen from Portugal, and on many fibrolite hatchets from Spain. [136] Dr. Keller has noticed the process, and suggests that the incisions on the flat surface of the stone chosen for the purpose of being converted into a celt were made sometimes on one side, and sometimes on both, by means of a sharp saw-like tool. He has since [137] gone more deeply into the question, and has suggested that the stone to be sawn was placed on the ground near a tree, and then sawn by means of a splinter of flint fixed in the end of a staff, which at its other end was forked, and as it were hinged under one of the boughs of the tree sufficiently flexible to give pressure to the flint when a weight was suspended from it. The staff was, he supposed, to have been grasped in the hand, and moved backwards and forwards while water was applied to the flint to facilitate the sawing. The objection to this suggestion is, that in case of the flint being brought to the edge of the stone it would be liable to be driven into the ground by the weight on the bough, and thus constantly hinder the operation; nevertheless some such mechanical aids in sawing may have been in use.

M. Troyon [138] considered that the blade of flint was used in connection with sand as well as water. This latter view appears, at first sight, far more probable, as the sawing instrument has in some instances cut nearly 3/4 of an inch into the stone, which, it would seem, could hardly have been accomplished with a simple flint saw; and the sides of the saw-kerf or notch show, moreover, parallel striæ, as if resulting from the use of sand. The objection that at first occurred to my mind against regarding the sawing instrument as having been of flint was of a negative character only, and arose from my not having seen in any of the Swiss collections any flint flakes that had indisputably been used for sawing by means of sand. At one time I fancied, from the character of the bottom and sides of the notches, that a string stretched like that of a bow might have been used with sand in the manner in which, according to Oviedo, [139] the American Indians sawed in two their iron fetters, and I succeeded in cutting off the end of an ancient Swiss hatchet of hard steatite by this means. I found, however, that the bottom of the kerf thus formed was convex longitudinally, whereas in the ancient examples it was slightly concave. It is therefore evident that whatever was used as the saw must have been of a comparatively unyielding nature, and probably shorter than the pebble or block of stone it was used to saw, for even the iron blades used in conjunction with sand and water by modern masons become concave by wear, and, therefore, the bottom of the kerf they produce is convex longitudinally. I accordingly made some further experiments, and this time upon a fragment of a greenstone celt of such hardness that it would readily scratch window-glass. I found, however, that with a flint flake I was able to work a groove along it, and that whether I used sand or no, my progress was equally certain, though it must be confessed, very slow. I am indeed doubtful whether the flint did not produce most effect without the sand, as the latter to become effective requires a softer body in which it may become embedded;

while by working with the points and projections in the slightly notched edge of the flake, its scratching action soon discoloured the water in the notch. What was most remarkable, and served in a great measure to discredit the negative evidence to which I before referred, was that the edges of the flake when not used with sand showed but slight traces of wear or polish.

On the whole, I am inclined to think that both the Swiss antiquaries are in the right, and that the blocks of stone were sawn both with and without sand, by means of flint flakes, but principally of strips of wood and bone used in conjunction with sand. [140] The reader may consult Munro's Lake-Dwellings, 1890, p. 505.

Professor Flinders Petrie, in addition to the flint implements of the "New Race," which he discovered near Abydos, found a number of stone implements at Kahun, and Mr. F. C. J. Spurrell has contributed to his [141] book an interesting chapter on their character and the method of their manufacture.

Most of the jade implements from New Zealand and N.W. America have been partially shaped by sawing, and in the British Museum is a large block of jade from the former country deeply grooved by sawing, and almost ready to be split, so as to be of the right thickness for a *mere*. The natives [142] use stone hammers for chipping, flakes of trap or of some other hard rock for sawing, and blocks of sandstone and a micaceous rock for grinding and polishing. Obsidian is said to be used for boring jade. I have a flat piece of jade, apparently part of a thin hatchet, on one face of which two notches have been sawn converging at an angle of 135° and marking out what when detached and ground would have formed a curved ear-ring. It was given me by the late Mr. H. N. Moseley, who brought it from New Zealand.

There is another peculiarity to be seen in some of the greenstone hatchets and perforated axes, of which perhaps the most characteristic examples occur in Switzerland, though the same may occasionally be observed in British specimens. It is that the blocks of stone have been reduced into form, not only by chipping with a hammer, as is the case with flint hatchets, but by working upon the surface with some sort of pick or chisel, which was not improbably formed of flint. In some instances, where the hatchets were intended for insertion into sockets of stag's horn or other materials, their butt-end was purposely roughened by means of a pick after the whole surface had been polished. Instances of this roughening are common in Switzerland, rare in France, and rarer still in England. The greenstone hatchet found in a gravel-pit near Malton [143] (Fig. 81) has its butt-end roughened in this manner. The shaft-holes in some few perforated axes appear to have been worked out by means of such picks or chisels, the hole having been bored from opposite sides of the axe, and generally with a gradually decreasing diameter. In some rare instances the perforation is oval. The cup, or funnel-shaped depressions, in some hammer-stones seem to have been made in a similar manner. The inner surface of the shaft holes in perforated axes is also frequently ground, and occasionally polished. This has in most cases been effected by turning a cylindrical grinder within the hole; though in some few instances the grinding instrument has been rubbed backwards and forwards in the hole after the manner of a file. M. Franck de Truguet, [144] of Treytel, in Switzerland, thinks he has found in a lake-dwelling an instrument used for finishing and enlarging the holes. It is a fragment of sandstone about 2 1/2 inches long, and rounded on one face, which is worn by friction.

But, besides the mode of chipping out the shaft-hole in perforated implements, several other methods were employed, especially in the days when the use of bronze was known, to which period most of the highly-finished perforated axes found in this country are to be referred. In some cases it would appear that, after chipping out a recess so as to form a guide for the boring tool, the perforation was effected by giving a rotatory motion, either constant or intermittent, to the tool. I have, indeed, seen some specimens in which, from the marks visible in the hole, I am inclined to think a metallic drill was used. But whether, where metal was not employed, and no central core, as subsequently mentioned, was left in the hole, the boring tool was of flint, and acted like a drill, or whether it was a round stone used in conjunction with sand, as suggested by the late Sir Daniel Wilson [145] and Sir W. Wilde, [146] so that the hole was actually ground away, it is impossible to say. I have never seen any flint tools that could unhesitatingly be referred to this use; but Herr Grewingk, in his "Steinalter der Ostseeprovinzen," [147] mentions several implements in the form of truncated cones, which he regards as boring-tools (*Bohrstempel*), used for perforating stone axes and hammers. He suggests the employment of a drill-bow to make them revolve, and thinks that, in some cases, the boring tools were fixed, and the axe itself caused to revolve. Not having seen the specimens, I cannot pronounce upon them; but the fact that several of these conical pieces show signs of fracture at the base, and that they are all of the same kinds of stone (diorite, augite, porphyry, and syenite) as those of which the stone axes of the district are made, is suggestive of their being merely the cores, resulting from boring with a tube, in the manner about to be described, in some cases from each face of the axe, and in others where the base of the cone is smooth, from one face only. One of these central cores found in Lithuania is figured by Mortillet, [148] and is regarded by him as being probably the result of boring by means of a metal tube; others, from Switzerland, presumably of the Stone Age, are cited by Keller. [149] Bellucci [150] thinks that he has found them in Northern Italy.

Worsaae [151] has suggested that in early times the boring may have been effected with a pointed stick and sand and water; and, indeed, if any grinding process was used, it is a question whether some softer substance, such as wood, in which the sand or abrasive material could become imbedded, would not be more effective than flint. By way of experiment I bored a hole through the Swiss hatchet of steatite before mentioned, and I found that in that case a flint flake could be used as a sort of drill; but that for grinding, a stick of elder was superior to both flint and bone, inasmuch as it formed a better bed for the sand.

Professor Rau, of New York, has made some interesting experiments in boring stone by means of a drilling-stock and sand, which are described in the "Annual Report of the Smithsonian Institute for 1868." [152] He operated on a piece of hard diorite an inch and three-eighths in thickness, and employed as a drilling agent a wooden wand of ash, or at times, of pine, in conjunction with sharp quartz sand. Attached to the wand was a heavy disc, to act as a fly-wheel, and an alternating rotatory motion was obtained by means of a bow and cord attached at its centre to the apex of the drilling-stock, and giving motion to it after the manner of a "pump-drill," such as is used by the Dacotahs [153] and Iroquois [154] for producing fire by friction, or what is sometimes called the Chinese drill. So slow was the process, that two hours of constant drilling added, on an average, not more than the thickness of an ordinary lead-pencil line to the depth of the hole.

The use of a drill of some form or other, to which rotatory motion in alternate directions was communicated by means of a cord, is of great antiquity. We find it practised with the ordinary bow by the ancient Egyptians; [155] and Ulysses is described by Homer [156] as drilling out the eye of the Cyclops by means of a stake with a thong of leather wound round it, and pulled alternately at each end, "like a shipwright boring timber." The "fire-drill," for producing fire by friction, which is precisely analogous to the ordinary drill, is, or was, in use in most parts of the world. Among the Aleutian Islanders the thong-drill, and among the New Zealanders a modification of it, is used for boring holes in stone. Those who wish to see more on the subject must consult Tylor's "Early History of Mankind" [157] and a "Study of the Primitive Methods of Drilling," [158] by Mr. J. D. McGuire.

Professor Carl Vogt [159] has suggested that the small roundels of stone (like Worsaae, "Afb." No. 86) too large to have been used as spindle-whorls, which are occasionally found in Denmark, may have been the fly-wheels of vertical pump-drills, used for boring stone tools. They may, however, be heads of war-maces.

In the case of some of the unfinished and broken axes found in the Swiss lakes, and even in some of the objects made of stag's horn, [160] there is a projecting core [161] at the bottom of the unfinished hole. This is also often seen in [162] Scandinavian and German specimens. Dr. Keller has shown that this core indicates the employment of some kind of tube as a boring tool; as indeed had been pointed out so long ago as 1832 by Gutsmuths, [163] who, in his paper "Wie durchbohrte der alte Germane seine Streitaxt?" suggested that a copper or bronze tube was used in conjunction with powdered quartz, or sand and water. In the Klemm collection, formerly at Dresden, is a bronze tube, five inches long and three quarters of an inch in diameter, found near Camenz, in Saxony, which its late owner regarded [164] as one of the boring tools used in the manufacture of stone axes. This is now in the British Museum, but does not appear to me to have been employed for such a purpose. The Danish antiquaries [165] have arrived at the same conclusion as to tubes being used for boring. Von Estorff [166] goes so far as to say that the shaft-holes are in some cases so regular and straight, and their inner surface so smooth, that they can only have been bored by means of a metallic cylinder and emery. Lindenschmit [167] considers the boring to have been effected either by means of a hard stone, or a plug of hard wood with sand and water, or else, in some cases, by means of a metallic tube, as described by Gutsmuths. He engraves some specimens, in which the commencement of the hole, instead of being a mere depression, is a sunk ring. Similar specimens are mentioned by Lisch. [168] Dr. Keller's translator, Mr. Lee, cites a friend as suggesting the employment of a hollow stick, such as a piece of elder, for the boring tool. My experience confirms this; but I found that the coarse sand was liable to clog and accumulate in the hollow part of the stick, and thus grind away the top of the core. If I had used finer sand this probably would not have been the case.

Mr. Rose [169] has suggested the use of a hollow bone; but, as already observed, I found bone less effective than wood, in consequence of its not being so good a medium for carrying the sand.

Mr. Sehested, [170] however, who carried out a series of interesting experiments in grinding, sawing, and boring stone implements, found dry sand better than wet, and a bone of lamb better than either elder or cow's-horn for boring.

Most of the holes drilled in the stone instruments and pipes of North America appear to have been produced by hollow drills, which Professor Rau [171] suggests may have been formed of a hard and tough cane, the *Arundinaria macrosperma*, which grows abundantly in the southern parts of the United States. He finds reason for supposing that the Indian workmen were acquainted with the ordinary form of drill driven by a pulley and bow. The tubes of steatite, one foot in length, found in some of the minor mounds of the Ohio Valley, [172] must probably have been bored with metal.

Dr. Keller, after making some experiments with a hollow bone and quartz-sand, tried a portion of ox-horn, which he found surprisingly more effective, the sand becoming embedded in the horn and acting like a file. He comments on the absence of any bronze tubes that could have been used for boring in this manner, and on the impossibility of making flint tools for the purpose. The perishable nature of ox-horn accounts for its absence in the Lake settlements. [173] On the whole this suggestion appears to me the most reasonable. Experiments have also been made in boring with stag's-horn. [174]

M. Troyon [175] considered that these holes were not bored by means of a hollow cylinder, inasmuch as this would not produce so conical an opening, and he thought that the axe was made to revolve in some sort of lathe, while the boring was effected by means of a bronze tool used in conjunction with sand and water. He mentions some stone axes found in Bohemia, and in the collection of the Baron de Neuberg, at Prague, which have so little space left between the body of the axe and the central cores, that in his opinion they must have been bored by means of a metal point and not of a hollow cylinder. Mortillet [176] thinks that some of the Swiss axes were bored in a similar manner. The small holes for suspension, drilled through some of the Danish celts, he thinks were drilled with a pointed stone. [177] Not having seen the specimens cited by M. Troyon, I am unable to offer any opinion upon them; but it appears to me very doubtful whether anything in character like a lathe was known at the early period to which the perforated axes belong, for were such an appliance in use we should probably find it extended to the manufacture of pottery in the shape of the potter's wheel, whereas the contemporary pottery is all hand-made. M. Desor, [178] though admitting that a hollow metallic tube would have afforded the best means of drilling these holes, is inclined to refer the axes to a period when the use of metals was unknown. He suggests that thin flakes of flint may have been fastened round a stick and thus used to bore the hole, leaving a solid core in the middle. I do not however think that such a method is practicable. In some of the Swiss [179] specimens in which the boring is incomplete there is a small hole in advance of the larger, so that the section is like that of a trifoliated Gothic arch. In this case the borer would appear to have somewhat resembled a centre-bit or pin-drill. In others [180] the holes are oval, and must have been much modified after they were first bored. The process of boring holes of large diameter in hard rocks such as diorite and basalt by means of tubes was in common use among the Egyptians. These tubes are supposed to have been made of bronze, and corundum to have been employed with them. Professor Flinders Petrie [181] has suggested that they had jewelled edges like the modern diamond crown drill, and that they could penetrate diorite at the rate of one inch in depth for 27 feet of forward motion. I think, however, that this is an over-estimate. Saws of the same kind were also used.

Kirchner, [182] the ingenious but perverse author of "Thor's Donnerkeil," considers that steel boring tools must have been used for the shaft-holes in stone axes; and even Nilsson, [183] who comments on the rarity of the axes with the central core in the holes, is inclined to refer them to the Iron Age. He [184] considers it an impossibility to bore "such holes" with a wooden pin and wet sand, and is no doubt right, if he means that a wooden pin would not leave a core standing in the centre of the hole.

The drilling the holes through the handles of the New Zealand [185] *meres* is stated to be a very slow process, but effected by means of a wetted stick dipped in emery powder. I have seen one in which the hole was unfinished, and was only represented by a conical depression on each face.

In some stones, however, such holes can be readily bored with wood and sand; and in all cases where the stone to be worked upon can be scratched by sand, the boring by means of wood is possible, given sufficient time, and the patience of a savage.

To what a degree this extends may be estimated by what Lafitau [186] says of the North American Indians sometimes spending their whole life in making a stone tomahawk without entirely finishing it; and by the years spent by members of tribes on the Rio Negro [187] in perforating cylinders of rock crystal, by twirling a flexible leaf-shoot of wild plantain between the hands, and thus grinding the hole with the aid of sand and water. The North American [188] tobacco-pipes of stone were more easily bored, but for them also a reed in conjunction with sand and water seems to have been employed.

On the whole, we may conclude that the holes were bored in various manners, of which the principal were—

- 1. By chiselling, or picking with a sharp stone.
- 2. By grinding with a solid grinder, probably of wood.
- 3. By grinding with a tubular grinder, probably of ox-horn.
- 4. By drilling with a stone drill.
- 5. By drilling with a metallic drill.

Holes produced by any of these means could, of course, receive their final polish by grinding.

With regard to the external shaping of the perforated stone axes not much need be said. They appear to have been in some cases wrought into shape by means of a pick or chisel, and subsequently ground; in other cases to have been fashioned almost exclusively by grinding. In some of the axe-hammers made of compact quartzite, the form of the pebble from which they have been made has evidently given the general contour, in the same manner as has been observed on some fibrolite hatchets, which have been made by sawing a flat pebble in two longitudinally, and then sharpening the end, or ends, the rest of the surface being left unaltered in form. This is also the case with some stone hatchets, to form which a suitable pebble has been selected, and one end ground to an edge.

Such is a general review of the more usual processes adopted in the manufacture of stone implements in prehistoric times, which I have thought it best should precede the account of the implements themselves. I can hardly quit the subject without just mentioning that here, as elsewhere, we find traces of improvement and progress, both in adapting forms to the ends they had to subserve, and in the manner of treating the stubborn materials of which these implements were made. Such progress may not have been, and probably was not, uniform, even in any one country; and, indeed, there are breaks in the chronology of stone implements which it is hard to fill up; but any one comparing, for instance, the exquisitely made axe-hammers and delicately chipped flint arrow-heads of the Bronze Age, with the rude implements of the Palæolithic Period—neatly chipped as some of these latter are—cannot but perceive the advances that had been made in skill, and in adaptation of means to ends. If, for the sake of illustration, we divide the lapse of time embraced between these two extremes into four Periods, it appears—

- 1. That in the Palæolithic, River-gravel, or Drift Period, implements were fashioned by chipping only, and not ground or polished. The material used in Europe was, moreover, as far as at present known, mainly flint, chert, or quartzite.

- 2. That in the Reindeer or Cavern Period of Central France, though grinding was almost if not quite unused, except in finishing bone instruments, yet greater skill in flaking flint and in working up flakes into serviceable tools was exhibited. In some places, as at Laugerie-haute, surface-chipping is found on the flint arrow-heads, and cup-shaped recesses have been worked in other hard stones than flint, though no other stones have been used for cutting purposes.

- 3. That in the Neolithic or Surface Stone Period of Western Europe, other materials besides flint were largely used for the manufacture of hatchets; grinding at the edge and on the surface was generally practised, and the art of flaking flint by pressure from the edge was probably known. The stone axes, at least in Britain, were rarely perforated.

- 4. That in the Bronze Period such stone implements, with the exception of mere flakes and scrapers, as remained in use, were, as a rule, highly finished, many of the axes being perforated and of graceful form, and some of the flint arrow-heads evincing the highest degree of manual skill. The subsequent manufacture of stone implements in Roman and later times needs no further mention.

Having said thus much on the methods by which the stone implements of antiquity were manufactured, I pass on to the consideration of their different forms, commencing with those of the Neolithic Age, and with the form which is perhaps the best known in all countries—the celt.

IMPLEMENTS OF THE NEOLITHIC PERIOD.

CHAPTER III.
CELTS.

The name of Celt, which has long been given to hatchets, adzes, or chisels of stone, is so well known and has been so universally employed, that though its use has at times led to considerable misapprehension, I have thought it best to retain it. It has been fancied by some that the name bore reference to the Celtic people, by whom the implements were supposed to have been made; and among those who have thought fit to adopt the modern fashion of calling the Celts "Kelts" there have been not a few who have given the instruments the novel name of "kelts" also. In the same manner, many French antiquaries have given the plural form of the word as *Celtæ*. Notwithstanding this misapprehension, there can be no doubt as to the derivation of the word, it being no other than the English form of the doubtful Latin word *Celtis* or *Celtes*, a chisel. This word, however, is curiously enough almost an ἅπαξλεγόμενον in this sense, being best known through the Vulgate translation of Job, [189] though it is repeated in a forged inscription recorded by Gruter and Aldus. [190] The usual derivation given is à *cælando*, and it is regarded as the equivalent of *cælum*. The first use of the term that I have met with, as applied to antiquities, is in Beger's "Thesaurus Brandenburgicus," [191] 1696, where a bronze celt, adapted for insertion in its haft, is described under the name of *Celtes*.

I have said that the word *celte*, which occurs in the Vulgate, is of doubtful authenticity. Mr. Knight Watson, [192] in a paper communicated to the Society of Antiquaries, has shown that the reading in many MSS. is *certe*, and the question has been fully discussed by Mr. J. A. Picton, [193] Mr. E. Marshall, [194] Dr. M. Much, [195] and others. K. v. Becker [196] suggests that the error in writing *celte* for *certe* originated between A.D. 800 and 1400, and he points out that Conrad Pickel, the poet laureate, who died in 1508, latinized his surname by *Celtes*. Treating the subject as one of probability, it appears much more unlikely that a scribe should place a newfangled word *celte* in the place of such a well-known word as *certe*, than that *certe* should have been substituted for a word that had become obsolete. I am, therefore, unwilling absolutely to condemn the word, especially having regard to there being a recognized equivalent in Latin, *Cælum*.

It has been suggested that there may originally have been some connection between the Latin *celtis* and the British or Welsh *cellt*, a flint; but this seems rather an instance of fortuitous resemblance than of affinity. [197] A Welsh triad says there are three hard things in the world—*Maen Cellt* (a flint stone), steel, and a miser's heart.

The general form of stone celts is well known, being usually that of blades, approaching an oval in section, with the sides more or less straight, and one end broader and also sharper than the other. In length they vary from about two inches to as much as sixteen inches. I do not, however, propose to enter at once into any description of the varieties in their form and character, but to pass in review some of the opinions that have been held concerning their nature and origin.

One of the most universal of these is a belief, which may almost be described as having been held "*semper, ubique et ab omnibus*," in their having been thunderbolts.

"The country folks [198] of the West of England still hold that the 'thunder-axes' they find, once fell from the sky." In Cornwall [199] they still have medical virtues assigned to them; the water in which "a thunderbolt," or celt, has been boiled being a specific for rheumatism. In the North of England, and in parts of Scotland, they are known as thunderbolts, [200] and, like flint arrow-heads, are supposed to have preservative virtues, especially against diseases of cattle. In Ireland the same superstition prevails, and I have myself known an instance where, on account of its healing powers, a stone celt was lent among neighbours to place in the troughs from which cattle drank.

In the British Museum is a thin highly polished celt of jadeite, reputed to be from Scotland, in form like Fig. 52, mounted in a silver frame, and with a hole bored through it at either end. It is said to have been attached to a belt and worn round the waist as a cure for renal affections, against which the material nephrite was a sovereign remedy.

In most parts of France, [201] and in the Channel Islands, the stone celt is known by no other name than "*Coin de foudre*," or "*Pierre de tonnerre*"; and Mr. F. C. Lukis [202] gives an instance of a flint celt having been found near the spot where a signal-staff had been struck by lightning, which was proved to have been the bolt by its peculiar smell when broken. M. Ed. Jacquard has written an interesting paper on "Céraunies ou pierres de tonnerre." [203]

In Brittany [204] a stone celt is frequently thrown into the well for purifying the water or securing a continued supply; and in Savoy it is not rare to find one of these instruments rolled up in the wool of the sheep, or the hair of the goat, for good luck, or for the prevention of the rot or putrid decay.

In Sweden [205] they are preserved as a protection against lightning, being regarded as the stone-bolts that have fallen during thunderstorms.

In Norway they are known as Tonderkiler, and in Denmark the old name for a celt was Torden-steen. [206] The test of their being really thunderbolts was to tie a thread round them, and place them on hot coals, when, if genuine, the thread was not burnt, but rather rendered moist. Such celts promote sleep.

In Germany [207] both celts and perforated stone axes are regarded as thunderbolts (*Donnerkeile* or *Thorskeile*); and, on account of their valuable properties, are sometimes preserved in families for hundreds of years. I possess a specimen from North Germany, on which is inscribed the date 1571, being probably the year in which it was discovered. The curious perforated axe or hammer found early in the last century, now preserved in the Museum of Antiquities at Upsala, [208] seems to have been a family treasure of the same kind. It bears upon it, in early Runes, an inscription thus interpreted by Professor Stephens—"Owns Oltha this Axe." Another, with four [209] Runic characters upon it, was found in Denmark, and it has been suggested that the letters on it represent the names of Loki, Thor, Odin, and Belgthor. [210] The appearance of the American inscribed axe from Pemberton, [211] New Jersey, described by my namesake, Dr. J. C. Evans, and published by Sir Daniel Wilson, is not calculated to inspire confidence in its authenticity.

The German belief is much the same as the Irish. Stone celts are held to preserve from lightning the house in which they are kept. They perspire when a storm is approaching; they are good for diseases of man and beast; they increase the milk of cows; they assist the birth of children; and powder scraped from them may be taken with advantage for various childish disorders. It is usually nine days after their fall before they are found on the surface.

In the ruins of a Cistercian nunnery, Martha's Hof, at Bonn, [212] a large polished celt of jadeite, like Fig. 52, was found, which had been presumably brought there as a protection against lightning. It had been placed in the roof of a granary.

In Bavaria [213] and Moravia [214] stone axes, whether perforated or not, are regarded as thunderbolts.

In Holland, [215] in like manner, they are known as *donder-beitels*, or thunder-chisels.

In Spain they are known as *rayos* or *centellos*, and are regarded as thunder-stones, while among the Portuguese [216] and in Brazil [217] the name for a stone axe-blade is *corisco*, or lightning.

In Italy [218] a similar belief that these stone implements are thunderbolts prevails, and Moscardo [219] has figured two polished celts as *Saette o Fulmini*; and in Greece [220] the stone celts are known as *Astropelekia*, and have long been held in veneration.

About the year 1081 we find the Byzantine emperor, Alexius Comnenus, [221] sending, among other presents, to the Emperor Henry III. of Germany, ἀστροπέλεκυν δεδεμένον μετὰ χρυσαφίου, an expression which appears to have puzzled Ducange and Gibbon, but which probably means a celt of meteoric origin mounted in gold. About 1670 [222] a stone hatchet was brought from Turkey by the French Ambassador, and presented to Prince François de Lorraine, bishop of Verdun. It still exists in the Musée Lorrain at Nancy.

Nor is the belief in the meteoric and supernatural origin of celts confined to Europe. Throughout a great part of Asia the same name of thunderbolts or lightning-stones is applied to them. Dr. Tylor [223] cites an interesting passage from a Chinese encyclopædia of the seventeenth century respecting lightning-stones, some of which have the shape of a hatchet.

In Japan [224] they are known as thunderbolts, or as the battle-axe of Tengu, [225] the Guardian of Heaven. They are there of great use [226] medicinally; in Java [227] they are known as lightning-teeth. The old naturalist Rumph, [228] towards the end of the seventeenth century, met with many such in Java and Amboyna, which he says were known as "Dondersteenen."

In Burma [229] and Assam [230] stone adzes are called lightning-stones, and are said to be always to be found on the spot where a thunderbolt has fallen, provided it is dug for, three years afterwards. When reduced to powder they are an infallible specific for ophthalmia. They [231] also render those who carry them invulnerable, and possess other valuable properties. The same is the case in [232] Cambodia.

Among the Malays [233] the idea of the celestial origin of these stones generally prevails, though they are also supposed to have been used in aërial combats between angels and demons [234]; while in China they are revered as relics of long-deceased ancestors.

I am not aware whether they are regarded as thunderbolts in India, [235] though a fragment of jade is held to be a preservative against lightning. [236] Throughout the whole of Hindostan, however, they appear to be venerated as sacred, and placed against the Mahadeos, or adorned with red paint as Mahadeo.

It is the same in Western Africa. [237] Sir Richard Burton [238] has described stone hatchets from the Gold Coast, which are there regarded as "Thunder-stones." Mr. Bowen, a missionary, states that there also the stones, or thunderbolts, which Saugo, the Thunder god, casts down from heaven, are preserved as sacred relics. Among the Niam-Niam, [239] in central Africa, they are regarded as thunderbolts. An instructive article by Richard Andrée on the place of prehistoric stone weapons in vulgar beliefs will be found in the *Mittheilungen* of the Anthropological Society of Vienna, [240] and an article [241] by Dr. A. Bastian on "Stone Worship in Ethnography" in the *Archiv für Anthropologie*.

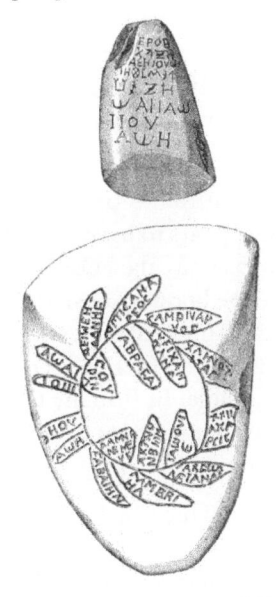

Fig. 11.—Celt with Gnostic Inscription. (The upper figure actual size, the lower enlarged.)

The very remarkable celt of nephrite (now in the Christy collection), procured in Egypt many years ago by Colonel Milner, and exhibited to the Archæological Institute in 1868 [242] by the late Sir Henry Lefroy, F.R.S., affords another instance of the superstitions attaching to these instruments, and has been the subject of a very interesting memoir by the late Mr. C. W. King, [243] the well-known authority on ancient gems. In this case both faces of the celt have been engraved with gnostic inscriptions in Greek, arranged on one face in the form of a wreath; and it was doubtless regarded as in itself possessed of mystic power, by some Greek of Alexandria, where it seems to have been engraved. It is shown in Fig. 11, here reproduced from the *Archæological Journal*. Another celt not from Egypt, but from Greece proper, with three personages and a Greek inscription engraved upon it, is mentioned by Mortillet. [244] It seems to reproduce a Mithraic [245] scene. A perforated axe, with a Chaldæan [246] inscription upon it, is in the Borgia collection, and has been figured and described by Lenormant.

Curiously enough, the hatchet appears in ancient times to have had some sacred importance among the Greeks. It was from a hatchet that, according to Plutarch, [247] Jupiter Labrandeus received that title; and M. de Longpérier [248] has pointed out a passage, from which it appears that Bacchus was in one instance, at all events, worshipped under the form of a hatchet, or πέλεκυς. He has also published a Chaldæan cylinder on which a priest is represented as making an offering to a hatchet placed upright on a throne, and has shown that the Egyptian hieroglyph for *Nouter*, God, is simply the figure of an axe.

In India the hammer was the attribute of the god Indra [249] as Vágrâkarti. A similar worship appears to have prevailed in the North. Saxo Grammaticus mentions that the Danish prince Magnus Nilsson, after a successful expedition against the Goths, brought back among his trophies some Thor's hammers, "malleos joviales," of unusual weight, which had been objects of veneration in an island in which he had destroyed a temple. In Brittany the figures of stone celts are in several instances engraved on the large stones of chambered tumuli and dolmens.

There are two [250] deductions which may readily be drawn from the facts just stated; first, that in nearly, if not, indeed, all parts of the globe which are now civilized, there was a period when the use of stone implements prevailed; and, secondly, that this period is so remote, that what were then the common implements of every-day life have now for centuries been regarded with superstitious reverence, or as being in some sense of celestial origin, and not the work of man's hands.

Nor was such a belief even in Europe, and in comparatively modern times, confined to the uneducated. On the contrary, Mercati, [251] physician to Clement VIII., at the end of the sixteenth century, appears to have been the first to maintain that what were regarded as thunderbolts were the arms of a primitive people unacquainted with the use of bronze or iron. Helwing [252] at Königsberg in 1717 showed the artificial character of the so-called thunderbolts, and in France, De Jussieu in 1723, and Mahudel, [253] about 1734, reproduced Mercati's view to the Académie des Inscriptions. In our own country, Dr. Plot, in his "History of Staffordshire" [254] (1686), also recognized the true character of these relics; and, citing an axe of stone made of speckled flint ground to an edge, says that either the Britons or Romans, or both, made use of such axes; and adds that "how they might be fastened to a helve may be seen in the Museum Ashmoleanum, where there are several Indian ones of the like kind fitted up in the same order as when formerly used." Dr. Plot's views were not, however, accepted by all his countrymen, for in the *Philosophical Transactions of the Royal Society*, [255] we find Dr. Lister regarding unmistakeable stone weapons as having been fashioned naturally and without any artifice. Some of the old German [256] authors have written long dissertations about these stone hatchets and axes under the name of Ceraunia, and given representations of various forms, which were known as *Malleus fulmineus*, *Cuneus fulminis*, Donnerstein, Strahlhammer, &c. Aldrovandus says that these stones are usually about five inches long and three wide, of a substance like flint, some so hard that a file will not touch them. About the centre of gravity of the stone is usually a hole an inch in diameter, quite round. They all imitate in form a hammer, a wedge, or an axe, or some such instrument, with a hole to receive a haft, so that some think them not to be thunderbolts, but iron implements petrified by time. But many explode such an opinion, and relate how such stones have been found under trees and houses struck by lightning; and assert that trustworthy persons were present, and saw them dug out, after the lightning had struck. [257] Kentmann informs us how, in the month of May, 1561, there was dug out at Torgau such a bolt projected by thunder. It was five inches long, and of a stone harder than basalt, which in some parts of Germany was used instead of anvils. He also relates how near Jülich another stone was driven by thunder through an enormous oak, and was then dug up. Aldrovandus gives a highly philosophical view as to the formation of these stones. He regards them as due to an admixture of a certain exhalation of thunder and lightning with metallic matter, chiefly in dark clouds, which is coagulated by the circumfused moisture and conglutinated into a mass (like flour with water), and subsequently indurated by heat, like a brick.

Georgius [258] Agricola draws a distinction between the *Brontia* and the *Ceraunia*. The former, he says, is like the head of a tortoise, but has stripes upon it, the latter is smooth and without stripes. The *Brontia* seems to be a fossil echinus, and the *Ceraunia* a stone celt, but both are thunderbolts. Going a little further back, we find Marbodæus, [259] Bishop of Rennes, who died in the year 1123, and who wrote a metrical work concerning gems, ascribing the following origin and virtues to the *Ceraunius*:——

"Ventorum rabie cum turbidus æstuat äer,

Cum tonat horrendum, cum fulgurat igneus æther,

Nubibus elisus cœlo cadit ille lapillus.

Cujus apud Græcos extat de fulmine nomen:

Illis quippe locis, quos constat fulmine tactos,

Iste lapis tantum reperiri posse putatur,

Unde κεράυνιος est Græco sermone vocatus:

Nam quod nos fulmen, Græci dixere κεραυνὸν.

Qui caste gerit hune à fulmine non ferietur,

Nec domus aut villæ, quibus affuerit lapis ille:

Sed neque navigio per flumina vel mare vectus,

Turbine mergetur, nec fulmine percutietur:

Ad causas etiam, vincendaque prælia prodest,

Et dulces somnos, et dulcia somnia præstat."

It was not, however, purely from the belief of his own day that Marbodæus derived this catalogue of the virtues of the Cerauniæ, but from the pages of writers of a much earlier date. Pliny, [260] giving an account of the precious stones known as Cerauniæ, quotes an earlier author still, Sotacus, who, to use the words of Philemon Holland's translation, "hath set downe two kinds more of Ceraunia, to wit, the blacke and the red, saying that they do resemble halberds or axeheads. And by his saying, the blacke, such especially as bee round withall, are endued with this vertue, that by the meanes of them, cities may be forced, and whole navies at sea discomfited; and these (forsooth) be called [261] Betuli, whereas the long ones be named properly Cerauniæ." Pliny goes on to say, "that there is one more Ceraunia yet, but very geason [262] it is, and hard to be found, which the Parthian magicians set much store by, and they only can find it, for that it is no where to bee had than in a place which hath been shot with a thunderbolt." There is a very remarkable passage in Suetonius [263] illustrative of this belief among the Romans. After relating one prodigy, which was interpreted as significant of the accession of Galba to the purple, he records that, "shortly afterwards lightning fell in a lake in Cantabria and twelve axes were found, a by no means ambiguous omen of Empire." The twelve axes were regarded as referring to those of the twelve lictors, and were therefore portentous; but their being found where the lightning fell would seem to have been considered a natural occurrence, except so far as related to the number. It appears by no means improbable that if the lake could be now identified, some ancient pile settlement might be found to have existed on its shores.

The exact period when Sotacus, the most ancient of these authorities, wrote is not known, but he was among the earliest of Greek authors who treated of stones, and is cited by Apollonius Dyscolus, and Solinus, as well as by Pliny. We cannot be far wrong in assigning him to an age at least two thousand years before our time, and yet at that remote period the use of these stone "halberds or axeheads" had so long ceased in Greece, that when found they were regarded as of superhuman origin and invested with magical virtues. We have already seen that flint arrow-heads were mounted, probably as charms, in Etruscan necklaces, and we shall subsequently see that superstitions, almost similar to those relating to celts, have been attached to stone arrow-heads in various countries.

To return from the superstitious veneration attaching to them, to the objects themselves. The materials [264] of which celts in Great Britain are usually formed are flint, chert, clay-slate, porphyry, quartzite, felstone, serpentine, and various kinds of greenstone, and of metamorphic rocks. M. A. Damour, [265] in his "Essays on the Composition of Stone Hatchets, Ancient and Modern," gives the following list of materials: quartz, agate, flint, jasper, obsidian, fibrolite, jade, jadeite, chloromelanite, amphibolite, aphanite, diorite, saussurite, and staurotide; but even to these many other varieties of rock might be added.

The material most commonly in use in the southern and eastern parts of Britain was flint derived from the chalk; in the north and west, on the contrary, owing to the scarcity of flint, different hard metamorphic and eruptive rocks were more frequently employed, not on account of any superior qualities, but simply from being more accessible. So far as general character is concerned, stone celts or hatchets may be divided into three classes, which I propose to treat separately, as follows:—

- 1. Those merely chipped out in a more or less careful manner, and not ground or polished;
- 2. Those which, after being fashioned by chipping, have been ground or polished at the edge only; and
- 3. Those which are more or less ground or polished, not only at the edge, but over the whole surface.

In describing them I propose to term the end opposite to the cutting edge, the butt-end; the two principal surfaces, which are usually convex, I shall speak of as the faces. These are either bounded by, or merge in, what I shall call the sides, according as these sides are sharp, rounded, or flat. In the figures the celts are all engraved on the scale of half an inch to the inch, or half linear measure, and are presented in front and side-view, with a section beneath.

CHAPTER IV.
CHIPPED OR ROUGH-HEWN CELTS.

Celts which have been merely chipped into form, and left unground, even at the edge, are of frequent occurrence in England, especially in those counties where flint is abundant. They are not, however, nearly so common in collections of antiquities as those which have been ground either wholly or in part; and this, no doubt, arises from the fact that many of them are so rudely chipped out, that it requires a practised eye to recognize them, when associated, as they usually are, with numerous other flints of natural and accidental forms. No doubt many of these chipped celts, especially where, from the numbers discovered, there appears to have been a manufactory on the spot, were intended to be eventually ground; but there are some which are roughly chipped, and which may possibly have been used as agricultural implements without further preparation; and others, the edges of which are so minutely and symmetrically chipped, that they appear to be adapted for use as hatchets or cutting-tools without requiring to be farther sharpened by grinding. There are others again, as already mentioned at page 32, the edges of which have been produced by the intersection of two facets only, and are yet so symmetrical and sharp, that whetting their edge on a grindstone would be superfluous.

Of this character I possess several specimens from Suffolk, of which one from Mildenhall is engraved in Fig. 12. As will be observed, the edge is nearly semicircular, but it is nevertheless formed merely by the intersection of two facets, each resulting from a single chip or flake of flint having been removed. I have in my collection another hatchet from the same place, which is so curiously similar to this in all respects, that it was probably made by the same hand. I am not, however, aware whether the two were found together.

There is in these implements a peculiar curvature on one face, as shown in the side view, which, I think, must be connected with the method by which they were attached to their handles. From the form, it seems probable that they were mounted as adzes, with the edge transversely to the line of the handle, and not as axes. I have a more roughly-chipped specimen of the same type, found near Wanlud's Bank, Luton, Beds, by Mr. W. Whitaker, F.R.S., in which the same curvature of one of the faces is observable. It is not so conspicuous in a larger implement of the same class, also from Mildenhall (Fig. 13), but this likewise is slightly curved longitudinally. In the Christy Collection is another, found at Burwell,

Cambridgeshire, of the same type. It is rounded at the butt, but nearly square at the cutting edge, which is formed by the junction of two facets, from which flakes have been struck off. I have seen others of the same character from near the Bartlow Hills, Cambs, and from Sussex. Others, from 4 3/4 to 6 inches in length, from Burwell, Wicken, and Bottisham Fens, are preserved in the museum of the Cambridge Antiquarian Society, and in my own collection. In the Greenwell collection is a specimen 7 3/4 inches long, from Burnt Fen. I have also a French implement of this kind from the neighbourhood of Abbeville.

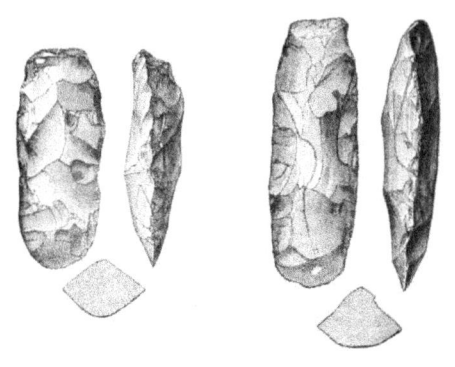

Fig. 12.—Near Mildenhall. 1/2

Fig. 13.—Near Mildenhall. 1/2

Implements with this peculiar edge, are found in Denmark. Indeed, the edges of the common form of Kjökken-mödding axes [266] are usually produced in the same manner, by the intersection of two facets, each formed by a single blow, though the resulting edge is generally almost straight.

Closely approaching this Danish form, is that of a celt of brown flint, shown in Fig. 14, and found near Thetford by the late Mr. J. W. Flower, F.G.S., with one face nearly flat, and the edge formed by a single transverse facet. The implements, however, of this type, with the chisel edge, are rarely met with in this country; and, generally speaking, axes similar to those which occur in such numbers in the Danish Kjökken-möddings and Coast-finds are of very rare occurrence elsewhere. I have, however, a small nearly-triangular hatchet of the Danish type, and with the sides bruised in the same manner (probably with a view of preventing their cutting the ligaments by which the instruments were attached to their handles, or, possibly, to prevent their cutting the hand when held), which I found in the circular encampment known as Maiden Bower, near Dunstable.

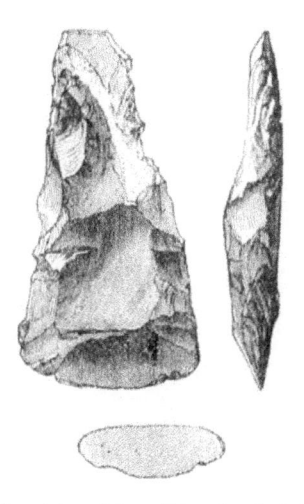

Fig. 14.—Near Thetford. 1/2

Hatchets of this type have also been found in some numbers in the valley of the Somme, at Montiers, near Amiens, as well as in the neighbourhood of Pontlevoy (Loir et Cher), in the Camp de Catenoy (Oise), and in Champagne. [267] I have also specimens from the neighbourhood of Pressigny-le-Grand and of Châtellerault. It would therefore appear that this form of implement is not confined to maritime districts, and that it can hardly be regarded as merely a weight for a fishing-line, [268] as has been suggested by Professor Steenstrup. [269]

A few of the large Polynesian adzes of basalt have their edges produced by a similar method of chipping and are left unground.

Capt. G. V. Smith [270] has experimented in Jutland with the Kjökken-mödding axes, and has cut down fir-trees of seven inches diameter with them. The trees for Mr. Sehested's [271] wooden hut were cut down and trimmed with stone hatchets ground at the edge.

In the British Museum are several roughly-chipped flints that seem to present a peculiar type. They are from about 4 to 6 inches long, nearly flat on one face, coarsely worked to an almost semicircular bevel edge at one end, and with a broad rounded notch on each side, as if to enable them to be secured to a handle, possibly as agricultural implements. They formed part of the Durden collection, and were found in the neighbourhood of Blandford.

Another and more common form of roughly-chipped celt is that of which an example is given in Fig. 15, from my own collection. It was found at Oving, near Chichester, and was given me by Professor W. Boyd Dawkins, F.R.S. The edge, in this instance, is formed in the same manner, by the intersection of two facets, but the section is nearly triangular. If attached to a handle it was probably after the manner of an adze rather than of an axe. I have a smaller specimen of the same type, and another, flatter and more neatly chipped, 7 3/4 inches long, from the Cambridge Fens.

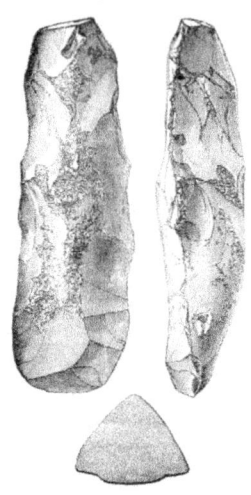

Fig. 15.—Oving, near Chichester. 1/2

I have seen implements of much the same form which have been found at Bemerton, near Salisbury (Blackmore Museum); at St. Mary Bourne, Andover; at Santon Downham, near Thetford; at Little Dunham, Norfolk; near Ware; and near Canterbury; but the edge is sometimes formed by several chips, in the same manner as the sides, and not merely by the junction of two planes of fracture.

There are also smaller rough celts with the subtriangular section, of which I have a good example, 4 1/2 inches long, found by Mr. W. Whitaker, F.R.S., near Maiden Castle, Dorsetshire. It is curiously similar to one that I found near Store Lyngby, in Denmark.

The same form occurs in France.

Other roughly-chipped implements are to be found in various parts of Britain, lying scattered over the fields, some of them so rude that they may be regarded as merely flints chipped into form, to serve some temporary purpose; as wasters thrown away as useless by those who were trying to manufacture stone implements which were eventually destined to be ground; or as the rude implements of the merest savage. Certainly some of the stone hatchets of the Australian natives are quite as rude or ruder, and yet we find them carefully provided with handles. In Hertfordshire, I have myself picked up several such implements; and they have been found in considerable numbers in the neighbourhood of Icklingham in Suffolk, near Andover, and in other places. An adze-like celt of this kind (4 1/2 inches) is recorded from Wishmoor, [272] Surrey. Were proper search made for them, there are probably not many districts where it would be fruitless. In Ireland they appear to be rare; but numerous roughly-shaped implements of this class have been found in Poitou and in other parts of France. They are also met with in Belgium and Denmark.

As has already been suggested, it is by no means improbable that some of these ruder unpolished implements were employed in agriculture, like the so-called shovels and hoes of flint of North America, described by Professor Rau. I have a flat celt-like implement about 6 1/2 inches long and 3 inches broad, found in Cayuga County, New York, which, though unground, has its broad end beautifully polished on both faces, apparently by friction of the silty soil in which it has been used as a hoe. It is, as Professor Rau has pointed out in other cases, slightly striated in the direction in which the implement penetrated the ground. [273] I have also an Egyptian chipped flint hoe from Qûrnah, polished in a precisely similar manner. It is doubtful whether many of the rough implements from the neighbourhood of Thebes are Neolithic or Palæolithic. [274]

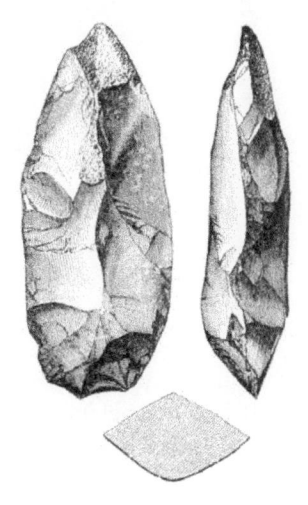

Fig. 16.—Near Newhaven. 1/2

The implement represented in Fig. 16, rude as it is, is more symmetrical and more carefully chipped than many of this class. I found it, with several other worked flints, on the surface of the soil in a field between Newhaven and Telscombe, Sussex, where had formerly stood a barrow, one of a group of four, the positions of which are shown on the Ordnance Map, though they are now all levelled to the ground. It is, of course, possible that such an implement may have been merely blocked out, with the intention of finishing it by subsequent chipping and grinding, and that it was not intended for use in its present condition; or it may possibly have been deposited in the tumulus as a votive offering, or in compliance with some ancient custom, as suggested hereafter. (See p. 282.) It will be observed that the original crust of the block of flint from which it was fashioned is left at the butt end. A somewhat similar specimen, from the neighbourhood of Hastings, and another from a tumulus at Seaford are figured in the *Sussex Archæological Collections* [275]; and I have one from the Thames at Battersea, and others from Suffolk and from the Cambridge Fens. The late Sir Joseph Prestwich, F.R.S., found one of the same character at Shoreham, near Sevenoaks, and the late Mr. J. F. Lucas had another, 4 inches long, from Arbor Low, Derbyshire. A small chipped celt was found in a barrow at Pelynt, [276] Cornwall.

Fig. 17.—Near Dunstable. 1/2

Fig. 18.—Burwell Fen. 1/2

Fig. 17 shows an implement found by my eldest son, at the foot of the Downs, near Dunstable. It has been chipped from a piece of tabular flint, and can hardly have been intended to be ground or polished. It is more than usually oval in form, and in general character approaches very closely to the ovate implements from the River gravels; from the manner in which it is fashioned, and from its being found in company with worked flints unquestionably belonging to the Surface Period, I regard it, however, as of Neolithic and not of Palæolithic age. [277] Another implement of much the same form, found near Grime's Graves, in Norfolk, [278] has been figured by Canon Greenwell, F.R.S. Others were found at Cissbury, [279] Sussex, and at Dunmer, [280] and near Ellisfield Camp, Hants. Mr. C. Monkman had another, 5 3/4 inches long, and rather narrower in its proportions, found at Bempton, Yorkshire. I have implements of much the same shape, though larger, from some of the ancient flint-implement manufactories of Belgium.

The next specimen (Fig. 18) is from Burwell Fen, Cambridge, and is in my own collection. It is of beautiful workmanship, most skilfully and symmetrically chipped, and thinner than is usual with implements of this class. The edge is perfectly regular, and has been formed by delicate secondary chipping. So sharp is it, that I should almost doubt its ever having been intended to be ground or polished. That a sufficient edge for cutting purposes could be obtained by careful chipping without grinding, seems to be evinced by the fact that some stone celts, the whole body of which has been polished, are found with the edge merely chipped and not ground. No doubt when these blades were new, they were polished all over; but as the edge became broken away by wear, it would appear as if the owners had contented themselves by chipping out a fresh edge, without taking the trouble of grinding it. Still it must be borne in mind, that a vast amount of labour in grinding was saved by the implement being brought as nearly to the required shape as possible by chipping only, so that the circumstance of polished celts having unground edges may be due to merely accidental causes.

Fig. 19.—Mildenhall. 1/2

Fig. 20.—Bottisham Fen. 1/2

These neatly-chipped flint celts are found also in Ireland. I have one of the same section as Fig. 18, but longer and narrower. It was found in Ulster. I have also specimens from Poitou.

They are of occasional but rare occurrence with this section in Denmark.

A neatly-chipped flint hatchet of small size and remarkably square at the edge is shown in Fig. 19. It was found at Mildenhall, Suffolk, and is in the Greenwell collection, now Dr. Sturge's. There are traces of grinding on some portions of the faces. In the same collection is another hatchet of the same character from Ganton Wold, Yorkshire, the edge of which is ground. I have an unground example of this type from Lakenheath.

The original of Fig. 20 is in the Museum of the Cambridge Antiquarian Society, and was found in Bottisham Fen. In neatness of workmanship it much resembles the last; but it is slightly curved longitudinally, and has the inner face more ridged than the outer. It was probably intended to be mounted as an adze.

I have a beautiful implement of the same general form, but nearly flat on one face, found in Burwell Fen. It has been manufactured from a large flake.

The hatchet engraved as Fig. 21, was found in ploughing near Bournemouth, and was kindly brought under my notice by the late Mr. Albert Way, F.S.A. Its principal peculiarity is the inward curvature of the sides, rendering it somewhat narrower in the middle than at either end. Its greatest expansion is, however, at what appears to have been intended for the cutting edge, so that at this end its outline much resembles that of one of the Scandinavian forms. The sides, however, instead of being square are sharp. The specimen from Burwell Fen, Fig. 36, exhibits nearly the same form, but has the edge ground. A thinner specimen, also from Burwell Fen, and in the Museum of the Cambridge Antiquarian Society, is unground. It is 5 3/8 inches long, 2 1/8 inches broad at one end and 1 1/2 inches at the other, but only 1 1/4 inches broad towards the middle of the blade. Mr. T. Layton, F.S.A., possesses a celt found in the Thames, that presents this peculiarity in a still more exaggerated manner. It is 6 3/4 inches long, 2 3/4 inches broad at one end and 2 1/4 inches at the other, but only 1 1/2 inches in width at the middle of the blade.

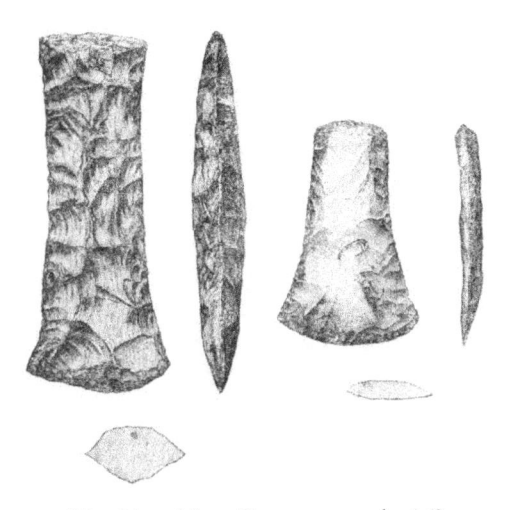

Fig. 21.—Near Bournemouth. 1/2

Fig. 22.—Thetford. 1/2

A remarkably elegant specimen of similar character is shown in Fig. 22. It was found on the surface at Thetford Warren, Suffolk, and was formerly in the collection of Mr. J. W. Flower, F.G.S., but now in mine. It is of grey flint, and has been formed from a large flake, a considerable portion of the flat face of which has been left untouched by the subsequent working. All along the sides, however, as well as at the ends, it has been chipped on both faces to a symmetrical form. The outer surface of the original flake has almost entirely disappeared during the process of manufacturing the adze, for such it appears to have been rather than an axe. The form is suggestive of the tool having been copied from one in metal, and is very like that of the flat bronze celts. It may belong to the transitional period, when bronze was coming into use, but was still too scarce to have superseded flint.

The commonest form of the symmetrically-chipped but unground celts is that shown in Fig. 23. The particular specimen engraved is in my own collection; and, like so many other antiquities of this class, came from the Fen district, having been found in Reach Fen in 1852.

It is equally convex on both faces, and, from its close resemblance in form to so many of the polished celts, it was probably destined for grinding. I have another of the same form, 6 1/2 inches long, from the neighbourhood of Thetford.

A magnificent specimen of this class, but wider in proportion to its length, found near Mildenhall, is preserved in the Christy Collection.

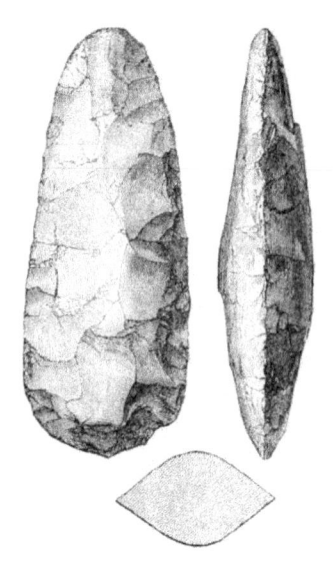

Fig. 23.—Reach Fen, Cambridge. 1/2

I have a very fine specimen 9 inches long, from the Thames, and others 6 1/2 and 5 1/4 inches long, of a wider form, and delicately chipped all round, from Burwell Fen. The late Mr. James Carter, of Cambridge, had one of the narrower kind, 9 inches long, found at Blunt's Hill, near Witham, Essex. The same form, with numerous modifications, was found in the pits at Cissbury, [281] which will shortly be described. One about 8 1/4 inches long, in outline like Fig. 20, was found in Anglesea. [282] Another 9 1/2 inches long, was found near Farnham, [283] Dorset.

One of the most remarkable discoveries of celts of this character, is that of which I have seen a MS. memorandum in the hands of the late Mrs. Dickinson, [284] of Hurstpierpoint, Sussex, who herself had four of the implements. According to this account, a man digging flints on Clayton Hill, on the South Downs, Sussex, in 1803, found near the windmill, just beneath the sod, and lying side by side, eight celts of grey flint, chipped into form and not ground. One of these was as much as 13 inches long. Those in Mrs. Dickinson's collection were—(1) 11 3/4 long by 3 1/2 broad and 2 1/8 thick, (2) 9 1/2 by 3 1/4 by 1 3/4, (3) 7 1/2 by 3 1/8 by 2 1/8, and (4) 6 1/2 by 3 by 1 5/8. Four such, 7 1/4 to 9 inches long, chipped only, were found buried in a row at Teddington. [285]

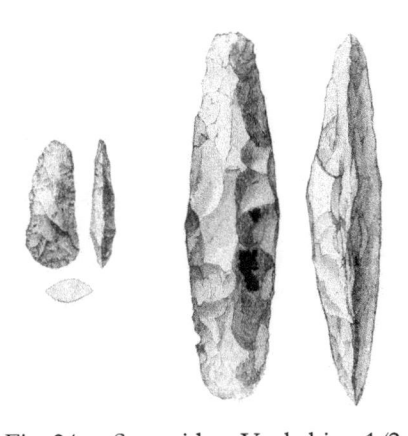

Fig. 24.—Scamridge, Yorkshire. 1/2

Fig. 25.—Forest of Bere, near Horndean. 1/2

These deposits seem to have been intentional. "In the Hervey Islands [286] it was customary on the eve of battle to bury the stone adzes of the family in some out-of-the-way place. Beds of these (in heathen times) priceless treasures are still occasionally discovered. About a dozen adzes, large and small, were arranged in a circle, the points being towards the centre. The knowledge of the localities where to find them was carefully handed down from one generation to another." At Northmavine, [287] Orkney, seven celts were found, arranged in a circle with the points towards the centre. From two to eight flint axes are sometimes found together in Denmark, and by Dr. Sophus Müller [288] are regarded as funeral offerings or ex-votos.

Such roughly-chipped celts have been found in immense numbers in the neighbourhood of Eastbourne. A large collection of them is in the Museum at Lewes. I have seen a large celt of this section, but with flatter edge [289] and straighter sides, which was found in peat at Thatcham, near Newbury, Berks. Of the same class is a celt found near Norwich, engraved in the *Geologist*. [290] I have seen several other specimens from Norfolk, as well as from Wilts, Cambridgeshire, Dorsetshire, and other counties. Some specimens from the neighbourhood of Grime's Graves, Norfolk, have been figured. [291] Flint celts of this class are occasionally found in Yorkshire, but the edge is usually less round in outline than Fig. 23. In some cases it is straight, like Fig. 19. Some of those from Yorkshire are extremely small, as will be seen by Fig. 24, from Scamridge, in the North Riding. I have other specimens, 2 and 2 1/2 inches long and about 1 1/2 inches broad, from the Yorkshire

Wolds. I have also one of the ordinary form from Lough Neagh, Ireland; but it has been slightly ground near the edge.

Though rare in Ireland, flint celts of this form and character are of common occurrence in France [292] and Belgium. Many such have been found at Spiennes, near Mons, where there appears to have been a manufactory, as already mentioned; and I have specimens from Amiens (including one from Montiers, 10 inches), from various parts of Poitou, and from the Seine, at Paris. A broad, thin instrument of this class, made of Silurian schist, and found in the dolmen of Bernac, Charente, [293] is engraved by De Rochebrune.

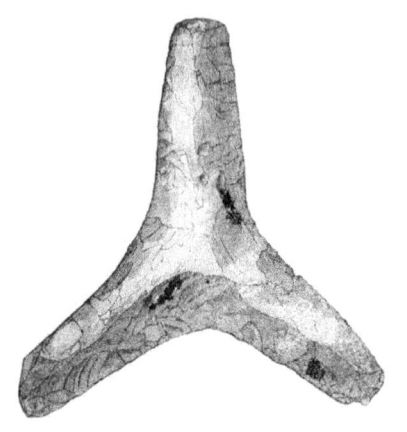

Fig. 25A.—Isle of Wight. 1/2

They occur also in Denmark and Sweden in considerable numbers.

A slightly different and narrower form of implement is shown in Fig. 25, which first appeared in the *Archæological Journal*, vol. xx., p. 371. The original is of yellow flint, and was found in the Forest of Bere, Hampshire. I may add that I have picked up several in the parish of Abbot's Langley, Herts. One like Fig. 25, but smaller, found at Bedmond, [294] has been figured. A narrow specimen (6 inches, like Fig. 25) from Aldbourne, Hungerford, is in the collection of Mr. J. W. Brooke, of Marlborough.

Many of the other forms of polished celts occur in the unground condition, of the same shape, for instance, as Fig. 35. It is needless to multiply illustrations, though I must mention a remarkable instrument of this character preserved in the Greenwell collection. It is of flint 6 1/4 inches long, and in outline closely resembling Fig. 35. It is, however, much curved longitudinally, the curve being more rapid towards the butt-end, which is also somewhat thickened. The chord of the rather irregular arc thus produced is 1/2 an inch. Such a tool can only have been mounted as an adze or hoe with the concave face towards the helve. It was found at Kenny Hill, Mildenhall.

A singular instrument chipped out of flint, like three celts conjoined into one, so as to form a sort of tribrach, is said to have been found in the Isle of Wight. It is shown in Fig. 25A, kindly lent by the Society of Antiquaries. [295] In form it is of much the same character as some of the implements from Yucatan, [296] and from Vladimir, [297] Russia. It may be compared with some examples of strange forms from Honduras. [298]

I have already spoken of the method in which these and other allied forms of stone implements were manufactured; but, before quitting the subject of chipped or rough-hewn celts, I must devote a little space to the interesting discovery made by General Pitt Rivers, F.R.S., on the site of an ancient manufactory of flint implements, among which celts predominated, within the entrenchment known as Cissbury, near Worthing, where Colonel Ayre, R.A., [299] found, some years ago, a very perfect flint celt. The entrenchment has now been proved to be of more recent date than the pits shortly to be mentioned.

Accounts of the investigations of General Pitt Rivers and of some subsequently carried on by Mr. Ernest Willett are given in the *Archæologia*, [300] from which most of the following particulars are abstracted. Canon Greenwell, F.R.S., also assisted at a part of the exploration, and some of my illustrations are taken from specimens in his collection. The earthwork, of irregularly oval form, surrounds the summit of a chalk hill, near Worthing, in Sussex, on the western slope of which, within the rampart, are some fifty funnel or cup-shaped depressions, some of small size, but others about seventy feet in diameter and twelve feet in depth. At the base of these there seem to have been originally shafts sunk into the chalk, and similar shafts have now been found beneath the rampart. Many of these were opened, and were found to contain, amongst the rubble with which they were partially filled, well-chipped celts and ruder implements, quantities of splinters and minute chippings of flint; flakes, some worked on one or both faces; some few boring-tools and scrapers; and many stones that had been used as hammers. Most of the flints had become quite white on the surface, as is often the case when they rest in a porous soil. Parts of antlers of red deer, remains of horse, goat, boar, and ox (*Bos longifrons*), oyster and a few other marine shells and snail-shells, as well as fragments of charcoal and rude pottery, were also found. At the base of one of the pits explored by Mr. Willett, galleries were found of precisely the same character as those at Grime's Graves, near Brandon, and at Spiennes, near Mons, in Belgium, which I have already described, and it is evident that they were excavated for the purpose of procuring flint, to be chipped into the form of implements upon the spot. It does not appear certain that the portions of antler which were found had been used, as in the other cases, as picks for digging in the chalk; but, possibly, some of the roughly-chipped flints, adapted for being held in the hand, [301] and not unlike in form to the chopper-like flints from the far older deposit in the cave of Le Moustier, Dordogne, [302] may have been thus used, or as wedges to split the chalk. This is by no means inconsistent with their having been originally flints partially trimmed into shape, in order to be made into celts, and used for a secondary purpose when it was found that they were not adapted for what they were at first intended to be. In chipping them out, the part of the nodule best suited for being held in the hand would be thus grasped, and the opposite edge be trimmed by the hammer, and in this manner the semblance of a chopper would be produced in what was merely an inchoate celt. I have found flints on the Sussex Downs, with one side trimmed in much the same manner as the Cissbury specimens, but which, from their form, can hardly have been intended for "choppers."

Looking at a series of the worked flints from Cissbury, exclusive of flakes and mere rough blocks, the general *facies* is such as to show that the ordinary forms of celts, or hatchets, were those at which, in the main, the workmen aimed. A small proportion of them are highly finished specimens, not improbably hidden away in the loose chalk when chipped out and accidentally left there. Others are broken; not, I think, in use, but in the process of manufacture. A great proportion are very rude, and ill-adapted for being ground. They are, in fact, such as may be regarded, if not as wasters, yet, at all events, as unmarketable; for it seems probable that at Cissbury, as well as at other manufactories of flint implements, they were produced, not for immediate use by those who made them, but to be bartered away for some other commodities. In Central America, [303] at the present day, the natives use cutting instruments of flint, which must, apparently, have been brought from a distance of four hundred miles; while, among the aborigines of Australia, [304] flints were articles of barter between distant tribes; and some of the chalcedony implements in the early Belgian caves are made of material presumed to have come from the south of France. Mr. W. H. Holmes, [305] has described an ancient quarry in the Indian territory, Missouri, from which chert was obtained and roughed out on the spot. Some of the rude forms exactly resemble the "turtle backs" of Trenton, by many regarded as palæolithic. The antiquity of the quarry does not, however, exceed two hundred years. Only a single fragment of a polished celt was found by General Pitt Rivers within the inclosure; though another was found by Lord Northesk in a pit that he subsequently opened. They are equally rare in proportion at Spiennes. This fact, and the absence of grinding-stones, also seem to show that the process of grinding was carried on elsewhere, in cases where a ground edge was required.

General Pitt Rivers suggests a question, whether the implements found at Cissbury belong to the Neolithic or Palæolithic age, and seems almost to regard the distinction between the implements of those two ages as founded merely on the minor point of whether they are chipped simply, or also polished. The associated fauna in this case is however purely Neolithic or, as Professor Boyd Dawkins would call it, Pre-historic; and whatever may be the case with a few of the specimens which resemble in form implements from the River Drift, the greater number are unmistakeably of forms such as are constantly found polished, and are undoubtedly Neolithic. Indeed, as already stated, a portion of at all events one polished specimen has been found in one of the pits. I need not, however, dwell longer on the circumstances of this discovery, nor on the speculations to which it may give rise, but will proceed to give illustrations of a few of the forms of implements found at Cissbury, referring for others to the memoirs already cited. A fine series of the implements has been presented to the Christy Collection, now in the British Museum.

One of the most highly-finished forms, of which, in all, a considerable number were found, is a long, narrow instrument, as shown in Fig. 26. So narrow and pointed are they, that General Pitt Rivers thought that they may have been intended to be used with the pointed end as spear-heads. Such instruments, however, are occasionally found with the broad end ground to an edge. It is also to be observed that this circular edge is generally more carefully chipped into form than the pointed butt, and was therefore considered of more importance.

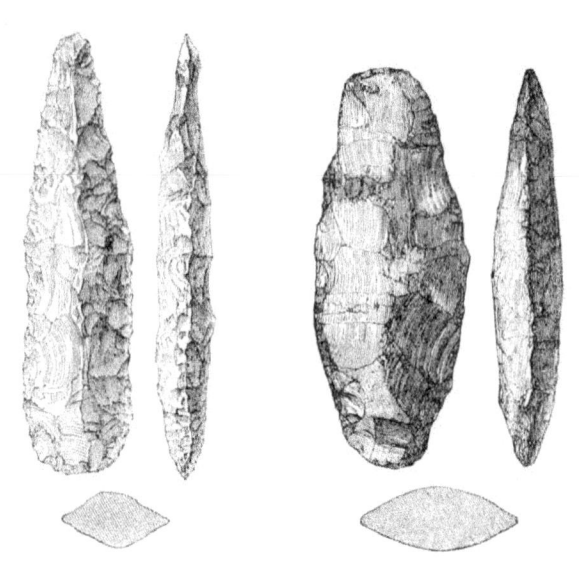

Fig. 26.—Cissbury. 1/2

Fig. 27.—Cissbury. 1/2

Another specimen is figured in the *Archæologia*; [306] and a narrow flint celt of this character, 5 1/4 inches long, found with a larger celt in a barrow in Hampshire, [307] is in the British Museum.

Another rough-hewn celt is shown in Fig. 27. Like several others, both from Cissbury and Spiennes, the two ends are almost similar in form, so that it is difficult to say at which extremity the cutting edge was intended to be. Possibly it was found convenient to fashion some of the implements, in the first instance, into this comparatively regular oval contour, and subsequently to chip an edge at whichever end seemed best adapted for the purpose. This instrument is not unlike that from the Forest of Bere, Fig. 25. Another from Cissbury, with more parallel sides, has been figured. [308] Others from the same place are like Figs. 16, 17, and 23, and like Fig. 35, though not ground at the edge.

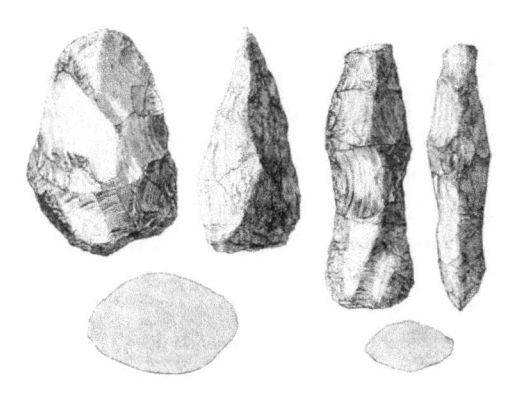

Fig. 28.—Cissbury. 1/2

Fig. 29.—Cissbury. 1/2

Others, again, but much fewer in number, are of a wedge-shaped form, with the thin end rounded. The specimen of this kind shown in Fig. 28 is in the Greenwell Collection, and is very symmetrical. The butt-end is considerably battered at one part, but not at its extremity; so that this bruising may possibly have been on the block of flint before the implement was chipped out. A less symmetrical specimen is figured by General Pitt Rivers, having the butt formed of the natural crust of the flint. That here engraved appears well adapted for holding in the hand, so as to be used as a kind of chopper: but the rounded edge is uninjured. Can it have been used as a wedge for splitting open the chalk? or is it to be regarded as a special form of implement? If so, it seems singular that, if such a form was in use in Britain, no specimens have hitherto been met with having the edge ground. I should be more satisfied as to the form being intentional and for a certain purpose, had it occurred elsewhere than among what is evidently the refuse of a manufactory; and yet a somewhat similar hand-tool is in use among the natives of Australia. A polished implement of analogous form is moreover shown in Fig. 83A. Two or three pointed implements, in form like Fig. 417, were found at Cissbury. Judging from shape alone, they might be regarded as being of Palæolithic age, but their surroundings prove them to be Neolithic.

Fig. 29 also forms part of the Greenwell Collection, and presents a very remarkable form, which, at first sight, has the appearance of being a chisel or hatchet, with a large tang, intended for insertion in a socket. The lower part is symmetrically chipped, like the cutting end of a narrow celt, with sharp sides, such as Fig. 26; but at a point a little more than half way along the blade, it rapidly expands, so as to have an almost circular section. Much as I am tempted to regard this as presenting a special type, I am almost convinced that the form is due rather to accident than design. It appears to me, that a piece of flint, partially chipped into shape for a larger and thicker celt, had been broken in the process of manufacture, and a second attempt had been made to convert it into a celt, this time of smaller size. The lower part of this was successfully chipped out, but on arriving at that portion of the blade where the section was nearly circular, the flint was either so refractory, or the projections on which blows could be administered to detach splinters were so small, that the manufacture was abandoned, not, however, before many blows had been fruitlessly struck, as the sides and projections of the face of the celt at this part are considerably battered.

Dr. C. B. Plowright has described a number of rough-hewn instruments of flint from what seems to have been the site of an ancient flint manufactory on Massingham Heath, in West Norfolk. He has figured several, including a wedge-formed implement like Fig. 28, and one of shoe-shape, not unlike a palæolithic form. [309]

An interesting instance of the discovery of a flint celt, merely chipped out, but associated with polished celts, and other objects, is that recorded in the *Archæologia*, [310] and Hoare's "Wiltshire." [311] In a barrow opened by Mr. W. Cunnington, in 1802, was a grave of oval form, containing a large skeleton lying on its back, and slightly on one side, and above it a smaller skeleton in a contracted posture. At the feet of the larger skeleton were more than three dozen perforated pins and other instruments of bone, and three celts of white flint, two of which were neatly polished, with a fine circular edge; and the third was "only chipped to the intended form and size." With these lay what was apparently a grinding stone to polish the celts or similar implements; and some grooved sandstones, like Fig. 185. About the legs were several boars' teeth perforated, and some cups made of hollow flints; near the breast was a flat circular stone, and a perforated stone axe, shown in Fig. 141, and two dozen more of the bone instruments. Some jet or cannel-coal beads and a ring of the same substance were also found, as well as a small bronze awl; but it is doubtful to which of the bodies this belonged.

It will subsequently be seen that perforated axes similar to that in this barrow are frequently associated with bronze daggers, so that we seem to have, in this instance, evidence of the contemporaneous use of unground, polished, and perforated stone axes at a period when bronze was at all events not unknown in this country.

If the chipped celt is to be regarded as unfinished, it may be that the survivors, in burying it, together with the grinding and polishing stones, in company with the original occupant of the barrow, entertained a belief that in some future state of existence he might be at leisure to complete the process of polishing.

Very roughly-chipped pieces of flint, apparently blocked-out celts, are occasionally found in barrows. Two such, 8 inches by 3 1/2, and 7 by 3 1/2, from a barrow near Alfriston, Sussex, examined by Dr. Mantell, are in the British Museum. They may have been deposited under a similar belief, or as votive offerings. Possibly this custom of placing roughly-chipped implements, like, for instance, Fig. 16, in graves, may be a "survival" from the times when warriors or hunters were buried with the arms or weapons they had worn when living, and the burials which they accompany may belong to a late part of the stone period. It is worthy of notice that in the cemetery of Hallstatt, which belongs to a date when iron was just coming into use, many of the ornaments appear to have been manufactured expressly for funereal purposes, being like the gold wreaths in Etruscan tombs, almost too light and fragile to be worn by the living. In Denmark, however, the weapons of flint which accompanied interments seem usually to have been highly finished and perfect.

Celts, merely chipped into form and unground, occur also in other kinds of stone. They are, however, much rarer than those of flint. One of iron-stone, from Sussex, 8 inches long and 3 1/4 wide at the broad end, is in the Blackmore Museum. A very fine specimen from Anglesey, formed of felstone, is preserved in the Museum of Economic Geology, in Jermyn Street. I have a fragment of one in greenstone, found by Mr. R. D. Darbishire, F.G.S., at Dwygyfylchi, Carnarvonshire, and another of felstone, extremely rude, found by him on Pen-maen-mawr. Some rough celts of greenstone, found in barrows near St. Just, Cornwall, are in the Truro Museum.

In Ireland, where flint celts are comparatively rare, those in the unpolished condition appear to be relatively more abundant in that material than in other rocks. In the large collection of the Royal Irish Academy there are but few of either class, and I certainly have seen some hundreds of Irish stone celts with the edges ground, for one in which it had been left as originally chipped out.

In France the chipped celts of flint are not uncommon, but those of other materials are extremely rare.

In Denmark, and Sweden also, the unpolished celts of flint are abundant, but principally of a class not found in Britain, with square sides and neatly worked wavy angles. Some of the other forms, however, also occur, as has been already mentioned. In other materials than flint they are almost unknown.

In North America the roughly-chipped hatchets are scarce, but are more common in flint or horn-stone than in other materials.

In Western Australia, where the hatchets are made of rough splinters of basalt and of silicious rocks, grinding seems but little practised. Hatchets ground at the edge seem more common in Northern Australia. It is, however, by no means improbable that in many countries the ruder forms of stone implements have to a great extent escaped observation. I much doubt whether the stone blades of the Australian hatchets, one of which is engraved in Fig. 106, would, if detached from their handles, be thought worthy of notice by the large majority of travellers, or even be regarded as of human workmanship.

However this may be, it appears that in Western Europe the practice of grinding the edges of hatchets and adzes was more universal in the case of those formed of other stones than flint, than with those of purely silicious material. This circumstance rather strengthens the probability of some of the flint implements which are found in the unground condition, having been destined for use in that state, as was the case with the North American hoe-like implements already mentioned.

It seems almost demonstrable that some at least of these unpolished celts must be among the earliest of the Neolithic implements of this country; for though, in Neolithic times, some naturally-shaped stones have been sharpened for use by grinding only, yet the art of chipping stone into shape must in all probability have preceded that of grinding or polishing its edges. So far as at present ascertained, the practice of sharpening stone tools on the grindstone was unknown in Palæolithic times; and, assuming the occupation of this country to have been continuous, into Neolithic times the transition from one stage of civilization to the other has still to be traced. Under any circumstances, we have as yet, in Britain, no means at command for assigning with certainty any of these roughly-chipped forms to an antiquity more remote than that of the carefully finished celts with their edges sharpened by grinding, though in all probability some of them must date back to a far remoter period.

We have, on the contrary, good evidence that whatever may have been the date when the roughly-chipped implements of this form were first manufactured, they continued to be chipped out in much the same manner at a time when the practice of sharpening by grinding was well known. Though some may have been used without being ground, they bear, for the most part, the same relation to the finished forms, as the blade of steel rough from the forge bears to the polished knife.

CHAPTER V.
CELTS GROUND AT THE EDGE ONLY.

The implements belonging to this class testify to a greater amount of pains having been bestowed upon them than on those which have been chipped only; yet the labour in grinding them has been far less than with those which are polished over their entire surface. There are some which occupy an intermediate position between those ground at the edge only, and those which are polished all over; inasmuch as not only has their edge been sharpened by grinding, but the principal asperities both of the sides and faces have been removed in a similar manner, yet without polishing anything like the entire surface. These may be classed among polished celts; and, indeed, any distinction that can be drawn between celts partly and wholly polished is imaginary rather than real, as it is only a difference in degree. The specimens of this class which I have selected for engraving present, as a rule, some slight peculiarity either in form or in other respects.

The first of these, Fig. 30, is remarkable for the extremely rude manner in which it is chipped out, and for the small portion of its surface which is polished. So rude, indeed, is it, that an inexperienced eye would hardly accept it as being of human workmanship. The edge, however, has unmistakeably been ground. Possibly the implement may have been chipped out from a fragment of a larger polished celt, of which the edge had been preserved. It is of flint, quite whitened by exposure, and was found by myself upon the Downs, near Eastbourne, on September 12th, 1852, being the first stone implement I ever discovered. I have since found a similar but larger celt in a field of my own at Abbot's Langley, Herts. It is 4 1/2 inches long, and the edge has been intentionally blunted by grinding, so that it was possibly a battle-axe. I have some other specimens which appear to have been made from fragments of larger polished celts. One of these, found near Icklingham, 2 1/4 inches wide and 2 3/4 inches long, is almost pear-shaped in outline, but truncated at the butt, where it is about an inch wide. I have several similar implements from France and Belgium, the butt-ends of which are battered, as if they had been used as wedges.

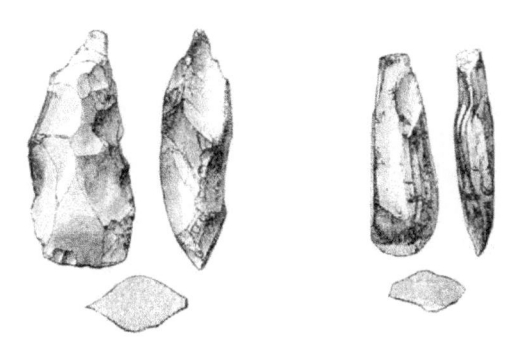

Fig. 30.—Downs near Eastbourne. 1/2

Fig. 31.—Culford, Suffolk. 1/2

The original of Fig. 31 is curious in another aspect, it having been shaped, with the exception of the edge, entirely by nature, and not by art. The tendency of certain kinds of flint to split up into more or less regular prisms by assuming a sort of columnar structure, much like that which is exhibited by starch in drying, is well known. The maker of this implement has judiciously selected one of these prisms, which required no more than a moderate amount of grinding at one end to convert it into a neat and useful tool. It was found at Culford, in Suffolk, and formerly belonged to Mr. Warren, of Ixworth, but is now in my own collection.

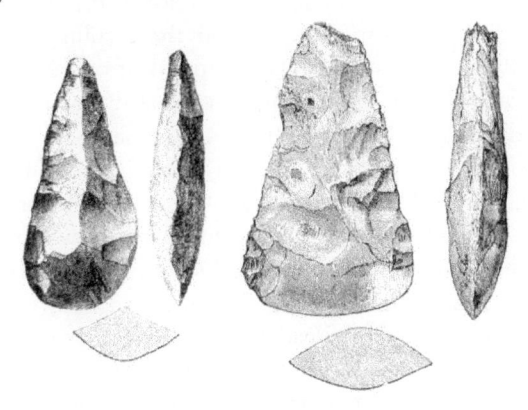

Fig. 32.—Near Mildenhall, Suffolk. 1/2

Fig. 33.—Sawdon, North Yorkshire. 1/2

The celt represented in Fig. 32 is also mine, and was found in the same neighbourhood, near Mildenhall. It is pointed and entirely unpolished at the butt-end, which, had that part only been preserved, would have had all the appearance of being the point of an implement of the Palæolithic period. It is, however, ground to a thin circular edge at the broad end. Another, nearly similar, from Burwell Fen, is in the Museum of the Cambridge Antiquarian Society. I have another, rather straighter at the edge, but even more sharply pointed at the butt, from Reach Fen, and several others from the Eastern Counties. One [312] of the three celts found in the Upton Lovel Barrow was of much the same shape, only larger and more rudely chipped. It had also apparently more of its surface polished. General Pitt Rivers has a large Indian celt of this character, but broader in its proportions, found in Bundelcund. It is not of flint. I have smaller specimens from Madras, but more like Fig. 33.

Approaching to the form of Fig. 32, but rather broader at the edge and more truncated at the butt, where a cavity in the flint has interfered with the symmetry, is another celt in my own collection, found at Sawdon, in the North Riding of Yorkshire, and engraved as Fig. 33. It has been skilfully rubbed to a sharp segmental edge, but no labour has been wasted in grinding any portion of the face beyond what was necessary to produce the edge. Towards the butt-end some few of the facets and projections are, however, highly polished, but by friction only, as the surface is still uneven and not ground down. These polished patches, as has been pointed out by Professor Steenstrup, are probably significant of the blade having been mounted in a horn or wooden socket, though not so firmly but that there was some little motion in it, so that the resulting friction produced the polish. A celt of this class, formed of ochreous flint, with a semicircular edge, the sides straight, and partly ground away, is in the Fitch Collection at Norwich. It is 6 1/2 inches long, and was found at Martlesham Hill, Suffolk. A good example found in 1880 at Hinchcombe, [313] Gloucestershire has been figured. Another, about 9 inches long, rounded at the sides, and partly ground on the faces, was found in a barrow at Hartland, Devon, and is preserved in the museum at Truro. One of black flint, 4 1/8 inches long, was found at Pen-y-bonc, [314] Holyhead Island, in 1873. It is curved, and may have been used as an adze. Small specimens of this form are occasionally found in Suffolk. In Yorkshire, they occur of still smaller size. In the Greenwell Collection is one from Willerby Wold, 2 inches long and nearly triangular in outline; and another with an oblique edge from Helperthorpe, 2 1/8 inches long. One from Ganton Wold, 2 3/4 inches long, has a straight edge. I have a very rude specimen from the Yorkshire Wolds about 1 3/4 inches long, 1 3/4 inches wide at the edge, and 1 inch at the butt. They occur also in Scotland. The late Dr. John Stuart showed me a sketch of a flint celt of this type, 4 3/4 inches long, from Bogingarry, Old Deer, Aberdeenshire. Another, 1 5/8 inches by 1 inch, was found near Dundee. [315] One very like the figure was found at Urquhart, [316] Elgin. I have a celt of this character (4 inches), from the neighbourhood of Mons, in Belgium.

Another much more elongated form, but still belonging to the same class of implements, is that represented by Fig. 34. The original is of grey flint, and was found at Weston, Norfolk. The grinding is continued farther along the body of the implement than in the former examples, especially on one of the faces, and the asperities of the sides have in places been removed by the same process. About half-way along the blade, some of the facets have been polished by friction.

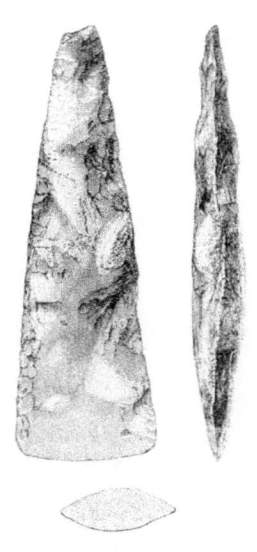

Fig. 34.—Weston, Norfolk. 1/2

In the Greenwell Collection is a beautiful specimen, 8 1/4 inches long, 2 inches broad at edge, and 3/4 inch at butt, and nowhere more than 5/8 inch thick. It is most skilfully chipped, and the grinding extends only 1/2 inch back from the edge. The sides have been made straight by grinding, and are slightly rounded. It was found at Kinlochew, Ross-shire. Another in the same collection, 9 1/4 inches long, was found at Kilham, in the East Riding of Yorkshire. I have seen one 8 inches long from Leighton Buzzard. One of the same length from Fordoun, [317] Kincardineshire, has been figured.

I have two shorter specimens, about the same breadth as Fig. 34 at the cutting edge, from the neighbourhood of Bury St. Edmunds and

Mildenhall. They do not, however, present any of the polished marks. The sides of both have to a certain extent been made straight by grinding. One of these with the natural crust of the flint still left at the butt-end is shown in Fig. 35. I have several others from the Eastern Counties, and two of much the same form from Carnaby Moor and King's Field, near Bridlington. The Greenwell Collection has specimens found at Woodhall, near Harbottle, Northumberland, and at Stanford, Norfolk. The latter is sharp at the butt. Others have been found in the Thames, and are now in the British Museum. I have a note of one 6 inches long from the Priory Valley, Dover.

Others from Debenham, Suffolk, from Dunham, Norfolk, and from Thorpe, are in the Norwich Museum.

One of white flint 4 1/2 inches long, with square butt, made straight by grinding, and with the faces chipped in such a manner as to form a central ridge, so that the grinding at the edge shows an almost triangular facet, was found at Kirby Underdale, and is in the Greenwell Collection. The sides in this specimen curve slightly inward.

The two celts found by the late Mr. Bateman, in Liff's Low, [318] near Biggin, in company with a curious cup, a stag's horn hammer, and numerous worked flints, including two flakes ground at the edge, were of this form and character. The larger of the two is about 7 inches long.

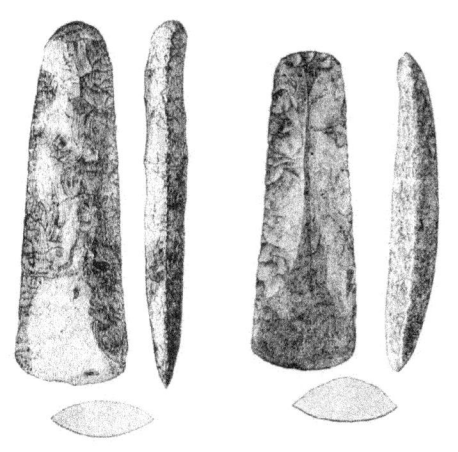

Fig. 35.—Mildenhall. 1/2

Fig. 35A.—Reach Fen. 1/2

Mr. Cunnington, F.G.S., has a small celt of this kind from Morton, near Dorchester. Messrs. Mortimer, of Driffield, have specimens of the same class. One of these (4 3/4 inches) is from Garton, Yorkshire; another similar, but less taper (4 3/8 inches), is from Lady Graves, near Fimber, where also a ruder celt of the same character was found. I have a small celt 3 inches long of the same class, from Seamer, Yorkshire. One of dark flint, slightly curved (5 1/4 inches), found at South Slipperfield, West Linton, Peeblesshire, is preserved in the National Museum at Edinburgh. [319]

It was the cutting end of a celt of this class, sharp at the sides, and ground at the edge only, which is said to have been found embedded in the skull of a *Bos primigenius*, [320] in a fen near Cambridge. The skull and implement are in the Woodwardian Museum. In the Fitch Collection is a small flint adze of this character, but rather narrower, and very much thinner in proportion. It is 4 1/2 inches long, about 1 3/8 inches broad, and only 1/4 inch thick. It is considerably curved in the direction of its length, and bears only slight traces of grinding at the edge, which is segmental. It was found at Santon Downham, Suffolk. I have two such thin adzes nearly flat (4 3/4 and 4 1/4 inches) from West Stow, Suffolk, and Thetford. They are both ground to a sharp edge.

A celt, in form like Fig. 35, found with flint knives and other implements in some beds of sand near York, has been figured by Mr. C. Monkman. [321] Similar implements are found in Ireland. I have two such, almost identical in form with those from Suffolk. They are both from Ulster. The same form occurs in Belgium.

One of these more adze-like implements with a considerable part of the convex face polished, was found in Reach Fen, and is shown in Fig. 35A. Fig. 84A, which is polished all over, belongs to the same class.

I have a fine bowed narrow adze (7 inches) ground at the edge only, from Hampshire.

The celt represented in Fig. 36 is of remarkable form, inasmuch as, like the unground specimen, Fig. 21, the sides expand at the butt-end. It was found in Burwell Fen, and is in the collection of the Cambridge Antiquarian Society. It is formed of chalcedonic flint, and the sharp sides are partially smoothed by grinding. It is slightly curved in the direction of its length, and may have been used as an adze. I have one of the same character (5 5/8 inches) from Swaffham, Cambs, and another (4 3/4 inches) from Oldbury, Ightham, given me by Mr. B. Harrison, in which the narrowing in the middle of the blade is even more conspicuous. One much like the figure, but with shorter sides (5 7/8 inches) was found near Dundee. [322] Another smaller, and somewhat similar implement, but expanding more towards the edge and less at the butt, was found at Bridge Farm, near North Tawton, Devon, and was in the possession of Mr. W. Vicary, F.G.S., of Exeter.

A few celts expanding at the edge, and polished all over, will be subsequently described.

In Fig. 37 is shown a flint celt, found near Thetford, and formerly in the collection of Mr. J. W. Flower, F.G.S. It is partially ground at the edge and on the projecting portion of one face, which is curved lengthwise. The other face is rather ogival, and much resembles that of the chipped celt from Mildenhall, Fig. 12. I have a shorter specimen of the same character from Icklingham.

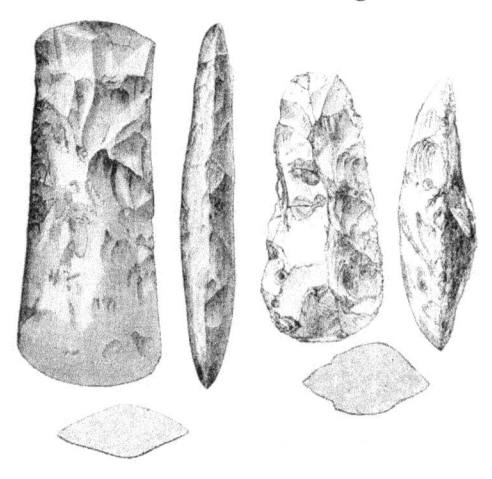

Fig. 36.—Burwell Fen. 1/2

Fig. 37.—Thetford. 1/2

Flint celts of the form of Fig. 23, but having the edge ground, frequently occur. I have specimens from Burwell Fen, Icklingham, and other places in the Eastern Counties. One was found at Stifford, near Gray's Thurrock, Essex, 6 1/2 inches long. [323] The late Mrs. Dickinson, of Hurstpierpoint, had another, 6 inches long, found at Pycombe Hill, Sussex. The late Mr. Durden, of Blandford, had one, now in the British Museum, from the encampment on Hod Hill, Dorsetshire. I have one or two such from the site of the ancient manufactory at Spiennes, near Mons, and others from the North of France.

The next specimen, Fig. 38, I have engraved on account of the peculiarity in its form. The butt-end, for nearly 2 1/2 inches along it, has the sides nearly parallel, the blade then suddenly expands with a rounded shoulder, and terminates in a semicircular edge, which is neatly ground, the rest of the celt being left in the state in which it was chipped out. From the form, it would appear as if this implement had been intended to be mounted by the insertion of the butt-end in a socket, like that shown in Fig. 98, so that it could be used as an axe. The axis of the butt is not quite in the same line as that of the rest of the blade. It was found at Undley Common, near Lakenheath, and is in the Greenwell Collection.

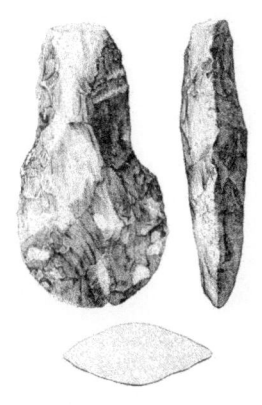

Fig. 38.—Undley Common, Lakenheath. 1/2

A remarkable specimen of an allied kind is shown in Fig. 38A. The edge only is ground and a flat surface has been left at the butt-end, which is almost circular. It was found on Ringwood Gore Farm, East Dean, Sussex, and was given to me by Mr. R. Hilton.

Another form, apparently intended for use as an adze, is also of rare occurrence. The specimen shown in Fig. 39 was found at Ganton, Yorkshire, and is in my own collection. It is very much more convex on one face than the other, which, indeed, is nearly flat. The grinding is confined to the edge, but some parts of the flat face are polished as if by friction.

The late Dr. John Stuart, F.S.A.Scot., showed me a sketch of a large implement of this type, and considerably bowed longitudinally, found at Bogingarry, Old Deer, Aberdeenshire. It is of flint, 4 1/2 inches long, and 2 inches wide.

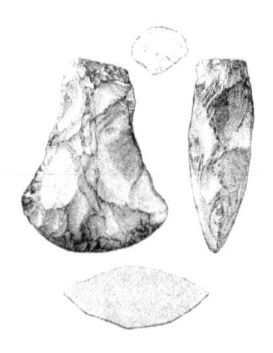

Fig. 38A.—East Dean. 1/2

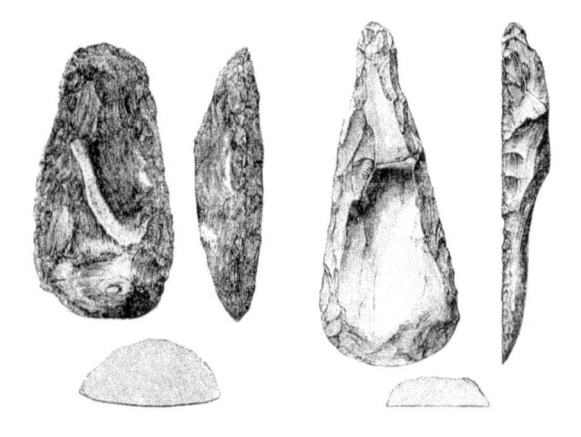

Fig. 39.—Ganton. 1/2

Fig. 40.—Swaffham Fen. 1/2

Another form of adze, if such it be, remarkably flat on one face and narrow at the butt, is shown in Fig. 40. This specimen was found in Swaffham Fen, Cambridge, and is in my own collection. The flat face has been produced at a single blow, and has been left almost untouched, except where trimmed by chipping to form the edge, which, however, has been rendered blunt by grinding. The sides are very minutely chipped along the angles, and there seems some possibility of the instrument having been used as a rimer or boring tool.

The celts of other materials than flint, and ground only at the edge, are of rarer occurrence than those in flint. That engraved as Fig. 41 was found at Grindale, near Bridlington. It is of felstone, and is remarkable as being so much curved in the direction of its length. I have another smaller specimen from the same place, but the blade is straight. The edge, however, is slightly gouge-like.

Mr. J. W. Brooke has a small adze of flint (2 1/4 inches) in outline almost identical with Fig. 41. It came from near Aldbourne, Wilts.

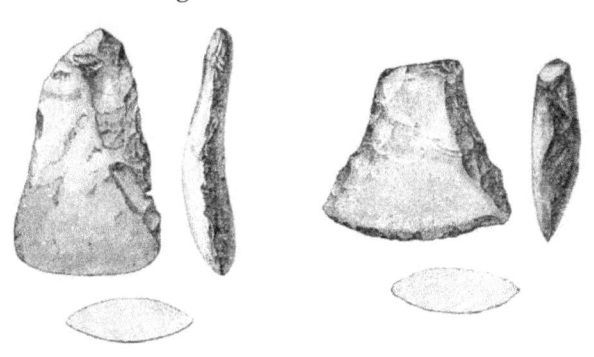

Fig. 41.—Grindale, Bridlington. 1/2

Fig. 42.—North Burton. 1/2

Another of these instruments expanding towards the edge, and apparently adapted for insertion in a socket, is shown in Fig. 42. It is made of hone-stone, and the flat butt is the result of a natural joint in the stone. It was found at North Burton, in the East Riding of Yorkshire, and is in the Greenwell Collection, where is also a celt of greenstone much like Fig. 41, found in a barrow with a burnt interment on Seamer Moor, Yorkshire; and another of the same class, 3 3/4 inches long and 2 3/4 inches wide, also from Seamer Moor. A third specimen, rather smaller, was found in a barrow at Uncleby, Yorkshire. One of greenstone, 2 1/2 inches long, and nearly triangular in outline, was found near Keswick, and is in the Blackmore Museum. A longer adze of greenstone, considerably curved in the blade, lay in company with various implements of flint in some sand-beds near York. [324] In the Mayer Collection at Liverpool is a celt of clay-slate, 4 inches long and ground at the edge, found at Toxteth. In the collection of the late Mr. J. F. Lucas, of Fenny Bentley Hall, near Ashbourne, were two celts (5 1/2 and 7 inches) of the same type as Fig. 35, but more adze-like in character, and formed of felstone. They were found on Middleton Moor, and at Wormhill, near Buxton, Derbyshire.

In my own collection, is a greenstone celt with the sides sharp and nearly parallel, 7 1/2 inches long and nearly 3 inches broad, with a semicircular edge partly ground, found at Shrub Hill, Feltwell, Norfolk.

I have also a large specimen in form more resembling Fig. 23, six inches long. It is ground at the edge, which is nearly semicircular, and along the sides. It was found at Thurston, Suffolk, and is formed of a piece of tough mica-schist, with garnets [325] in it, a material, no doubt, derived from the Glacial beds of that district. Another from Troston, in the same neighbourhood, is formed from a rough fragment of micaceous grit ground to an edge at one end. In Scotland some wedge-shaped blades of granite, exhibiting traces of a very small amount of artificial adaptation, have been found. Two such, from Aberdeenshire, described as axes, have been figured. [326] The small stone celts found in Orkney, [327] though tolerably sharp at the edge, are described as rough on the sides.

Turning to foreign countries, the discovery of flint instruments of this class, ground at the edge only, or on some small portions of their surface, is, as has already been observed, not uncommon in France and Belgium. In Denmark they are also very abundant, but the most common Danish form with a thick rectangular section does not appear to occur in Britain. Among the North American stone hatchets, many present this feature of being ground at the edge only, and the same is the case with some of the tools of the native Australians, such as that engraved in Fig. 105. A rough celt from Borneo, ground at the edge only, has been engraved by General Pitt Rivers. [328] The type also occurs in India and Japan.

In all European countries instruments of this form and character, but made of other materials than flint, are, like those entirely unground, of very rare occurrence. This rarity may arise from two causes, the one, that the tools or weapons made of these materials have not so sharp a cutting edge produced by chipping only as those formed of flint; and the second, that being usually somewhat softer than flint it required less time and trouble to grind them all over.

None of the rough celts, nor those ground at the edge only, seem so well adapted for use as hand-tools without a haft, as do some of those which are polished all over. Looking, however, at some of the rough Australian tools which are hafted with gum in a piece of skin, and thus used in the hand, it is hardly safe to express a decided opinion. The majority were, notwithstanding, in all probability, mounted with shafts after the manner of axes or adzes.

CHAPTER VI.
POLISHED CELTS.

The last of the three classes into which, for the sake of convenience of arrangement, I have divided these instruments, viz., that comprising the celts ground or polished, not only at the edge, but over a great portion, or the whole, of their surface, is also that which is usually most numerously represented in collections of antiquities. Whether this excess in number over the other classes arises from the greater original abundance of these polished implements, or from their being better calculated to attract observation, and, therefore, more likely to be collected and preserved than those of a less finished character, is a difficult question. From my own experience it appears that, so far as relates to the implements of this character formed of flint, and still lying unnoticed on the surface of the soil, the proportions which usually obtain in collections are as nearly as may be reversed, and the chipped, or but partially polished, celts are in a large majority.

Among the polished celts there is a great range in size, and much variation in form, though the general character is in the main, uniform. The readiest method of classification is, I think, in accordance with the section presented by the middle of the blade, and I, therefore, propose to arrange them as follows:—

- 1. Those sharp or but slightly rounded at the sides, and presenting a pointed oval or *vesica piscis* in section.
- 2. Those with flat sides.
- 3. Those with an oval section.
- 4. Those presenting abnormal peculiarities.

In each subdivision there will, of course, be several varieties, according as the sides are more or less parallel, the blade thicker or thinner, the butt-end more or less pointed, and the edge flat, segmental, or oblique. There are also intermediate forms between these merely arbitrary classes.

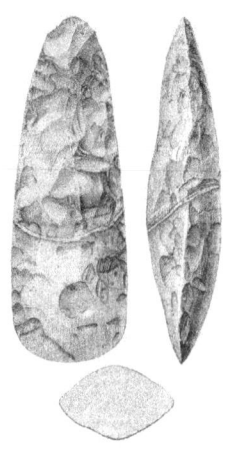

Fig. 43.—Santon Downham, Suffolk. 1/2

I commence with those of the first sub-division, in flint. The first specimen I have engraved, Fig. 43, is a representative of a common type, and was found at Santon Downham, between Brandon and Thetford, on the borders of Norfolk and Suffolk, where, also, implements belonging to the Palæolithic Period have been discovered. The sides were originally sharp, but have been slightly rounded by grinding. The faces still show, in many places, the surface originally produced by chipping, but all projections have been ground away.

I have also a larger specimen, 9 1/2 inches long, from the same spot, and found, I believe, at the same time.

This form is of common occurrence in the Eastern Counties. I have specimens from Hilgay Fen, Norfolk (8 1/2 inches), and Botesdale (7 inches), Hepworth (6 1/4 inches), Undley Hall, near Lakenheath (5 3/4 inches), in Suffolk. Some of these are ground over almost the entire face. A fine specimen (10 inches) is in the Woodwardian Museum, at Cambridge. In the Fitch Collection is a fine series of them. One of these, 9 3/4 inches long, 3 1/2 inches broad, and 2 1/2 inches thick, weighing 3 lbs. 6 1/2 ozs., was found at Narborough, near Swaffham. Another (9 1/2 inches), weighing 3 3/4 lbs., was found near Ipswich. A third (8 3/4 inches) was discovered at Bolton, near Great Yarmouth. Others from 5 3/4 inches to 7 1/4 inches long, are from Beachamwell, Elsing, Grundisburgh, Aylsham, and Breccles, in the counties of Suffolk and Norfolk. That from the last-named locality has one face flatter than the other.

There are others in the Norwich Museum, including one from Blofield, 8 1/2 inches long.

There are numerous specimens of this type in the British Museum. One from Barton Bendish, Norfolk, is 7 3/4 inches long; another from Oxburgh, in the same county, 6 3/4 inches. Others, 6 1/2 inches and 5 1/2 inches long, are from Market Weston and Kesgrave, Suffolk. The former is semicircular at both ends.

Mr. A. C. Savin has a well-finished example (6 1/2 inches) from Trimingham, five miles south of Cromer.

The Rev. S. Banks, of Cottenham, had a fine specimen, of white flint, 8 1/2 inches long, found at Stow Heath, Suffolk.

Several celts of this form found in the Fen district are in the Museum of the Cambridge Antiquarian Society. I have some from the same neighbourhood, of which two are unusually wide in proportion to their length, and in outline much resemble Fig. 48, though the edge is more semicircular. One of these is 7 inches long, 3 1/4 inches wide, and 1 3/4 inches thick; the other 5 1/2 inches long, 2 3/4 inches wide, and 1 3/8 inches thick.

I have seen a celt presenting a narrow variety of this form, which was found at Albury, near Bishop's Stortford. It is 6 3/4 inches long, and 1 5/8 inches wide, and polished all over.

The ordinary form, though apparently of most frequent occurrence in the East Anglian counties, is not by any means confined to that district. One, 8 1/2 inches long, the sides very slightly flattened; and three others, 6 inches and 5 inches long, with the sides more rounded, all found in the Thames, at London, are in the British Museum. I have one from the Thames, at Teddington (6 inches), and three, 5 1/4 to 6 inches long, found together in [329] Temple Mills Lane, Stratford, Essex, in 1882. In the Greenwell Collection is one 7 1/2 inches long, found at Holme, on Spalding Moor, Yorkshire.

A flint celt of this form (6 1/2 inches), from Reigate, [330] is in the British Museum, as well as another (6 1/4 inches), rather oblique at the edge, found in a barrow in Hampshire, engraved in the *Archæologia*. [331] Another, 7 inches long, was found near Egham, [332] Surrey. Two from Ash [333] near Farnham, and Wisley in the same county have been figured. I have a short, thick specimen (4 1/2 inches) found at Eynsham, Oxfordshire. It sometimes happens that celts of this general character have one side much curved while the other is nearly straight, so that in outline they resemble Fig. 86. One such, 5 inches long and 2 inches broad in the middle, found at Bishopstow, is in the Blackmore Museum. Another (6 1/2 inches) with the sides less curved, from Stanton Fitzwarren, Wilts, has been engraved by the Archæological Institute. [334] Two, 7 1/4 and 5 1/4 inches long, were found at Jarrow. [335]

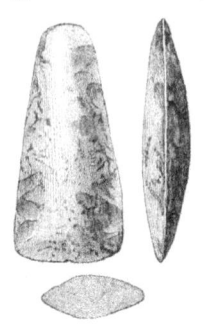

Fig. 44.—Coton, Cambridge. 1/2

The same type as Fig. 43 occasionally occurs in other materials than flint. The late Mr. James Wyatt, F.G.S., had a celt of greenstone 9 3/4 inches long, 3 1/2 inches wide at the edge, which is slightly oblique, found many years ago in Miller's Bog, Pavenham, Beds. There is an engraving of it, on which it is described as of flint, but such is not the fact. The form is also sometimes found in France and Belgium. I have specimens from both countries; and one from Périgord, 8 inches long, is in the Museum at Le Puy.

Allied to this form, but usually more rounded at the sides, and flatter on the faces, are the implements of which an example is given in Fig. 44. The original was found at Coton, Cambridgeshire, in 1863. The type is the same as that of Fig. 35; but in this case the celt is polished all over. The butt-end is ground to a semicircular outline, but is, like the sides, rounded. The same is the case with some of the thicker celts of the form last described. A celt of much the same character, but with the sides apparently rather flatter (7 1/3 inches), was found at Panshanger, Herts. [336] One (5 inches), from the Isle of Wight, is in the British Museum. The edge is oblique, as is that of another of the same length found on the South Downs, and now in the Museum at Lewes. Another of grey flint, 7 inches long, tapering from 2 inches at edge to 1 inch at butt, 7/8 inch thick, semicircular at the butt and edge, the faces polished nearly all over, but the sides sharp and left unground, was found during the Main Drainage Works for London, and is also in the British Museum. Others have been described from Playford, [337] Suffolk (6 7/8 inches) and

Chalvey Grove, [338] Eton Wick, Bucks (7 3/8 inches), and part of one from Croydon. [339]

I have seen specimens of the same kind, with the sides straight and sharp though slightly rounded, tapering towards the butt which is semicircular, and varying in length from 5 1/4 inches to 7 1/4 inches, found at Alderton, Suffolk; Thorn Marsh, Yorkshire; Norton, near Malton; Westacre Hall, Norfolk; and elsewhere. The late Mr. J. Brent, F.S.A., showed me a drawing of one about 7 inches long, found at Bigborough Wood, Tunford, Canterbury.

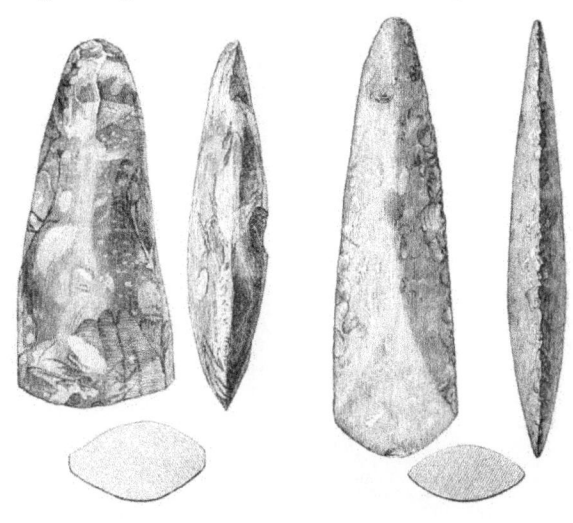

Fig. 45.—Reach Fen, Cambridge. 1/2

Fig. 46—Great Bedwin, Wilts. 1/2

The celt shown in Fig. 45 belongs to the same class, though it is rather flatter at the sides. It is polished over the greater part of its surface, but is on one face quite unpolished at the edge. I have engraved it as an example of the manner in which, after the edge of a hatchet of this kind had become damaged by use, a fresh edge was obtained by chipping, which, in some instances, the owner of the implement was not at the pains to sharpen by grinding.

Fig. 46 gives another variety of the flint celts with sharp or slightly rounded sides. It is slightly ridged along each face, and the faces instead of being uniformly convex to the edge have at the lower part a nearly flat facet of triangular form, the base of which forms the edge. This specimen was found at Great Bedwin, Wilts, and is in the Greenwell Collection.

I have a nearly similar specimen (6 1/4 inches) from Northwood, Harefield, Middlesex, and another of the same length, found at Hepworth, Suffolk, but the facet at the edge is not quite so distinct. A third from Abingdon is only 4 1/2 inches long.

A long narrow chisel-like celt of this pointed oval section (8 inches) from Aberdeenshire [340] has been figured. A flint celt from Chiriqui, [341] found with a sort of flint punch and some burnishing pebbles in a grave, presumed to be that of one of the native workers in gold, is remarkably like Fig. 46 in form.

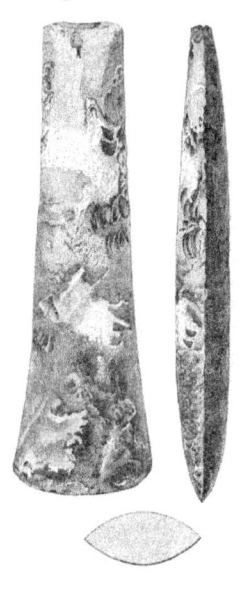

Fig. 47.—Burradon, Northumberland. 1/2

In the Fitch Collection is a large thick specimen (9 5/8 inches) found at Heckingham Common, Norfolk, and a shorter, broader one with a faceted edge, from Pentney. Another of flint (6 1/2 inches) with the sides much rounded, but with a similar facet at the edge, was found at Histon, Cambs, and belonged to the late Rev. S. Banks.

It seems probable that these instruments when first made did not exhibit the facet at the edge, but that it has resulted from repeated grinding as the edge became injured by wear.

A celt, apparently of this section, but more truncated at the butt, and with a narrow facet running along the centre of the face, was found in Llangwyllog, [342] Anglesey. It is not of flint but of "white magnesian stone."

Fig. 47 exhibits a beautiful implement of a different character, and of a very rare form, inasmuch as it expands towards the edge. It is of ochreous-coloured flint polished all over, and is in the Greenwell Collection. It was found at Burradon, Northumberland, and in outline much resembles that from Gilmerton, Fig. 76, but this latter has the sides flat and a cutting edge at each end.

A celt of similar form, but only 6 1/2 inches long, found at Cliff Hill, is in the Museum at Leicester. Four flint hatchets, found at Bexley, Kent, seem from the description given of them to be nearly of this type. [343]

A few specimens of this form, both unground and ground merely at the edge, have already been mentioned, and specimens engraved, as Figs. 21 and 36. Hatchets expanding towards the edge are of more common occurrence in Denmark than in this country, though even there they are rather rare when the expansion is well-defined.

In the British Museum is a magnificent celt of this section, but in outline like Fig. 77. It is ground over nearly the whole of its surface, but the edge at each end has only been chipped out. It is made of some felspathic rock, and is no less than 14 5/8 inches in length. It was found near Conishead Priory, Lancashire.

The next specimens that I shall describe are also principally made of other materials than flint.

Fig. 48.—Coton, Cambridge. 1/2

Fig. 48, in my own collection, is of porphyritic greenstone, and was found at Coton, Cambridgeshire. It is polished all over, equally convex on both faces, and has the sides rather more rounded than most of those of nearly similar section in flint. The butt is rather sharper than the sides. I have an analogous implement, found at Nunnington, Yorkshire, but with the sides straighter and rather more converging towards the butt. Others have been found in the same district.

Other specimens made of greenstone have been found in the Fens, some of which are in the Museum of the Cambridge Antiquarian Society.

Some "stone" celts from Kate's Bridge [344] and Digby Fen have been figured in Miller and Skertchly's "Fenland." One (7 inches) of greenstone, and apparently of this type, was found at Hartford, [345] Hunts, and is now in the Ashmolean Museum at Oxford.

In the Newcastle Museum is a compact greenstone celt of this character (5 3/4 inches) with the edge slightly oblique, found at Penrith Beacon, Cumberland. Some celts of the same general character have been found in Anglesea.

Implements of this class are frequently more tapering at the butt than the one shown in the figure. I have several such from the Cambridge Fens, and have seen an example from Towcester. One of flint (4 inches), so much rounded at the edge as to be almost oval in outline, found near Mildenhall, is in the Christy Collection. One of greenstone (4 1/4 inches) was found at Wormhill, Buxton, Derbyshire.

Fig. 49, of dark-grey whin-stone, is of much the same character, but has an oblique cutting edge. The butt-end is ground to a blunted curve. The original is in the Greenwell Collection, and was dug up in draining at Ponteland, Northumberland. Another, in the same collection, similar, but much rougher (6 inches) was found at Halton Chesters, in the same county. I have one of the same kind (6 5/8 inches) found near Raby Castle, Durham.

A flint hatchet of nearly the same form, 4 1/2 inches long, was found at Kempston, near Bedford. The Earl of Ducie, F.R.S., has another of flint (5 inches) from Bembridge, Isle of Wight. A celt, from Andalusia, of this character, but with the edge straighter, has been figured. [346]

Fig. 49.—Ponteland, Northumberland. 1/2

Fig. 50.—Fridaythorpe, Yorkshire. 1/2

The celt engraved in Fig. 50 is likewise in the Greenwell Collection, and was found at Fridaythorpe, in the East Riding of Yorkshire. It is formed of green hone-stone. Another, similar but thicker, and having the sides more convergent and the edge less oblique, was found at the same place and is in the same collection, in which also is the fragment of a larger implement of the same class from Amotherby, near Malton, Yorkshire. With these is another (4 3/4 inches) which was found in a barrow with a burnt interment on Seamer Moor, Yorkshire. It is apparently of clay-slate which has become red by burning with the body.

Messrs. Mortimer have one of this form in greenstone (5 3/8 inches) found near Malton, and also one in flint (4 1/8 inches) found near Fimber.

I have a well-finished celt of hone-stone, rather thicker proportionally than that figured (5 5/8 inches), probably found in Cumberland, it having formed part of the Crosthwaite Collection at Keswick. In the Greenwell Collection is another of basalt, with straight sides, tapering from 2 3/4 inches at edge to 1 3/4 at butt, 9 1/2 in length, and 1 3/4 thick, from a peat moss at Cowshill-in-Weardale, Durham.

A thin, flat form of celt, still presenting the same character of section, is represented in Fig. 51. The original is formed of a hard, nearly black clay-slate, and was found at Oulston, in the North Riding of Yorkshire. Like many others which I have described, it is in the Greenwell Collection.

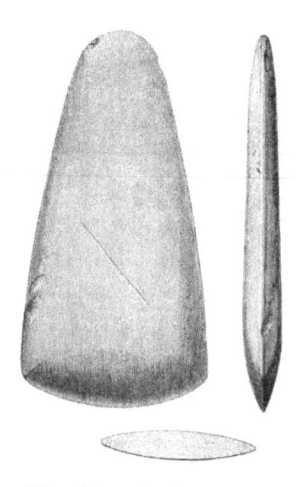

Fig. 51.—Oulston. 1/2

One of flint like Fig. 51 (5 inches) was found at Shelley, [347] Suffolk.

A celt of greenstone (4 3/4 inches), of the same character but thicker and with straighter sides, from Newton, Aberdeenshire, is in the National Museum at Edinburgh, where is also another, in outline more like the figure, but broader at the butt-end, and with one side somewhat flattened. It is 4 3/8 long, and was found at Redhall, near Edinburgh.

Some Irish celts, formed of different metamorphic rocks, present the same forms as those of Figs. 48 to 51. As a rule, however, the sides of Irish specimens are more rounded.

Fig. 52 represents an exquisitely polished celt, of a mottled, pale green colour, found in Burwell Fen, Cambridge, and, through the kindness of Mr. Marlborough Pryor, now in my own collection. The material appears to be a very hard diorite; and as both faces are highly polished all over, the labour bestowed in the manufacture of such an instrument must have been immense. It is somewhat curved lengthways, and on the inner face is a slight depression, as if, in chipping it out, one of the lines of fracture had run in too far; but even this depression is polished, and no trace of the original chipped surface remains. The point is quite sharp, and the sides are only in the slightest degree rounded.

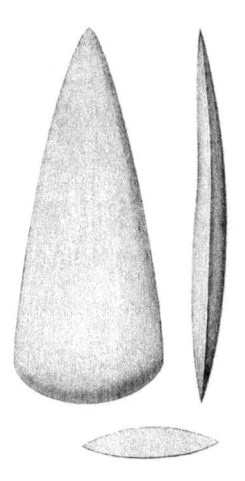

Fig. 52.—Burwell Fen. 1/2

A beautiful example of the kind is said to have been found in a barrow near Stonehenge. [348] Another of a green-grey colour (6 1/2 inches) was found at Lopham Ford, near the source of the Waveney, and was submitted to me in 1884, by the late Mr. T. E. Amyot, of Diss.

The late Mr. J. W. Flower, F.G.S., bequeathed to me a somewhat larger specimen of the same character, found at Daviot, Inverness. It is slightly broken at the pointed butt, but must have been about 8 inches long and 3 5/8 broad. The material may be a diorite, but perhaps more nearly approaches what the French term jadeite. In the Truro Museum is another highly polished celt of the same form, and similar material, found near Falmouth.

Mr. J. W. Brooke has a beautifully polished specimen, made of a green transparent stone, from Breamore, Salisbury. It has lost a small piece at the butt-end, but is still 8 inches long. It is only 2 5/8 inches broad at the cutting end.

Another celt, 7 3/4 inches long, "the edges thin, rising gradually to about the thickness of half an inch in the middle," was found in 1791 near Hopton, Derbyshire. [349] The material is described as appearing "to be marble, of a light colour tinged with yellow, and a mixture of pale red and green veins."

In the collection of the late Mr. J. F. Lucas was a celt of this type 5 1/2 inches long, slightly unsymmetrical in outline, owing to the cleavage of the stone. It is said to have been found near Brierlow, Buxton. The material is a green jade-like stone, but so fibrous in appearance as to resemble fibrolite.

Another, of "a fine granite stone, highly polished, 9 inches long, 4 1/4 broad at one end, tapering to the other, its thickness in the middle 3/4 of an inch, and quite sharp at the edges all round," was found at Mains, [350] near Dumfries, in 1779. It was discovered in blowing up some large stones, possibly those of a dolmen, and is now in the possession of Sir R. S. Riddell, Bart., of Strontian.

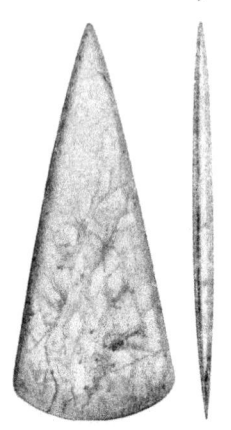

Fig. 52A.—Berwickshire. 1/2

Several other specimens have been found in Scotland. A beautiful celt from Berwickshire [351] is, through the kindness of the Society of Antiquaries of Scotland, shown in Fig. 52A. It is made of green quartz and has the edge intentionally blunted. A smaller celt (7 1/2 inches) was found at Cunzierton near Jedburgh [352]; another (8 inches) at Rattray, [353] Perthshire; another (8 1/4 inches), only 3/4 inch thick at most, near Glenluce, [354] Wigtownshire; and others (8 inches) at Aberfeldy, [355] Perthshire, and Dunfermline. [356]

Several of these highly polished jadeite celts have been found in dolmens in Brittany and there are some fine specimens in the museum at Vannes. Some of them [357] have small holes bored through them. The various types of Brittany celts have been classified by the Société Polymathique du Morbihan. [358] In the Musée de St. Germain is a specimen (unbored) 9 inches long, found near Paris, [359] as also a hoard of fifteen, originally seventeen, mostly of jadeite and fibrolite, some perforated, found at Bernon, [360] near Arzon, Morbihan, in 1893. I have one 7 1/2 inches long from St. Jean, Châteaudun, and others 5 3/8 to 7 inches in length, of beautiful varieties of jade-like stone, found at Eu (Seine Inférieure), Miannay, near Abbeville (Somme), and Breteuil (Oise). The two latter are rounded and not sharp at the sides. One about

6 1/2 inches long, from the environs of Soissons, is in the museum at Lyons.

One of jade, of analogous form to these, and found near Brussels, is engraved by Le Hon. [361] Another was found at Maffles. [362]

Five specimens of the same character, of different sizes, the longest about 9 1/2 inches in length, and the shortest about 4 inches, are said to have been found with Roman remains at Kästrich, near Gonsenheim, [363] and are preserved in the museum at Mainz. The smallest is of greenstone, and the others of chloritic albite. They are said to have been buried in a sort of leather case, arranged alternately with the pointed and broad ends downwards, and in accordance with their size.

Eight specimens from museums at Weimar, Rudolstadt, and Leipzig were exhibited at Berlin. [364] in 1880. One from Wesseling, [365] on the Rhine (8 inches), is thought to have been associated with Roman remains.

Both with the English and Continental specimens, there appears to be considerable doubt as to the exact localities whence the materials were derived from which these celts are formed.

Instruments for which such beautiful and intractable materials were selected, can hardly have been in common use; but we have not sufficient ground for arriving at any trustworthy conclusion as to the purpose for which they were intended. I have, however, a short celt, 3 1/2 inches long, from Burwell Fen, and made of this jade-like material, which has evidently been much in use, and was once considerably longer. It appears, indeed, to be the butt-end of an instrument like Fig. 52.

A detailed account of the jade and jadeite celts in the British Museum is given in the *Zeitschrift für Ethnologie*. [366]

It was formerly supposed that the jade of which many hatchets found in Switzerland and other European countries are made, came of necessity from the East, and theories as to the early migrations of mankind have been based upon this supposition. As a fact, jade has now been found in Europe, and notably in Styria [367] and Silesia. [368] Below [369] are given some references to comments on the sources of jade. An account of the method of working jade in Western Yun-nan is given in Anderson's Report [370] on the Expedition to that country; and a complete and well-illustrated catalogue of objects in jade and nephrite, by Dr. A. B. Meyer, forms part of the publications of the Royal Ethnographical Museum, at Dresden, for 1883.

I now come to the second of the subdivisions under which I have arranged this class of implements, viz., those having the sides flattened. The flat sides, of course, taper away to a point at the cutting edge of the celts, and usually diminish much in width toward the butt-end, which is commonly ground to a semicircular blunted edge. The implements of this kind are generally very symmetrical in form.

I have selected a large specimen for engraving in Fig. 53. It is of grey mottled flint, ground all over to such an extent, that hardly any traces of the original chipping remain. It was found at Botesdale, Suffolk, and was formerly in the collection of Mr. Warren, of Ixworth, but is now in my own. I have another (4 3/4 inches) from Redgrave, Suffolk, and a third (5 1/2 inches) from Bottisham Lode, Cambs.

One of the same form, found near Stowmarket, is engraved in the *Archæologia*. [371] If the account there given be correct, it was 12 3/4 inches long. A specimen from Cardiff, now in the British Museum (4 1/2 inches), has lost a considerable portion of its original length by use, and is ground so that the edge bounds a facet on the face. The sides at the butt-end are somewhat rounded, but near the edge they are flat and 1/4 inch wide.

A fine specimen of this character, formed of ochreous flint (9 inches), found in Swaffham Fen, Cambridgeshire, is in the Christy Collection, as well as one from Mildenhall (5 1/2 inches), the butt-end of which is sharper than is usual.

In the Fitch Collection is a flint celt of this type, 7 1/2 inches long and 2 1/2 broad at the edge, which however, has been broken off. It is said to have been found in a tumulus at Swannington, Norfolk, in 1855. In the Northampton Museum is a specimen (6 inches) of ochreous flint, found at Gilsborough, Northamptonshire. The late Mr. James Wyatt, F.G.S., had a beautiful implement of this type, but narrower in proportion to its length, being 7 inches long and only 1 3/4 wide at the edge, found in the Thames at Coway Stakes, near Egham. I have one (6 inches) from the Thames at Hampton Court. A fine specimen, 9 1/2 inches long, and 3 wide at the edge, with the sides quite flat, but less than 1/4 inch wide, of ochreous flint, polished all over, was found at Crudwell, Wilts.

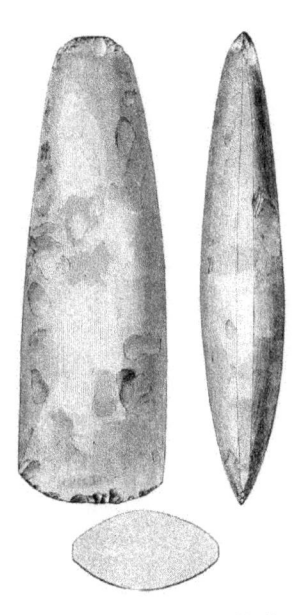

Fig. 53.—Botesdale, Suffolk. 1/2

Others, in flint, have been found at Sutton, Suffolk (8 inches); Wishford, Great Bedwin, Wilts [372] (7 inches); Portsmouth; [373] Cherbury Camp, Pusey, Faringdon [374] (5 1/2 inches long, edge faceted), and Rampton, Cambridge. [375] I have seen one (5 1/2 inches) that was found near Loughborough. Mr. G. F. Lawrence has a fine specimen (7 5/8 inches) from the Lea Marshes.

In the National Museum at Edinburgh is one of white flint (10 inches) from Fochabers, [376] Elginshire, and another from the same place (7 1/4 inches). They are in shape much like Fig. 61. There is another of grey flint, from Skye (7 1/2 inches). One 5 1/2 inches long, in the same museum, from Roxburghshire, has the middle part of the faces ground flat, so that the section is a sort of compressed octagon; the edge is nearly straight.

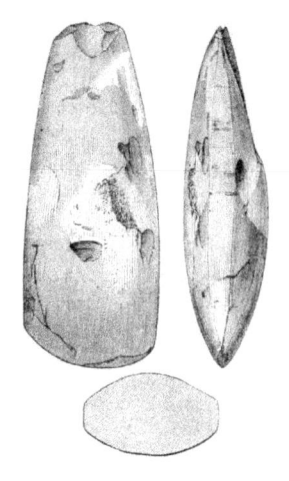

Fig. 54.—Lackford, Suffolk. 1/2

Much the same form occurs in other materials than flint. I have a specimen, formed of flinty clay-slate, with one side less flat than the other, 10 1/4 inches long, 3 wide, and 1 5/8 thick, said to have been found with four others in a cairn on Druim-a-shi, Culloden, Inverness. I have another of whin-stone (9 1/4 inches) from Kirkcaldy, Fife.

The fine celt from Gilmerton, Fig. 76, is of the same class, but has a cutting edge at each end. Some Cumberland and Westmorland specimens partake much of this character.

Implements of nearly similar form to that last described, but having the edge oblique, are also met with. That engraved in Fig. 54 was found at Lackford, Suffolk, and was formerly in the collection of Mr. Warren, of Ixworth, but is now in mine. It is of grey flint. I have another, of white flint, of the same length but a trifle narrower, and with the grinding for the edge forming more of a facet with the body of the celt. It was found in the Isle of Portland. The obliquity of the edge was no doubt intentional, and may have originated in the manner in which these hatchets were mounted with hafts. Professor Nilsson [377] has suggested that the obliquity is due to the front part of the blade being worn away in use more quickly than the back.

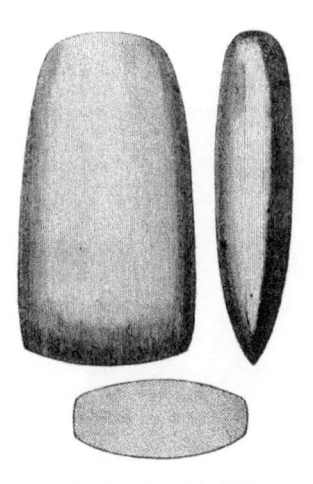

Fig. 55.—Dalmeny, Linlithgow. 1/2

To this class, though very different in appearance, belongs a beautifully made celt of grey flint, in the British Museum. It is probably of English origin, though the place of finding is unknown. The sides are straight and flat, but only about 1/16 of an inch wide, the faces equally convex and polished all over. It is 9 inches long, and tapers from 1 1/2 inches wide at the edge, which is broken, to 5/8 at the butt. Its greatest thickness is 1/2 an inch. It is engraved in the *Archæological Journal.* [378]

Flint celts of the type of both Fig. 53 and 54 are not uncommon in France and Belgium. They are also found, though rarely, in Ireland.

The cutting end of one formed of nearly transparent quartz, and found in Egypt, is in the Museum at Geneva.

Celts with the sides flattened are of not unfrequent occurrence in other materials than flint. That figured as No. 55 is of ochreous-coloured quartzite, and was found at Dalmeny, Linlithgow. It is preserved in the National Museum at Edinburgh. The form is remarkable, as being so broad in proportion to the length. The sides are flat, but the angles they make with the faces are slightly rounded. The butt-end is rounded in both directions, and appears to have been worked with a pointed tool or pick.

Another celt, of greenstone, of much the same form but with the sides more tapering, 6 inches long and 3 1/4 wide, which was found in Lochleven [379] in 1860, is in the same museum. This latter more nearly resembles Fig. 51 in outline. A small highly-polished celt of flinty slate (2 5/8 inches), found near Dundee, [380] has been figured. Another, more triangular in outline, 6 1/2 inches long, was found at Barugh, Yorkshire, and is in the Greenwell Collection. I have a celt of rather narrower proportions that was found between Hitchin and Pirton, Herts. It is made of a kind of *lapis lydius*.

Many of the Danish greenstone celts, which are perforated at the butt, present much the same outline and section.

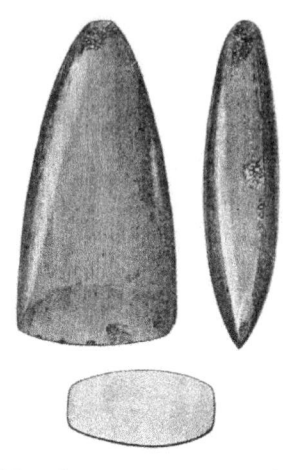

Fig. 56.—Sprouston, near Kelso. 1/2

Stone hatchets of this character occur, though rarely, in France. I have seen one in the collection of the late M. Aymard, at Le Puy. Dr. Finlay, of Athens, had a thin, flat hatchet of this form made of heliotrope, 3 1/2 inches long, with flat sides, found in Greece. The form occurs also in Sicily. [381]

Several celts of this type have been brought from different parts of Asia. One, of basalt, 2 inches long, wedge-shaped, found at Muquier, [382] in Southern Babylonia, is in the British Museum; and several of jade, 3 to 4 inches long, procured by Major Sladen from the province of Yun-nan in Southern China, are in the Christy Collection. By Major Sladen's kindness, I have also a specimen. Mr. Joseph Edkins has published some notes on "Stone Hatchets in China." [383] Others from Perak [384] have also been described.

The same form, also in jade, has been found in Assam. [385] Some from Java, in the museum at Leyden, formed of flint, present the same section, but the sides expand towards the edge. A nearly similar form occurs in Japan. [386]

Fig. 56 is of the same character as Fig. 55, but narrower at the butt-end. The original is in the Greenwell Collection, and is formed of Lydian stone. It was found at Sprouston, near Kelso, Roxburghshire.

Though flat at the sides along most of the blade, the section becomes oval near the butt-end.

I have a smaller example of this type in clay-slate, 3 1/2 inches long and 1 3/4 wide at the edge, found at Carnaby, near Bridlington. The butt-end is in this case rectangular in section. It closely resembles the flat-sided hatchets so commonly found in France. I have an Irish celt of the same form found near Armagh, and made of clay-slate. Flat-sided celts are, however,rare in Ireland.

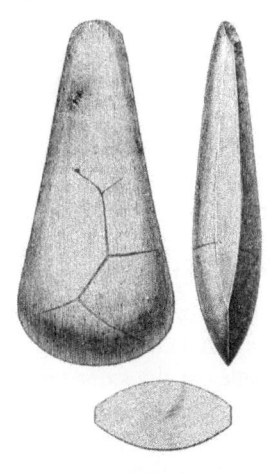

Fig. 57.—Nunnington, Yorkshire. 1/2

A celt of grey flint, 4 1/2 inches long, of much the same outline, but having the sides rounded and not flat, and the butt brought to a straight sharp edge, was found in Burwell Fen, and is now in the Christy Collection.

A celt of the same section, but of peculiar form, with the sides curved slightly inwards, and tapering considerably to the butt, is shown in Fig. 57. The sides are flat, but have the angles slightly rounded; a narrow flattened face is carried round the butt-end. It would appear to have been made from a calcareous nodule found in some argillaceous bed, like the septaria in the London clay. Both of its faces present a series of diverging cracks, of slight depth, apparently resulting from the dissolution of calcareous veins in the stone. It was found at Nunnington, Yorkshire, and now forms part of the Greenwell Collection.

The original of Fig. 58 was discovered at Burradon, Northumberland, where also the fine flint celt, Fig. 47, was found. This likewise is in the Greenwell Collection. It is of porphyritic stone, and has the angles of the flat sides slightly rounded. Another, in the same collection, 4 inches long, from Doddington, in the same county, is of similar character. Celts of much the same shape and size have been found in the Shetland Isles; one of these, 5 1/2 inches long, from West Burrafirth, is in the British Museum. A similar form is found in Japan. [387]

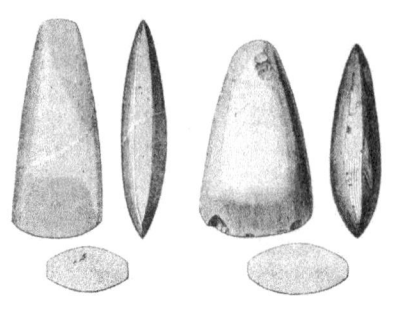

Fig. 58.—Burradon, Northumberland. 1/2

Fig. 59.—Livermere, Suffolk. 1/2

Fig. 59 shows a celt of much the same kind, found at Livermere, near Bury St. Edmunds. It is formed of a close-grained greenstone, and is in my own collection. The angles at the sides are slightly rounded. I have others of nearly the same size and of similar material, found near Cirencester, and at Soham and Bottisham, Cambs. Greenstone celts of about this size, and with the sides more or less flat, so as to range between Figs. 48 and 58, are of not uncommon occurrence in the Fen country. Mr. Fisher, of Ely, has one, found near Manea, and several from Bottisham. I have one, of felstone, 3 1/2 inches long, found at Coton, Cambs., one side of which presents a flat surface 3/8 inch wide, while the other is but slightly flattened. One (4 3/10 inches) was found near Torquay, Devon. [388]

A still more triangular form, more convex on the faces, and having the flat sides much narrower, is shown in Fig. 60, from a specimen in the Greenwell Collection, found at Ilderton, Northumberland. It is formed of a hard, slaty rock or hone-stone. The angles of the sides are rounded.

In the National Museum at Edinburgh are two implements of greenstone (2 3/4 and 3 inches) of nearly similar form to Fig. 60, but having the sides sharp. They were found in the Isle of Skye. [389]

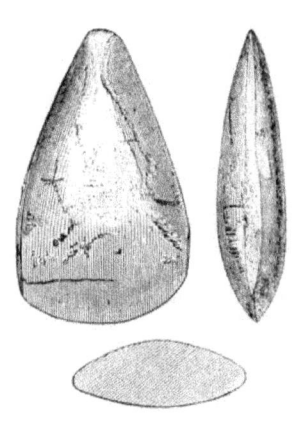

Fig. 60.—Ilderton, Northumberland.

A smaller celt of the same character, 2 1/2 inches long, found in a cairn at Brindy Hill, Aberdeenshire, [390] is in the British Museum.

One 2 5/8 inches long, from Sardis, [391] in Lydia, and in the same collection, is of much the same form, but rounder at the sides and less pointed at the butt.

Implements of the form represented in Fig. 61 occur most frequently in the northern part of Britain, especially in Cumberland and Westmorland, in consequence, it may be supposed, of the felspathic rocks, of which they are usually formed, being there found in the greatest abundance. That here figured is in the British Museum. It is of mottled close-grained stone, beautifully finished, and was found in a turf pit on Windy Harbour Farm, near Pendle, Lancashire. [392] It is more slender than the generality of the implements of this class, which in outline usually more closely resemble Fig. 77, which, however, has a cutting edge at each end. They sometimes slightly expand towards the butt-end.

I have a more roughly-finished implement of this class, with the two faces faceted longitudinally, found near Wigton, Cumberland, and formerly in the Crosthwaite Museum, at Keswick. It is of felspathic ash, much decomposed on the surface, and 9 inches long. I have also a small example of the type (7 1/2 inches) made of whin-stone, and found by Mr. W. Whitaker, F.R.S., near Sudbury, Suffolk, in 1873. Some larger specimens of similar character are in the Christy Collection. One of them is 13 3/4 inches in length.

In the Greenwell Collection is an implement of this type, but with the sides straighter, and the angles rounded, found at Holme, on Spalding Moor, Yorkshire. It is of hone-stone, 7 inches long, 2 1/2 inches broad at the edge, but tapering to 1 1/4 inches at the butt. There is also another of felstone, 12 3/4 long, found at Great Salkeld, Cumberland.

There is a celt of this type in the Blackmore Museum (13 1/8 inches), the butt-end round and sharpened, though the edge has been removed by grinding. It is said to have been found, 5 or 6 feet deep in gravel, at Shaw Hall, [393] near Flixton, Lancashire. Another, in the same collection (8 inches), was found near Keswick.

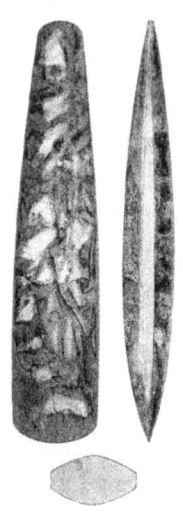

Fig. 61.—Near Pendle, Lancashire. 1/2

What from the engraving would appear to be a large implement of this kind, has been described by Mr. Cuming [394] as a club. "It is wrought of fawn-coloured hone-slate, much like that obtained in the neighbourhood of Snowdon. It weighs 6 1/4 pounds, and measures 17 5/8 inches in length, nearly 3 3/4 inches across its greatest breadth, and nearly 2 1/8 inches in its greatest thickness. The faces are convex, the edges blunt and thinning off at both of the rounded extremities." It was found near Newton, Lancashire. Another so-called club is mentioned as having been found near Keswick. [395]

Clumsy and unwieldy as implements of such a length appear to be if mounted as axes, there can be no doubt of their having been intended for use as cutting tools; and though, from their size, they might be considered to be clubs, yet their form is but ill-adapted for such a weapon, even if we assume that, as is said to be the case with the New Zealand *mere*, they were sometimes employed for thrusting as well as for striking, and, therefore, had the broad end sharpened.

The Stirlingshire specimen, Fig. 77, which is 13 1/4 inches long, is, however, sharp at both ends. There have been, moreover, discovered in Denmark what are indubitably celts, longer than the Newton so-called club. They are sometimes more than 18 inches long, and I have myself such an implement from Jutland, of ochreous flint, 16 inches long and 3 inches broad at the edge, which is carefully sharpened. I have another roughly-chipped Danish celt of flint, 14 1/2 inches long, which weighs 6 lbs. 14 oz., or more than that from Newton.

The celt found in Solway Moss, with its handle still preserved, as will subsequently be mentioned, is of the form of Fig. 61. It is of felspathic rock, 9 1/2 inches long and 2 1/4 inches broad, the edge slightly oblique.

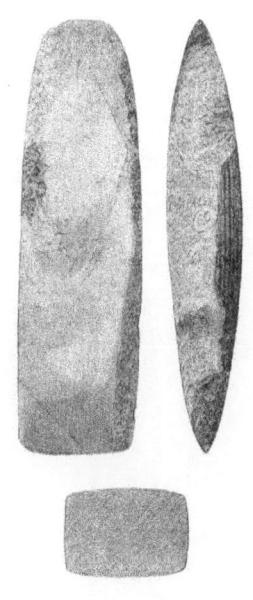

Fig. 62.—Ness. 1/2

One of felstone (15 1/2 inches), was found at Drumour, [396] in Glenshee, Forfarshire, with another 13 inches long. This latter widens out suddenly at the butt. The larger of these two presents on its surface a transverse mark, not unlike that on the Solway Moss specimen, such as may have resulted from that portion of the surface having been protected for a time by a wooden handle, which eventually decayed and perished.

Another from Lempitlaw, in the Kelso Museum, is 13 inches long.

The flattening of the sides and faces of celts is sometimes, though rarely, carried to such an extent that they become almost rectangular in section.

That shown in Fig. 62 was found near the Rye bank, at Ness, [397] in the North Riding of Yorkshire, and is formed of a dark, much altered slaty rock, containing a good deal of iron. The butt-end, though brought to an edge, is not so sharp as the broader or cutting end. The surface is somewhat decomposed. It is in the Greenwell Collection, in which also is the somewhat analogous implement shown in Fig. 63.

This also is from the same part of Yorkshire, having been found, in 1868, at Gilling, [398] in the Vale of Mowbray, 4 ft. deep in peaty clay. It is formed of clay iron-stone, and has the angles somewhat rounded. The edge is oblique and slightly chipped away. Another celt of close-grained schist (5 3/4 inches), found in the same parish, and preserved in the same collection, more resembles in outline that from Ness, though not sharp at the butt, and having an oblique edge. In the Greenwell Collection is a thinner celt of the same type, found at Heslerton Carr.

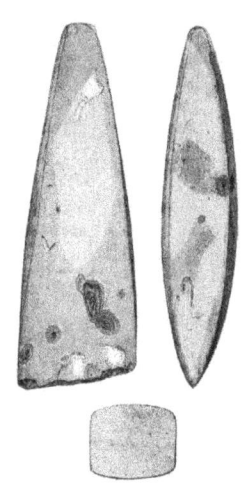

Fig. 63.—Gilling. 1/2

I have a specimen (5 1/4 inches) of hone-stone, rather flatter on one face than the other, from Kirkcaldy, Fife.

An Italian celt, of much the same character as Fig. 62, but of greenstone, has been figured by Gastaldi. [399]

The next celt which I have to describe is even more chisel-like in appearance, both the faces and sides being almost flat and nearly parallel. This peculiarity of form is no doubt mainly due to the schistose character of the rock from which the implement is made; which, in the case of the original of Fig. 64, is a close-grained slate or hone-stone. It was found at Swinton, near Malton, Yorkshire, and was given to me by the late Mr. C. Monkman. The angles are slightly rounded, and the butt-end is tapered off as if to an edge, which, however, is now broken away.

Long, narrow celts of this rectangular section are of very rare occurrence both in Britain and Ireland, and, so far as I am aware, have never been found of flint. In Denmark, on the contrary, they are common in flint, but generally of a larger size than the specimen here engraved. The faces also are usually rather more convex.

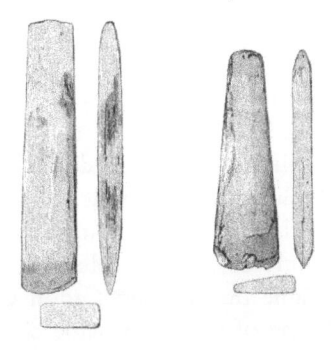

Fig. 64.—Swinton, near Malton. 1/2

Fig. 65.—Scamridge Dykes, Yorkshire. 1/2

They are to be found among the North American [400] forms, sometimes with a hole towards the butt-end, as if for suspension.

Somewhat the same form occurs in Siam and in the Malay Peninsula.

The next specimen, shown in Fig. 65, is of the same material as the last, and was found in the same neighbourhood, at the Dykes, Scamridge, in the North Riding of Yorkshire. Owing to the irregular fissure of the stone, it is considerably thicker at one side than the other. The broader side is flat with the angles chamfered, and the narrower side is rounded. The faces taper at the butt-end, which is ground to a regular curve and blunted. This also was given to me by the late Mr. C. Monkman, of Malton.

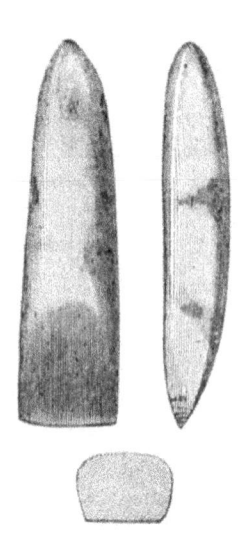

Fig. 66.—Whitwell, Yorkshire. 1/2

A curious variety of celt is shown in Fig. 66, the original of which was found at Whitwell, in the North Riding of Yorkshire, and forms part of the Greenwell Collection. It is made of a hard, shelly limestone, apparently of Oolitic age, the surface of which has been partially eroded. It is nearly flat on one face, and seems to have been intended for mounting as an adze. Other celts of similar material have been found in the same district, and Canon Greenwell has kindly presented me with one of much the same character as this, though far broader in proportion to its thickness. This specimen, which was found at Osgodby, closely resembles in section that from Truro, Fig. 84.

A specimen of the type of Fig. 66 (7 1/4 inches) is in the British Museum. It was found at Creekmoor, near Poole, Dorset.

Some of the large celts from the Shetland Isles present the same peculiarity of being flat on one face, but, as the sides are much rounded, I shall include them among those of oval section.

These, of oval section, form the third subdivision of polished celts, which I now proceed to describe.

It will be observed that implements of this character, formed of flint, are extremely rare. The reason for this appears to be, that from the method in which, in this country, flint celts were chipped out, the sides were in all cases originally sharp, and they had a pointed oval, or *vesica piscis*, section. In polishing, this form was to a great extent preserved, though the edges were, as has been seen, sometimes ground flat and sometimes rounded. It rarely happens, however, that the rounding is carried to so great an extent as to produce such a contour that it is impossible to say within a little where the faces end and the sides begin; though this is often the case with celts of greenstone and other materials, which were shaped out in a somewhat different manner, and in the formation of which grinding played a more important part. It is almost needless to say that I use the word oval in its popular sense, and not as significant of a mathematically true ellipse. At the part where the edge of the celts commences, the section is of course a *vesica piscis*.

The first specimen engraved, Fig. 67, is in my own collection, and was found in the Thames at London. It is of dark greenstone, and, owing to a defect in the piece of stone of which it was made, there is a hollow place in one of the faces. General Pitt Rivers has a similar but more symmetrical celt, of the same material, also found in the Thames. Another, smaller, from the same source, is in the British Museum; and another (8 inches) from the collection of the late Rev. T. Hugo, F.S.A., [401] is now mine. Its edge is rather oblique. I have another from the Thames (7 1/2 inches) with a symmetrical edge.

Fig. 67.—Thames, London. 1/2

Large implements of this form are of not uncommon occurrence in Scotland and in the Shetland Isles. There are several in the National Museum at Edinburgh, and also in the British Museum, and in that of Newcastle. The butt-end is occasionally pointed, and the faces in broad specimens, flatter than in Fig. 67. Several of these celts in the British Museum were found in the middle of the last century, in

Shetland. The largest is 11 inches long, 3 inches wide at the edge, and 1 3/4 inches thick. It was found in Selter, [402] parish of Walls. Others are from 8 inches to 9 inches long. In the case of one, 12 inches long, from Shetland, and in the Edinburgh Museum, the edge is oblique.

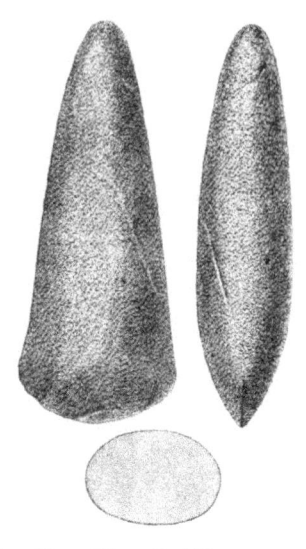

Fig. 68.—Near Bridlington. 1/2

Mr. J. W. Cursiter, of Kirkwall, has a beautiful, long, narrow celt of oval section, from Lunnasting, Shetland. It is formed of spherulitic felstone, and is 9 1/4 inches long, but only 2 1/8 inches wide at the broadest part. Another, 12 inches long, from Trondra, is of felstone, and slightly curved longitudinally, so that it was probably an adze.

Others [403] (14, 11, 10 1/2, and 9 inches) have been figured.

In the Greenwell Collection is a celt of this kind formed of porphyritic greenstone, 13 inches long, from Sandsting, Shetland.

A celt of greenstone (8 inches), in outline much resembling Fig. 72, was found, in 1758, at Tresta, in the parish of Aithsting, Shetland, and is now in the British Museum. It is flat on one face, the other being convex, so that the section is an oval with a segment removed. Such an instrument must, in all probability, have been mounted as an adze, though the flat face may have originally been due to the cleavage of the material, which is a porphyritic greenstone.

Another celt (6 1/4 inches), flat on one face, so that the section presents little more than half an oval, was found in the island of Yell, and is now in the Newcastle Museum.

I have a large heavy celt less tapering at the butt than Fig. 67, 8 1/2 inches long, 3 1/2 inches wide, and 2 1/4 inches thick, said to have been found at Spalding, Lincolnshire. One of flint (7 inches) nearly oval in section, and found at Northampton, is in the museum at that town.

Celts of the same form and character as Fig. 67 are found both in Ireland and in France.

Fig. 68 shows another variety of this type, which becomes almost conical at the butt. The original was found near Bridlington, and is now in my own collection. The material is greenstone. Implements of this form, but rarely expanding at the edge, are of common occurrence in that part of Yorkshire. Some of them have been made of a variety of greenstone liable to decomposition from atmospheric or other causes, and the celts when found present a surface so excessively eroded that their form can with difficulty be recognized. In the Greenwell Collection are celts of the type of Fig. 68, from Willerby, in the East Riding (6 1/4 inches and 5 1/2 inches), and Crambe, in the North Riding of Yorkshire (6 1/4 inches), as well as another (5 3/4 inches) from Sherburn, Durham. I have one nearly 8 inches long, from Speeton, near Bridlington, and several (5 1/2 to 6 inches) from the Cambridge Fens. The surface of one of them is for the most part decomposed, but along a vein of harder material the original polish is preserved.

Mr. F. Spalding has found one (8 inches), with a sideways curve, on the shore at Walton-on-the-Naze.

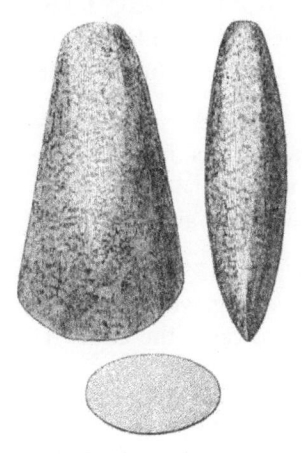

Fig. 69.—Lakenheath, Suffolk. 1/2

A greenstone celt of this form (8 1/2 inches) was found at Minley Manor, [404] Blackwater, Hants.

In the Fitch Collection is one of serpentine (6 1/4 inches), from Dull's Lane, near Loddon, Norfolk, and the late Mr. J. W. Flower had one of greenstone (4 1/4 inches), found at Melyn Works, Neath. The greenstone celt found in Grime's Graves, [405] Norfolk, was of this form, but rather longer in its proportions, being 7 1/2 inches long and 2 1/4 inches broad at the edge, which is oblique. The late Mr. H. Durden, of Blandford, had a greenstone celt of this type (5 inches), found at Langton, near Blandford, the butt-end of which is roughened by picking, probably for insertion in a socket; and the late Rev. E. Duke, of Lake, near Salisbury, had a celt of this character, found in a tumulus in that parish. I have both French and Danish specimens of the same form at the butt, though narrower at the edge.

Another variety, in which the butt-end is less pointed and more oval, is given in Fig. 69. The original is of dark green hornblende schist, and was found at Lakenheath, Suffolk. I have a large implement of similar form and material (5 1/2 inches), with the edge slightly oblique, from Swaffham, Cambridgeshire; another of serpentine (3 1/4 inches), from Coldham's Common, Cambridge; others of greenstone (4 and 3 3/4 inches), from Kempston, Bedford, and Burwell Fen, Cambs.; as well as one of greenstone (4 3/8 inches), from Standlake, Oxon. A celt of this type, of porphyritic stone (5 1/2 inches), found at Branton, Northumberland, is in the Greenwell Collection. It is slightly oblique at the edge. Another of the same character, of greenstone (6 3/4 inches), found at Sproughton, Suffolk, is in the Fitch Collection. Another, 5 inches long, found at Kingston-on-Thames, is in the Museum of the Society of Antiquaries.

Another of green serpentine, faceted to form the edge, and rounded at butt, 4 inches long, was found in a cairn in Fifeshire, and is preserved in the National Museum at Edinburgh.

In the Blackmore Museum is a celt of granite tapering to the rounded point at the butt, 6 1/2 inches long, which has been roughened at the upper end, and is polished towards the edge. It was found in the River Lambourn, Berks.

I have seen another of this form, but of flint (4 1/2 inches), with the sides much rounded, so as to be almost oval, found near Eastbourne, where also this form has occurred in greenstone. The late Mr. H. Durden, of Blandford, had a celt of greenstone of this form 4 3/8 inches long, found at Tarrant Launceston, Dorset. Many of the celts found in India are of this type.

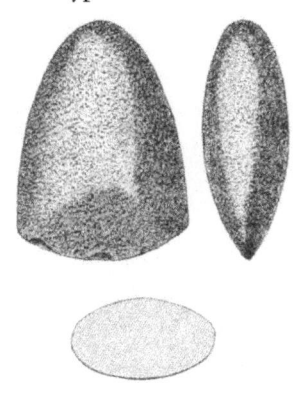

Fig. 70.—Seamer, Yorkshire. 1/2

A shorter form, which also seems to be most prevalent in Yorkshire, is represented in Fig. 70. The specimen figured is from Seamer, formed of greenstone, and belongs to the Greenwell Collection. In the same collection is another (4 inches), rather larger and thicker, from Scampston. Another of quartzite (5 inches), polished all over, but showing traces of having been worked with a pick, was found at Birdsall, near Malton, and is in the collection of Messrs. Mortimer, of Driffield. I have one of greenstone (4 1/2 inches), also from Seamer.

A celt of greenstone, of the same section, but broader and more truncated at the butt, 3 inches long, and found near Bellingham, North Tyne, is in the Newcastle Museum. Another (4 inches), in outline more like Fig. 60, was found in a sepulchral cave at Rhos Digre, [406] Denbighshire.

Some of the stone celts from Italy, Greece, Asia Minor [407] and India, are of much the same form, but usually rather longer in their proportions. I have some Greek specimens more like Fig. 71— kindly given to me by Captain H. Thurburn, F.G.S. Celts of this character are said to have been in use among the North American Indians [408] as fleshing instruments, employed by the women in the preparation of skins. They were not hafted, but held in the hand like chisels. I have a celt almost identical in form and material with Fig. 70, but from Central India.

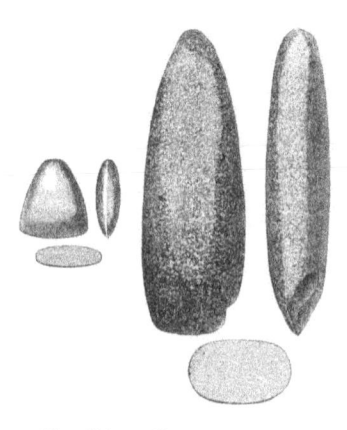

Fig. 71.—Guernsey. 1/2

Fig. 72.—Wareham. 1/2

The form shown in Fig. 71 is inserted among those of Britain, though geographically it may be regarded as French rather than British, having been found in Guernsey. I have engraved it from a cast presented to the Society of Antiquaries by the late Mr. F. C. Lukis, F.S.A. The form occurs in various materials—rarely flint—and is common through the whole of France. A specimen from Surrey is in the British Museum. I have seen one which was said to have been found in the neighbourhood of London, but it was not improbably an imported specimen.

Should authenticated instances of the finding of celts of this class in our southern counties be adduced, they will be of interest as affording *primâ facie* evidence of intercourse with the Continent at an early period.

Small hatchets, both oval and circular in section, have been found at Accra, [409] West Africa, and others, larger, on the Gold Coast. [410] The same form is not uncommon in Greece and Asia Minor.

Major Sladen brought several small jade celts of this form, but flatter at the sides, from Yun-nan, in Southern China. Through his liberality several are in the Christy Collection, and one in my own. Some hæmatite celts found in North America [411] are of much the same size and form.

The specimen engraved as Fig. 72 was found in the neighbourhood of Wareham, Dorsetshire, and is in my own collection. It is formed of syenite, and, unlike the instruments previously described, is narrower at the edge than in the middle of the blade; the section shows that the faces are nearly flat. I have another celt, in which these peculiarities are exaggerated, the faces being flatter, the blade thinner, and also wider in the middle in proportion to the edge, it being 5 1/2 inches long, 2 1/4 inches wide in the middle, and 1 1/2 inches at the edge, and rather less than an inch in thickness. The material is a *Serpula* limestone, and the celt was no doubt formed from a travelled block, as it was found in a Boulder-clay district at Troston, near Bury St. Edmunds. I have a much heavier implement from the same locality, and formed of the same kind of stone. It is 10 inches long, and rather wider in proportion than Fig. 72. It does not narrow towards the edge, but in section and general form may be classed with the specimen there figured.

A large celt, 10 inches long, of the same section, but thinner proportionally, and with straighter and more parallel sides, in outline more like Fig. 79, was found at Pilmoor, in the North Riding of Yorkshire, and forms part of the Greenwell Collection. It is of clay-slate. Another in the same collection, and from North Holme, in the same Riding (10 inches), is broader and flatter, with the sides somewhat more square, and the edge more curved. One face is somewhat hollowed towards one side, possibly to grind out the trace of a too deep chip. A third is from Barmston, in the East Riding (10 1/2 inches), and a beautiful celt of hornblendic serpentine (10 5/8 inches), oval in section and pointed at the butt, was found at Cunningsburgh, [412] Shetland, and another of diorite (10 1/8 inches), rather broader in its proportions than Fig. 72, on Ambrisbeg Hill, [413] Island of Bute. An analogous form from Japan is in the museum at Leyden.

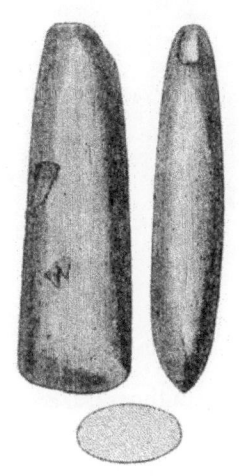

Fig. 73.—Forfarshire. 1/2

A long narrow chisel-like celt, with an oval section, is given in Fig. 73. The original is of dark greenstone, and was found in Forfarshire. It is in the National Museum at Edinburgh. I have a larger celt of the same form (5 1/2 inches), formed of a close-grained grit, and found at Sherburn, Yorkshire. Messrs. Mortimer have another of schist (4 1/2 inches), from Thixendale, Yorkshire. This form occurs, though rarely, in Ireland.

A much larger celt, of metamorphic rock, 8 1/2 inches long, 3 inches broad at the edge, and 1 3/4 inches at the butt, 1 3/8 inches thick, was found on Throckley Fell, Northumberland, and is in the Museum at Newcastle.

Fig. 74 gives a shorter form of implement truncated at the butt. The original, which is in my own collection, is formed of greenstone, and was found at Easton, near Bridlington. It is carefully polished towards the edge, but at the butt it is roughened, apparently with the intention of rendering it more capable of adhesion to its socket. The celt from Malton, Fig. 81, is roughened in a similar manner, and the same is the case with many of the hatchets from the Swiss lake-dwellings, which have been frequently found still fixed in their sockets of stag's horn.

I have another specimen, from South Back Lane, Bridlington, which, however, is not roughened at the butt, and the sides of which have had a narrow flat facet ground along them. It is 6 inches long, and 3 1/2 inches wide at the edge. Mr. W. Tucker has shown me a broken specimen like Fig. 74, found near Loughborough.

Fig. 74.—Bridlington. 1/2

Fig. 75.—Caithness. 1/2

Another form presents a rather pointed, and unusually elongated oval in section, and is pointed at the butt. Fig. 75 represents a highly-finished celt of this kind made of light green, almost jade-like stone, preserved in the National Museum at Edinburgh, and said to have been found in Caithness. It is so thoroughly Carib in character, and so closely resembles specimens I possess from the West Indian Islands, that for some time I hesitated to engrave it. There are, however, sufficiently numerous instances of other implements of the same form having been found in this country for the type to be accepted as British. The celt found at Glasgow, [414] in a canoe at a depth of twenty-five feet below the surface, was of this kind. In the Greenwell Collection is one of porphyritic greenstone (7 inches), and of nearly this form, found at Grantchester, Cambridge. Two celts of this character, the one from Jamaica and the other from the North of Italy, are engraved in the *Archæologia*. [415] Both are in the British Museum.

A celt like Fig. 75 (4 1/2 inches), of a material like jadeite, is said to have been found about 60 years ago at King's Sutton, [416] Northamptonshire. It has much the appearance of being Carib.

Four greenstone celts of this type, one of them rather crooked laterally, were found in 1869 at Bochym, [417] Cury, Cornwall.

Another of aphanite (11 1/2 inches) from Cornwall [418] is in the Edinburgh Museum, where is also one of the same material and form (10 1/2 inches) from Berwickshire, [419] two others of grey porphyritic stone (9 inches) from Aberdeenshire, [420] and another of porphyrite (10 inches) found near Lerwick, [421] Shetland.

I have specimens of the same type from various parts of France. In the Greenwell Collection is a Spanish celt of the same form found near Cadiz.

The bulk of the celts found in Ireland, and formed of other materials than flint, approximate in form to Figs. 69 to 75, though usually rather thinner in their proportion. They range, however, widely in shape, and vary much in their degree of finish.

I now come to the fourth of the subdivisions under which, mainly for the sake of having some basis for classification, I have arranged the polished celts. In it, I have placed those which present any abnormal peculiarities; and the first of these which I shall notice are such as do not materially affect the outline of the celts; as, for instance, the existence of a second cutting edge at the butt-end, at a part where, though the blade is usually tapered away and ground, yet it very rarely happens that it has been left sharp. Indeed, in almost all cases, if in shaping and polishing the celt the butt-end has at one time been sharpened, the edge has been afterwards carefully removed by grinding it away.

The beautifully-formed implement of ochreously-stained flint represented in Fig. 76, was found at Gilmerton, in East Lothian, and is preserved in the National Museum at Edinburgh. The sides are flat with the angles rounded off, and the blade expands slightly at the ends, both of which are sharpened. It is carefully polished all over, so as to show no traces of its having been chipped out, except a slight depression on one face, and this is polished like the rest of the blade. It is upwards of a century since this instrument was turned up by the plough, as described in the *Minutes of the Society of Antiquaries of Scotland* [422] for April 2, 1782, where it is mentioned as the "head of a hatchet of polished yellow marble, sharpened at both ends."

Another from Shetland [423] (11 1/2 inches) is made of serpentine and has both ends "formed to a rounded cutting edge."

A celt from Kirklauchline, Wigtownshire, mentioned at page 135, is much like Fig. 76 in outline.

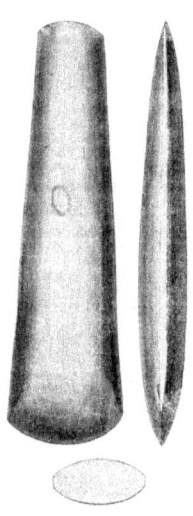

Fig. 76.—Gilmerton, East Lothian

A somewhat similar instrument, but narrower at the butt, formed of jade (?) and 11 inches long, found at Nougaroulet, is engraved in the *Revue de Gascogne.* [424]

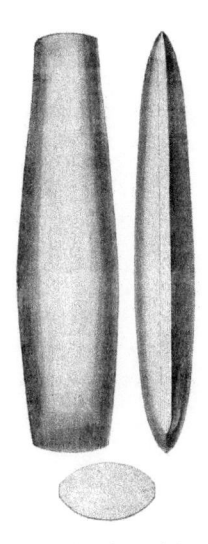

Fig. 77.—Stirlingshire. 1/2

Fig. 77 represents another celt, in the Edinburgh Museum, of similar section, but expanding only at the butt-end, which is sharpened, and contracting from the middle towards the broader end, which, as usual, seems to have been the principal cutting end. It is formed of compact greenstone, and was found in Stirlingshire. In general outline, it closely resembles a common Cumberland form, of which, however, the butt is not sharp. Several such were found in Ehenside Tarn, [425] Cumberland, varying in length from 6 to 14 1/2 inches. One of them was in its original haft. The whole are now in the British Museum. Another celt (10 3/4 inches), made of a fine volcanic ash, was found in 1873 near Loughrigg Tarn, [426] Westmorland. Two celts of much the same form from Drumour, [427] Glenshee, Forfarshire, in 1870, are mentioned on page 119.

Celts with an edge at each end are rare on the Continent, though they are of more frequent occurrence in Ireland. One of this character, found in Dauphiné, France, [428] has been engraved by M. Chantre.

Another from Portugal [429] has been described by myself elsewhere.

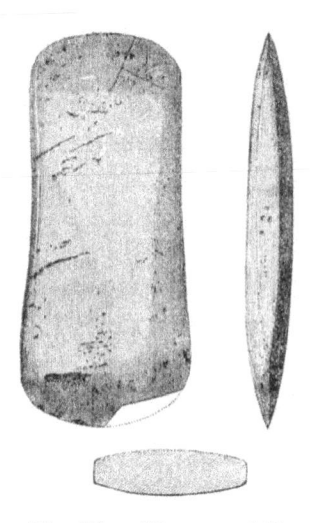

Fig. 78.—Harome. 1/2

A celt of shorter proportions, but also provided with a cutting edge at each end, is shown in Fig. 78. It is in the Greenwell Collection, and was found at Harome, in the North Riding of Yorkshire, where several stone implements of rare form have been discovered. The material is a hard clay-slate. The tool seems quite as well adapted for being used in the hand without any mounting, as for attachment to a haft.

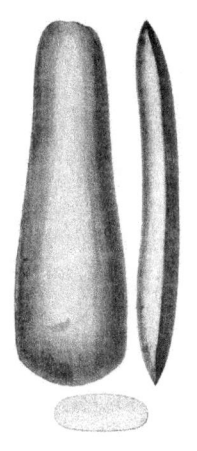

Fig. 79.—Daviot, near Inverness.

Another of these implements, with a cutting edge at either end, is shown in Fig. 79.

As will be observed, it is curved longitudinally, so that if attached to a handle, it must have been after the manner of an adze and not of an axe. The sides curve slightly inwards, which would render any attachment to a handle more secure.

The material of which it is formed is a dark green porphyry. It was found in a cairn at Daviot, [430] near Inverness, in company with a celt of oval section, and pointed at the butt (9 1/2 inches); and also with a greenstone pestle (?) (10 1/4 inches), rounded at each end. This latter was probably formed from a long pebble. They are all preserved in the National Museum at Edinburgh. A curved celt of this character but pointed at the butt-end (14 inches), formed of indurated clay-stone, was found in Shetland. [431] A straighter celt of felstone (13 inches), blunt at the butt-end, was found at Kirklauchline, [432] Wigtownshire.

The next peculiarity which I have to notice, is that of the tapering sides of the celt being curved inwards, as if for the purpose of being more securely fixed either to a handle or in a socket. In the last implement described, the reduction in width towards the middle of the blade would appear to have been intended to assist in fastening it at the end of a handle, as an adze cutting at each end. In Fig. 80 the reduction in width is more abrupt, and the blade would appear to have been mounted as an axe. It is formed of a compact light grey metamorphic rock, and was formerly in the collection of the Rev. S. Banks, of Cottenham, Cambridgeshire. I have a greenstone celt found at Carnac, Brittany, with shoulders of the same character about the middle of the blade. A form of celt expanding into a kind of knob at the butt-end is peculiar to the Lower Loire. [433] It is known as the *"hâche à bouton,"* or *"hâche à tête."*

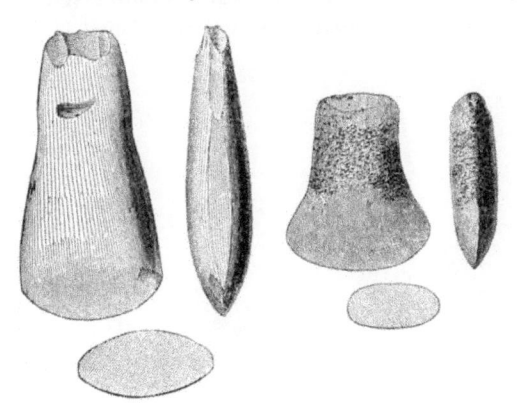

Fig. 80.—Near Cottenham. 1/2

Fig. 81.—Near Malton. 1/2

The original of Fig. 81 was found in a gravel-pit near Malton, Yorkshire. It was at first supposed to have been found in undisturbed drift, and some correspondence upon the subject appeared in the Times newspaper. [434] The gravel, however, in which it was found seems to belong to the series of Glacial deposits, and if so, is of considerably greater antiquity than any of the old River-gravels, in which the unpolished flint implements have been discovered. This celt is of greenstone, carefully polished at the edge, and towards the butt slightly roughened by being picked with a sharp pointed tool. This roughening is in character similar to that which has been observed on many of the celts from the Swiss Lake-dwellings and from France, [435] and was no doubt intended in their case to make the stone adhere more firmly in the socket of stag's horn in which it was inserted. The object in this case would appear to be the same; and, like other polished celts, it belongs to the Neolithic Period. The expansion of the blade towards the edge is very remarkable.

A celt of the same type as that from Malton, but somewhat oblique at the edge, and formed of quartz containing pyrites, found at Soden, is in the Museum at Bonn.

A flat form of stone hatchet, expanding rapidly from a slightly tapering butt about half the entire length of the blade, so as to form a semicircular cutting-edge, has been found in South Carolina. [436] There is a small perforation in the centre, as if for a pin, to assist in securing it in its handle.

Another form, with the blade reduced for about half its length, so as to form a sort of tang, is engraved by Squier and Davis. [437]

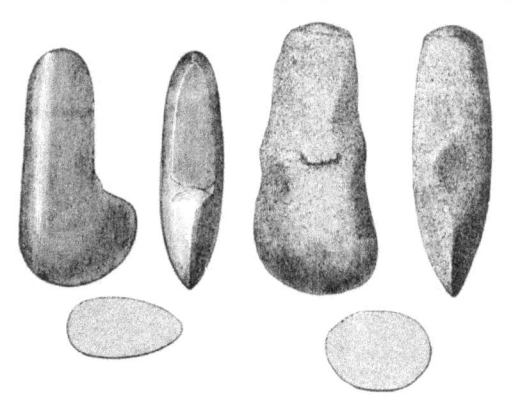

Fig. 82.—Mennithorpe, Yorkshire. 1/2

Fig. 83.—Middleton Moor.

The celt engraved in Fig. 82 presents an abrupt shoulder on one side only, which, however, is in this case probably due to the form of the pebble from which it was made, a portion of which had split off along a line of natural cleavage. It is formed of a reddish, close-grained porphyritic rock, and is subquadrate in section at the butt. It was found at Mennithorpe, Yorkshire, and is in the Greenwell Collection. In the same collection is a thin celt of clay-slate, 4 3/4 inches long, of much the same form, but rounded at the shoulder. It was found at Ryedale, in the North Riding of Yorkshire.

Some of the shouldered implements may have been intended for use in the hand, without hafting. This appears to be the case with the greenstone celt shown in Fig. 83. It was found on Middleton Moor, Derbyshire, and was in the collection of the late Mr. J. F. Lucas. The shallow grooves at the sides seem intended to receive the fingers much in the same manner as the grooves in the handles of some of the tools of the Eskimos or the handles of the bronze sickles of the Swiss Lake-dwellers. [438] An Irish celt, 8 inches long, and now in the Blackmore Museum, has two notches on one side only, and more distinctly formed, "seemingly to receive the fingers and give a firmer hold when used in the hand without a haft."

Another peculiar instrument adapted for being held in the hand is shown in Fig. 83A. It was found at Keystone, Huntingdonshire, [439] and is now in the British Museum. It is made of greenstone, and in form resembles the sharp end of a celt with flat sides let into a spherical handle. Some hand-hatchets from Australia are of much the same character, but in their case the knob is distinct from the blade, and formed of hard *xanthorrhœa* gum.

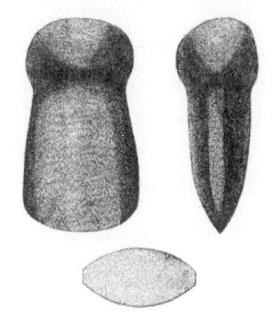

Fig. 83A.—Keystone. 1/2

The original of Fig. 84 is in the Greenwell Collection, and was found near Truro. It is of serpentine, with an oblique edge, and seems to have been formed from a pebble with little labour beyond that of sharpening one end. Though much flatter on one face than the other, it would appear, from the slanting edge, to have been used as an axe and not as an adze, unless indeed it were a hand-tool.

A beautiful adze formed of chalcedonic flint is shown in Fig. 84A. kindly lent by the Society of Antiquaries of Scotland. The original was found at Fernie Brae, [440] Slains, Aberdeenshire. It is 7 inches long, and of nearly triangular section. A somewhat similar adze of greenstone was found at Little Barras, [441] Drumlithie, Kincardineshire. I have a flint adze (5 inches) of much the same character, but not so flat and blunt at the butt-end, and ground at the edge only, which was found in Reach Fen, Cambs. It is shown in Fig. 35A at page 92.

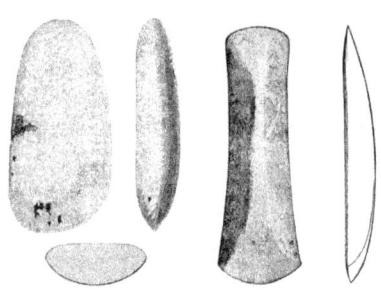

Fig. 84.—Near Truro.

Fig. 84A.—Slains (7 inches long).

Another peculiarity of form is where the edge, instead of being as usual nearly in the centre of the blade, is almost in the same plane as one of the faces, like that of a joiner's chisel. An implement of this character, from a "Pict's castle," Clickemin, near Lerwick, Shetland, is shown in Fig. 85.

It was presented to me by the late Rev. Dr. Knowles, F.S.A. The material appears to be a hard clay-slate. The form is well adapted for being mounted as an adze, much in the same manner as the nearly similar implements in use by the South Sea Islanders. A New Zealand [442] adze of precisely the same character has been figured.

Sometimes the edge of a celt, instead of being sharp, has been carefully removed by grinding, so as to present a flat or rounded surface. In Fig. 86 is represented a singular implement of this kind in flint. It is polished all over; one side is straight, and the other curved; both ends are curved, but one is rounded at the edge and the other flat. It is difficult to understand for what purpose such an instrument can have been intended. There is no reason for supposing that the grinding at the ends was later in date than the formation of the other parts. I have others like Fig. 30 with the edge also flattened, one of these I found, as already mentioned, at Abbot's Langley; and I have seen another flint celt of much the same form, found at Chesterford, Cambs., with a somewhat flat edge, but rounded and worn away, as if by scraping some soft substance. Small transverse *striæ*, such as might have been caused by particles of sand, are visible on the worn edge. In the Greenwell Collection is a portion of a celt of greenstone, the fractured face ground flat and a portion of the edge also ground away.

Fig. 85.—Near Lerwick. 1/2

Fig. 86.—Weston, Norfolk. 1/2

A small flint celt, with a round polished edge instead of a cutting one as usual, was found, with other objects, in a barrow on Elton Moor, Derbyshire. [443] I have seen a small flint celt like Fig. 33, with the edge perfectly rounded by grinding. It was found between Deal and Dover, near Kingsdown, by Mr. Hazzeldine Warren, of Waltham Cross.

It is hard to say for what purpose the edge was thus made blunt. In some cases, however, the instruments may have been used as battle-axes, the edges of which when of the perforated forms are usually flattened or rounded, probably with the view of preventing accidental injury to those who carried them. In some celts, however, the broad end is so much rounded that they can hardly be said to have an edge, and they have more the appearance of having-been burnishing or calendering tools. I have observed this rounding of the end in some Irish and French specimens, not made of flint, as well as in one from India.

Occasionally, but very seldom, a circular concave recess is worked on each face of the celt, apparently for the purpose of preventing it from slipping when held in the hand and used either as a chopping or cutting instrument. That engraved as Fig. 87 was kindly lent me by Mr. J. R. Mortimer, who found it on Acklam Wold, Yorkshire. It is of greenstone, and has been polished over almost the entire surface. The butt-end is nearly flat transversely, and ground in the other direction to a sweep, so as to fit beneath the forefinger, when held by the thumb and middle-finger placed in the recesses on the faces. Such recesses are by no means uncommon on the stones intended for use as hammers, and farther on (p. 242) I have engraved a hammer-stone of this class which would seem to have been originally a celt such as this, but which has entirely lost any approach to an edge by continual battering. In Mr. Mortimer's specimen the edge is fairly sharp, though it has lost some splinters from it in ancient times.

Fig. 87.—Acklam Wold. 1/2

Fig. 88.—Fimber. 1/2

In the same collection is another specimen, found near Fimber, formed of a green metamorphic rock. The butt-end is ground flat, and the sides nearly so. There is a slight depression worked on each face. The edge is slightly rounded, and shows longitudinal *striæ*. By the owner's kindness I am able to engrave it as Fig. 88.

In General Pitt Rivers's Collection is a celt from Hindostan, with a cup-shaped depression on one of its faces. A celt of basalt from Portugal [444] has such a depression on each face.

In the fine and extensive Greenwell Collection, so often referred to, is another remarkable celt, Fig. 89, which, though entirely different in character from those last described, may also have been intended for holding in the hand. It is of greenstone, the surface of which is considerably decomposed, and was found at Duggleby, in the East Riding of Yorkshire. On each side is an elongated concavity, well adapted for receiving the end of the forefinger when the instrument is held in the hand with the thumb on one face and the middle finger on the other. At first sight it might appear that the depressions had been made with the view of perforating the blade, so as to make it like Fig. 133. It is, however, too thin for such a purpose, and as the depressions can hardly be connected with any method of hafting, it appears probable that they are merely for the purpose of giving the hand a secure grip, when using the instrument as a cutting tool. This form is not uncommon in India.

Some of the stone hatchets from British Guiana [445] have a notch on either side, apparently to assist in fastening them to their haft. A form with projecting lugs half-way down the blade has been found in Armenia. [446]

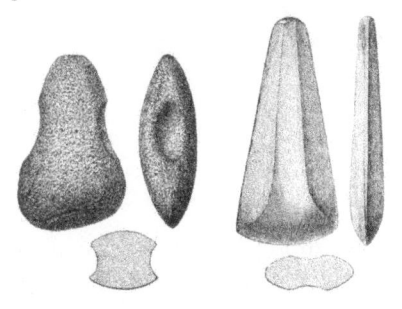

Fig. 89.—Duggleby. 1/2

Fig. 90.—Guernsey. 1/2

The last peculiarity I have to notice is when the blade of the celt assumes an ornamental character, by being fluted or otherwise ornamented. That represented in Fig. 90 is deeply fluted on either face. I have engraved the figure from a cast in the Museum of the Society of Antiquaries, the original of which was in the possession of F. C. Lukis, Esq., M.D. It was found at St. Sampson, Guernsey. Assuming the figure given by M. Brouillet to be correct, a somewhat similar celt of red flint was found with skeletons in the Tombelle de Brioux, Poitou. [447] Another with three hollow facets on the lower parts of one face was found in Finistère. [448] I have a small celt of nearly similar form, but not so hollow on the faces, from Costa Rica. Such specimens are extremely rare, and I cannot at present point to any other examples. Indeed, it may be questioned how far the implements found in the Channel Islands come within the scope of the present work. The grooves in the faces of the celt found at Trinity, near Edinburgh, [449] can hardly have been intended for ornament.

A kind of celt, not uncommon in Denmark, like Fig. 55, but with a small hole drilled through it at the butt-end, as if for suspension, like a sailor's knife, has very rarely been found in England, but I have a broken specimen from Cavenham, Suffolk, formed of greenstone. When perfect the celt must have been in outline like Fig. 69, but thinner.

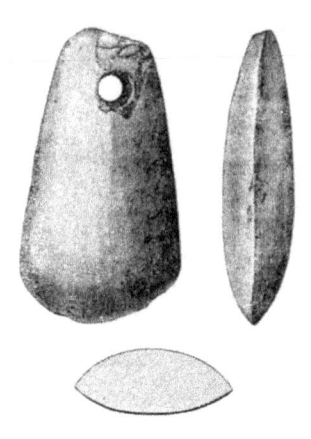

Fig. 90A.—Wereham. 1/2

A perfect example is shown in Fig. 90A. It is formed of whin-stone and was found in 1896 at Wereham, near Stoke Ferry, Norfolk. It is in the collection of Mr. E. M. Beloe, F.S.A., who has kindly permitted me to figure it. It is curiously striated towards the butt-end, possibly from friction in a socket. One from Thetford, perforated through the centre of the face, is in the National Museum at Edinburgh. Another of felstone (11 1/4 inches), oval in section, found at Melness, Sutherlandshire, was exhibited to the Society of Antiquaries of Scotland in March, 1897. Bored celts, though rare in Britain, occur in Brittany [450] and other parts of France, as well as in Italy. [451] A few have also been found in Ireland. [452] A stone hatchet from Quito in the Christy Collection, though of somewhat different form, is perforated at the end in this manner.

A vastly greater number of instances of the discovery in Britain of stone hatchets or celts might have been cited; but inasmuch as in most cases where mention is made of celts, no particulars are given of their form, and as they occur in all parts of the country, it seems needless to encumber my pages with references. As an instance of their abundance, I may mention that the late Mr. Bateman [453] records the discovery of upwards of thirty, at fourteen different localities within a small district of Derbyshire. Numerous discoveries in Yorkshire are cited by Mr. C. Monkman. [454]

Dr. Joseph Stevens has recorded several from the Thames near Reading, [455] and a very large number of those in my own and various public collections I have had to leave unnoticed for want of space.

The circumstances under which stone celts of various forms have been discovered must now be considered, with a view of throwing some light on their antiquity, and the length of time they have remained in use. And it must at the outset be confessed that we have but little to guide us on these points. We have already seen that they have been found with objects of bronze; for in the barrow on Upton Lovel Down, [456] examined by Sir R. Colt Hoare, flint celts, both rough and polished, were discovered in company with a perforated stone axe, and a bronze pin, though in this instance there were two interments. The Ravenhill tumulus, near Scarborough, [457] is more conclusive; for in it was an urn containing burnt bones, a broken flint celt, flint arrow-heads, and a beautiful bronze pin one and a-half inches long. The evidence of other recorded cases is but weak. Near Tynewydd, in the parish of Llansilin, Denbighshire, [458] a greenstone celt and a bronze socketed celt were found together in moving an accumulation of stones, which did not, however, appear to have been a cairn. In another instance, [459] three stone celts, one roughly chipped, the others polished, are stated to have been found with a bronze socketed celt in the parish of Southend, Kintyre, Argyllshire. At Campbelton, in the same district, [460] were found two polished stone celts, and with them, on the same spot, two stone moulds for casting looped spear-heads of bronze.

Though there may be doubts as to the true association of stone celts with instruments of bronze in some of these cases, the presumptive evidence is strong of their having remained in use, as might indeed have been reasonably expected, after the introduction of bronze for cutting-tools. By the time bronze knife-daggers had become common, perforated battle-axes had also come to form part of a warrior's ordinary equipment. These are often found with the daggers in graves, and there can be no doubt of the ordinary form of stone hatchet having preceded that with a shaft-hole. There are, however, a number of facts in connection with the occurrence of the ordinary stone celt that must not be passed over, inasmuch as at first sight they tend to raise a presumption of celts having remained in use even during the period of the Roman occupation of this country. I will shortly recapitulate the principal facts to which I allude.

In excavating a Roman building at Ickleton, [461] Cambs., the late Lord Braybrooke found a greenstone celt; and another is said to have been found with Roman remains at Alchester, Oxfordshire. [462] A flint celt is also described as having been found with Roman antiquities at Eastbourne. [463]

Among the relics discovered by Samuel Lysons, F.R.S., in the Roman villa at Great Witcombe, [464] Gloucestershire, is described "a British hatchet of flint." Another flint celt was found close by a Roman villa at Titsey. [465] Flint celts and scrapers were found in the Romano-British village in Woodcuts Common, [466] Dorset, by General Pitt Rivers.

A stone celt, like Fig. 70, has been engraved by Artis [467] as a polishing stone used in the manufactory of Roman earthen vessels, but no evidence is given as to the cause of its being thus regarded.

At Leicester, a fragment of a flint celt was found at a depth of twelve feet from the surface on an old "ground line," and accompanied by bone objects which Sir Wollaston Franks assigned to a late Roman or even possibly to an early Saxon period. [468]

In the Saxon burial-place at Ash, in Kent, were found a polished flint celt, "a circular flint stone," and a Roman fibula. [469]

In 1868, a fibrolite hatchet was found within a building at Mont Beuvray, the ancient Bibracte, [470] with three Gaulish coins of the time of Augustus.

Others of flint were found in a Merovingian cemetery at Labruyère, in the Côte d'Or. [471]

The occurrence at Gonsenheim, near Mainz, of a series of thin polished celts with remains presumably Roman, has already been mentioned. In two, if not more, instances in Denmark, [472] fragments of iron have been found in tumuli, and apparently in association with polished hatchets and other instruments of flint and stone. It seems doubtful, however, whether in these cases the iron was not subsequently introduced.

The association of these stone implements with Roman, and even Post-Roman, remains in so many different places, would at first sight appear to argue their contemporaneity; but in the case of the celts being found on the sites of Roman villas, two things are to be remarked—First, that sites once occupied may, and constantly do, continue in occupation for an indefinite length of time, so that the imperishable relics of one age, such as those in stone, may become mixed in the soil with those of a long subsequent date; and second, that had these stone implements been in common use in Roman times, their presence among Roman remains would have been the rule and not the exception, and we should have found them mentioned by Latin authors. Moreover, if their use had survived in this manner into Roman times, we should expect to find them still more abundantly associated with tools of the Bronze Age. We have, however, seen how rarely this class of stone instruments is found with bronze.

As to the stone celt discovered at Ash, Mr. Douglas remarks it may not "be improbable that this stone instrument was deposited with the dead, as an amulet; and which the owner had found and preserved with a superstitious reverence." In a tumulus in Flanders, [473] six celts were found placed upright in a circle round the interment, but from the difference in the condition of their surface they appeared to be of different ages, so that it has been suggested that they also were gathered from the surface of the soil and placed in the tomb as amulets. We shall subsequently see that flint arrow-heads were frequently thus preserved in Merovingian cemeteries.

In many cases in Germany, [474] stone axes, for the most part perforated, are said to have been found in association with objects of iron; but the proofs of the contemporaneity of the two classes of objects are not satisfactory. The religious veneration attaching to the Thor's hammers may, however, have had to do with their interment in graves, at a time when they had ceased to be in ordinary use. Moreover, the axes may have been preserved to ward off lightning.

Another argument in favour of these instruments having remained in use in Britain until a comparatively late period, has been derived from the circumstance of the words *stan-æx* and *stan-bill*, occurring in Ælfric's Saxon glossary. These words are translated by Lye [475] as a stone axe, a stone bill—terms which have naturally been regarded as referring to axes and bills made of stone, which, therefore, it might be reasonably inferred were in use at the time when the glossary was written, or about A.D. 1000. On examination, however, it appears that no such inference is warranted. The glossary is Latin with the Saxon equivalents annexed to each word, and the two words referred to are *Bipennis*, rendered *twibille* and *stan-æx*; and Marra, rendered *stan-bill*. Now *Bipennis* is an axe cutting at either end, and the word is accurately rendered by "twibille;" [476]—the axe having "bill" or steel at its two edges. But a double-cutting axe in stone is a form of very rare occurrence, and this alone raises a presumption of the *stan* in *stan-æx* referring to stone in some other manner than as the material of which the axe was made. The second word, *Marra*, seems to clear up the question, for this was a mattock or pick-axe, or some such tool, and this is rendered *stan-bill*,—the steel for use on or among stones. The stone axe may be one for cutting stones, like the mill-bill of the present day, which is used for dressing mill-stones, and this being usually sharp at each end, might not inaptly be regarded as the equivalent of the ancient *bipennis*. An axe is still a bricklayer's tool, and is also occasionally used by stone-cutters. It seems, then, that the "*stan*" in these two Saxon words refers, not to the material of which the axes or bills were made, but to the stones on or among which they were used. In Halliwell's "Dictionary of Archaic and Provincial Words," [477] the interpretation of Stone-axe is given as "A stone-worker's axe," but it is not stated where the term occurs.

In the "*Matériaux*" [478] M. Soreil has called attention to a very early German poem, possibly of the fifth century, in which the heroes are described as contending with stone axes. The subject has been discussed by Dr. Much, [479] who suggests that the name survived long after the actual use of the weapons, and points out that the modern word Hellebarde (halberd) has the same meaning, *hella* in Old German signifying "stone," and *barte* being still used to signify an "axe" or "chopper." He also hints at a connection between the *scrama-seax* or large knife, with *saxum*. The whole paper is worth reading.

In the Song of Hildebrand and Hadubrand, probably of the eighth century, stone hammers, *staim-borts*, are also mentioned.

"Do stoptun tosamane staimbort chludun

Hewun harmlicco huitte scilti." [480]

The passage in "William of Poitiers," [481]—"Jactant cuspides ac diversorum generum tela, sævissimas quasque secures ac lignis imposita saxa,"—which has been cited as proving that some of the Anglo-Saxons fought with weapons of stone at the battle of Hastings, seems only to refer to stone missiles probably discharged from some engines of war, and serving the same purpose as the stone cannon-balls of more recent times. Professor Nilsson [482] has pointed out that *jactare* often signifies to brandish, and argues that the large stone axes were too heavy either for brandishing or throwing as weapons. It seems to me, however, that *jactare* in this passage is used in the sense of throwing, the same as in Virgil, [483]—

"Deucalion vacuum lapides jactavit in orbem,

Unde homines nati, durum genus."

If it be uncertain to how late a period these Neolithic implements remained in use in this country, it is still more uncertain to how early a period their introduction may be referred. If we take the possible limits in either direction, the date at which they fell into disuse becomes approximately fixed as compared with that at which they may first have come into use in Britain. For we may safely say that the use of bronze must have been known in this country 500 or 600 years B.C., and, therefore, that at that time cutting tools of stone began to be superseded; while by A.D. 1100, it will be agreed on all hands that they were no longer in use. We can, therefore, absolutely fix the date of their desuetude within at the outside two thousand years; but who can tell within any such limits the time when a people acquainted with the use of polished stone implements first settled in this island, or when the process of grinding them may have been first developed among native tribes? The long duration of the period which intervened between the deposit of the River-gravels (containing, so far as at present known, implements chipped only and not polished), and the first appearance of polished hatchets, is not in this country so well illustrated as in France; but even there, all that can be said as to the introduction of polished stone hatchets, is that it took place subsequently to the accumulation in the caves of the south of France, of the deposits belonging to an age when reindeer constituted one of the principal articles of food of the cave-dwellers. As to the date at which those cave-deposits were formed, history and tradition are silent, and at present even Geology affords but little aid in determining the question.

But though we cannot fix the range in time of these implements, it will be well to notice some of the circumstances under which they have been found, if only as illustrative of the habits and customs of the ancient people who used them. Of course the most instructive cases are those in which they have occurred with interments, and some of these I have already incidentally mentioned; as, for instance, the discovery in a barrow on Upton Lovel Down of a roughly chipped celt, with others polished at the edge, and other objects; and that of two very roughly chipped flint celts found by Dr. Mantell, in a barrow at Alfriston, Sussex.

A celt of greenstone, ground at the edge only, was found in a barrow with a burnt body on Seamer Moor, Yorkshire, by the Rev. F. Porter; and in another [484] barrow on the same moor, Canon Greenwell found a celt of clay-slate, like Fig. 50, burnt red, in association with a deposit of burnt bones. In a third tumulus on the same moor, opened by the late Lord Londesborough, there were numerous interments, but one of these consisted of a small portion of human bones, [485] four flint celts, five beautifully formed arrow-heads of flint, two rude spear-heads of flint, two well-formed knives and spear-heads of flint, two very large tusks of the wild boar, and a piece of deer-horn, perforated at the end and drilled through, which was thought to be the handle for one of the celts.

In these three instances the polished celts accompany interments by cremation, and probably belong to a late period of the Stone Age in Britain. They have, however, been frequently found with the remains of unburnt bodies. In one of the banks of an ancient settlement near Knook Castle, Upton Lovel, Sir R. Colt Hoare [486] discovered a skeleton with its head towards the north and at its feet a fine black celt. In a barrow about seven miles east of Pickering, [487] besides other interments is said to have been one of a skeleton with the head towards the south, and a "beautiful stone adze or celt, 3 1/2 inches long, wrought in green basalt, and a very elaborately chipped spear of flint, near four inches long, near its right hand."

In another barrow in the same district [488] the skeleton was accompanied by "a very small celt or chisel of grey flint, smoothly rubbed, and a plain spear-head of the same material."

In another barrow on Elton Moor, Derbyshire, [489] there lay behind the skeleton a neatly ornamented "drinking cup," containing three pebbles of quartz, a flat piece of polished iron ore, a small celt of flint, with a rounded instead of a cutting edge, a beautifully chipped cutting tool, twenty-one circular-ended instruments, and seventeen rude pieces of flint.

In Liffs Low, near Biggin, [490] Mr. Bateman found a skeleton in the contracted position, and with it two flint celts beautifully chipped and polished at the cutting edges; two flint arrow-heads delicately chipped, two flint knives polished on the edge, and one of them serrated on the back to serve as a saw; numerous other objects of flint, some red ochre, a small earthenware cup, and a hammer-head of stag's horn.

In Cross Low, near Parwich, [491] a fragment of a celt and a small piece of chipped flint were with a human skeleton in a cist; and a kind of flint axe or tomahawk is reported to have been similarly found in a barrow near Pickering. [492]

In the Gospel Hillock barrow, near Buxton, Captain Lukis, F.S.A., found near the shoulder of a contracted skeleton, a polished flint celt, of which an engraving is given in the *Reliquary*. [493]

In what appears to have been a tumulus at Seaford, [494] Sussex, celts both whole and broken, and other forms of worked flint, were found, but the account given of the exploration is rather confused.

It will be observed that in these cases stone celts accompany the earliest form of interment with which we are acquainted, that in which the body is deposited in the contracted position. The reason why bodies were interred in that posture appears to be that it was in all probability the usual attitude of sleep, at a period when the small cloak of the day must generally have served as the only covering at night.

In Scotland stone celts seem to be of frequent occurrence in cairns. I have one, already mentioned, [495] which is said to have been found with four others in a cairn on Druim-a-shi, near Culloden.

Three others, of which two have been already described, [496] were discovered in a cairn in Daviot parish, Inverness, together with a cylindrical implement, possibly a pestle, and are now in the National Museum at Edinburgh. Not improbably my specimen came from the same cairn.

Another [497] was found in the Cat's Cairn, Cromartyshire. A second, [498] pointed at the butt, is said to have been found in a "Druidical circle," Aberdeenshire. A third, [499] of black flint, from the parish of Cruden, Aberdeenshire, would seem to have accompanied an interment, as with it was found a necklace of large oblong beads of jet, and rudely shaped pieces of amber.

None, however, of these instances afford any absolute testimony as to their exact or even approximate age, unless, indeed, the jet and amber, if they really accompanied the flint celt, point in that case to a date at all events not far removed from that of the bronze objects with which such necklaces have frequently been found.

In the other cases of interments in barrows, however ancient they may be, it seems probable that they are not those of the earliest occupants of this country, by whom polished stone celts, or those of the same character rough hewn only, were in use. The labour bestowed in the formation of the graves and the erection of the barrows must have been immense, and could hardly have been undertaken until a stage of civilization had been reached higher than that of some of the ruder savage races of the present day.

It may be mentioned that stone celts are not unfrequently found in the soil of which barrows are composed, but in no way connected with the interments in the barrow.

There are a few instances of the finding of these instruments, not in association with interments, where the circumstances under which they have been discovered testify to a great, though still indeterminate antiquity. One, for instance, of greenstone, in the Museum of the Society of Antiquaries, is stated to have been "found deep in the clay whilst digging the Chelsea Waterworks at Kingston." [500] Others in a sand-bed near York [501] were 6 or 7 feet below the surface, and nearly a quarter of a mile from the river which is thought to have deposited the sand.

In Wilson's "Prehistoric Annals of Scotland" [502] is recorded the finding of a greenstone celt in a primitive canoe, formed of a hollowed trunk of oak, at a depth of 25 feet from the surface, at Glasgow; and in the Norwich Museum is one of brown flint, ground all over, 4 1/4 inches long, similar to Fig. 54, but with facets towards the edge, as if from repeated grinding, which is stated to have been found fixed in a tree in the submarine forest at Hunstanton, by the Rev. George Mumford, of East Winch, in the year 1829.

On the whole evidence it would appear, from the number of implements of this class which has been discovered, from the various characters of the interments with which they are associated, and from the circumstances under which they have been found, that these stone celts must have been in use in this country during a long period of years; though we still revert to our first confession, that it is impossible to determine at how early a date this period commenced, or to how late a date it may have extended. If, however, the occupation of this part of the globe by man was continuous from the period of the deposit of the old River-gravels unto the present day, it seems probable that some of these implements may claim an almost fabulous antiquity, while in certain remote districts of Britain into which civilization made but a tardy approach, it is possible that their use may have lingered on to a time when in other parts of the country, owing to the superiority and abundance of metallic tools, these stone hatchets had long fallen into disuse.

Instances of this comparatively late use of stone celts appear to be afforded by some of the discoveries made in the Orkney and Shetland Isles; and it is doubtful whether in Ireland the use of stone implements did not survive in some parts of the country to a far more recent date than would at first sight appear probable. I have, however, remarked on this subject elsewhere. [503] Sir Arthur Mitchell's book, "The Past in the Present," may also be consulted.

The methods in which these instruments were used and mounted must to some extent have varied in accordance with the purposes to which they were applied. In describing the forms, I have pointed out that in some cases they were used as axes or hatchets, and in other cases as adzes, and that there are some celts which not improbably were used in the hand without any handle at all, or else were mounted in short handles, and used after the manner of chisels or knives.

The instances of their being found in this country still attached to their handles are rare. In the case of the celt found near Tranmere, [504] Cheshire, and now in the Mayer Museum at Liverpool, "the greater part of the wood had perished, but enough remained to show that the handle had passed in a slightly diagonal direction towards the upper end of the stone." In the Christy Collection is a large felstone celt 12 1/4 inches long and 3 1/4 inches broad, of the same section as Fig. 43, slightly flattened at the sides, on the face of which the mark of the handle is still visible, crossing it obliquely near the middle. This specimen was found at Pentney, Norfolk. Similar marks may not improbably be observed on other specimens, like that from Drumour already mentioned at page 119.

Fig. 91.—Solway Moss.

In the Solway Moss, near Longtown, a hafted hatchet was found by a labourer digging peat, at the depth of rather more than six feet, but the handle appears to have been broken, even at the time when the sketch was made from which the woodcut given in the *Proceedings of the Society of Antiquaries* [505] was engraved, which is, by permission, here reproduced. The instrument is now in the British Museum, but the haft, in drying, has, unfortunately, quite lost its form, and is still further broken. The process of preserving wood when in the tender condition in which it is found after long burial in peat was probably not known at the time. It has been adopted with great success by Mr. Engelhardt in preserving the wooden antiquities from the Danish peat bogs, and consists in keeping the objects moist until they have been well steeped, or even boiled, in a strong solution of alum, after which they are allowed to dry gradually, and are found to retain their form in a remarkable manner.

It is probably owing to the broken and distorted condition of the wood that the sketch was inaccurate as to the position of the blade with regard to the handle, for the mark of the wood where it was in contact with the stone is still visible, and proves that the central line of the blade was inclined outwards at an angle of about 100° to the haft, instead of being nearly vertical, as shown. The edge of the hatchet is oblique to nearly the same extent as the inclination of the blade to the haft. It would seem from this, that the obliquity of the edge was in some cases connected with the method of hafting, and not always, as suggested by Nilsson, [506] the result of the blade being most worn away in the part farthest from the hand holding the shaft.

The preservation of the wooden handle has been more successfully effected in the case of the celt shown in Fig. 92, engraved from a photograph kindly supplied me by Mr. R. D. Darbishire, F.G.S. It is figured on a larger scale in the *Archæologia*, [507] where all the circumstances of the discovery are set forth in detail. The axe was found, in the year 1871, in peat which had once formed the bed of a small lake, known as Ehenside Tarn, near Egremont, in Cumberland, which has now been drained. With it were found another haft of the same character, and several stone celts, one of them 14 1/2 inches in length, with the sides but slightly curved, and almost equally broad at each end. Some wooden paddles and clubs formed of beech and oak, pottery and other objects, were also found. The farmer who cultivates the former bed of the lake had previously discovered some stone antiquities which were brought under the notice of Sir Wollaston Franks, who induced Mr. Darbishire to make the search which was so amply rewarded. The haft is formed of a hard root of beech-wood, and has been most carefully carved, the surface exhibiting alternate cuts and ridges forming small concave facets about 1/8-inch apart, and arranged spirally. The other haft for a celt is of oak-wood, and is not so well preserved. It will be noticed that the end of the beech-wood handle has originally been recurved, possibly with a view of steadying the butt-end of the celt.

Fig. 92.—Cumberland. 1/4

Curiously enough, in the outline of a celt in its handle, carved on the under side of the roof-stone of a dolmen, known as La Table des Marchands, near Locmariaker, Brittany, [508] the end of the handle seems also to be curved back beyond the socket for the blade, which however it does not touch. At the other end of the handle there is a loop like a sword guard, for the insertion of the hand. There is some little difficulty in determining the exact form of this incised carving, as the lines are shallow, and the light does not fall upon them. I speak from a sketch I made on the spot in 1863. Other such representations occur in Brittany. [509]

In a paper [510] on a neolithic flint weapon in a wooden haft, Mr. C. Dawson has given an account of a discovery made by Mr. Stephen Blackmore, a shepherd of East Dean, near Eastbourne, of a flint hatchet at Mitchdean. It was lying in its wooden haft which was perfectly carbonized, but Mr. Blackmore made a drawing of it, apparently from memory. He describes the blade, which seems to have been unground, as lying in a horizontal groove cut in one side of the shaft, which was 2 feet 6 inches long. At one end of the shaft were two projections supposed to serve for holding the ligatures by which the blade was attached, and nearer the hand were a number of grooves running round the haft. Neither the description nor the drawings of this and other objects found with it are such as to inspire complete confidence.

About 1822, in sinking a well at Ferry Harty, Isle of Sheppey, [511] there were found, according to newspaper reports, the remains of a hut, two skeletons, and "flints and hard stones, apparently intended for axes and cutting implements, with handles of wood quite complete and in good preservation." Nothing farther seems to be known of this discovery.

At Ervie, [512] near Glenluce, Wigtownshire, a celt of indurated clay-stone in form like Fig. 77 (8 inches) was found, which shows a band of dark colour about 1 1/2 inch wide and about 2 inches from the butt-end, crossing it at an angle of about 20°. This band probably shows the position of the haft in which the blade was fixed. Another celt from Glenshee, Forfarshire, likewise in the Edinburgh Museum, shows a fainter mark of the kind. On a third from Dolphinton, [513] Lanarkshire, the mark is very distinct and at a right angle to the axis of the blade. Montelius [514] mentions a Swedish specimen, and A. de Mortillet [515] a French one of flint similarly marked.

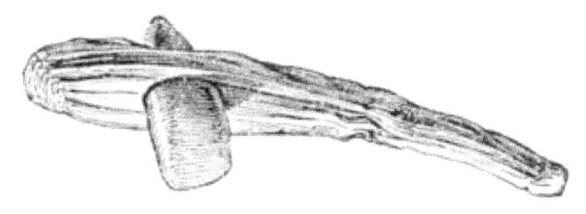

Fig. 93.—Monaghan.

In the Museum of the Royal Irish Academy [516] is a drawing of a celt in its handle (which is apparently of pine) found in the county of Monaghan. This handle was 13 1/2 inches long, and more clumsy at the socketed end than that from Solway Moss. The woodcut given by Sir W. Wilde is here, by permission, reproduced as Fig. 93.

Another nearly similar specimen was discovered near Cookstown, [517] in the county of Tyrone. What may be the haft of a stone hatchet was found in another Irish crannog. [518] Another is in the collection of General Pitt Rivers, F.R.S. Some of the hatchets from the Swiss Lake-dwellings were hafted in a similar manner. In one such haft, formed of ash, from Robenhausen, [519] the blade is inclined towards the hand; in another, also of ash, the blade is at right angles to the shaft. [520] Some of these club-like hafts resemble in character those in use for iron blades in Southern and Central Africa. [521] The copper or bronze axes of the Mexicans [522] were hafted in the same manner.

A method of hafting, which implies fixity of residence, is said to have been in use among the Caribs [523] of Guadaloupe. The blade of the axe had a groove round it at the butt-end, and a deep hole having been cut in the branch of a growing tree, this end of the blade was placed in it, and as the branch grew became firmly embedded in it, the wood which grasped it having formed a collar that filled the groove. The Hurons [524] are said to have adopted the same plan.

Fig. 94.—Axe from the Rio Frio. 1/6

I have engraved in Fig. 94, an extremely rude example of hafting by fitting the blade into a socket, from an original kindly lent me by the late Mr. Thomas Belt, F.G.S., who procured it among the Indians of the Rio Frio, a tributary of the San Juan del Norte in Nicaragua. The blade is of trachyte entirely unground and most rudely chipped. The club-like haft is formed of some endogenous wood, and has evidently been chopped into shape by means of stone tools.

Fig. 95.—War-axe—Gaveoë Indians, Brazil.

In these instances Clavigero's [525] remark with regard to the copper or bronze axes of the Mexicans holds good; they are like "those of modern times, except that we put the handle in an eye of the axe while they put the axe in an eye of the handle." A similarly hafted hatchet with the blade ground is in use among the Botocudo Indians. In the Island of New Hanover [526] the axe blade is inserted about the middle of the club-like haft. Some hatchets from the Admiralty Islands [527] are curiously like those from the Swiss Lake-dwellings. Excessively long hafts in which the blades are let into a socket are occasionally in use among the Chamacocos [528] of south-east Bolivia.

Many stone and metallic axes in use among other modern savages are hafted in much the same manner by insertion in a socket. In some instances it would appear as if the hole for receiving the stone did not extend through the haft, but was merely a shallow depression—even a notch. Such seems to be the case with a war-axe of the Gaveoë Indians of Brazil in the British Museum, figured in the *Proceedings of the Society of Antiquaries*, [529] and here, by permission, reproduced, as Fig. 95. Some of their axes have longer hafts. In the Over Yssel Museum is a Brazilian stone axe with a blade of this kind, which is said to have been used in an insurrection at Deventer [530] in 1787.

Fig. 96.—Axe of Montezuma II.

The "securis lapidea in sacrificiis Indorum usitata," engraved by Aldrovandus, [531] seems to have the blade inserted in a socket without being tied, but in most axes of the same kind the blade is secured in its place by a plaited binding artistically interlaced. The stone axe said to be that of Montezuma II., preserved in the Ambras Museum at Vienna, is a good example of the kind. [532] I have engraved it as Fig. 96, from a sketch I made in 1866.

In some cases the whole handle is covered with the binding. Two such in the Dresden Historical Museum are engraved by Klemm. [533] Others have been figured by Prof. Giglioli. [534]

Some of the war-axes (called taawisch or tsuskiah) in use among the natives of Nootka Sound [535] are mounted in this manner, but the socket end of the shaft is carved into the form of a grotesque human head, in the mouth of which the stone blade is secured with cement, as in Fig. 97. In another instance the handle is carved into the form of a bird [536] and inlaid with mother-of-pearl, or, more properly speaking, shell of *haliotis*. The blade of basalt projects from the breast of the bird, the tail of which forms the handle. In some the blade goes right through the handle, so as to project equally on both sides of it, and is sharpened at both ends.

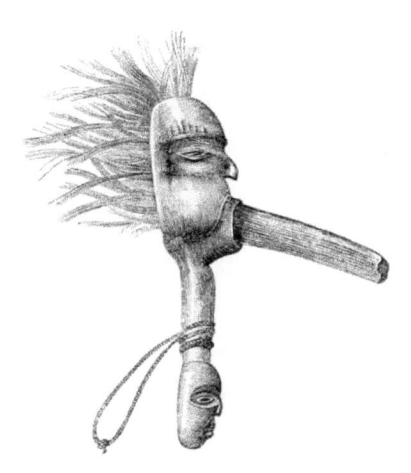

Fig. 97.—Axe—Nootka Sound.

Fig. 98.—Axe in stag's-horn socket—Concise. 1/2

The socket in all these handles is usually at some little distance from their end, but even with this precaution, the wedge-like form of the celt must have rendered them very liable to split. It was probably with a view of avoiding this, that the intermediate socket of stag's horn, so common in the Lake-dwellings of Switzerland, was adopted. The stone was firmly bedded in the horn, the end of which was usually worked into a square form, but slightly tapering, and with a shoulder all round to prevent its being driven into the wood. In the annexed woodcut (Fig. 98) is shown one of these sockets with the hatchet inserted. It was found at Concise, in the Lake of Neuchâtel. An analogous system for preventing the stone blade from splitting the haft was adopted in Burma, Cambodia, and Eastern India, but the shoulders were there cut in the stone-blades themselves. One of the Swiss instruments in its complete form is shown in Fig. 99, which I have copied from Keller. [537] It was found at Robenhausen, and the club-like handle is of ash. Several other specimens are engraved by the same author and Professor Desor, [538] and by other more recent writers.

In some instances the stone was inserted lengthways [539] into the end of a tine of a stag's horn at the part where it had been severed from the antler, so as to form a sort of chisel. [540] In other cases the socket was worked through the tine, and the stone blade fixed in it after the manner of an axe, though the handle was too short for the tool to be used for chopping. Some wooden handles [541] are also but a few inches long, so that the celts mounted in them must have been used for cutting by drawing them along the object to be cut.

Fig. 99.—Axe—Robenhausen. 1/1

Such stag's-horn sockets have occurred, though rarely, in France. M. Perrault found some in his researches in the Camp de Chassey, (Saône et Loire). [542] Some seem to have been found at Vauvray, [543] in making the railway from Paris to Rouen. Others were discovered in company with arrow-heads, celts, and trimmed flakes of flint, in the Dolmen, [544] or *Allée couverte*, of Argenteuil (Seine et Oise). These are now in the Musée de St. Germain. Others were found in a cavern on Mont Sargel (Aveyron). [545] They occasionally occur in Germany. One from Dienheim is in the Central Museum at Mayence.

Discoveries of these stag's-horn sockets for stone tools in England seem to be extremely rare. Mr. Albert Way describes one, of which a woodcut is given in the *Archæological Journal*. [546] It is formed of the horn of the red deer (which is erroneously described as being extinct), and is said to have been found with human remains and pottery of an early character at Cockshott Hill, in Wychwood Forest, Oxfordshire. It seems better adapted for mounting a small celt as a chisel, like that of bronze found in a barrow at Everley, [547] than for forming part of a hatchet. Mr. Way [548] cites several cases of the discovery of these stag's-horn sockets in France and elsewhere on the continent of Europe. I may add, by way of caution, that numerous forgeries of them have been produced at Amiens. In some of the genuine specimens from the peat of the valley of the Somme, [549] the stone was fixed in a socket bored in one end of the piece of stag's horn, and the shaft was inserted in another hole bored through the horn. M. Boucher de Perthes describes the handle of one as made of a branch of oak, burnt at each end.

An example of this method of mounting is given in Fig. 99A. The original was found at Penhouet, Saint Nazaire sur Loire, [550] in 1877. The length of the haft is 19 1/2 inches. A fine socket with the blade still in it, but without the shaft, has been figured by the Baron Joseph de Baye. [551] It was found in La Marne, in which department funereal grottoes have been discovered, at the entrances of which similar hafted axes were sculptured.

Fig. 99A.—Penhouet. 1/6

The socket discovered by the late Lord Londesborough in a barrow, near Scarborough, [552] appears to have been a hammer, although he describes it as a piece of deer horn, perforated at the end, and drilled through, and imagined it to have been the handle for one of the celts found with it, "much in the manner of that in the museum of M. de Courvale, at his Castle of Pinon, in France," of which he sent a drawing to the Archæological Association. A stag's-horn socket, with a transverse hole for the haft, and a circular socket bored in the end, from which the main body of the horn was cut off, was found in the Thames, near Kew, and is in the possession of Mr. Thomas Layton, F.S.A. In the circular socket was a portion of a tine of stag's horn, so that it seems rather to have been intended for mounting such tines for use as picks, than for hafting celts.

Fig. 99B.—New Guinea.

A celt, mounted in a socket of stag's horn, bored through to receive the wooden shaft, found in the Lake-dwellings at Concise, and in the collection of Dr. Clément, has been engraved by Desor; [553] and another, found near Aerschot, [554] in Belgium, by Le Hon. A hatchet, mounted in a socket of this kind, is figured by Dupont [555] and Van Overloop. [556] Some of the stag's-horn sockets are ornamented by having patterns engraved upon them. [557]

In New Guinea and Celebes a plan has been adopted of inserting the stone blade into the end of a tapering piece of wood, which is securely bound round to prevent its splitting. The small end of this fits in a hole in the club-like haft. An example is shown in Fig. 99B, [558] obligingly lent by the Society of Antiquaries of Scotland. By turning round the pivot an axe is converted into an adze. In some New Guinea and New Caledonia adzes and axes the blade is let into a socket at a nearly right angle to the haft, and either forming part of it or attached to it. Such an adze is shown in Fig. 99C, kindly lent by the same Society. A similar method of hafting is in use in the Entrecasteaux Islands. [559]

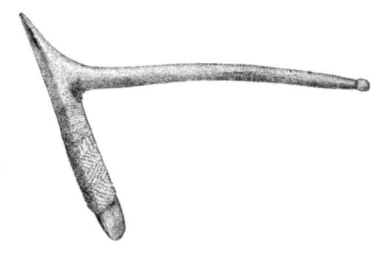

Fig. 99C.—New Guinea Adze.

Some ingenious suggestions as to the probable method of mounting stone implements in ancient times have been made by the Vicomte Lepic. [560] With a polished Danish flint hatchet 8 inches long, hafted in part of the root of an oak, an oak-tree 8 inches in diameter was cut down without injury to the blade.

Another method of hafting, adopted by the Swiss Lake-dwellers for their stone hatchets, is described by Dr. Keller, [561] from whose work I have copied the annexed woodcut, Fig. 100.

The haft was usually formed of a stem of hazel, "with a root running from it at right angles. A cleft was then made in this shorter part, forming a kind of beak in which the celt was fixed with cord and asphalte." A woodcut of a handle of the same character, found near Schraplau, in company with its stone blade, is given by Klemm, [562] and is here reproduced as Fig. 101. A handle of much the same kind, consisting of a shaft with a branch at right angles to it, in which was fixed a flint axe, was found with a skeleton and a wooden shield in a tumulus near Lang Eichstätt, in Saxony, [563] and has been engraved by Lindenschmit. Another is said to have been found at Winterswyk.

Fig. 100.—Axe—Robenhausen.

Fig. 101.—Schraplau.

The discovery in the district between the Weser and the Elbe of several stone hatchets mounted in hafts of wood, stag's-horn, and bone, has been recorded by Mr. A. Poppe, [564] but the authenticity of the hafting seems to me open to question. The compound haft of a stone axe, said to have been found at Berlin, [565] is also not above all suspicion. The handles of bronze palstaves, found in the salt mines near Salzburg, Austria, are forked in the same manner as Figs. 100 and 101. One of them, formerly in the Klemm Collection, is now in the British Museum.

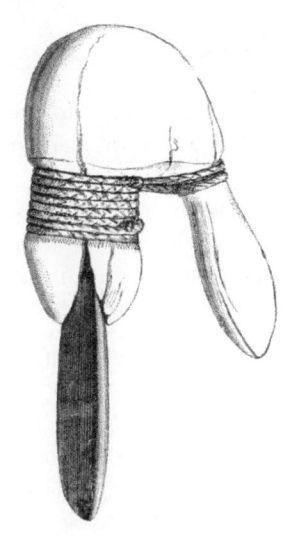

Fig. 102.—Adze—New Caledonia.

The same system of hafting has been in use among the savages in recent times, as will be seen from the annexed figure of a stone adze from New Caledonia, [566] Fig. 102, lent to me by the late Mr. Henry

Christy. Another is engraved in the *Proceedings of the Society of Antiquaries of Scotland*. [567] Several other varieties of New Caledonian and Fiji handles have been engraved by M. Chantre. [568] In some countries, probably in consequence of the difficulty of procuring forked boughs of trees of the proper kind, the wood which forms the socket for the blade is bound on at the desired angle to the end of the wooden handle. An adze of stone from the Caroline Islands, thus mounted, is engraved in the *Comptes Rendus*; [569] and a handle of this kind from North America, but with a small iron blade, is figured by Klemm. [570]

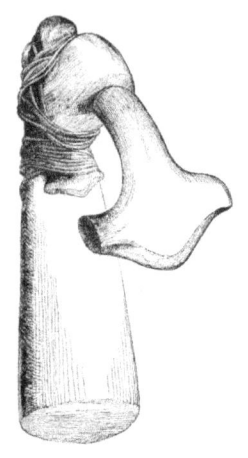

Fig. 103.—Adze—Clalam Indians.

We are left in a great degree to conjecture as to the other methods of mounting stone hatchets and adzes on handles in prehistoric times; but doubtless some besides those already mentioned were practised. A very common method among existing savages is to bind the blade of stone on to the face of a branch at the end of the handle, which in some cases projects upwards, and in others downwards, and is inclined at an angle more or less perpendicular to the handle.

Figs. 103 and 104 are kindly lent me by the Society of Antiquaries of Scotland. [571] The short-handled adze, Fig. 103, is one used by the Schlalum or Clalam Indians, of the Pacific Coast, to the south of the Straits of De Fuca and on Puget's Sound, to hollow out their canoes. The group, Fig. 104, exhibits various methods of attachment of stone adzes to their handles employed by the South-Sea Islanders.

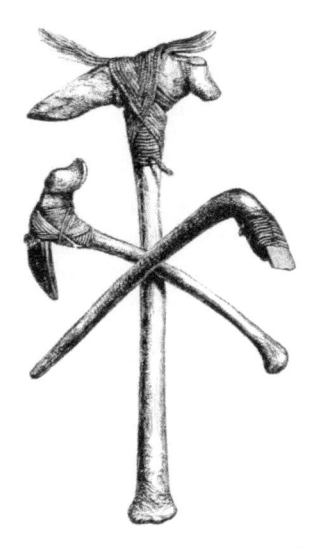

Fig. 104.—South-Sea Island Axes.

The Australians occasionally mounted their tomahawks in much the same manner as that shown in the central figure. An example has been engraved by the Rev. J. G. Wood. [572] The right-hand figure probably represents an adze from the Savage Islands. Some Brazilian and Aleutian Island adzes are mounted in much the same fashion.

The jade adzes of the New Zealanders are hafted in a somewhat similar manner; but the hafts are often beautifully carved and inlaid. A fine example is in the Blackmore Museum, and a handle in the Christy Collection. I have also a haft with the original jade blade, but the binding has been taken off. One of them is engraved by the Rev. J. G. Wood. [573] The axe to the left, in Fig. 104, as well as that in the centre, is from Tahiti. The axes from Mangaia, so common in collections, exhibit great skill in the mounting and in the carving of the handles. Some have been engraved by the Rev. J. G. Wood. [574] A ceremonial stone adze with a very remarkable carved haft from New Ireland [575] has been figured by Professor Giglioli.

In some instances the ligaments for attaching the stone blade against the end of the handle pass through a hole towards its end. A North American adze in the Ethnological Museum, at Copenhagen, is thus mounted, the cord being apparently of gut.

A similar method of mounting their adzes, by binding them against the haft, was in use among the Egyptians. [576] Although it is extremely probable that some of the ancient stone adzes of other countries may have been mounted in this manner, there have not, so far as I am aware, been any of the handles of this class discovered. I have, however, two Swiss celts of Lydian stone, and of rectangular section, found at Nussdorf and Sipplingen, in the Ueberlinger See, and on the flatter of the two faces of each, there is a slight hollow worn away apparently by friction, which was, I think, due to their having been attached against a handle in this manner. The blade in which the depression is most evident has lost its edge, seemingly from its having been broken in use. I have not up to the present time found any similarly worn surfaces upon British celts.

Another method of hafting adopted by various savage tribes is that of winding a flexible branch of wood round the stone, and securing the two ends of the branch by binding them together in such a manner as tightly to embrace the blade. A stone axe from Northern Australia thus hafted, is figured in the *Archæologia*, [577] whence I have borrowed the cut, Fig. 105. Another used by natives on the Murray river [578] has been figured by the Society of Antiquaries of Scotland. This method of hafting has been mentioned by White, [579] who describes the binding as being effected by strips of bark, and in his figure shows the two ends of the stick more firmly bound together.

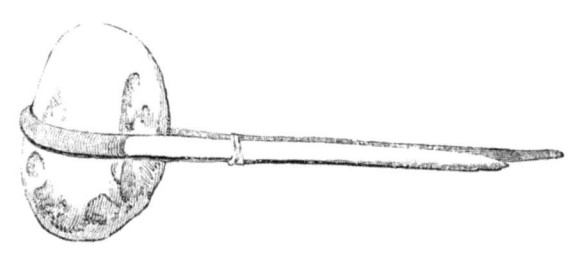

Fig. 105.—Axe—Northern Australia.

Another example has been engraved by the Rev. J. G. Wood. [580] This mode is very similar to that in common use among blacksmiths for their chisels and swages, which are held by means of a withy twisted round them, and secured in its place by a ring.

It seems extremely probable that so simple a method may have been in use in early times in this country, though we have no direct evidence as to the fact. A "fancy sketch" of a celt in a withy handle will be found in the *Archæologia*. [581] It resembles in a singular manner the actual implements employed by the Ojibway Indians, [582] of which there is a specimen in the Christy Collection, engraved by the Rev. J. G. Wood. [583] Some of the other North American tribes [584] mounted their hatchets in much the same manner. A hatchet thus hafted is engraved by Schoolcraft. [585]

In some instances a groove of greater or less depth has been worked round the axes mounted in this manner, though undoubtedly British examples are scarce. An axe-hammer of diorite (13 inches), found near Newburgh, [586] Aberdeenshire, has a groove round it instead of the usual haft-hole. The blade engraved in the *Archæological Journal* [587] and found near Coldstream, Northumberland, is probably of Carib origin, like others which have also been supposed to have been British. Another from the Liverpool Docks is mentioned by Mr. H. Ecroyd Smith. [588] In the British Museum are two such axes, and some other stone implements, found near Alexandria, but which probably are Carib, as would also seem to be those in the Museum of Douai, [589] on which are sculptured representations of the human face.

Stone axe-heads with a groove round their middle, for receiving a handle, have been found in Denmark, [590] but are of rare occurrence. The form has been found in the salt-mines of Koulpe, [591] Caucasus, and in Russian Armenia. The large stone mauls found so commonly in the neighbourhood of ancient copper-mines, in this and many other countries in both hemispheres, were hafted much in the same manner as the Australian axe.

In other cases axe-heads are mounted by being fixed in a cleft stick for a handle, the stick being then lashed round so as to secure the stone and retain it in its place. This method was employed by some of the North American Indians, [592] and the aborigines in the colony of Victoria. [593] In the Blackmore Museum is a stone axe thus mounted, from British Guiana. There is a small hole through the butt which is carved into a series of small spikes. Others from Guiana [594] have notches at the sides to receive a cord which bound the haft in a groove running along the butt-end. The same form has been found in Surinam. [595] An Egyptian [596] stone hammer is mounted in much the same way. The notches practically produce lugs at the butt-end of the blade. I have an iron hatchet, edged with steel, brought home by the late Mr. David Forbes, F.R.S., from among the Aymara Indians of Bolivia, which is mounted in a stick cleft at the end. The blade is T-shaped at the butt, and is tied in such a manner, by means of a strip of leather, that the arms of the T rest on two of the coils, so as to prevent its falling out, while other two coils pass over the butt and prevent its being driven back, and the whole binds the two sides of the cleft stick together so as tightly to grasp the blade and prevent lateral or endways motion. The ancient Egyptian bronze hatchets were merely placed in a groove and bound to the handle by the lugs, and sometimes by the cord being passed through holes in the blade. The same shape is found in flint hatchets ascribed by Professor Flinders Petrie [597] to the twelfth dynasty. What may be a stone hatchet mounted occurs in a painting at Medum. [598]

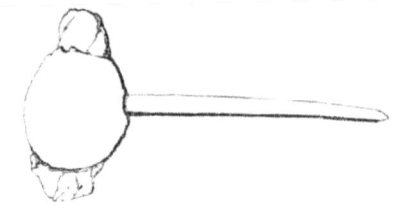

Fig. 106.—Hatchet—Western Australia.

Another Australian method of mounting implies the possession of some resinous material susceptible of being softened by heat, and again becoming hard and tough when cold. This mode is exhibited in Fig. 106, which represents a rude instrument from Western Australia, now in my collection, engraved in the *Archæologia*. [599] It is hammer-like at one end, axe-like at the other, and is formed of either one or two roughly chipped pieces of basalt-like stone entirely unground, and secured in a mass of resinous gum, in which the handle is inserted. In most implements of this kind there appear to be two separate stones used to form the double blade, and these are sometimes of different kinds of rock. It would seem that the shaft, either cleft or uncleft, passed between them, and that the stones, when bound with string to hold them in their places, were further secured with a mass of the gum of the *Xanthorrhæa* or grass-tree. [600]

Such a method of hafting cannot, I think, have been in general use in this country, for want of the necessary cementing material, though, from discoveries made in Scandinavia, it would appear that a resinous pitch was in common use for fixing bronze implements to their handles; so that the practice may also have applied to those of stone. In the Swiss Lake-dwellings, bitumen was used as a cement for attaching stone to wood. In the case of the axes of the Indians on the River Napo, [601] Ecuador, the binding of the blades, which are formed with lugs like those of Guiana, is covered with a thick coating formed of bees-wax and mastic.

Besides those that were hafted as axes or adzes, it seems probable that not a few of the implements known as celts may have been for use in the hand as cutting tools, either mounted in short handles or unmounted. There can be but little doubt that the tools, Fig. 83 and 83A, were thus used in the hand, as also the implement with a depression on each face (Fig. 87), and that with the notches at the side (Fig. 89); and they can hardly have been unique of their kind.

Dr. Lukis, [602] indeed, at one time expressed an opinion that the stone celt was not intended to be secured "in a handle, but was held in the hand and applied to particular uses which are not now evident, but to which neither the hammer nor the hatchet were applicable." But in the face of the fact that numerous handles have since been found, such an opinion is no longer tenable except in a very limited sense.

Among modern savages we have instances of similar tools being used in the hand without the intervention of any haft, giving a form much like that of Fig. 83A, though among the Australians the butt-end is sometimes enveloped in a mass of resinous matter, so as to form a knob which fits the hand. According to Prinz Neuwied, [603] the Botocudos used their stone blades both unmounted in the hand and hafted as hatchets. The South Australians [604] and Tasmanians [605] likewise use celts in a similar manner.

There are cases in which the hatchet and haft have been formed from one piece of stone. Such a one, of chloritic stone, found in a mound in Tennessee, [606] is in outline like Fig. 92, and has a small loop for suspension at the end of the handle. Mr. Cursiter, of Kirkwall, has an instrument of the same kind from Orkney, formed of hard slate. In extreme length it measures 9 3/4 inches. It cannot, however, be assigned to a very early date. For a comparison of celts from different countries Westropp's "Prehistoric Phases" [607] may be consulted.

With regard to the uses to which these instruments were applied, they must have been still more varied than the methods of mounting, which, as we have seen, adapted them for the purposes of hatchets and adzes; while, mounted in other ways, or unmounted, they may have served as wedges, chisels, and knives. The purposes which similar instruments serve among modern savages must be much the same as those for which the stone celts found in this country were employed by our barbarian predecessors. An admirable summary of the uses to which stone hatchets—the "Toki" of the Maori—are, or were applied in New Zealand, has been given by Dr. W. Lauder Lindsay. [608] They were used chiefly for cutting down timber, and for scooping canoes [609] out of the trunks of forest trees; for dressing posts for huts; for grubbing up roots, and killing animals for food; for preparing firewood; for scraping the flesh from the bones when eating, and for various other purposes in the domestic arts. But they were also employed in times of war, as weapons of offence and defence, as a supplementary kind of tomahawk.

For all these purposes stone celts must also have been employed in Britain, and some may even have been used in agriculture. We can add to the list at least one other service to which they were applied, that of mining in the chalk in pursuit of flint, as the raw material from which similar instruments might be fashioned.

CHAPTER VII.
PICKS, CHISELS, GOUGES, ETC.

I now come to several forms of implements which, though approximating closely to those to which the name of celts has been applied, may perhaps be regarded with some degree of certainty as forming a separate class of tools. Among these, the long narrow form to which, for want of a better name, that of "Picks" has been given, may be first described. It is, however, hard to draw a line between them and chisels.

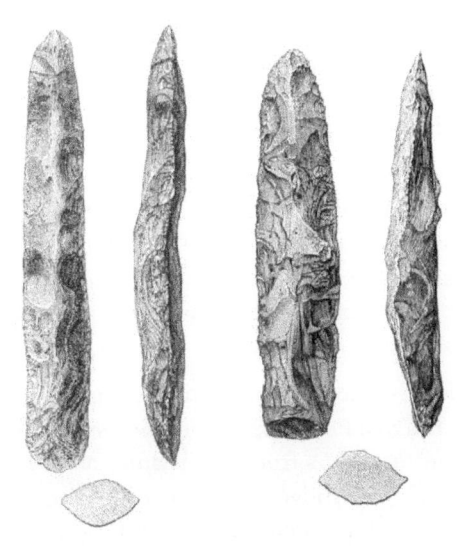

Fig. 107.—Great Easton. 1/2

Fig. 108.—Bury St. Edmunds. 1/2

An idea of the prevailing form will be gathered from Fig. 107, which represents a specimen in my own collection found at Great Easton, near Dunmow, Essex, and given me by Colonel A. J. Copeland, F.S.A. Its surfaces are partially ground, especially towards the upper end, which appears to have been pointed, though now somewhat broken. The lower end is chipped to a rounded outline, but this end is not ground, and the outer or more convex face of the implement, in one part shows the original crust of the flint.

In the Fitch Collection is a finer and more symmetrical specimen of the same kind from North Walsham. It is 7 1/2 inches long, rather more than 1 inch wide, and 7/8 inch thick. It is polished nearly all over, both faces are ridged, so that it is almost rhomboidal in section, though the angles are rounded; one face is curved lengthways much more than the other, which is nearly straight. At one end it is ground to a semicircular edge, but at the other it is merely chipped, and still shows part of the original crust of the flint. Another implement of this character, but 11 1/2 inches long, and 2 7/8 inches wide in the broadest part, was found at Melbourn, [610] Cambridgeshire, and was in the collection of the late Lord Braybrooke.

I have seen another nearly 6 inches long, but little polished, and almost oval in section, which was found at Melton, near Woodbridge, Suffolk. This also is blunt at one end, and ground to a semicircular edge at the other. A fragment of a tool of this class, found near Maidenhead, is in the Geological Museum in Jermyn Street. Another, more roughly chipped out and but partially polished, was found on Mount Harry, near Lewes, and is preserved in the Museum in that town. It is narrow at one end, where it is ground to a sharp edge.

The late Mr. H. Durden, of Blandford, had another, found on Iwerne Minster Down, Dorset, 5 1/2 inches long and 1 1/4 inches broad, more celt-like in type. One face is more convex than the other; the sides are sharp, and one end is squarer than the other, which comes to a rounded point.

In my own collection is one of oval section (5 inches), polished nearly all over, from Burwell Fen, Cambridge; another (4 3/8 inches), much polished on the surface, is from the Thames at Twickenham. A third, from Quy Fen, Cambridge (4 7/8 inches), is rather broader in its proportions, and of pointed oval section. A fourth, from Bottisham Fen (4 3/4 inches), has a narrow segmental edge, and is rounded at the butt, where it is slightly battered. These may perhaps be regarded as chisels.

In the Greenwell Collection is what appears to be a fragment of a chisel, still about 4 inches long, found at Northdale, Bridlington. The same form of implement is found in France. I have a fragment of one which was found by M. Dimpre, of Abbeville, in the old encampment known as the Camp de César, near Pontrémy.

In the case of some very similar implements of flint from Scandinavia it is the broad end that is usually sharp, though some are entirely unground.

Occasionally these implements occur in this country in the same unpolished condition, like Fig. 108, from the neighbourhood of Bury St. Edmunds. This also presents on the more highly ridged face the same curvature in the direction of its length as is to be observed on the polished specimens, and the pointed end seems the sharper and the better adapted for use.

I have a fine unground specimen (6 inches) from Feltwell, Norfolk, and another (4 1/2 inches) from Chart Farm, Ightham, Kent, given to me by Mr. B. Harrison.

Unfortunately there are no indications by which to judge of the method of hafting such instruments. It appears probable, however, that the broader end may have been attached at the end of a handle, like those in Fig. 104, and that the tool was a sort of narrow adze or pick, adapted for working out cavities in wood, or it may be for grubbing in the ground. Some rough instruments of this character are found in Ireland, [611] but are usually more clumsy in their proportions than the English specimens that I have figured. They are often of a sub-triangular section, and pointed at one or both ends, though rarely ground. I have, however, a tapering pointed tool of black chert, and belonging to the same class of implements, found in Lough Neagh. [612] It appears adapted for boring holes in leather or other soft substances.

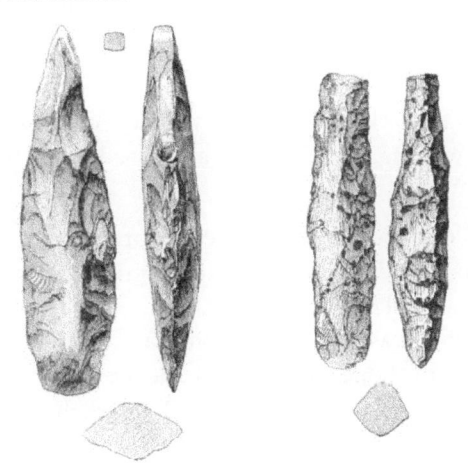

Fig. 109.—Burwell.

Fig. 110.—Near Bridlington. 1/2

A very remarkable implement belonging to the same group is shown in Fig. 109. It was found in the Fen country near Burwell, Cambridge, and was given me by the late Mr. J. W. Flower, F.G.S. At the broad end it is much like the instruments just described. A portion of both faces has been polished, the sides have been rounded by grinding, and though it has been chipped to an edge at the broad end, this also has been rendered blunt in the same manner, possibly with the view of preventing it from cutting the ligaments by which it was attached to a handle. The narrow end is ground to a chisel edge, which is at right angles to that of the broad end. In form and character this chisel end is exactly like that of a narrow "cold chisel" of steel, in use by engineers. Whether it was used as a narrow adze or axe, or after the manner of a chisel, it is difficult to say.

Fig. 110 is still more chisel-like in character. It is of flint weathered white, but stained in places by iron-mould, from having been brought in contact with modern agricultural implements, while lying on the surface of the ground. It was found at Charleston, near Bridlington. It is unground except at the edge, where it is very sharp, and at one or two places along the sides, where slight projections have been removed or rounded off by grinding. The butt-end is truncated, but is not at all battered, so that if a hammer or mallet was used with it, without the intervention of a socket or handle, it was probably of wood. I have another specimen of rather smaller size from the same locality. It is, however, of porphyritic greenstone, and the butt-end, instead of being truncated, has been chipped to a comparatively sharp edge, which has subsequently been partially rounded by grinding. If used as a chisel at all, this implement must have been inserted in a socket.

Mr. H. Durden had a chisel of the same character found at Hod Hill, Dorset, 5 1/2 inches long, and 1 3/8 inches broad, with the sides ground straight.

The Greenwell Collection contains a flint chisel of this form 5 inches long and 1/2 inch broad, found near Icklingham, Suffolk. It is ground at the sides as well as at the edge. Another, 4 3/4 inches long, in the same collection, was found at North Stow, Suffolk. There is also a small chisel of hone-stone, 2 7/8 inches long, found at Rudstone, near Bridlington, and another 3 3/4 inches long, of subquadrate section, found in a barrow at Cowlam, [613] Yorkshire.

The form occurs in France. A beautiful chisel (7 inches), polished all over, and brought to a narrow edge at either end, was found in the Camp de Catenoy (Oise). [614] It is nearly round in section. Another, of dark jade-like material (4 inches), polished all over, was obtained from a dolmen at Pornic [615] (Loire Inférieure).

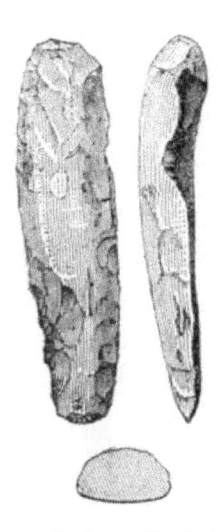

Fig. 111.—Dalton, Yorkshire. 1/2

There are occasionally found some small chisels apparently intended for holding in the hand, as if for carving wood. One of these, from Dalton, on the Yorkshire Wolds, and in the collection of Messrs. Mortimer, is shown in Fig. 111. It is of grey flint, slightly curved longitudinally, nearly semicircular in section, with the side angles rounded, the butt truncated, but all its sharp angles worn or ground away, and with a circular edge slightly gouge-like in character. It has been ground transversely or obliquely on both faces, but the *striæ* from the grinding are at the edge longitudinal. I have a nearly similar tool from West Stow, Suffolk (5 1/4 inches), and one from the neighbourhood of Bridlington, Yorkshire, but the butt-end is broken.

Another flint chisel, from the same neighbourhood, 3 1/2 inches long and 7/8 inch wide, in my collection, presents the peculiarity of having the butt-end ground to a sharp narrow semicircular edge, the principal edge at the other end being broader and less curved. There can be little doubt of this having been merely a hand tool. A portion of the edge at the narrow end is worn away as if by scraping bone or something equally hard. This wearing away does not extend to the end of the tool. Another specimen from Yorkshire is in the Blackmore Museum. [616]

A chisel from Suffolk, [617] ground at both ends, has been figured.

The implement shown in Fig. 112 appears to belong to this same class of tools, though closely resembling some of those which will hereafter be described as "arrow-flakers," from which it differs only in not showing any signs of being worn away at the ends. It is of flint neatly chipped, and was found at Helperthorpe, Yorkshire. I have another of the same form, but a trifle longer, found by Mr. W. Whitaker, F.R.S., near Baldock, Herts. Neither of them shows any traces of grinding.

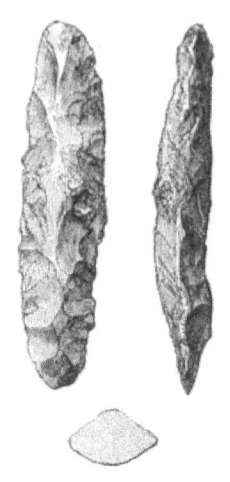

Fig. 112.—Helperthorpe. 1/2

A similar chisel of flint, square at the edge, and found near Londinières [618] (Seine Inférieure), is engraved by the Abbé Cochet.

Implements, which can without hesitation be classed as chisels, are rare in Ireland, though long narrow celts approximating to the chisel form are not uncommon. These are usually of clay-slate, or of some metamorphic rock. I have, however, specimens of oval section not more than an inch wide, and as much as 5 inches long, with narrow straight edges, which seem to be undoubtedly chisels. I do not remember to have seen a specimen in flint, those described by Sir W. Wilde [619] being more celt-like in character.

Narrow chisels, occasionally 10 and 12 inches long, and usually square in section, and either polished all over or merely ground at the edge, are of common occurrence in Denmark and Sweden. [620] They are sometimes, but more rarely, oval in section.

In Germany and Switzerland the form is scarce, but one from the Sigmaringen district is engraved by Lindenschmit, [621] and a Swiss specimen, in serpentine, by Perrin. [622]

Some of the small celts found in the Swiss lakes appear to have been rather chisels than hatchets or adzes, as they were mounted in sockets [623] bored axially in hafts of stag's horn. In some instances the hole was bored transversely through the piece of horn, but even then, the tools are so small that they must have been used rather as knives or drawing chisels than as hatchets. Chisels made of bone are abundant in the Swiss Lake-settlements. They are also plentiful in some of the caverns in the French Pyrenees, which have been inhabited in Neolithic times. Several have also occurred in the Gibraltar caves.

Fig. 113.—New Zealand Chisel. 1/2

Among the Maories of New Zealand small hand-chisels of jade are used for carving wood and for other purposes. They are sometimes attached to their handles by a curiously intertwined cord, [624] and sometimes by a more simple binding. For the sketch of that shown in Fig. 113, I am indebted to the late Mr. Gay. The original is in the British Museum. [625] It will be observed that the end of the handle, which has been battered in use, is tied round with a strip of bark to prevent its splitting. The blade seems to rest against a shoulder in the handle, to which it is firmly bound by a cord of vegetable fibre. A stone chisel from S. E. Bolivia [626] is mounted in the same fashion, but the blade is shorter. The stone chisels in use in ancient times in Britain were, when hafted at all, probably mounted in a somewhat analogous manner.

Considering the great numbers of gouges or hollow chisels of flint which have been found in Denmark and Sweden, their extreme rarity in Britain is remarkable. It seems possible that the celts with an almost semicircular edge, some of which, when the two faces of the blade are not equally convex, are of a gouge-like character, may have answered the same purpose as gouges. It is to be observed that this class of celts is scarce in Denmark, where gouges are abundant; but possibly the ancient inhabitants of that country may have been more of a canoe-forming race than those of Britain, so that, in consequence, implements for hollowing out the trunks of trees were in greater demand among them. The best-formed gouges discovered in England, have, so far as I am aware, been found in the Fen country, where it is probable that canoes would be in constant use.

Two such, found in Burwell Fen, are preserved in the Museum of the Cambridge Antiquarian Society, one of which is shown in Fig. 114. The other is rather smaller, being 5 1/4 inches long and 1 7/8 inches broad. They are entirely unpolished, with the sides nearly straight and sharp, and one face more convex than the other. At the butt-end they are truncated, or show the natural crust of the flint. The cutting edge at the other end is approximately at right angles to the blade, and is chipped hollow, so that the edge is like that of a carpenter's gouge.

In Fig. 114A, is shown a fine gouge of white flint in my own collection. It was found in 1871 on the Westleton Walks, Suffolk, and was ceded to me by Mr. F. Spalding. It has been most skilfully and symmetrically chipped out, but both the surface and the edge are left entirely unground. What may be termed the front face is flatter than in the specimens last described. The cutting edge is more rounded.

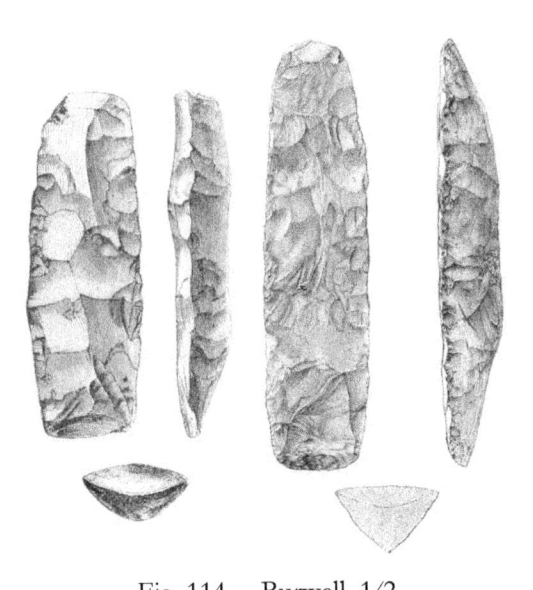

Fig. 114.—Burwell. 1/2

Fig. 114A.—Westleton Walks. 1/2

The next specimen, Fig. 115, is less decidedly gouge-like in character. It is of grey flint, and was in the collection of the late Mr. Caldecott, of Mead Street, having been found at Eastbourne, Sussex. The sides are sharp, but rounded towards the butt, which is also round. A large flake has been taken lengthways off the hollow face, and it may be mainly to this circumstance rather than to original design, that the gouge-like character of the implement is due.

Most of the Danish gouges have a rectangular section at the middle of the blade, and the butt-end is usually truncated, and sometimes shows marks of having been hammered, so that these implements were probably used without hafting and in conjunction with a mallet or hammer of wood or stag's horn. Another and rarer form of gouge with a sharp elliptical section, tapers to the butt, and may have been used for paring away charred surfaces without the aid of a mallet. Some small examples of this class show, however, polished markings, as if from having been inserted in handles.

Under the head of gouges I must comprise a few of those celt-like implements already mentioned, which, without being actually ground hollow, yet, by having one of their faces much flatter transversely than the other, present at the edge a gouge-like appearance, somewhat after the manner of the "round-nosed chisels" of engineers. One of these was discovered in a barrow on

Willerby Wold, [627] Yorkshire, by Canon Greenwell, F.R.S., though it was not associated with any burial.

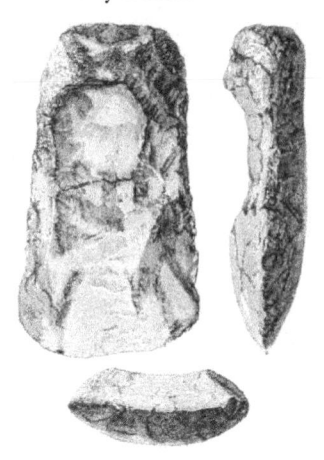

Fig. 115.—Eastbourne.

It is shown in Fig. 116, and is formed of a light green hone-stone, carefully ground and even polished, and presents a beautifully regular and sharp cutting edge. It would appear to have been intended for mounting as a hollow adze rather than as a gouge, and would when thus mounted have formed a useful tool for hollowing canoes, or for other similar purposes.

In the Greenwell Collection is also another implement of the same character and material, but smaller, being 4 inches long and 2 3/8 inches broad. It was found at Ganthorpe, Yorkshire. The sides in this case are flat.

The implement shown in Fig. 117 has, when the convex face is seen, much the same appearance as Fig. 68. The other face, however, is slightly hollowed towards the middle longitudinally, and is nearly flat transversely, so that the edge presents a gouge-like appearance. It was found at Huntow, near Bridlington, and is in my own collection. The material is greenstone, the surface of which is somewhat decomposed, and seems in places to have been scratched by the plough or the harrow.

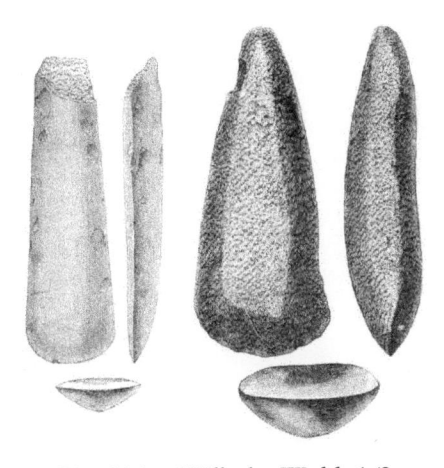

Fig. 116.—Willerby Wold. 1/2

Fig. 117.—Bridlington. 1/2

A considerable number of gouges of this bastard kind have been found in Ireland, and I have figured one from Lough Neagh. [628] A few of the Irish celts are actually hollowed at the edge, so as to become more truly gouge-like in character.

Besides occurring in abundance in Scandinavia, gouges, properly so called, are also found in Northern Germany and Lithuania. They also occur in Russia, [629] Finland, and Western Siberia, and even in Japan and Cambodia.

One of flint, 5 inches long, from the neighbourhood of Beauvais (Oise), is in the Blackmore Museum. The same form has also been found in Portugal [630] and Algeria. [631]

A stone implement, [632] "a square chisel at one end and a gouge at the other," was found in one of the Gibraltar caves.

In North America, [633] including Canada and Newfoundland, gouges formed of other varieties of stone than flint are by no means uncommon, and among the Caribs of Barbados, where stone was not to be procured, we find gouge-like instruments formed from the *columella* of the large *Strombus gigas*. On the western coast of North America, mussel-shell adzes are still preferred by the Ahts [634] to the best English chisels, for canoe-making purposes.

Some narrow bastard gouges, almost semicircular on one face and flat transversely on the other, but not hollowed, have been found in the Swiss Lake-settlements. I have one of diorite, 5 3/4 inches long and 1 inch broad, from Sipplingen. The butt is roughened as if for insertion in a socket. A similar form is found in Germany. I have a specimen 9 1/2 inches long found in the neighbourhood of Mainz.

A bastard form of gouge, mounted as an adze, is in use in the Solomon Islands. One tied to its haft with rattan is in the Christy Collection.

CHAPTER VIII.
PERFORATED AXES.

I now come to a very important class of antiquities, the stone axes and axe-hammers with a hole for the insertion of a shaft, like the ordinary axes and hammers of the present day. As to the method by which these shaft-holes were bored, I have already spoken in a previous chapter. I have also mentioned that many of them appear to belong to a time when bronze was already in use, at all events for knife-like daggers, and that they have in many countries shared with the more simply-formed celts the attribution of a heavenly origin as thunderbolts, together with the superstitious reverence due to their supernatural descent. I have, therefore, but little here to add beyond a classification and description of the various forms; but I may mention that the name by which such implements were "popularly known in Scotland almost till the close of last century was that of the Purgatory Hammer," buried with its owner that he might have the wherewithal "to thunder at the gates of Purgatory till the heavenly janitor appeared." [635]

They are for the most part made from metamorphic or volcanic rocks, and occasionally from quartzite, but I have never seen a British perforated axe made from ordinary flint, though hammers of this material are known. Stukeley, [636] indeed, mentions that in cleansing the moat at Tabley, near Knutsford, "they found an old British axe, or some such thing, made of large flint, neatly ground into an edge, with a hole in the middle to fasten into a handle; it would serve for a battle-axe." Stukeley was probably mistaken as to the material; but there are in the Museum at Copenhagen one or two flint axes ground to an edge, the shaft-holes in which are natural, and no doubt led to the stones being selected for the purpose to which they were applied. An artificially-perforated French specimen will subsequently be mentioned. Flints both naturally and artificially perforated, have also been occasionally converted into hammers and maces.

In Scandinavia and Northern Germany, perforated axes and axe-hammers are frequently known as Thor's hammers, as already mentioned, [637] and some authors have maintained that they were in use for warlike purposes so late as eight or ten centuries after our era. Kruse, [638] however, has urged that though found in the neighbourhood of graves of the Iron Age in Livonia and Courland, they are never found in the graves themselves, and that their use is not mentioned in any ancient histories.

The principal forms may be classified as follows:—

- 1. Double-edged axes, or those with a cutting, or but slightly blunted edge at either end.

- 2. Adzes, or implements with the edge at right angles to the shaft-hole.

- 3. Axes with the edge at one end only, the hole being near the other end, which is rounded. These shade off into—

- 4. Axe-hammers sharp at one end, and more or less hammer-like at the other, the shaft-hole being usually near the centre.

To the weapons of the first of these classes the name of Amazon Axe has been applied by Professor Nilsson; [639] but the Scandinavian axes expanding considerably at the cutting ends, resemble the *Amazonia securis* of classical sculpture more than do the English specimens.

Fig. 118 represents a beautifully formed axe of the first class, in my own collection. It is of greenstone, and was found near Hunmanby, Yorkshire. The two sides are concave longitudinally, so that it expands towards the edges. They are also slightly concave transversely. The angles are rounded, and the edges are blunt, especially that at the shorter end. The shaft-hole is oval, and tapers slightly from each end towards the middle. It would appear to have been worked out with some sort of chisel, and to have been afterwards made smoother by grinding.

A broader weapon of granite, expanding more at the ends (5 1/2 inches) was found in the Tay, [640] near Newburgh, Fife. A flatter specimen of porphyritic stone (4 inches) was found on the shore of Cobbinshaw Loch, [641] West Calder, Midlothian, in 1885.

A specimen of nearly the same type, found near Uelzen, Hanover, is engraved by von Estorff; [642] another from Sweden, by Sjöborg. [643]

In the Museum at Geneva is a very similar axe of greenstone (5 1/4 inches), found in the neighbourhood of that town. One of serpentine, much longer in its proportions (9 1/4 inches), and with an oval shaft-hole, is in the Museum at Lausanne. It was found at Agiez, Canton de Vaud.

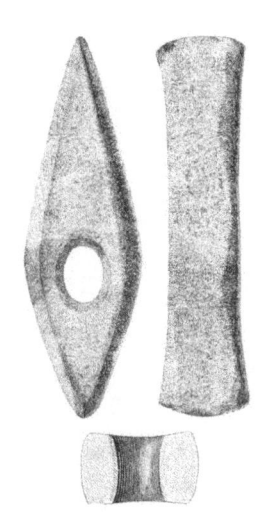

Fig. 118.—Hunmanby. 1/2

In the *Collections* [644] published by the Sussex Archælogical Society is a figure, obligingly lent to me, of a beautiful axe-head of this class (Fig. 119) found with the remains of a skeleton, an amber cup (Fig. 307), a whetstone (Fig. 186), and a small bronze dagger with two rivet holes, in an oaken coffin in a barrow at Hove, near Brighton. The axe-head is said to be formed of some kind of ironstone, and is 5 inches long. The hole is described as neatly drilled. A weapon of the same kind (3 1/2 inches) blunter at the ends and described as a hammer, was found with a deer's-horn hammer, and a bronze knife in a barrow at Lambourn, Berks. [645] A small black stone axe-head of nearly similar form was found near the head of a contracted skeleton at a depth of 12 feet in a barrow in Rolston Field, Wilts. [646] A somewhat similar specimen, with the sides faceted and blunt at one end, has been engraved as having been found in Yorkshire. [647] It is, however, doubtful whether, like many other objects in the same plate, it is not foreign. The original is now in the Christy Collection.

A double-edged axe-head of basalt, injured by fire, and 4 1/2 inches long, was found by the late Mr. Bateman, in a large urn with calcined bones, bone pins, a tubular bone laterally perforated, a flint "spear-head," and a bronze awl, in a barrow near Throwley, Derbyshire. [648] This was the only instance in which he found a perforated stone axe accompanying an interment by cremation.

An axe-head of basalt, with a double edge to cut either way, was also dug up in the neighbourhood of Tideswell, Derbyshire. [649]

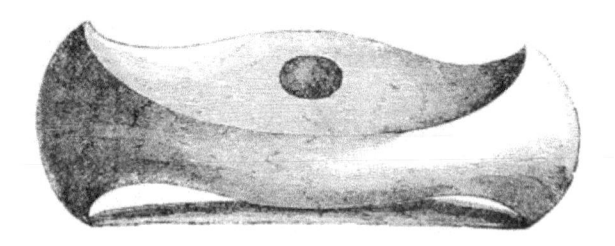

Fig. 119.—Hove. 1/2

A specimen of this kind (5 inches), edged at both ends, but "the one end rather blunted and lessened a little by use," was found near Grimley, Worcestershire, and is figured by Allies. [650]

I have a specimen (5 1/8 inches), much weathered, which is said to have come from Bewdley in that county, but which may be that from Grimley.

An example, 5 inches long, engraved in the Salisbury volume [651] of the Archæological Institute, from a barrow on Windmill Hill, Abury, Wilts, is described as double-edged. [652]

The Danish and German axe-heads of this form have usually, but not always, one edge much more blunted than the other. Occasionally there is a ridge on each side at the blunt end, which shows that this thickening was intentional. A fine double-edged axe-head of this form from Brandenburg is engraved in the "Horæ Ferales." [653] The double-edged form is found also in Finland. [654]

The form likewise occurs in France, but the faces are usually flatter. I have one from the Seine at Paris (5 1/2 inches). Another from the department of the Charente is engraved by de Rochebrune; [655] and a third from the department of Seine et Oise is in the Musée de St. Germain. [656] A fine example of the same form is in the Museum at Tours, and another in that of Blois. In the collection of M. Reboux [657] was a curious implement from the Seine, formed of flint, pointed at each end, and perforated in the middle. Another, in flint, from Mesnil en Arronaise [658] (Somme) (8 1/2 inches), has been figured. The perforations may be natural, though improved by art. In my own collection is one of the finest specimens that I have ever seen. It is also from the Seine at Paris. It is 9 3/4 inches long, and slightly curved in the direction of its length; on either side there is a long sunk lozenge, in the centre of which is the cylindrical shaft-hole, and the ends expand into flat semicircular blades about 2 1/4 inches across. The material is a hard basaltic rock, and the preservation perfect. It was found in 1876.

A stone axe in the Museum of the Royal Institution at Swansea, and found at Llanmadock, in Gower, has been kindly lent me for engraving, and is shown in Fig. 120. It expands at the sharper end much more suddenly and to a much greater extent than does that from Hunmanby. The edge at that end, which is almost semicircular in outline, has suffered from ill-usage since it was discovered; the material of which it is made being felspathic ash, the surface of which has become soft by decomposition. The other and narrower end is flattened to about half an inch in width. The implement has already been engraved on a smaller scale. [659]

In Bartlett's "History and Antiquities of Manceter, Warwickshire," [660] is engraved an axe of the same character as this, but expanding at the blunter end almost as much, as it does at the edge, which is described as being very sharp. It is said to have been formed of the hard blue stone of the country, but "from age or the soil in which it has lain" to be "now coloured with an elegant olive-coloured patina." It was found on Hartshill Common, in 1770, where a small tumulus had been cut through, "the bottom of which, was paved with brick, which by the heat of the fire had been nearly vitrified." There is probably some mistake as to the bricks.

Another axe-head like Fig. 120, 8 inches in length, and more distinctly hammer-like at the narrow end, was found in the parish of Abernethy, Perthshire, and has been engraved by Wilson. [661]

In character these axes with expanded ends more nearly resemble some of the Scandinavian and North German types than do most of the other British forms. Broken stone axes expanding at the edge have been found on the site of Troy.

In the Museum of the Leeds Philosophical Society is a double-edged axe-head of a larger and coarser kind, which, is said to have been found near Whitby. Its authenticity was strongly vouched for by the late Mr. Denny, but I fear that it is a modern fabrication.

An implement of the same form, from Gerdauen, East Prussia, is preserved in the Berlin Museum; and another of greenstone was found at Hallstatt. [662] A singular variety from the same spot has the edge at one end at right angles to that at the other.

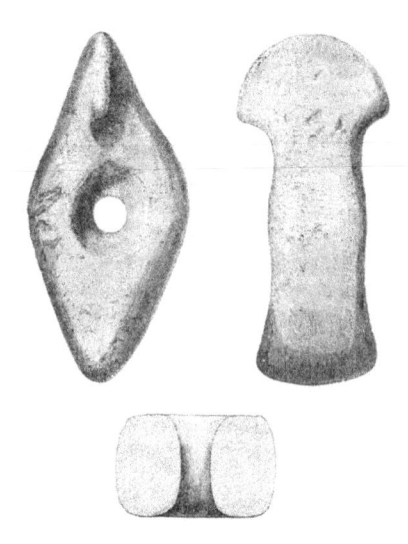

Fig. 120.—Llanmadock. 1/2

A small sketch of a very remarkable curved blade, pointed at one end and with an axe-like edge at the other, is given in the *Journal of the Archæological Association*. [663] It is of greenstone, 11 inches long and 2 1/2 inches across, and was found in Guernsey. By the kindness of the late Rev. W. C. Lukis, F.S.A., of Wath, I am enabled to give an engraving of the type in Fig. 121. A number of specimens have been found in the Channel Islands, to which the form seems peculiar.

The second class into which I proposed to divide these implements consists of adzes, or blades having the edge at right angles to the shaft-hole. Apart from a short notice by Mr. Monkman, I believe that attention was for the first time called in the former edition of this book, to the occurrence of this form in Britain.

The specimen I have selected for engraving, as Fig. 122, gives a good idea of the typical character. It is of greenstone, with the shaft-hole tapering inwards from both faces, one of which is less convex than the other. It was found at Fireburn Mill, near Coldstream, Berwickshire, and is in the Greenwell Collection. In the same collection is another of similar character, but having the butt-end broken off and the edge more circular, found at Willerby Carr, in the East Riding of Yorkshire.

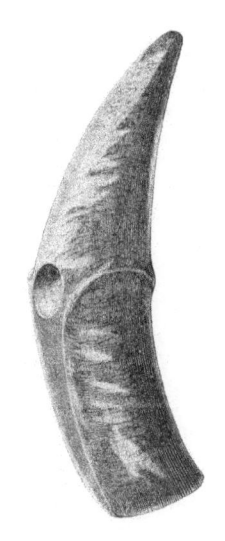

Fig. 121.—Guernsey. 1/2

I have a smaller specimen (4 3/4 inches), of a hard micaceous grit, found at Allerston, in the North Riding; as also a remarkably fine and perfect adze of porphyritic greenstone (6 3/8 inches), ground to a rounded edge at the butt, instead of being truncated like Fig. 122. The shaft-hole, like that of all the others, tapers inwards from both faces, in this instance from 1 3/8 inch to 7/8 inch. This specimen was found at South Dalton, near Beverley. An adze or hoe of the same kind, found at Wellbury, [664] near Offley, Herts, is in the collection of Mr. W. Ransom, F.S.A.

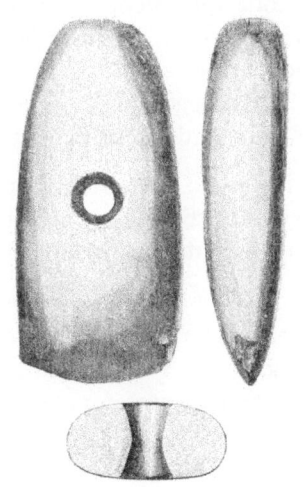

Fig. 122.—Fireburn Mill, Coldstream. 1/2

Another implement of the same class (9 inches), flat on one face, and much like Fig. 122, is in the National Museum at Edinburgh. It is of greenstone, much decomposed, and was found at Ormiston Abdie, Fife. A shorter specimen (3 3/4 inches) sharpened at each end, found at Sandwick, Shetland, is in the fine collection of Mr. J. W. Cursiter, at Kirkwall.

Another, in outline more like the celt Fig. 57, though sharp at the sides, is also in the Greenwell Collection. It is formed of red micaceous sandstone (6 3/4 inches), and was found at Seackleton, in the North Riding of Yorkshire. A rough sketch of it has been published by Mr. Monkman. [665] In the same collection is another, rather narrower in its proportions, being 7 1/2 inches long and 3 inches broad, found at Pilmoor, as well as one 6 inches long and 2 3/8 inches broad, found at Nunnington.

Another, 5 1/2 inches long, square at both ends, found near Whitby, is in the Museum at Leeds.

The form is known in Denmark, but is rare. A more celt-shaped specimen is engraved by Worsaae. [666] He terms it a hoe (*hakke*), and it is, of course, possible that these instruments may have been used for digging purposes.

Two short, broad hoes (*hacken*), of Taunus slate, found near Mainz, are given by Lindenschmit. [667] Another is in the Museum at Brunswick.

Some hoe-like, perforated stone implements from Mexico, are in the Ethnological Museum at Copenhagen. The so-called stone hoes of North America [668] are not perforated, though sometimes notched at the sides. Dr. Keller [669] has suggested that a circular perforated disc from one of the Swiss Lake-settlements may have been a hoe.

In the Museum of the Deutsche Gesellschaft at Leipzig, is a greenstone implement resembling these adzes or hoes at its broader end, but at the other, instead of being square or rounded, presenting an axe-like edge.

A narrow, thick adze of this character, flat on one face, rounded on the other, 4 1/2 inches long, found at Scudnitz, near Schweinitz, Prussian Saxony, is in the Berlin Museum. A rather similar form has been found in Bohemia. [670]

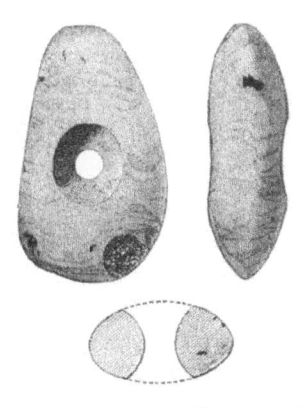

Fig. 123.—Burwell Fen. 1/2

An intermediate form between a hammer and an adze will be subsequently described at p. 231.

A small perforated adze in the Museum of the Cambridge Antiquarian Society, Fig. 123, is more truly celt-like in character, and appears, indeed, to have been made from an ordinary celt by boring a shaft-hole through it. It is formed of a hard, green, slaty rock, and was found in Burwell Fen. I believe that another, but larger, specimen of the same type, was found in the same district in Swaffham Fen.

The late Mr. G. W. Ormerod, F.G.S., brought under my notice another specimen found, in 1865, at North Bovey, Devon. It is of greenstone, about 3 3/4 inches long. The sides taper towards the butt-end, which is rounded, and the hole in the middle appears to be only about 1/2 inch in diameter, but bell-mouthed at each face. It is now in the Museum at Exeter. Another (3 7/8 inches) was found at Ugborough, Devon. [671]

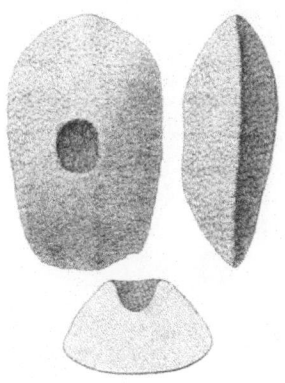

Fig. 124.—Stourton. 1/2

The implement shown in Fig. 124 seems to be an unfinished specimen belonging to this class. It is formed of greenstone, portions of the natural joints of which are still visible on its surface. It seems to have been worked into shape by picking rather than by grinding; but the hole appears, from the character of the surface, to have been ground. Had it been continued through the stone, it would probably have been considerably enlarged in diameter, and if so, the implement would have been much weakened around the hole. It seems possible that it was on this account that it was left unfinished. It was found near Stourton, on the borders of Somerset and Wilts.

The third of the classes into which, for the sake of convenience, I have divided these instruments, consists of axe-heads with a cutting edge at one end only, the shaft-hole being near the other end, which is rounded.

Fig. 125 represents an elegant specimen of this class, found at Bardwell, in Suffolk, and formerly in the collection of Mr. Joseph Warren, of Ixworth, but now in my own. The material appears to be felstone. The edge is slightly rounded, the shaft-hole carefully finished, and the two faces ground hollow, probably in the manner suggested at p. 43.

I have another made from a quartzite pebble (4 5/8 inches) with the sides hollowed transversely, but rounded longitudinally, found with an urn on Wilton Heath, near Brandon, in 1873. The blunt end is bruised and flattened by wear. I have a second, also of quartzite (5 3/8 inches), rounded in all directions, found near Ipswich, in 1865. It retains much of the form of the original pebble.

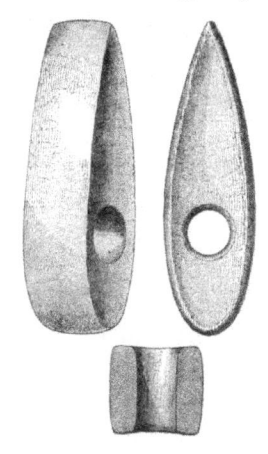

Fig. 125.—Bardwell. 1/2

In the Museum at Newcastle is preserved a specimen very similar to Fig. 125, of mottled greenstone, beautifully finished; the sides are, however, flat and not hollowed. It is 6 1/2 inches long, the faces are rounded, and the hole, which is about 7/8 inch in diameter, tapers slightly towards the middle. It was found in the River Wear at Sunderland. Another of the same character, formed from a beautifully veined stone, accompanied a bronze dagger in a barrow near East Kennet, Wilts. [672]

I have another axe of the same kind, with both sides flat, 6 1/8 inches long, formed of porphyritic greenstone, and found near Colchester. Another, formed of basalt, 6 1/4 inches long, the sides slightly hollowed, from Chesterford, Cambridge, [673] was in the possession of the late Mr. Joshua Clarke, of Saffron Walden.

Another, 5 inches long, was found in the Thames off Parliament Stairs, and passed with the Roach Smith Collection into the British Museum. One, 5 3/4 inches long, from Cumberland, is in the Christy Collection.

One of sandstone (4 1/2 inches) was discovered at Northenden, [674] Cheshire, in 1883.

In the Greenwell Collection is one of greenstone, 6 3/4 inches long, found at Millfield, near Sunderland. The hole is somewhat oval, and tapers inwards from each side. There is also one of basalt, 4 1/4 inches long, with an oval hole and slightly convex sides, from Holystone, Northumberland. The edge, as usual, is blunt.

An axe-head of this kind, from a chambered tumulus or dolmen at Craigengelt, near Stirling, Scotland, is engraved by Bonstetten. [675]

One with flat sides (6 1/4 inches) was found in the Tay, near Mugdrum Island, Perth, [676] and another (7 inches) at Sorbie, Wigtownshire. [677]

Implements or weapons of this character occasionally occur in Ireland, [678] but the sides are usually flat.

The exact form is rare in Denmark and North Germany. Lindenschmit [679] engraves a thin specimen from Lüneburg. It occurs also in Styria. A specimen from Lithuania, more square at the butt, is engraved by Mortillet. [680] I do not remember to have met with it in France.

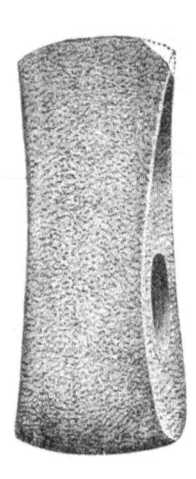

Fig. 126.—Potter Brompton Wold. 1/2

In one of the barrows on Potter Brompton Wold, [681] Yorkshire, explored by Canon Greenwell, accompanying an interment by cremation, he found a beautifully-formed axe-head of serpentine(?) the surface of which was in places scaling off from decomposition, arising from its having been partly calcined. A single view of it is given in Fig. 126. The hole is about 1 1/4 inches in diameter on each side, but rather smaller in the middle. The cutting edge has been rounded as well as the angles round the sides, but this process has been carried to a greater extent on one than the other; possibly this was the outer side.

A somewhat similar, but rather broader, axe-head of basalt, 5 1/4 inches long, was found by the late Mr. T. Bateman in a barrow called Carder Low, [682] near Hartington, in company with a small bronze dagger, and near the elbow of a contracted skeleton.

Another, expanding rather more at the edge, from a barrow in Devonshire, [683] was in the Meyrick Collection.

A somewhat similar axe-head, more rounded at the butt and rather more expanded at the cutting edge, was found in Annandale in 1870, and was described to me by the late Mr. Joseph Clarke, F.S.A.

One of granite, much like Fig. 126, came to light in a cairn at Breckigoe, [684] Caithness.

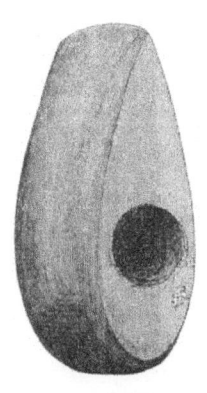

Fig. 127.—Rudstone.

In the same barrow at Rudstone, [685] near Bridlington, as that in which the block of pyrites and flint scraper, subsequently to be described (Fig. 223), were found, but with a different interment, Canon Greenwell discovered the beautifully formed axe-hammer shown in Fig. 127. It is of very close-grained, slightly micaceous grit, and presents the peculiarity of having the rounded faces slightly chamfered all round the flat sides. The edge is carefully rounded, and the broad end somewhat flattened. It lay behind the shoulders of the skeleton of an old man lying on his left side, with his right hand on his head, and his left to his face. Before the face, was a bronze knife 4 inches long, with a single rivet to fasten it to its handle, and close to the axe-hammer lay a pointed flint flake re-chipped on both faces. In a barrow at Sledmere [686] with burnt bones lay a weapon of this kind battered at the blunt end.

An axe-head (6 1/4 inches), with convex faces, rounded at the butt, and with an oval shaft-hole, was dredged from the Thames at London, [687] and is now in the British Museum.

It seems almost indisputable that these elegantly formed axe-heads belong to the period when bronze was in use, and from their occurrence in the graves they appear to have formed part of the equipment of warriors.

The careful manner in which their edges are blunted shows that they cannot have been intended for cutting tools, but that they must have been weapons of war. A blow from a battle-axe with a blunted edge would be just as fatal as if the edge had been sharp and trenchant, while the risk of accidental injury to the scantily-clothed warrior who carried the axe was next to none when the edge of the weapon was thus blunted. The practice of removing the edge by grinding was, no doubt, introduced in consequence of some painful experience.

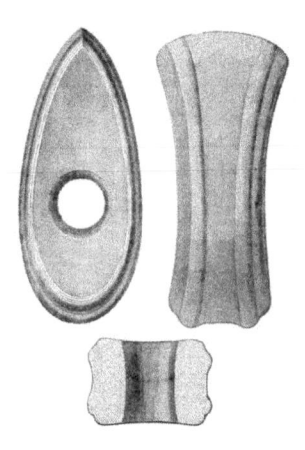

Fig. 128.—Borrowash. 1/2

Fig. 128 is of still more ornamental character, having a beaded moulding towards each edge of the faces and following the curvature of the sides. The drawing is taken from a cast in the Museum of the Society of Antiquaries, presented by Sir W. Tite. M.P. [688] The original is said to have been found near Whitby. A fine axe-head "of red granite, ornamented with raised mouldings," was, however, found with human bones near Borrowash, Derbyshire, in 1841, [689] and is in the Bateman Collection, now at Sheffield. To judge from the woodcut in the Catalogue, the cast must have been taken from this specimen.

"A very elegant axe-head, 5 inches long, of reddish basalt, beautifully wrought, with a slight moulding round the angles, and a perforation for the shaft," is described by Mr. Bateman [690] as having been found on a barrow eleven miles E. of Pickering, Yorkshire.

Mouldings of various kinds occur on Danish and German axe-hammers of the Bronze Age, [691] but this form of small axe with a rounded butt is of rare occurrence. The longitudinal line in relief which occurs on the sides of some German battle-axes [692] has been regarded as an imitation of the mark left on bronze axes by the junction of the two halves of the mould. The small axe-heads from Germany [693] are wider at the butt, and more like Figs. 118 and 120 in outline.

Fig. 129.—Crichie, Aberdeenshire.

The beautiful battle-axe, formed of fine-grained mica schist, found placed on burnt bones in a "Druidical" circle at Crichie, near Inverurie, Aberdeenshire, [694] and presented by the Earl of Kintore to the National Museum at Edinburgh, has deeply-incised lines round the margins of the hollow sides at the mouth of the shaft-hole. This weapon is 4 inches in length, and is considerably sharper at the broader end than at the other, though the edge is well rounded. For the loan of Fig. 129 I am indebted to the Society of Antiquaries of Scotland. In general character this specimen approximates to a somewhat rare Irish form, shortly to be mentioned, of which I possess a specimen. The battle-axe from the barrow at Selwood, Fig. 140, is also slightly ornamented by lines on the sides, and that from Skelton Moors, Fig. 139, is fluted.

Two axe-hammers of granite and greenstone (4 1/2 and 5 inches) of much the same type as Fig. 129, but more elongated, so as in form to resemble Fig. 136, were found near Ardrossan, [695] Ayrshire.

An unfinished axe-head of the same kind was found at Middleton, [696] Stevenston, Ayrshire.

An axe-head of porphyritic greenstone (7 3/4 inches long), from Stainton Dale, near Scarborough, [697] is said to resemble in form an Irish axe-head engraved in the *Ulster Journal of Archæology.* [698] If so, the sides through which the hole is bored were hollow, as in Fig. 129, and there was also a moulding round them. This Irish axe-head is formed of a kind of pale green hone-stone, and is now in the British Museum. Instead of incised lines there are raised flanges on each face, bordering the concave side in which is the shaft-hole. The length is 5 1/4 inches, and the butt-end is half an oval, just flattened at the end. It was found in the river Bann.

Axe-heads of a much more clumsy character than any of those last described are of more frequent occurrence in this country. The one I have selected for illustration as Fig. 130, is rather small of its kind.

It is made of greenstone, the surface of which has considerably suffered from weathering, and was found in draining at Walsgrave-upon-Sowe, near Coventry. It was presented to my collection by the late Mr. J. S. Whittem, F.G.S. The shaft-hole, as usual, tapers inwards from both sides; its surface is more polished than that of the exterior of the implement. A small portion of the end of the butt is flat, but this appears due to accident rather than design. I have a rather longer axe-head, of porphyritic greenstone, which was washed out of the ground by a brook at Ayside, near Newby Bridge, Windermere, and was given to me by Mr. Harrison, of Manchester. It is considerably rounded in both directions at the butt, the edge is narrow, and one side, probably the outer, much more rounded than the other. The edge is carefully ground, but farther up the face, the surface shows that it has been picked into form. The shaft-hole is much like that of Fig. 130.

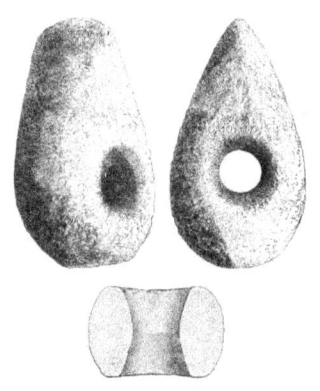

Fig. 130.—Walsgrave-upon-Sowe. 1/2

I have another specimen from Plumpton, near Penrith (9 1/2 inches), rounded at the butt, but unsymmetrical, owing to a natural plane of cleavage interfering with the shape, and, as it were, taking off a slice of the stone. The shaft-hole is oval, the longer diameter being lengthwise of the blade, and the edge is oblique. The sides are flatter than those of Fig. 130. In my collection are others from Mawbray and Inglewood Forest, Cumberland (7 1/2 and 8 inches), and one (7 inches) from Cader Idris, Merionethshire. Another (10 inches) was found at Llanfairfechan, [699] Carnarvonshire, another at Llanidloes, [700] Montgomeryshire, and a third in Anglesey. [701] The late Mr. Llewellynn Jewitt, F.S.A., had a flatter and longer specimen of this form (10 inches), found at Winster, Derbyshire. Implements of this character, but often approximating in shape to Fig. 131, have been found in considerable numbers, though as isolated specimens, in the North. One found in Aberdeenshire (8 1/2 inches long), of this class, but with the butt-end slightly hollowed, and having a well-marked shoulder on each face, as if by continual reduction by sharpening at the edge, is engraved in the *Archæological Journal*. [702] One from Scotland [703] (10 1/4 inches) was exhibited by the Marquis of Breadalbane at Edinburgh, in 1856, and one (12 inches) from Alnwick. [704] Others have been found at Tillicoultry Bridge, [705] Clackmannan; Kelton, [706] Kircudbrightshire; in Wigtownshire [707]; Silvermine, [708] Torphichen, Linlithgow; and Laurie Street, [709] Leith; another from the coast of Scotland is engraved in Skelton's "Meyrick's Armour," [710] but is there regarded as having been brought over by Danish invaders. Other Scottish [711] specimens are numerous. There are thirteen in the Grierson Museum, Thornhill, Dumfriesshire. One of the same form as the figure (9 3/8 inches) was found at Dean, [712] near Bolton, Lancashire, and others at Hopwood and Saddleworth in the same county. One of grit (7 1/2 inches) was found at Siddington, [713] near Macclesfield. Another (8 inches), found at Kirkoswald, Cumberland, is in the museum at Newcastle, together with a similar specimen from Haydon Bridge; and others have been found at Thirstone, Shilbottle, Barrasford, [714] and Hipsburn, [715] Northumberland; and in Yorkshire. [716] One (10 1/2 inches) was found at Ehenside Tarn, [717] Cumberland. Others at Rusland, North Lonsdale, and Troutbeck. A long list of stone-hammers, &c., found in Cumberland and Westmorland, has been given by Chancellor R. S. Ferguson, F.S.A., [718] and a similar list has been compiled for Lancashire and Cheshire. [719] They occur also in more southern districts. I have seen one (8 inches) from the neighbourhood of Glastonbury. Another of the same length was found on Dartmoor, near Burnt Tor. Others (8 1/2 and 9 inches) from Ashbury and Holsworthy, [720] Devon, are in the Museum of the Plymouth Institute. One was found at Withycombe Raleigh, [721] Devon. A fine specimen (8 inches long), with the sides somewhat hollowed, was found at Tasburgh, Norfolk. Another of greenstone (5 1/2 inches), and rather curved longitudinally, was found in the same parish. Other specimens from Norfolk are mentioned in the Norwich volume of the Archæological Institute. I have one of serpentine from Chatteris Fen, which has been broken diagonally, and had a fresh edge ground quite away from the middle. The Rev. S. Banks had one of hard sandstone (7 3/4 inches), found in Cottenham Fen. Its faces are more parallel, so that the edge is more obtuse. I have seen one, found near Stourton (9 1/2 inches), Somersetshire, straighter at the sides, and having the angles rounded.

They occur in Leicestershire. [722] One (7 inches) from the Cemetery at Leicester, and one (9 1/2 inches) from Barrow-on-Soar, are recorded. An axe of the same kind, but smaller, found near Imola, has been engraved by Gastaldi. [723]

Perhaps the more common variety, in Cumberland, is that which is somewhat flattened at the butt, like Fig. 131, and which is, more properly speaking, an axe-hammer. This specimen was found near Bed Dial, Wigton, Cumberland, and is in my own collection. The two sides are nearly flat and parallel, and the edge appears to have been re-sharpened since the axe-head was first formed, as it is ground away to a shoulder a little below where it is perforated. It is formed of an igneous rock. A very symmetrical example, 8 1/2 inches long, with the sides nearly flat, from Aikbrae, Culter, Lanarkshire, is engraved in the *Journal of the Archæological Association.* [724]

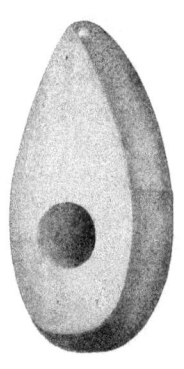

Fig. 131.—Wigton. 1/2

A very similar specimen, 11 inches long, found in a turf moss near Haversham, Westmorland, is engraved in the *Archæologia*, [725] as is another from Furness. [726] Another, with the sides more parallel, and rounder at the end, 8 inches in length, was found near Carlisle upwards of a century ago, and forms the subject of an interesting paper by Bishop Lyttelton. [727] Two also were found at Scalby, [728] near Scarborough. In the Greenwell Collection are several implements of this character, obtained in the North of England. They are 8 to 9 inches long, and 4 to 5 inches broad. One (10 inches) is from Helton, in the parish of Chalton, Northumberland; and another, of nearly the same size and form as Fig. 131, from Castle Douglas, Kircudbrightshire; another of greenstone (6 inches) from Brompton Carr, Yorkshire; and others, varying in form, from Ousby Moor, Cumberland, and Heslerton

Wold, Yorkshire. A fine example (8 inches), truncated at the butt, from Dunse Castle, [729] Berwickshire, has been figured.

In the British Museum are several axe-heads of this form. One, 9 inches long, of a porphyritic rock, is said to have been found in a barrow on Salisbury Plain. One, 12 inches long, is from Stone, Staffordshire, as well as another in which the boring is incomplete, there being only a conical depression on each side. A third, thinner (8 inches), was found near Hull. A fourth, of compact felspathic material, 8 1/4 inches long, is from the parish of Balmerino, Fife. A fifth, of similar material, 8 inches long, is from Llanbrynmair, Montgomeryshire. [730] It is worked to a flat oval at the butt-end, but with the angles rounded. The hole, as usual, tapers inwards from each side, but is not at right angles to the central line of the axe. I have a fine implement of this class, but larger and narrower than the figure, and concave on the sides, so that the edge is wider than the butt. It is of basalt, much eroded on the surface, and was found at Hardwick, near Bishop's Castle, Shropshire. It is 10 1/2 inches long, about 4 1/4 inches wide at the butt, where it is 3 inches thick. The shaft-hole is nearly 2 inches in diameter, and almost parallel; the weight, 8 1/2 lbs.

One (9 1/2 inches) was found at Grimley, [731] Worcestershire. Another, of porphyry, nearly triangular in outline (7 inches), from Necton, Norfolk, is in the Norwich Museum. The shaft-hole, in this case, is parallel, but in most, it tapers both ways, contracting from about 1 3/4 or 2 inches on each face to about 1 1/4 inches in diameter in the middle. One of greenstone (6 inches), found near Ely, has an oval hole.

Fig. 132.—Wollaton Park. 1/2

The late Mr. Llewellynn Jewitt, F.S.A., had an axe-hammer of this class (7 1/2 inches), but still more flattened at one end, found in Cambridgeshire. At the edge the faces form an angle of 45° to each other, and there is little doubt that the implement has lost much of its original length through continual sharpening. He also kindly lent me for engraving the curious axe-hammer shown in Fig. 132, and has made use of my wood-cut in his "Grave Mounds and their Contents." [732] It is formed of a very fine-grained, hard, and slightly micaceous grit, and its weight exceeds 7 3/4 lbs. It is somewhat rounded at the hammer-end, which appears to have lost some splinters by use, though the broken surface has since been partially re-ground. The blade is slightly curved longitudinally, and both the outer and inner sides have been hollowed from the point, as far as the perforation. The faces have each four parallel grooves worked in them, so that they are, as it were, corrugated into five ribs, extending from near the edge to opposite the centre of the hole. The hollows on the sides also show two slight ribs parallel with the faces of the blade, the angles of which are rounded. The shaft-hole tapers slightly in both directions towards the centre, where it is about 1 3/8 inch in diameter. The grooves seem to have been produced by picking, but have subsequently been made smoother by grinding. It was found at a spot known as the Sand Hills, in Lord Middleton's Park, [733] near Wollaton, Notts. The Rev. W. C. Lukis, F.S.A., had a closely similar specimen (10 inches), found at Jervaux, near Bedale, Yorkshire. It is not, however, fluted on the faces.

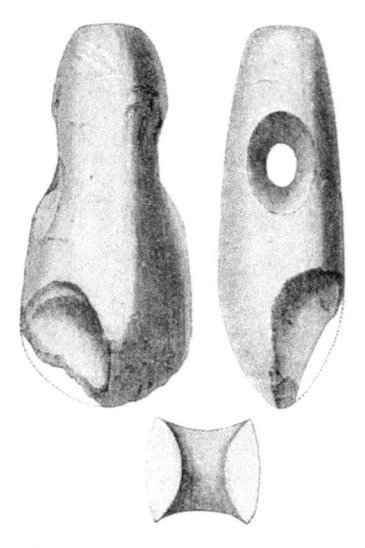

Fig. 133.—Buckthorpe. 1/2

Some of these instruments are so heavy that they can hardly have been wielded in the ordinary manner as axes, though they may have served for splitting wood, either by direct blows or by being used as wedges. Bishop Lyttelton thought they might have been battle-axes, but Pegge [734] pointed out that they were too heavy for such a purpose or for use as missiles, and came to the conclusion "that these perforated stones were not originally applied to any warlike purpose, but rather to some domestic service, either as a hammer or beetle for common use." Professor Nilsson, [735] at a later date, has arrived at the same conclusion, and considers them most suitable for being held in the left hand by a short handle, and driven into wood by blows from a club held in the right hand. He has suggested for them the name of "handled wedges." In some parts of France I have seen extremely heavy iron axes, much resembling these stone implements in form, used for splitting wood. It seems possible that in old times these heavy stone implements may also have been employed in agriculture.

Axes of this character, usually formed of greenstone, are very common in Denmark and Northern Germany. They are much rarer in France, partly, no doubt, in consequence of the less abundance of suitable material. They also occur in Russia [736] and in Italy. [737]

A small specimen of the same form but rather more square at the butt than Fig. 131, made of dark serpentine, and only 3 5/8 inches long, was found at Tanagra, in Bœotia, and was formerly in the collection of Dr. G. Finlay, [738] of Athens.

Some of the forms last described, having square butt-ends, might, perhaps, with greater propriety, have been included in the fourth class into which I have proposed to divide these instruments, viz., axe-hammers, sharpened at one end and more or less hammer-like at the other, and with the shaft-hole usually about the centre.

One of the simplest, and at the same time the rarest varieties of this class, is where an implement of the form of an ordinary celt, like Fig. 69, has been bored through in the same direction as the edge. Fig. 133 represents such a specimen, in the collection of Messrs. Mortimer, of Driffield. It was found at Buckthorpe, Yorkshire, and is formed of close-grained greenstone. The butt-end is circular and flat, and the shaft-hole, which is oval, tapers considerably both ways.

An axe-hammer of diorite, of nearly similar form, found at Groningen, in the Netherlands, is in the museum at Leyden.

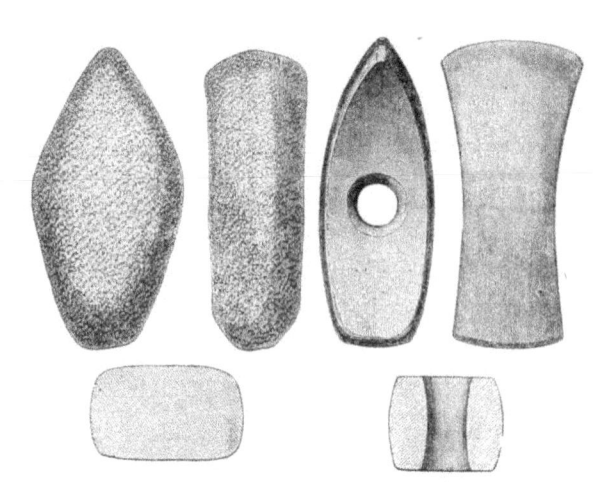

Fig. 134.—Aldro'. 1/2

Fig. 135.—Cowlam. 1/2

Another simple form is that exhibited in Fig. 134, taken from a specimen in greenstone found at Aldro', near Malton, Yorkshire, and in the possession of Mr. Hartley, of Malton. Its principal interest consists in its having been left in the unfinished state, previous to its perforation. We thus learn that the same practice of working the axe-heads into shape before proceeding to bore the shaft-hole, prevailed here as in Denmark. In that country numerous specimens have been found, finished in all respects except the boring, and in many instances this has been commenced though not completed. It would appear from this circumstance that the process of boring was one which required a considerable amount of time, but that it was most satisfactorily performed after the instrument had been brought into shape; the position of the hole being adjusted to the form of the implement, and not the latter to the hole. In the extensive Greenwell Collection is the cutting end of an axe which has been broken half-way across the hole, which, though commenced on both faces, was never finished. The conical, cup-shaped depressions produced by the boring instrument, extend to some depth in the stone, but are still 1/4 inch from meeting. The fragment is 3 1/8 inches long, and was found at Sprouston, near Kelso.

In the same collection is a small unfinished axe-head of greenstone, 4 inches long, in which the hole has not been commenced. It was found at Coxwold, in the North Riding of Yorkshire.

An unpierced axe-head of greenstone, 4 inches long, in form much like Fig. 136, but with the hollowed face shorter, was found in a grave in Stronsay, one of the Orkney islands, and is now in the National Museum at Edinburgh. There are slight recesses on each face, showing the spots at which the perforation was to have been commenced.

A perforated axe of serpentine, of the same character as Fig. 134, but wider at the butt, was found in the Thames, and is now in the British Museum. It is 4 inches long and has the peculiarity of being much thicker at the cutting end than at the butt; the two sides tapering from 1 1/2 inch at the edge to 3/4 inch at the butt.

A similar feature is to be observed in another axe of hornblende schist (5 3/4 inches), and of rather more elongated form than Fig. 134, found at Cawton, in the North Riding of Yorkshire, and in the Greenwell Collection.

A partially-finished axe-head, with one side and about two-thirds of the width of the faces worked into form, is engraved in the "Horæ Ferales." [739] It is not a British specimen, but its place of finding is unknown. Perforated hammers, in form much like Fig. 134 and 135, occurred among the early remains at Troy. [740]

A rather more elaborate form, having the two sides curved longitudinally inwards, and the edge broader than the hammer-end, is shown in Fig. 135. The cutting edge is carefully removed, so that it was probably a battle-axe. The original, which is of porphyritic greenstone, was discovered by Canon Greenwell, in a barrow at Cowlam, [741] near Weaverthorpe, Yorkshire. It lay in front of the face of a contracted skeleton, the edge towards the face, and the remains of the wooden handle still grasped by the right hand. Connected with this grave was that of a woman with two bronze ear-rings at her head.

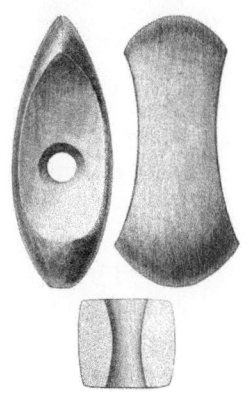

Fig. 136.—Seghill. 1/2

Another of much the same form, but of coarser work and heavier, was found near Pickering, and is preserved in the Museum at Scarborough.

I have seen a small axe of similar type, but with the edge almost semicircular, and the hole nearer the butt, found at Felixstowe, Suffolk. It is of quartzite, 4 1/2 inches long. The hole, though 1 3/4 inch in diameter at the sides, diminishes to 1/2 an inch in the centre. In this respect it resembles some of the hammer-stones shortly to be described.

Fig. 136 presents a rather more elaborate form, which is, however, partly due to that of the flat oval quartzite pebble from which this axe-hammer was made. The hammer-end seems to preserve the form of the pebble almost intact; it is, however, slightly flattened at the extremity. The original is preserved in the Greenwell Collection, and was found in a cist at Seghill, [742] near Newcastle, in 1866. The bones, by which it was no doubt originally accompanied, had entirely gone to decay. A Scotch example, made of basalt, the sides of which are much more concave, is shown in Fig. 136A, kindly lent by the Society of Antiquaries of Scotland. It was found at Wick, [743] Caithness.

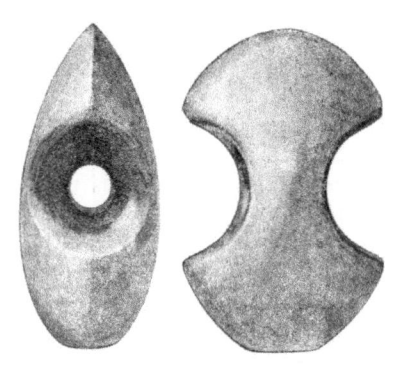

Fig. 136A.—Wick, Caithness. 1/2

It was an axe-head somewhat of the character of Fig. 136, but sharper at the hammer-end, that was found in an urn, near Broughton in Craven, in 1675, and with it a small bronze dagger (with a tang and single rivet hole) and a hone. It is described and figured by Thoresby. [744] Hearne [745] regarded it as Danish. It is described as of speckled marble polished, 6 inches long and 3 1/2 inches broad, with the edge at one end blunted by use. A nearly similar form (4 1/2 inches) has occurred in Shetland. [746] What appears to be an unbored axe of this kind is in the Powysland Museum. [747]

A still greater elaboration of form is exhibited in Fig. 137, from an implement found at Kirklington, Yorkshire, and in the Greenwell Collection. It is of basalt, worked to a flat oval at the hammer-end, and to a curved cutting edge at the other. The two sides are ground concave, and the shaft-hole is nearly parallel. This axe-hammer is of larger size than usual when of this form, being 8 inches in length.

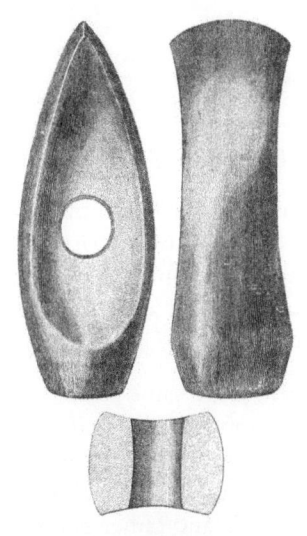

Fig. 137.—Kirklington. 1/2

Nearly similar weapons have been frequently found in barrows. One such, of greenstone, about 4 inches long, was found by the late Mr. Charles Warne, F.S.A., in a barrow at Winterbourn Steepleton, near Dorchester, associated with burnt bones. He has given a figure [748] of it, which, by his kindness, I here reproduce, as Fig. 138. Another (4 inches) was found in a barrow at Trevelgue, [749] Cornwall, in 1872.

An extremely similar specimen, found near Claughton Hall, Garstang, Lancashire, has been figured. [750] It is said to have been found, in cutting through a tumulus in 1822, in a wooden case, together with an iron axe, spear-head, sword, and hammer. There must, however, be an error in this account; and as an urn, containing burnt bones, was found in the same tumulus with the Saxon or Danish interment, it seems probable that the objects belonging to different burials, primary and secondary in the barrow, became mixed during the twenty-seven years that elapsed between their discovery and the communication to the Archæological Institute. Another weapon of much the same shape, but 4 3/4 inches long, and formed of dark greenstone, is in the British Museum. It was found in the Thames, at London. The process by which these hollow sides appear to have been ground will be described at page 266.

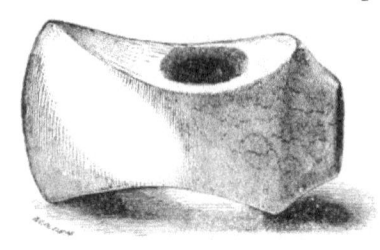

Fig. 138.—Winterbourn Steepleton. 1/2

Sir R. Colt Hoare has engraved two axe-hammers of this form, but slightly varying in size and details, from barrows in the Ashton Valley. [751] In both cases they accompanied interments of burnt bones, in one instance placed beneath an inverted urn; in the other there was no urn, but an arrow-head of bone lay with the axe.

An axe (5 1/4 inches), of nearly the same form, but having a small oval projection on each face opposite the shaft-hole, was found in the bed of the Severn, at Ribbesford, Worcestershire, and is now in the Museum of the Society of Antiquaries. It has been somewhat incorrectly figured by Allies, [752] and rather better by Wright. [753]

An axe-head (5 4/10 inches), of the same character as Fig. 138, but in outline more nearly resembling Fig. 137, found near Stanwick, Yorkshire, is in the British Museum. [754] The cutting end of such a weapon was dredged with gravel from the Trent, at Beeston, near Nottingham, in 1862.

Another axe-hammer of greenstone, with projections on the faces opposite the centre of the hole, and with a hollow fluting near each margin, that is carried round on the sides below the holes, is shown in Fig. 139. The original was found by the Rev. J. C. Atkinson, who kindly lent it me for engraving. It lay in an urn about 17 inches high, containing burnt bones and some fragments of burnt flint, in a large barrow on the Skelton Moors, Yorkshire. In the same barrow were found eight other urns, all containing secondary interments. In another barrow, on Westerdale Moors, Mr. Atkinson found a second axe-hammer of nearly the same size and form, but more hammer-like at the end. This also has the channels on the faces. It is of fine-grained granite, and lay in an urn with burnt bones, a small "incense-cup," and a sort of long bone bead, having a spiral pattern upon it and a transverse orifice into the perforation, about the centre. In this case, also, the interment was not that over which the barrow was originally raised. In another barrow, on Danby North Moors, also opened by Mr. Atkinson, a rather larger axe-hammer of much the same outline, lay with the hole in a vertical position, about 15 inches above a deposit of burnt bones. It is of basalt much decayed. An axe-hammer from Inveraray, [755] Argyllshire (5 3/4 inches), in outline rather like Fig. 143, has small projections on each face opposite to the centre of the shaft-hole.

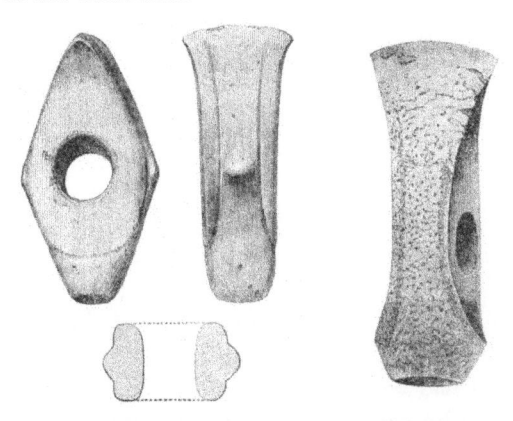

Fig. 139.—Skelton Moors. 1/2

Fig. 140.—Selwood Barrow. 1/2

A longer and more slender form has also occasionally been found in tumuli. Sir R. Colt Hoare has given an engraving of a beautiful specimen from the Selwood Barrow, [756] near Stourton, which is here reproduced as Fig. 140. The axe is of syenite, 5 1/2 inches long, and lay in a cist, in company with burnt bones and a small bronze dagger, which in the description is erroneously termed a lance-head. Parallel with each side, there appears to be a small groove worked on the face of the weapon. A very pretty example of the same form accompanied an interment in a barrow at Snowshill, [757] Gloucestershire. With it were associated two bronze daggers and a bronze pin.

In the Christy Collection is a similar but larger specimen, 7 inches long, formed of dark greenstone. It also has the grooves along the margin of the faces, and has an oval flat face about 1 inch by 7/8 inch at the hammer-end. The hole, which is 1 1/8 inch full in diameter at one side, contracts rather suddenly to 1 inch at the other. This weapon was formerly in the Leverian Museum, and is said to have been found in a barrow near Stonehenge, which, from its similarity to Sir R. C. Hoare's specimen, there seems no reason to doubt.

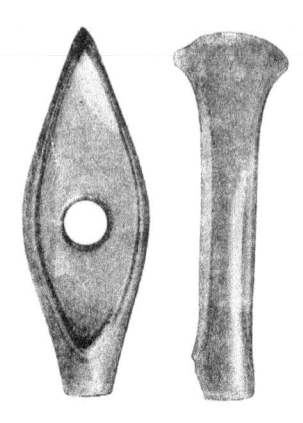

Fig. 140A.—Longniddry. 1/2

An axe-hammer of clay-stone porphyry, 4 3/4 inches long, and in form the same as those last described—except that there appears to be more of a shoulder at the hammer-end—was found in a barrow at Winwick, [758] near Warrington, Lancashire. It was broken clean across the hole, and had been buried in an urn with burnt bones. With them was also a bronze dagger with a tang, and one rivet hole to secure it in the handle.

An axe-hammer of much the same proportions, but more square at the hammer-end, was discovered in a dolmen near Carnac, [759] in Brittany. A beautiful axe of the same character with ornamental grooves and mouldings is in the Museum at Edinburgh, and is here, by favour of the Society of Antiquaries of Scotland, shown as Fig. 140A. The original is of diorite, and was dug up in 1800 at Longniddry, [760] East Lothian.

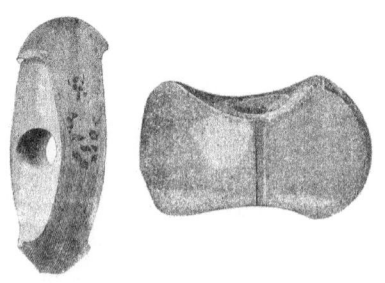

Fig. 141.—Upton Lovel. 1/2

Fig. 142.—Thames, London. 1/2

Another variety of form is shown in Fig. 141, reduced from Sir R. Colt Hoare's great work. [761] In this case the hammer-end would appear to be lozenge-shaped, as there is a central ridge shown on the face. It was found in the Upton Lovel barrow, on the breast of the larger skeleton, near the feet of which the flint celts, polished and unpolished, and various other objects in bone and stone, were found, as previously mentioned. [762] The engraving of this weapon in the *Archæologia* differs considerably from that given by Sir R. C. Hoare.

In Fig. 142 is shown another form, in which the hammer-end, though flat in one direction, forms a semicircular sweep, answering in form to the cutting edge at the other end. The two faces are ornamented with a slight groove, extending across them parallel to the centre of the shaft-hole. The material of which this axe-hammer is made appears to be serpentine. It was found in the Thames, at London, and is in the British Museum. A "hammer" from a barrow at Wilsford, [763] Wilts, which was associated with a flat bronze celt and other articles of bronze, was of the same type as Fig. 142, but without the grooves.

The very neatly formed instrument represented in Fig. 143, seems to occupy an intermediate place between a battle-axe and a mace or fighting hammer. It is rounded in both directions at the butt-end, but instead of having a sharp edge at the other end it is brought to a somewhat rounded point. The inner side is concave, though hardly to the extent shown by the dotted line in the cut. The shaft-hole is nearly parallel, though somewhat expanding at each end. The material is greenstone. This weapon was found in the middle of a barrow, or rather cairn, formed of stones, in the parish of Pelynt, Cornwall. [764] It lay among a considerable quantity of black ashes, which had evidently been burnt on the natural surface of the ground at the spot. There was no urn, nor any other work of art in company with it. In another barrow, in the same field, was a bronze dagger with two rivets. I have never seen any other stone hammer of this form found in Britain, nor can I call to mind any such in continental museums. The nearest approach to it is to be observed in some of the Scandinavian weapons, in which the outer side is much more rounded than the inner, but in these there is usually an axe-like edge, though very narrow. A shuttle-shaped weapon of porphyritic stone, found in Upper Egypt, [765] is not unlike it, but is equally pointed at both ends. The perforation narrows from 3/4 inch to 1/4. The concave side of the Pelynt weapon is so much like that of some of the battle-axes, such as Fig. 137, as to suggest the idea that originally it may have been of this form, but having in some manner been damaged, it has been re-worked into its present exceptional shape.

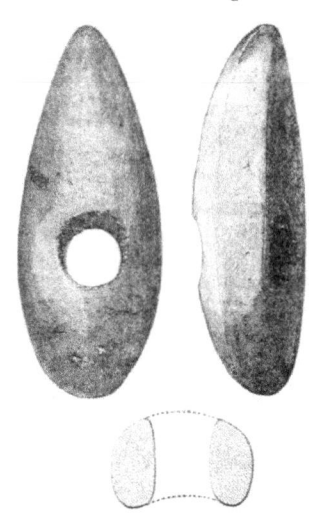

Fig. 143.—Pelynt, Cornwall. 1/2

It will have been observed that instruments, such as most of those engraved, have accompanied interments both by cremation and inhumation, and have, in some cases, been found in association with small daggers, celts, and pins or awls of bronze. Other instances may be adduced from the writings of the late Mr. T. Bateman, though sometimes the exact form of the weapons is not recorded. In the Parcelly Hay Barrow, [766] near Hartington, an axe-head of granite, with a hole for the shaft, and a bronze dagger, with three rivets for fastening the handle, had been buried with a contracted body, above the covering stones of the primary interment. [767] Another, of basalt, apparently like Fig. 126, broken in the middle, is said to have lain between two skeletons at full length, placed side by side in a barrow at Kens Low Farm. [768] On the breast of one lay a circular brooch of copper or bronze. With the axe was a polished porphyry-slate pebble, the ends of which were ground flat.

Looking at the whole series, it seems probable that they were intended to serve more than one purpose, and that while the adze-like instruments may have been tools either for agriculture or for carpentry, and the large heavy axe-hammers also served some analogous purposes, the smaller class of instruments, whether sharpened at both ends or at one only, may with some degree of certainty be regarded as weapons. That the perforated form of axe was of later invention than the solid stone hatchet is almost self-evident; and that many of the battle-axe class belong to a period when bronze was coming into use is well established. That all instruments of this form belong to so late a period there is no evidence to prove; but in other countries where perforated axes are common, as in Scandinavia and Switzerland, those who have most carefully studied the antiquities, find reason for assigning a considerable number to a period when the use of bronze was unknown. On the other hand, it is possible that in some instances the large heavy axe-hammer may have remained in use even in the days when bronze and iron were well known. Sir W. Wilde mentions one in the museum of the Royal Irish Academy, 10 3/4 inches long, which is said to have been recently in use. Canon Greenwell had another which was used for felling pigs in Yorkshire. Such, however, may be but instances of adapting ancient implements, accidentally met with, to modern uses.

I have already, in the description of the various figures, mentioned when analogous forms were found in other parts of Western Europe, so that it is needless again to cite instances of discoveries on the Continent. I may, however, notice a curious series from Northern Russia and Finland. [769] They are for the most part pointed at one end, the other being sometimes carved to represent the head of an animal. Some are pointed at each end. In several there is a projection on both sides of the shaft-hole, designed to add strength to a weak part, but at the same time made ornamental. The animal's head occurs also on bronze axes.

Out of Europe this class of perforated instruments is almost unknown.

Turning to modern savages, the comparative absence of perforated axes is striking. In North America, it is true that some specimens occur, but the material is usually too soft for cutting purposes, and the haft-holes are so small that the handles would be liable to break. It has therefore been inferred that they were probably used as weapons of parade. They are, however, occasionally formed of quartz. [770] Schoolcraft, [771] moreover, regards the semilunar perforated maces as actual weapons of war. One of them, pointed at each end, he describes as being 8 inches long, and weighing half a pound. The more hatchet-like forms he considers to be tomahawks. In some instances [772] the hole does not extend through the blade.

In Central America, Southern Africa, and New Zealand, where the art of drilling holes through stone is, or was, well known, perforated axes appear to be absent. I have, however, heard of an instrument of the kind having been discovered in New Zealand, but have not seen either the original or a sketch. Some perforated hoe-like implements have been found in Mexico.

The nearest approach to such instruments is perhaps afforded by the sharp-rimmed perforated discs of stone, mounted on shafts so as to present an edge all round, which are in use, apparently as weapons, in the Southern part of New Guinea, and Torres Straits. Some perforated sharp-rimmed discs of flint and serpentine, have been found in France. [773] They are probably heads of war-maces. In New Caledonia, [774] flat discs of jade, ground to a sharp edge all round, are mounted as axes, being let into a notch at the end of the haft and secured by a lashing that passes through two small holes in the edge of the blade.

The cause of this scarcity of perforated weapons appears to be, that though it might involve rather more trouble and skill to attach a solid hatchet to its shaft, yet this was more than compensated by the smaller amount of labour involved in making that kind of blade, than in fashioning and boring the perforated kind. These latter, moreover, would be more liable to break in use. Looking at our own stone axes from this point of view, it seems that with the very large implements the shaft-hole became almost a necessity; while with those used for warlike purposes, where the contingencies of wear and breakage were but small, it seems probable that the possession of a weapon, on the production of which a more than ordinary amount of labour had been bestowed, was regarded as a mark of distinction, as is the case among some savages of the present day.

CHAPTER IX.
PERFORATED AND GROOVED HAMMERS.

Closely allied to the axe-hammers, so closely indeed that the forms seem to merge in each other, are the perforated hammer-heads of stone, which are found of various shapes, and are formed of several different kinds of rocks. In many instances, the whole of the external surface has been carefully fashioned and ground into shape, but it is at least as commonly the case that a symmetrical oval pebble has been selected for the hammer-head, and has been thus used without any labour being bestowed upon it, beyond that necessary for boring the shaft-hole. By some antiquaries, these perforated pebbles have been regarded as weights, for sinking nets, or for some such purpose; but in most cases this is, I think, an erroneous view—firstly, because the majority of these implements show traces, at their extremities, of having been used as hammers; and, secondly, because if wanted as weights, there can be no doubt that the softer kinds of stone, easily susceptible of being pierced, would be selected; whereas these perforated pebbles are almost invariably of quartzite or some equally hard and tough material.

There are some instances, indeed, in which the perforation would appear to be almost too small for a shaft of sufficient strength to wield the hammer, if such it were; but even in such cases, where hard silicious pebbles have been used, they must, in all probability, have been intended for other purposes than for weights. I am inclined to think that some means of hafting, not now in use, may have been adopted in such cases, and that possibly the handles may have been formed of twisted hide or sinews, passed through the hole in a wet state, secured by knots on either side, and then allowed to harden by drying. Such hafts would be more elastic and tough than any of the same size in wood; but it must be confessed that there is no evidence of their having been actually employed, though there is of the stones having been in use as hammers. I have an Irish specimen, 3 3/4 inches long, with the perforation tapering from about 1 3/4 inch diameter on either side, to less than 1/2 an inch in the middle, and yet each end of the stone is worn away by use, to the extent of 1/4 inch below the original oval contour. It is possible that these deep cavities may have been intended to assist in keeping a firm hold of the stone when used in the hand as a hammer without any shaft, in the same manner as did the shallow indentations, which occasionally occur on the faces of pebbles which thus served; but this is hardly probable when the cavities meet in the centre to form a hole exactly like the ordinary shaft-holes, except in its disproportionately small size. It is worthy of notice, that even in axe-hammers the shaft-hole appears to be sometimes absurdly small for the size of the implement. I have a Danish specimen of greenstone, carefully finished, 6 3/4 inches long, and weighing 1 lb. 15 ozs. avoirdupois, and yet the shaft-hole is only 3/4 inch in diameter on either side, and but 1/2 an inch in the centre. The axe from Felixstowe, already mentioned, presents the same peculiarity.

It has been suggested that one of the methods of hafting these implements with the double bell-mouthed perforations, was by placing them over a branch of a tree, and leaving them there until secured in their position by the natural growth of the wood, the branch being then cut off at the proper places, and serving as a handle. I have, however, found by experience that even with a fast-growing tree, such a process requires two or three years at the least, and that when removed, the shrinkage of the branch in drying, leaves the hammer-head loose on its haft. Such a system of hafting would, moreover, imply a fixity of residence on the part of the savage owners of the tools, which appears hardly compatible with the stage of civilization to which such instruments are probably to be referred.

At the same time, it must be remembered that the Caribs of Guadaloupe and the Hurons are, as has been mentioned at page 155, credited with an analogous system of hafting imperforate hatchets.

It has also been suggested that some of these pierced stones were offensive weapons, having been attached by a thong of leather to a handle, [775] and used as "flail-stones," after the manner of the "morning-stars" of the middle ages. Such a method of mounting, though possible, appears to me by no means probable in the majority of cases, though among the Eskimos [776] a weapon has been in use, consisting of a stone ball with a drilled hole, through which a strip of raw hide is passed to serve as a handle.

The first specimen that I have selected for illustration, Fig. 144, might, with almost equal propriety, have been placed among the perforated axes, though it has three blunt edges instead of one or two. It was found at Balmaclellan, in New Galloway, and is now in the National Museum at Edinburgh. It is of very peculiar triangular form, 1 1/2 inches in thickness, and with a perforation expanding from an inch in diameter in the centre, to 1 3/4 inches on each side. An engraving of it is given in the *Proceedings of the Society of Antiquaries of Scotland*. [777] This I have here reproduced on a larger scale, so as to correspond in its proportions with the other woodcuts.

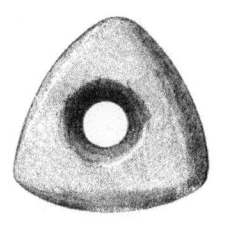

Fig. 144.—Balmaclellan.

A curious hammer, of brown hæmatite, not quite so equilateral as the Scotch specimen, and much thicker in proportion, found in Alabama, has been engraved by Schoolcraft. [778] The holes, from each side, do not meet in the middle.

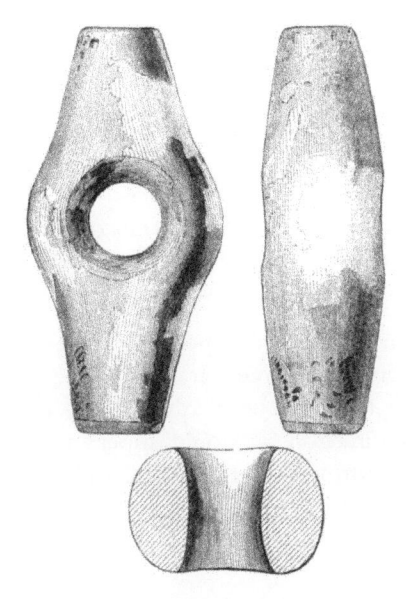

Fig. 145.—Thames, London. 1/2

The specimen shown in Fig. 145 was found in the Thames, at London, and is now in the British Museum. In form it is curiously like a metallic hammer, swelling out around the shaft-hole, and tapering down to a round flat face at each extremity. So far as I know, it is unique of its kind in this country. It is more probably the head of a war mace than that of an ordinary hammer. A somewhat similar hammer, of porphyry, is in the museum of the Deutsche Gesellschaft at Leipzig. It is, however, shorter in its proportions.

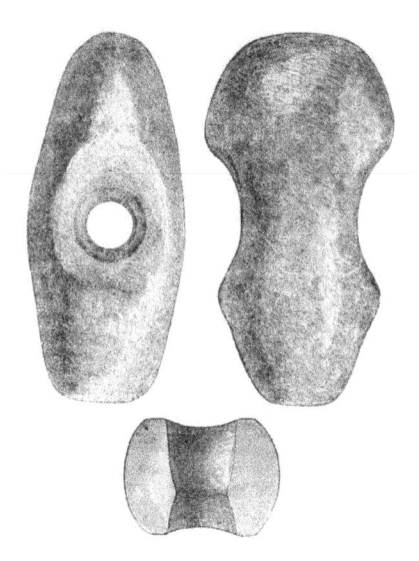

Fig. 145A.—Kirkinner. 1/2

A stone hammer found at Claycrop, Kirkinner, [779] Wigtownshire, is, by the courtesy of the Society of Antiquaries of Scotland, shown in Fig. 145A. In form, it is very like Fig. 136A from Wick, but blunter at the edge.

The instrument shown in Fig. 146 is perhaps more like a blunted axe-hammer than a simple hammer. It has at one end a much-rounded point, and at the other is nearly straight across, though rounded in the other direction. It would appear to be a weapon rather than a tool. It is formed of greenstone, and was found near Scarborough, being now in the museum at the Leeds Philosophical Hall. A similar form has been found in Italy. [780]

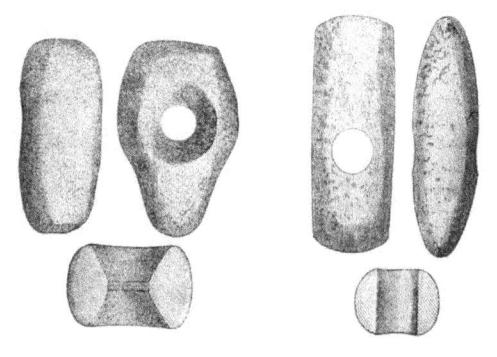

Fig. 146.—Scarborough. 1/2

Fig. 147.—Shetland. 1/2

A beautifully finished hammer-head, cross-paned at both ends, and with a parallel polished shaft-hole, is shown in Fig. 147. It is of pale mottled green gneissose rock, with veins of transparent pale green, like jade, and was found in a barrow in Shetland. It is preserved in the National Museum at Edinburgh, where is also another of the same form, but broader and much more weathered, which was found at Scarpiegarth, [781] also in Shetland. Mr. J. W. Cursiter has another of these ruder examples (3 1/2 inches) from Firth. He has also a very highly polished specimen made of serpentine (4 inches) subquadrate in section, and with hemispherical ends, from Lingrow, Orkney. The perforation is conical, being 1 inch in diameter on one face and only 1/2 inch on the other. A remarkably elegant instrument of this kind, formed of a quartzose metamorphic rock, striped green and white, and evidently selected for its beauty, is in the well-known Greenwell Collection. It was found in Caithness. It is polished all over, and 4 1/4 inches long, of oval section, with the ends slightly rounded. The shaft-hole is parallel, 1/2 inch in diameter, and about 3/4 inch nearer to one end than to the other. In the same collection is another specimen, rather more elongated in form, and of more ordinary material, found near Harome, in Yorkshire, in a district where a number of stone implements of rare types have been discovered. It is of clay-slate, 5 1/4 inches long, and of oval section. The shaft-hole tapers from 1 inch at the faces to 9/16 inch in the centre. A shorter hammer, of gneiss, 3 3/4 inches long, and of similar section, with a parallel shaft-hole 5/8 inch in diameter, was found near Blair-Drummond, and is now in the National Museum at Edinburgh. It has a thin rounded edge at one end, and is obtuse at the other, as if it had been broken and subsequently rounded over. The form occasionally occurs in the South of England. In the British Museum is a beautiful specimen (4 1/4 inches) from Twickenham, and another of more ordinary stone from the Thames, which was formerly in the Roots Collection.

Another polished hammer (of grey granite) with curved sides, and narrower at one end than the other, was found in a cairn in Caithness, [782] in company with a flint flake ground at the edge, some arrow-heads, and scrapers. By permission of the Society of Antiquaries of Scotland, it is shown in Fig. 148. A somewhat similar form of hammer has been obtained in Denmark. [783]

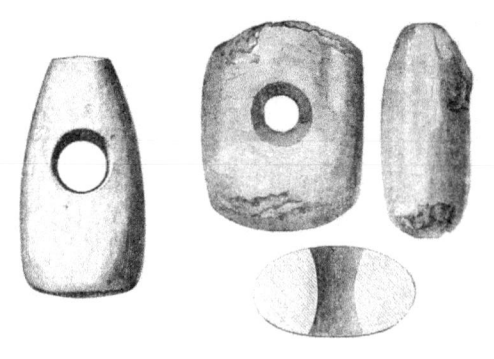

Fig. 148.—Caithness. 1/2

Fig. 149.—Leeds. 1/2

The hammer-head shown in Fig. 149 resembles the Shetland implements in character, though, besides being far less highly finished, it is shorter and broader, and shows more wear at the end. The hole, also, is not parallel, but tapers from both faces. It is stated to have been found 12 feet deep in gravel, while sinking for foundations for the works of the North-Eastern Railway in Neville Street, Leeds. It is formed of greenstone, and has all the appearance of having been made out of a portion of a celt.

I have a somewhat smaller hammer-head, of much the same form, from Reach Fen, Cambridge, which also seems to have been made from a fragment of a broken celt. I have seen one of the same kind, found near Brixham, in Devonshire.

I have another specimen, from Orwell, Wimpole, Cambs., in which a portion of an implement of larger size has also been utilized for a fresh purpose. In this case the sharper end of a large axe-head of stone, probably much like Fig. 131, having been broken off, the wedge-shaped fragment, which is about 3 inches long and 2 inches broad, has been bored through in a direction at right angles to the edge, and probably to the original shaft-hole, and a somewhat adze-like hammer-head has been the result, what was formerly the edge of the axe being rounded and battered.

Fragments of celts which, when the edge was lost, subsequently served as hammers, but without any perforation, have not unfrequently been found, both here and on the Continent. The Eskimo hammer, already mentioned, has much the same appearance and character as if it had been made from a portion of a jade celt.

The form of hammer shown in Fig. 150, may be described as a frustum of a cone with convex ends. The specimen here figured is of quartzite, and was found near Rockland, Norfolk. It is preserved in the Norwich Museum. The hole, as usual with this type, is nearly parallel. The lower half of a similar hammer, but of flint, 2 inches in diameter, and showing one-half of the shaft-hole, which is 5/8 inch in diameter, is in the British Museum. It came from Grundisburgh, Suffolk.

A more conical specimen, tapering from 2 3/8 inches to 1 7/8 inches in diameter, and 3 inches long, with a shaft-hole 7/8 inch in diameter within 3/4 inch of the top, is in the Greenwell Collection. It is of basalt, and was found at Twisel, in the parish of Norham, Northumberland.

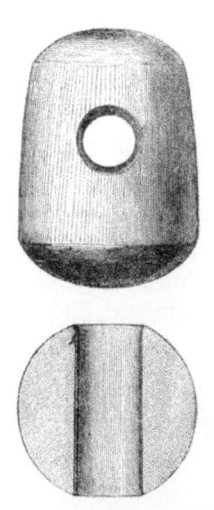

Fig. 150.—Rockland. 1/2

Some rather larger and more cylindrical instruments of analogous form have been obtained in Yorkshire. One such, about 4 inches long, and with a small parallel shaft-hole about 3/4 inch in diameter, was found with an urn in a barrow at Weapon Ness, and is in the museum at Scarborough. With it was a flint spear-head or javelin-head. It is described as rather kidney-shaped in the *Archæologia*. [784] I have the half of another, made of compact sandstone, and found on the Yorkshire Wolds.

The same form occurs in Ireland, but the sides curve inwards and the section is somewhat oval. Sir W. Wilde [785] describes two such of polished gneiss, and a third is engraved in Shirley's "Account of Farney." [786] Sir William suggests that such implements were, in all probability, used in metal working, especially in the manufacture of gold and silver. Certainly, in most cases, they can hardly have been destined for any ordinary purposes of savage life, as the labour involved in boring such shaft-holes in quartzite, and especially in flint, must have been immense. It seems quite as probable that these were weapons as tools, and, in that case, we can understand an amount of time and care being bestowed on their preparation such as in modern days we find savages so often lavishing on their warlike accoutrements. Another argument in favour of these being weapons, may be derived from the beauty of the material of which they are sometimes composed. That from Farney is of a light green colour and nicely polished, and one in my own collection, found near Tullamore, King's County, is formed of a piece of black and white gneissose rock, which must have been selected for its beauty. One in the British Museum from Lough Gur is of black hornblende.

The type with the oval section is not, however, confined to Ireland. In the Greenwell Collection is a beautiful hammer of this class, which is represented in Fig. 151. It is made of a veined quartzose gneiss, and was found on Heslerton Wold, Yorkshire. As will be seen, it is somewhat oval in section. The sides are straight, but the faces from which the hole is bored are somewhat hollow. I have a specimen of the same form, but made of greenstone (3 inches), from the neighbourhood of Sutton Coldfield, [787] Warwickshire.

A barrel-shaped hammer (3 3/4 inches) was found on the hill of Ashogall, [788] Turriff, Aberdeenshire, and a rude triangular hammer on the Gallow Hill of Turriff.

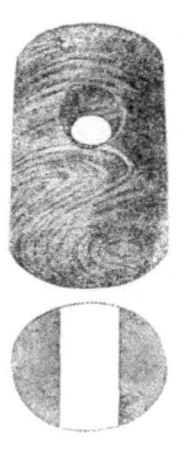

Fig. 151.—Heslerton Wold. 1/2

A smaller hammer-head, curiously like those from Farney and Tullamore, both in form and material, was found with a small "food vessel" accompanying an interment near Doune, [789] Perthshire. It is 2 5/8 inches long, with a parallel shaft-hole 5/8 inch in diameter.

Another, of small-grained black porphyry, neatly polished, and about 3 1/4 inches long, similar in outline to Fig. 150, but of oval section, and little more than an inch in thickness, was dredged up in the Tidal Basin, at Montrose, and is preserved in the local museum.

A cylindrical hammer of grey granite (2 3/4 inches) only partially bored from both faces, was found in the parish of Glammis, [790] Forfarshire. Mr. J. W. Cursiter, of Kirkwall, has a beautiful specimen formed of striped gneiss (3 1/4 inches) with well-rounded ends, and the sides much curved inwards. It was found at Whiteness, Shetland. Another of his hammers (2 3/4 inches) with a parallel hole (7/8 inch) has the sides straight and is of oval section. It is of beautifully mottled gneiss.

Another variety, allied to the last, has an egg-shaped instead of a quasi-conical form; the shaft-hole being towards the small end of the egg. The specimen here engraved, Fig. 152, is apparently of serpentine, and was found at Hallgaard Farm, near Birdoswald, Cumberland. It is in the Greenwell Collection.

I have a smaller but nearly similar specimen in greenstone, from the neighbourhood of Flamborough, Yorkshire. The hole in this is more bell-mouthed than in the other specimen, and a little nearer the centre of the stone.

One of nearly similar form, but rather flatter on one face, 3 1/4 inches long, found in Newport, Lincoln, is engraved in the *Archæological Journal*. [791]

Another in size and shape, much like Fig. 152, was dug up at Llanrhaiadr-yn-Mochnant, Montgomeryshire. [792] Another in the British Museum came from the neighbourhood of Keswick.

An egg-shaped hammer, 3 inches long, of mica schist, and found in the Isle of Arran, [793] is in the National Museum at Edinburgh. The shaft-hole is in the centre.

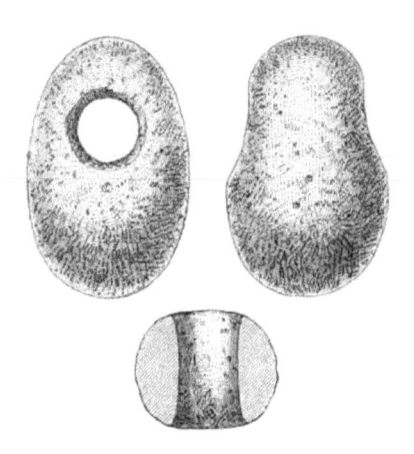

Fig. 152.—Birdoswald. 1/2

Sometimes these hammer-heads are, in outline, of an intermediate form between Figs. 151 and 152, being oval in section, and more rounded at the smaller end than the larger, which is somewhat flattened. One such, in the Christy Collection, is formed of granite, and was found at Burns, near Keswick, Cumberland. Another, of quartzite, 3 1/4 inches long, found on Breadsale Moor, is in the Museum at Derby. Neither of them presents the same high degree of finish as Fig. 151. They seem, indeed, to have been made from pebbles, which were but slightly modified in form by their conversion into hammer-heads.

Occasionally, though rarely, flint pebbles naturally perforated have been used as hammers. In excavating a barrow at Thorverton, [794] near Exeter, the Rev. R. Kirwan discovered a flint pebble about 3 3/4 inches long, with a natural perforation rather nearer one end than the other, but which on each face has been artificially enlarged. Each end of the pebble is considerably abraded by use. No other relics, with the exception of charcoal, were found in the barrow. Mr. Kirwan suggests that the stone may have been used by placing the thumb and forefinger in each orifice of the aperture; but not improbably it may have been hafted. In the Museum at Copenhagen are one or two axes of flint, ground at the edge, but with the shaft-holes formed by natural perforations of the stone. And in M. Boucher de Perthes' Collection [795] were two hammer-heads, with central holes of the same character.

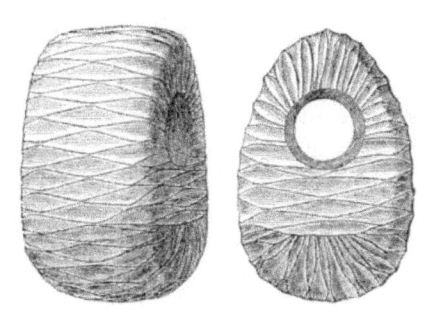

Fig. 153.—Maesmore, Corwen.

The beautiful and elaborately finished hammer-head found at Maesmore, near Corwen, Merionethshire, and now in the National Museum at Edinburgh, is to some extent connected in form with those like Fig. 152. It is shown in Fig. 153, on the scale of 1/2 linear, but a full size representation of it is given elsewhere. [796] It is of dusky white chalcedony, or of very compact quartzite, and weighs 10 1/2 ounces. "The reticulated ornamentation is worked with great precision, and must have cost great labour. The perforation for the haft is formed with singular symmetry and perfection; the lozengy grooved decoration covering the entire surface is remarkably symmetrical and skilfully finished." The Rev. E. L. Barnwell, [797] who presented it to the Society of Antiquaries of Scotland, has observed that "the enormous amount of labour that must have been bestowed on cutting and polishing, would indicate that it was not intended for ordinary use as a common hammer." "Some have considered it as the war implement of a distinguished chief; others, that it was intended for sacrificial or other religious purpose, or as a badge of high office." Other conjectures are mentioned which it is needless to repeat. My own opinion is in favour of regarding it as a weapon of war, such as, like the jade *mere* of the New Zealander, implied a sort of chieftainship in its possessor. At the time of its discovery it was unique of its kind. But since then a second example has been found, though in an unfinished condition, [798] at Urquhart, near Elgin, and has also been placed in the museum at Edinburgh. It is rather smaller, but of similar type and material to the Welsh specimen. The shaft-hole is finished, but the boring process has not been skilfully carried out, the meeting at the centre of the holes bored from either face not having been perfect; and though the hole has been made straight by subsequent grinding out, there is still a lateral cavity left. The faceted pattern is complete at the small end, and commenced on both sides. Along the edge of the face small notches are ground, showing the manner in which the pattern was laid out before grinding the hollow facets.

A third but ruder example of the same kind was found in the Thames, at Windsor, [799] and was exhibited to the Society of Antiquaries in 1895 by Mr. F. Tress Barry, F.S.A., who has kindly presented it to me. It is of nearly the same size as the others, but the perforation is natural, and there is no attempt at ornamentation, though much of the surface has been ground in irregular facets.

The end of a naturally perforated flint nodule from Aldbourne, Wilts, in the collection of Mr. J. W. Brooke, seems to be part of a hammer. It is neatly faceted like the nucleus, Fig. 189, and has been rounded by grinding. The hole has been partially ground.

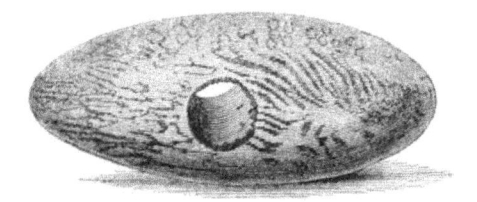

Fig. 154.—Normanton, Wilts. 1/2

A very peculiar hammer, discovered by Sir Richard Colt Hoare, [800] in Bush barrow, near Normanton, Wilts, is reproduced in Fig. 154. It lay on the right side of a skeleton, which was accompanied by a bronze celt without side flanges, a magnificent bronze dagger, the handle of which was ornamented with gold, a lance-head of bronze, and a large lozenge-shaped plate of gold. The hammer-head is "made out of a fossil mass of *tubularia*, and polished, rather of an egg form," or "resembling the top of a large gimlet. It had a wooden handle, which was fixed into the perforation in the centre, and encircled by a neat ornament of brass, part of which still adheres to the stone." As it bore no marks of wear or attrition, Sir Richard hardly considered it to have been used as a domestic implement, and thought that the stone as containing a mass of *serpularia*, or little serpents, might have been held in great veneration, and therefore have been deposited with the other valuable relics in the grave. Judging from the other objects accompanying this interment, it seems more probable that this hammer was a weapon of offence, though whether the material of which it was formed were selected from any superstitious motive, rather than for the beauty of the stone, may be an open question. I have already mentioned instances of *serpula* [801] limestone having been employed as a material for celts of the ordinary character. The hole in this instrument appears to be parallel, and may possibly have been bored with a metallic tool. The occurrence of this hammer in association with such highly-finished and tastefully-decorated objects of bronze and gold, shows conclusively that stone remained in use for certain purposes, long after the knowledge of some of the metals had been acquired.

The hammer-heads of the next form to be noticed are of a simpler character, being made from ovoid pebbles, usually of quartzite, by boring shaft-holes through their centres. The specimen I have selected for illustration, Fig. 155, is in my own collection, and was found in Redgrave Park, Suffolk. It is said to have been exhumed ten feet below the surface, by men digging stone in Deer's Hill. The pebble is of quartzite, probably from one of the conglomerates of the Trias, but more immediately derived from the gravels of the Glacial Period, which abound in the Eastern Counties. The hole as usual tapers towards the middle of the stone. The pebble is battered at both ends, and slightly worn away by use. I have a rather smaller, and more kidney-shaped hammer, also slightly worn away at the ends, found at Willerby Carr, in the East Riding of Yorkshire, and one (4 inches), that is considerably worn at both ends, from Stanifield, Bury St. Edmunds. An example was found at Normandy, [802] near Wanborough, Surrey. I have seen one formed from a sandstone pebble (4 1/2 inches) found near Ware.

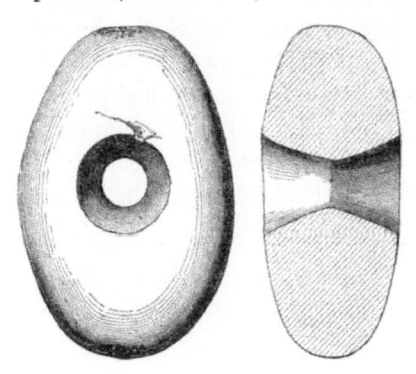

Fig. 155.—Redgrave Park. 1/2

In the Greenwell Collection is a large specimen, made from a flat pebble (7 1/2 inches) obtained at Salton, York, N.R.

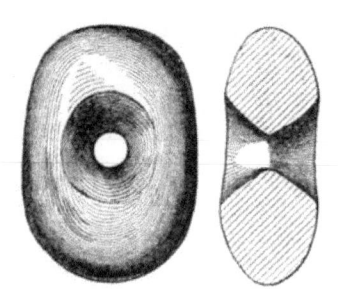

Fig. 156.—Redmore Fen. 1/2

Fig. 156 shows a smaller variety of the same type, but rather square in outline, and with the shaft-hole much more bell-mouthed. The original is in my own collection, and was found in Redmore Fen, near Littleport, Cambridgeshire. I have others from Icklingham (2 3/8 inches) and Harleston, Norfolk (3 1/4 inches). Hammers of this and the preceding type are by no means uncommon. Mr. Joshua W. Brooke has one (3 1/4 inches) from Liddington, Wilts. One of quartzite, 5 inches long, was found in a vallum of Clare Castle, Suffolk, [803] and is in the Museum of the Society of Antiquaries; another (4 1/2 inches) at Sunninghill, Berks; [804] another (2 1/2 inches) near Reigate. [805] One, in form like Fig. 156 (4 1/4 inches), was discovered in Furness. [806] Others were found at Pallingham Quay, [807] and St. Leonard's Forest, [808] Horsham (5 inches), both in Sussex. What seems to be a broken hammer (2 3/8 inches) and not a spindle-whorl was obtained at Mount Caburn, [809] Lewes. Another, circular in outline, and 3 inches in diameter, was found at Stifford, [810] near Grays Thurrock, and is engraved in the *Archæological Journal*. [811] I have here reproduced the figure (Fig. 157), though the scale is somewhat larger than that of my other illustrations.

In the British Museum is a specimen, originally about 3 1/2 inches by 2 1/4 inches, and 3/4 inch thick, with the end battered, which was found in a tumulus at Cliffe, near Lewes. Another, 3 3/4 inches in diameter, from the Thames; a subtriangular example from Marlborough (4 1/4 inches); and an oval one (3 7/8 inches) from Sandridge, Herts, are in the same collection.

Fig. 157.—Stifford.

A longer form (6 1/4 inches by 3 1/8) was found at Epping Uplands, Essex, [812] and another about 5 inches, rather hoe-like in form, in the Lea, at Waltham. Another (4 1/2 inches) was found in London. [813]

In the Norwich Museum are two hammer-heads of this type, one from Sporle, near Swaffham (3 1/8 inches), of quartzite; and the other of jasper, from Eye, Suffolk, 5 inches by 2 3/4 inches. In the Fitch Collection are also specimens from Yarmouth (3 1/2 inches), from Lyng (5 inches), and Congham, Norfolk (6 inches), as well as a fragment of one found at Caistor.

The late Mr. Warren, of Ixworth, had one from Great Wratting, near Haverhill (4 inches), and the late Mr. James Carter, of Cambridge, one 3 1/4 inches in diameter, from Chesterton.

In the Museum of the Cambridge Antiquarian Society is one of irregular form, found near Newmarket. A thin perforated stone, 6 inches by 3 inches, from Luton, [814] in Bedfordshire, may belong to this class, though it was regarded as an unfinished axe-head.

In the collection formed by Canon Greenwell is one found at Coves Houses, Wolsingham, Durham (3 1/2 inches), and another of quartzite (4 1/2 inches), with both ends battered, from Mildenhall Fen. He discovered another of small size, only 2 1/4 inches in length, with the perforation not more than 7/16 inch in diameter in the centre, in the soil of a barrow at Rudstone, [815] near Bridlington.

The late Mr. H. Durden, of Blandford, had two fragments of these hammers, made from quartzite pebbles, one of them from Hod Hill, Dorset, and the other from the same neighbourhood. A perforated oval boulder of chert was also found near Marlborough. [816]

Both round and oval hammer-stones are in the Leicester Museum. [817] One (6 1/2 inches) was found at Doddenham,

Worcestershire, and others (3 3/8 inches) at Silverdale, [818] Torver, [819] and elsewhere in Lancashire. [820] A large specimen (8 inches) was found at Abbey Cwm Hir, [821] Radnorshire, and a small one near Rhayader, [822] Montgomeryshire. A circular example (4 1/4 inches), with a very small central hole, was discovered in Pembrokeshire. [823] Quartzite pebbles converted into hammerheads occur also in Scotland. The hole in one from Pitlochrie [824] is only 1/8 inch in diameter at its centre. In one from Ythanside, Gight, [825] Aberdeenshire (4 3/4 inches), it is only 1/4 inch.

Besides quartzite and silicious pebbles, these hammer-heads were made from fragments of several other rocks. The Rev. S. Banks had one of greenstone, 5 3/4 inches by 3 1/4 inches, found at Mildenhall. A disc of dolerite [826] (4 inches) with convex faces and perforated in the centre in the usual manner, was found at Caer Leb, in the parish of Llanidan, Anglesea. Several hammer-stones of this kind were obtained by the late Hon. W. O. Stanley, M.P., in his researches in the Island of Holyhead. [827] One of them, now in the British Museum, is of trap, 4 1/2 inches long and 3 inches broad, somewhat square at the ends; another is of schist, 3 3/8 inches long, and much thinner in proportion. Both were found at Pen-y-Bonc. A fragment of a third, formed of granite (?), was found at Ty Mawr, in the same island. One of granite (?) [828] was found at Titsey Park, Surrey. A small one of "light grey burr stone," 2 3/8 inches in diameter, was found at Haydock, [829] near Newton, Lancashire. I have a subquadrate example (4 inches) of felsite, from Belper, Derbyshire. The Scottish specimens are often of other materials than quartzite. A circular "flailstone," found at Culter, Lanarkshire, has been figured, [830] but the material is not stated. The same is the case with an oval one, 4 inches long, found near Longman, [831] Macduff, Banff; another from Forfarshire; [832] and a third, 4 inches by 3 inches, from Alloa. [833]

Others from Portpatrick [834] (6 3/4 inches), and from a cist at Cleugh, [835] Glenbervie, Kincardineshire, have been figured. I have a disc (3 inches), nearly flat round the circumference like a Danish "child's wheel" from Ballachulish, Inverness. It is formed of hornblendic gneiss. A hammer-stone of this kind from Poyanne, Landes, [836] has been recorded.

Some of these circular pebbles may have formed the heads of war-maces, such as seem to have been in use in Denmark in ancient times and in a modified form, among various savage tribes in recent days.

A curious variety of this type, flat on one face and convex on the other, is shown in Fig. 158. It is made from a quartzite pebble, that has in some manner been split, and was found at Sutton, near Woodbridge. It is now in the collection of General Pitt Rivers, F.R.S.

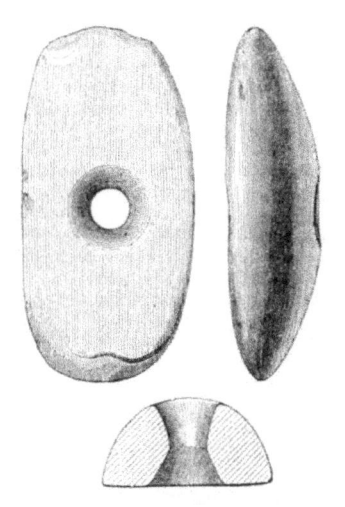

Fig. 158.—Sutton. 1/2

In the Christy Collection is another implement of much the same size, material, and character, which was found at Narford, Norfolk. The ends are somewhat hollowed after the manner of a gouge, but the edges are rounded. It seems to occupy a sort of intermediate position between a hammer and an adze.

One of similar, but more elongated form, found at Auquemesnil [837] (Seine Inférieure), has been figured by the Abbé Cochet.

It is difficult to say for what purpose hammers of this perforated kind were destined. I can hardly think that such an enormous amount of labour would have been bestowed in piercing them, if they had merely been intended to serve in the manufacture of other stone implements, a service in which they would certainly be soon broken. If they were not intended for weapons of war or the chase, they were probably used for lighter work than chipping other stones; and yet the bruising at the ends, so apparent on many of them, betokens their having seen hard service. We have little, in the customs of modern savages, to guide us as to their probable uses, as perforated hammers are almost unknown among them. The perforated spheroidal stones of Southern Africa [838] act merely as weights to give impetus to the digging sticks, and such stones are said to have been in use in Chili [839] and California. [840] The perforated discs of North America appear to be the fly-wheels of drilling sticks. Some quartz pebbles perforated with small central holes, and brought from the African Gold Coast, [841] seem to have been worn as charms.

In Ireland, perforated hammer-stones are much more abundant than in England. They are usually formed of some igneous or metamorphic rock, and vary considerably in size, some being as much as 10 or 12 inches in length. Sir W. Wilde observes that stone hammers, and not unfrequently stone anvils, have been employed by smiths and tinkers in some of the remote country districts until a comparatively recent period. If, however, these hammers were perforated, there can be but little doubt that they must have been ancient tools again brought into use, as the labour in manufacturing a stone hammer of this kind would be greater than that of making one in iron, which would, moreover, be ten times as serviceable. If, however, the stone hammers came to hand ready made, they might claim a preference. For heavy work, where iron was scarce, large mauls, such as those shortly to be described, might have been in use rather than iron sledges; but the more usual form of stone hammer would probably be a pebble held in the hand, as is constantly the case with the workers in iron of Southern Africa. Even in Peru and Bolivia, the late Mr. David Forbes, F.R.S., informed me that the masons skilful in working hard stone with steel chisels, make use of no other mallet or hammer than a stone pebble held in the hand. The anvils and hammers used in Patagonia [842] in working silver are generally of stone, but the latter are not perforated.

In Germany, as already [843] incidentally remarked, anvils formed of basalt were in frequent use in the sixteenth century.

In Scandinavia and Germany the same forms of hammers as those found in the British Isles occur, both in quartzite and in other kinds of stone. They are not, however, abundant. Worsaae does not give the type in his "Nordiske Oldsager," and Nilsson gives but a single instance. [844] Lindenschmit [845] engraves a specimen from Oldenstadt, Lüneburg, and another from Gelderland. [846]

In Switzerland they are extremely rare. In the Neuchâtel Museum, however, is a perforated hammer, formed from an oval pebble, and found in the Lake-habitations at Concise; another, 2 inches in diameter, with a small perforation deeply countersunk on each face, has been regarded by M. de Mortillet [847] as a sink-stone for a net.

I have a lenticular mace-head, 3 inches in diameter and 2 inches thick, formed of a silicious breccia from Pergamum. The hole tapers from 3/4 inch to 1/2 inch.

The half of a small perforated hammer made of greenstone and polished is recorded to have been found at Arconum, [848] west of Madras. A perforated stone, possibly a hammer, was found in the Jubbulpore district, Central India; [849] and a fine example from the Central Provinces, [850] rather more oval than Fig. 157, has been figured by the late Mr. V. Ball.

In the British Museum is a perforated ball of hard red stone of a different type from any of those which I have described, which came from Peru. It is about 3 inches in diameter, with a parallel hole an inch across. Around the outside are engraved four human faces, each surmounted by a sort of mitre. It may be the head of a mace.

Spherical mace-heads of marble and of harder rocks occur among Egyptian antiquities. They are sometimes decorated by carving.

In this place perhaps it will be well to mention a class of large hammer-stones, or mauls, as they have been termed, which, though belonging to a period when metal was in use, are in all probability of a high degree of antiquity. They consist, as a rule, of large oval pebbles or boulders, usually of some tough form of greenstone or grit, around which, somewhere about the middle of their length, a shallow groove has been chipped or "picked," from 3/4 inch to 1 inch in width. On the two opposite sides of the pebble, and intersecting this groove, two flat or slightly hollowed faces have often been worked, the purpose of which is doubtless connected with the method of hafting the stones for use as hammers. This was evidently by means of a withe twisted round them, much in the same manner as a blacksmith's chisel is mounted at the present day. In the case of the mauls, however, the withe appears to have been secured by tying, like the haft of one form of Australian stone hatchets (Fig. 105), and then to have been tightened around the stone by means of wedges driven in between the withe loop and the flat faces before mentioned.

A [851] German stone axe seems to have been fastened to its haft in the same manner.

In many of the Welsh specimens about to be mentioned, the flat faces are absent, and the notch or groove does not extend all round the stone, but exists only on the two sides through which the longer transverse axis of the pebble passes. In this case the wedges, if any, were probably driven in on the flatter side of the boulder.

The ends of the pebbles are usually much worn and broken by hammering, and not unfrequently the stone has been split by the violence of the blows that it has administered. It is uncertain whether they were merely used for crushing and pounding metallic ores, or also in mining operations; but with very few exceptions they occur in the neighbourhood of old mines, principally copper-mines.

In some copper mines at Llandudno, [852] near the great Orme's Head, Carnarvonshire, an old working was broken into about sixty years ago, and in it were found a broken stag's horn, and parts of what were regarded as of two mining implements or picks of bronze, one about 3 inches and the other about 1 inch in length. In 1850, another ancient working was found, and on the floor a number of these stone mauls, described as weighing from about 2 lbs. to 40 lbs. each. They had been formed from water-worn boulders, probably selected from the beach at Pen-maen-mawr. One of the mauls in the Warrington Museum [853] is 6 5/8 inches long, and weighs 3 lbs. 14 ozs. One of basalt, measuring nearly a foot in length, was found in ancient workings at Amlwch Parys Mine, [854] in Anglesea. Others have been discovered in old workings in Llangynfelin Mine, [855] Cardiganshire, and at Llanidan, [856] Anglesea.

A ponderous ball of stone, about 5 inches in diameter, probably used in crushing and pounding the ore, a portion of stag's horn, fashioned so as to be suited for the handle of some implement, and an *iron* pick-axe, were found in some old workings in the Snow Brook Lead Mines, Plinlimmon, Montgomeryshire. [857]

Two of these hammer-stones, 4 1/2 and 5 inches in length, were obtained by the late Hon. W. O. Stanley, within hut circles, possibly the remains of the habitations of copper miners in ancient times, at Ty Mawr, in the Island of Holyhead. Some of these mauls are figured in the *Archæological Journal*, [858] and are of much the same form as Fig. 159, the original of which probably served another purpose. Others of the same character, formed of quartzite, were found at Pen-y-Bonc, [859] Holyhead, and Old Geir, [860] Anglesea. They have also been found at Alderley Edge, [861] Cheshire.

A boulder, like those from Llandudno, but found at Long Low, near Wetton, Staffordshire, is in the Bateman Collection. [862] One from Wigtownshire [863] has been regarded as a weight.

They are of not uncommon occurrence in the south of Ireland, [864] especially in the neighbourhood of Killarney, where, as also in Cork, many of them have been found in ancient mines. They have, in Ireland, been denominated miners' hammers. One of them is engraved in "Flint Chips." [865] I have seen an example from Shetland.

They have also been found in ancient copper mines in the province of Cordova, [866] at Cerro Muriano, Villanueva del Rey, [867] and Milagro, in Spain; in those of Ruy Gomes, [868] in Alemtejo, Portugal; and at the salt mines of Hallstatt, [869] in the Salzkammergut of Austria, and at Mitterberg, [870] near Bischofshofen.

A large hammer of the same class, but with a deeper groove all round, has been recorded from Savoy. [871]

They are not, however, confined to European countries, for similar stone hammers were found by Mr. Bauerman in the old mines of Wady Maghara, [872] which were worked for turquoises (if not also for copper ore) by the ancient Egyptians, so early as the third Manethonian Dynasty. It is hard to say whether the grooved stone found by Schliemann at Troy [873] was used as a hammer or a weight.

What is more remarkable still, in the New World similar stone hammers are found in the ancient copper mines near Lake Superior. [874] As described by Sir Daniel Wilson, [875] "many of these mauls are mere water-worn oblong boulders of greenstone or porphyry, roughly chipped in the centre, so as to admit of their being secured by a withe around them." They weigh from 10 to 40 lbs., and are found in enormous numbers. M. Marcou [876] has given an account of the discovery of some of those mauls in the Mine de la Compagnie du Nord-Ouest, at Point Kievenau, Lake Superior. He describes them as formed of leptynite (quartz and felspar), quartz, and porphyry, and weighing from 5 to 8 lbs. each; and mentions having seen one of quartz weighing about 5 lbs., which was in the possession of some Kioway Indians, and was bound to a handle with a strip of bison skin.

This similarity or identity in form of implements used in countries so wide apart, and at such different ages, does not, I think, point of necessity to any common origin, nor to any so-called "continuity of form," but appears to offer another instance of similar wants with similar means at command, resulting in similar implements for fulfilling those wants. Grooved hammers for other purposes, as evinced by their smaller size, and a few grooved axes, occur in Scandinavia. An example among one of the lower races in modern times is afforded by a large crystal of quartz, with its terminal planes preserved at both ends, which has been slightly grooved at the sides for the purpose of attaching it to a handle, and was brought by Captain Cook, from St. George's Sound, where it appears to have been used as a hammer or pick. It is now in the British Museum, and has been described by Dr. Henry Woodward. [877]

Even in Britain the hammer-stones of this form are not absolutely confined to mining districts. Canon Greenwell, in one of the barrows at Rudstone, [878] near Bridlington, found on the lid of a stone-cist two large greenstone pebbles 8 and 9 3/4 inches long, each with a sort of "waist" chipped in it, as if to receive a withe, and having marks at the ends of having been in use as hammers.

Closely connected in form and character with the mining hammers, though as a rule much smaller in size, and in all probability intended for a totally different purpose, is the class of stone objects of one of which Fig. 159 gives a representation, reproduced from the *Archæological Journal*. [879] This was found in company with two others at Burns, near Ambleside, Westmorland; and another, almost precisely similar in size and form, was found at Percy's Leap, and is preserved at Alnwick Castle. Another, from Westmorland, is in the Liverpool Museum, and they have, I believe, been observed in some numbers in that district. A stone of the same character, but more elaborately worked, having somewhat acorn-shaped ends, was found by the late Hon. W. O. Stanley, at Old Geir, [880] Anglesea. Others from Anglesea, [881] one of them ornamented, have been figured. They were originally regarded as hammer-stones, but such as I have examined are made of a softer stone than those usually employed for hammers, and they are not battered or worn at the ends. It is, therefore, probable that they were used as sinkers for nets or lines, for which purpose they are well adapted, the groove being deep enough to protect small cord around it from wear by friction. They seem also usually to occur in the neighbourhood either of lakes, rivers, or the sea. A water-worn nodule of sandstone, 5 inches long, with a deep groove round it, and described as probably a sinker for a net or line, was found in Aberdeenshire, [882] and is in the National Museum at Edinburgh; and I have one of soft grit, and about the same length, given me by Mr. R. D. Darbishire, F.G.S., and found by him near Nantlle, Carnarvonshire.

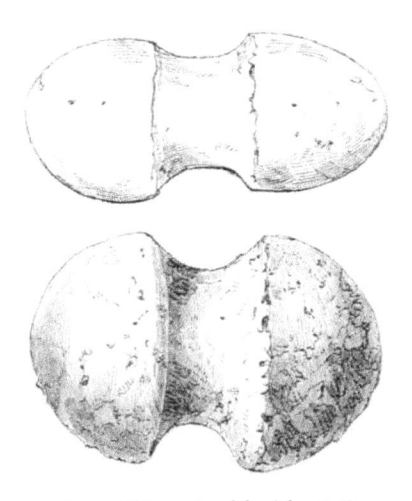

Fig. 159.—Ambleside. 1/2

Many of these sink-stones are probably of no great antiquity. With two transverse grooves, they are still in use in Shetland. [883]

The Fishing Indians of Vancouver's Island [884] go out trolling for salmon in a fast canoe, towing behind them a long line made of tough seaweed, to which is attached, by slips of deer hide, an oval piece of granite perfectly smooth, and the size and shape of a goose's egg. It acts as a sinker, and is said to spin the bait. A net-sinker, formed of a pebble slightly notched or grooved, is among the antiquities from Lake Erie, engraved by Schoolcraft. [885] Others have been found in the State of New York. [886] See C. Rau's "Prehistoric Fishing." [887]

Sink-stones are by no means rare in Ireland, and continue in use to the present day. One of the same class as Fig. 159, but grooved round the long axis of the pebble, is engraved by Sir W. Wilde. [888] Similar stones occur in Denmark, and were regarded by Worsaae [889] as sink-stones, though some of them, to judge from the wear at the ends, and the hardness of the material, were used as hammers. I have seen, in Sweden, the leg bones of animals used as weights for sinking nets.

Another form of sink-stone, weight, or plummet, was formed by boring a hole towards one end of a flattish stone. Such a one, weighing 14 1/4 oz., was dredged from the Thames at Battersea. [890]

Another, of oval form, pierced at one end, from Tyrie, [891] Aberdeenshire, is in the National Museum at Edinburgh; and a wedge-shaped perforated stone from Culter, Lanarkshire, [892] was probably intended for the same purpose. These may have been in use for stretching the warp in the loom when weaving. They are found of this form with Roman remains. [893]

CHAPTER X.
HAMMER-STONES, ETC.

Under this head I propose to treat of those implements which have apparently been used as hammers, but which, for that purpose, were probably held in the hand alone, and not provided with a shaft, as the groove or shaft-hole characteristic of the class last described, is absent. At the same time there are some hammer-stones in which there are cavities worked on either face, so deep and so identical in character with those which, in meeting each other, produce the bell-mouthed perforations commonly present in the hammers intended for hafting, that at first sight it seems difficult to say whether they are finished implements, or whether they would have become perforated hammer-heads had the process of manufacture been completed. Certainly in some cases the cavities appear to be needlessly deep and conical for the mere purpose of receiving the finger and thumb, so as to prevent the stone slipping out of the hand; and yet such apparently unfinished instruments occur in different countries, in sufficient numbers to raise a presumption that the form is intentional and complete. There are some instances where, as was thought to be the case with a quartz pebble from Firth, [894] in Orkney, the unfinished implements may have been cast aside owing to the stone having cracked, or to the holes bored on each face not being quite opposite to each other, so as to form a proper shaft-hole.

In other instances, as in Figs. 160 and 161, the battering of the end proves that the stones have been in actual use as hammers. It is of course possible that these cavities may have been worked for the purpose of mounting the stones in some other manner than by fixing the haft in a socket. A split stick may, for instance, have been used, with a part of the wood on each side of the fissure worked away, so as to leave projections to fit the cavities, and have then been bound together so as to securely grasp the pebble. A stone mallet, consisting of a large pebble mounted between two curved pieces of wood, somewhat resembling the hames of a horse collar, and firmly bound together at each end, is still used by the quarrymen of Trichinopoly, [895] in India. Another method of hafting stones, by tying them on to the side of a stick with little or no previous preparation, is practised by the Aymara Indians of Bolivia and Peru. [896] Mr. D. Forbes, F.R.S., in his interesting account of this people, has engraved a pebble thus mounted, which was in use as a clod crusher. One of them is preserved in the Christy Collection.

Among the Apaches, [897] in Mexico, hammers are made of rounded pebbles hafted in twisted withes.

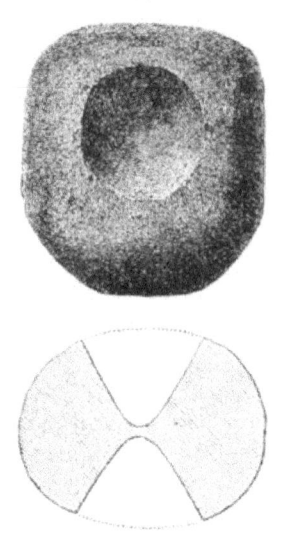

Fig. 160.—Helmsley. 1/2

A remarkable hammer-head, found at Helmsley, in the North Riding of Yorkshire, is in the collection formed by Canon Greenwell. It is shown in Fig. 160, and has been made from a rather coarse-grained quartzite pebble, both ends of which have, however, been worn away by use to an extent probably of an inch in each case, or of two inches in the whole pebble. The worn ends are rounded, but somewhat hollow in the middle, as if they had at that part been used for striking against some cylindrical or sharp surface. The funnel-shaped cavities appear almost too deep and too sharp at their edges to have been intended merely to assist in holding the hammer in the hand, and it seems possible that their original purpose may have been in connection with some method of hafting. The hammer has, however, eventually been used in the hand alone, for the wear of the ends extends over the face, quite to the margin of one of the cavities, and at such an angle, that it would have been almost impossible for any handle to have been present. But if the stone be held in the hand, with the middle finger in the cavity, the wear is precisely on that part of the stone which would come in contact with a flat surface, in hammering upon it. What substance it was used to pound or crush it is impossible to determine, but not improbably it may have been animal food; and bones as well as meat may have been pounded with it.

A quasi-cubical hammer-stone, with recesses on two opposite faces, found at Moel Fenlli, [898] Ruthin, Denbighshire, has been figured. It is now in my collection.

The specimen engraved as Fig. 161 has been made from a quartzite pebble, and has the conical depression deeper on one face than the other. It was found at Winterbourn Bassett, Wilts, and is now in the British Museum.

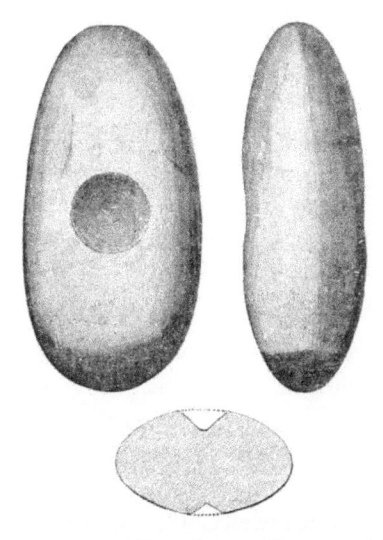

Fig. 161.—Winterbourn Bassett. 1/2

In the Norwich Museum is a similar pebble, from Sporle, near Swaffham. It is 3 3/4 inches long, recessed on each face, with a conical depression, the apex rounded. These cavities are about 1 1/4 inches diameter on the face of the stone, and about 3/4 inch in depth. The Rev. W. C. Lukis, F.S.A., had a hammer-stone of this kind, 3 inches long, found at Melmerby, Cumberland. One (6 inches) was found at Langtree, [899] Devon, another (3 1/8 inches) at Trefeglwys, [900] Montgomeryshire. I have one (3 inches) from Ryton-on-Dunsmore, Coventry, and a thinner example, 2 3/4 inches, much worn at the ends, from Litlington, Cambs.

A circular rough-grained stone, 3 inches in diameter, with deep cup-like indentations on each face, found on Goldenoch Moor, Wigtownshire, [901] is in the National Museum at Edinburgh; where is also another hammer formed of a greenstone pebble (3 1/2 inches), with broad and deep cup-shaped depressions on each face, and much worn at one end, which came from Dunning, Perthshire. There are other examples of the same kind in the same museum.

Many have, indeed, been found in Scotland. A good example from Machermore Loch, [902] Wigtownshire, and several others, [903] have been figured.

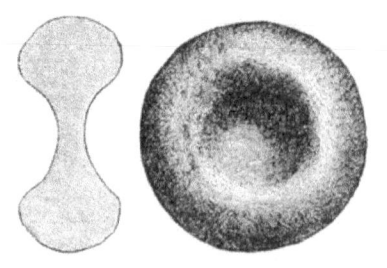

Fig. 161A.—Goldenoch. 1/2

That from Goldenoch, shown in Fig. 161A, [904] has a deep recess on each face. Others from Fife [905] have the recess on one face only. In the case of one from the Island of Coll [906] the recesses are at the sides instead of on the faces.

In some cases the depressions are shallower, and concave rather than conical. I have a flat irregular disc of greenstone, about 2 1/4 inches diameter and 5/8 inch thick, thinning off to the edges, which are rounded, and having in the centre of each face a slight cup-like depression, about 5/8 inch in diameter. It was found in a trench at Ganton, Yorkshire. In the Greenwell Collection is a somewhat larger disc of sandstone, worn on both faces and round the whole edge, and with a slight central depression. It was found in a cairn at Harbottle Peels, Northumberland. In form, these instruments are identical with the *Tilhuggersteene* [907] of the Danish antiquaries, and it is possible that some of them, especially those of the circular form, may have been used for the purpose of chipping out other kinds of stone implements.

The type is not of uncommon occurrence in Ireland. [908] It is rare in France, but a broken example from the neighbourhood of Amiens is in the Blackmore Museum.

I have a specimen which might be mistaken for Danish or Irish, but which was brought me from Port Beaufort, Cape of Good Hope, by Captain H. Thurburn, F.G.S. It must have been in use there at no very remote period.

An oval stone, with what appears to be a cup-shaped depression on one face, 3/8 inch deep, is engraved by Schoolcraft [909] as a relic of the Congarees. Another, from the Delaware River, of the Danish form, is described by Nilsson [910] as a tool for making arrow-points. He also engraves one from Greenland. Other so-called hammer-stones in the same plate are more probably "strike-a-light" stones, and under any circumstances belong to the Early Iron Period. Abbott [911] and Rau [912] also describe Indian hammer-stones, some like Fig. 161.

Highly polished, and deep cup-shaped or conical depressions are occasionally to be observed occurring on one or both faces of large pebbles, usually of quartz, and sometimes in two or three places on the same face. Though very similar to the hollows on the hammer-stones, they are due to a very different cause, being merely the results of stone bearings or journals having been employed, instead of those of brass, for the upright spindles of corn mills. It seems strange that for such a purpose stone should have gone out of use, it being retained, and indeed regarded as almost indispensable for durability, in the case of watches, the pivot-holes of which are so frequently "jewelled."

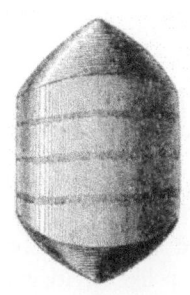

Fig. 162.—St. Botolph's Priory. 1/2

Fig. 162, which I have reproduced from the Sussex Archæological Collections [913] on the same scale as the other figures, shows a pivot-stone of quartzite (?) found in the ruins of St. Botolph's Priory, Pembrokeshire, a few yards from a pebble (4 1/2 inches) of similar material, in which a hole had been bored to the depth of half an inch apparently by the friction of the pointed end of the smaller pebble. Another pivot-stone of the same kind was found at Bochym, [914] Cornwall. Such socket-stones were, until recently, in use in Scotland [915] and Piedmont [916] for the iron spindles of the upper mill-stones of small water-mills. Pivot-stones with larger socket-stones were also used for field-gates. Similar socket-stones occur in Switzerland, [917] and have puzzled Dr. Keller.

Fig. 163.—Bridlington. 1/2

A stone, with a well-polished cavity, found on the site of an old mill near Carluke, Lanarkshire, [918] was exhibited at Edinburgh in 1856. Another was found in Argyllshire; and I have seen other specimens from Ireland. The socket of the hinge of the great gate at Dunnottar Castle is said to have consisted of a similar stone. Stones with highly-polished hollows in them, in which apparently the ends of drill-sticks revolved, are common on the site of ancient Naukratis. [919]

As has already been observed at page 223, it is by no means uncommon to find portions of polished celts which, after the edge has been by some means broken away, have been converted into hammers. Very rarely, there is a cup-like cavity worked on either face in the same manner as in the celts shown in Figs. 87 and 88. A specimen of this character, from the neighbourhood of Bridlington, is shown in Fig. 163. It is of close-grained greenstone, and, to judge from the thickness of the battered end, the celt, of which this originally formed the butt, must have been at least half as long again as it is in its present form. The cavities have been worked out with some kind of pick or pointed tool, and from their position so near the butt-end, it seems probable that they did not exist in the original celt, but were subsequently added when it had lost its cutting edge, and was destined to be turned into a hammer-stone. In the Greenwell Collection is a similar specimen, 4 inches long, found at Wold Newton, in the East Riding of Yorkshire. In the celts with cup-shaped depressions on their faces, but still retaining their edge, the depressions are nearer the centre of the blade.

This hollowing of a portion of the surface is sometimes so slight as to amount to no more than a roughening of the face, such as would enable the thumb and fingers to take a sufficiently secure hold of the stone, to prevent its readily falling out of the hand when not tightly grasped; a certain looseness of hold being desirable, to prevent a disagreeable jarring when the blows were struck. If, as seems probable, many of these hammers or pounders were used for the purpose of splitting bones, so as to lay bare the marrow, we can understand the necessity of roughening a portion of the greasy surface of the stone, to assist the hold.

Fig. 164.—Bridlington. 1/2

Fig. 165.—Bridlington. 1/2

In Fig. 164 I have represented a large quartz pebble found in Easton Field, Bridlington, which has the roughened depression on both faces rather more strongly marked than usual, especially on the face here shown. It is more battered at one end than the other, and has evidently been long in use. It shows some traces of grinding at the lower end in the figure, as if it had been desirable for it to have a sort of transverse ridge at the end, to adapt it to the purpose for which it was used.

Canon Greenwell found in a barrow at Weaverthorpe, [920] Yorkshire, a hammer-stone of this kind, but nearly circular in form. It is a flat quartz pebble, about 1 3/4 inches in diameter, battered all round, and broken at one part, and having the centre of one face artificially roughened.

A round hammer (2 1/2-inches), with depressions on each face, was found at Gatley, [921] Cheshire. Hammer-stones of the same character occurred abundantly on the site of ancient Naukratis. [922] The *wallong*, [923] or stone used by the Australian natives for grinding nardoo seeds on the *yow wi*, a large flat stone, is curiously like Fig. 164.

To the same class, belongs the hammer-stone shown in Fig. 165, found at Huntow, near Bridlington. It has been made from a quartz pebble, of the original surface of which but little remains, and has a well-marked depression about 1/8 inch deep in the centre of each face. The periphery is much worn away by use.

A fine-grained sandstone pebble, in form like a small cheese, about 3 inches in diameter, having the two faces smooth and perfectly flat, was found at Red Hill, [924] near Reigate, and was regarded as a muller or pounding-stone used possibly in husking or bruising grain; or even for chipping flint, its surface bearing the mark of long-continued use as a pestle or hammer. [925] "Precisely similar objects have been found in Northumberland, and other parts of England."

Canon Greenwell informs me that about twenty such, differing in size and thickness, were found on Corbridge Fell, together with several stone balls. He thinks they may possibly have been used in some game. A paper on the stone hammer and its various uses has been published by Mr. J. D. McGuire. [926]

The circular stone from Upton Lovel Barrow, [927] engraved by Sir R. Colt Hoare, appears to be a hammer or, more probably, a rubbing-stone, but it is worn to a ridge all round the periphery. I have a precisely similar instrument from Ireland. Other mullers from Wiltshire [928] barrows have been figured by Dr. Thurnam. Several such discoidal stones, somewhat faceted on their periphery, were found by the late Hon. W. O. Stanley, in his examination of the ancient circular habitations in Holyhead Island, and some have been engraved. [929]

An almost spherical stone, but flattened above and below, where the surface is slightly polished, was found in Whittington Wood, Gloucestershire, and exhibited to the Society of Antiquaries in 1866. [930] It is of quartzite, about 3 inches in diameter. Another, of the same size, of depressed, spherical form, was found in Denbighshire, [931] and another flat disc of quartz in Aberdeenshire. [932]

Pebbles that have been used in this way, as pounders or mullers, belong to various ages and different degrees of civilization. Some well worn have been found in Yorkshire [933] barrows and elsewhere. [934] One from Philiphaugh, [935] Selkirkshire, has been figured. I have one such, worn into an almost cubical form, which was found with Roman remains at Poitiers, and I have seen several others said to be of Roman date. A pounding-stone of much the same form as Fig. 165, found on the summit of the Mont d'Or, Lyonnais, [936] has been engraved by M. Chantre, with others of the same character. I have seen examples in Germany.

I have a flat granite pebble, about 3 1/2 inches by 3 inches, the sides straight, the ends round, and with well-marked circular depressions in each face, from Cayuga County, New York. It has certainly been used as a hammer-stone. Such mullers are by no means uncommon in North America. Some of the American [937] stone discs, which are occasionally pierced, appear to have been more probably used in certain games.

Cup-shaped cavities occasionally occur on stones which have not apparently been intended for use as hammers. In the soil of one of the barrows at Rudstone, near Bridlington, Canon Greenwell found a fragment of a greenstone pebble, nearly flat on one face, in which a concave depression, about an inch over and 1/4 inch deep, had been picked. In the National Museum at Edinburgh is a subquadrate flat piece of grit, 1 inch thick and about 3 1/2 inches long, on each face of which is a cup-shaped depression about 1 1/4 inches in diameter. It does not appear to have been used as a hammer. Mr. James Wyatt, F.G.S., had a piece of close-grained grit, in shape somewhat like a thick axe-head, 4 1/2 inches long, 3 inches wide, and 3 inches thick, with four concave depressions, one on each face and side, found at Kempston Road, near Bedford. What purpose these hollows fulfilled, it is difficult to guess. The stones in which they occur may, however, have been used as anvils or mortars on which to hammer or pound; or the cavities may have served to steady objects of bone, stone, or wood in the process of manufacture. Anvil stones, with pits worn on their faces, probably by flints having been broken upon them, have been found in Scotland. [938] A sandstone [939] with a concave depression on each of its six faces has been regarded by Mortillet as a grindstone for fashioning stone buttons or the convex ends of other implements. I have seen analogous cavities produced, on a larger scale, on blocks of granite which have been used as anvils, on which to break road materials. The cup and ring cuttings [940] common on ancient stone monuments, especially in Scotland, do not come within my province. Flat stones, with cup-shaped markings upon them, sometimes as many as seven on a stone, were found in considerable abundance in some of the Yorkshire [941] barrows examined by Canon Greenwell.

The stones with cup-shaped [942] depressions in them, found in the caves of the Reindeer Period in the south of France, have the hollows, in nearly all instances, upon one of their faces only, and have therefore more probably served as mortars than as hammers. The pebbles, from the same caves, which have been used as knapping or chipping stones, are usually left in their natural condition on the faces, though worn away at the edges, sometimes over the whole periphery. A very few of the hollowed stones show signs of use at the edges.

Stones with cup-shaped [943] depressions, like those from the French caves, are in use in Siberia for crushing nuts and the seeds of the Cembro Pine; and among the natives of Australia [944] for pounding a bulbous root called *bellilah*, and the roasted bark of trees and shrubs for food. Some Carib examples of the same kind are in the Ethnological Museum at Copenhagen, as well as some from Africa, used in the preparation of poison.

Some of the so-called corn-crushers [945] and mealing-stones from the Swiss Lake-dwellings have shallow depressions on the faces, but for the most part they belong to the class to be subsequently described. I have one of granite, from Nussdorf, with a depression on one face, in which the thumb can be placed, while the forefinger lies in a groove, like that of a pulley, which extends about half-way round the stone. The opposite part of the edge is much worn by hammering. It approximates in form to the pulley-like stones to which the name of sling-stones has been given, but the use of which is at present a mystery.

A hammer-stone, curiously like that which I have engraved as Fig. 165, is among those found in the settlements of the Lac du Bourget, [946] by M. Rabut. This or a similar one is in the British Museum. Another from Picardy [947] has been figured.

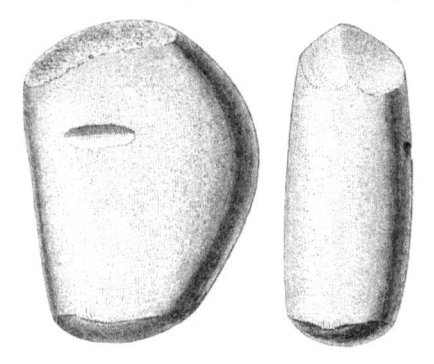

Fig. 166.—Scamridge. 1/2

A hammer-stone, if so it may be called, of bronze, is among the antiquities from Greenland in the Ethnological Museum at Copenhagen.

Occasionally the depression is reduced to a minimum, and consists of merely a slight notch or roughening on one or both faces of the pebble which has served as a hammer or pounding-stone.

The irregular, flat greenstone pebble, worn away at both ends, shown in Fig. 166, has on one face only a notch, apparently intended to receive the thumb. It was found at Scamridge, Yorkshire, and is in the Greenwell Collection. It will be observed that it is worn into a curved ridge at one end. In the same collection is an oval quartzite pebble (4 1/2 inches), battered at both ends, and with a slight diagonal ridge at that most worn away. This was found in a barrow at Weaverthorpe, [948] with an unburnt body. I have a flat greenstone pebble from Scamridge, Yorkshire, worn away at one end to a curved ridge somewhat oblique to the faces of the pebble, one of which is slightly polished as if by constant rubbing. There is in the Greenwell Collection a granite pebble (3 1/2 inches), from the same place, battered at one end, and the other much worn away by use, which also has one face flat and slightly polished. In the camp at Little Solsbury Hill, [949] near Bath, I found two quartzite implements of rudely quadrangular prismatic form, each having one end worn away to a ridge. Another quartzite pebble, rubbed to an obtuse edge at one end, was found by General Pitt Rivers, F.R.S., [950] within an ancient earthwork at Dorchester, Oxfordshire.

A hammer-stone of close-grained grit, having a ridge all round the periphery, was found in Anglesea. [951] Others with ridged ends have occurred in crannogs at Lochlee, [952] Ayrshire, and in Wigtownshire. [953] Some of them seem to belong to the Iron Age.

Among the specimens just described, there are three peculiarities which, though not occurring together on all, are worthy of notice—the notch on the face, the ridge at the end, and the polished face.

There can be no doubt of the notch on the face being, like the cup-shaped depressions, merely intended as an aid in holding the stone. On the hammer-stones discovered by the late Mr. J. W. Flower, F.G.S., in a post-Roman kjökken-mödding, in the island of Herm, [954] there were usually one or two rough notches or indentations on each face, exactly adapted to receive the ends of the thumb and some of the fingers; and, curiously enough, I have a pebble notched in precisely the same manner from Delaware Water Gap, Pennsylvania, and no doubt intended for a hand-hammer or pounder.

In the same kjökken-mödding at Herm were several [955] celt-like implements of porphyry and greenstone which, instead of an edge, had the end blunt, but with a ridge obliquely across it, as on these pebbles. Somewhat similar pounding-stones have been found by the late Hon. W. O. Stanley, at Pen-y-Bonc, [956] Holyhead, in some instances provided with a depression fitting the thumb or finger, and several having the ridge at the end.

The same sort of ridge occurs on pounding-stones from Denmark, Portugal, [957] Spain, [958] Ireland, and elsewhere, and occasionally extends all round the stone when it happens to be disc-shaped, like those already mentioned from Upton Lovel and elsewhere. Hammer-stones worn to a ridge are also found in Egypt. [959] It would appear that the face of the hammer was ground away, either by a rocking motion on a flat stone, or by the blows given with it being administered alternately from the right and from the left, so as to keep any matter that was being pounded with it from being driven out of position.

I have, lastly, to notice the more or less polished condition of one of the faces of these stones, which may be due to their being used for grinding the material already pounded by their edges to a finer powder on the slab, which served instead of a mortar. One of the flat pebbles found in the Cave of La Madelaine, Dordogne, appears to have served as a muller for grinding the hæmatite used as paint.

Sometimes these hammer-stones are mere pebbles without any previous preparation, and indeed it is but natural that such should have been the case. Canon Greenwell has found pebbles of quartz and greenstone, worn and battered at the ends, accompanying interments on the Yorkshire Wolds, and such are also occasionally present on the surface, though they are, of course, liable to escape observation. A quartzite pebble that has served as a hammer-stone, and is much worn and fractured by use, was found at Ty Mawr, and is figured in the *Archæological Journal*, [960] as are also several from hut-circles in Holyhead and Anglesea. [961] A large sarsen-stone pebble, weighing 4 3/4 lbs., and which had obviously been used as a hammer, was found in the Long Barrow, at West Kennet, [962] Wiltshire. A large conical sort of muller of sarsen-stone, [963] weighing 12 1/2 lbs., was discovered with twenty-two skeletons, various animal remains, and pottery, in a large cist, in a barrow near Avebury. Mr. G. Clinch has a hammer from West Wickham, made from a nearly cylindrical quartz pebble, much worn at both ends, one of which is more rounded than the other.

Figs. 167 and 168.—Yorkshire Wolds. 1/2

On the Downs of Sussex, in the pits of Cissbury, in Yorkshire, Suffolk, Dorsetshire, and other counties, hammer-stones of flint, apparently used for chipping other flints, have been found, but from their rudeness it seems hardly worth while to engrave any specimens. At Grime's Graves the hammer-stones consisted principally of quartzite pebbles, though some were of flint. In many instances the hammers made of flint seem to be cores from which flakes have been struck, but which, proving to be of refractory stone, have been found more serviceable as hammers. Some of the cores found at Spiennes, near Mons, have been thus used, as well as fragments of celts. Some of the hammer-stones from the French caves consist also of such cores. Stone mullers are in common use in most countries at the present day, for grinding paint and similar purposes. They occur at the Cape of Good Hope, [964] but were there, no doubt, originally intended for other uses.

The general character of the chipped flint hammer-stones will be gathered from Figs. 167 and 168, both from the Yorkshire Wolds. Neither of them shows any trace of the original surface or crust of the flint from which it has been fashioned. The larger one has been chipped with numerous facets somewhat into the shape of a broad bivalve shell, and is much battered round the margin. Fig. 168 is much smaller than usual, and is more disc-like in character.

Fig. 168A.—Culbin Sands. 1/2

A large number of discoidal stones, formed from flattish quartzite pebbles, have been found on the Culbin Sands, [965] Elginshire. By the kindness of the Society of Antiquaries of Scotland, one of them is shown in Fig. 168A. They may be hammer-stones, but show no traces of use.

Fig. 169.—Bridlington. 1/2

More commonly, perhaps, the form is approximately spherical. Fig. 169 is, however, a more symmetrical specimen than usual. It was found by Mr. E. Tindall at Grindale, near Bridlington, and its surface is battered all over by continual pounding. I have others of similar character from Icklingham, Suffolk; Jordan Hill, Weymouth; and elsewhere. Two from Old Geir, Anglesea, are engraved in the *Archæological Journal*. [966]

Others were found in a tumulus at Seaford, [967] and at Mount Caburn, [968] Sussex.

Numerous rude hammer-stones have been found at Carnac, [969] Brittany.

One of chert, 3 inches in diameter, was found in the Isle of Portland, [970] and several have been found in Dorsetshire [971] which were supposed to have been used in fashioning flint implements; and balls of chert, 2 1/2 inches and 2 1/4 inches in diameter, found at West Coker, Somersetshire, [972] and another from Comb-Pyne, Devonshire, [973] have been thought to have been "intended for the sling, or else to be tied up in a leather thong attached to a staff, and employed as a sort of mace."

A globular nodule of flint, one pound in weight, and chipped all over, found with numerous flint flakes in the long-chambered barrow at West Kennet, [974] appeared to Dr. Thurnam to have been used in their production. Several others found together in the parish of Benlochy, [975] near Blairgowrie, were regarded as sling-stones. A lump of red flint found in a barrow near Pickering, [976] in company with a flint spear-head and two arrow-heads at the right hand of a skeleton, was considered by Mr. Bateman to have been used as a hammer for chipping other flints. A more highly-decorated class of stone balls will be described at a subsequent page. Stone balls, such as were in common use for cannon in the Middle Ages, and those thrown by catapults and other military engines, do not come within my province.

Judging from the battered surface of the spherical stones now under consideration, there can be no doubt of their having been in use as hammers or pounders; but they were probably not in all cases used merely for fashioning other implements of stone, but also for triturating grain, roots, and other substances for food, in the same manner as round pebbles are still used by the native Australians. [977] One such root, abundant in this country, is a principal article of food consumed by the Ahts [978] of North America, among whom "the roots of the common fern or bracken are much used as a regular meal. They are simply washed and boiled, or beaten with a stone till they become soft, and are then roasted." In New Zealand also fern roots are pounded for food, with pestles of basalt. The corn-crushers and mealing-stones found in the Swiss Lake-dwellings have evidently been intended for the purposes which their names denote; and at the present day among many savage tribes, the only form of mill that is known is that of a flat or slightly concave bed-stone, with a stone rolling-pin or muller. Among the Kaffirs [979] and in West Africa the mill is of this character, the bed-stone being large and heavy, slightly hollowed on its upper surface; the muller, a large oval pebble which is used with a peculiar rocking and grinding motion. The corn (maize or millet) is often boiled before grinding. In Abyssinia [980] the bed-stone of gneiss or granite is about 2 feet in length and 14 inches in width. The face of this is roughened by beating it with a sharp-pointed piece of harder stone, such as quartz or hornblende, and the grain is reduced to flour by repeated grinding or rubbing with a stone rolling-pin. Such mealing-stones are also in use in South America. [981] They have been occasionally found in Britain, and the annexed figure shows a pair found in a hut-circle at Ty Mawr, [982] in the island of Holyhead. Others have been found in Anglesea. [983] Similar specimens have been obtained in Cambridgeshire and Cornwall, and Mr. Tindall had a pair found near Bridlington. A mealing-stone with the muller was found in Ehenside Tarn, [984] Cumberland. I have myself found a muller at Osbaston, Leicestershire. A pair of stones from the Fens [985] is in the museum of the Cambridge Antiquarian Society. Some large blocks of flint, having a flat face bruised all over by hammering, have also been found in the Fens, and may have served as mealing-stones.

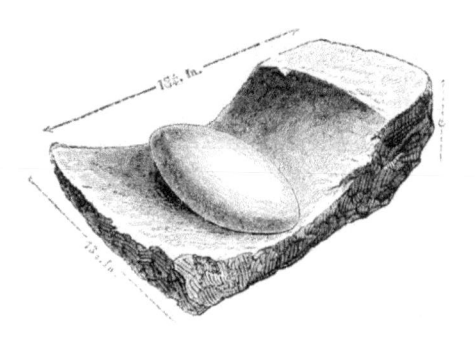

Fig. 170.—Holyhead.

The same form of mill is found also in Ireland, [986] and not improbably remained in occasional use until a comparatively late period. Fynes Moryson [987] mentions having seen in Cork "young maides, stark naked, grinding corne with certaine stones, to make cakes thereof;" and the form of the expression seems to point to something different from a hand-mill or quern, which at that time was in common use in England. The name of saddle-quern has been given to this form of grinding apparatus. In the Blackmore Museum is one from the pit-dwellings at Highfield, [988] near Salisbury, which are not improbably of post-Roman date; and in the British Museum is one found near Macclesfield.

They are also known in Scotland. One of granite, found near Wick, [989] is in the National Museum at Edinburgh; as is also another, 20 inches by 12 inches, with a rubber 12 inches by 8 inches, found in a cave near Cullen, Banffshire. [990]

They likewise occur in Shetland. [991] Mr. J. W. Cursiter has a long narrow muller with a curved back, in which are five grooves to receive the fingers, so as to give it the appearance of being a fragment of an ammonite.

Saddle-querns of the same character occur also in France. [992] I have a small example from Chateaudun. One from Chassemy [993] (Aisne) has been figured.

Some were likewise found in the Genista Cave at Gibraltar. [994] They are common in West Prussia and in the Island of Rügen, as well as in Scandinavia generally.

A German saddle-quern, from the ancient cemetery at Monsheim, has been engraved by Lindenschmit. [995] Others are mentioned by Klemm. [996] MM. Siret have also found them in their explorations in Spain.

It will have been observed, in the instances I have cited, that the movable muller or grinding-stone is not spherical, but elongated; but what is possibly the more ancient form approached more closely to a pestle and mortar in character, and consisted of a bed-stone with a slight concavity in it, and a more or less spherical stone for a pounder.

A grinding-stone of granite, with a cavity, apparently for bruising grain by a globular stone, was found in Cornwall, [997] and undressed slabs with concavities of the size and shape of an ordinary soup-plate, are of frequent occurrence in the Hebrides. [998] Others have been found in company with stone balls, in the ancient habitations in Anglesea.

Fig. 171 shows a trough of stone, found at Ty Mawr, [999] Holyhead, by the late Hon. W. O. Stanley, who kindly lent me the wood-cuts of Figs. 170 and 171. The cylindrical grinding-stone or muller was found within it, and has a central cavity on each face, to give the hand a better hold in grinding. A similar appliance was found at Pen-y-Bonc [1000] in the same island.

A triturating trough from Cleveland [1001] has been figured.

They have been found in Cornwall [1002] and in Ireland. [1003]

Others have been discovered in Brittany.

Hand-mills of granite formed in much the same manner have been in use until lately in Brandenburg. The lower stones are described as from 2 feet to 4 feet long, and nearly as wide, with channels, after long use, as much as 6 inches deep; the mullers are either spherical or oval, and of such a size that they can be held in the hand. [1004]

A large sandstone, with a small bowl-shaped concavity worked in it, was found near burnt bones, in a barrow at Elkstone, [1005] Staffordshire; and two others in barrows near Sheen. [1006] Another, with a cup-shaped concavity, 2 1/2 inches in diameter, occurred in a barrow near Pickering; [1007] and in other barrows were found sandstone balls roughly chipped all over, from 4 inches to 1 inch in diameter, in one instance associated with a bronze dagger. A ball of sandstone, 2 1/2 inches in diameter, was found with flint instruments accompanying a contracted skeleton in a barrow near Middleton. [1008] A round stone like a cannon-ball was also found in a barrow near Cromer, [1009] and three balls of stone, from 2 1/4 inches to 1 3/4 inches in diameter, were picked up in a camp at Weetwood, [1010] Northumberland.

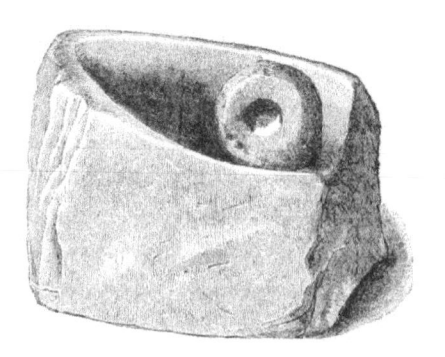

Fig. 171.—Ty Mawr.

Mealing-stones, both flat and hollowed, were found in Schliemann's [1011] excavations at Troy.

In grinding and pounding a considerable amount of grit must have been worn off the stones and been mixed with the meal. The usual worn condition of the teeth in the skulls from ancient barrows may be connected with this attrition. Mr. Charters-White, [1012] by examination of some teeth from a long barrow at Heytesbury, Wilts, was able to show the presence of grains of sand of different kinds in the dental tartar.

Fig. 172.—Holyhead.

There are two other forms of grinding apparatus still in use—the pestle and mortar, and the rotatory mill—both of which date back to an early period, and concerning which it will be well to say a few words in this place. The ordinary form of pestle—a frustum of a very elongated cone with the ends rounded, is so well known that it appears needless to engrave a specimen on the same scale as the other objects. In Fig. 172 is shown one of a more than usually club-shaped form, 11 inches long, found in Holyhead Island. [1013]

Fig. 173.—Pulborough.

This cut originally appeared in illustration of an interesting paper by Mr. Albert Way, F.S.A., on some relics found in and near ancient circular dwellings in Holyhead Island, in which paper some of the other discoveries about to be mentioned are also cited. A pestle like a small club, 9 1/4 inches long, was found in a gravel-pit near Audley End, [1014] with a Roman cinerary urn. Another, of grey granite, more cylindrical in form, and flatter at one end, 11 1/2 inches long and 2 inches in diameter, was found at Pulborough, [1015] Sussex, and is engraved in Fig. 173. A limestone pestle of the same character, 12 inches long and 2 1/2 inches in diameter, found at Cliff Hill, is in the museum at Leicester. A fine pestle of granite or gneiss (12 5/8 inches) from Epping Forest [1016] has been figured, as has been a shorter one from a barrow at Collingbourn Ducis, [1017] Wilts. Another of greenstone, probably a naturally-formed pebble, 10 1/4 inches long and 2 1/2 inches in diameter, rounded at both ends, was found with three porphyry celts in a cairn at Daviot, [1018] near Inverness. It is now in the National Museum at Edinburgh. Another of greenstone, 16 inches long, was found near Carlisle [1019]; and the late Mr. J. W. Flower, F.G.S., had one of the same material 10 inches long, tapering from 2 inches in diameter to 1 1/4 inches, found in Hilgay Fen, Norfolk. A similar pestle-like stone, 6 inches long, found in Styria, is engraved by Professor Unger. [1020] Another of the same length was among the objects found in the Casa da Moura, [1021] Portugal. Many pestles, more or less well finished in form, have been discovered by the late Dr. Hunt, Dr. Mitchell, Mr. Petrie, Mr. Long, and others in the Orkney and Shetland Isles, and in different parts of Scotland.

Those who wish to make themselves thoroughly acquainted with the different circumstances of these discoveries, and with the various forms of rough implements brought to light, will have to consult the original memoirs [1022] which have been written concerning them. Both in cists or graves, and in the remains of ancient circular habitations, have numerous hammer-stones and pestles been found, associated with various other articles manufactured from stone and bone. Some of these are extremely rude, and appear hardly deserving of the names of spear-heads, knives, chisels, battle-axes, &c., which have been bestowed upon them. There can, however, be no doubt of their being of human manufacture, whatever purpose they may have served. A few well-formed and polished stone celts were found in company with the objects of this class in the "Underground House of Skaill," Orkney, which, however, was not, strictly speaking, subterranean. In the building, and in the midden around it, were very great numbers of oval sandstone pounding-stones and of large sandstone flakes, probably knives of a rude kind, a pebble with a groove round it like a ship's block, and a few celts. In Shetland these rude stone implements have been found with human skeletons interred in cists, sometimes with polished weapons. [1023] A very curious implement, somewhat T-shaped, with pointed extremities, and grooves round the transverse part, was found in the broch of Quoyness, [1024] Sanday, Orkney, and has been figured.

Many of the pestle-like stones are merely chipped into a somewhat cylindrical form, but others have been picked or ground all over, so as to give them a circular or oval section. The ends in many instances are more or less splintered, as if by hammering some hard substance rather than by pounding, and the exact purpose to which they were applied it is extremely difficult to divine.

Four of them are shown, on a small scale, in Figs. 174 to 177.

Fig. 174.—Shetland. 20 1/2 in.

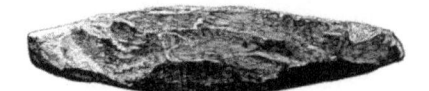

Fig. 175.—Shetland. 19 in.

Fig. 176.—Shetland.

Fig. 177.—Shetland.

Fig. 178.—Shetland. 21 in.

Some are more club-like [1025] in character, as in Fig. 178, and are even occasionally wrought to a handle at one end, as was the case with one found in the heart of a burnt stone tumulus at Bressay [1026] (Fig. 179), so as to give them much of the appearance of the short batlet or batting-staff used in the primitive mode of washing linen, such as is still so commonly practised in many parts of the Continent. Nearly similar rough instruments have been found at Baldoon, [1027] Wigtownshire. Is it possible that these stone bats can have served a similar purpose? In the Northern counties [1028] a large smooth-faced stone, set in a sloping position by the side of a stream, on which washerwomen beat their linen, is still called a battling-stone, [1029] and the club is called a batter, batlet, battledore, or battling-staff. Such clubs may also have been used in the preparation of hemp and flax.

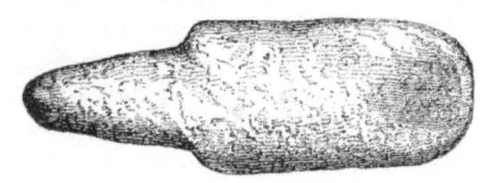

Fig. 179.—Shetland.

A stone club, from St. Isabel, [1030] Bahia, Brazil, is described as 13 3/8 inches long, 2 1/2 inches wide, and 1 1/4 inch thick. It may, however, be a celt, like the supposed clubs from Lancashire [1031] and Cumberland.

There can be no doubt of several of the pestles, though probably not all, belonging to the same period as stone implements of other forms. The mortars in which they were used, were probably merely depressions in blocks of stone, or even of wood. Some rude mortars have, as already mentioned, been found in Holyhead Island, and Anglesea, but it is uncertain to what age they belong. A portion of a mortar of granite, with a channelled lip, found with fragments of urns and calcined bones in a grave at Kerris Vaen, Cornwall, is engraved in the *Archæologia Cambrensis*. [1032]

Very similar stone pestles to those from Orkney were in use among the North American Indians [1033] for pounding maize, and some are engraved by Squier and Davis. [1034]

They also employed [1035] a small form of mortar for pounding quartz, felspar, or shell, with which to temper the clay for pottery. Stone mortars and pestles were in use among the Toltecs and Aztecs in making tortillas, and are found in South Carolina, [1036] and elsewhere in the United States. Among the ancient Pennacooks [1037] of the Merrimac valley, the heavy stone pestle was suspended from the elastic bough of a tree, which relieved the operator in her work; and among the Tahitians [1038] the pestle of stone, used for pounding the bread fruit on a wooden block, is provided with a crutch-like handle.

Some large circular discs of stone, apparently used for grinding, and others with deep cup-shaped depressions in them, found on Dartmoor, and probably connected with some ancient metallurgical operations on the spot, have been engraved and described in the *Transactions of the Devonshire Association*. [1039]

The hand-mill formed with an upper rotatory stone is a mere modification of the pestle and mortar, and dates back to a very early period, though it has continued in use in some parts of the British Isles even unto our own day. The name quern, by which such mills are usually known, occurs in closely similar forms, in all the Teutonic dialects. In Anglo-Saxon it appears under the form Cweorn or Cwyrn, and in modern Danish as Qværn. An excellent example of this instrument, which had been, up to 1850, in use in the cabin of a Kilkenny peasant, was presented by the Rev. J. Graves to the Archæological Institute, and is described and engraved in their Journal. [1040] The upper stone is of granite, the lower of millstone grit. The lower stone is recessed to receive the upper, and has a central depression, in which a small block of oak is fixed, from which projects a small pin—also of oak—to carry the upper stone. This is about 2 feet in diameter, and is perforated at its centre with a hopper-like hole, across the bottom of which a small bar of oak is secured, having a recess in it to receive the pin, but only of such a depth as to keep the upper stone at a slight distance from the lower. Through the upper stone, and near its verge, a vertical hole is drilled to receive a peg, which forms the handle for turning it. When in use it is worked, as in ancient times among the Jews, by two women seated opposite each other, who alternately seize and propel the handle, so as to drive the stone at considerable speed. The corn, highly dried, is fed by handfuls into the hopper in the runner or upper stone, and the meal passes out by a notch in the rim of the nether stone. Pennant, [1041] in his "Tour in Scotland," describes querns as still in use in the Hebrides in 1772. They were said to cost about fourteen shillings, and to grind a bushel of corn in four hours, with two pair of hands. He gives a representation of a quern at work, with a long stick, hanging from the branch of a tree, inserted in the hole in the runner, so as to form the handle. A somewhat similar method of driving the hand-mill indoors, taken from a German MS. of the fourteenth century, has been reproduced from a work by Drs. Von Hefner and Wolf in the *Archæological Journal*. [1042]

A sketch of a hand-mill in use at the present day, at Abbeville, is given in C. Roach Smith's "Collectanea Antiqua." [1043]

Even in the neighbourhood of water-mills, when the charge for grinding was at all high, we find these hand-mills in use in mediæval times. Such use, by the townsmen of St. Albans, was, in the beginning of the fourteenth century, a fruitful source of litigation between them and the abbots, who claimed the monopoly of grinding for their tenants. [1044] Thirteen of these, however, maintained their right of using hand-mills, as having been enjoyed of old, and some claims were raised to the privilege of grinding oatmeal only, by means of a hand-mill.

It seems probable that these mediæval hand-mills were of large size, and with a comparatively flat upper stone, like the modern Irish form, which is sometimes 3 feet 6 inches in diameter. One, 3 feet in diameter, found near Hollingbourne, [1045] Kent, was probably of no great antiquity. The same may be said of a six-sided quern, with an iron pivot, found in Edinburgh. [1046] A quern, found at West Coker, [1047] Somerset, with a fleur-de-lis over the passage by which the meal escaped, has been assigned to the thirteenth century. The lower stone of a quern accompanied an apparently Saxon interment at Winster, [1048] Derbyshire. It was of the beehive [1049] shape, and made of millstone grit. Similar querns, with iron pins, have been found at Breedon, [1050] Leicestershire, as well as others with the upper stone more conical. One of this class was also found near Rugby. [1051] They frequently accompany Roman [1052] remains, but these are generally of smaller size, and of a more hemispherical form, the favourite material being the Lower Tertiary conglomerate, or Hertfordshire pudding-stone. Those of Andernach lava, from the Rhine, are usually flat.

A complete quern was found at Ehenside Tarn, [1053] Cumberland. The upper half of another was in a post-Roman circular dwelling, near Birtley, [1054] Northumberland.

Querns of various forms are of frequent occurrence in Wales, especially in Anglesea. An upper stone from Lampeter, [1055] Cardiganshire, has a semicircular projection at the margin round the hole for the handle. In some districts [1056] they have been in use until quite recent times. [1057]

In Scotland, querns are of frequent occurrence in the ancient brochs and hill forts. In one of the former, at Kettleburn, [1058] Caithness, a stone in preparation for a quern was found; in another, in Aberdeenshire, an upper stone, 18 inches in diameter, was discovered. Another stone of the same size, surrounded by four border stones to prevent the scattering of the grain in grinding, was discovered in a subterranean chamber in a hill fort at Dunsinane, [1059] Perth. A curious pot-quern, the lower stone decorated with a carved human face, was found in East Lothian, and is engraved by Wilson. [1060]

Some interesting notices of Scottish querns have been given by Sir Arthur Mitchell. [1061]

The upper stone, ornamented with raised lines, shown in Fig. 180, from a cut kindly lent me by the Society of Antiquaries of Scotland, was found in trenching a moss in the parish of Balmaclellan, New Galloway, with some curious bronze objects of "late-Celtic" workmanship. [1062]

An upper stone (18 inches), ornamented in a nearly similar way, was found near Stranraer, [1063] Wigtownshire, and another, with a tribrach instead of a cross, at Roy Bridge, [1064] Inverness-shire.

Some ornamentally carved upper stones of querns, one of them with spiral and leaf-shaped patterns upon it, much like those on the bronze ornaments of the "late-Celtic" Period, have been discovered in Anglesea. [1065]

Fig. 180.—Balmaclellan.

Querns of green sandstone are stated, by Sir R. Colt Hoare, [1066] to be numerous in British villages and pit-dwellings in Wiltshire, as indeed they are in other counties, [1067] though formed of various kinds of grit. They rarely occur in barrows, though burnt granite querns have been found with burnt bones in cromlechs in Jersey. [1068]

Some observations on querns by the Rev. Dr. A. Hume, are published in the *Archæologia Cambrensis*. [1069] As these utensils belong, for the most part, to Roman and post-Roman times, I have thought it needless to enter into any more minute description of their forms, or of the circumstances under which they have been found.

CHAPTER XI.
GRINDING-STONES AND WHETSTONES.

Before proceeding to the consideration of other forms of implements, it will be well to say a few words with regard to those which have served for grinding, polishing, or sharpening tools and weapons, and more especially such as there is every reason to suppose, were employed to give an edge or finish to other materials than metal, though the whetstones of the Bronze Period must not be passed by unnoticed.

I have already mentioned the fact that the grindstones on which stone celts and axes were polished and sharpened, were not like those of the present day, revolving discs against the periphery of which the object to be ground was held; but stationary slabs on which the implements to be polished or sharpened were rubbed. Considering the numbers of polished implements that have been discovered in this country, it appears not a little remarkable that such slabs have not been more frequently noticed, though not improbably they have, from their simple character, for the most part escaped observation; and even if found, there is usually little, unless the circumstances of the discovery are peculiar, to connect them with any particular stage of civilization or period of antiquity. In Denmark and Sweden, however, these grinding-stones, both of the flat and polygonal forms already described, are of comparatively frequent occurrence. Specimens are figured by Worsaae, [1070] Sophus Müller, and others, and were also given by Thomsen, [1071] so long ago as 1832. He states that they have been found in Scandinavia, in barrows and elsewhere in the ground, with half-finished stone celts lying with them, so that there can be no doubt as to the purpose for which they were intended. They are also described by Nilsson [1072] and Montelius. [1073] Both slabs and prismatic pieces of sandstone have been found in the Swiss Lake-dwellings, [1074] several of the former with concavities on one or both faces, resulting from stone hatchets having been ground upon them. [1075]

In France the discovery of numerous *'polissoirs'* has been noticed, some of them of very large dimensions. They are abundant in the Departments of la Charente [1076] and la Dordogne, [1077] and some fine examples are in the Museum of Troyes (Aube). One, nearly 3 feet long, with hollows of different characters, apparently for grinding different parts of tools and weapons, is figured by M. Peigné Delacourt; [1078] an oval concavity upon it is 2 feet 3 inches long by 1 foot wide, and seems well adapted for grinding the faces of large celts. Another fine example was in the possession of Dr. Léveillé, [1079] at Grand Pressigny, and a large specimen, also from Poitou, is in the Musée de St. Germain. Several have been found in Luxembourg [1080] and Belgium.

Flat grinding-stones of smaller dimensions have been found in the turbaries of the Somme and in the Camp de Catenoy. [1081] A narrow sharpening stone 5 inches long is recorded to have been found with stone hatchets and other implements in the Cueva de los Murciélagos, in Spain. [1082] *Polissoirs* have also been observed in India. [1083]

The Carreg y Saelhau, [1084] or Stone of the Arrows, near Aber, Carnarvonshire, has numerous scorings upon it, a quarter or half an inch in depth; and, though doubtless used for sharpening tools and weapons of some kind, it seems to belong to the metallic age. Canon Greenwell informs me that he observed a rock close to a camp on Lazenby Fell, Cumberland, with about seventy grooves upon it from 4 to 7 inches long and about 1 inch wide and deep, pointed at either end, as if from sharp-ended tools or weapons having been ground in them. The grooves are in various directions, though sometimes in groups of four or five together, which are parallel with each other. In the course of his investigations in the barrows on the Yorkshire Wolds [1085] he has found a few of the flat slabs for grinding or polishing, though of small size. One of them, formed of a flat piece of red sandstone about 4 1/2 inches by 3 1/2 inches, with both faces bearing marks of having been in use for grinding, lay close to a deposit of burnt bones. Another somewhat similar fragment of sandstone (2 3/4 inches by 2 1/2 inches), which also bore traces of attrition, was found in a barrow at Helperthorpe.

In another barrow at Cowlam, [1086] Yorkshire, E. R., was a rough piece of grit, 2 1/4 inches long, with one end slightly hollowed, apparently by grinding celts, and a large flat compact laminated red sandstone pebble about 8 3/4 inches by 3 inches, with both faces ground away, the one being evenly flat and the other uneven. In the same barrow occurred one of the flint rubbers to be subsequently described, and also a quartzite pebble (2 1/2 inches long) that had been used as a hammer-stone. A portion of a whetstone of Pennant or Coal-measure sandstone was found in the long barrow at West Kennet, Wiltshire, [1087] in which also occurred a thin ovoidal knife of flint, ground at the edges.

I have in my own collection a very interesting specimen of this kind from Burwell Fen, near Cambridge. It is a thin slab of close-grained micaceous sandstone, about 5 1/2 by 4 inches, slightly hollowed and polished on both faces by grinding. With it were found two celts of flint, 4 1/2 and 5 inches long, of pointed oval section, one of them polished all over, and the other at the edge only, which in all probability had been sharpened on this very stone. In the same place were two long subangular fragments of greenstone of the right form, size, and character to be manufactured into celts, and which had no doubt been selected for that purpose.

A grinding-stone with a celt lying in it, found at Glenluce, [1088] Wigtownshire, has been figured.

On the Sussex Downs I have found flat pebbles 3 or 4 inches long, which have evidently been used as hones, but whether for stone or metallic tools it is impossible to say. Fragments of polished celts and numerous flakes and "scrapers" of flint were, however, in their immediate neighbourhood. Among the modern savages of Tahiti [1089] who used hatchets of basalt, a whetstone and water appear to have been always at hand, as constant sharpening was necessary. It seems probable therefore that there must have been a constant demand for such sharpening-stones in this country, and that many of them ought still to exist. With flint hatchets, the constant whetting was, however, no doubt less necessary than with those of the different kinds of basalt. Their edges, if carefully chipped, will indeed cut wood without being ground at all.

Mr. Bateman mentions "a flat piece of sandstone rubbed hollow at one side" as having been found in a barrow at Castern, Staffordshire, [1090] but it is uncertain whether this was a grindstone. It may have been used only as a mortar, for with it was a round piece of ruddle or red ochre, "which from its abraded appearance must have been in much request for colouring the skin of its owner." [1091] In a barrow on the West Coast of Kintyre, there also occurred a piece of red Lancashire or Westmoreland iron-ore or hæmatite worn flat on the side, apparently by having been rubbed upon some other substance. Nodules of ruddle are also said to have occurred, interspersed with the charcoal in a barrow at Broad Down, near Honiton. [1092]

In one of the ancient habitations in Holyhead, [1093] was a large stone 11 inches long, probably used for grinding hæmatite, with which it was deeply tinged; and a small stone box found with celts and other relics at Skara, Skaill, Orkney, [1094] contained a red pigment.

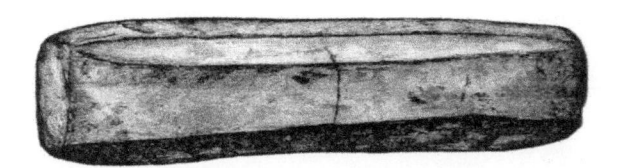

Fig. 180A.—Lamberton Moor.

There can be little doubt of this red pigment having been in use for what was considered a personal decoration by the early occupants of Britain. But this use of red paint dates back to a far earlier period, for pieces of hæmatite with the surface scraped, apparently by means of flint-flakes, have been found in the French and Belgian caves of the Reindeer Period, so that this red pigment appears to have been in all ages a favourite with savage man. The practice of interring warpaint with the dead is still observed among the North American Indians. [1095]

> "The paints that warriors love to use
>
> Place here within his hand,
>
> That he may shine with ruddy hues
>
> Amidst the spirit land."

Some few of the grinding-stones found in this country resemble those of polygonal form found in Denmark, [1096] in so far as they are symmetrically shaped and have been used on all their faces. One 13 1/2 inches long, found on Lamberton Moor, [1097] Berwickshire, is shown in Fig. 180A., kindly lent by the Society of Antiquaries of Scotland.

In the Christy Collection is such a sharpening-stone, nearly square in section, about 9 1/4 inches long, and of the form shown in Fig. 181. Both the faces and sides are worn slightly concave, as if from grinding convex surfaces such as the edges of celts, though it is impossible to say with any degree of certainty that this was really the purpose to which it was applied. It is said to have been found near Barcoot, in the parish of Dorchester, Oxon, in 1835, not far from a spot where a stone celt had been found a few years previously. In the same collection is a Danish whetstone of precisely the same character, but rather broader at one end than at the other.

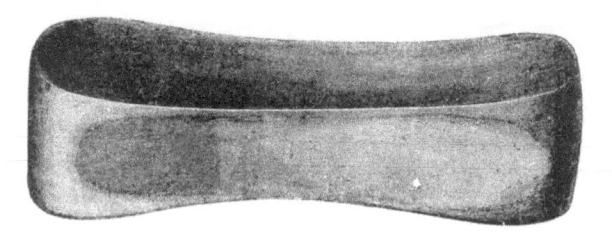

Fig. 181.—Dorchester. 1/2

A grinding-stone, 26 inches long, was found at Ehenside Tarn, [1098] Cumberland.

Fig. 182.—Rudstone. 1/1

In Fig. 182 is shown, full size, a very curious object formed of compact mica-schist, which has the appearance of having served as a whetstone or hone. It has been ground over its whole surface. The flatter face is towards the middle somewhat hollowed—rather more so than is shown in the section—and shows some oblique scratches upon it as if from rubbing a rather rough object upon it. It was found in 1870 by Canon Greenwell, with other relics accompanying an unburnt body in a barrow at Rudstone, near Bridlington. [1099] About midway between the head and the knees was a series of articles in this descending order. On the top was this whetstone—if such it be—resting on a carved jet ring, like Fig. 372, which lay on the boss of a large jet button. Below this was another jet button, like

Fig. 371, face downwards. Close by lay a half-nodule of pyrites and a round-ended flint flake, which will be subsequently noticed. Nearer the face was a dagger-knife of bronze, with three rivets through it, and two more for fastening together the two plates of ox-horn of which the hilt had been composed. The whetstone may have been that used for sharpening this instrument.

An instrument of slate of nearly the same form was found in a cairn at Penbeacon, [1100] Dartmoor, and was regarded by Mr. Spence Bate as a tool used in fashioning clay vessels. Dr. Thurnam [1101] has suggested that if covered with leather these stones may have served as bracers or arm-guards for archers.

Two pieces of a dark-coloured slaty kind of stone, of nearly the same form and size as the Yorkshire specimen, and lying parallel with each other, were found by Sir R. Colt Hoare [1102] at the feet of a skeleton, together with a little rude drinking-cup, in a barrow near Winterbourn Stoke. A stud and ring of jet, probably of the same character as those from Rudstone, and a piece of flint rudely chipped, as if intended for a dagger or spear, were also found. No bronze objects were discovered, but the cist appears to have been imperfectly examined.

Fig. 183.—Fimber. 1/2

I have already mentioned [1103] that in grinding and polishing the concave faces of different forms of perforated stone axes, it is probable that stone rubbers were used in conjunction with sand. Even the smaller flat and rounded faces may have been wrought by similar means. That rubbers of some kind must have been used, is, I think, evident from the character of the surfaces, especially of those which are hollowed; and the most readily available material for the formation of such rubbers, was doubtless stone. There is therefore an *à priori* probability of such stone grinding-tools having been in use; and if we find specimens which present the conditions which such tools would exhibit, we are almost justified in assuming them to have served such purposes. Now in the collection of Messrs. Mortimer, of Driffield, Yorkshire, are several pieces of flint and portions of pebbles of schist, flint, and quartz found in that neighbourhood, which are ground at one end into a more or less rounded form, and exhibit striæ running along, and not across, the rounded surface. They have, in fact, all the appearance of having been used with coarse sand for grinding a concavity in another stone, such, for instance, as the concave face of the stone axe shown in Fig. 125. I am indebted to their kindness for the specimen shown in Fig. 183, which consists of a short piece of a conical nodule of flint, the large end of which has been used for grinding in ancient times, the striated face being now considerably weathered. In the Greenwell Collection is a rubber of the same kind from Weaverthorpe on the Yorkshire Wolds. Mr. H. S. Harland [1104] has found other specimens in Yorkshire, of which he has kindly given me several. Polishers [1105] are also found in Scotland. A polisher of somewhat similar character, but made of serpentine, was found in the Lago di Varese, near Como, where a number of stone implements were also discovered.

At a later period larger rubbers of the same kind were used to smooth the flutings of Doric columns. I have seen some among the ruins of the temples at Selinunto, in Sicily.

Some long narrow rubbers, apparently intended for grinding out the shaft-holes of perforated axes, have been found in the Swiss Lake-dwellings; and I have a slightly conical stone, about an inch in diameter, from Mainz, which may have been used for the same purpose.

In the barrow at Cowlam, already mentioned, besides the grinding-stones of grit, there was a piece of flint roughly chipped into a cubical form, and having one face partly ground smooth. It may have been used for polishing the surfaces of other stone implements, or possibly merely as a muller. It is shown in Fig. 184. The striæ run diagonally of the square face.

In the collection formed by Canon Greenwell, is also a sandstone pebble, 2 1/2 inches in diameter, which has been "picked" into shape, and has one face smooth as if used for grinding. It was found in a barrow on Ganton Wold, East Riding. A roughly conical piece of oolitic sandstone, 2 1/2 inches high, in places "picked" on the surface, and with the base apparently used for grinding, was found with a contracted body and some flint flakes, in another barrow on Ganton Wold. [1106]

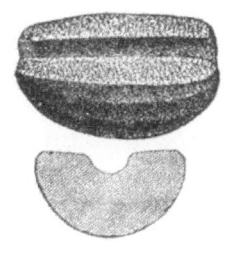

Fig. 184.—Cowlam. 1/2

Fig. 185.—Amesbury. 1/2

In the Wiltshire barrows several rubbing-stones (or what appear to be such) of a peculiar form have been found, of which one is shown in Fig. 185. It is of close-grained grit, possibly from the Lower Greensand, and was discovered with two others in a barrow on Normanton Down, near Amesbury. Two more were in the collection of the late Rev. Edward Duke, of Lake, near Salisbury, to whose kindness I am indebted for the loan of the specimen. Both are now in the British Museum. These instruments vary but little in shape, size, or character, being usually of a truncated half-ovoid form, with a rounded groove along the flat surface, and are formed of sandstone.

One was found in a barrow at Upton Lovel, [1107] with flint celts, a perforated stone axe-head, various implements of bone, a bronze pin or awl, and other objects. Another occurred in a barrow at Everley, [1108] with a bronze chisel, an unused whetstone of freestone, and a hone of bluish colour; and another with a skeleton, a stone hammer, a bronze celt, a bone tube, and various other articles in a barrow at Wilsford. [1109] Two or three of these sharpening stones, found in a barrow at Roundway, near Devizes, are in the Museum of the Wilts Archæological Society. One of these has been figured. [1110] A pebble with shallow grooves on each face found at Mount Caburn, Lewes, [1111] may possibly belong to this class of implements, though it may have been a hammer. A rubbing-stone of this kind was found at Topcliffe, [1112] Yorkshire, but not in a barrow.

Sir R. C. Hoare considered whetstones of this kind to have been used for sharpening and bringing to a point, pins and other implements of bone, and they seem well adapted for such a purpose, and are still so used by the Eskimos. They may also have served for smoothing the shafts of arrows. Serpentine pebbles with a groove in them are used for straightening arrow-shafts by the Indians of

California, [1113] and shaft rubbers of sandstone have been found in Pennsylvania. [1114]

The Rev. W. C. Lukis found a similar stone (4 1/4 inches) in a barrow in Brittany. It is now in the British Museum. Another from a dolmen in Lozère [1115] has been thought to be for sharpening the points of bone instruments. Stones of the same form have been found in Germany; two from the cemetery near Monsheim [1116] are preserved in the Museum at Mainz. They are rather more elongated than the English examples. A specimen very like Fig. 185 has been found in Denmark. [1117] They seem also to occur in Hungary. [1118] I have a grooved stone of this kind from the Lago di Varese, Como, where the manufacture of flint arrow-heads was carried on extensively. An object found with polished stone instruments in the cave Casa da Moura, Portugal, [1119] not improbably belongs to this class of grooved sharpening stones.

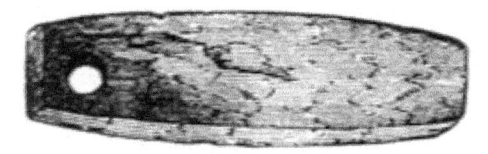

Fig. 186.—Hove. 1/2

From their association with bronze objects, they appear to belong to the Bronze rather than to the Stone Period; and the same holds good with the more ordinary form of whetstone, of which an example is given in Fig. 186. The original was found in the tumulus at Hove, [1120] near Brighton, which contained the stone axe-head already mentioned, a beautiful amber cup, and a bronze dagger. Another, of compact red sandstone, 3 3/8 inches long, with the perforated end rounded, was found in a barrow on Bow Hill, [1121] Sussex, and is now in the British Museum. Another, 3 inches long, bluish grey in colour, was found with a bronze dagger and a stone axe-hammer in an urn at Broughton [1122] in Craven, in 1675.

Two perforated whetstones were found with a bronze dagger and pin in the Silk Hill Barrow, [1123] Wilts. Another, with the perforation in a sort of loop at the end, was found with two daggers and a crutched pin of bronze, associated with burnt bones in a barrow at Normanton. [1124] Whetstones, in some cases not perforated, have occurred in other Wiltshire barrows, associated with bronze daggers at Wilsford [1125] and Lake, [1126] and with flint daggers or spear-heads at Durrington. [1127] The smooth stone found with a flint dagger in a barrow near Stonehenge, [1128] may also possibly have been a whetstone. Two from barrows at Knowle, [1129] Dorset, and Camerton, Somerset, have been figured by Dr. Thurnam. Another of the same kind was found in a barrow at Tregaseal, [1130] St. Just, Cornwall, and two others with urns at Brane Common, [1131] in the same neighbourhood. Others not perforated are recorded from Cottenham, [1132] Cambs. One from Anglesea [1133] has been figured.

Two of greenish stone (chlorite?) one 2 5/8 inches long, perforated at the end, were found at Drewton, [1134] near North Cave, Yorkshire; and another of similar material, 2 inches long, was found near some "Picts' houses," [1135] Shapinsay, Orkney. Half of a whetstone was found with a bronze dagger and numerous flint flakes by Mr. Morgan in a barrow at Penhow, [1136] Monmouthshire; and a much-used whetstone was found in a barrow near Scarborough, [1137] but the form of neither is specified. Several, both pierced and otherwise, have been recorded from Scotland. [1138] One with the boring incomplete was found with a flint knife in a cist at Stenton, [1139] East Lothian, and another, perforated, with a thin bronze blade and an urn at Glenluce, [1140] Wigtownshire. It appears possible that some of the stones found in Scotland and perforated at one end, described by Wilson [1141] as flail-stones, may after all be merely whetstones. The perforated form is common in Ireland, and is usually found in connection with metal objects. [1142] I have a narrow hone of rag-stone, perforated at one end, which was found with a remarkable hoard of bronze objects, including moulds for socketed celts and for a gouge, in the Isle of Harty, Sheppey. An almost identical whetstone is in the Zurich Museum.

Whetstones, perforated at one end, have occurred in the Swiss Lake-dwellings. [1143] Most of those found in the ancient cemetery of Hallstatt, [1144] in the Salzkammergut, were perforated in the same manner, and in some cases provided with an iron loop for suspension. They are usually of sandstone, and not formed from slaty rocks.

A whetstone, 5 1/4 inches long, the two flat faces of which had evidently been used for sharpening flat blades, while in the centre of each is a deep groove, probably caused by sharpening pointed tools, such as awls or needles of bronze, was found at Ty Mawr, Anglesea, near a spot where a number of bronze celts, spear-heads, &c., had previously been dug up. It has been figured by the late Hon. W. O. Stanley, [1145] whose cut is here reproduced as Fig. 187. The ends of the stone are somewhat battered from its having been also used as a hammer.

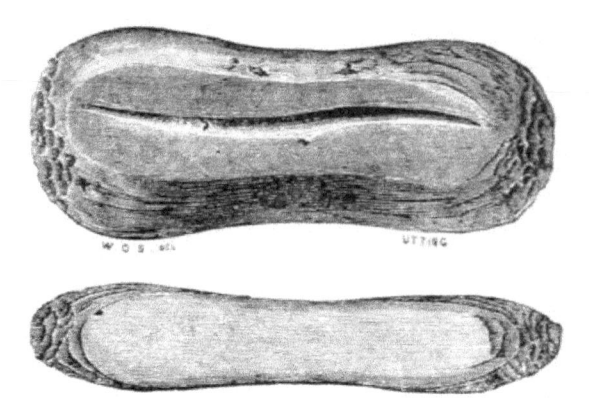

Fig. 187.—Ty Mawr.

The same explorer discovered in hut-circles in Holyhead Island [1146] other whetstones of the same character, in one instance with two principal grooves and minor scorings crossing each other at an acute angle, and in another with three parallel grooves in the face of the stone. There can be little doubt that these sharpening stones belong to a period when the use of metal for cutting and piercing instruments was fully established.

There are frequently found in Ireland and Scotland flat pebbles of quartz and quartzite, sometimes ground on the edges or faces, or on both, and having on each face an indentation running in a somewhat oblique direction to the longer axis of the pebble. Specimens [1147] have been figured by Sir William Wilde, who describes them as slingstones. The flat faces of some have all the appearance of having been abraded by a pointed instrument. I have never met with this form in England, but in the National Museum at Edinburgh is a grooved pebble exactly like those found in Ireland, from the broch, at Kintradwell, [1148] Sutherlandshire, and another from that at Lingrow, Orkney. One from Borness, [1149] Kirkcudbrightshire, has been figured. Others have been found at Dunino, [1150] Fife, and Dunnichen, [1151] Forfarshire. This latter has an oval hollow on one face and a groove on the other.

This pebble variety is rarely found in Scandinavia, but another and probably rather later form, in which the pebbles have been wrought into a long shuttle-like shape, is abundant. Some of these are provided with a groove along the sides, which would admit of a cord being fastened round them, by which to suspend them from the girdle. On one or both faces there is often a similar indentation to those on the Irish specimens, on which, however, it is, as a rule, deeper than on the Scandinavian. On the latter, the grooves have sometimes more the appearance of having been produced by repeated slight blows than by friction. Specimens are engraved by Worsaae [1152] and Nilsson. [1153] The latter regards them as belonging to the Stone Age. They occurred, however, with numerous objects of the early Iron Age at Thorsbjerg, [1154] and have even been found with remains of both bronze and iron bands around them, instead of any more perishable cord.

These grooved stones are not to be confounded with the ordinary form of hammer-stone, [1155] but belong to a distinct category. They were, in all probability, used as a means for obtaining fire, by striking them with a pointed piece of iron. They constitute, in fact, the "flint" part of a modification of the ordinary "flint and steel."

Whetstones are, of course, commonly found with Roman domestic antiquities; with Saxon, which are usually of a more purely sepulchral character, they are rarely discovered. Canon Greenwell found, however, two whetstones, one as much as 24 inches long, in graves of this period, at Uncleby, Yorkshire.

In one of the German cemeteries on the Rhine, corresponding to ours of Anglo-Saxon date, a small rubbing or sharpening stone, almost celt-like in form, was found. [1156]

In Dutch Guiana [1157] a small form of grinding-stone of quartz, apparently of the same age as the stone hatchets of that country, is known as a thunderstone, and great medicinal powers are ascribed to it by the natives. I must, however, return to the sharper forms of stone implements.

CHAPTER XII.
FLINT FLAKES, CORES, ETC.

The different forms of implements and weapons which have been treated of in the preceding pages have, for the most part, been fashioned from larger or smaller blocks of stone, reduced into shape by chipping; the chips having apparently been mere waste products, while the block from which they were struck was eventually converted into the tool or weapon required. With the majority, though by no means all, of the Neolithic forms which we still have to pass in review, the reverse holds good; for the raw materials, if I may so term them, from which the bulk of them were made, were flakes or splinters of flint struck off from larger blocks, in such a manner that it was the splinters that were utilized. The block from which they were struck, instead of being the object of the manufacture, became, when all the available flakes had been removed from it, mere refuse, to be thrown away as useless.

Before considering any of the various tools and weapons into which these flakes or splinters were converted by subsequent or secondary working, it will be well to say a few words about the simpler forms of flakes, and the cores or *nuclei* from which they were struck.

I have already, in speaking of the manufacture of stone implements, described the manner in which flakes or spalls are, at the present day, struck off by successive blows from the parent block or core, and have suggested the probable methods employed in ancient times for producing similar results. Remarks on the method of production of flint flakes have also been made by Sir W. Wilde, [1158] Sir John Lubbock, [1159] Mr. S. J. Mackie, [1160] Prof. T. McK. Hughes, [1161] and others. I need not, therefore, re-open the subject, though it will be well again to call attention to some of the distinctive marks by which artificially formed flakes may be distinguished from mere splinters of natural origin. The formation of these latter is usually due either to the flint, while still embedded in the chalk, having received some violent shock from disturbance of the stratum; or to unequal expansion, which sometimes causes flints to split up into rudely prismatic forms, much like those assumed by starch in drying, and sometimes causes cracks on the surface, which enable water and frost to complete the work of splitting them. Occasionally, nearly flat planes of fissure are caused by the expansion of some small included particle of a different mineralogical character from the surrounding flint. In such cases a series of concentric and more or less circular rings may usually be traced on the surface surrounding the central particle, which apparently mark the intervals of repose, when its expansion had ceased for a time to exert sufficient force to continue the fissure. This kind of fracture is most prevalent in flints upon or near the surface of the ground, such as those in drift-deposits.

In hardly any instances of natural fracture does the surface of the splinter show any trace of its having been produced by a blow, though the violent impact of one stone upon another, by means of a fall from a cliff, or of other natural causes, might produce a splinter of the same form as if it had been struck off by a hammer. There would, however, be the mark of the blow on one face only of such a splinter, whereas in a perfectly artificial flake the traces of the blow by which each facet was produced would be discernible. On the seashore, natural splinters of flint, resulting from the blow of one wave-borne pebble on another, may occasionally be found, some of them having a kind of secondary working at the edges, the result of attrition among the pebbles on the shore.

If a blow from a spherical-ended hammer be delivered at right angles on a large flat surface of flint, the part struck is only a minute portion of the surface, which may be represented by a circle of very small diameter. If flint were malleable, instead of being slightly elastic, a dent would be produced at the spot; but, being elastic, this small circle is driven slightly inwards into the body of the flint, and the result is that a circular fissure is produced between that part of the flint which is condensed for the moment by the blow, and that part which is left untouched. As each particle in the small circle on which the hammer impinges may be considered to rest on more than one other particle, it is evident that the circular fissure, as it descends into the body of the flint, will have a tendency to enlarge in diameter, so that the piece of flint it includes will be of conical form, the small circle struck by the hammer forming the slightly truncated apex. That this is not mere theory will be seen from the annexed woodcut, Fig. 188, showing a cone of flint produced by a single blow of a hammer. [1162]

Fig. 188.—Artificial Cone of Flint.

Sometimes, as has been shown by Prof. T. McK. Hughes, F.R.S., the sides of the cone are in steps, the inclination varying from 30° to 110°. This is probably to some extent due to the character of the blow, and the form of the hammer.

If the blow be administered near the edge, instead of in the middle of the surface of the block, a somewhat similar effect will be produced, but the cone in that case will be imperfect, as a splinter of flint will be struck off, the fissure probably running along the line of least resistance; though, owing to the suddenness of the blow, the conical character of fracture is at first produced at the point of impact. This fracture will vary to some extent in accordance with the angle at which the blow is given, and the character of the hammer; but in all cases where a splinter of flint is struck off by a blow, there will be a bulb or projection, of a more or less conical form, at the end where the blow was administered, and a corresponding hollow in the block from which it was dislodged. This projection is usually known as the "bulb of percussion," a term, I believe, first applied to it by the late Dr. Hugh Falconer, F.R.S.; and on every flake, all the facets of which are purely artificial, this bulb will be found at the butt-end of the larger flat face, and the hollow depressions, or portions of depressions, on all the other facets. If on a splinter of flint such a bulb occurs, it proves that it must have resulted from a blow, in all probability, but not of necessity, given by human agency; but where the bulb is on the principal face, and analogous depressions, or portions of them, are visible on the several other faces, and at the same end of a flake, all of them presenting the same character, and in a definite arrangement, it is in the highest degree probable that such a combination of blows must be the result of design, and the features presented are almost as good a warrant for the human origin of the flake as would be the maker's name upon it. When, however, several of such flakes are found together, each bearing these marks of being the result of several successive blows, all conducing to form a symmetrical knife-like flake, [1163] it becomes a certainty that they have been the work of intelligent beings.

In size and proportions flakes vary considerably, the longest English specimens that I have seen being as much as 8 or 9 inches long, while some, which still appear to have been made use of as tools, are not more than an inch in length. Their proportional breadth is almost as variable.

With regard to the classification and nomenclature of these objects, I would suggest that the name of flake should be limited to such artificial splinters of flint as, either in their section or outline, or in both, present a certain amount of symmetry, and appearance of design; and that the ruder forms, such as would result from chipping some large object into shape, without any regard to the form of the parts removed, should be called chips or spalls. [1164] Such as show no bulb of percussion may be termed splinters. The Scottish name for flakes is "skelbs."

The inner, or flat face of a flake, is that produced by the blow which dislodged it from the parent block, core, or nucleus. The outer, ridged or convex face comprises the other facets, or, in some instances, the natural surface of the flint. The base, or butt-end of a flake, is that at which the blows to form it were administered; the other end is the point.

Flakes may be subdivided into—

- 1. External, or those which have been struck off by a single blow from the outer surface of a nodule of flint. Many of these are as symmetrical as those resulting from a more complicated process of manufacture, and they have frequently been utilized, especially for scrapers.

- 2. Ridged flakes, or those presenting a triangular section. One face of these sometimes presents the external crust of the flint, as in Fig. 190. In others, the ridge has been formed by transverse chipping, as is the case with the long flakes from Pressigny (Fig. 6), but this method appears to have been almost unknown in Britain.

- 3. Flat, where the external face is nearly parallel to the internal, and the two edges are formed by narrow facets, as in Fig. 200.

- 4. Polygonal, where the external face consists of many facets, as in Fig. 192.

These several varieties may be long or short, broad or narrow, straight or curved, thick or thin, pointed or obtuse. The character of the base may also vary, being rounded or flat, thick or thin, broad or narrow.

The cores from which flakes have been struck are, of course, of various forms, some having had only one or two flakes removed from them, and others several. In the latter case they are often more or less regularly polygonal, though only few of the facets will be of the full breadth of the flakes, as the external face of every successive flake carries off some part of the traces of those previously struck off. Not unfrequently some of the facets are arrested at a little distance from the end where the blows were struck, in consequence of the flake having broken short off, instead of the fissure continuing to the end of the block. Occasionally, and more especially on the Yorkshire Wolds, the nuclei are very small, and much resemble in character those found, with numerous flakes, in India, in the neighbourhood of Jubbulpore. [1165]

It has been suggested [1166] that cores were occasionally made on purpose for use as tools; but this appears very doubtful. Of course, if a core were at hand, and seemed capable of serving some special purpose, it would be utilized.

Fig. 189.—Weaverthorpe. 1/1

The core here engraved of the full size in Fig. 189 was found by myself at Weaverthorpe, Yorkshire. I have already suggested that in striking off such small flakes as those removed from this core, some sort of punch may have been used, instead of the blows being administered directly by a hammer. We have no conclusive evidence as to the purpose to which such minute flakes were applied, but they may have been fashioned into drills or scraping or boring tools, of very diminutive size. Such small objects are so liable to escape observation, that though they may exist in considerable numbers, they are but rarely found on the surface of the ground. Numerous flakes, however, quite as minute, with their edges showing evident signs of wear, are present among the refuse left by the cave-dwellers of the Reindeer Period of the South of France. As will subsequently be seen, these minute flakes have been also found in Egypt and in Asia, as well as in Britain. See Fig. 232 A to 232 F. There is a class of ancient Scandinavian harpoon-heads, the stems of which are formed of bone with small flint flakes cemented into a groove on either side so as to form barbs. Knives of the same kind are subsequently mentioned.

Among the Australians [1167] we find very minute splinters of flint and quartz secured to wooden handles by "black-boy" gum, and forming the teeth of rude saws and the barbs of javelins. Some remarkably small flakes have also been found in the diamond-diggings of South Africa in company with fragments of ostrich-egg shell, such as with the aid of the flakes might have been converted into the small perforated discs still worn as ornaments by the Bushmen.

There are but few published notices of the discovery of English cores of flint, though they are to be found in numbers over a considerable tract of country, especially where flint abounds.

I have recorded their finding at Redhill, [1168] near Reigate, and at Little Solsbury Hill, [1169] near Bath. I also possess numerous specimens from Herts, Gloucestershire, Sussex, Bedfordshire, Suffolk, and Yorkshire. In several instances two series of flakes have been struck off, the one set at right angles to the other. More rarely the flakes have been obtained from both ends of the block.

A core from the Fens [1170] is in the Museum of the Cambridge Antiquarian Society, and several were found, with other worked flints, in the chambered Long Barrow at West Kennet, Wiltshire.

Numerous specimens from Peter's Finger, near Salisbury, and elsewhere, are in the Blackmore Museum; and a number were found by General Pitt Rivers in his researches at Cissbury, Sussex, and by Canon Greenwell at Grime's Graves. [1171] Mr. Joseph Stevens has described specimens from St. Mary Bourne, [1172] Hants. They are recorded also as found with flakes at Port St. Mary, [1173] Isle of Man.

A long bludgeon-shaped nodule of flint, from one end of which a succession of flakes had been struck, was found in a grave, with a contracted skeleton, in a barrow near Winterbourn Stoke, [1174] Wilts.

Illustrations of cores, and of the manner in which flakes have been struck from them, have been given by various authors. [1175]

The existence of flakes involves the necessity of there having been cores from which they were struck; and as silicious flakes occur in almost all known countries, so also do cores. A series of French *nuclei* is figured by Mortillet, [1176] and a fine example from Olonetz, [1177] Russia, by Worsaae. They have also been found in the Arabian desert. [1178] Those of large size and of regular polygonal form are rare in Britain and Ireland, and, indeed, generally in Europe. Some of the largest and most regular occur in Scandinavia. I have also some good examples from Belgium. Many of the cores from Spiennes, near Mons, were subsequently utilized as celts; and the same was the case to some extent at Pressigny, the large cores from which have already been described. The Mexican [1179] and East Indian [1180] forms, in obsidian and cherty flint, have also been mentioned. They are unsurpassed for symmetry and for the skill exhibited in removing flakes from them.

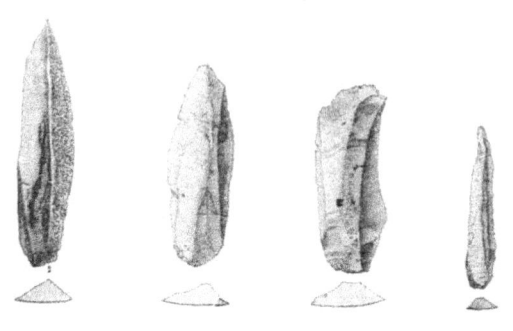

Fig. 190.—Newhaven. 1/2

Fig. 191.—Redhill. Reigate. 1/2

Fig. 192.—Icklingham. 1/2

Fig. 193.—Seaford. 1/2

It is worthy of remark that cores and flakes of obsidian, almost identical in character with those from Mexico, but generally of small size, have been found in Greece, principally in the island of Melos. [1181] Specimens are in the Christy Collection, and I possess several. Obsidian nuclei are also found in Hungary.

Simple flakes and splinters of flint have been found in considerable numbers over almost the whole of Britain. Of the four here shown, Fig. 190 was found near Newhaven, Sussex; Fig. 191 near Reigate, Surrey; Fig. 192 near Icklingham, Suffolk; and Fig. 193 at Seaford, Sussex. At each of these places they occur in great numbers on the surface, and near Reigate some thousands were collected nearly forty years ago by Mr. Shelley, [1182] of whose discoveries I have given an account elsewhere. The counties in which they principally abound are perhaps Cornwall, [1183] Devonshire, [1184] Dorsetshire, Wilts, Hants, [1185] Surrey, [1186] Oxfordshire, [1187] Sussex, Suffolk, Norfolk, Derbyshire, Lancashire, [1188] and Yorkshire; but they may be said to be ubiquitous. In some parts of Devonshire, and especially near Croyde, they occur in great numbers, so great, indeed, as to have led Mr. Whitley [1189] to suppose them to have been formed by natural causes rather than by human agency. Far more rational accounts of them have been given by Mr. Townshend M. Hall, [1190] Mr. H. S. Ellis, [1191] and Mr. C. Spence Bate. [1192]

Flakes and splinters of flint frequently occur in and around ancient encampments and settlements, as well as in association with interments both by cremation and inhumation. Many of the immense number of "spear-heads" collected by Mr. Bateman in his investigations were of the simple flake form, and others were flakes with but slight secondary working at the edges, such as will hereafter be noticed. Many other instruments which he discovered were merely flakes, such as the thick-backed cutting instrument of flint three inches long, with a bronze dagger and two small balls of stone, in a barrow containing a skeleton near Pickering, [1193] which would appear to have been of this character. They occurred with burnt bones in cinerary urns at Broughton, [1194] Lincolnshire, in one case with a flat bronze arrow-head; at Summer Hill, [1195] near Canterbury; with a flint arrow-head at Sittingbourne; [1196] with burnt bones and bronze daggers in a barrow at Teddington, [1197] Middlesex; at Penhow, [1198] Monmouth; and in the Gristhorpe Barrow, [1199] near Scarborough; with burnt bones in a circle of stones near Llanaber, [1200] Merionethshire, where no flint occurs naturally; with burnt bones in an urn beneath a tumulus at Brynbugeilen, [1201] Llangollen; in a barrow near Blackbury Castle, [1202] Devon; and in one on Dartmoor; [1203] and at Hollingsclough and Upper Edge, [1204] Derbyshire. Flakes, not of flint, but of a hard silicious grit, occurred in a cist with burnt bones near Harlech; [1205] and of some other hard stone in a cist in Merionethshire. [1206] Other instances have been cited by General Pitt Rivers, [1207] who found several rough flakes and splinters of grit and felspathic ash in cairns near Bangor, North Wales. Some of these showed signs of rubbing and use on their edges; in some cases they had the appearance of having been scraped by metal. Whether they were the weapons and tools of the people buried in the cairns, or merely votive offerings, appeared to be somewhat doubtful. The urns associated with them were such as might well belong to the Bronze Period.

Flint flakes are described as found in graves with contracted interments at Amble, [1208] Northumberland; Driffield, [1209] Yorkshire; Ballidon Moor, [1210] Derbyshire; Littleton Drew, [1211] and Winterbourn Stoke, [1212] Wilts. Canon Greenwell [1213] has also found them in great numbers with interments of different characters. They occurred with extended burials at Oakley Park, [1214] near Cirencester. In some of the long barrows they are especially numerous, upwards of three hundred having been found by Dr. Thurnam at West Kennet, [1215] while there were three only in that of Rodmarton, [1216] and two were found at the base of the cairn in the chambered tumulus at Uley, [1217] Gloucestershire. Another accompanied a skeleton in a long barrow near Littleton Drew. [1218] Sir Richard Colt Hoare speaks of a great quantity of chipped flints, prepared for arrows or lances, as having been found in barrows on Long Street Down, [1219] and at Brigmilston, Wilts; [1220] but, as a rule, he seems not to have taken much notice of such simple forms. Others have been discovered with ashes at Helmingham, [1221] Suffolk.

It is, however, needless, to cite more instances of their occurrence with interments belonging to the Stone and Bronze Ages, as the presence of flakes and chippings of flint is in such cases the rule rather than the exception.

In Scotland, where flint is a scarcer natural product, they are also found. As instances, I may cite one found in an urn within a cist at Tillicoultry, [1222] Clackmannanshire; and in a cist in Arran. [1223] In some parts of Aberdeenshire [1224] and Banffshire they are numerous, and in the Buchan district are associated with shell mounds, or kjökken-möddings. They occur also in Lanarkshire and Elgin. [1225] In Orkney [1226] they abound: as also at the Bin of Cullen, [1227] where a manufactory of arrow-heads seems to have existed. In cists in Roxburghshire [1228] were sepulchral urns and numerous flint flakes; and in Argyllshire [1229] there were in a cist with a skeleton flint flakes in such numbers as to form a heap from eighteen inches to two feet in height. Some of white quartz have been found associated with arrow-heads in Banffshire. [1230] Little heaps [1231] of six or eight were found in each corner of a grave at Clashfarquhar, Aberdeen. They abound on the sand-hills near Glenluce and on the Culbin Sands.

Of ancient encampments or settlements where flint flakes occur in numbers, I may mention Maiden Bower, near Dunstable; Pulpit Wood, near Prince's Risborough; Cissbury, [1232] Beltout Castle, and other encampments in Sussex; Little Solsbury Hill, near Bath; Castle Ring, [1233] Cannock Chase; Avebury, [1234] Wilts; and Callow Hill, [1235] Oxfordshire. They have been found in wonderful abundance on the surface in the counties already mentioned, and their occurrence has been noticed near Bradford Abbas; [1236] near Folkestone; [1237] at Possingworth Manor, [1238] Uckfield; near Hastings; [1239] at Stonham [1240] and Icklingham, Suffolk; near Grime's Graves, Norfolk; [1241] at St. Mary Bourne, [1242] Hants;

and in a turbary at Heneglwys, [1243] Anglesea, an island in which no flint occurs naturally. Two from Carno, Montgomeryshire, are engraved in the *Archæologia Cambrensis*. [1244] They have also been found under a submerged forest on the coast of West Somerset. [1245] I have seen a few flakes made from Lower Tertiary conglomerate.

In districts where flint was an imported luxury, other stones, usually containing a large proportion of silica, and when broken presenting a conchoidal fracture, served, so far as the material allowed, the same purposes as flint. Of this a few instances have already been given. In some cases even laminated sandstones, shales, and slates seem to have been utilized. Numerous relics of this kind, some so rude that their purposes may appear doubtful, were found by the late Mr. S. Laing, [1246] in Caithness. Large oval flakes, made from sandstone pebbles, occurred in very great numbers in and around the ancient dwelling at Skaill, Orkney. In form, however, these approximate more nearly to the Pict's knives, of which hereafter, than to ordinary flakes. The method of their manufacture has been described by Mr. Laing. [1247]

A curious stone knife or dagger, found beside a stone cist in Perthshire, [1248] is described as a natural formation of mica-schist, the peculiar shape of which has suggested its adaptation as a rude but efficient implement.

Some rude spear-heads of flint and greenstone are said to have been found near Pytchley, [1249] Northamptonshire; and some of Kentish rag at Maidstone. [1250] I have also seen them made of Oolitic flint.

Flakes of quartzite have been found, together with some of flint and quartz and with polished celts, in some of the caverns inhabited during the Neolithic Period in the Pyrenees of the Ariège, [1251] and also in the Lake Settlement of Greug. [1252]

When we consider how well adapted for cutting purposes were these simple flakes of flint, and how they constituted, as it were, the raw material for so many of the more finished forms, such as arrow-heads, of which the consumption in ancient times must have been enormous; and when, moreover, we take into account that in producing a well-formed flake many waste flakes and mere splinters must probably have been struck off, and that in forming the large implements of flint almost innumerable chips or spalls must have been made, their abundance on the sites of ancient dwelling-places is by no means surprising, especially as the material of which they are formed is almost indestructible.

Such fragments of flint must have been among the daily necessities of ancient savage life, and we can well understand the feeling which led the survivors of the departed hunter to place in his grave not only the finished weapons of the chase, but the material from which to form them, as a provision for him in "the happy hunting grounds," the only entrance to which was through the gate of Death.

The occurrence of flint chips and potsherds in the soil of which barrows are composed, may in some cases be merely the result of their being made up of earth gathered from the surface of the ground, which from previous occupation by man was bestrewn with such remains. It is, however, often otherwise, especially when the flakes are in immediate association with the interment. The practice of throwing a stone on a cairn is no doubt a relic of an ancient custom. [1253] The "shards, flint, and pebbles" which Ophelia should have had thrown on her in her grave may, as has been suggested by Canon Greenwell, [1254] point to a sacred Pagan custom remembered in Christian times, but then deemed irreligious and unholy.

The presence of flint flakes in ancient graves is not, however, limited to those of the so-called Stone and Bronze Periods, but they occur with even more recent interments. For it seems probable that the flint was in some cases buried as a fire-producing agent, and not as the material for tools or weapons. In a cist at Lesmurdie, [1255] Banffshire, apparently of early date, were some chips of flint which appeared to the discoverer to have been originally accompanied by a steel or piece of iron and tinder. The oxide of iron may, however, have been merely the result of the decomposition of a piece of iron pyrites. At Worle Hill, [1256] Somersetshire, "flint flakes, prepared for arrow-heads," were found with iron spear-heads and other objects, though it is very doubtful whether they were in true association. In Saxon graves, [1257] however, small nests of chipped flints are not unfrequent, and the same is the case with Merovingian and Frankish interments, sometimes accompanied by the steels or *briquets*, [1258] at other times without them. I have a wrought flint of this class, curiously like a modern gun-flint, from an early German grave near Wiesbaden. Occasionally flakes of other materials than flint occur. Their presence in graves is regarded by M. Baudot as due to a reminiscence of some ancient rite of sepulchre. In the Anglo-Saxon burial-ground at Harnham Hill, [1259] near Salisbury, and at Ozengal, steels were also found. Canon Greenwell found a steel, in form much like those of modern date, in a Saxon grave at Uncleby in the East Riding of Yorkshire. As has been pointed out by Mr. Akerman, Scheffer [1260] informs us that so late as the seventeenth century, the Lapps were buried with their axe, bow, and arrows, and a flint and steel, to be used both in a life to come and in finding their way to the scene of their future existence.

Flakes and rudely chipped pieces of flint are also of very common occurrence on the sites of Roman occupation, as, for instance, at Hardham, [1261] Sussex, where Prof. Boyd Dawkins found them associated with Roman pottery. At Moel Fenlli, [1262] also, in the vale of Clwyd, there occurred with Roman pottery some flint flakes which have been figured as arrow-heads, and with them what is termed a stone knife, but which is, however, more probably a whetstone used to sharpen those of steel. I have myself noticed flint flakes at Regulbium (Reculver), Verulamium (St. Alban's), and on other Roman sites. Many of them were no doubt used for producing fire, but the more finished flakes may possibly have served as carpenters' tools for scraping, in the same way as fragments of glass are in use at the present day.

There is, however, another cause why rude splinters of flint should accompany Roman remains, especially in the case of villas in country districts, for the *tribulum*, or threshing implement employed both by the Romans and other ancient civilized nations, was a "sharp threshing instrument having teeth," [1263] in most cases of flint. Varro [1264] thus describes the *tribulum*:—"Id fit e tabulâ lapidibus aut ferro exasperatâ, quæ imposito auriga aut pondere grandi trahitur jumentis junctis ut discutiat e spicâ grana." Another form of the instrument was called *traha* or *trahea*. In the East, in Northern Africa, Spain, Portugal, Madeira, Teneriffe, and probably other parts of the world, threshing implements, which no doubt closely resemble the original *tribula*, are still in use. The name is still preserved in the Italian *trebbiatrice*, the Spanish *trilla*, and the Portuguese *trilho*, but survives, metaphorically alone, in our English *tribulation*. In Egypt their name is *nureg*, and in Greece ἀλωνίιστρα, from ἀλωνία, a threshing-floor. Drawings of various *tribula* have been given by various travellers, [1265] and the implements themselves from different countries may be seen in the Christy Collection and in the Blackmore Museum. They are flat sledges of wood, five to six feet in length, and two or three in breadth, the under side pitted with a number of square or lozenge-shaped holes, mortised a little distance into the wood, and having in each hole a flake or splinter of stone. I have seen them in Spain mounted with simple pebbles. In those from Madeira the stone is a volcanic rock, but in that from Aleppo—preserved in the Christy Collection, [1266] and shown in Fig. 194—each flake is of cherty flint and has been artificially shaped. Occasionally there are a few projecting ribs or runners of iron along part of the machine, but in most instances the whole of the armature is of stone. As each *trilho* is provided with some hundreds of chipped stones, we can readily understand what a number of rough flakes might be left in the soil at places where they were long in use, in addition to the flakes and splinters which for centuries have been used for striking a light.

Fig. 194.—Tribulum from Aleppo.

Flakes and splinters of silicious stone, whether flint, jasper, chert, iron-stone, quartzite, or obsidian, are to be found in almost all known countries, and belong to all ages. They are in fact the most catholic of all stone implements, and have been in use "semper, ubique, et ab omnibus." Whether we look in our old River-gravels of the age of the mammoth, in our old cave-deposits, our ancient encampments, or our modern gun-flint manufactories, there is the inevitable flake. And it is almost universally the same in other countries—in Greenland or South Africa, on the field of Marathon or in the backwoods of Australia, among the sands of Arabia [1267] or on the plains of America,—wherever such flakes and splinters are sought for, they are almost sure to be found, either in use among the savage occupants of the country at the present day, or among civilized nations, left in the soil as memorials of their more or less remote barbarian ancestors.

Flint flakes are found in great abundance in Ireland, especially in Ulster, where the raw material occurs in the chalk. At Toome Bridge, on the shores of Lough Neagh, many thousands have been found, and they occur in abundance in the valley of the Bann, [1268] and in slightly raised beaches along the shores of Belfast Lough. They are rarely more than 4 or 5 inches in length; and symmetrical, flat, parallel flakes are extremely rare. Many pointed flakes have been slightly trimmed [1269] at the butt-end, and converted into a sort of lance-head without further preparation. Such flakes may have pointed fishing-spears. They are occasionally formed of Lydian stone.

In Scandinavia, the art of flaking flint attained to great perfection, and flat or ridged symmetrical flakes, as much as 6 inches long, and not more than 3/4-inch wide, are by no means uncommon. Occasionally they are no less than 13 inches long. [1270] Two in the Museum at Copenhagen [1271] (9 inches) fit the one on the other. The ridge is sometimes formed by cross-chipping. The bulk of the flakes from the kjökken-möddings are of a rude character, though very many show traces of use.

In Germany, long flakes of flint are rare, but one about 6 1/2 inches long, found in Rhenish-Hesse, is engraved by Lindenschmit. [1272]

In some parts of France they are extremely plentiful, especially on and around the sites of ancient flint *ateliers*. Some flakes, like those produced at Pressigny, were of great length. One not less than 13 1/4 inches long, and not more than 1 1/2 inches broad at the butt, found at Pauilhac, in the Valley of the Gers, has been figured in the *Revue de Gascogne*. [1273] A flake from Gergovia, 9 inches long, is in the Museum at Clermont Ferrand.

One 8 3/4 inches long was found in the Camp de Catenoy [1274] (Oise).

Long flakes found in France have been engraved by numerous authors, [1275] and some from Belgium by Le Hon. [1276]

Obsidian cores and flakes have been found in Lorraine, [1277] the material having been brought from Auvergne.

Flakes occur, but not so abundantly, in Spain and Portugal. A fragment of a ridged flake of jasper, found in the cave of Albuñol in Spain, [1278] is 1 1/2 inches long. In one of the Genista Caves [1279] at Gibraltar there was found one of the long flakes, but of which a part had been broken off. Another was 6 1/2 inches long and 5/8 inch wide. In Algarve, [1280] Portugal, they have been found up to 15 inches in length; some of them are beautifully serrated at the edges.

In Italy they are by no means uncommon, sometimes of great length. One, 7 inches long, is figured by Nicolucci. [1281]

Among the Swiss Lake-dwellers considerable use was made of flint flakes, not only as the material for arrow-heads, but for cutting tools. So great was the abundance of flint left on the site of some of their habitations, as at Nussdorf, [1282] that in after ages the spot was resorted to for generations, in order to procure flints for use with steel. It was by their being thus known as flint-producing spots that some of the Lake-dwellings were discovered. A flake nearly 7 inches long, from peat, in the Canton de Vaud, has been engraved by De Bonstetten. [1283]

A flake 9 inches long from Transcaucasia [1284] has been figured.

In Egypt [1285] flakes of flint have been found in considerable numbers in certain localities, some of them associated with polished stone hatchets; others are possibly of no extreme antiquity, though undoubtedly of artificial origin, and not of merely natural formation, as has been suggested by Lepsius. [1286] That distinguished antiquary has, however, found a number of well-formed ridged and polygonal flakes in Egypt, some of them in a grave which he has reason to assign to about 2500 B.C.

A vast number of discoveries of flint flakes and other forms of worked flints has, of late years, been made in Egypt. It will probably be sufficient to indicate in a note [1287] some of the principal memoirs relating to the subject. They are found also in the Libyan [1288] desert. The discoveries at Helouan will be subsequently mentioned.

The presence of numerous flakes, scrapers and other forms of flint instruments, has also been noticed in Algeria. [1289] They are for the most part rude and small.

Flint flakes and tools are found on Mount Lebanon, [1290] and on the Nablus [1291] road from Jerusalem there are mounds entirely composed of flint chippings.

Fig. 195.—Admiralty Islands.

In Southern Africa, [1292] near Capetown and Grahamstown, flakes abound on the surface of the ground, sometimes of chert or flint, but often of basaltic rock. I have one from Grahamstown 8 inches in length.

Their occurrence in India has already been noticed. The flakes from Jubbulpore [1293] are for the most part of small size, but some of those removed from the cores found in the river Indus must have been at least 5 or 6 inches long.

In America, flint, or rather horn-stone flakes, are not uncommon, though not so often noticed as the more finished forms. Some found in the mounds of Ohio are of considerable length, one engraved by Squier and Davis [1294] being 5 1/2 inches long. Some of the Mexican flakes of obsidian are fully 6 inches in length.

In ancient times the Ichthyophagi are described by Diodorus [1295] as using antelopes' horns and stones broken to a sharp edge in their fishing, "for necessity teaches everything." Flakes are still in some cases used without any secondary chipping or working into form.

We find, for instance, flakes of flint or obsidian, and even of glass, almost in the condition in which they were struck from the parent block, employed as lance and javelin-heads, among several savage people, such as the natives of Australia, [1296] and of the Admiralty Islands. [1297] One of those said to be in use among the latter people is shown, half-size, in Fig. 195, [1298] and exhibits the method of attachment to the shaft. The butt-end of the flake is let into a socket in a short tapering piece of wood, into the other extremity of which the end of the long light shaft is inserted; both flake and shaft are next secured by tying, and then the whole of the socket and ligatures is covered up with a coating of resinous gum, occasionally decorated with zigzag and other patterns. Some flakes are mounted as daggers.

Some of the long parallel flakes also appear to have been hafted. One such, probably from Mexico, has been engraved by Aldrovandus as a *culter lapideus*. [1299] A tool in use among the natives of Easter Island [1300] consisted of a broad flake of obsidian, with a roughly chipped tang which was inserted in a slit in the handle to which it was bound, the binding being tightened by means of wooden wedges driven in under the string.

To return, however, to the flakes of flint which were used in this country for scraping or cutting purposes, at an early period, when metal was either unknown or comparatively scarce. Each flake, when dexterously made, has on either side a cutting edge, so sharp that it almost might, like the obsidian flakes of Mexico, be used as a razor. Some flakes indeed seem to have served as surgical instruments, as the practice of trephining was known in the Stone Period. So long as the edge is used merely for cutting soft substances it may remain for some time comparatively uninjured, and even if slightly jagged its cutting power is not impaired. If long in use, the sides of the blade become rather polished by wear, and I have specimens, both English and foreign, on which the polish thus produced can be observed. If the flake has been used for scraping a surface, say, for instance, of bone or wood, the edge will be found to wear away, by extremely minute portions chipping off nearly at right angles to the scraping edge, and with the lines of fracture running back from it. The coarseness of these minute chips will vary in accordance with the amount of pressure used, and the material scraped; but generally speaking, I think that I am right in saying that they are more delicate and at a more obtuse angle to the face, than the small chipping produced by the secondary working of the edge of a flake, of which I shall presently speak. In all cases where any considerable number of flakes of flint occur, such as there appears to be good reason for attributing to a remote period, a greater or less proportion of them will, on examination, be found to bear these signs of wear upon them, extending over, at all events, some portion of their edges.

It is, however, difficult if not impossible, always to determine whether the chipping away of the edge of a flake is merely the result of use, or whether it is intentional. There can be no doubt that for many purposes the acute edge of a flake, as originally formed, was too delicate and brittle, and that it was therefore re-worked by subsequent chipping, so as to make the angle more obtuse, and thus strengthen the edge of the tool. It is curious to observe how rarely the edges of flakes were sharpened by grinding. It was probably considered less troublesome to form a new flake than to sharpen an old one; in the same way as it is recorded that the Mexican barbers threw away their obsidian flakes as soon as they were dull and made use of new ones. Dr. E. B. Tylor, in the free translation of the passage in Torquemada relating to these razors, appears, as has been pointed out by Messrs. Daubrée and Roulin, [1301] to have fallen into a mistake in representing them to have been sharpened on a hone, the original author having merely said that the edge of the obsidian flakes was as keen as if they had been forged in iron, ground on a stone, and finished on a hone.

British flakes with ground edges are by no means common. One from Yorkshire, in my own collection, is a thin, flat, external flake, having both edges (which are parallel) ground from both faces to an angle of about 60°. It has, unfortunately, been broken square across, about 2 inches from the butt-end, and is 1 inch wide at the fracture. Another, from Bridlington, is an ovate flat external flake, produced, not by art, but by natural fracture, and having one side brought to a sharp edge by grinding on both faces. With the exception of its being partially chipped into shape at both ends, this grinding is all that has been done to convert a mere splinter of flint into a serviceable tool. It is an interesting example of the selection of a natural form, where adapted for a particular purpose, in preference to making the whole implement by hand. The small celt, Fig. 31, affords an analogous instance. In the Greenwell Collection are also two or three very rude flakes from the Yorkshire Wolds, which are ground at some portion of their edges.

In a barrow on Seamer Moor, Yorkshire, the late Lord Londesborough [1302] found, with other relics, a delicate knife made from a flake of flint, 4 1/4 inches long, and dexterously ground. A trimmed flake, like Fig. 239, some small celts, and delicate lozenge-shaped arrow-heads, like Fig. 276, were also present. The whole are now in the British Museum.

A flake, from Charleston, in the East Riding, presented to me by Canon Greenwell, is shown in Fig. 196. It is of thin triangular section, slightly bowed longitudinally, having one edge, which appears to have been originally blunt, sharpened by secondary working. The other edge has been sharpened to an angle of about

45° by grinding both on the inner and outer faces of the flake. The point, which is irregular in shape, is rounded over either by friction or by grinding. It seems well adapted for use as a knife when held between the ball of the thumb and the end of the first finger, without the intervention of any handle.

Fig. 196.—Charleston. 1/2

Another specimen, 4 inches long, ground to a sharp edge along one side, was in the collection of the late Mr. J. W. Flower, F.G.S., and is now in mine. It was found near Thetford.

Mr. Flower had also a flake from High Street, near Chislet, Kent, with both edges completely blunted by grinding, perhaps in scraping stone.

I have two trimmed flakes with the edges carefully ground, from the neighbourhood of Icklingham, Suffolk, and another ridged flake, 2 3/8 inches long, pointed at one end and rounded at the other, one side of which has been carefully ground at the edge. I found it in a field of my own, in the parish of Abbot's Langley, Herts. Canon Greenwell obtained another 2 1/2 inches long, ground on both edges, from Mildenhall Fen.

I have seen a flake about 3 inches long, with the edge ground, that had been found on the top of the cliffs at Bournemouth; and another, from a barrow near Stonehenge, in the possession of the late Mr. Frank Buckland.

A flat flake, with a semicircular end, and ground at the edges so as to form "a beautiful thin ovoidal knife three and a half inches long," was found by Dr. Thurnam, [1303] with many other worked flints, in the chambered long barrow at West Kennet, Wilts. Another, carefully ground at one edge, was found by Sir R. Colt Hoare, [1304] at Everley.

An oval knife, about 2 inches long, ground at the edge and over a great part of the convex face, found at Micheldean, Gloucestershire, is in the museum at Truro.

A cutting instrument, with a very keen edge, nicely polished, is recorded as having been found, with twenty other flint implements or tools of various shapes, accompanying a skeleton, in a barrow near Pickering. [1305] A so-called spear-head, neatly chipped and rubbed, was found with burnt bones in another barrow near the same place. [1306]

A few flat flakes, ground at the edge, have been discovered in Scotland. One 2 1/2 inches long was found at Cromar, [1307] Aberdeenshire; and a portion of another in a cairn in Caithness, [1308] in company with a polished perforated hammer and other objects.

Irish flakes are rarely sharpened by grinding. I have, however, one of Lydian stone, [1309] found in Lough Neagh, and ground to an edge at the end.

Fig. 197.—Nussdorf. 1/2

In form the Charleston flake, Fig. 196, much resembles some of the Swiss flakes, which, from examples that have been found in the Lake-dwellings, are proved to have been mounted in handles. One of these, from Nussdorf, in the Ueberlinger See, [1310] is in my own collection, and is shown in Fig. 197. It is fastened into a yew-wood handle by an apparently bituminous cement. The edge has been formed by secondary chipping on the ridged face of the flake. I am unable to say whether the edge of the flake still embedded in the wood is left as originally produced or no, but several unmounted flakes from the same locality have been re-chipped on both edges. In some instances, however, only one edge is thus worked. In the case of many of the small narrow flakes from the Dordogne caves, one edge is much worn away, and the other as sharp as ever, as if it had been protected by being inserted in a wooden handle.

From the hole in the handle, this form of instrument would appear to have been carried attached to a string, like a sailor's knife at the present day—a similarity probably due to the somewhat analogous conditions of life of the old Lake-dwellers to those of seamen. In some French and Swiss flakes [1311] which seem to have been used in a similar manner, the ends are squared, and a central notch worked in each, apparently for the reception of a cord. In this case, a loop at the end of the cord would answer the same purpose as the hole in the handle, which with these flakes seem to have been needless. They are abundant at Pressigny.

A pointed flake in the museum at Berne [1312] is hafted like a dagger, in a wooden handle, which is bound round with a cord made from rushes.

Some of the Swiss handles are not bored, and occasionally they are prolonged at one end to twice the length of the flint, so as to form a handle like that of a table-knife, the flint flake, though let in to a continuation of the handle, projecting and forming the blade. In some cases there is a handle at each end, like those of a spoke-shave. The handles are of yew, deal, and more rarely of stags'-horn; and the implements, though usually termed saws, are not regularly serrated, and may with equal propriety be termed knives.

The late Sir Edward Belcher showed me an Eskimo "flensing knife," from Icy Cape, hafted in much the same manner. The blade is an ovate piece of slate about 5 inches long, and is let into a handle made of several pieces of wood, extending along nearly half the circumference, and secured together by resin. Other specimens of the same kind are in the British Museum, and in the Ethnological Museum at Copenhagen. The stone blades are more like the flat Picts' [1313] knives, such as Fig. 263, than ordinary flint flakes. An iron blade, hafted in a closely analogous manner by the Eskimos, is engraved by Nilsson. [1314]

As already mentioned, some of the Australian savages about King George's Sound make knives or saws on a somewhat similar plan; but instead of one long flake they attach a number of small flakes in a row in a matrix of hard resin at one end of a stick. Spears are formed in the same manner.

In other cases, however, flakes are differently hafted. One such is shown in Fig. 198, from an original in the Christy Collection. One edge of this flake has been entirely removed by chipping so as to form a thick, somewhat rounded back, not unlike that of an ordinary knife-blade, though rather thicker in proportion to the width of the blade. The butt-end has then had a portion of the hairy skin of some animal bound over it with a cord, so as to give it a sort of haft, and effectually protect the hand that held it. The material of the flake appears to be horn-stone. Another knife of the same character, from Queensland, is in the Museum of the Hartley Institution at Southampton.

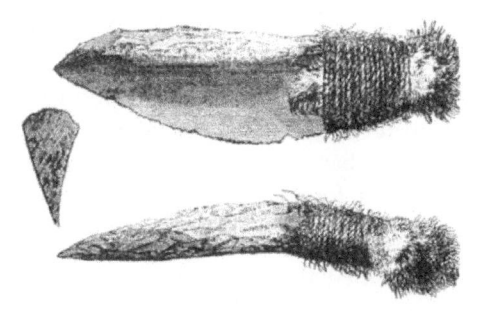

Fig. 198.—Australia. 1/2

Another example, from the Murray River, [1315] but without the skin handle, has been figured.

A friend in Queensland tried to procure one of these knives for me, but what he obtained was a flake of glass made from a gin bottle, and the wrapping was of calico instead of kangaroo-skin. Iron blades [1316] are sometimes hafted in the same way with a piece of skin. Some Australian jasper or flint knives, [1317] from Carandotta, are hafted with gum, and provided with sheaths made of sedge. These gum-hafted knives are in use on the Herbert River [1318] for certain surgical operations.

Some surface-chipped obsidian knives from California are hafted by having a strip of otter skin wound round them, and Prof. Flinders Petrie [1319] has found an Egyptian flint knife hafted with fibre lashed round with a cord.

Occasionally flakes of quartz or other silicious stone were mounted at the end of short handles by the Australians, so as to form a kind of dagger or chisel. One such has been engraved by the Rev. J. G. Wood. [1320] Another is in the Museum of the Hartley Institution at Southampton.

In the Berlin Museum [1321] is a curious knife, found, I believe, in Prussia, which shows great skill in the adaptation of flint for cutting purposes. It consists of a somewhat lanceolate piece of bone, about 7 1/4 inches long, and at the utmost 1/2 inch wide, and 1/4 inch thick. The section is approximately oval, but along one of the narrow sides a groove has been worked, and in this are inserted a series of segments of thin flakes of flint, so carefully chosen as to be almost of one thickness, and so dexterously fitted together that their edges constitute one continuous sharp blade, projecting about three-sixteenths of an inch from the bone. In some examples from Scandinavia the flint flakes are let in on both edges of the blade. [1322] The flakes sometimes form barbs, as already mentioned.

The Mexican [1323] swords, formed of flakes of obsidian attached to a blade of wood, were of somewhat the same character, and remains of what appears to have been an analogous sword, armed with flint flakes, have been found in one of the mounds of the Iroquois country.

Another use to which pointed flint flakes have occasionally been applied is for the formation of fishing-hooks. Such a hook, the stem formed of bone, and the returning point made of flint bound at an acute angle to the end of the bone, has been engraved by Klemm. [1324] It was found in a grave in Greenland. Fishhooks formed entirely of flint, and found in Sweden, have been engraved by Nilsson, [1325] and others, presumed to have been found in Holderness, by Mr. T. Wright, F.S.A. [1326] These latter are, however, in all probability, forgeries.

Besides the flakes which may be regarded as merely tools for cutting or scraping, there are some which may with safety be reckoned as saws, their edges having been intentionally and regularly serrated, though in other respects they have been left entirely unaltered in form.

Fig. 199.—Willerby Wold. 1/1

Fig. 200.—Yorkshire Wolds. 1/1

A specimen, found in a pit which appeared to have been excavated by the primitive inhabitants of the district, at Brighthampton, Oxon, has been figured; [1327] and another oblong flint flake, with a regularly serrated edge, but the teeth not so deep or well defined as in this instance, was found by Dr. Thurnam in a chambered long barrow at West Kennet, Wilts, with numerous flakes and "scrapers." [1328]

Figs. 199 to 201 represent similar instruments in my own collection from the Yorkshire Wolds. The largest has been serrated on both edges, but has had the teeth much broken and worn away on the thinner edge.

Fig. 200 is very minutely toothed on both edges, and has a line of brilliant polish on each margin of its flat face, showing the friction the saw had undergone in use, not improbably in sawing bone or horn.

Fig. 201 is more coarsely serrated, and shows less of this characteristic polish, which is observable on a large proportion of these flint saws. The teeth are on many so minute that without careful examination they may be overlooked. Others, however, are coarsely toothed. Canon Greenwell has found saws in considerable numbers, and varying in the fineness of their serration, in the barrows on the Yorkshire Wolds, near Sherburn and elsewhere. In the soil of a single barrow at Rudstone there were no less than seventy-eight of these saws. Some have been found by Mr. E. Tindall in barrows near Bridlington, [1329] as well as on the surface. Some well-formed flint saws have also been found near Whitby, [1330] and some of small size at West Wickham, [1331] Kent. In the Greenwell Collection is a finely-toothed saw, made from a curved flake, found at Kenny Hill, Mildenhall.

Five flint saws, finely serrated, were found in a barrow at Seaford, [1332] and another on St. Leonard's Forest, [1333] Horsham. One was also found in a barrow on Overton Hill, [1334] Wilts. Seven saws, thirteen scrapers, and other worked flints were among the materials of another barrow at Rudstone. [1335]

The teeth are usually but not universally worked in the side edges of the flakes. In Fig. 202 it is the chisel-like broad end of a flake that has been converted into a saw. This specimen was found by the late Mr. J. W. Flower, F.G.S., in a barrow at West Cranmore, Somerset, in company with numerous flint flakes and "scrapers." A bronze dagger was found in the same barrow.

Near Newhaven, Sussex, I found on the downs a flat flake, about 2 1/2 inches long, and slightly curved sideways towards the point. At this part the inner curve is neatly worked into a saw, and the outer curve carefully chipped into a rounded edge as a scraping tool.

A flint knife serrated at the back to serve as a saw was found by Mr. Bateman in Liff's Low, near Biggin. [1336]

In Scotland several saws have been procured from the Culbin Sands, [1337] and near Glenluce. [1338] They are also recorded from Forglen, [1339] near Banff, and Craigsfordmains, [1340] Roxburghshire.

In Ireland, flakes converted into saws are scarce; they occur occasionally, though but rarely, with neolithic interments in France. In the Museum at le Puy is a very good specimen of a flat flake, neatly serrated with small teeth, found with a skeleton near that town. Another, found in a dolmen in Poitou, [1341] has been published by M. de Longuemar. Mortillet [1342] includes several forms under the general denomination of *scies*.

Fig. 201.—Scamridge. 1/1

Fig. 202.—West Cranmore. 1/1

Similar saws to those first described, and made from flakes more or less coarsely toothed, have been found in the cave-deposits of the Reindeer Period of the South of France, but in some caves, as, for instance, that at Bruniquel explored by M. V. Brun, they were much more abundant than in others. In the Vicomte de Lastic's cave at the same place but few occurred, and in most of the caves of the Dordogne they appear to be absent. An irregularly-notched flake was probably almost as efficient a saw as one more carefully and uniformly toothed.

Flakes of flint, carefully serrated at the edge, have been found in the Danish kjökken-möddings [1343]; in Posen, [1344] Prussia; and with relics of the Early Bronze Period in Spain. [1345] One is recorded from the Algerian Sahara. [1346] It has been suggested that some serrated flints were potters' tools, by which parallel mouldings were produced on vessels. [1347]

Among the more highly finished Scandinavian stone implements there is some difficulty in determining exactly which have served the purpose of saws. The flat, straight tapering instrument, with serrated edges, which, from its many teeth at regular distances from each other, Nilsson [1348] is disposed to think has probably been a saw, Worsaae [1349] regards as a lance-point. I am inclined to think that they were not saws, for on such specimens as I have examined minutely I find no trace of the teeth being polished by use. They cannot, however, in all cases have been lance-heads, as I have one of those serrated instruments, 8 1/4 inches long, with the sides nearly parallel and both ends square.

Some of the crescent-shaped [1350] blades have almost similar teeth on the straighter edge, and some of these are polished on both faces as if by being worked backwards and forwards in a groove, and have no polish between the teeth, such as would result from their being used crossways like combs. From this I infer that such specimens at all events have been used for cutting purposes, and not, as may have been the case with others, as instruments [1351] for dressing skins, or heckling flax or hemp. As has been pointed out by Professor J. J. Steenstrup, many of these crescent-shaped blades seem to have had their convex edges inserted in wooden handles, which would render them convenient for use as saws. Their action on wood, though not rapid, is effectual, and with the aid of a little water I have with one of them cut through a stick of dry sycamore seven-eighths of an inch in diameter in seven minutes. In Thomsen's [1352] opinion, these implements with teeth were intended for saws. Nilsson [1353] also regards some of them in the same light. The form seems to be confined to the North of Germany and Scandinavia. [1354] They are frequently found in pairs, one being smaller than the other. Mr. T. Wright, [1355] after engraving one of these Danish saws as a British specimen, remarks that several have been found in different parts of England. I believe this statement to be entirely without foundation, so far as this particular form is concerned.

I have left what I originally wrote upon this subject with very little modification, but Prof. Flinders Petrie's [1356] discoveries have thrown a flood of light upon the purposes for which serrated flints were used. We now know that the Egyptian sickle was formed of a curved piece of wood in shape much like the jaw-bone of a horse, armed along the inner edge with a series of serrated flint flakes, cemented into a groove. Not only are there numerous pictorial representations of such instruments going back so far as the 4th dynasty, but the sickles themselves have been found in a complete state, as well as numbers of the serrated flakes that formed their edge. Similar flakes, which no doubt served the same purpose, were found by Schliemann on the site of Troy. [1357] Others have been found at Helouan. [1358] The whole subject has been treated exhaustively by Mr. Spurrell, [1359] to whose paper the reader is referred. [1360] Dr. Munro is, however, inclined to regard most European examples as saws.

I now pass on to an instrument of very frequent occurrence in Britain.

CHAPTER XIII.
SCRAPERS.

One of the simple forms into which flakes are susceptible of being readily converted has, in consequence of its similarity in character to a stone implement in use among the Eskimos for scraping skins and other purposes, received the name of a "scraper," or to use the term first I believe employed by the late M. E. Lartet, a *grattoir*. A typical scraper may be defined as a broad flake, the end of which has been chipped to a semicircular bevelled edge round the margin of the inner face, similar in character to that of a "round-nosed turning chisel."

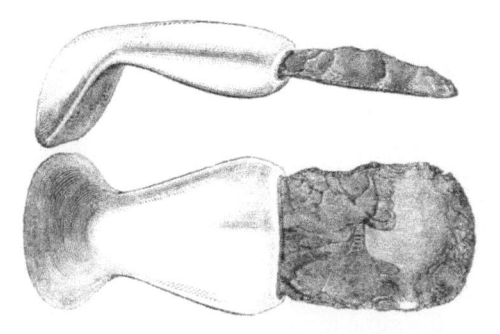

Fig. 203.—Eskimo Scraper.

A very good specimen of an Eskimo scraper of flint, mounted in a handle of fossil ivory, is in the Christy Collection, and has been engraved for the "Reliquiæ Aquitanicæ." [1361] For the loan of the woodcut, Fig. 203, there given, I am indebted to the representatives of the late Mr. Christy. Sometimes the hafts are of wood, and they have frequently indentations intended to receive the ends of the fingers and thumb, so as to secure a good grasp. In the collection of Sir John Lubbock is another specimen much like Fig. 203, with a flint blade almost like a lance-head in character, but with the more pointed end inserted in the handle; there is also another short straight-sided blade of jade bound in a wooden haft, which is notched along one side to receive the fingers, and recessed on the face for the thumb. This latter seems well adapted for use as a knife or chisel; in fact, Sir John Lubbock, who has figured the instruments in his "Prehistoric Times," [1362] terms them both knives. Another example has been engraved by the Rev. J. G. Wood. [1363]

These instruments are said to be used for scraping skins, [1364] for which indeed they seem well suited, if the flat face of the stone be held vertically to the hide that is to be scraped. The handles, however, are better adapted for pushing the scrapers forward on a flat surface, and judging from the wear upon them they must have been so used. The late Sir Edward Belcher [1365] has described them as Eskimo planes, for the manufacture of bows and other articles of wood, but in this respect he may have been mistaken.

The scrapers in use among the Fuegians [1366] are drawn towards the operator and not pushed. Some North American varieties are mounted after the manner of adzes. [1367] Mr. Otis T. Mason in his Paper "on Aboriginal skin-dressing" has exhaustively treated the subject.

A form of Skin-scraper, straight at the edge, was in use among the Pennacook tribe [1368] of North America, and though some of the Eskimo instruments may have been used as planes, no doubt many were employed in dressing hides. A peculiar form in use among the Gallas [1369] of Southern Shoa has been figured by Giglioli, [1370] who has also recorded the fact that flat scrapers of stone are still in use in Italy and France for dressing hides.

Whether the instruments were used vertically as scrapers, or horizontally as planes, the term "scrapers" seems almost equally applicable to them; and there appears no valid reason why, for the sake of convenience, the same term should not be extended to their ancient analogues, especially as their edges, as will subsequently be seen, are in many cases worn away in a manner indicative of their having been used for scraping.

The names of "thumb-flints" and "finger-flints" which have sometimes been applied to the shorter and longer varieties of these instruments, though colloquially convenient, appear to me not sufficiently definite in meaning to be worthy of being retained.

Scrapers may be classified and described—firstly, in accordance with the character of the flakes from which they have been made; and, secondly, in accordance with the outline of the portion of the margin which has been chipped into form, and the general contour of the implement.

Fig. 204.—Weaverthorpe.

Their outline is in some cases horseshoe-shaped or kite-shaped, in others it is discoidal or nearly circular, and in others again it may be compared with that of a duck's bill or of an oyster-shell. To these may be added side-scrapers, or such as are broader than they are long, and the hollow scrapers with a rounded notch in them instead of a semicircular end.

When the flakes have been chipped into the scraper form at both ends they may be termed double-ended scrapers—to which class circular scrapers also belong; where a sort of handle has been worked they may be termed spoon-shaped, and where the butt has been chipped to a sharp chisel-edge, at right angles to the flat face, they have been called tanged scrapers.

In speaking of the sides as right or left, I do it with reference to the flat face of the scraper, as shown in the first of the three views of Fig. 204.

It will be well to pass some of the forms in review before entering into any more general considerations.

The figures are all of full size, Fig. 204, from Weaverthorpe, on the Yorkshire Wolds, is a good example of a symmetrical horseshoe-shaped scraper. It is made from a broad flat flake, of rather pink flint, with the point chipped to a neat semicircular bevelled edge, and one of the sides trimmed so as to correspond with the other. The bulb of percussion visible on the flat face and side views has been slightly splintered by the blow. It gives a graceful ogee curve to the face longitudinally, which brings forward the scraping or cutting edge at the end. In the centre this is slightly rounded and worn away by use.

I have other specimens almost identical in form from other parts of the Yorkshire Wolds, from Suffolk, Sussex, and Dorsetshire. They are abundantly found of smaller dimensions, and occasionally of larger, sometimes as much as 2 1/2 inches in diameter.

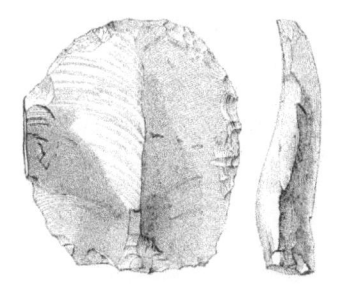

Fig. 205.—Sussex Downs.

Fig. 205 shows another horseshoe-shaped scraper, which has become white and grey by exposure. I picked it up on the Downs near Berling Gap, on the Sussex coast, a few miles west of Eastbourne; a district so prolific, that I have there found as many as twenty of these instruments, of various degrees of perfection, within an hour. In this case the scraper has been made from a broad ridged flake, and it will be observed that not only the end but one of the sides has been carefully trimmed, while the other has been left untouched, and has, moreover, a flat facet on it, as shown in the side view. It would appear from this that probably the side as well as the end was used for scraping purposes, that whoever used it was right-handed and not left-handed, and, moreover, that it is doubtful whether the implement was ever inserted in a handle, at all events at the butt-end. I have a nearly similar specimen, but trimmed at the end only, which I found in the *vallum* of the camp of Poundbury, near Dorchester, Dorset. I have smaller instruments of the same form which I have found on the surface of the ground at Abbot's Langley, Herts; at Oundle, Northamptonshire; and in the ancient encampment of Maiden Bower, near Dunstable. Large scrapers are abundant in some parts of Suffolk.

The form is of common occurrence in Yorkshire, in all sizes from 2 1/2 inches to one inch in length. To show the great range in size, and the variations in the relative thickness of the instruments, I have engraved, in Fig. 206, a small specimen from the Yorkshire Wolds.

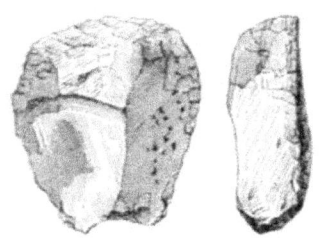

Fig. 206.—Yorkshire.

When the chipping to an edge is continued beyond a semicircle, in the case of scrapers made from broad short flakes, an almost circular instrument is the result. These discoidal scrapers are of extremely common occurrence on the Yorkshire Wolds. Fig. 207 shows a specimen from Helperthorpe.

Fig. 207.—Helperthorpe.

They are not unfrequently formed from external flakes or splinters, and are sometimes made from fragments broken from long flakes, inasmuch as there is no bulb of percussion on the flat face. In rare cases the flat face is the result of a natural fracture, and, more rarely still, it is the external face of a flint nodule.

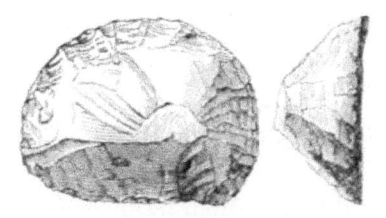

Fig. 208.—Weaverthorpe.

When the instrument is broader than it is long, it has been termed a side scraper. One in what is now white flint, made from a portion of a flake, and showing no bulb on the flat face, is engraved in Fig. 208. It was found at Weaverthorpe. Occasionally the arc is flatter and longer in proportion to the height than in this instance.

Fig. 209 may be called a long horseshoe-shaped scraper. It has been made from a thick flat flake, which there had evidently been some difficulty in shaping, as at least two blows had failed of their desired effect before the flake was finally dislodged. The back of the scraper is disfigured by the marks of the abortive flakes produced by these two blows. The end, and part of the right side are neatly trimmed into form. This specimen also I found on the Sussex Downs, near Berling Gap.

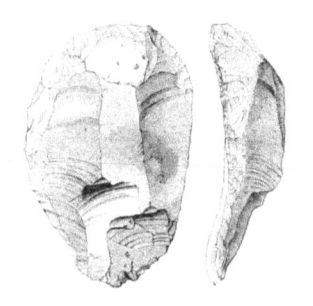

Fig. 209.—Sussex Downs.

Fig. 210.—Yorkshire.

Fig. 211.—Yorkshire Wolds.

The implements of this form are often neatly chipped along both sides as well as at the end. An example of the kind is given in Fig. 210, the original of which is in milky chalcedonic flint, and was found on the Yorkshire Wolds.

Fig. 211 shows another specimen from the Yorkshire Wolds. It is made from a flat flake, considerably curved longitudinally, and trimmed at the end as well as along a small portion of the left side. Some are more oval in form, and have been chipped along the sides, and somewhat rounded at the butt. In several instances the chipped edge at the butt-end is slightly worn away by friction, the edge of the rounded end being unworn.

Fig. 212.—Yorkshire Wolds.

Fig. 213.—Sussex Downs.

Fig. 212 gives a kite-shaped scraper from Yorkshire, also made from a flat flake, but showing a considerable extent of the original crust of the flint of which it was made. It comes almost to a point at the butt-end, and both edges are somewhat chipped away as if the instrument had at that end been used as a boring tool. The point is somewhat rounded by friction. Occasionally, scrapers of this form are chipped on both faces at the pointed base, so as to make them closely resemble arrow-heads. It seems possible that this pointing was for the purpose of hafting the tool more readily in wood.

Fig. 213 shows one of what may be termed the duck-bill scrapers. It is made from a flat flake as usual, somewhat curved, and showing all along one side the original crust of the flint. It is neatly worked to a semicircular edge at the end, but the sides are left entirely untouched. I found it on the Sussex Downs, near Cuckmare Haven.

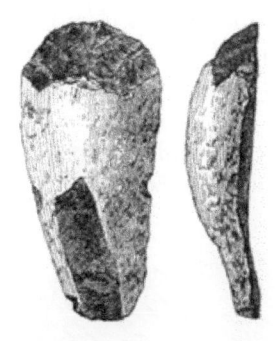

Fig. 214.—Yorkshire Wolds.

A smaller analogous instrument, from the Yorkshire Wolds, is shown in Fig. 214. It is made from an external flake, struck from a nodule of flint of small diameter. The end alone is trimmed. Scrapers made from such external flakes and splinters of flint are by no means uncommon. I have one which appears to have been made from a splinter of a hammer-stone—a portion of the surface being bruised all over.

In Fig. 215 is shown another duck-bill scraper, with parallel sides, found by myself on the Sussex Downs, near Berling Gap. It is a thick instrument, with both sides and end trimmed into form, the flake from which it is made having in all probability been originally much broader, and more circular. The bulb of percussion is not in the middle of the butt, but within three-eighths of an inch of the left side.

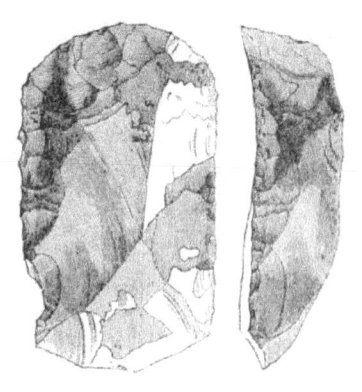

Fig. 215.—Sussex Downs.

Another form of these instruments is not unlike the flat valve of an oyster shell, being usually somewhat unsymmetrical either to the right or to the left. A specimen of this class from the Downs, near Berling Gap, is shown in Fig. 216. The end is neatly chipped to an almost elliptical sweep, but the sides in this instance are left untrimmed; the right side shown in the side view being flat and almost square with the face. In some instances the trimming of the sides extends all the way round to the butt.

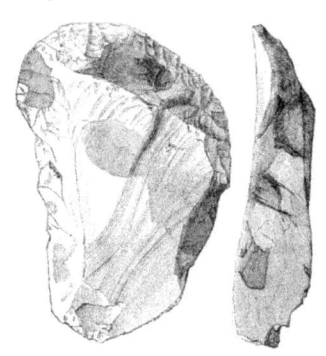

Fig. 216.—Sussex Downs.

Occasionally, though rarely, one of the sides, either right or left, is trimmed in such a manner that its more or less straight edge meets the curved edge of the end at an angle, so as to form an obtuse point. An example of this kind is shown in Fig. 217, from the Downs, near Berling Gap. This instrument is made from an external splinter of flint, the edge at the end and front of one side alone being carefully chipped into shape. It approaches in form to the *grattoir-bec* [1371] of French antiquaries.

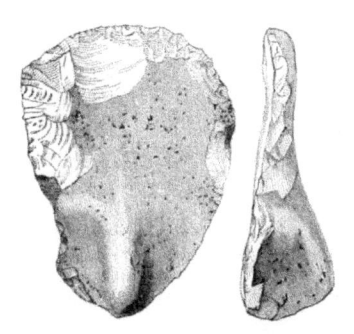

Fig. 217.—Sussex Downs.

In most scrapers the bulb of percussion of the flake from which they have been made is, as has already been said, at the opposite end to that which has been trimmed to form the curved edge; but this is by no means universally the case, for sometimes the bulb is at the side of the scraper, and sometimes, though more rarely, it has been at the end which has been worked to the scraper edge.

It seems needless to engrave examples of these varieties, which are only indicative of the manufacturers of the implements having made use of that part of the piece of flint which seemed best adapted to be chipped into the form they required. For the same reason we find scrapers of an endless variety of forms, some of them exceedingly irregular, as any one who has examined a series from the Yorkshire Wolds will know. I have not, however, thought it necessary to give representations of all these minor varieties, as even more than enough are engraved to show the general character of the instruments. It is perhaps worth mentioning, that the flakes selected for conversion into scrapers are usually such as expand in width at the point. It is doubtful whether the long narrow flakes worked to a scraper-like termination at one or both ends properly come under the category of scrapers. I shall consequently treat of them under the head of wrought flakes.

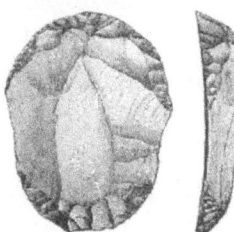

Fig. 218.—Bridlington.

Fig. 219.—Bridlington.

I must now pass on to the consideration of the forms showing a greater extent of trimming at the edge than those hitherto described. Of these the double-ended scrapers, or those presenting a semicircular edge at either end, first demand notice. They are of by no means common occurrence. Those I have seen have been for the most part found in Yorkshire and Suffolk. Fig. 218 exhibits a specimen from Bridlington. As is not unfrequently the case, it is rather thinner at the end nearest to what was the butt-end of the flake. The sides are left almost untrimmed, but each end is worked to a nearly semicircular curve. In the Greenwell Collection is a specimen from one of the barrows at Rudstone; as well as a large one from Lakenheath, and others from Suffolk. Occasionally the length and breadth are so nearly the same, that the scraper assumes the form of a disc, with sharp edges—a kind of plano-convex lens. A specimen of this form from Bridlington is shown in Fig. 219. It is, however, exceptionally regular in form. I have another smaller specimen, not quite so circular or so well chipped, which I found on the Downs between Newhaven and Brighton, and I have others from Suffolk. Such a form was probably not intended for insertion in a haft.

Fig. 220.—Yorkshire Wolds.

Sometimes, where the scraper has been made from a flat flake, the trimmed edge curves slightly inwards at one part, so as to produce a sort of ear-shaped form. I have such, both with the inward curve on the left side, as shown in Fig. 220, and also with it on the right side.

A deeply-notched tool, to which the name of hollow scraper has been applied, will be subsequently mentioned. [1372]

There are some scrapers which at the butt-end of the flake are chipped into what has the appearance of being a kind of handle, somewhat like that of a short spoon. That engraved in Fig. 221 is from the Yorkshire Wolds, and is in the collection of Messrs. Mortimer, of Driffield. It is chipped from both faces to an edge at each side in the handle-like part. I have an implement of the same character, found at Sewerby, the handle of which is slighter but less symmetrical. I have from the same district another large discoidal scraper, 1 3/4 inches in diameter, and chipped all round, with a rounded projection, about 3/4 of an inch wide, left at the thicker end of the flake.

The Greenwell Collection contains specimens of the same character as Fig. 221, found near Rudstone.

A nearly similar implement, in the Museum of the Royal Irish Academy, has been engraved by Sir W. Wilde. [1373]

Some of the large Danish scrapers are provided with a sort of handle, and have been termed by Worsaae [1374] "skee-formet," or spoon-shaped.

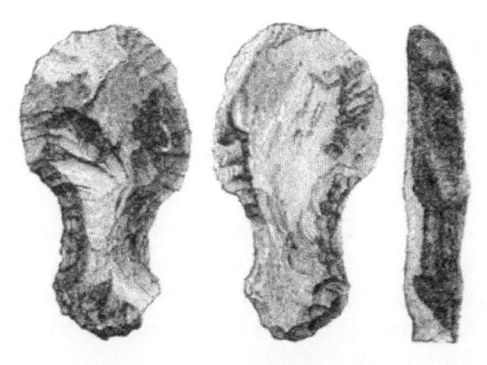

Fig. 221.—Yorkshire Wolds.

It will be well now to refer to some of the published notices of the discovery of these implements, which seem to have met with little attention from antiquaries until within the last forty years. There is, however, in the British Museum a fine horseshoe-shaped scraper, which was found long ago by the late Dr. Mantell, in company with broken urns and ashes, in a barrow on Windore Hill, near Alfriston. In the same collection are four or five others of various sizes from barrows on Lambourn Downs, Berks, as well as those from the Greenwell Collection. Sir R. Colt Hoare has recorded the discovery of what appear to be two discoidal scrapers, with a flint spear-head or dagger, a small hone or whetstone, and a cone and ring of jet, like a pulley, accompanying an interment, near Durrington Walls. [1375] He terms them little buttons of chalk or marl; but from the engraving it would seem that they were scrapers—probably of flint, much weathered, or altered in structure. It seems likely that many more may have escaped his notice, as they are of common occurrence in the tumuli in Wiltshire, as well as in the other parts of Britain. They are also recorded from Morgan's Hill [1376] and Winterbourn Stoke. The late Dean Merewether [1377] found several in barrows on Avebury Down, together with numerous flint flakes.

Some were found with burnt bodies in barrows at Cockmarsh, [1378] Berks, and others in a barrow at Great Shefford. [1379]

They occurred in barrows at Seaford, [1380] Sussex, and Lichfield, [1381] Hants, as well as in Devonshire [1382] barrows.

Ten or twelve were also found by Dr. Thurnam in the chambered Long Barrow, at West Kennet, [1383] with about three hundred flint flakes. There was no trace of metal, nor of cremation in this barrow.

A neat scraper was found in a hut-circle on Carn Brê, [1384] Cornwall.

In the Yorkshire barrows they abound in company both with burnt and unburnt bodies, [1385] without any metal being present. Canon Greenwell has in some cases found them with the edge worn smooth by use.

Mr. Bateman found many in Derbyshire barrows, as, for instance, at the head of a contracted skeleton on Cronkstone Hill, [1386] and with another contracted skeleton with two sets of Kimmeridge coal beads, at Cow Low, Buxton, [1387] and with four skeletons in a cist, in a barrow near Monsal Dale. [1388]

They not unfrequently occur with interments in association with bronze weapons. In a barrow on Parwich Moor, Staffordshire, [1389] called Shuttlestone, Mr. Bateman found a skeleton, with a bronze dagger at the left arm, and a plain flat bronze celt at the left thigh, and close to the head a jet bead and a "circular flint." As before stated, the late Mr. J. W. Flower, obtained three, and a bronze dagger, from the same barrow as the saw engraved at p. 266. They were also found with bronze in barrows in Rushmore Park. [1390]

They are frequently to be seen on the surface of the ground. One such, found by the late Mr. C. Wykeham Martin, F.S.A., at Leeds Castle, Kent, [1391] has been figured. Others from the neighbourhood of Hastings, [1392] the Isle of Thanet, [1393] and Bradford Abbas, Dorset, [1394] have also been engraved. Many of those from Bradford are said to have a notch on the left side, but I am doubtful whether it is intentional. Gen. Pitt Rivers has found them at Callow Hill, Oxon, [1395] and at Rotherley. They are also recorded from Holyhead Island, [1396] Anglesea, [1397] Tunbridge, [1398] Milton, [1399] and West Wickham, [1400] Kent; Stoke Newington, [1401] Middlesex; and Walton-on-the-Naze, [1402] Essex.

I have found them in considerable numbers in and near ancient encampments. At Maiden Bower, near Dunstable, a party of three or four have on more than one occasion picked up upwards of forty specimens. I have examples from Hod Hill, Badbury Rings, and Poundbury Camp, Dorsetshire; from Little Solsbury Hill, Bath; Pulpit Wood, near Wendover, Bucks, and several localities in Suffolk, Cambs, and other counties. Some are very thick, though quite symmetrical in outline. On the Yorkshire Wolds, the Sussex Downs, [1403] and in parts of Wilts and Suffolk, they are extremely numerous; but in any chalk country where flint is abundant, this form of implement can be found. In other districts, into which flint has to be imported, they are of course more scarce. They seem, however, to occur in greater or less abundance over the whole of England.

They are very numerous in Scotland, and extensive collections of them from Elgin, Wigtown, and other counties are to be seen in the National Museum at Edinburgh.

Specimens from a crannog in Ayrshire, [1404] Urquhart, Elgin, [1405] and Gullane Links, [1406] Haddingtonshire, have been published.

They are found of nearly similar forms in Ireland, but are there rarer than in England, though fairly numerous in Antrim. [1407]

In France the same form of instrument occurs, and I have a number of specimens from different parts of Belgium.

A spoon-shaped scraper from Neverstorff, [1408] Schleswig Holstein, is figured. They are likewise found in South Russia. [1409]

In Denmark scrapers of various forms are found, and are not uncommon in the kjökken-möddings and coast-finds. Sir John Lubbock [1410] records having picked up as many as thirty-nine scrapers at a spot on the coast of Jutland, near Aarhuus.

In the Swiss Lake-dwellings they occasionally occur. I have a fine, almost kite-shaped, specimen from Auvernier, given me by Professor Desor, and others from Nussdorf. Some are engraved by

Keller. They are also found in Italy. I have a small specimen from the Isle of Elba.

I possess specimens formed of obsidian, from Mexico; and instruments of jasper, of scraper-like forms, have been found at the Cape of Good Hope. [1411] As already mentioned, they are well known in America. Some are found in Newfoundland. [1412]

Instruments of the same character date back to very remote times, as numbers have been found in the cave deposits of the Reindeer Period of the South of France, as well as in a few in our English bone caves, as will subsequently be mentioned. A somewhat similar form occurs, though rarely, among the implements found in the ancient River Gravels.

Besides being used for scraping hides, and preparing leather, it has been suggested, by Canon Greenwell, [1413] that they might have served for making pins and other small articles of bone, and also for fabricating arrow-heads and knives of flint. As to this latter use I am doubtful, but before entering into the question of the purposes which implements of the "scraper" form were in ancient times intended to serve, it will be well to examine the evidence of wear afforded by the implements themselves. This evidence is various in its character, and seems to prove that the implements were employed in more than one kind of work.

Among some hundreds of scrapers, principally from the Yorkshire Wolds, I have met with between twenty and thirty which show decided marks of being worn away along the circular edge, by friction. In some, the edge is only worn away sufficiently to remove all keenness or asperity, and to make it feel smooth to the touch, and this perhaps along one part only of the arc. In others, the whole edge is completely rounded, and many of the small facets by which it was originally surrounded, entirely effaced. The small striæ, resulting from the friction which has rounded the edge, are at right angles to the flat face of the implement, and the whole edge presents the appearance of having been worn away by scraping some comparatively soft substance—such, for instance, as leather. When we consider what an important part the skins of animals play in the daily life of most savage tribes, and especially of those exposed to a cold climate; and when we remember the amount of preparation, in the way of dressing and scraping, the hides require before they can be available for the purposes of clothing, or even tent making, it becomes evident that some instruments must have been in use by the ancient occupants of the country for the purpose of dressing skins; and the probability of these scrapers having been devoted to this purpose is strengthened by their being worn in just such a manner as they would have been, had they been in use for scraping some greasy dressing off not over-clean leather. The scrapers thus worn away are for the most part of the horseshoe form. There are some, however, which have the edge worn away, not at the circular end but along the edge towards the butt. In this case also they appear to have been employed for scraping, but the evidence as to the character of the substance scraped is not so distinct. It is, however, probable that in the fashioning of perforated axes and other implements, made of greenstone and other rocks not purely silicious, some scraping as well as grinding tools may have been employed, and possibly the wear of the edge of some of these tools may be due to such a cause. Even among the cave-dwellers of the Dordogne we find scrapers bearing similar marks of attrition, and we also know that flint flakes were used for scraping the hard hæmatitic iron ore, to produce the red pigment—the paint with which the men of those times seem to have adorned themselves. [1414]

It will of course be urged that it is, after all, only a small proportion of these implements which bear these unmistakeable marks of wear upon them. It must, however, be remembered, that to produce much abrasion of the edge of an instrument made of so hard a material as flint, an enormous amount of wear against so soft a substance as hide would be necessary. It is indeed possible that the edge would remain for years comparatively unworn were the substance to be scraped perfectly free from grit and dirt. If we find identically the same forms of instruments, both worn and unworn, there is a fair presumption that both were intended for the same purpose, though the one, from accidental causes, has escaped the wear and tear visible on the other.

There are, however, circumstances which in this case point to an almost similar form having served two totally distinct purposes; for besides those showing the marks of use already described, we find some of these instruments with the edge battered and bruised to such an extent that it can hardly have been the result of scraping in the ordinary sense of the word.

To account for such a character of wear, there seems no need of going so far afield as among the Eskimos, or any other semi-civilized or savage people, to seek for analogies on which to base a conclusion—how far satisfactory it must be left to others to judge. Among the primary necessities of man (who has been defined as a cooking animal) is that of fire. It is no doubt a question difficult of solution whether our primitive predecessors were acquainted with any more ready means of producing it than by friction of two pieces of wood, especially at a time when there is reason to suppose they were unacquainted with the existence of iron as a metal. I have, however, already mentioned [1415] that for the purpose of producing sparks, pyrites is as effective as iron, and was indeed in use among the Romans. Now the lower beds of our English chalk are prolific of pyrites, though not to the same extent as the upper beds are of flint; and it is not impossible that the use of a hammer-stone of pyrites, in order to form some instrument of flint, gave rise to the discovery of that method of producing fire, the invention of which the old myth attributed to Pyrodes, the son of Cilix. When exposed upon or near the surface of the ground, pyrites is very liable to decomposition, and even if occurring with ancient interments it would be very likely to be disregarded. This may account for the paucity of the notices of its discovery. Some, however, exist, and I have already mentioned [1416] instances where nodules of pyrites have been discovered on the Continent in association with worked flints, both of Neolithic and Palæolithic age.

There are also instances of its occurrence in British barrows. That careful observer, the late Mr. Thomas Bateman, found, in the year 1844, in a barrow on Elton Moor, [1417] near the head of a skeleton, "a piece of spherical iron pyrites, now for the first time noticed as being occasionally found with other relics in the British tumuli. Subsequent discoveries," he says, "have proved that it was prized by the Britons, and not unfrequently deposited in the grave, along with the weapons and ornaments which formed the most valued part of their store." With the same skeleton, in a "drinking-cup," with a small celt and other objects of flint, was a flat piece of polished iron ore, and twenty-one "circular instruments." In another barrow, Green Low, [1418] Mr. Bateman discovered a contracted skeleton, having behind the shoulders a drinking-cup, a splendid flint dagger, a piece of spherical pyrites or iron ore, and a flint instrument of the circular-headed form. Lower down were barbed flint arrow-heads and some bone instruments. In Dowe Low, [1419] a skeleton was accompanied by a bronze dagger and an "amulet or ornament of iron ore," together with a large flint implement that had seen a good deal of service. A broken nodule of pyrites showing signs of friction was found with a bronze dagger in a barrow at Angrowse [1420] Mullion, Cornwall. In a barrow at Brigmilston, [1421] between Everley and Amesbury, Sir R. Colt Hoare found, with an urn containing ashes, "the fragment of a bone article like a whetstone, some chipped flints prepared for arrow-heads, a long piece of flint and a *pyrites*, both evidently smoothed by usage."

A piece of iron pyrites with a groove worn in it and a peculiarly shaped implement of flint with evident marks of use at the larger end were found with an interment near Basingstoke Station. [1422] Flint arrow-heads and flakes were also present.

Nodules of pyrites occurred in such numbers in a barrow on Broad Down, [1423] near Honiton, as to suggest the idea of their having been placed there designedly, but none of them are described as abraded.

We have here, at all events, instances of the association of lumps of iron pyrites with circular-ended flint instruments in ancient interments. Can they have been in use together for producing fire? In order to judge of this our best guide will probably be, so far at all events as the flints are concerned, those in use for the same purpose in later times, and even at the present day.

In the Abbé Hamard's researches at Hermes [1424] (Oise), two flint scrapers mounted in wooden handles round which were iron ferrules are said to have been discovered in Merovingian graves.

Fig. 222.—French "Strike-a-Light."

The Abbé Cochet [1425] describes some of the flints found with Merovingian interments as resembling gun-flints; one of these was apparently carried at the waist, in a purse with money and other necessaries. A steel and a small piece of flint were found in a Saxon grave at High Down, Ferring, [1426] Sussex. A similar practice of carrying in the pocket a piece of flint and some prepared tinder prevails in some parts of Europe to the present day; and, as I have before remarked, flints for this purpose are articles of sale. Fig. 222 shows one of these modern "strike-a-lights" which I purchased some years ago at Pontlevoy, in France. It is made of a segment of a flake, one edge and the sides of which have been trimmed to a scraper-like edge, and the other merely made straight. The resemblance between this and some of the ancient "scrapers" is manifest. Another strike-a-light flint, which I bought at a stall in Trier, is about 2 inches long by 1 3/8 inches broad, and is made from a flat flake, trimmed to a nearly square edge at the butt-end, and to a very flat arc at the point, both the trimmed edges being of precisely the same character as those of scrapers. I find, moreover, that by working such a flint and a steel or *briquet* together, much the same bruising of the edge is produced as that apparent on some of the old "scrapers." I come, therefore, to the conclusion, that a certain proportion of these instruments were in use, not for scraping hides like the others, but for scraping iron pyrites, and not improbably, in later days, even iron or steel for procuring fire. Were they used for such a purpose we can readily understand why they should so often present a bruising of the edge and an irregularity of form. We can also find a means of accounting for their great abundance.

Looking at the question from a slightly different point of view, this method of solution receives additional support. Everyone will, I think, readily concede that, putting for the moment pyrites out of the question, the inhabitants of this country must have been acquainted with the method of producing fire by means of flint and steel or iron, at all events so long ago as when their intercourse with the Romans commenced, if not at an even earlier period. We may, in any case, assume that flints have been in use as fire-producing agents for something like 2,000 years, and that consequently the number of them that have thus served must be enormous. What has become of them all? They cannot, like some antiquities, be "only now rare because they were always valueless," for in their nature they are almost indestructible. Many, no doubt, were mere irregular lumps of flint, broken from time to time to produce such an edge as would scrape the steel; but is it not in the highest degree probable that many were of the same class as those sold for the same purpose at the present day—flakes chipped into a more or less scraper-like form at one end?

There is yet another argument. In many instances these circular-ended flints, when found upon the surface, have a comparatively fresh and unweathered appearance; and, what is more, have the chipped parts stained by iron-mould. In some cases there are particles of iron, in an oxidized condition, still adherent. Such iron marks, especially on flint which has weathered white, may, and indeed commonly do, arise from the passage of harrows and other agricultural implements, and of horses shod with iron, over the fields; but did the marks arise merely from this cause, it appears hardly probable that in any instance they should be confined to the chipped edge, and not occur on other parts of the flint.

Fig. 223.—Rudstone.

I had written most of the foregoing remarks when, in November, 1870, an interesting discovery, made by Canon Greenwell, F.R.S., in his exploration of a barrow [1427] at Rudstone, near Bridlington, in Yorkshire, came to corroborate my views. I have already described a whetstone found with one of the interments in this barrow, and mentioned that between the knees and the head were found, with other objects, the half of a nodule of iron pyrites, and a long round-ended flake of flint which lay underneath it. They are both represented full size in accompanying figure (Fig. 223). A portion of the outside of the pyrites has been ground smooth, and a projecting knob has been worked down, so as to bring it to an approximately hemispherical shape, and adapt it for being comfortably held in the hand. The fractured surface, where the nodule was broken in two, is somewhat oval, and in the centre, in the direction of the longer diameter, is worn a wide shallow groove, of just the same character as would have been produced by constant sharp scraping blows from a round-ended flake or scraper, such as that which was found with it. The whole surface is somewhat worn and striated, in the same direction as the principal central groove; and the edge of the flat face of the pyrites is more worn away at the top and bottom of the groove than at the other parts.

The scraper is made from a narrow thick external flake, the end of which has been trimmed to a semicircular bevelled edge—a portion of one side has also been trimmed. At the end, and along some parts of the sides, this edge is worn quite smooth, and rounded by friction, and there are traces of similar wear at the butt-end. In a second grave in the same barrow there lay, behind the back, two jet buttons and a similar pyrites and flint. There can, I think, be no reasonable doubt of their having been, in these instances, fire-producing implements, used in the manner indicated in the annexed figure. The finding of the two materials together, in two separate instances, in both of which the pyrites and the flint presented the same forms and appearance, establishes the fact of their connection; and it is hard to imagine any other purpose for which pyrites could be scraped by flint except that of producing fire. Moreover, in another barrow on Crosby Garrett Fell, [1428] Westmoreland, Canon Greenwell found a piece of iron ore (oxidized pyrites) held in the hand of a skeleton, and a long thick flake of flint, evidently a "flint and steel."

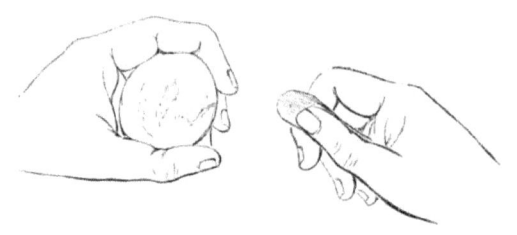

Fig. 224.—Method of using Pyrites and "Scraper" for Striking a Light.

It cannot have been merely for the purpose of producing a paint or colour that they were brought together, as though the outer crust of a nodule of pyrites might, if ground, give a dull red pigment, yet the inner freshly-broken face would not do so; and, if it would, the colour would be more readily procured by grinding on a flat stone than by scraping. It would be interesting to compare these objects with the pyrites and pebbles in use among the Fuegians [1429], who employ dried moss or fungus by way of tinder, but appear to find some difficulty in producing fire. The Eskimos [1430] and some North American tribes also obtain fire from pyrites.

Sir Wollaston Franks has called my attention to another half nodule of pyrites preserved in the British Museum, which is somewhat abraded in the middle of its flat face, though not so much so as that from Yorkshire. It was discovered with flint flakes in a barrow on Lambourn Down, [1431] Berkshire, by Mr. E. Martin Atkins, in 1850. In a barrow at Flowerburn, [1432] Ross-shire, in 1885, a similar half nodule and a flint scraper were found, and a discovery of the same kind was made by Lord Northesk, at Teindside, [1433] near Minto, Roxburghshire, about 1870. A fine piece of pyrites in company with worked flints was found in 1881, in a ruined dolmen, in the Ile d'Arz, [1434] Brittany, by the Abbé Luco. A well striated block of pyrites was also found with numerous objects formed of flint and other kinds of stone, on the Rocher de Beg-er-Goallenner, Quiberon, by M. F. Gaillard. [1435]

A nodule of pyrites, with a deep scoring upon it, and found in one of the Belgian bone caves, the *Trou de Chaleux*, has been engraved by Dr. E. Dupont, [1436] who regards it as having been used as a fire-producing agent. The flint that produced the scoring appears to have had a pointed, rather than a rounded end. Possibly the wearing away of the ends of certain flakes, for which it has been difficult to account, may be due to their having been used in this manner for striking a light.

There are yet some other long flakes which are trimmed to a scraper-like edge at one or both ends; but in these cases the trimming appears to have been rather for the purpose of enabling the flake to be conveniently held in the hand, so as to make use of its cutting edge, than with the intention of converting the trimmed end into a scraping or cutting tool. The ends of some of the hafted knives or saws found in the Swiss Lake-dwellings are thus trimmed.

On the whole, we may conclude, with some appearance of probability, that a certain proportion of these instruments, and more especially those of regular shape, and those of large size, were destined to be used as scrapers in the process of dressing hides and for other purposes; that others again, and chiefly those of moderate size with bruised and battered edges, were used at one period with iron pyrites, and at a subsequent date with iron or steel, for the production of fire; and lastly that others have had their ends trimmed into shape, so as to render them symmetrical in form, or to enable them to be conveniently handled or hafted.

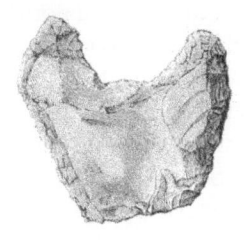

Fig. 225.—Yorkshire Wolds.

Fig. 226.—Yorkshire Wolds.

There are still one or two other forms to which, from the character of their edge, the designation of scraper may be given. The instrument from the Yorkshire Wolds, shown in Fig. 225, may, for instance, be called a straight scraper. It is made from a broad flat flake, with a well-developed bulb of percussion on the face, and the counterpart of another at the back, so that the section at the base is much curved. The point of the flake and its left side have been chipped away, so that they are nearly straight, and form between them an angle of about 60°. The edge is sharper, and the form, I think, more regular than if it had been used in conjunction with pyrites or steel, and I am therefore inclined to regard it as a tool. The late Mr. Charles Monkman, who gave me this specimen, also gave me another, more crescent-shaped in form, the base being roughly chipped to a regular sweep. I have another larger flint, similar to Fig. 225, found by the late Mr. Whitbourn, F.S.A., in the neighbourhood of Godalming. Before pronouncing definitely as to the degree of antiquity to be assigned to such instruments, it will be well to have authenticated instances of their discovery in association with other remains, and not merely on the surface. In character, however, they much resemble other flint instruments of undoubtedly high antiquity, though they present the peculiarity of having the edge at right angles to the axis of the flake from which they are made, instead of being parallel to it.

A singular flint instrument of a rudely heart-shaped form, with one straight serrated edge, is figured with other tools, &c., from the Culbin Sands. [1437]

To another of these forms, of which a not very first-rate example is given in Fig. 226, the designation of hollow scraper may be applied, the scraping edge being concave, instead of as usual, convex. This specimen also is from the Yorkshire Wolds. I have, however, found analogous instruments on the Sussex Downs, the hollowed edges of which appear to have been used for scraping some cylindrical objects. In Ireland this form not unfrequently occurs. I have several specimens with the hollow as regular in its sweep as any of the scrapers of the ordinary form, and I have thought it advisable to figure a typical example as Fig. 226A. They seem well adapted for scraping into regular shape the stems of arrows or the shafts of spears, or for fashioning bone pins. Among modern artificers in wood, bone, ivory, or metal, scraping tools play a far more important part than would at first sight appear probable, looking at the abundance and perfection of our cutting tools and files. The latter, indeed, are merely compound forms of "scrapers."

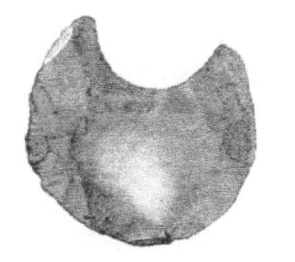

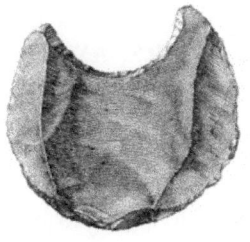

Fig. 226A.—North of Ireland.

A less symmetrical hollow scraper from the Culbin Sands [1438] has been engraved; as has been another which Dr. Joseph Anderson [1439] used in the production of an arrow-shaft, and which he found to be a very efficient tool. Some writers have regarded these hollow-edged scrapers as saws [1440], but I think erroneously.

Implements of the same character have been found in Egypt [1441], and in France, and probably exist in other countries.

CHAPTER XIV.
BORERS, AWLS, OR DRILLS.

Another of the purposes to which flint flakes were applied appears to have been that of boring holes in various materials. Portions of stags' horns, destined to serve either as hammers, or as sockets for hatchets of stone, had either to be perforated or to have recesses bored in them; and holes in wood were, no doubt, requisite for many purposes, though in this country we have but few wooden relics dating back to the time when flint was the principal if not the only material for boring-tools. To form some idea of the character of the objects in the preparation of which such tools were necessary, we cannot do better than refer to the vivid picture of ancient life placed before us by the discoveries in the Swiss Lake-dwellings. Besides perforated stone axes and hammers, such as have been already described in these pages, we find stag's horn and wooden hafts or helves, with holes and sockets bored in them, plates of stone, teeth of animals, bone and stag's horn instruments, and wooden knife handles pierced for suspension, and portions of bark perforated, so as to serve like corks for floating fishing-nets.

Even in the caverns of the Reindeer Period of the South of France we find the reindeer horns with holes bored through them in regular rows, and delicate needles of hard bone with exquisitely formed eyes drilled through them—one of which has also been found in Kent's Cavern—as well as teeth, shells and fossils perforated for suspension as ornaments or amulets. So beautifully are the eyes in these ancient needles formed, that I was at one time much inclined to doubt the possibility of their having been drilled by means of flint flakes; but the late Mons. E. Lartet demonstrated the feasibility of this process, by himself drilling the eye of a similar needle with a flint borer, found in one of the French caves. I have myself bored perfectly round and smooth holes through both stag's horn and wood with flint flakes, and when a little water is used to facilitate the operation, it is almost surprising to find how quickly it proceeds, and how little the edge of the flint suffers when once its thinnest part has been worn or chipped away, so as to leave a sufficient thickness of flint to stand the strain without being broken off.

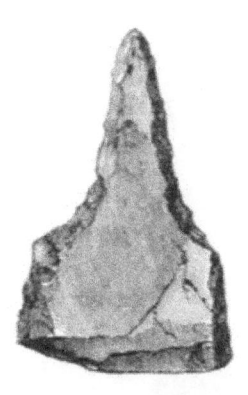

Fig. 227.—Yorkshire Wolds. 1/1

The most common form of boring tool, to which by some writers the name of awl or drill [1442] has been given, is that shown in Fig. 227, from the Yorkshire Wolds. It is formed from a flat splinter of flint, and shows the natural crust of the stone at the broad end. At the other, each edge has been chipped away from the flat face, so as to reduce it by a rapid curve on each side to a somewhat tapering blade, with a sharp point. The section of this portion of the blade is almost of the form of half a hexagon when divided by a line joining opposite angles. A borer of this kind makes a very true hole, as whether turned round continuously or alternately in each direction, it acts as a half-round broach or rimer, enlarging the mouth of the hole all the time it is being deepened by the drilling of the point. The broad base of the flake serves as a handle by which to turn the tool. Several boring instruments of this form were found in the pits at Grime's Graves, [1443] already so often mentioned.

A borer of this kind has been experimentally [1444] tried and found efficient for drilling a hole in jet.

Fig. 228. Bridlington. 1/1

Borers of the same character occur in Ireland [1445] and in Scotland, [1446] where natural crystals [1447] of quartz seem also occasionally to have been used as drills. I have also seen several found near Pontlevoy, France, in the collection of the Abbé Bourgeois.

Similar boring instruments of flint have been found in Denmark, in company with scrapers and other tools. Two of them have been engraved by Mr. C. F. Herbst. [1448]

They are common in some parts of North America, and finely chipped tools of the kind occur in Patagonia. [1449] They are also found in Natal [1450] and in Japan.

Sometimes the borer consists of merely a long narrow pointed flake, which has had the point trimmed to a scraping edge on either side. A specimen of the kind, found near Bridlington, is shown in Fig. 228. The point, for about a sixteenth of an inch in width, has been ground to a nearly square edge, so that it acts like a drill. Such a form was probably attached to a wooden handle for use, but I doubt whether any mechanical means were used for giving it a rotary motion as a drill, and regard these borers rather as hand-tools to be used much in the same way as a broach or rimer.

Some implements from the lake settlement at Meilen, regarded by Dr. Keller [1451] as awls or piercers, are perforated at one end, and appear to be ground over their whole surface.

Occasionally some projecting spur at the side of the flake has been utilized to form the borer, as is the case in Fig. 229, also from the

Yorkshire Wolds. In this instance, the two curved sweeps, by which the boring part of the tool is formed, have been chipped from the opposite faces of the flake, so that the cutting edges are at opposite angles of the blade, which is of rhomboidal section. This is the case with some of the Scottish specimens, [1452] which closely resemble Fig. 229. Such a tool seems best adapted for boring by being turned in the hole continuously in one direction. In some instances the projecting spur is so short that it can have produced but a very shallow cavity in the object to be bored.

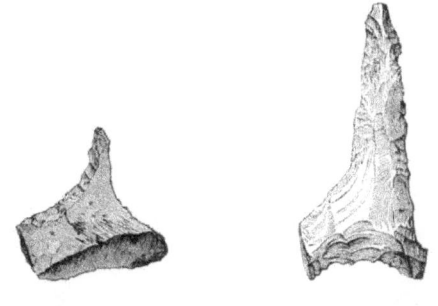

Fig. 229.—Yorkshire Wolds. 1/1

Fig. 230.—Bridlington. 1/1

The tools, of which a specimen is shown in Fig. 230, also appear to have been intended for boring. It is, however, possible that after all they may have served some other purpose. That here engraved was found near Bridlington, and is weathered white all over. It is made from a flake, and the edge of the blade on the left in the figure is formed as usual by chipping from the flat face. The other edge is more acute, and has been formed by secondary chipping on both faces. The spur to the left, which may have served as a handle for turning the tool round when in use, has originally been longer, but the end has been lost through an ancient fracture. The edges at the point of the tool are somewhat worn away by friction.

I am uncertain whether the instruments shown in Figs. 231 and 232 can be with propriety classed among boring tools, as it is possible that they may have been intended and used for some totally different purpose, such, for instance, as forming the tips of arrows, for which, from their symmetrical form, they are not ill adapted. Though the points of those, like Fig. 231, are much rounded, it may be that they were mounted like the chisel-edged Egyptian flint arrow-heads, of which hereafter. A number of instruments of this form have been found in Derbyshire and Suffolk, but that here figured came from the Yorkshire Wolds, and has been made from a part of a thin flat flake, one edge of which forms the base opposite to the semicircular point. The side edges, which expand with a sweep to the base, are carefully chipped to a sharp angle with the face of the flake; but in some instances this secondary working extends over a greater or less portion of both faces. Some specimens are also much longer in their proportions. The original edge of the flake, which extends along the base, is usually unworn by use, so that if these objects were boring tools this part may have been protected by being inserted in a notch in a piece of wood, which in such a case would serve as a handle for using the tool after the manner of an auger. A few examples of this kind have been found on the Culbin Sands [1453], Elginshire. The same form has been found in the Camp de Chassey [1454] (Saône et Loire).

Fig. 231.—Yorkshire Wolds. 1/1

Fig. 232.—Yorkshire Wolds. 1/1

Fig. 232 is also from the Yorkshire Wolds. Though more acutely pointed than Fig. 231, it seems to have been intended for much the same purpose, and it has been formed in a similar manner. The secondary working is principally on the convex face of the flake, but owing to an irregularity in the surface of the flat face, a portion of it has been removed by secondary chipping along one edge, so as to bring it as nearly as possible in the same plane as the other. For whatever purpose this instrument may have been designed, its symmetry is remarkable.

I have a somewhat similar instrument from Bridlington, but triangular in form, with the sides curved slightly inwards, and the two most highly wrought edges produced by chipping almost equally on both faces of the flake. Such a form approximates most closely to some of those which there appears reason for regarding as triangular arrow-heads. In America, some forms which might be taken for arrow-heads have been regarded as drills.

There is a series of minute tools of flint to which special attention has been called by Mr. J. Allen Brown, F.G.S., the Rev. Reginald A. Gatty [1455], and Mr. W. J. Lewis Abbott, F.G.S. [1456] Through the kindness of the last, specimens from a kjökken mödding at Hastings are shown in Figs. 232A, 232B, and 232C. They have been made from small flakes and are of various forms, though I have only selected three for illustration. In two of these the end of the flake has been chipped into a straight scraping edge at an acute angle to the body of the flake, so as to form a tool which can be held in the hand and used for scraping a flat surface, perhaps of bone. Whether the chipping of the edge is intentional or the result of wear, or arising partly from both of these causes, is a question of secondary importance. The oblique ends resemble those of the flakes from Kent's Cavern, Figs. 398–400, and the *selci romboidale* [1457] of Italian antiquaries. In the other form, one side of a flake has been chipped in a similar manner, so as to form a segment of a circle, or occasionally an obtuse angle; the other side being left intact. This may possibly have been inserted in wood, and the tool thus formed may have been used for scraping or carving. Mr. Abbott disagrees with this view, and thinks that many of the flakes may have been utilized in the formation of fish-hooks. Such tools have been found in Lancashire, far from the sea, and a series from hills in the eastern part of that county has been presented to the British Museum by Dr. Colley March. Owing to their diminutive size they may readily escape observation. Mr. Gatty has found some thousands of these "Pygmy flints" on the surface in the valley of the Don between Sheffield and Doncaster. They no doubt exist in many other districts.

Fig. 232A.	Fig. 232B.	Fig. 232C.	Fig. 232D.	Fig. 232E.	Fig. 232F.
Hastings. 1/1			Vindhya Hills. 1/1		

Curiously enough, identical forms have been found in some abundance on the Vindhya Hills [1458] and the Banda district, India; at Helouan, [1459] Egypt, in France, and in the district of the Meuse, [1460] Belgium. Such an identity of form at places geographically so remote does not imply any actual communication between those who made the tools, but merely shows that some of the requirements of daily life, and the means at command for fulfilling them being the same, tools of the same character have been developed, irrespective of time or space.

CHAPTER XV.
TRIMMED FLAKES, KNIVES, ETC.

Besides being converted into round-ended scrapers, and pointed boring-tools, flint flakes were trimmed on one or both faces into a variety of forms of cutting, scraping, and piercing tools, and weapons. In one direction these forms pass through daggers and lance-heads, into javelin and arrow heads; and in another through cutting tools, wrought into symmetrical shape, and ground at the edges, into hatchets or celts adapted for use in the hand without being hafted.

Fig. 233.—Cambridge (1). 1/2

The first I shall notice are flakes trimmed into form by secondary working on both edges, but only on the convex face, the flat face being left either almost or quite intact. The illustrations of these forms are no longer full size, but on the scale of one half, linear measure.

The simplest form of such instruments is when merely the edge of the flake is worked, so as to reduce it to a regular leaf-like shape. A beautiful specimen of this kind is preserved in the Christy Collection, and is shown in Fig. 233. It was probably found in the neighbourhood of Cambridge, having formed part of the collection of the late Mr. Litchfield of that town. It is of grey flint, curved lengthwise, as is usually the case with flint flakes, and worked to a point at each end, though rather more rounded at the butt-end of the flake. Such instruments have sometimes been regarded as poignards, though not improbably they were used for various cutting and scraping purposes.

They rarely occur in Britain of so great a length as this flake, which is 5 1/2 inches long, but those of shorter proportions are not uncommon.

In Ireland also the long flakes are scarce.

In France they are more abundant, though still rare. Some of those formed from the Pressigny flints were, judging from the cores, as much as 12 inches long, but none have as yet been found of this length. One trimmed on both edges, and 8 1/4 inches long, was dredged from the bed of the Seine [1461] at Paris, and is now in the Musée d'Artillerie, with another nearly as long found about the same time in the same place. Both appear to be of Pressigny flint. Others have been found in different parts of France. [1462] A beautiful flake, 8 3/4 inches long, trimmed on its external face, and found near Soissons, [1463] was in the collection of M. Boucher de Perthes. I have one of the same character, 8 1/2 inches long and 1 3/8 inches broad in the middle, most symmetrically shaped and perfectly uninjured, which was formerly in the collection of M. Meillet, of Poitiers. It is said to have been found at Savanseau, and in places has a red incrustation upon it, as if it had been embedded in a cave. In the Grotte de St. Jean d'Alcas, [1464] was found a blade of the same kind, together with some lance-heads of flint worked on both faces. Occasionally they are found in the dolmens. The *Allée couverte* [1465] of Argenteuil furnished one, 7 1/4 inches long; and one of the dolmens in the Lozère [1466] another, 8 inches in length. One almost 10 inches long and 1 inch broad, found at Neuilly-sur-Eure, [1467] has on the convex face the delicate secondary working, like ripple marks, such as is seen in perfection on some of the Danish and Egyptian blades of flint.

Others have been found in the dolmen at Caranda [1468] (Aisne), du Charnier [1469] (Ardèche), and in the Grotte Duruthy (Landes). [1470]

Curiously enough, the long flakes found in some abundance in Scandinavia are rarely, if ever, worked on the convex face alone, but are either left in their original form, or converted by secondary working on both faces, into some of the more highly finished tools or weapons.

In the Swiss Lake-dwellings flakes trimmed at the edges and ends are of not unfrequent occurrence. Some of these, as already described, have been regarded as saws.

Two long trimmed flakes, from Chevroux, tied to wooden handles, both string and handle partially preserved, are in the Museum at Lausanne. [1471] There is a small pommel at the end of the handle.

A remarkably fine Italian specimen of a ridged flake, 11 inches in length, and carefully trimmed along both edges, is in the British Museum. It is stated to have been found at Telese, near Pæstum. [1472]

Many of these trimmed flakes, as well as in some cases those entirely untrimmed, have been called by antiquaries spear-heads and lance-heads. They have frequently been found with interments in barrows.

Not to mention numerous instances recorded by Mr. Bateman, I may cite a flake found in company with a barbed flint arrow-head at the foot of a contracted skeleton in a barrow [1473] at Monkton Down, Avebury, and a "triangular spear-head of stone curiously serrated at the edges," found with a flint arrow-head and perforated boar's tusk, in an urn at the foot of a skeleton, in a barrow on Ridgeway Hill, [1474] Dorsetshire.

Among the flint implements occurring on the surface of the Yorkshire Wolds and elsewhere, flakes trimmed to a greater or less extent along both edges, and over the convex face, are frequently found. The point as well as the base is often neatly rounded, though the former is sometimes chipped to a sharp angle.

There is a considerable difference in the inclination of the edge to the face, it being sometimes at an angle of 60° or upwards, like the edge of some scrapers, at other times acute like a knife-edge.

There is so great a range in the dimensions and proportions of this class of instruments that it is almost impossible to figure all the varieties. I have, therefore, contented myself with the selection of a few examples, and will commence with those having the more obtuse edges.

Fig. 234.—Yorkshire Wolds. 1/2

Fig. 234, from the Yorkshire Wolds, is an external flat flake, weathered white, and trimmed all round the face, showing the natural crust of the flint, to a point in form like a Gothic arch. A part of the edge is bruised, but it is impossible to say for what weapon such an instrument was intended. It can hardly have been for a javelin-head, though from the outline it would seem well adapted for such a weapon; for in that case the edge would not have become bruised. It may possibly be an abnormal form of scraper.

A nearly similar specimen, but narrower in proportion, was found by the late Lord Londesborough [1475] in a barrow near Driffield, and is described as a spear-head.

Fig. 235. Yorkshire. 1/2

Another form, usually very thick in proportion to its breadth, and neatly worked over the whole of the convex face, is shown in Fig. 235. This specimen, also from the Yorkshire Wolds, is in the Greenwell Collection, now Dr. Sturge's. I have seen another from a barrow near Hay, Breconshire; and in the National Museum at Edinburgh is a specimen found near Urquhart, Elgin. In an implement of the same form in my own possession some small irregularities on the flat face have been removed by delicate chipping. I have several examples from Suffolk. There is nothing to guide us in attempting to determine the use of such instruments, but if inserted in handles they would be well adapted for boring holes in wood or other soft substances. The same form occurs in Ireland. In the Greenwell Collection is an Irish specimen ground all along the ridge, and over the whole of the butt-end. A pointed flattish flake (4 1/2 inches), worked over the whole of the outer face, from Rousay, [1476] Orkney, has been figured.

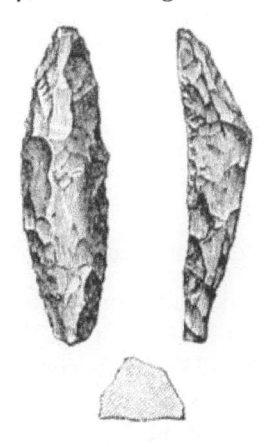

Fig. 236.—Bridlington. 1/2

Another much coarser but somewhat similar form is shown in Fig. 236. The instrument in this case is made from a very thick curved flake, roughly chipped into a boat-like form, and then more carefully trimmed along the edges. It may possibly have been used as a borer, as the edges near the point show some signs of attrition. It is of flint weathered grey, and was found near Bridlington. I have found a similar scaphoid form in Ireland. [1477]

A rather thick external flake, worked over nearly the whole of its convex face and reduced to about half its breadth for about a third of its length from the point, is shown in Fig. 237. The narrower part is nearly semicircular in section. It is difficult to imagine a purpose for this reduction in width; and it hardly seems due to wear. I have, however, another specimen, also from the Yorkshire Wolds, reduced in the same manner along fully three-quarters of its length.

Some of the worked flakes from the Dordogne Caves [1478] show a somewhat similar shoulder, but it seems possible that with them the broader part may have been protected by some sort of handle, as the original edge of the flake is there preserved.

Fig. 237. 1/2 Yorkshire.

Fig. 238. 1/2 Bridlington.

Fig. 239. 1/2 Castle Carrock.

I now come to the instruments with more acute edges, made by dressing the convex face of flint flakes. Of these the form shown in Fig. 238 is allied to that of Fig. 235, but is considerably flatter in section and more distinctly oval in outline. The original was found near Bridlington. A hard particle of the flint has interfered with the regular convexity of the worked face, but in some specimens the form is almost as regular as a slice taken lengthways off a lemon, though in others the outline presents an irregular curve. The flat face is generally more or less curved longitudinally, and the ends are sometimes more pointed than in the specimen engraved. I have an exquisitely chipped and perfectly symmetrical implement of this character (3 inches) from the neighbourhood of Icklingham, Suffolk, in which county the type is not uncommon. The flaking on the convex surface is very even and regular, and produces a slightly corrugated surface, with the low ridges following each other like ripple marks on sand. The edge is minutely and evenly chipped, and is very sharp. The instrument may perhaps be regarded as a sort of knife.

The form is well known in Ireland, but I do not remember to have seen it in foreign collections.

The beautifully wrought blade of flint, shown in Fig. 239, presents a more elongated variety of this form. It was found by Canon Greenwell, with a burnt body, in a barrow at Castle Carrock, [1479] Cumberland. Another blade, curiously similar in workmanship and character, was found by the same explorer in a barrow near Rudstone, Yorkshire, but in this case the body was unburnt. Another, with both ends rounded and the edges more serrated, was found in a barrow at Robin Hood Butts, near Scarborough, and is preserved in the museum of that town. Mounted with it on the same card are arrow-heads—leaf-shaped, lozenge-shaped, and stemmed and barbed. Mr. Carrington [1480] describes a flake flat on one face, and laboriously chipped to a convex shape on the other, as found with burnt bones in a barrow at Musdin, Staffordshire. A similar specimen in Ribden Low accompanied a contracted interment. Mr. Bateman terms them lance-heads. In the Greenwell Collection is a leaf-shaped blade of this kind, flat on one face, found in Burnt Fen. A knife of the same kind (2 inches) was found with an interment at Chollerford, [1481] Northumberland.

Fig. 240.—Ford, Northumberland.

Fig. 240A.—Etton. 1/1

The skilful character of the surface chipping on these blades is perhaps better shown in Fig. 240, which is drawn full-size from another specimen, also in Canon Greenwell's collection, which was found in a cist with the remains of a burnt body, on Ford Common, Northumberland. [1482]

Fig. 241.—Weaverthorpe. 1/2

Canon Greenwell found other knives in barrows at Sherburn [1483] and Etton, [1484] Yorkshire. The latter is beautifully serrated and I am enabled to reproduce his figure of it as Fig. 240A. [1485] He found another of the same character in a barrow at Bishop's Burton, [1486] Yorkshire. Knives not serrated have been found at Carn Brê, [1487] Cornwall; Chagford, [1488] Devon; and Grovehurst [1489] near Milton, Kent.

A serrated knife was found in a barrow at Dalmore, [1490] Alness, Ross-shire, and another, less distinctly serrated, at Tarland, [1491] Aberdeenshire. In some instruments, evidently belonging to the same class, the secondary flaking does not extend over the whole of the convex surface of the blade, but some of the facets of the original flake are still visible, or if it has been an external flake, some portion of the original crust of the flint remains. This is the case with the blade engraved in Fig. 241, which was found by Canon Greenwell in a barrow near Weaverthorpe, [1492] Yorkshire. In another barrow at Rudstone, Yorkshire, also opened by him, was a rather smaller but similar instrument, very neatly formed, and somewhat serrated at the edge. It lay at the feet of a skeleton. General Pitt Rivers found one nearly similar in a pit in the Isle of Thanet. [1493]

Knives of much the same form, but more rudely chipped, from Udny, Aberdeenshire, and Urquhart, Elgin, are in the National Museum at Edinburgh. They have also been found on the Culbin Sands, Elginshire. [1494]

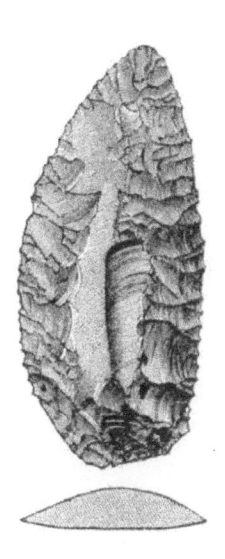

Fig. 242.—Wykeham Moor. 1/2

Some of these blades are left blunt at the butt-end of the flake, or else not so carefully worked round at that end, but that the square end of the original flake may be discerned. A very fine specimen of this kind was obtained by Canon Greenwell in a barrow on Wykeham Moor, Yorkshire, [1495] and is shown in Fig. 242. It was found lying side by side with a fluted bronze dagger, affording, as Canon Greenwell observes, a valuable illustration of the contemporaneous use of bronze and stone. He has found others, both with burnt and unburnt bodies, in barrows in Yorkshire and Northumberland. I have a beautiful blade of the same general form, but rather more rounded at the point and curved slightly in the other direction, and but little more than half the length of this specimen, which was found by Mr. E. Tindall, with another nearly similar, in a barrow near Bridlington. Dr. Travis in 1836 described another (2 3/4 inches) from a barrow near Scarborough. Another (2 inches) was found with food-vessels in a barrow at Marton, [1496] Yorkshire, E.R. A knife of the same kind from a cave at Kozarnia, [1497] Poland, has been figured by Dr. F. Römer.

Among other English examples I may mention a thin flake (4 1/4 inches), somewhat curved laterally, and trimmed along both edges and rounded at the point, found in Burwell Fen, Cambridge. Another from the same locality (3 3/4 inches) is even more curved on the concave edge. A recurved flake or knife of flint, 3 1/2 inches long, finely chipped at the sharp convex edge, was found with jet ornaments and an ovoid instrument of serpentine, accompanying a skeleton, in a barrow near Avebury, Wilts. [1498] I have several from the surface, Suffolk, and from the Cambridge Fens. In a larger instrument from Icklingham, both edges are worn smooth and rounded by use, as if in scraping some soft but gritty substance, possibly hides in the process of preparation as leather.

In some of these instruments the point is sharp instead of being rounded. One of them, found by Canon Greenwell in a barrow on Potter Brompton Wold, [1499] is shown in Fig. 243.

I have a more triangular form of implement, of the same kind, 3 3/4 inches long, showing the crust of the flint at the base, found near Icklingham, Suffolk. Another from the same locality is of the same form as the figure.

Instruments of the same character as these were discovered by the late Mr. Bateman in many of the Derbyshire Barrows. What appears to be one of the same kind was found with a flake and burnt bones in an urn at Broughton, Lincolnshire. [1500] It may, however, have been convex on both faces. A fragment of another was found at Dorchester Dykes, [1501] Oxfordshire, by General Pitt Rivers.

Fig. 243.—Potter Brompton Wold. 1/2

The sharp-edged instruments of the forms last described seem to have been intended for use as cutting, or occasionally as scraping tools, and may not improperly be termed knives, as has been proposed by Canon Greenwell. [1502] Even the last described, though sharply pointed, cannot with certainty be accepted as a spear-head. To regarding the other form, Fig. 242, as such, Canon Greenwell objects that "the people who fashioned the arrow-heads so beautifully, if they fabricated a spear-head in flint, would not have made one side straight, the other curved, and carefully rounded it off at the sharper end." One of these pointed instruments (3 inches), trimmed on one face and slightly curved, was found with an urn and a whetstone in a cairn at Stenton, [1503] East Lothian.

Sometimes the secondary working extends over part of both faces of the flake, the central ridge of which is still discernible. Canon Greenwell found a fine instrument of this kind (3 1/4 inches), made from a ridged flake, with neat secondary chipping along both sides, and on both faces, with a burnt body, in a barrow on Sherburn Wold. [1504] The flint itself is partially calcined. It is difficult to determine the claims of such an instrument to be regarded as a knife or as a lance-head.

Fig. 244.—Snainton Moor. 1/2

Fig. 245.—Ford. 1/2

The pointed instrument from Snainton Moor, Yorkshire, which is shown in Fig. 244, and was kindly lent to me by the late Mr. C. Monkman, of Malton, has more the appearance of having been a lance-head. A fragment of another weapon of this kind was found in Aberdeenshire. [1505] Larger lance-heads of this form have been found in tumuli in the South of France. [1506] A closely similar javelin-head, found at Vercelli, has been engraved by Gastaldi, [1507] as well as another longer and more distinctly tanged, from Telese. [1508] A third from Tuscany has been engraved by Cocchi. [1509] A fourth of the same form, but slightly notched on each side near the base, was found with skeletons in Andalusia. [1510] In the English specimen the secondary flaking extends over the whole, or nearly the whole, of both faces of the original flake; and the same is the case with the other instruments of this class which I am now about to describe.

Fig. 245 represents an implement of dark grey almost unweathered flint, found with burnt bones in a barrow at Ford. [1511]

Northumberland, examined by Canon Greenwell. It has been made from an external flake subsequently brought into shape by working on both faces. Judging from its form only, it would appear to have been a lance-head; but there are some signs of wear of the edge at the butt-end, which seem hardly compatible with this assumption, unless, indeed, like the natives of Tierra del Fuego, [1512] who are said to make use of their arrow-heads for cutting purposes, its owner used it also as a sort of knife. Mr. C. Monkman had a blade of this character (3 3/8 inches) from Northdale, Yorkshire. Some lance-heads (3 and 2 1/2 inches) have been found at West Wickham, [1513] Kent; and Carn Brê, [1514] Cornwall.

The original of Fig. 246 was found at West Huntow, near Bridlington. It is boldly chipped on both faces, so that hardly any portion of the original surface of the flake remains. It has a sharp edge all round, which is, however, slightly abraded at the blunter end; a small portion of the point at the other end has been broken off. In character it so closely resembles a leaf-shaped arrow-head that there seem some grounds for regarding this form as that of a lance-head, though from the doubtful character of other specimens of nearby similar form I have thought it better to place it here. A much larger specimen of brown flint (3 3/4 by 2 3/8 inches), but of nearly the same form and character, was found by the late Rev. J. C. Clutterbuck, at Hounslow Heath. In the Greenwell Collection is one of almost the same dimensions found on Willerby Wold, and others not quite so large from Rudstone, Yorkshire.

Some blades, similar in general form, were found, with various other stone implements, in sand-beds, near York, and have been described by Mr. C. Monkman. [1515]

Fig. 246.—Bridlington. 1/2

Fig. 247.—Cambridge Fens. 1/2

Fig. 248.—Scamridge. 1/2

I have collected somewhat similar blades to that here engraved, though of rather smaller dimensions, in the ancient encampment of Maiden Bower, near Dunstable; and I have several found on the surface near Lakenheath and Icklingham, Suffolk. I have seen one of the same character, which was found near Ware, Herts. General Pitt Rivers found in the Isle of Thanet [1516] two lance-heads, curiously like this and the preceding figure.

A far more highly-finished blade, but still preserving the same general character, is shown in Fig. 247. The original, of brown flint, was found in the Cambridge Fens, and is now in my own collection. Though ground on some portions of both faces, apparently for the purpose of removing asperities, the edges are left unground. They are, however, very carefully and delicately chipped by secondary working to a regular sweep. I think this instrument must be regarded rather as a form of knife than as a head for a javelin or lance. In size, and to some extent in shape, it corresponds with the more crescent-like or triangular tools described under Fig. 256. I have a rather smaller example from Bottisham, ground along one side only.

This correspondence is still more evident in a blade now in the Blackmore Museum, Salisbury, of nearly the same shape but somewhat less curved on one edge than the other, which has been ground along the more highly curved edge. It was found at Hamptworth, near Salisbury.

A narrower form of blade is shown in Fig. 248. The original, of flint weathered nearly white, was found at Scamridge, Yorkshire, and is preserved in the Greenwell Collection. It is, as will be observed, slightly unsymmetrical in form, so that it would appear to have been intended for a knife rather than for a lance-head. A remarkably fine specimen in the same collection, found at Flixton, Yorkshire [1517] (5 1/8 inches), is in form much like that from Scamridge. A part of the edge towards the point on the flatter side is slightly worn. There is a considerable diversity of form amongst the instruments of this character, some having the sides almost symmetrical, while others have them curved in different degrees, so much so as to make the instrument resemble in form some of the crescent-shaped Danish blades. In a specimen which I possess, from Ganton Wold, one side presents the natural crust of the flint along the greater part of its length, and has been left unworked; the other side has been chipped to an obtuse edge, which is considerably bruised and worn. I have others from Suffolk, sharpened by cross-flaking on one edge only. Some such knives are rounded at one or both ends instead of being pointed. A blade from the neighbourhood of Bridlington, in my collection, is pointed at one end but rounded at the other, where also the edge is completely worn away by attrition. In the case of another symmetrical and flat blade, from Icklingham (3 3/4 inches), rather more convex on one face than the other, the edge on one side at the more pointed end is also completely rubbed away. I have as yet been unable to trace on the face of any of these pointed specimens signs of those polished markings which occur so frequently at a little distance within the more highly curved margin of the Danish semi-lunar blades, and from which Professor Steenstrup has inferred that they were inserted in handles of wood or bone. A specimen from Craigfordmains, [1518] Roxburghshire, has been figured.

A blade of the same kind as Fig. 248, 3 5/8 inches long, found in the Department of the Charente, is engraved by de Rochebrune. [1519] Others of larger size were found in the Grotto des Morts, Durfort (Gard). [1520]

The view that many of these blades were used as knives rather than as lance-heads, seems to be supported by a specimen from Burwell Fen, in the Museum of the Cambridge Antiquarian Society, and engraved in Fig. 249. This blade is rather more convex on one face than the other, and shows along half of its flatter face the original inner surface of the flake from which it was made. One of its side edges has been rounded by grinding along its entire length, so that it can be conveniently held in the hand; the other edge is left sharp, and is polished as if by use.

A remarkably large specimen of this kind, but with no traces of grinding upon it, was found in digging the foundations of a house on Windmill Hill, Saffron Walden, and was in the possession of Mr. William Tuke, [1521] of that town. It is shown in Fig. 250. One face is somewhat flatter than the other, but both faces are dexterously and symmetrically chipped over their whole surface. The small flakes have been taken off so skilfully and at such regular intervals, that, so far as workmanship is concerned, this instrument approaches in character the elegant Danish blades. The form seems well adapted for a lance-head, but on examination the edges appear to be slightly chipped and worn away, as if by scraping some hard material. It would appear, then, more probably to have been used in the hand. In the often-cited Greenwell Collection is a blade of grey flint, also 5 3/8 inches long, but rather narrower than the figure, and straighter on one edge than the other, found in Mildenhall Fen. In the same collection is a large thin flat blade of flint, 8 3/8 inches long and 3 inches broad, more curved on one edge than the other, and rounded at one end. The straighter edge is also the sharper. It was found at Cross Bank, near Mildenhall. In general outline it is not unlike some of the Danish lunate implements. It may, however, be only the result of a somewhat unskilful attempt to produce a symmetrical dagger or spear-head, such as Fig. 264. I have several instruments of this kind, found near Icklingham and at other places in Suffolk.

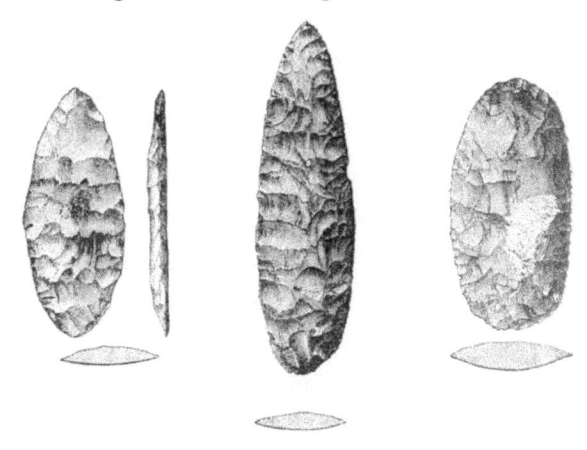

Fig. 249.—Burwell Fen. 1/2

Fig. 250.—Saffron Walden. 1/2

Fig. 251.—Fimber. 1/2

A lance-head of almost the same size and form as Fig. 250, from the neighbourhood of Brescia, has been engraved by Gastaldi. [1522] They are also said to be found in Greece. [1523]

They sometimes occur among American antiquities. One of them, 11 inches in length, pointed at each end, is engraved by Squier and Davis. [1524] I have a beautiful blade of pale buff chalcedony, acutely pointed at one end and rounded at the other, which was found in company with a second of the same size and character, near Comayagua, in Spanish Honduras. It is 6 3/8 inches long and 1 1/8 inches broad. Other lance-heads from Honduras have been published. [1525] A flint sword or spear-head 22 inches long, serrated at the end towards the point, is said to have been found in Tennessee. [1526] Lance-heads of flint, not unlike Figs. 249 and 250, are found in South Africa. [1527]

Messrs. Mortimer, of Driffield, Yorkshire, have in their collection a remarkable specimen belonging to this class of instrument, which instead of being pointed is almost semicircular at both ends. They have kindly allowed me to engrave it in Fig. 251. It has been neatly chipped from a piece of tabular flint, and not from a flake, and is equally convex on both faces; some of the salient parts along both edges are polished, as if by wear, and on either face are some of the polished "Steenstrup's markings," possibly arising from its having been inserted in a handle. This form is perhaps more closely connected with some of those which will shortly follow than with those which precede it. A somewhat similar oval blade 3 3/4 inches long and 2 3/4 inches wide, found in the Thames at Long Wittenham, and formerly belonging to the Rev. J. C. Clutterbuck, is ground along both sides, and is now in the Oxford Museum.

A blade of the same form was found in the Grotte des Morts, Durfort (Gard). [1528]

In none of the specimens hitherto figured in this chapter, have the edges been sharpened by grinding; in the only instances where that process has been used, it has been for the purpose of removing, not of sharpening the edge. In the case of the next examples which I am about to describe, one or both edges, and in some the whole of both faces, have been ground.

I have already mentioned instances of untrimmed flakes of flint having been ground on the edge, but knives of a similar character made from carefully chipped blades also occur, though so far as I have at present observed, principally in Scotland.

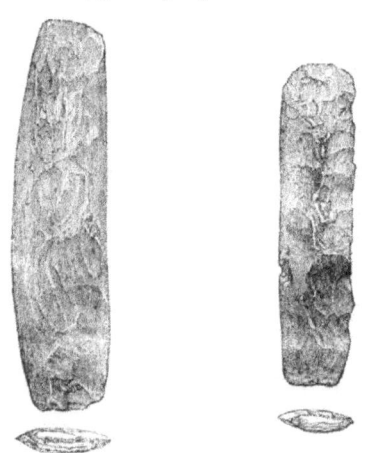

Fig. 252.—Argyllshire. 1/1

Fig. 253.—Glen Urquhart.

One of these, carefully worked on both faces, and with one edge sharpened by grinding, was found at Strachur, [1529] Argyllshire, and is shown full size in Fig. 252. Another, 2 1/2 inches long and 7/8 inch broad, with less grinding on the surface, was found at Cromar, Aberdeenshire. A third, of almost the same size, with the edge nearly straight and the back curved, and with neatly chipped faces but little ground, was found in a chambered cairn at Camster, [1530] Caithness. A nodule of iron ore was found with it, but whether this was for fire-producing purposes is not apparent. A fragment of another knife of the same kind was found, in 1865, by Messrs. Anderson and Shearer in a cairn at Ormiegill Ulbster, Caithness; and among the numerous articles of flint found at Urquhart, [1531] Elgin, is a very perfect knife of this kind, which is shown in Fig. 253. All five specimens are in the National Museum at Edinburgh. I have two English specimens of the same kind but pointed at the butt, from the neighbourhood of Icklingham.

The sharpened ends of stone celts, when broken off, have occasionally been converted into knives. One such, from Gilling, Yorkshire, with the fractured surface rounded by grinding, is in the Greenwell Collection.

Another form of knife closely allied to the type of Fig. 251, is broader, and has all its edges sharpened. The instrument shown in Fig. 254 was found near Bridlington. It is made from a large broad flake, the outer face of which has been re-worked to such an extent that not more than one-fourth of the original surface remains intact. The inner face, on the contrary, is left almost untouched, except just at the two ends. As will be seen from the engraving, a portion of the original edge has been chipped away, apparently in modern times, by the first finder having used it as a "strike-a-light" flint. What remains of the original edge has been carefully sharpened, and the angles between some of the facets on the convex face have also been removed by grinding. An example of the same kind from Butterlaw, [1532] near Coldstream, has been figured.

Fig. 254.—Bridlington. 1/2

Fig. 255.—Overton. 1/2

Others more or less perfect have been found at Glenluce, [1533] Earlston, and on the Culbin Sands. [1534]

A nearly similar instrument, from Sweden, has been engraved by Nilsson, [1535] but its edges are not described as ground.

A more highly finished form of the same implement is shown in Fig. 255. The original was found at Pick Rudge Farm, [1536] Overton, Wilts, in company with the large barbed arrow or javelin-head, Fig. 305, and both are now in the Blackmore Museum. Like Fig. 254, it is flatter on one face than the other; it is, however, polished all over as well as ground at the edges. These are rather sharper at the two ends than at the sides. Another specimen of the same form, and of almost identically the same dimensions, was found at Pentrefoelas, [1537] Denbighshire. A third specimen, 3 1/2 inches long and 2 1/4 inches wide, was found at Lean Low, near Newhaven, Derbyshire, and is in the Bateman collection. [1538]

In my own collection are two very fine and perfect specimens of this class of instrument, both from the neighbourhood of Cambridge. The larger of these is 4 1/4 inches long, 2 3/4 inches broad at one end, and 2 5/8 inches at the other. The ends are ground to a regular sweep, and the sides are somewhat hollowed. It has been made from a very broad thin flake, and is ground over nearly the whole of the outer and over part of the inner face, and brought to a sharp edge all round. It was found in Burwell Fen. The smaller instrument has been even more highly finished in the same manner, every trace of the original chipping of the convex face having been removed by grinding. The edge is sharp all round, but the ends are more highly curved than in the larger instrument. It is 3 1/4 inches long, 2 1/8 inches broad at one end, and 1 7/8 inches at the other, and was found in Quy Fen. In the Greenwell Collection is a portion of what appears to have been another of these instruments, ground on both faces and sharp at the edges, from Lakenheath.

Fig. 256.—Kempston. 1/2

I have the half of another, 2 inches wide, found near Bridlington, and one of the same character, but oval in outline, from the same place. The latter has lost one of its ends. Its original dimensions must have been about 3 inches in length by 1 7/8 inches in extreme breadth, and 3/16 inch in thickness. Both faces are coarsely ground, the striæ running crossways of the blade. The edges appear to have been sharpened on a finer stone. It has been supposed that these instruments were intended to serve for dressing [1539] the flesh side of skins, or for flaying-knives. [1540] Mr. Albert Way has called attention to the analogy they present to an unique bronze implement found at Ploucour, [1541] Brittany.

The beautifully-formed instrument shown in Fig. 256 belongs apparently to the same class. It was found at Kempston, near Bedford, and was kindly lent to me for engraving by the late Mr. James Wyatt, F.G.S., who afterwards presented it to the Blackmore Museum. [1542] It is of dark flint, the two faces equally convex, and neatly chipped out but not polished. Regarding it as of triangular form, with the apex rounded, the edges on what may be described as the two sides in the [1543] engraving have been carefully sharpened, while that of the base has been removed by grinding. In the same field was found a flint lance-head or dagger of fine workmanship, which will subsequently be mentioned.

Messrs. Mortimer, of Driffield, possess an instrument of the same character found near Fimber. It is more equilaterally triangular in form than the Kempston specimen, though the sides are all curved and the angles rounded. It is polished all over on one face, though some traces of the original flaking are still apparent. On the other face, which is rather more convex, the grinding is confined to two sides of the triangle, which are thus brought to a sharp edge. The edge on the third side, which is rather straighter than the others, is very slightly rounded. It seems probable that this blunter edge was next the hand when the instrument was in use.

Fig.—256A.—Eastbourne. 1/2

Another specimen, even more triangular in outline, was found in the Thames, at Windsor; it is of ochreous flint, and the base, which is 3 3/8 inches long, exhibits the natural crust of the flint; each of the other two sides, which are ground to a sharp edge, is about 2 3/4 inches long. Another from Lakenheath, 3 1/4 inches long and 3 inches wide at the unground base, was in the collection of the late Rev. W. Weller Poley, of Brandon.

I have an implement of this kind, much like that from Kempston, but more curved at what is the base in the figure. All along this sweep the edge produced by chipping out the form has been removed by grinding. All round the other sweep the edge has been carefully sharpened by the same means. A portion only of each face is ground. This specimen was found near Mildenhall. I have another, more curved both at the edge and the base, found near Icklingham. From the same district I have the form entirely unground. Other specimens found in Derbyshire are preserved in the Bateman Collection. There are several in the Museum at Oxford.

In Fig. 256A is shown an almost circular knife of this kind found at Willington Mill, near Eastbourne, which was kindly given to me by Mr. R. Hilton, of East Dean.

In the Greenwell Collection is another nearly circular tool, about 2 inches in diameter, ground to an edge along most of the periphery, and found in Yorkshire. Another rather smaller disc, in the same collection, and found at Huntow, near Bridlington, is partly ground on both faces, but not at the edge. A circular knife of the same kind was found at Trefeglwys, [1544] Montgomeryshire. It is 2 3/4 inches in diameter and ground to an edge all round except at two places at opposite ends of one of its diameters, where for a short distance the edge is left as it was originally chipped out. It is now in the Powysland Museum. A circular knife from Mam Tor, [1545] Derbyshire, is in the Castleton Museum.

Fig. 257.—Kintore. 1/2

Fig. 258.—Newhaven, Derbyshire.

In the Greenwell Collection is an implement, about 2 inches in diameter, found at Sherburn Carr, Yorkshire, and in outline like a scraper, but with the greater part of the semicircular edge sharpened by grinding. In character it much resembles some instruments occasionally found both in Britain and Ireland, of which an example is given in Fig. 257. This is a horseshoe-shaped blade of flint, 3 inches over, with the rounded part of the circumference ground to a fine cutting edge, so that it was probably used as a knife. It is in the National Museum at Edinburgh, and was presumably found near Kintore, Aberdeenshire. In the same Museum is another instrument of the same kind, but somewhat kidney-shaped in outline, found in Lanarkshire. It is 3 3/8 inches in length, and 2 5/8 inches in extreme width. On a part of the hollowed side it shows the natural crust of the flint, but the rest of the periphery is ground to a sharp edge, and the projections on the faces have been removed by grinding. Others were found at Pitlochrie, [1546] Kincardineshire, and Turriff, [1547] Aberdeenshire. Mr. C. Monkman, of Malton, had a knife much like Fig. 257, 2 3/4 inches across, which was found at Huntow, near Bridlington. I have an Irish specimen from near Ballymena almost like that from Kintore, as well as one of longer horseshoe shape found at Swan Brake, North Stow, Bury St. Edmunds, another large one more subtriangular (3 8/10 by 3 1/2 inches) found near Wallingford, and a broad hatchet-shaped one from the Cambridge Fens.

In the collection (now in the British Museum) of the late Mr. J. F. Lucas, is an instrument of this kind, 3 inches over, found at Arbor Low, Derbyshire, in 1867. He kindly presented me with another, closely resembling Fig. 257, and found at Mining Low. He also possessed a remarkably fine knife of this form, but with the edge unground, which was found at Newhaven, Derbyshire, and is shown in Fig. 258. An example more pear-shaped in outline and ground half-way round the edge, found near Whitby, has been figured. [1548] I have a fine one (4 inches) more rhomboidal from Swaffham Fen, Cambridge, and another smaller from Burwell. From the latter place I have an oval knife made from a broad external flake (2 3/4 inches) ground along one side, and a thick one also of oval form from Icklingham.

In all the specimens with the circular edge sharpened by grinding, the flat side has been purposely made blunt, as if for being held in the hand. The backs, however, may have been let into wooden handles, in which case these instruments would have been the exact counterparts of the Ulus, or Women's knives of the Eskimos. [1549]

Fig. 259.—Harome, Yorkshire. 1/2

Though not formed of flint, but of a hard slaty rock of the nature of hone-stone, an implement of much the same form as that from Fimber [1550] may be here described. It was found at Harome, in Ryedale, Yorkshire, and is in the Greenwell Collection, now Dr. Allen Sturge's. As will be seen from Fig. 259, it approximates in form to an equilateral spherical triangle with the apices rounded. It is carefully polished over the whole of both faces, except where small portions have broken away, owing to the lamination of the stone. Each of the three sides is ground to a cutting edge, which however is not continued over the angles; these are rounded in both directions, as each would probably be in contact with the palm of the hand when the opposite edge was used for cutting.

There can be no doubt that all these triangular instruments, whether of flint or other material, were used as cutting tools; and the name of skinning-knife, which has been applied to them as well as to the quadrangular instruments, not improbably denotes one of the principal purposes for which they were made.

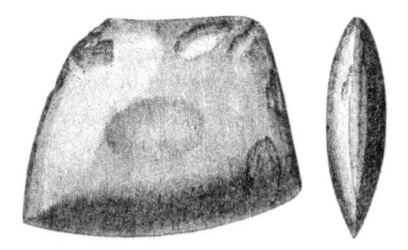

Fig. 260.—Harome, Yorkshire. 1/2

In the Greenwell Collection is another curious instrument, from the same locality as that last described, which is shown in Fig. 260. It is formed of a hard slaty stone, having one side ground to a regularly curved and sharp edge, and the others rounded by grinding. The two faces, which are equally convex, are also ground to such an extent that but little of the original chipped surface can be discerned. In the face shown in the figure there is a slight central depression, and on the other face two such at about 2 inches apart, and in a line parallel with the top or back of the instrument. When it is held in the right hand, with the fore-finger over the end, the thumb fits into the depression on the one face and the middle and fourth fingers into those on the other, so that it is firmly grasped. It is evident that this must have been a cutting or chopping tool: but the materials on which it was employed would seem to have been soft, as the edge is by no means sharp, and is also entirely uninjured by use. These depressions for the thumb and fingers resemble in character those on the handles of some of the Eskimo [1551] scrapers and knives already described.

Another implement, of nearly the same form, but rather longer and narrower, is in the same collection, and was found in Ryedale, Yorkshire. It is of hard clay-slate, 5 1/8 inches long at the blade and 2 1/2 inches wide, with a curved sharp edge, and a straight back rounded transversely. It is bevelled at one end, which is flat, apparently owing to a joint in the slate; and somewhat rounded at the other, where it fits the hand. Neither in this nor in a third instrument of the same class, also from Harome, are there any depressions on the face. This last has been formed from a flat kidney-shaped pebble of clay-slate, the hollow side and one end left almost in the natural condition so as to fit the hand, and the curved side ground to a sharp edge, which is returned round the end almost at a right angle. The edge at the end is polished as if by rubbing, and looks as if it might have been used in the same manner as bookbinders' tools for indenting lines on leather. This instrument is 6 inches long, 3 inches wide at the butt-end, and 2 1/2 inches at the sharp end. It is nearly 1 1/4 inches thick.

Besides the three which I have mentioned several other instruments of the same description have been found in the same part of Yorkshire.

I have never seen any specimens of precisely this character from other localities; but they were apparently destined for much the same purposes as the "Picts' knives," shortly to be mentioned, unless possibly they were merely used in the manner just indicated. It is very remarkable that the form should appear to be limited to so small an area in England; and though the specimens occur under the same circumstances as polished celts, it seems probable that for stone antiquities they belong to a late period.

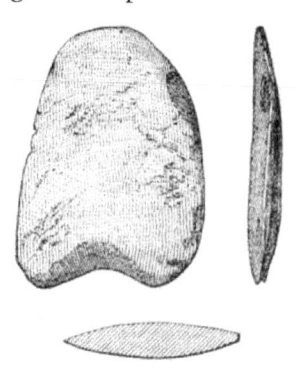

Fig 261.—Crambe. 1/2

The large thin flat blades, usually subquadrangular or irregularly oval in form, of which a large number has been found in the Shetland Islands, and which are known as "Pech's knives," or "Picts' knives," apparently belong to the same class of instruments as the quadrangular and triangular tools lately described, and this would therefore appear to be the proper place for making mention of them. They are never formed of flint; the principal materials of which they are made being slate and compact greenstone, porphyry, and other felspathic rocks, and madreporite. Their usual length is from 6 inches to 9 inches, and the breadth from 3 inches to 5 inches; their thickness is rarely more than 1/2 inch in the middle, and sometimes not more than 1/10 of an inch. They are usually polished all over, and ground to an edge all round. Sometimes, however, the edge on one or more sides is rounded, and occasionally an end or side is left of the full thickness of the blade, and rounded as if for being held in the hand. I have a specimen, 4 1/2 inches long, and 3 1/4 inches wide at the base, formed of porphyritic greenstone, and found at Hillswick, in Shetland, which was given me by the late Mr. J. Gwyn Jeffreys, F.R.S. Its cutting edge may be described as forming nearly half of a pointed ellipse, of which the thick side for holding forms the conjugate diameter. This side is rounded and curved slightly inwards; one of the angles between this base and the elliptical edge is rounded, and a portion of the edge is also left thick and rounded, so that when the base is applied to the palm of the hand the lower part of the forefinger may rest upon it. When thus held it forms a cutting tool not unlike a leather-cutter's knife. Instruments of this character are extremely rare in England, but in the extensive Greenwell Collection is a specimen which I have engraved as Fig. 261. It was found at

Crambe, in the North Riding of Yorkshire, and is formed of an oolitic shelly limestone, a material also used for the manufacture of celts in that district. Though smaller, and rather more deeply notched at the base than my Shetland knife, it is curiously like it in general form. The edge, however, only extends along one side, and is not carried round the point.

Fig. 262.—Walls, Shetland. 1/2

The specimens that I have engraved as Figs. 262 and 263, are in the Museum of the Society of Antiquaries of London. They are formed of thin laminæ of what is said to be madreporite, and are sharp all round. [1552] They were found with fourteen others at the depth of six feet in a peat-moss, the whole of them being arranged in a horizontal line, and overlapping each other like slates upon the roof of a house. There are several specimens formed of felspathic rocks, and from various localities in Shetland, preserved in the British Museum. A note attached to one of them states that twelve were found in Easterskild, in the parish of Sandsting. An engraving of one of them is given in the "Horæ Ferales." [1553] I possess several; one of porphyritic stone, oval, 8 inches long, is polished all over both faces, one side is sharp and the other rounded.

In the National Museum at Edinburgh [1554] are other examples, also from Shetland. Several have been figured. [1555] Some have a kind of haft. [1556] They occasionally have a hole for suspension. [1557] Sir Daniel Wilson [1558] states that a considerable number of implements, mostly of the same class, were found under the clay in the ancient mosses of Blairdrummond and Meiklewood, but in this he was in error. There are some fine specimens from Shetland in the Ethnological Museum at Copenhagen. Mr. J. W. Cursiter, of Kirkwall, has fine examples of such knives from Shetland. One in his collection is 8 inches long and 5 3/4 inches broad, being in form much like Fig. 262.

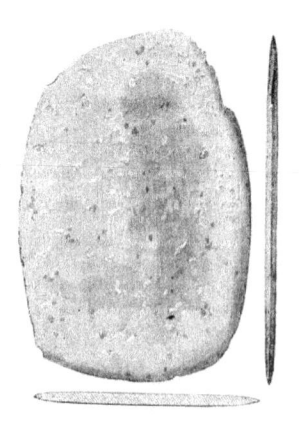

Fig. 263.—Walls, Shetland. 1/2

There can be little doubt of these implements having been cutting tools for holding in the hand, though they have been described by Dr. Hibbert and Mr. Bryden [1559] in "The Statistical Account of the Shetland Isles" as double or single-edged battle-axes. They appear, however, as Mr. Albert Way [1560] has pointed out, to be too thin and fragile for any warlike purpose. Those with the cutting edge all round were probably provided with a sort of handle along one side, like the flensing-knife from Icy Cape in the possession of Sir Edward Belcher, of which mention has already been made. This is a flat thin blade, about 5 inches long, and of subquadrangular form. It is sharp at the edge, but has a guard or handle along the opposite side, made of split twigs attached by resinous gum. In some Eskimo knives of the same kind in the Christy Collection and in the Ethnological Museum at Copenhagen the wooden back is tied on by a cord which passes through a hole in the blade. It is possible that the "Picts' knives" may in some cases have been used, like those of the Eskimos, for removing the blubber from whales.

It is difficult to assign a date to these instruments, which are almost peculiar to the Shetland Islands. There are traditions extant of their having been seen in use within the present century, in one instance by an old woman for cutting kail, and in Lewis, [1561] a sharp stone was used in 1829, for cutting out a wedding dress. In the latter case the reason assigned was the want of scissors, but it would appear to have probably been merely an experimental trial of the cutting powers of a stone which may not have been one of these primitive tools. The occurrence of Picts' knives under so thick a deposit of peat shows, however, that they do not belong to any recent period, though five or six feet of peat do not of necessity indicate any very high degree of antiquity.

When the Princess Leonora Christina [1562] was imprisoned in Copenhagen in 1663 and she was deprived of scissors and cutting instruments, she records, in 1665, that, "Christian had given me some pieces of flint which are so sharp that I can cut fine linen with them by the thread. The pieces are still in my possession, and with this implement I executed various things."

Stone knives of any form, having the edges ground, are of rare occurrence on the Continent, though in Norway and Sweden [1563] those of what have been termed Arctic types are found. Nearly similar forms occur in North America. A peculiar knife, with a rectangular handle, much like a common table-knife, has been found in the Lake Settlement of Inkwyl. [1564]

A North American knife, [1565] with a somewhat similar handle, has a curved blade very thick at the back.

To return to the implements made of flint. Those which I have next to describe have been termed spear-heads, lance-heads, knives, and daggers. Their ordinary length is from 5 to 7 inches, and their extreme width from 1 1/2 to 2 1/2 inches. Their general form is lanceolate, but the greater breadth is usually nearer the point of the blade than the butt, which is in most instances either truncated or rounded. They exhibit remarkable skill in the treatment of flint in their manufacture, being as a rule symmetrical in form, with the edge in one plane, and equally convex on the two faces—which are dexterously chipped into broad flat facets—while the edges are still more carefully shaped by secondary working. Towards the butt, the converging sides are usually nearly straight, and in many, the edge at this part has been rounded by grinding, and the butt-end has had its angles removed in a similar manner. This may have been done either with the view of rendering the instrument more convenient for holding in the hand, or in order to prevent the blade from cutting the ligaments by which it was attached to a handle. For the latter purpose, however, there would be no advantage in rounding the butt-end; and as this, moreover, is frequently the thickest part of the blade, it seems probable that the majority of the instruments were intended for holding in the hand, so that the term dagger appears most appropriate to this form.

Other blades, with notches on the opposite sides, seem to have been mounted with handles or shafts, and may have served either as daggers or possibly as spear-heads.

I have figured four specimens showing some difference in shape, mainly in consequence of the different relative positions of the broadest part of the blades. This in Fig. 265 may be, to some extent, due to the point having been chipped away by successive sharpening of the edge by secondary chipping, in the same manner as we find some of the Danish daggers worn to a stump, by nearly the whole of the blade having been sharpened away.

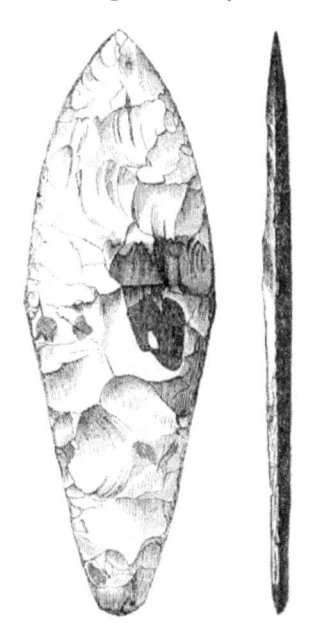

Fig. 264.—Lambourn Down. 1/2

In Fig. 264 is shown a beautiful dagger of white flint, which was found in a barrow on Lambourn Down, Berks, in company with a celt and some exquisitely-finished stemmed and barbed arrow-heads of the same material. It is now in the British Museum. Its edges are sharp all along, and not blunted towards the butt-end. It may have been an entirely new weapon, buried with the occupant of the barrow for use in another state of existence, or it may have had moss wrapped round that part, so as to protect the hand; like the blade [1566] of flint with *Hypnum brevirostre* wrapped round its butt-end to form a substitute for a handle, which was found in the bed of the River Bann, in Ireland. Some North American implements of similar character are, as Sir Wollaston Franks [1567] has pointed out, hafted by insertion into a split piece of wood in which they are bound by a cord. One from the north-west coast, thus mounted, is in the British Museum.

Professor Nilsson [1568] has engraved another American knife, in the same collection, but erroneously refers it to New Zealand.

A good specimen (6 1/2 inches) was found in 1890 in a field known as Little Wansford, near Great Weldon, Northamptonshire. I have specimens (6 1/4 inches) from Fiskerton, Lincolnshire, and from Bottisham Fen, Cambs (4 5/8 inches). There is a slight shoulder on the latter rather nearer the butt than the point. A beautiful specimen (6 3/4 inches) from a barrow at Garton. [1569] Yorkshire, E. R., has been figured.

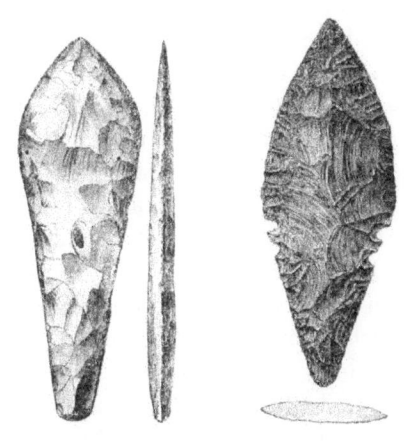

Fig. 265.—Thames. 1/2

Fig. 266.—Burnt Fen.

The blade shown in Fig. 265 is in the British Museum, having been formerly in the Roach Smith Collection. It is of nearly black flint, and was found in the Thames. Its length is still 7 inches, but from the form of the point it seems possible that it may, as already suggested, originally have been even longer. There is in the Museum another specimen from the Thames, [1570] 5 3/4 inches long, in form like Fig. 264. Both of these have the edges towards the butt rendered more or less blunt, and have had any prominences removed by grinding. The same is the case with a blade 6 inches long and 2 3/8 inches wide, found in Quy Fen in 1849, and now in the Museum of the Cambridge Antiquarian Society. In the same collection is a smaller specimen, 4 3/4 inches long and 1 5/8 inches wide, from Burwell Fen. This has its edges sharp, and shows the natural crust of the flint at the butt, as does also one 7 inches long by 2 1/2 inches wide, found at Jackdaw Hill, near Cambridge. [1571] Another blade (5 3/8 inches) found at Wolseys, near Dunmow, Essex, is in the British Museum. A blade of this type from a garden at Walton-on-Thames [1572] is recorded.

A remarkably fine spear-head of the notched class, 6 3/4 inches long, was exhibited some years ago to the British Archæological Association, and their *Proceedings*, [1573] without giving any information as to the size, shape, or character of the specimen, record as an interesting fact that it weighs nearly four ounces. It was found in Burnt Fen, Prickwillow, Ely, and is now in my own collection. It is engraved as Fig. 266. It is of black flint, and has in the first instance been boldly chipped into approximately the requisite form, and then been carefully finished by neat secondary working at the edges, no part of which has been rounded by grinding. On either side, at rather less than half way along the blade from the base, are two deep rounded indentations not quite half an inch apart, in character much like the notches between the barbs and stems of one form of flint arrow-heads. The same peculiarity is to be observed in a somewhat smaller spear-head found at Carshalton, [1574] in Surrey, and forming part of the Meyrick Collection. Of this it is observed that it "was let into a slit in the wooden shaft, and bound over with nerves diagonally from the four notches which appear on the sides." There can, I think, be little doubt of the correctness of this view, nor of the method of attachment to the shafts or handles having been much the same as that in use among the American tribes for their arrow-and lance-heads with a notch on either side. Whether the British blades were mounted with a short handle or a long shaft, we have no means of judging; but if those with the edges rounded towards the butt were knives or daggers, there seems some probability of these also having served the same purpose, though provided with handles like some North American and Mexican examples, and of their not having been spear-or lance-heads.

I have another blade of this kind found in Burwell Fen, Cambridge, about 5 3/4 inches in length, and 1 7/8 inch in width. At about 3 1/2 inches from the point there is on either side a slight notch; beyond this there is a narrow projection, and then the width of the blade is suddenly reduced by a full eighth of an inch on either side, so as to leave a sort of shoulder. Between this and the butt, at intervals of about an inch, there are on each side two other notches, as if to assist in fastening the blade into a shaft or handle. There has in this case been no attempt to remove the edges by grinding.

A flint dagger (6 3/8 inches) found in the Thames, [1575] near London Bridge, has a notch on each side 2 7/8 inches from the base. A smaller notched example was found at Hurlingham.

In the Christy Collection is another of these blades, 5 3/8 inches long, with a notch on either side about 1 3/4 inches from the butt. It is uncertain where it was found.

One with a notch at each side about mid-length was found at Hare Park, [1576] Cambridge.

A blade remarkably like Fig. 266 was found in the Dolmen of Vinnac [1577] (Aveyron).

A beautifully formed blade, chipped square at the base, and with a series of notches along the sides towards the butt, was found at Arbor Low, Derbyshire. [1578] The late Mr. J. F. Lucas obligingly lent it to me for engraving, as Fig. 267. It is now preserved in the British Museum.

Fig. 267.—Arbor Low. 1/2

In the Wiltshire Barrows, explored by Sir R. Colt Hoare, were several of these daggers. One, [1579] 6 1/2 inches long, was found with a skeleton beneath a large "sarsen stone" near Durrington Walls, in company with a small whetstone, a cone and ring of jet like a pulley, and two small discoidal scrapers. Another, [1580] of much the same form and size as Fig. 264, occurred in company with a drinking-cup, and what was probably a whetstone of "ligniformed asbestos," at the feet of a skeleton in a barrow near Stonehenge.

Others have been found in the barrows of Derbyshire and Yorkshire. In Green Low, on Alsop Moor, [1581] a dagger-blade of flint, 6 inches long, stemmed and barbed arrow-heads, a bone pin, and other bone instruments, were associated with a contracted interment. It was in this barrow also that the pyrites and scrapers, previously mentioned at p. 313, were found. Another leaf-shaped dagger of white flint, 4 1/2 inches long, with the narrow half curiously serrated—as boldly as Fig. 266, but with many more notches—was found by Mr. Bateman beneath the head of a contracted skeleton in Nether Low, [1582] near Chelmorton. Another, 4 1/4 inches long, was found with burnt bones in one of the Three Lows, [1583] near Wetton. A flint dagger, [1584] elegantly chipped, 5 1/4 inches long, was found on Blake Low, near Matlock, in 1786. Fragments of similar daggers have been found with interments in barrows near Pickering; [1585] and in Messrs. Mortimer's rich collection is a fine specimen from a barrow on the Yorkshire Wolds.

One like Fig. 264, but of coarser workmanship, 5 3/4 inches long and 2 3/8 inches wide, was found in 1862, with a skeleton and an earthen vessel, at Norton, near Daventry, and particulars sent to me by the late Mr. S. Sharp, F.S.A., F.G.S.; and what would appear to have been an instrument of the same character, 8 inches long, was found near Maidstone. [1586] A very good specimen, of fine workmanship, is in the Museum at Canterbury, but its place of finding is unknown.

Another, more like Fig. 267, but not serrated, 6 3/4 inches long and 2 inches broad, was found with an urn at Ty ddu Llanelieu, [1587] Brecon, and has been engraved.

In the Greenwell Collection is a blade like Fig. 264, 6 inches long and 2 1/4 inches wide, finely chipped along the edges for 4 inches from the point, which was found at Kempston, near Bedford, in the same field as that shown in Fig. 256. There is also a specimen rather more rudely chipped, and pointed at each end, from Irthington, Cumberland, which has more of the character of a spear-head. In the Fitch Collection is a fine but imperfect dagger from the neighbourhood of Ipswich, and I have one in similar condition from Peasemarsh, near Godalming.

In Scotland one has been found in a cairn at Guthrie, Forfarshire, 6 3/4 inches long and 1 1/2 inches wide, which is engraved in the *Gentleman's Magazine*. [1588] Sir Daniel Wilson [1589] also mentions one 15 inches long, found in a cairn at Craigengelt, near Stirling, but I think there must be some error as to the length.

Mr. J. W. Cursiter, of Kirkwall, has a very symmetrical blade like Fig. 264, but smaller, found in Blows Moss, South Ronaldsay, Orkney. A blade from Nunraw, [1590] Haddingtonshire (7 1/4 inches) with notches at the side for hafting, has been engraved. Another (3 3/8 inches), was found in a cairn near Kirkmichael, Ayrshire. [1591]

Though occurring in so many parts of England and Scotland, these daggers appear to be unknown in Ireland, where, however, some large lozenge-shaped blades, ground on both faces, occur. Sword-like blades made of slaty stone are also found in Ireland [1592] and in Shetland. [1593] I have Irish specimens up to 15 inches in length, and have seen the sketch of one of subquadrate section, and pointed at each end, 20 3/4 inches in length. It was found in the Lower Bann, near Portglenone, co. Antrim.

In some Continental countries, and especially in Denmark, Sweden, and Northern Germany, similar weapons are far more abundant than here. The shape is somewhat different, for the English specimens are as a rule broader in proportion, and more obtusely pointed than the Scandinavian. These latter frequently exhibit the blunting at the edges towards the butt-end, such as has been already mentioned. Occasionally they have the notches at the sides. Daggers with square or fish-tailed handles, like Worsaae, Nos. 52 and 53, some of which present delicately ornamented and crinkled edges, have not as yet been found in Britain, though somewhat analogous forms occur in Honduras and in North America. The crinkling is seen on some Egyptian knives.

Nearly similar blades to those from Britain are found in other parts of Europe. Two lance-heads, made from flakes 5 1/4 inches and 5 3/4 inches long, more or less worked on both faces, and reduced in width at the butt, so as to facilitate insertion in a handle, were found in the sepulchral cave of St. Jean d'Alcas, [1594] in the Aveyron. Another, worked on both faces, about 7 inches long and 1 1/4 inches broad, notched in two or three places on each side at the base, was found in one of the dolmens of the Lozère. [1595] A third, shorter and broader, but also notched at the base, was in the dolmen [1596] of Grailhe (Gard).

A finely-worked, somewhat lozenge-shaped, blade of flint, 10 inches in length, was found at Spiennes, [1597] near Mons, in Belgium.

A lance-head (6 3/4 inches) from the Government of Vladimir, [1598] Russia, has been figured.

A lance-head of flint, 9 inches long and 2 1/8 broad, tanged at the butt, and with a notch on each side of the tang, has been figured by Gastaldi [1599] from a specimen in the Museum at Naples, found at Telese.

In Egypt, associated with other objects betokening a considerable civilization, have been found several thin blades of flint, of much the same character as the highly-finished European specimens. A magnificent lance-head (14 1/2 inches) has been presented to the Ashmolean Museum by Prof. Flinders Petrie [1600]. It is delicately serrated along the edges for most of its length. A smaller blade is more leaf-shaped and minutely serrated all round. Another appears to have been hafted as a dagger. In my own collection is a leaf-shaped blade 7 inches long, most delicately made and serrated. Others are, however, thick at the back, and provided with a tang like a metallic knife. Two of these in the Berlin Museum, [1601] are 7 1/4 inches and 6 3/4 inches long respectively, and 2 1/4 inches and 2 inches wide; I have one 5 1/8 inches in length. There are other specimens in the Egyptian Museums at Leyden and Turin, and in the National Museum [1602] at Edinburgh. A larger blade, and even more closely resembling some of the Scandinavian lunate instruments in form, being leaf-shaped, but more curved on one edge than the other, is also in the Berlin Museum. [1603] It is 9 inches long and 2 1/2 inches wide. A curved scimitar-like knife from Egypt [1604] is figured, as is one with a notch on each side of the butt. [1605] Another blade, of ovate form, and without tang, 2 3/4 inches long and 1 inch wide, is preserved in the Mayer Collection in the Museum [1606] at Liverpool.

Some other Egyptian blades will be subsequently mentioned.

A dagger-blade of flint, still mounted in its original handle, is in the British Museum, [1607] and has already been described.

Some of the dagger-blades in use in Mexico in ancient times were of much the same character as these, being in some cases of flint, in others of obsidian. A beautiful blade of chalcedony, 8 inches long, found at Tezcuco, is in the Christy Collection, as well as another of chert; but the most remarkable is of chalcedony, still in its original wooden handle in form of a kneeling figure, encrusted with precious materials, including turquoise, malachite, and coral. [1608] An almost similar specimen was engraved by Aldrovandus. [1609]

There are Japanese [1610] stone knives and daggers polished all over and with the blade and hilt in one piece. Some are as much as 15 inches long.

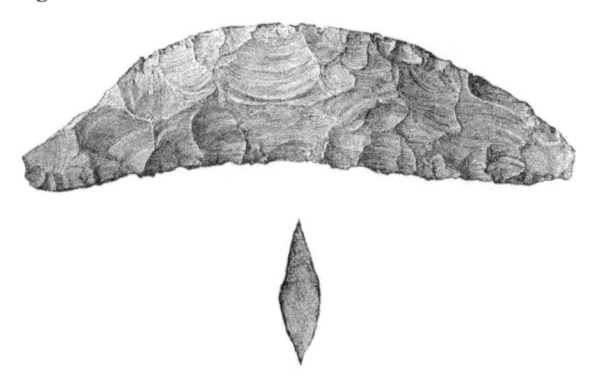

Fig. 267A.—Sewerby. 1/2

A peculiar form of knife, closely resembling in character some of the crescent-shaped blades from Scandinavia, is shown in Fig. 267A. It was found in the parish of Sewerby, [1611] near Bridlington, and somewhat resembles the blade from Balveny, subsequently mentioned. I have described it in some detail [1611] elsewhere. A similar form occurs in Arctic America. [1612] A wider form from New Jersey [1613] has been regarded as a scalping-knife.

Another form of curved knife—for as such it would seem the instrument must be regarded—seems to be more abundant in Britain than in other European countries, unless possibly in Russia. A somewhat similar form is known in Denmark, [1614] of which a highly finished variety is engraved by Worsaae [1615] from an almost, if not quite, unique example. Examples of analogous knives from other countries will also be subsequently cited. As the form has not hitherto received much attention from antiquaries, I have engraved three specimens slightly differing in character, and found in different parts of England.

Fig. 268 represents a beautifully formed knife, with a curved blade tapering to a point, and found in draining at Fimber, Yorkshire. It is preserved in the collection of Messrs. Mortimer, of Driffield, who have kindly allowed me to engrave it. It is about 7 inches in length, formed of flint, which has now become ochreous in colour, and exhibits a portion of the natural crust at the butt-end. The blade is nearly equally convex on the two faces, but thickens out at the butt, which seems to have formed the handle, as the side edges which are elsewhere sharp are there slightly blunted. The faces present no signs of having been ground or polished.

Fig. 268.—Fimber. 1/2

Fig. 269.—Yarmouth. 1/2

I have two or three fragments of similar knives also from the Yorkshire Wolds; and one almost perfect, but only 4 1/2 inches long, from Ganton Wold. In the Greenwell Collection is a fragment of one from Wetwang, and the point of another from Rudstone. I have one (5 inches) perfect except at the butt, found at North Stow, Bury St. Edmunds.

Fig. 269 represents a nearly similar knife, which has, however, been already described, though not figured, in the *Archæological Journal* [1616] and in the *Proceedings of the Society of Antiquaries.* [1617] It was found on Corton Beach, midway between Yarmouth and Lowestoft, and belonged to the late Mr. C. Cory, of Yarmouth, who kindly lent it to me for engraving. It has been suggested that it was fixed to a haft, possibly of stag's horn or of wood, but there are no *indiciæ* of this having been the case, though the side-edges are blunted towards the butt-end, where also remains a considerable portion of the crust of the long nodule of flint from which the instrument was chipped.

For the loan of the original of Fig. 270 I am indebted to the late Mr. Caldecott, of Mead Street, near Eastbourne, near which place it was found. It is of grey flint, and presents the peculiarity of having one face partially polished by grinding, which extends to the point, but does not touch the edges, which, as in the other instances, are produced by chipping only. It is rather more convex on the polished face than on the other, and it appears probable that recourse was had to grinding in order to remove a hard projection of the flint which had been too refractory to be chipped off. As usual, there is a portion of the crust of the original flint visible at the butt, where also the side edges have been blunted, in this case by grinding. This instrument has already been described and figured. [1618]

A curved knife (7 3/4 inches) now in the British Museum, much like Fig. 270, was found at Grovehurst, [1619] near Milton, Kent.

Fig. 270.—Eastbourne. 1/2

In the same museum is a beautifully-chipped knife, 8 1/4 inches long, without any traces of grinding, and of much the same form as this, but with the point more sharply curved. It was found in the Thames, at London, in 1868.

One from Bexley, Kent, is in the Ashmolean Museum at Oxford, and another from the Thames at Greenwich in the Jermyn Street Museum.

The Greenwell Collection contains an implement of this class, but of broader proportions, 4 inches long and 1 3/4 inches wide, with a portion of the natural crust of the flint left on the convex side, not far from the point. It is sharp at the base, which is semicircular, and the edge shows signs of wear. It was found on Heslerton Wold.

A thinner form of curved knife (6 1/2 inches), found at Balveny, [1620] Banffshire, has been figured.

The point of what appears to have been a curved knife of this character was found in the Lake-dwelling of Bodmann. [1621] Some curved knives from one at Attersee [1622] have been engraved. A long flint knife from Majorca, [1623] nearly straight at the edge, but curved at the back, may also be mentioned.

Some curved knives of polished slate, about 5 inches long, notched at the base as if for suspension by means of a string, have been found in Norway. Small blades of chipped flint with a neck for the same purpose are not uncommon in Japan, and occur more rarely in Russia. [1624] In the Greenwell Collection is preserved a curved knife of slate sharpened on the concave side, found in Antrim.

Curved knives of flint, as well as some of the crescent shape, have been found in Volhynia. [1625]

I have seen flint knives in outline very like Fig. 240 in the museums at Cracow, Moscow, and Kiev. Some are highly polished by friction and may have served as sickles.

It is difficult to assign any definite use to the British form of knife, but as the curvature is evidently intentional, and as probably it was more difficult to chip out such curved blades than it would have been to make them straight, there must have been some advantage resulting from the form. As both edges of the blade are sharp, it is hard to say whether the convex or concave edge was the principal object. But inasmuch as the convex edge might more readily be obtained, and that twice over, in a leaf-shaped blade, it appears that the concave edge was the desideratum. The blunting of the edges at the butt-end suggests the probability of the instruments having been held immediately in the hand without the intervention of any form of haft; and the view of the concave edge being the principal one is supported by the circumstance that in the short knife from Ganton Wold, already mentioned, a considerable portion of the crust of the round-ended nodule of flint from which it was made is left along the convex side at the butt-end, while on the opposite side the edge extends the whole length, so that it cannot be comfortably held in the hand except with that edge outwards from the palm. It seems, indeed, adapted for holding in the hand and cutting towards rather than from the operator; and looking at the form universally adopted for reaping instruments, which seem to require a concave edge, so as to gather within them all the stalks that have to be cut, I am inclined to think that these curved flint knives may not impossibly have supplied the place of sickles or reaping hooks, whether for cutting grass to serve as provender or bedding, or for removing the ears of corn from the straw. We know that amongst the inhabitants of the Swiss Lake-dwellings some who were unacquainted with the use of metals had already several domesticated animals, and cultivated more than one kind of cereal, and it is not unfair to infer that the same was the case in Britain. It has already been suggested that some serrated flint flakes may have served for the armature of another form of sickle, like that in use in Egypt at an early period.

The analogy in form between these flint blades and those of the bronze reaping-hooks occasionally found in Britain is striking, when we leave the sockets by which the latter were secured to their handles out of view. These also have usually the outer edge sharp as well as the inner, but for what purpose I cannot say.

This seems a fitting place to say a few words with regard to some Egyptian flint knives, for the knowledge of which we are mainly indebted to Prof. Flinders Petrie, and the workmanship of which is absolutely unrivalled. They are of two kinds, both presenting an outline curved on one or both sides. For the one kind a flake from 8 to 9 inches long of triangular section with a thick back and sharp edge has been taken: the back has been most carefully retouched and left slightly convex: the ridge of the flake has been wrought so as to show a crinkled line like that on the handles of some Danish daggers, the edge has been more or less re-worked, producing a bold convex sweep, and what was originally the inner face of the flake has first been delicately fluted by cross-flaking and then still more finely retouched along both the back and the edge.

For the other kind the whole surface of the original flake has, as Mr. Spurrell [1626] has pointed out, been carefully ground, one face being made rather more convex that the other. The flatter face has been left almost untouched, but one side has been trimmed by flaking at the edge into almost a straight or slightly concave line: the other side is boldly curved, the general outline having been produced during the grinding process. The more convex face has been fluted or "ripple-marked" by cross-flaking from either side in the most skilful manner, the whole of the original polished surface being sometimes removed. The projections at the butt-end between the successive flakes have next been levelled down by secondary chipping, and finally the curved edge has been minutely serrated, there being about 36 teeth to the inch. These blades are from 7 to 9 1/4 inches in length, and occasionally made of beautiful chalcedonic flint. They are attributed by Professor Flinders Petrie [1627] to a period between the fourth and the twelfth Dynasty, but may possibly be of even earlier date. As already mentioned, some beautiful leaf-shaped lance-heads with finely-serrated edges have been made in the same manner.

One of the fluted knives in the Ghizeh Museum [1628] is hafted for a distance of about 4 inches in a thin plate of gold, engraved on the one face with well-drawn figures of animals, and on the other with floral ornaments arranged between two serpents. The plates of gold are not soldered together, but sewn one to the other with gold wire.

CHAPTER XVI.
JAVELIN AND ARROW HEADS.

I now come to a series of flint weapons, small but varying in size, which though presenting a general resemblance in character to each other, are still susceptible of being classified under several types. The similarity is probably due to their having been all intended for the same purpose—that of piercing the skin, whether of enemies in war, or of animals in the chase; the differences may result from some of the weapons having served for warlike and others for hunting purposes. The variation in size probably arises from some of them having tipped spears to be held in the hand for close encounters, while others may have been attached to lighter shafts, and formed javelins to be thrown at objects at some distance; and the majority of the smaller kind were, beyond doubt, the heads of arrows discharged from bows.

The possibly successive ideas of pointing a stake as a weapon of offence, of hardening the point by means of fire, and of substituting a still harder point made of horn, bone, or stone, must have occurred to mankind at the earliest period of its history, and weapons of one or all of these kinds are to be found among savage tribes in all parts of the world. The discovery of the bow, as a means of propelling javelins on a small scale to a distance, seems to belong to a rather higher grade of culture, and its use is not universal among modern savages. The use of the bow and arrow was totally unknown to the aborigines of Australia, [1629] and even the Maories [1630] of New Zealand—who were by no means in the lowest stage of civilization—had, when first discovered, no bows and arrows, nor even slings; in fact, no missile weapon except the lance, which was thrown by hand.

In Europe, however, the use of the bow seems to date back to a very remote period, as in some of the cave-deposits of the Reindeer Period of the South of France, what appear to be undoubtedly arrow-heads are found. In other caves, possibly, though not certainly, inhabited at a somewhat later period, such arrow-heads are absent, though what may be regarded as harpoon-heads of bone occur; and in the River Gravel deposits, nothing that can positively be said to be an arrow-head has as yet been found, though it is barely possible that some of the pointed flakes may have served to tip arrows.

The Greek myth [1631] that bows and arrows were invented by Scythes, the son of Jove, or by Perses, the son of Perseus, though pointing to an extreme antiquity for the invention, not improbably embodies a tradition of the skill in archery of the ancient Scythians and Persians. [1632]

The simplest form of stone-pointed spear or lance at present in use among savages, consists of a long sharp flake of obsidian, or some silicious stone, attached to a shaft, like that shown in Fig. 195; and arrows, tipped with smaller flakes, having but little secondary working at the sides, beyond what was necessary to complete the point, and to form a small tang for insertion into the shaft, may also be seen in Ethnological collections. Between these almost simple flakes and skilfully and symmetrically-chipped lance and arrow heads, all the intermediate stages may be traced among weapons still, or until quite recently, in use among savages; as well as among those which once served to point the weapons of the early occupants of this country.

It is indeed probable that besides these stone-tipped weapons, other seemingly less effective, but actually more deadly missiles, were in use among them in the form of poisoned arrows; but as these at the present day are usually tipped with hard wood or bone, as better adapted than stone for retaining the poison, the same was probably the case in ancient times; and while those of wood have perished, those of bone, if found, have not as yet been recognized. Such arrow-heads of bone were also in use without being poisoned, as, for instance, among the Finns, or Fenni, as Tacitus calls them, whose principal weapons were, for want of iron, bone-pointed arrows. [1633] The use of poisoned arrows had, among the Greeks and Romans, long ceased in classical times, [1634] and is always represented by authors, from the time of Homer downwards, as a characteristic of barbarous nations; and yet, in our own language, a word in common use survives as a memorial of this barbarous custom having been practised by the Greeks probably long before the days of Homer. For from τόξον a bow (or occasionally an arrow [1635]), was derived τοξικόν—*toxicum*—the poison for arrows; a term which gradually included all poisons, even those of the milder form, such as alcohol, the too free use of which results in that form of poisoning still known among us as *intoxication*.

One of the first to mention the discovery of flint arrow-heads in Britain was Dr. Plot, who, in his "Natural History of Staffordshire" [1636] (1686), speaking of the use of iron by "the Britains" in Cæsar's time, observes: "we have reason to believe that, for the most part at lest, they sharpen'd their warlike instruments rather with stones than metall, especiall in the more northerly and inland countries, where they sometimes meet with flints in shape of arrow-heads, whereof I had one sent me by the learned and ingenious Charles Cotton, Esq., found not far from his pleasant mansion at Beresford, exactly in the form of a bearded arrow, jagg'd at each side, with a larger stemm in the middle, whereby I suppose it was fixt to the wood." "These they find in Scotland in much greater plenty, especially in the prefectury of Aberdeen, which, as the learned Sr Robert Sibbald [1637] informs us, they there call Elf-arrows—*Lamiarum Sagittas*—imagining they drop from the clouds, not being to be found upon a diligent search, but now and then by chance in the high beaten roads." "Nor did the Britans only head their arrows with flint, but also their *mataræ* or British darts, which were thrown by those that fought *in essedis*, whereof I guess this is one I had given me, found near Leek, by my worthy friend Mr. Thomas Gent, curiously jagg'd at the edges with such-like teeth as a sickle, and otherwise wrought upon the flat, by which we may conclude, not only that these arrow and spear-heads are all artificial, whatever is pretended, but also that they had anciently some way of working of flints by the toole, which may be seen by the marks, as well as they had of the Egyptian porphyry; which, as the aforesaid worthy Gent. Sir Robert Sibbald, thinks, they learned of the Romans, who, as Aldrovandus [1638] assures us, anciently used such weapons made of stones. However, still, it not being hence deducible, but they may be British, they are not ill-placed here, whatever original they have had from either nation."

Plot gives engravings both of a stemmed and barbed arrow-head, and of a leaf-shaped lance-head or knife.

Sir Robert Sibbald, in his [1639] "Scotia Illustrata," 1684, expresses his belief that the flint arrow-heads are artificial. He possessed two, one like the head of a lance and the other like the end of an anchor, or tanged and barbed. He also relates the account given him by the Laird of Straloch, in Aberdeenshire, which he had passed on to the historian of Staffordshire.

It will be observed that Plot alludes to different opinions regarding these instruments, it being a matter in dispute whether they were artificial, natural, or partly natural; in the same manner as at the time when the flint implements were first discovered in the River Gravels doubts were expressed by some as to their artificial origin, while others regarded them as fossils of natural formation; and others again carried their unconscious Manichæism so far as to ascribe all fossils, and we may presume these included, to diabolical agency. The old Danish collector, Olaf Worm, speaks of a flint of a dark colour [1640] exhibiting the form of a spear-head with such accuracy that it may be doubted whether it is a work of art or of nature, and of others like daggers, which, as being found in ancient grave-hills, are regarded by some as the arms of an early people; while others doubt whether they are the work of art or nature; and others consider them to be thunderbolts. One reason in former times for doubting the artificial origin of the most highly finished instruments was ignorance of how such objects could have been chipped out. After describing one of the beautiful Danish daggers, with the delicately "ripple-marked" blade and the square ornamented handle, Worm remarks—"si silex ullo modo arte foret tractabilis, potius Arte quam Naturâ elaboratum esse hoc corpus jurares." [1641]

Aldrovandus [1642] engraves a flint arrow-head as a Glossopetra— a stone which, according to Pliny, [1643] "resembleth a man's tongue, and groweth not upon the ground, but in the eclipse of the moone falleth from heaven," and which "is thought by the magicians to be verie necessarie for those that court faire women."

But perhaps one of the most curious of these early notices of flint arrow-heads is that given in the "Catalogue and Description of the Natural and Artificial Rarities belonging to the Royal Society and preserved at Gresham College," [1644] made by Nehemiah Grew, M.D., F.R.S. In Part III., Chap. V., Of Regular Stones, Dr. Grew speaks of "The flat Bolthead—*Anchorites*. Of affinity with that well described by Wormius [1645] with the title of *Silex venabuli ferreum cuspidem exacte referens*. By Moscardo [1646] with that of *Pietre Ceraunie*; who also figures it with three or four varieties. This like those of a perfect Flint and semiperspicuous. 'Tis likewise, in the same manner, pointed, like a *Speer*, having at the other end, like those of Moscardo, a short handle. But, moreover, hath this peculiar, that 'tis pointed or spiked also backward on both sides of the Handle, with some resemblance to an Anchor or the head of a Bearded Dart, from whence I have named it. 'Tis likewise tooth'd on the edges, and the sides as it were wrought with a kind of undulated sculpture, as those before mentioned. Another different from the former, in that it is longer, hath a deeper indenture, but no handle. Both of them strike fire like other *flints*." There is a representation given of this Anchorites, which shows it to have been a common barbed arrow-head with a central stem.

Moscardo's [1647] figures which are here cited represent for the most part tanged arrow-heads. He says that Bonardo relates that they fall from the clouds, and that those who carry them cannot be drowned or struck by lightning. They produce, moreover, pleasant dreams.

Mention has already been made of the superstition attaching to flint arrow-heads in Scotland, where they were popularly regarded as the missiles of Elves. In speaking of them Dr. Stuart [1648] quotes Robert Gordon of Straloch, the well-known Scottish geographer, who wrote about 1661. After giving some details concerning elf-darts, this writer says that these wonderful stones are sometimes found in the fields and in public and beaten roads, but never by searching for them; to-day, perhaps one will be found where yesterday nothing could be seen, and in the afternoon in places where before noon there was none, and this most frequently under clear skies and on summer days. He then gives instances related to him by a man and a woman of credit, each of whom while riding found an arrow-head in their clothes in this unexpected way. Mr. F. C. Lukis, F.S.A., [1649] draws a distinction between the elf-shot or elf-arrow and the elf-dart, the latter being of larger dimensions and leaf-shaped. He gives an engraving of one which has been mounted in a silver frame and worn as a charm. The cut is here reproduced, as Fig. 271. The initials at the back are probably those of the owner, who mounted the amulet in silver, and of his wife. It was worn by an old Scottish lady for half a century. Others thus mounted were exhibited in the Museum of the Archæological Institute at Edinburgh in 1856. [1650]

Fig. 271.—Elf-Shot.

Another arrow-head, also thus mounted, is engraved by Douglas, [1651] but in this instance it was found in Ireland, where "the peasants call them elf-arrows, and frequently set them in silver, and wear them on their necks as amulets against the AITHADH or elf-shot." Others are engraved in the *Philosophical Transactions* [1652] and in Gough's "Camden's Britannia." [1653] Sir W. Wilde [1654] informs us that in the North of Ireland, when cattle are sick and the cattle doctor or fairy doctor is sent for, he often says that the beast has been elf-shot, or stricken by fairy or elfin darts, and by some legerdemain contrives to find in its skin one or more poisoned weapons, which, with some coins, are then placed in the water which is given the animal to drink, and a cure is said to be effected. The Rev. Dr. Buick, [1655] in an article on Irish flint arrow-heads, has given some particulars as to their use in curing cattle that are bewitched, and the Folklore Society [1656] has published some details as to the beliefs still existing with regard to fairy darts. The same view of disease being caused by weapons shot by fairies at cattle, and much the same method of cure, prevailed, and indeed in places even now prevails, in Scotland. [1657]

The late Dr. J. Hill Burton informed me that it is still an article of faith that elf-bolts after finding should not be exposed to the sun, or they are liable to be recovered by the fairies, who then work mischief with them.

Mr. Llewellynn Jewitt has recorded a similar elf-arrow superstition [1658] as obtaining in Derbyshire, where flint arrow and spear heads are by some regarded as fairy darts, and supposed to have been used by the fairies in injuring and wounding cattle. It was with reference to discoveries near Buxton, in that county, that Stukeley wrote—"Little flint arrow-heads of the ancient Britons, called elfs'-arrows, are frequently ploughed up here." [1659]

The late Sir Daniel Wilson [1660] gives many interesting particulars regarding the elf-bolt, elf-shot, or elfin-arrow, which bears the synonymous Gaelic name of *Sciat-hee*, and cites from Pitcairn's "Criminal Trials," the description of a cavern where the archfiend carries on the manufacture of elf-arrows with the help of his attendant imps, who rough-hewed them for him to finish. He also mentions the passage in a letter from Dr. Hickes [1661] to Pepys, recording that my Lord Tarbut, or some other lord, did produce one of those elf-arrows which one of his tenants or neighbours took out of the heart of one of his cattle that died of an usual death (*sic*). Dr. Hickes had another strange story, but very well attested, of an elf-arrow that was shot at a venerable Irish bishop by an evil spirit, in a terrible noise louder than thunder, which shaked the house where the bishop was.

Similar superstitions prevailed among the Scandinavian [1662] nations, by whom a peculiar virtue was supposed to be inherent in flint arrow-heads, which was not to be found in those of metal.

The fact, already mentioned, of arrow-heads of flint being appended to Etruscan [1663] necklaces of gold, apparently as a sort of charm, seems to show that a belief in the supernatural origin of these weapons, and their consequent miraculous powers, was of very ancient date. It has still survived in Italy, [1664] where the peasants keep flint arrow-heads to preserve their houses from lightning, believing that the lightning comes down to strike with a similar stone—a superstition which Professor Gastaldi also found prevalent in Piedmont. In some instances they are carried on the person as preservatives against lightning, and in parts of the Abruzzo [1665] they are known as *lingue di S. Paolo,* and the countryman who finds one devoutly kneels down, picks it up with his own tongue, and jealously preserves it as a most potent amulet. In the Foresi Collection [1666] at the Paris Exhibition were some arrow-heads mounted in silver as amulets, like those in Scotland, but brought from the Isle of Elba. Another has been engraved by Dr. C. Rosa. [1667]

M. Cartailhac [1668] has published an interesting pamphlet on such superstitions, and Professor Bellucci has also dilated upon them. They are abundant in the neighbourhood of Perugia. [1669]

It is a curious circumstance, that necklaces formed of cornelian beads, much of the shape of stemmed arrow-heads, with the perforation through the central tang, are worn by the Arabs of Northern Africa at the present day, being regarded, as I was informed by the Rev. J. Greville Chester, as good for the blood. Similar charms are also worn in Turkey. I have a necklace of fifteen such arrow-head-like beads, with a central amulet, which was purchased by my son in a shop at Kostainicza, [1670] in Turkish Croatia. Among the Zuñis [1671] of New Mexico, stone arrow-heads are frequently attached to figures of animals so as to form charms or fetishes.

Enough, however, has been said with regard to the superstitions attaching to these arrow-heads of stone; the existence of such a belief in their supernatural origin, dating, as it seems to do, to a comparatively remote period, goes to prove that even in the days when the belief originated, the use of stone arrow-heads was not known, nor was there any tradition extant of a people whose weapons they had been. And yet it is probable that of all the instruments made of stone, arrow-heads would be among the last to drop out of use, being both well adapted for the purpose they served, and at the same time formed of a material so abundant, that with weapons so liable to be lost as arrows, it would be preferred to metal, at a time when this was scarce and costly. In this country, at all events, the extreme scarcity of bronze arrow-heads is remarkable, while we know from interments that flint arrow-heads were in common use by those who employed bronze for other weapons or implements. There appears to be some doubt as to whether the arrow-heads, or rather the flakes of black flint or obsidian which have been found in considerable numbers associated with bronze arrow-heads on the field of Marathon, were made in Greece, or whether they were not rather in use among some of the barbarian allies of the Persian King. M. Lenormant [1672] is clearly of the opinion that they are not of Greek origin, [1673] but this is contested by others, and probably with reason. Whatever their origin, there is a strong argument against stone arrow-heads having been in use among the Greeks at so late a period as the battle of Marathon, B.C. 490, in the fact that Herodotus, [1674] writing but shortly afterwards, records, as an exceptional case, that in the army of Xerxes, *circa* B.C. 480, the arrows of some of the Æthiopian contingent were tipped with stone, while those of some Indian nations were even pointed with iron. So early as the days of Homer the arrow-heads of the Greeks were of bronze, and had the three longitudinal ribs upon them, like those in that metal found at Marathon, for he speaks of the χαλκῆρε ὀϊστόν [1675] and applies to it the epithet τριγλώχιν. [1676]

Even among such rude tribes as the Massagetæ and Scythians, the arrow-heads, in the days of Herodotus, were of bronze; as he records an ingenious method adopted by one Ariantas, [1677] a king of the Scythians, to take a census of his people by levying an arrow-head from each, all of which were afterwards cast into an enormous bronze vessel.

Besides the Æthiopians there was another nation which made use of stone-pointed arrows in Africa, as is proved by the arrows from Egyptian tombs, of which specimens are preserved in several of our museums. The head, which is of flint, differs however from all the ordinary forms, inasmuch as it is chisel-shaped rather than pointed, and in form much resembles a small gun-flint. The tip of one of these, secured to the shaft by bitumen, is shown in Fig. 272. The original is in the British Museum. In my own collection are some specimens of such arrows. Their total length is about 35 inches and the shafts for about two-thirds of their length are made of reed, the remainder towards the point being of wood. Near the notch for the string are distinct traces of there having been a feather on either side, in the same plane as the notch. It is probable that arrow-heads of similar character may have been in use in Britain, though they have hitherto almost escaped observation, owing to the extreme simplicity of their form. To these I shall subsequently recur.

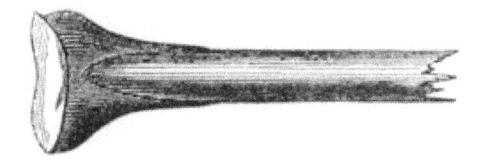

Fig. 272.—Egypt. 1/1

Some of the Egyptian arrows [1678] have supplemental flakes at the sides, so as practically to make the edge of the arrow-head wider.

In October, 1894, the Ghizeh Museum acquired from a Sixth Dynasty tomb at Assiut, two squadrons of soldiers, each of forty figures carved in wood. The figures of one set, presumed to be Egyptians, have a brown complexion and are armed with bronze-tipped spears and with shields. The figures are about 13 inches high. The other group is shorter, and the soldiers are black-skinned and armed with bow and arrows only; each has a bow in his left hand, and in his right four arrows with chisel-shaped heads of flint. [1679]

The better-known forms of arrow-heads which occur in Britain may be classed as the leaf-shaped, the lozenge-shaped, the tanged or stemmed, and the triangular, each presenting several varieties. The arrow-heads of the third class are in this country usually barbed; those of the fourth but rarely.

Whether the forms were successively developed in this order is a question difficult of solution; but in an ingenious paper by Mr. W. C. Little, of Liberton, published early in this century, being "An Inquiry into the Expedients used by the Scotts before the Discovery of Metals," [1680] the lozenge-shaped are regarded as the earliest; next, those barbed with two witters, [1681] but no middle tang; and last, the tanged. The same author argues from analogy that the ancients could extend this flint manufacture to other purposes, "as the same ingenuity which formed the head of an arrow could also produce a knife, a saw, and a piercer."

Colonel A. Lane-Fox, now General Pitt Rivers, in his second lecture on "Primitive Warfare," [1682] arranges the forms of arrow-heads in the same manner as I have here adopted, and shows that the transition from one form to the other is easy and natural. There are, indeed, some arrow-heads of which it would be impossible to say whether they were leaf-shaped or lozenge-shaped, or whether they were lozenge-shaped or tanged.

Sir William Wilde regards the triangular as the primary form, and the leaf-shaped and lozenge-shaped as the last.

Mr. W. J. Knowles [1683] has suggested a somewhat different classification, but it seems unnecessary to alter the arrangement here adopted. He does not enter into the question of the development of the forms. An exhaustive paper on Irish flint arrow-heads, by the Rev. Dr. Buick, [1684] may be usefully consulted.

Whatever may have been the order of the development of the forms, it would, in my opinion, be unwarrantable to attempt any chronological arrangement founded upon mere form, as there is little doubt of the whole of these varieties having been in use in one and the same district at the same time, the shape being to some extent adapted to the flake of flint from which the arrow-heads were made, and to some extent to the purposes which the arrows were to serve. The arrow-heads in use among the North American Indians, [1685] when intended for hunting, were so contrived that they could be drawn out of the wound, but those destined for war were formed and attached to the shaft in such a manner, that when it was attempted to pull out the arrow, its head became detached, and remained in the wound. The poisoned arrows of the Bushmen of South Africa [1686] are in like manner made with triangular heads of iron, which become detached in the body if an attempt is made to withdraw the arrow from the wound that it has caused.

I have already remarked on the difficulty of distinguishing between javelin and arrow heads; but, from their size, I think that the late Dr. Thurnam was justified in regarding those engraved as Figs. 273, 274, 275, as heads of javelins; and they may therefore be taken first in order. Two of them have already been engraved. [1687] Their beautifully worked surfaces had, however, hardly had justice done them, and, by the kindness of Dr. Thurnam, I was able to have them engraved afresh full size. They were found in 1864, in company with another almost identical in form with the middle figure, in an oval barrow on Winterbourn Stoke Down, about a mile and a half north-west of Stonehenge, close to the head of a contracted skeleton. They are most skilfully chipped on both faces, which are equally convex, and they are not more than a quarter of an inch in thickness. Three are leaf-shaped, and one lozenge-shaped, and this latter, though larger, is thinner and more delicate. They have acquired a milky, porcellanous surface while lying in the earth. They are all four now in the British Museum. As has been remarked by Dr. Thurnam, objects of this description have rarely been found in barrows.

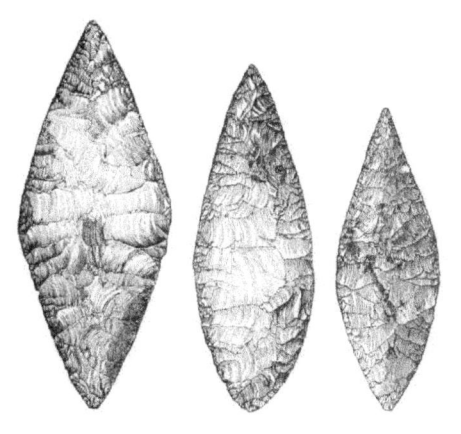

Fig. 273.

Fig. 274.

Fig. 275.

Winterbourn Stoke.

The two javelin-heads, if such they be, found by Mr. J. R. Mortimer in the Calais Wold barrow, near Pocklington, Yorkshire, [1688] are lozenge-shaped and much more acutely pointed, and were accompanied by two lozenge-shaped arrow-heads. By the kindness of the late Mr. Llewellynn Jewitt they are all four here reproduced as Figs. 276 to 279. A similar javelin-head to Fig. 277, 2 3/4 inches long, now in the British Museum, was found by the late Lord Londesborough in a barrow on Seamer Moor, near Scarborough. [1689] A fine lozenge-shaped javelin-head (5 inches) was found with arrow-heads, scrapers, and knives, near Longcliffe, [1690] Derbyshire, and some delicate arrow-heads, broken, at Harborough Rocks, [1691] in the same county. Javelin-heads of much the same form as those from Winterbourn Stoke and Calais Wold occur not unfrequently in Ireland, but are rarely quite so delicately chipped. Lozenge-shaped arrow-heads are recorded from a cairn at Unstan, [1692] Orkney, and from the Culbin Sands. [1693] The class having both faces polished, though still only chipped at the edges, like Wilde's [1694] Fig. 27, has not, except in Portugal, as yet occurred out of Ireland. A few of these may have served as knives or daggers, as they are intentionally rounded by grinding at the more tapered end, which at first sight appears to have been intended for the point and not for the handle. The long lozenge-shaped form is found in the Government of Vladimir, Russia. [1695]

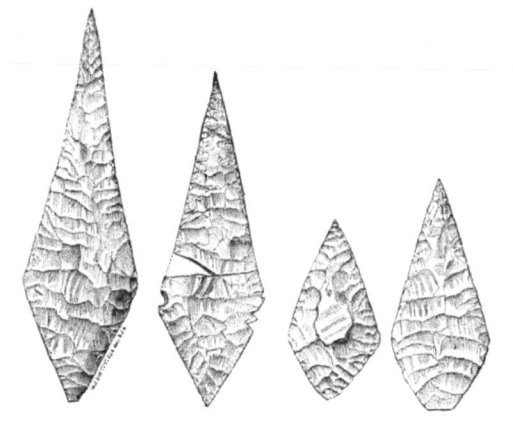

Fig. 276.

Fig. 277.

Fig. 278.

Fig. 279.

Calais Wold Barrow.

Large lozenge-shaped lance-heads were occasionally in use among the North American Indians; [1696] but the more usual form is a long blade, notched at the base to receive the ligature which binds it to the shaft.

Of leaf-shaped arrow-heads, which form the first class now to be described, there are several minor varieties, both in outline and section, some being longer in proportion to their breadth than others, rounder or more pointed at the base, thicker or thinner, or more carefully chipped on one face than the other. A few typical examples are given full size in the annexed woodcuts. The originals are all in my own collection, unless otherwise specified.

Fig. 280 is from the neighbourhood of Icklingham, Suffolk, of flint become nearly white by weathering, and carefully chipped on both faces, one of which is, however, more convex than the other. I have a larger but imperfect specimen of the same form from Oundle. A nearly similar arrow-head, of yellow flint, from Hoxne, Suffolk, has been figured. [1697] It was supposed to have occurred in the same deposit as that containing large palæolithic implements and elephant remains; but nothing certain is known on this point, and from the form there can be no hesitation in assigning it to the Neolithic Period. A rather smaller arrow-head, but of much the same character, was found at Bradford Abbas, Dorset. [1698] Professor Buckman had several leaf-shaped arrows from the same neighbourhood. Some of them were long and slender, more like Fig. 286.

In Fig. 281 is shown an arrow-head of rather broader proportions, from Gunthorpe, Lincolnshire, which has been engraved in the *Reliquary*, [1699] whence the block is borrowed. I have specimens of the same form, delicately chipped on both faces, and found near Icklingham and Lakenheath, Suffolk. Occasionally, one face of the arrow-heads of this form is left nearly flat.

Fig. 280.—Icklingham.

Fig. 281.—Gunthorpe.

Fig. 282.—Yorkshire Wolds.

Fig. 282 shows a smaller specimen in the extensive Greenwell Collection. In this instance, the flake from which the arrow-head was made has been but little retouched on the flat face. It is slightly curved longitudinally, but probably not to a sufficient extent to affect the flight of the arrow. This form is of common occurrence on the Yorkshire Wolds, though very variable in its proportions, and also in point of symmetry, both as regards outline and similarity of the two faces.

Fig. 283.—Yorkshire Wolds.

Fig. 284.—Little Solsbury Hill.

Fig. 285.—Yorkshire Wolds.

Fig. 286.—Bridlington.

In Fig. 283 is shown another and broader form, from Butterwick, on the Yorkshire Wolds. It is in the same collection, and is worked on both faces. The sides are slightly ogival, so as to produce a sharper point.

Occasionally, instead of being sharply pointed, arrow-heads are more oval in form. An instance of this kind is given in Fig. 284, the original of which was found by Mr. Francis Galton, F.R.S., on the occasion of a visit with me to the camp of Little Solsbury Hill, near Bath. It is of flint that has become white with exposure, equally convex on the two faces, and rather thick in proportion to its size. I have a somewhat similar but broader specimen from the camp of Maiden Bower, near Dunstable, and others even more rounded at the point, and larger and thinner, from Willerby Wold, Yorkshire, and from Icklingham. I have one Yorkshire specimen, which is almost circular in form, and bears traces of grinding on one of its faces. In the Greenwell Collection are specimens of almost all intermediate proportions between an oval like Fig. 284 and a perfect circle.

More lanceolate forms are shown in Figs. 285 and 286, both from Yorkshire. Fig. 285, though worked on both faces, still exhibits portions of the original surface of the flake from which it was made; but Fig. 286, from Grindale, near Bridlington, is of transparent chalcedonic flint, beautifully and symmetrically worked over both faces. This elongated form is not of common occurrence. I have a beautiful example, of the same general character, but pointed at either end, found near Icklingham, Suffolk. A large example of this form, from Derbyshire, in the Bateman Collection, may have been a javelin-head.

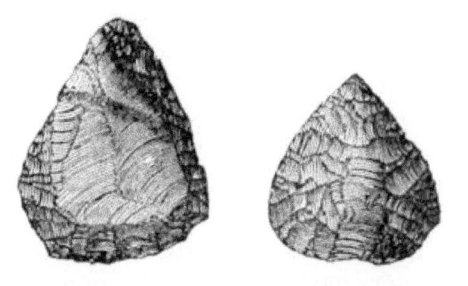

Figs. 287 and 288.—Yorkshire Wolds.

Other and shorter forms are shown in Figs. 287 and 288, the former of which has been made from a flat flake, the original surface of which remains intact on a large portion of each face. Fig. 288, on the contrary, is carefully chipped over the whole of both faces, which are equally convex. It has a slightly heart-shaped form.

It will have been observed that in all these specimens the base of the arrow-head is much more rounded that the point. This, however, is by no means universally the case with the leaf-shaped arrow-heads, the bases of which are in some instances almost, if not quite, as acute as the points. It is, in fact, sometimes difficult to say which of the ends was intended for the point.

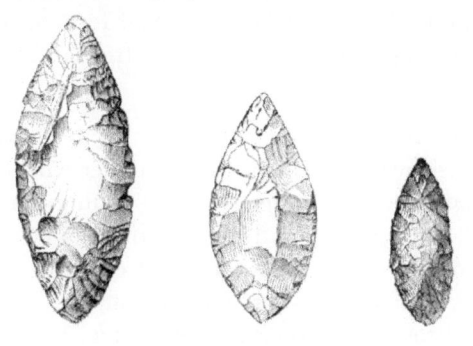

Fig. 289.—Lakenheath.

Figs. 290 and 291.—Yorkshire Wolds.

Fig. 289 shows a large arrow-head from Lakenheath, Suffolk, from the collection of the late Mr. J. W. Flower, F.G.S. It is equally convex on both faces, and almost equally sharp at both ends. In the Greenwell Collection are similar specimens from Burnt Fen, Cambs.

Others, of the same character, but of smaller size, are engraved in Figs. 290 and 291. Both the originals are from the Yorkshire Wolds.

That shown in Fig. 290 is in the Greenwell Collection. It is thin, slightly curved longitudinally, and very neatly worked into shape at the edges. It is a form of not unfrequent occurrence in the Yorkshire Wolds, sometimes of larger dimensions, and more roughly chipped, but more commonly of smaller size. I have a beautifully-made arrow-head of nearly the same size and shape, found at Lakenheath, Suffolk. It is not more than one-eighth of an inch in thickness. One of wider proportions from Burnt Fen is in the Greenwell Collection. Fig. 291 is thicker in proportion to its width, more convex on one face than the other, and less acutely pointed at the base.

In Figs. 292 and 293 are shown some more or less unsymmetrical varieties of form. Fig. 292 is, towards the point, equally convex on each face; but at the base the flat inner face of the original flake has been left untouched, so that the edge is like that of a "scraper," or of a round-nosed chisel. Though the point is, in all respects, identical with that of undoubted arrow-heads, and though I have placed it here among them, it is possible that that end may, after all, have been intended for insertion in a handle, and that it was a small cutting tool, and not an arrow-head.

There can be no doubt of the purpose of Fig. 293, which is of white flint delicately chipped, and is equally convex on the two faces. On one side the outline is almost angular, instead of forming a regular sweep, so that it shows how easy is the passage from the leaf-shape to the lozenge form.

There are often instances like that afforded by the arrow-head engraved in Fig. 294, where it is hard to say under which form a specimen should be placed. The original of this figure forms part of the Greenwell Collection, and is neatly worked on both faces. I have a somewhat broader arrow-head of the same character, which I found in the camp of Maiden Bower, near Dunstable. General Pitt Rivers found one of the same form, and one like Fig. 311, within an earthwork at Callow Hill, [1700] Oxfordshire. Another was found with a perforated hammer, a flint flake ground at the edge, some scrapers, and other objects, in a cairn in Caithness. [1701] One like Fig. 294, but smaller, was found in the Horned Cairn [1702] of Get, at Garrywhin, Caithness. A large specimen from Glenluce [1703] has been figured. Another, very thin, found at Urquhart, Elgin, is in the Edinburgh Museum.

Figs. 292 and 293.—Yorkshire Wolds.

Fig. 294.—Yorkshire Wolds.

Fig. 295.—Fyfield.

It is to arrow-heads of this leaf-shaped form, but approximating closely to the lozenge-shaped, that Dr. Thurnam [1704] is inclined to assign a connection with the class of tumuli known as long barrows; and in support of this view he has cited several cases of their discovery in this form of barrow, in which no barbed arrow-heads have hitherto been found. Some leaf-shaped arrow-heads were found in a long barrow at Walker's Hill, Wilts. [1705]

The annexed cut, kindly furnished by the Society of Antiquaries, shows an arrow-head from a long barrow near Fyfield, Wilts. It is delicately chipped, and weighs only forty-three grains. Another, 1 1/2 inches in length, from a long barrow on Alton Down, is of surprising thinness, and weighs only thirty grains. Others, it would seem purposely injured at the point, were found in the long chambered barrow at Rodmarton, Gloucestershire. [1706] Others, again, were found by Mr. Bateman in long barrows in Derbyshire and Staffordshire. One of these, from Ringham Low, is 2 1/4 inches long and 1 inch broad, yet weighs less than forty-eight grains. In Long Low, Wetton, [1707] were three such arrow-heads, and many flakes of flint. Dr. Thurnam, in speaking of the leaf-shaped as the long-barrow type of arrow-head, does not restrict it to that form of tumulus, but merely indicates it as that which is alone found there. The form indeed occurred elsewhere, thus, one was found in a bowl-shaped barrow at Ogbourne, [1708] Wilts.

The Calais Wold barrow, [1709] already mentioned as having produced four lozenge-shaped javelin and arrow heads, is circular, while that on Pistle Down, Dorsetshire, [1710] which contained four beautifully-chipped arrow-heads of this type, is oblong.

Leaf-shaped arrow-heads are mentioned as having been found with burnt bones in Grub Low, Staffordshire. [1711] The same forms, more or less carefully chipped, and occasionally almost flat on the face, are frequently found on the surface in various parts of Scotland, [1712] especially in the counties of Aberdeen, Banff, Elgin, and Moray. One not of flint, but apparently of quartzite, was found near Glenluce, [1713] Wigtownshire. Numbers have been found on the Culbin Sands, [1714] and at Urquhart. [1715] They are comparatively abundant in Yorkshire, Derbyshire, and Suffolk, but rarer in the southern counties of England. They have been found at Grovehurst, [1716] near Milton, Kent, and I have picked up a specimen near Kit's Coty House. I have seen specimens found at Redhill, near Reigate; [1717] near Bournemouth; at Prince Town, Dartmoor; and near Oundle; besides the localities already mentioned.

Fig. 296.—Bridlington.

Fig. 297.—Newton Ketton.

Figs. 298 and 299.—Yorkshire Wolds.

Typical lozenge-shaped arrow-heads are, in Britain, and, indeed, in other countries, rarer than the leaf-shaped. That shown in Fig. 296 has been made from a flat flake, and is nicely chipped on both faces, though not quite straight longitudinally. It was found at Northdale Farm, Grindale, Bridlington. A Scottish specimen, from Urquhart, [1718] Elginshire, slightly smaller, has been figured. The original of Fig. 297 forms part of the Greenwell Collection, and has been made from a very thin, transparent flake. It is rather less worked on the face opposite to that here shown. It was found at Newton Ketton, Durham. One like Fig. 297 was found on Bull Hill, [1719] Lancashire. A regularly-chipped arrow-head of lozenge shape is said to have been found at Cutterly Clump, Wilts; [1720] and I have seen a few specimens from Derbyshire. Those from the Calais Wold Barrow have already been mentioned.

A diamond-shaped arrow-head was found at Cregneesh, [1721] Isle of Man; and another, as well as one of leaf shape, within a stone circle near Port Erin. [1722] Lozenge-shaped arrow-heads are frequently found in Scotland.

A more elongated form is shown in Figs. 298 and 299, taken from specimens found on the Yorkshire Wolds. Both of them are neatly chipped on either face, and have but little left of the original surface of the flakes from which they were formed. One of the shorter sides of Fig. 299 is somewhat hollowed, *possibly* to give a slight shoulder, and thus prevent its being driven into the shaft.

This is more evidently the case with the arrow-head represented in Fig. 300, which, like so many others, comes from the Wolds of Yorkshire. It is made from a slightly curved flake, and is more convex on one face than the other, especially at the stem or tang.

In the collection of Messrs. Mortimer, of Driffield, is another Yorkshire arrow-head, which is leaf-shaped, but provided with a slight tang.

Leaf-shaped arrow-heads, with a decided stem like that of the leaf, found in Arabia and Japan, will be mentioned at a subsequent page.

Fig. 300.—Yorkshire Wolds.

Fig. 301.—Amotherby.

Fig. 302.—Iwerne Minster.

Another of these stemmed but barbless arrow-heads, from the same district, is shown in Fig. 301. It was found at Amotherby, near

Malton, and was given to me by the late Mr. Charles Monkman, of that place. It has been made from a flat flake, and has been worked into shape by a slight amount of chipping along the edges, which does not extend over the face. There are numerous arrow-heads of the same class, though not of the same form, which have been made from flakes of the proper thickness, by a little secondary working to give them a point, and by slightly trimming the butt-end of the flake. They usually approximate to the leaf-shape in form, but, as might be expected, vary considerably in size, proportions, and the amount of symmetry displayed. It seems needless to engrave specimens.

The weapon point shown in Fig. 302 is so large that possibly it may be regarded as that of a javelin, and not of an arrow. In was in the collection of Mr. H. Durden, of Blandford, and is now in the British Museum. It was found on Iwerne Minster Down, Dorsetshire. It is boldly and symmetrically chipped, thick in proportion to its breadth, and equally convex on both faces; though distinctly stemmed, it can hardly be said to be barbed. It much resembles an Italian specimen in the Arsenal of Turin. [1723]

A somewhat more distinctly-barbed arrow-head from the Yorkshire Wolds is represented in Fig. 303. Its thickness, 5/16 inch, is great in proportion to its size; the two faces are equally convex, and the stem widens out slightly at the base. The same is the case with a smaller and thinner arrow-head in my collection, of somewhat similar form, found near the camp of Maiden Bower, Dunstable. A third, from the Yorkshire Wolds, presents the same peculiarity, which is still more apparent in an arrow-head from a barrow on Seamer Moor, near Scarborough, [1724] if indeed it has been correctly figured.

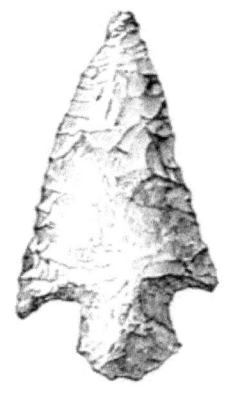

Fig. 303.—Yorkshire Wolds.

A magnificent specimen of much the same type as Fig. 303, but nearly twice as long, has been kindly lent me for engraving by Messrs. Mortimer, of Driffield, Yorkshire. It was found in the neighbourhood of Fimber, and is shown in Fig. 304. It is neatly chipped over both faces, which are equally convex, and the stem is carefully shaped and of considerable thickness. The edges, as is not unfrequently the case, are serrated.

The fine arrow-head engraved as Fig. 305 shows the barbs or "witters" still more strongly developed. One of them is, however, less pointed than the other. From its size, this and others may have formed the heads of javelins rather than of arrows, though arrow-heads as large are still in use among some savage tribes. It was found at Pick Rudge Farm, [1725] Overton, Wilts, in company with the oblong implement engraved as Fig. 255. It is now in the Blackmore Museum, the Trustees of which kindly allowed me to figure it.

I have a very fine specimen with even longer barbs, from Ashwell, Herts, which is shown in Fig. 305A.

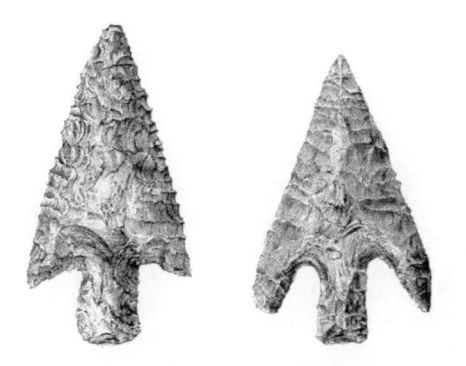

Fig. 304.—Yorkshire Wolds.

Fig. 305.—Pick Rudge Farm.

Fig. 306 represents another unusually large specimen, found on Sherburn Wold, Yorkshire. It is nicely worked on both faces, and the end of the stem or tang has been carefully chipped to a sharp semicircular edge, well adapted for fixing into the split shaft. One similar to it was found on Bull Hill, [1726] Lancashire. Mr. A. C. Savin, of Cromer, has a rather smaller arrow-head of this type, but with the sides more curved outwards, like Fig. 313, found near Aylsham. Barbed arrow-heads of various forms and sizes are of frequent occurrence in some parts of the Yorkshire Wolds and Moors, and in parts of Berkshire, Oxfordshire, Gloucestershire, Suffolk and Derbyshire.

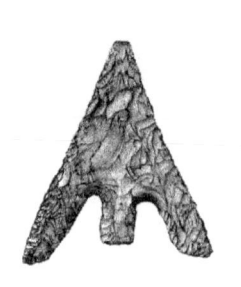

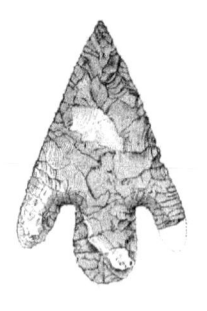

Fig. 305A.—Ashwell.

Fig. 306.—Sherburn Wold.

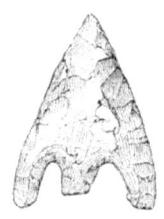

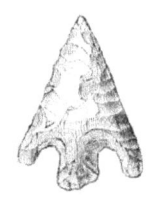

Fig. 307.

Fig. 308.

Fig. 309.

Yorkshire Wolds.

Fig. 310.

Fig. 311.

Fig. 312.

Yorkshire Wolds.

It would be tedious to attempt to exhibit all the different varieties, but specimens of the more ordinary forms are given in Figs. 307 to 312, from originals principally in the Greenwell Collection. As a rule, there is but little difference in the convexity of the two faces, though very frequently one face is decidedly flatter than the other; and occasionally the flat face of the original flake has been left almost untouched. Fig. 311 affords an example of this kind, being nearly flat on the face not shown, while the other face still retains part of the crust of the flint nodule from which the flake was struck. The central stem or tang varies much in its proportions to the size of the arrow-head, and occasionally forms but an inconsiderable projection, as in Fig. 309, making the form approximate to the triangular. Sometimes, as in Fig. 312, the ends of the barbs are carefully chipped straight, as is the case with many arrow-heads from the more southern parts of England, some of which will shortly be noticed. An arrow-head like Fig. 312 was found near Ashwell, [1727] Herts.

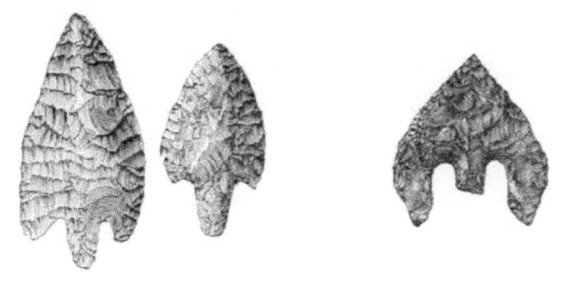

Figs. 313 and 314.—Yorkshire Wolds.

Fig. 314A.—Icklingham.

Before quitting the arrow-heads of the Yorkshire Wolds, I must insert figures of two other specimens illustrative of another form. Of these, that shown in Fig. 313 was found at Northdale Farm, Grindale, Bridlington. It is thick in proportion to its size, and skilfully chipped on both faces. The tang is thin and slight. The other arrow-head Fig. 314 is not so thick in proportion. In both, if the sweep of the outline were continued past the barbs, it would about meet the extremity of the tang, and give a leaf-shaped form; so that it seems probable that this class was made by first chipping out the simple leaf-shaped form, and then working in a notch on either side to produce the tangs and barbs. The same type occurs in Suffolk. An exaggerated example, rather like Fig. 320 but broader, found near Icklingham, is shown in Fig. 314A.

The next specimen that I have selected for engraving, Fig. 315, is from another part of the country, having been found by myself in 1866 on the surface of a field, at the foot of the Chalk escarpment between Eddlesborough and Tring, Herts. It can hardly be regarded as unfinished, though one of the surfaces is very rough and the outline far from symmetrical. It rather shows how rude were some of the appliances of our savage predecessors in Britain. Curiously enough, some barbed flint arrow-heads of nearly similar form, and but little more symmetrical (to judge from the engravings), were found in 1763 at Tring Grove, Herts, [1728] with an extended skeleton. They lay between the legs, and at the feet were some of the perforated plates of greenish stone of the character of Fig. 354. An arrow-head of much the same form was found in a barrow near Tenby, [1729] with human bones and a part of a curious ring-shaped ornament, supposed to be of ivory. The long tapering arrow-head shown in Fig. 316 affords a contrast to this broad form. Its barbs are unfortunately not quite perfect, but the form being uncommon I have engraved it. It was found in Reach Fen, Cambridgeshire. A ruder example of the same form as Fig. 316, from Bourn Fen, has been figured in Miller and Skertchly's "Fen-land." [1730] A longer specimen, almost as acutely pointed, and with square-ended barbs, found on Lanchester Common, [1731] Durham, is in the Museum of the Society of Antiquaries of Newcastle. I have several others of the same type from Suffolk, some with the sides curved slightly inwards.

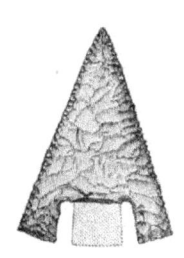

Fig. 315.—Eddlesborough.

Fig. 316.—Reach Fen.

Fig. 317.—Isleham.

The next Figure (317) is illustrative of the extraordinary amount of care and skill that was sometimes bestowed on the manufacture of objects so liable to be broken or lost in use as arrow-heads. This specimen was found at Isleham, Cambridgeshire, and has unfortunately lost its central stem, the outline of which I have restored from a nearly similar arrow-head found at Icklingham, Suffolk, which has lost both its barbs. It is very thin, so much so that its weight is only thirty-eight grains, but it is neatly chipped over the whole of both faces. Nothing, however, can exceed the beautiful regularity of the minute chipping by which the final outline was given to the edges, extremely small flakes having been removed at regular intervals so close to each other that there are twenty of them in an inch. The inner sides and ends of the barbs are worked perfectly straight, the ends forming right angles to the sides of the arrow-head, and the inner sides being nearly parallel with each other, so that the barbs are somewhat dovetailed in form.

The broader, but almost equally beautiful arrow-head shown in Fig. 318 was found in front of the face of an unburnt body, in a barrow at Rudstone, near Bridlington, by Canon Greenwell. I have a beautiful specimen of the same type from Dorchester Dykes, Oxon, given to me by the late Mr. Davey, of Wantage. It is shown in Fig 318A. A less highly finished example from Chatteris Fen [1732] has been figured.

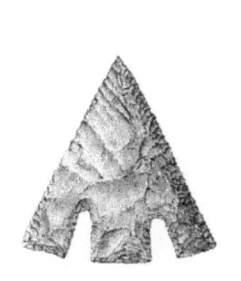

Fig. 318.—Rudstone.

Fig. 318A.—Dorchester Dykes.

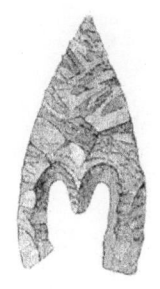

Fig. 319.—Lambourn Down.

Fig. 320.—Fovant.

The ends of the barbs thus chipped straight sometimes, as in Fig. 312, form a straight line. Occasionally, as in the arrow-heads found by Sir R. Colt Hoare [1733] in one of the Everley barrows, the base of the barbs forms an obtuse angle with the sides of the arrow-head, so that there is a sharp point at the inner side of the barbs. In others the end forms an acute angle with the sides of the arrow-head, so that the point of each barb is at the outer side. A beautiful specimen of this kind is shown in Fig. 319. It is one of six, varying in size and somewhat in shape, but all beautifully worked, found in barrows on

Lambourn Down, Berks, and now in the British Museum. In some few instances the sides of the arrow-head are rather ogival in form (like the Scotch specimen, Fig. 326), which adds to the acuteness of the point. In one of this character from a barrow on the Ridgeway Hill, [1734] Dorsetshire, and others from one of the Woodyates barrows, [1735] the barbs are also acutely pointed at the outer side. I have a rather smaller specimen than that figured, from Lakenheath, Suffolk, and others from Thetford and Reach Fen, with the sides even more ogival than in Fig. 326. Others of the same character, found in Derbyshire, are in the Bateman Collection. In some of the arrow-heads [1736] from the Wiltshire barrows the barbs are inordinately prolonged beyond the central tang, which is very small. Fig. 320, copied from Hoare, [1737] gives one of those from a barrow near Fovant, found with a contracted interment, in company with a bronze dagger and pin, and some jet ornaments. One of similar character was found in a barrow on Windmill Hill, [1738] Avebury, but its barbs are not so long. An arrow-head with equally long barbs, but with the central tang of the same length as the barbs, was found in a dolmen in the Morbihan, and is in the Musée de St. Germain.

Fig. 321.—Yorkshire Moors.

Figs. 322 and 323.—Yorkshire Wolds.

Before proceeding to notice one or two Scottish specimens, I must devote a short space to an exceptional form of arrow-head shown in Fig. 321. Like so many others, it is from the Yorkshire Moors, and was probably either barbed on both sides or intended to have been so. But one of the barbs having been broken off, possibly in the course of manufacture, the design has been modified, and the stump, so to speak, of the barb, has been rounded off in a neat manner by surface-flaking on both faces. The one-barbed arrow-head thus resulting presents some analogies with several of the triangular form, such as Figs. 336 to 338, about to be described.

Arrow-heads either accidentally lost before they were finished, or thrown away as "wasters," in consequence of having been spoilt in the making, are occasionally found. Examples, apparently of both classes, are shown in Figs. 322 and 323. The originals form part of the Greenwell Collection. Fig. 322, from Sherburn Wold, appears to have been completely finished, with the exception of the notch on one side of the central tang. The face not shown in the figure exhibits on the left side a considerable portion of the surface of the original flake, the edge of which has been neatly trimmed along the right side of the face here shown. The base has been chipped on both faces to a sharp hollow edge, in which one notch has been neatly worked to form the barb and one side of the stem. There is no apparent reason why the other notch should not have been formed, so that the probability is that the arrow-head was lost just before completion. In the other case the arrow-head, after being skilfully chipped on both faces into a triangular form, has had one of the notches worked in its base; but in effecting this the tool has been brought so near the centre of the head as to leave insufficient material for the tang, and the barb has also been broken off. In this condition it appears to have been thrown away as a waster.

Whether these views be correct or not, one deduction seems allowable, viz., that the barbed flint arrow-heads were, as a rule, finished at their points, and approximately brought into shape at their base, before the notches were worked to form the central tang and develop the barbs.

A curious double-pointed arrow-head from Brompton, [1739] Yorkshire, is, by the kindness of the Society of Antiquaries, shown in Fig. 323A. It had probably at first only a single point, and having been broken was trimmed into its present shape. Some of the "exceptional" forms from Brionio, in the Veronese, approximate to this, but with all respect to the Italian archæologists, I agree with Mr. Thomas Wilson, [1740] and cannot accept these forms as genuine.

Fig. 323A. Brompton. 1/1

I must now give a few examples of the stemmed and barbed flint arrow-heads found in Scotland, which, however, do not essentially differ in character from those of the more southern part of Britain. First among them I would place a remarkably fine specimen found in the Isle of Skye, [1741] which has already been published more than once. It is very acutely pointed, and expands at the base so as to give strength to the barbs, which are slightly curved inwards. From its size it may have served to point a javelin rather than an arrow.

The edges of some of the Scottish arrows are sometimes neatly serrated. An example of this kind is given in Fig. 325, from a specimen in the National Museum at Edinburgh. It is formed of chalcedonic flint, and was found with others of ordinary types at Urquhart, [1742] Elgin.

The original of Fig. 326 is in the Museum of the Society of Antiquaries of London, and was found in Aberdeenshire. Its sides (like those of some in the National Museum at Edinburgh) are slightly ogival, so as to give sharpness to the point. Another from Urquhart, [1743] Elgin, has been figured, as well as one from Ballachulish, [1744] with straighter sides. One from Montblairy, Banff, [1745] is of the same type, as is one from Kilmarnock. [1746] The sides of Fig. 327 are curved outwards. This arrow-head was found in Glenlivet, Banff, a district where arrow-heads are common, and is in the Greenwell Collection, now the property of Dr. Allen Sturge, at Nice.

I have already mentioned the counties of Scotland in which "elf-bolts" are most abundantly found. I may now enumerate a few of the spots, and the characters of the specimens of this form. One much like Fig. 327, but with the barbs more pointed, is figured by Wilson, [1747] as well as another [1748] like Fig. 305, found in a tumulus at Killearn, Stirlingshire. One from the Isle of Skye, [1749] like Fig. 316, and another from Shapinsay, Orkney, [1750] like Fig. 312, have been figured by the Society of Antiquaries of Scotland. Others, found with burnt bones in an urn deposited in a cairn in Banff, have been engraved by Pennant, [1751] and some from Lanarkshire are given in the *Journal of the Archæological Association*. [1752]

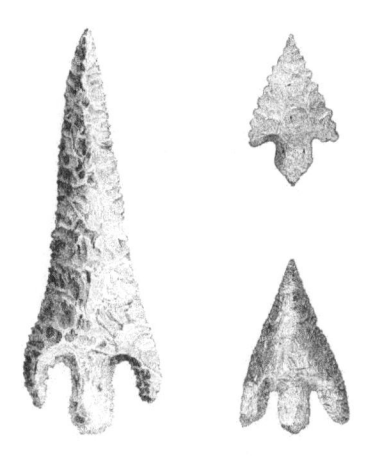

Fig. 324.—Isle of Skye.

Fig. 325.—Urquhart.

Fig. 326.—Aberdeenshire.

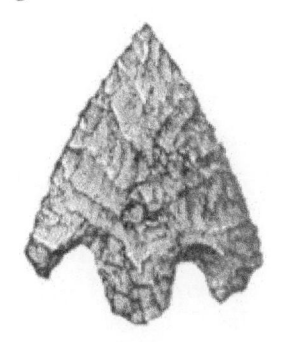

Fig. 327.—Glenlivet.

Stemmed and barbed arrow-heads are recorded to have been found in Aberdeenshire at the following localities:—Slains, [1753] Forgue, [1754] Kintore; [1755] Kildrummy, [1756] Strathdon, [1757] and Cruden; [1758] one 3 inches long and 2 1/2 inches wide, at Tarland, [1759] and a large number at Cloister-Seat Farm, [1760] Udny.

In Banff, at Mains of Auchmedden, [1761] Eden [1762] and Bowiebank, King Edward; Cullen of Buchan, [1763] Glen Avon, [1764] Alvah, [1765] and Longman, [1766] Macduff.

In Elgin, at St. Andrew's, Lhanbryd; [1767] Urquhart, and elsewhere.

In Forfarshire, at Carmyllie [1768] and elsewhere. Some Ayrshire [1769] specimens have been figured.

They have also been found near Gretna Green [1770] and Linton, [1771] Peebles, and in numbers on the Culbin Sandhills, [1772] Morayshire, and Killearn, [1773] Stirlingshire. In Fifeshire, in a cist at Dairsie; [1774] near Fordoun, [1775] Kincardineshire; Glenluce, [1776] Wigtownshire; and stemmed but not barbed, at Philiphaugh, [1777] Selkirkshire. This last is shown in Fig. 327A.

Fig. 327A. Philiphaugh.

Other specimens, of which the form is not mentioned, were exhibited in a temporary Museum of the Archæological Institute at Edinburgh from the following localities:—Caithness, [1778] Cruden, Cromar, Kinellar, Aberdeenshire; Robgill, Ruthwell, Dumfriesshire; Arbuthnot, Bervie and Garvoch, Kincardineshire; Braidwood and Carluke, Lanarkshire; and Burgh-head, Wigtownshire.

Other have been found at Elchies, Keith, [1779] and Oldtown of Roseisle, [1780] Morayshire; Abernethy, [1781] Inverness; and at Mortlach [1782] and Lesmurdie, [1783] Banff.

In this place, also, it will be well to mention some of the discoveries of stemmed and barbed flint arrow-heads in England which have not already been cited. The following have been engraved:—One much like Fig. 303, found in the Kielder Burn, [1784] North Tyne; one like Fig. 327, found with burnt bones in an urn on Baildon Common, [1785] Yorkshire; another from Lake, Wilts; [1786] others, like Figs. 312 and 319, from the Green Low Barrow, [1787] Derbyshire; one like Fig. 308, from Hastings; [1788] one like Fig. 307, found near urns, scrapers, &c., at Wavertree, near Liverpool; [1789] some like Fig. 307, with ashes, at Carno, [1790] Montgomeryshire; and several others from barrows in Wilts, [1791] Dorsetshire, and Derbyshire. A considerable number of flint arrow-heads are engraved in a plate in the *Transactions of the Historical Society of Lancashire and Cheshire*. [1792] They are, however, for the most part forgeries. Others from East Lancashire [1793] and Rochdale [1794] have been described. Besides the discoveries recorded by Hoare and Bateman, and those made in Yorkshire, [1795] such arrow-heads are mentioned as having been found in the Thames; [1796] in the cemetery at Standlake, [1797] Oxon; in West Surrey, [1798] from which a number of arrow-heads of various forms have been figured by Mr. F. Lasham; St. Leonard's Forest, [1799] Horsham; Plymouth, [1800] on Dartmoor, [1801] Devonshire; at Horndean, [1802] Hants; and in large numbers in Derbyshire, especially on Middleton Moor. [1803] Both the leaf-shaped and the barbed forms have been found near Leicester. [1804] A number have been found at Carn Brê, [1805] Cornwall.

Arrow-heads, of which the form is not specified, have been found at Wangford, [1806] Suffolk; Cliffe, [1807] near Carlebury, on the Yorkshire side of the Tees; Priddy, [1808] Somerset; Sutton Courtney, [1809] Berks; Lingfield Mark Camp, [1810] Surrey; near Ramsgate; [1811] Bigberry Hill, [1812] near Canterbury; Manton, [1813] Lincolnshire; Anstie Camp [1814] and Chart Park, Dorking.

Besides specimens already cited, and many from the Yorkshire Wolds and Moors, there are in my collection stemmed and barbed arrow-heads from the following localities:—One much like Fig. 307, from Staunton, near Ixworth, Suffolk; many others from West Stow, Lakenheath, and Icklingham, in the same county; from Hunsdon, near Ware, Brassington, Derbyshire, and Turkdean, Gloucestershire, much like Fig. 308; one from Abingdon, like Fig. 327; and one from St. Agnes, Truro, of the same form as Fig. 317, but not so delicately worked; and others from Wicken and Reach Fens, Cambs. I have also numerous examples of different forms from Stow-on-the-Wold, Gloucestershire, and from the neighbourhood of Wallingford. The Earl of Ducie has a series found near Sarsden House, Chipping Norton.

In the British Museum is a stemmed and barbed arrow-head, rather more curved at the sides than Fig. 307, found at Hoxne, Suffolk. Another of the same class, from Necton, Norfolk, is in the Norwich Museum, together with a smaller specimen like Fig. 308, from Attleborough. In the Cambridge Antiquarian Society's Museum is one like Fig. 306, but with one of the barbs square-ended. It is 2 5/8 inches long, and 1 1/2 inch wide, and very thin, and was found in Burwell Fen. Another, like it, but 2 1/4 inches long, was found near Aldreth, Cambs., and was in the collection of the Rev. S. Banks.

Canon Greenwell obtained one of somewhat similar character, but narrow, from Barton Mills, Suffolk; and the Rev. C. R. Manning found one like Fig. 311 on a tumulus near Grime's Graves, Norfolk. One of the same class is in the Penzance Museum; and Mr. Spence Bate, F.R.S., has shown me a broken one like Fig. 308, found under six feet of peat at Prince Town, Dartmoor, where also a leaf-shaped arrow-head was found. Prof. Buckman had one much like Fig. 327, found at Barwick, Somersetshire. One like Fig. 309, from Milton, near Pewsey, Wilts, is in the collection of Mr. W. H. Penning, F.G.S. Mr. Durden had one rather smaller than Fig. 308 from the neighbourhood of Blandford. I have seen them both stemmed and barbed and leaf-shaped, found near Bournemouth. Sir John Lubbock has one with square-ended stem, and barbs separated from it by a very narrow notch, found at Shrub Hill, Feltwell, Norfolk; and numerous specimens exist in other collections.

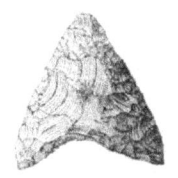

Fig. 328.—Icklingham.

Fig. 329.—Langdale End.

Fig. 330.—Amotherby.

Before entering into the circumstances under which flint arrow-heads have been discovered, it will be well to describe the remaining class—the triangular. Some of these differ only from those last described in the absence of the central stem. Although this form is very common in Ireland and in Scandinavia, it occurs but rarely in Britain. The arrow-head shown in Fig. 328 was found near Icklingham, Suffolk, and was formerly in the collection of Mr. H. Trigg, of Bury St. Edmunds. Messrs. Mortimer possess a very similar specimen from the Yorkshire Wolds near Fimber. One has also been figured by Mr. C. Monkman [1815] as from Yorkshire. An arrow-head from Forfarshire, and one or two others of this type, are in the National Museum at Edinburgh. One from Ellon, [1816] Aberdeenshire, has been engraved, as well as one of much more elongated form, with a semicircular notch at the base, from Glenluce, [1817] Wigtownshire. A broader arrow-head of the same type was found by the Rev. James M. Joass at Golspie, Sutherland, and is now in the Dunrobin Museum. An example was also found by Canon Greenwell in the material of a barrow at Childrey, [1818] Berks. Prof. Flinders Petrie has found the type in Egypt. [1819]

A beautiful specimen of another double-barbed triangular form is shown in Fig. 329. It was found at Langdale End, on the Moors of the North Riding of Yorkshire, and is in the Greenwell Collection. It has been surface-chipped over part of one face, but on the other it still shows the central ridge of the flake from which it was made. The sides are neatly serrated.

Fig. 330 represents a broader and less distinctly barbed form. The original was found at Amotherby, near Malton, and is chipped over both faces. I have another longer specimen from Sherburn, the base of which is less indented. Allied to this longer form, but having the sides more curved, is that shown in Fig. 331. The original was found by Canon Greenwell in one of the barrows examined by him at Weaverthorpe, Yorkshire. Varieties of this form, with the sides more or less straight, are of not unfrequent occurrence in Yorkshire. The same type has been found near Mantua. [1820]

Fig. 331.—Weaverthorpe.

Fig. 332.—Lakenheath.

Fig. 333.—Yorkshire Wolds.

The more perfectly triangular form shown in Fig. 332 is of rather rare occurrence. This arrow-head was found near Lakenheath, Suffolk, and is now in the Greenwell Collection. It is neatly chipped over both faces, which are equally convex. I possess other specimens from Suffolk. Some arrow-heads of the same shape from Gelderland are in the Christy Collection.

In many instances rude triangular arrow-heads have been formed from flakes and splinters of flint, which were evidently selected as being nearly of the desired form, and were brought into shape by the least possible amount of subsequent chipping. The secondary working on Fig. 333 nowhere extends back so much as an eighth of an inch from the edges, and the bulb of percussion of the splinter of flint from which it was made is at the right-hand angle of the base, but not on the face here figured.

In Fig. 334 the bulb is at the back of the left-hand angle, but this specimen is much thicker, and shows a considerable amount of skilful chipping on both faces. The angle at the bulb is rounded, while on the opposite side of the base it is somewhat curved downwards, so as to form a kind of barb. This obliquity of the face is more apparent in Fig. 335, though the barb is less pronounced. The flat face of the original flake is in this instance left nearly untouched, but the ridge side has been neatly wrought by removing a series of minute parallel flakes. This form occurs in Ireland, [1821] and has been regarded as rather a knife than an arrow-head. I have seen an arrow-head of much the same form found at Bournemouth.

Fig. 334.—Yorkshire Wolds.

Fig. 335.—Yorkshire Wolds.

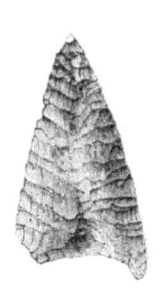

Fig. 336.—Bridlington.

Fig. 337.—Bridlington.

The character of surface-flaking, observable in Figs. 335, 336 and 337, is almost peculiar to Yorkshire; and one of the most beautiful examples that I have seen of it is on the arrow-head engraved as Fig. 336, which was found on Northdale Farm, Grindale, Bridlington. The ripple-like flaking extends over nearly two-thirds of one face, the remainder of which is a flat portion of the original surface of the flake from which the arrow-head was made. On the other face a rather larger portion of the original surface is left, but the surface-chipping, though, neat, is not of this regular character. The base is chipped on both faces, so as to leave a sharp edge with a delicate projecting barb at one angle only. The other angle is perfect, and has never been continued so as to form a barb. I have fragments of other arrow-heads of the same kind, from the same neighbourhood, and on some the fluting along the base is as regular as that on the side, and the two series of narrow shallow grooves "mitre" together with great accuracy. I have arrow-heads of the same general form and character from the neighbourhood of Icklingham, Suffolk; and in the Greenwell Collection is a small and elegant example from Lakenheath; but these are devoid of the parallel flaking, as are also some of the Yorkshire specimens. The late Mr. J. F. Lucas, however, had an arrow-head of this form, with the fluted chipping, from Middleton Moor, Derbyshire. Such regular fluting can, I think, only have been produced by pressure, probably with a pointed instrument of stag's-horn, as before described. It comes nearer in character to the wonderful "ripple-mark flaking" on some of the Danish daggers or lance-heads, and of the Egyptian knives, than the workmanship of any other British specimens.

The same style of work is observable on another arrow-head, Fig. 337, found on the same farm, though it is not of equal delicacy. In this case, however, the flaking extends along both sides, and the two series meet in the middle of the face, where but a very small portion of the original surface of the flake is visible. The face not shown is chipped in the same manner, but less neatly. One of the angles at the base has unfortunately been broken off, but there is no appearance of there having been more than one barb.

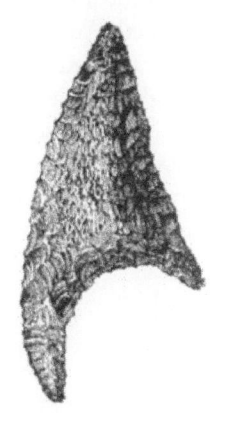

Fig. 338.—Fimber

In some Egyptian arrow-heads from Abydos the surface seems to have been made smooth by grinding before the final flaking, just as was the case with the large blades mentioned on p. 359.

Less finely executed arrow-heads, with a long projecting wing or barb at one of the angles of the base, are of common occurrence in Yorkshire and Suffolk. They usually retain a considerable portion of the surface of the flakes from which they have been manufactured. They are also found in Gloucestershire [1822] and Worcestershire. [1823]

An unusually well-finished specimen of this class is engraved as Fig. 338. It was found in the neighbourhood of Fimber, Yorkshire, and is in the collection of Messrs. Mortimer, who have kindly allowed me to figure it. It has been made from an external flake, as there is a portion of the crust of the flint visible on one of the faces, both of which are neatly chipped. It is barbed at both angles of the base, though the projection is far longer and more curved on the one side than on the other. In most instances, however, there can hardly be said to be any barb at all at one of the angles.

The form with the long single barb appears to be common on the Derbyshire Moors. In one instance a rectangular notch has been worked in the curved side, with what object it is hard to say. This specimen, shown in Fig. 339, was found in a barrow at Hungry Bentley, Derbyshire, by the late Mr. J. F. Lucas. It had been buried together with a jet ornament and beads, subsequently described, in an urn containing burnt bones.

The single-winged form is of rare occurrence in Scotland, but what appears to be an arrow-head of this kind, from Caithness, [1824] has been engraved by the Society of Antiquaries of Scotland, and the cut is here, by their kindness, reproduced. Another from Urquhart and several from the Culbin Sands, Elginshire, and Glenluce Sands, Wigtownshire, are in the Edinburgh Museum. By some [1825] they are regarded as knives, with the tang for insertion in a handle. The same form is found in greater abundance in the North of Ireland. A somewhat analogous shape from Italy has been figured by Dr. C. Rosa. [1826] The type also occurs in Egypt.

Fig. 339.—Hungry Bentley.

Fig. 340.—Caithness.

The varieties here engraved of single-barbed triangular arrow-headeds of flint are, I think, enough to establish them as a distinct class, though they have received but little attention among the antiquities of any other country than the United Kingdom, nor have they been observed in use among modern savages. Many of the early bone harpoons, as well as those of the Eskimos, are barbed along one side only; and some of the Persian iron arrow-heads, as well as those of the Mandingoes, [1827] and of some South American tribes, are also single-barbed. The same is the case with some arrow-heads of iron belonging to the Merovingian period. [1828]

Another form of triangular arrow-head is round instead of hollow at the base, and bears an affinity with the leaf-shaped rather than the barbed variety. One of these from the neighbourhood of Lakenheath, in the Greenwell Collection, is shown in Fig. 341. It is surface-chipped on both faces.

The chisel-ended type in use among the ancient Egyptians has already been mentioned, and a specimen engraved in Fig. 272.

Another and much longer [1829] Egyptian form has now become known. It approaches a triangle in form, but the base is indented like the tail of many homocercal fishes. The specimens vary in length from 3 or 4 inches to as much as 7 or 8 inches, so that some appear to have been javelin-heads. The flaking is wonderfully delicate, and the edges, for the most part, minutely serrated. Mr. Spurrell has described and figured a triangular blade, 4 1/2 inches long, which much resembles the Egyptian form so far as general character is concerned. It was found in Cumberland, [1830] and is now in the British Museum. I have specimens from Abydos of a small, narrow, pointed and tanged arrow-head beautifully serrated at the sides. Other forms are figured by De Morgan.

Fig. 341.—Lakenheath.

Fig. 342.—Urguhart.

In Fig. 342 is shown what appears to be a large example of the chisel-ended type, which was found at Urquhart, [1831] Elgin, and is in the National Museum at Edinburgh. The edge is formed by the sharp side of a flake, and the sharp angles at the two sides of the arrow-head have been removed by chipping, probably to prevent their cutting the ligaments that attached it to the shaft. Another was found at the same place. A small specimen from Suffolk is in the Christy Collection, and I have a few from the same county. Canon Greenwell has obtained others from Yorkshire. It is questionable whether the specimens like Fig. 231 ought not also to have been classed as arrow-heads.

A similar form to Fig. 342 occurs in France. In one of the dolmens on the plateau of Thorus, near Poitiers, I found a small chisel-ended wrought flint, closely resembling the Egyptian arrow-heads; and I have observed in the collection of the late Rev. W. C. Lukis, F.S.A., others of the same form from chambered tumuli in Brittany. They have been discovered with ancient interments in other parts of France, [1832] and I have specimens found on the surface of the soil near Pontlevoy, and given to me by the Abbé Bourgeois.

Baron Joseph de Baye has found them in considerable numbers in sepulchres of the Stone Age in the department of La Marne. [1833] One was found embedded in a human vertebra. They also occur in the Camp de Catenoy, Oise.

One from St. Clement's, Jersey, is in the British Museum.

Some are recorded from Namur and other parts of Belgium. [1834]

Two arrow-heads of this class, found in Denmark, have been engraved by Madsen; [1835] one of them, to which I shall again refer, was still attached to a portion of its shaft.

Nilsson [1836] has also engraved some specimens of this form found in Scandinavia. A considerable number of them were found at Lindormabacken in Scania, [1837] some of which, by the kindness of Dr. Hans Hildebrand, are in my collection. I have also specimens from Denmark. There are others from the same countries in the Christy Collection, where is also an example of the same kind from Southern Italy. Several are engraved by Bellucci. [1838]

They occur also in Germany, [1839] Spain, [1840] and Portugal. [1841] Some crescent-shaped flints with sharp edges and a central tang, found on an island in the Lake of Varese, [1842] may possibly be arrow-heads. Forms of nearly the same kind have been found near Perugia. [1843]

In General Pitt Rivers's collection are some Persian arrows with chisel-edged tips of iron. Crescent-like [1844] arrow-heads or bolt-heads, with a broad hollowed edge, were used in hunting in the Middle Ages, and some are preserved in museums. The Emperor Commodus [1845] is related to have shown his skill in archery by beheading the ostrich when at full speed with crescent-headed arrows.

There still remains to be noticed another form of triangular arrow-head, of which, however, I have never had the opportunity of seeing a British specimen. It has a notch on either side near the base, which is slightly hollowed, and in general form closely resembles a common type of North American arrow-heads. A specimen of this form, said to have been found at Hamden Hill, [1846] near Ilchester, has been engraved. Another, described as of much the same shape, was found in a barrow in Rookdale, Yorkshire. [1847] A broken specimen, with the base flat instead of hollowed, and found in Lanarkshire, [1848] has also been figured.

I am not, however, satisfied that this triangular form, with notches in the sides, is a really British type, though lance-heads notched in this manner have been found in France.

Both in Yorkshire and on the Wiltshire Downs arrow-heads have from time to time been found with their surface much abraded. There seems little doubt that this wearing away has been effected during their sojourn in the gizzards of bustards.

Having now described the principal types of arrow-heads found in Britain, it will be well to notice some of the circumstances of their discovery in barrows and with interments, which throw light on the manners and the stage of civilization of those who used them.

I am not aware of any well-established discovery of flint arrow-heads in this country in association with iron weapons, and certainly such a mixture of materials would require careful sifting of evidence to establish it. And yet we can readily conceive conditions under which flint arrow-heads might be present in Saxon graves, either from their having been dug in barrows of an earlier period, in which case a flint arrow-head might already exist in the soil with which the grave was filled; or from the occupant of the tomb having carried an "elf-bolt" as a charm, or even as the flint for his *briquet à feu*. In the Frankish cemetery of Samson, [1849] near Namur, a broken flint arrow-head, almost of a lozenge form, accompanied a human skeleton with an iron sword and a lance; and another stemmed arrow-head (now in the Namur Museum) was found in the soil. At Sablonnières [1850] (Aisne) flint arrow-heads were associated with Merovingian remains, and numerous instances of such associations have been adduced by the Baron de Baye. [1851] Even in modern times flint arrow-heads have served for this fire-producing purpose. The late Earl of Enniskillen informed me that with flint-guns and muskets in Ireland [1852] the gun-flint was frequently neither more nor less than an "elf-bolt" often but slightly modified in form.

The occurrence in Northern Italy of a flint arrow-head, in company with ten of the degenerate imitations of the gold coin of Philip II. of Macedon, known by the Germans as Regenbogen-schüsseln, recorded by Promis, [1853] may also have been accidental. I have in my own collection a stone celt which is said to have been found with a hoard of Anglo-Saxon coins of the tenth century in Ireland, [1854] but which can hardly be regarded as contemporaneous with them. There are, however, as I have already observed, many well-attested instances in which flint arrow-heads have been discovered in this and other countries in true association with weapons of bronze. Sir R. Colt Hoare records several such in his examination of the barrows of South Wilts. In one near Woodyates [1855] a skeleton in a contracted position was buried with a bronze dagger and pin or awl, a jet button and pulley-like ornament, four arrow-heads (one of them engraved as Fig. 320), and "some pieces of flint, chipped and prepared for similar weapons; in another bowl-shaped barrow at Wilsford an interment of burnt bones was accompanied by a small bronze dagger, some whetstones, and instruments formed of stag's horn, an arrow-head of flint, and another in an unfinished condition."

It is stated in the *Archæologia* [1856] that with the well-known interment in the hollowed oak-trunk found in the Gristhorpe tumulus, near Scarborough, were "a brass and a flint spear-head and flint arrow-heads," &c. The flints [1857] were, however, in this instance, merely flakes and the "brass spear-head" a bronze dagger.

In Borther Low, [1858] near Middleton, Derbyshire, Mr. Bateman found by the side of a skeleton a flint arrow-head, a pair of canine teeth of fox or dog, and a diminutive bronze celt; and in a barrow on Roundway Hill, [1859] North Wilts, a barbed flint arrow-head, like Fig. 327, was found close to the skull of a skeleton in a contracted posture, with a tanged bronze dagger at its left hand. Another bronze fragment, and a small plate of chlorite slate engraved as Fig. 355, were found at the same time. Similar plates, as well as flint arrow-heads, accompanied the skeleton at Tring Grove, [1860] Herts, and an interment at Cruden, Aberdeen. [1861]

A stemmed and barbed arrow-head of calcined flint was found in one of the urns containing burnt bones in the cemetery at Standlake, [1862] Oxfordshire. In another urn was a spiral finger-ring of bronze, the only fragment of metal brought to light during the excavations.

Flint arrow-heads have been so frequently found in barrows containing both burnt and unburnt interments, and in company with other implements of stone and with pottery, that it seems needless to adduce all the recorded instances of such discoveries. I give a few references below. [1863]

The stemmed and barbed variety is of the most common occurrence in tumuli; but, as has already been shown, one leaf-shaped form appears to be, to some extent, peculiar to a class of long barrows, though the stemmed and barbed, [1864] lozenge and leaf-shaped forms have been found in the soil of the same grave mound.

In several instances, stemmed and barbed arrow-heads have been discovered with skeletons, accompanied also by the finely-chipped leaf-shaped knife-daggers of flint. In Green Low, [1865] Alsop Moor, Derbyshire, the dagger-blade lay behind the shoulders, and three arrow-heads behind the back; in one, as already mentioned, on Seamer Moor, near Scarborough, [1866] "two beautifully formed knives and spear-heads of flint," and four flint celts, accompanied "beautifully formed arrow-heads of flint;" and the dagger (Fig. 264) appears to have been found in the same barrow as the arrow-heads, on Lambourn Down.

Occasionally arrow-heads are found in the "drinking-cups" accompanying the skeleton, as in Mouse Low, [1867] Staffordshire.

It remains for me to say a few words as to the points of difference and resemblance between the arrow-heads of Britain and those of other countries; [1868] and also as to the method of shafting in use in ancient times.

In comparing the arrow-heads of Great Britain with those of what is now the sister kingdom of Ireland, we cannot but be struck, in the first place, with the far greater abundance found in Ireland, especially in its northern parts. How far this is due to their use having come down into later times, and how far to the character of the country, it is difficult to say. It is, however, evident that over so large an area of morass and bog, the number of arrows lost in the chase during a long series of years must have been immense; that when once lost they would be preserved uninjured, and remain undiscovered until the operations of draining and obtaining peat for fuel again brought them to light; and further, that the former of these operations has only been carried on to a large extent within the last few years, while the latter has also in all probability increased. On hard and stony soil, on the contrary, even assuming an originally equal abundance of arrow-heads, agricultural operations, after being carried on for a few centuries, would infallibly destroy a large number of them, and what were left would not be so instantly apparent to the eye as those in a peaty soil, and would consequently be found in fewer numbers. In districts where flint is scarce many ancient arrow-heads must have been used as strike-a-lights and gun-flints. In Ireland, [1869] as already stated, they were highly esteemed for the latter purpose. Even on land recently enclosed, and where arrow-heads and worked flints may exist in abundance, unless some unusual inducement is offered, they remain unnoticed by the farm-labourers; and it is only owing to the diligence of local collectors that such numbers have been found on the Yorkshire Wolds, the Derbyshire Moors, and in parts of Gloucestershire, Oxfordshire and Suffolk. There seems, however, either from the character of the game pursued, or from some different customs of the early occupants of the country, to have been a far greater production of arrow-heads in these districts than in some other parts of Britain, such, for instance, as the Sussex Downs, [1870] where on land but recently enclosed, almost innumerable flakes, scrapers, and other instruments of flint may be found, but where I have hitherto never succeeded in finding a single arrow-point. It is possible that in some districts, bone may have been preferred to stone.

Apart from the greater general abundance in Ireland, there is a far greater relative abundance of some particular forms, especially of the barbed triangular arrow-heads without a central stem, and of the elongated form with the stem and barbs. Lozenge-shaped arrow-heads are also more frequent, and some of the varieties of this form do not appear to occur in Britain. As a rule, Irish arrow-heads are also of larger size than the British. Their forms have been described by Sir W. Wilde, [1871] Mr. Wakeman [1872] and others.

In France, flint arrow-heads are at least as rare as in England, if not indeed rarer. In some of the dolmens of Brittany explored by the Rev. W. C. Lukis, F.S.A., [1873] he has found them both leaf-shaped and stemmed and barbed. Among the latter there are some of extremely neat workmanship, and closely resembling in form Fig. 312. I have seen the same form from the Côtes du Nord. Some beautiful examples, more elongated than Fig. 319 and with very small tangs, were found in a tumulus at Cruguel, [1874] Morbihan. The more common French form is like Fig. 311, but with both stem and barb rather longer and the sides straighter. Specimens have been engraved from the neighbourhood of Londinières; [1875] from a dolmen at Villaigre, Poitou; [1876] a lake-habitation at La Péruse [1877] (Charente); the Valley of the Saône, [1878] the department of the Aisne, [1879] the Camp de Chassey, [1880] and other places.

Various forms from the Landes, [1881] Gironde, [1882] Marne, [1883] Gard, [1884] and other Departments [1885] have been figured. Dr. Leith Adams traced a manufactory of flint arrow-heads in Guernsey. [1886]

I have several tanged, and stemmed and barbed arrow-heads from Poitou, as well as some of triangular form, both with a rounded segmental base and with barbs. I have also leaf-shaped, lozenge-shaped, and tanged and barbed examples from the neighbourhood of Clermont Ferrand. Twenty-two of the latter form were found together, in company with a bronze dagger, in a cist in Brittany. [1887]

Another common variety is stemmed and but very slightly barbed. Some of these approximate in form to a lozenge, with two of its sides curved inwards. Specimens from the dolmen of Bernac [1888] (Charente), the Grotte de St. Jean d'Alcas, [1889] and Argenteuil (Seine et Oise), [1890] and the dolmens of Taurine, Pilande, and des Costes (Aveyron), may be cited. In several of the latter both leaf-shaped and lozenge-shaped specimens were also found. Many are neatly serrated at the edges, sometimes so as to form a sort of regular pattern, with only two or three projections on each of the sides. A pointed leaf-shaped arrow-head in a human vertebra was found in the Grotte du Castellet [1891] (Gard).

The same varieties, as well as some triangular arrow-heads, occurred in the Camp de Chassey. [1892] Some of them are barbed without having the central tang.

A large arrow-head from the dolmen of Bernac, with pointed barbs, has a strongly dovetailed central stem. I have seen other much more elongated javelin-heads, four and five inches long, and an inch or an inch and a quarter broad, with similar tangs, but without barbs, the tang being formed by notches on either side at the base, as is the case with so many North American specimens, which these resemble in form. They were found at Corente, in Auvergne, and were in the collection of M. Aymard at Le Puy, where was also a leaf-shaped arrow-head with side notches, from Clermont. Another of the same kind, 4 inches long, with a more dovetail-like tang and better-developed barbs, has been found near Laon. [1893] Others of smaller size were found in the Grotte des Morts, Durfort (Gard). [1894]

A somewhat similar form has occurred among the lake-dwellings of the Ueberlinger See. [1895]

A type much like Fig. 314 also occurs in the lake-habitations of Switzerland, [1896] where, as might have been expected, a large number of stone arrow-heads have been found. Some few of them are stemmed and barbed, much like Fig. 311, but with the tang and barbs rather longer and sharper. More of them are tanged only, or but slightly barbed, and in many, the tang has so slight a shoulder that the outline is almost, and in some quite, lozenge-shaped. The most common form, however, appears to be the triangular, with the sides slightly curved outwards and the base flat, or even slightly rounded outwards. Many are a little hollowed at the base, so much so, in some cases, as to be distinctly barbed. At Nussdorf one arrow-head was formed of serpentine, and another of translucent quartz. One or two specimens are of bone.

Leaf-shaped and stemmed arrows without barbs, from Hasledon and Yvoir, are in the Museum at Namur, in Belgium. Belgian arrow-heads have been described by Van Overloop. [1897]

In the lake-dwellings of Northern Italy, [1898] as, for instance, at Mercurago, near Arona, and Cumarola, near Modena, the tanged arrows prevail, though leaf-and lozenge-shaped also occur. The same is the case in the south, where numerous discoveries of arrow-heads have been recorded by Nicolucci. [1899] At Cumarola [1900] some skeletons were found interred with flint arrow-heads and weapons of stone, in company with others of copper and bronze.

In the valley of the Vibrata, [1901] in the Abruzzo, Dr. C. Rosa has found numerous arrow-heads, principally stemmed and barbed, but some also triangular and leaf-shaped. One specimen appears to be barbed on one side only, and a lance-head has a notch on each side near the base like those from Auvergne.

In the Lake of Varese, [1902] where the site of a manufactory of arrow-heads was discovered by Captain Angelucci, the principal forms were those with a pointed tang and barbs. The roughly-chipped-out blocks were of a leaf-shaped form. A fine specimen like Fig. 302, but rather longer, was found near Civitanova [1903] (Piceno), and the form occurs in Central Italy. A long leaf-shaped arrow from Italy is engraved by Lindenschmit, [1904] as well as a tanged form without barbs. The latter form occurs in the Isle of Elba. [1905] I have a series, from near Bergamo, nearly all of which are tanged, though few of them are distinctly barbed. The various forms of lance and arrow heads in the province of Perugia [1906] have been described by Prof. Bellucci. The stone arrow-heads frequently cited as having been found on the plains of Marathon [1907] appear to be only flakes, [1908] as are many of those from Tiryns. [1909] At Mycenæ, [1910] however, in the fourth sepulchre, Schliemann found thirty-five beautifully-wrought arrow-heads of obsidian. They are mainly of triangular form, hollowed at the base, though the long leaf shape is also present. In general *facies* they closely resemble the Danish forms.

In a dolmen in Andalusia [1911] a broken arrow-head of flint, with pointed stem and barbs, was found; and inasmuch as the fragment is engraved by Don Manuel de Gongora y Martinez as the head of a three-pointed dart, it appears that the form is not common in Spain.

A number of arrow-heads, mostly tanged, have, however, been found in the south-east of Spain by MM. Siret. [1912] In Portugal [1913] the arrow-heads are usually triangular, but often with long-projecting wings or barbs.

Returning northwards, I may cite a small series of flint arrow-heads in my collection, found near Luxembourg, where they appear to be not uncommon. They present the following forms: leaf-shaped, tanged, tanged and barbed, triangular with a straight base, and the same with barbs.

Numerous arrow-heads of flint have also been found in Gelderland, and a collection of them is to be seen in the Leyden Museum. Some are also in the Christy Collection. The most common forms are triangular, with barbs, or with a somewhat rounded base, and stemmed and barbed. Leaf-shaped and tanged arrow-heads appear to be rarer. Some scarce triangular forms are equilateral, and others long and somewhat expanding at the base. I have a series from Heistert, Roermond, Limburg.

In Central and Southern Germany flint arrow-heads appear to be rather scarce. In Pomerania the prevailing type is triangular hollowed at the base. The same form occurs in Thuringia. In the Königsberg Museum there are arrow-heads leaf-shaped pointed at both ends, lozenge-shaped, slightly tanged, tanged and barbed, and triangular with and without the hollowing at the base. Lindenschmit [1914] engraves specimens, like Figs. 311 and 327, from the Rhine and Oldenburg, and a tanged arrow-head of serpentine from Inzighofen, near Sigmaringen, on the Danube. [1915] Lisch also engraves a few specimens from North Germany, [1916] which resemble the Scandinavian in character. Near Egenburg, [1917] in Lower Austria, a considerable number have been found. Some Austrian [1918] arrow-heads are barbed, but without the central tang.

Considering the wonderful abundance of flint implements in Denmark and Southern Sweden, it is not a little singular that arrow-heads should be there comparatively so rare. The leaf-shaped form is extremely scarce, but a triangular form, resembling the leaf-shaped in all respects but in having a rounded notch at the base in lieu of a rounded end, is more common. Stemmed and barbed arrow-heads are also very scarce, and those merely tanged are usually flakes simply trimmed at the edges, with the exception of those of equilateral triangular section, which are peculiar to Scandinavia. The lozenge-shape appears to be unknown; and by far the greater number of arrow-heads are of the triangular form, sometimes but slightly, if at all, hollowed at the base, though usually furnished with long projecting wings or barbs. The same type occurs in Norway. [1919] Occasionally the notch between the barbs is square, and the ends of the barbs worked at an angle of about 45°, like Fig. 319, without the central stem. In some rare instances the barbs curve outwards at the points, giving an ogee form to the sides. In others the barbs curve inwards. In many, the sides are delicately serrated, and in most the workmanship is admirable. What appear to be lance-heads are sometimes notched on either side near the base, like the common

North American form, and like those already mentioned as occurring occasionally in France. [1920]

In Norway, [1921] and more rarely in Sweden, [1922] stemmed and acutely barbed arrow-and lance-heads, made of hard slate ground on the surface, are occasionally found. Knives of the same material also occur. They much resemble some of those from Greenland, and are probably of comparatively late date. Some spear-head-like implements of slate, ornamented with incised lines, have been found in a circular fort on Dunbuie Hill, [1923] near Dumbarton.

Triangular arrow-heads of flint, more or less excavated at the base like those from Scandinavia, are also sometimes found in Russia. Specimens from Ekaterinoslav in the South, and Olonetz in the North, were exhibited at Paris in 1867. Others from Archangel approach more nearly to the North American form. They are occasionally tanged. [1924]

In Northern Africa flint arrow-heads have been discovered, and the leaf-shaped, triangular, and tanged and barbed forms have been found in the dolmens of Algeria. [1925] Some have also been collected in Tunis, [1926] and simple tanged arrow-heads have been found in the Sahara. [1927]

But little is at present known of the stone antiquities of a great part of Asia; but an arrow-head from India [1928] was in the possession of Prof. Buckman, who obligingly furnished me with a sketch of it. It is acutely pointed, about 2 5/8 inches long, and tanged and barbed, though the barbs are now broken off. Some small leaf-shaped arrow-heads have been found at Ranchi, [1929] in the Chota-Nagpore district. Mr. Bauerman, F.G.S., found, at Ghenneh, in Wady Sireh, Sinai, a flint arrow-head, neatly chipped on both faces, of a very peculiar form, being leaf-shaped, with a tang attached. It is in all nearly 2 inches long, of which the leaf-shaped part occupies about 1 1/2 inches, and the slender tang or stalk the other 1/2 inch. It lay in a tomb [1930] with a lance-head of flint, a bracelet of copper, and a necklace of spiral shells. A very similar arrow-head, 2 1/2 inches long, from Wady Maghara, was presented by Major Macdonald [1931] to the British Museum. The form seems also to occur in North America. [1932]

The Abbé Richard found some very finely worked arrow-heads on and around Mount Sinai. [1933] Two [1934] from that locality were presented to the Society of Antiquaries in 1872. Flint arrow-heads have been found on Mount Lebanon, [1935] mostly tanged, but without pronounced barbs. A few are leaf-shaped and triangular.

Some obsidian arrow-heads from the Caucasus [1936] are triangular, with a semicircular notch at the base. Some of flint and of leaf-shaped form have been found at Hissar, [1937] near Damghan, Persia.

Arrow-heads from Japan [1938] are curiously like those from Europe, being triangular with or without barbs, and stemmed and slightly barbed. For the most part, they are narrower in their proportions than the European. Some are formed of obsidian. Besides these, the lozenge-shaped, the leaf-shaped, and a peculiar form with broad-ended barbs and no central tang, occur. There is a fine series in the Museum at Leyden and in the British Museum.

In Greenland flat arrow-heads and harpoon-points of chalcedony and slate are found, most of which approximate to ordinary North American forms. I have one triangular arrow-head with the sides curved outwards and delicately serrated. In Newfoundland [1939] a narrow, triangular form prevails, sometimes ground sharp at the base.

One of the ordinary types in North America, [1940] viz., that with a notch at the base on either side, has already been mentioned more than once. This form shades off into that with a central dovetailed tang, sometimes with well-developed barbs. Others again have merely a central tang, with little or no attempt at barbs. The triangular form, usually but little excavated at the base, is also common. A rare form terminates in a semicircular edge. The leaf-shaped form is rare. For the most part the chipping is but rough, as the material, which is usually chert, horn-stone, or even quartz, does not readily lend itself to fine work. They were made of various sizes, the smaller for boys, and those for men varying in accordance with the purpose to which they were to be applied. [1941] They have been so fully described by others that I need not dilate upon them. Some broken arrow-heads have been converted into scrapers.

As we proceed southwards in America, the forms appear more closely to resemble the European. Some of the obsidian and chalcedony arrow-heads from Mexico are stemmed and barbed, and almost identical in shape with English examples. Don Antonio de Salis [1942] relates that in the Palace of Montezuma there was one place where they prepared the shafts for arrows and another where they worked the flint (obsidian) for the points. In Tierra del Fuego [1943] the natives still fashion stemmed arrow-heads tanged and barbed, or of a triangular form, with a tang extending from the centre of the base. In Patagonia, [1944] triangular, stemmed, and stemmed and barbed arrow-heads occur in deposits analogous to the Danish kjökken-möddings. One brought from Rio Grande, and presented to me by Lieut. Musters, R.N., has a broad stem somewhat hollowed at the base. Mr. Hudson, [1945] in giving an account of arrow-heads from the valley of the Rio Negro, formed of agate, crystal, and flint of various colours, remarks that beauty must have been as much an aim to the worker as utility.

Some of the flint and chalcedony arrow-heads from Chili are beautifully made, and closely resemble those from Oregon, farther north. A tanged and barbed point, embedded in a human vertebra, was found in a burial mound near Copiapo. [1946]

A tanged arrow-head from Araucania, with a well-marked shoulder at the base of the triangular head, so that it might almost be called barbed, is engraved by the Rev. Dr. Hume. [1947] It is like an Italian form.

Stemmed arrow-or harpoon-heads of quartz are found in Chili and Peru of much the same form as Fig. 303. The barbs, if such they may be called, are usually at rather more than a right angle to the stem, and occasionally project considerably from the side of the blade, giving it a somewhat cruciform appearance. I have several which were dug out by the late Mr. David Forbes, F.R.S., from graves close to the shore, about two miles south of Arica. [1948] In some instances they are still attached to their shafts, which are unlike those of ordinary arrows, being shorter and clumsier. I have them of two sizes, the larger 10 1/2 inches long, about 5/8 inch in diameter at the end, where the head has been inserted in a socket, increasing to 7/8 in diameter towards the other end. At a distance of 2 inches from this, however, there is an abrupt shoulder, so that the diameter is increased by at least 1/4 of an inch, and the shaft then rapidly tapers in the contrary direction. The shafts have thus a stopper-like termination, which Mr. Forbes suggests may have been inserted in the end of a longer shaft of bamboo, so that the whole weapon was a sort of spear or javelin, and not, strictly speaking, an arrow. The smaller kind of shaft is of the same character, but only 6 inches long, and proportionately smaller. This may possibly have served as part of an arrow. The wood of all has been coloured with a red pigment.

One arrow-head from the same spot is of remarkably elegant form, and of wonderfully good workmanship. In general outline it is not unlike Fig. 324, but the blade expands more rapidly to form the barbs, which stand out well from the stem, and are separated from it by a slight hollow. It is 1 5/8 inches long. Its greatest width at the barbs is but 1/2 an inch; and the extreme acuteness and delicacy of the point may be judged of from the fact, that a distance of an inch from the apex the width is less than 1/4 of an inch. The heads appear to have been secured in their sockets by binding with thread formed of vegetable fibre. In some instances the wooden shaft is furnished with barbs made of bronze, tied on a little distance behind the stone point.

Leaf-shaped arrow-heads, as well as tanged and barbed, and barbed without a central tang, are found in Peru. [1949] Some leaf-shaped arrows with a stalk, from New Granada, are in the Albert Memorial Museum at Exeter.

It will, however, be thought that enough, and more than enough, has been said as to the forms of arrow-heads occurring in various parts of the world. Allowing for local differences, the general correspondence in form is so great that we cannot wonder at Dr. Woodward's [1950] suggestion that the first model of flint arrow-heads was probably brought from Babel, and preserved after the dispersion of mankind. To most, however, it will appear that this general similarity affords another proof that in all places, and in all times, similar circumstances and similar wants, with similar materials only at command for gratifying them, result in similar contrivances.

I must, in conclusion, say a few words as to the method of mounting these stone points upon the arrows; and here we are not left absolutely to conjecture, though the discoveries of flint arrow-heads still attached to their shafts, in any part of the United Kingdom, are extremely rare. But in Ballykillen Bog, King's County, a stemmed and barbed flint arrow-head was found, still remaining in a part of its "briar-wood" shaft, and with a portion of the gut-tying by which it had been secured, still attached. It is in the museum of Mr. Murray, of Edenderry, and has been figured by Sir W. Wilde. [1951] Another Irish example was found in Kanestown Bog, [1952] co. Antrim, and has been published by Mr. W. J. Knowles. In this case the head was barbed though not stemmed, but the shaft was cleft to receive it, and was bound round with gut or sinew for a length of about 4 inches. The shaft is thought to have been of ash.

A third example was found in a moss at Fyvie, [1953] Aberdeenshire, and has been described by Dr. Joseph Anderson. By the kindness of the Society of Antiquaries of Scotland it is shown in Fig. 342A. The point is leaf-shaped, approaching to a lozenge. It is inserted in a cleft in the tapering shaft, which extends almost to the point. The nature of the tough wood, of which the shaft is made, has not been determined, and the manner in which the head was secured in the shaft seems uncertain; but there may have been a binding which has perished. Dr. Anderson was able to reproduce the shaft in soft wood, making use of flint tools only.

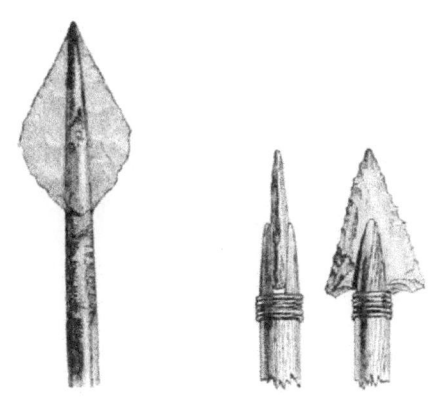

Fig. 342A.—Fyvie, Aberdeenshire. 1/1

Fig. 343.—Switzerland. 1/1

Specimens have also been found in Switzerland and Germany. One of the former has been figured by Dr. Keller, [1954] whose engraving I here reproduce, as Fig. 343, in the full size of the original arrow, instead of on the scale of one-half. It was found, not in any of the Lake habitations, but in the moss of Geissboden.

The arrow-heads found among the ancient Swiss lake-dwellings, often bear on their surface some portion of the bituminous cement which helped to attach them to the shafts. Dr. Clément [1955] possessed one, apparently tanged but not barbed, the base of which is completely incrusted with bitumen, with traces of the wood of the shaft upon it, and of the cord by which the whole was bound together. Another, leaf-shaped, similarly incrusted, is in the Museum at Lausanne. The attachment of a conical bone arrow-head to its shaft is of the same character. Some single-barbed [1956] arrows were made by tying a bone pin, pointed at each end, diagonally to the extremity of the shaft.

Fig. 344.—Fünen, Denmark. 1/1

Fig. 345.—Modern Stone Arrow-head.

Another specimen has been engraved by Madsen, [1957] who, however, does not appear to have recognised it as an arrow-head. He describes it as "a flint instrument, fastened by means of fine bast-fibre to a wooden shaft, of which only 1 1/2 inch remains." I have here reproduced his engraving, as Fig. 344, and there can I think be little doubt that it represents the point of an arrow of the same character as those in use among the ancient Egyptians. [1958] It was found in a peat moss in the parish of Vissenberg, Odense, in the Isle of Fünen.

Among modern savages, we find the stone points sometimes attached to the shafts by vegetable fibre, not unfrequently aided by some resinous gum, and also by means of animal sinew. The annexed woodcut, Fig. 345, kindly supplied by the Society of Antiquaries of Scotland, [1959] shows an arrow-head, stated to be from one of the South Sea Islands, but more probably from California, attached by means of tendon to a reed shaft. The Indians of California certainly affix their arrow-heads in a similar manner; but commonly there are notches on either side of the head at the base, to receive the sinew or split intestine, which is in the form of tape about 1/8 inch wide. The binding extends about an inch along the shaft, and is of the neatest description. North American [1960] arrow-heads, fastened in this manner, have been engraved by Sir John Lubbock and the Rev. J. G. Wood. The end of the shaft has a shallow notch in it to receive the flint, which is cemented into the notch before being bound on.

Among the Kaffirs, [1961] the iron heads of the assagais are usually bound to the shafts with strips of wet hide, which contract and tighten in drying.

The shafts of arrows are frequently of reed, in which case there is often a longer or shorter piece of solid wood joined on to the reed to which the head is attached. This is the case with the ancient Egyptian arrows, and with those of the Bushmen, [1962] in which, however, bone and ivory replace the wood; and the shaft generally consists of three pieces—reed, ostrich bone, and ivory, to which latter the head of iron is attached. In other cases the shafts consist of straight-growing shoots of trees. Among the Eskimos, [1963] where wood is so scarce, a peculiar tool—formed of bone, with an oval or lozenge-shaped hole through it—is used for the purpose of straightening arrow-shafts. The tang of their arrow-heads is inserted in a socket, and bound fast with sinew.

For harpoons there is often a hole in the triangular armature. One of these points was found in the body of a seal killed in Iceland [1964] in 1643, and Olaf Worm judiciously thought that the seal had been wounded by a Greenlander.

In most countries the shafts are feathered at the bow-string end, and such was the case in the earliest historical times. Hesiod [1965] describes the arrows of Hercules as feathered from the wings of a black eagle, and Homer [1966] speaks of the πτερόεντες ὀϊστοί—if indeed, as Mr. Yates suggests, this latter refers to the plumes. [1967] Herodotus, [1968] however, mentions, as a remarkable fact, that the arrows of the Lycians in the army of Xerxes, like those of the Bushmen and some other savages of the present day, had no feathers, so that this addition to the shaft was not indispensable. It is said that some North American arrow-heads are "bevelled [1969] off on the reverse sides, apparently to give them a revolving motion," so as to answer the same purpose as plumes. But this result seems very doubtful.

From what kind of wood the bows in Britain were made at the time when flint-pointed arrows were in use is uncertain; the yew, however, which is probably the best European wood for the purpose, is indigenous to this country. It is not probable that the cross-bow was known in these early times, though it was in use during the Roman period, as may be seen on a monument in the museum at Le Puy.

I need, however, hardly enter into further details with regard to arrows, and I therefore proceed to the consideration of other forms of stone implements, including those by which it seems probable that some of the arrow-heads were fashioned.

CHAPTER XVII.
FABRICATORS, FLAKING TOOLS, ETC.

In treating of the manufacture of stone implements in prehistoric times I have already (p. 41) described certain tools of flint with a blunted, worn, and rounded appearance at one or both ends, as if resulting from attrition against a hard substance, and I have suggested that their purpose may have been for chipping out arrow-heads and other small instruments of flint. As, however, it was not desirable to introduce unnecessary details when dealing only with the processes adopted in the manufacture of stone implements, the more particular description of some of the tools was deferred, until after an account had been given of the objects in the making of which they had probably assisted.

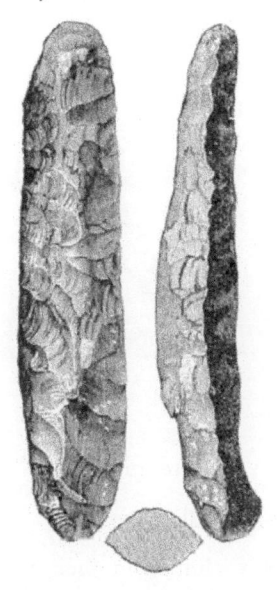

Fig. 346.—Yorkshire Wolds.

In Fig. 346 is shown, full size, a characteristic specimen of the tool to which I have provisionally assigned the name of "flaking tool," or fabricator. It is symmetrically chipped out of grey flint, and is curved at one extremity, probably with the view of adapting it for being better held in the hand. The side edges, which were originally left sharp, have been slightly rounded by grinding, apparently from the same motive. The angles at the curved end have been smoothed off, but the other end is completely rounded, and presents the half-polished, worn appearance characteristic of these tools. The curvature lengthways to some extent resembles that of the Eskimo arrow-flakers engraved as Figs. 8 and 9, and is of common occurrence among these tools. They vary much in the amount of workmanship they display; some being mere flakes with the edges rounded by chipping, and others as carefully wrought into form as any flint hatchet or chisel. These skilfully-chipped specimens are frequently much more convex on one face than the other. They vary in length from about 2 to 4 inches.

An unusually long example is, by permission of the Society of Antiquaries of Scotland, shown in Fig. 346A. It was found on the Hill of Corennie, [1970] Aberdeenshire, and closely resembles another implement of the same kind found near Fordoun, [1971] Kincardineshire.

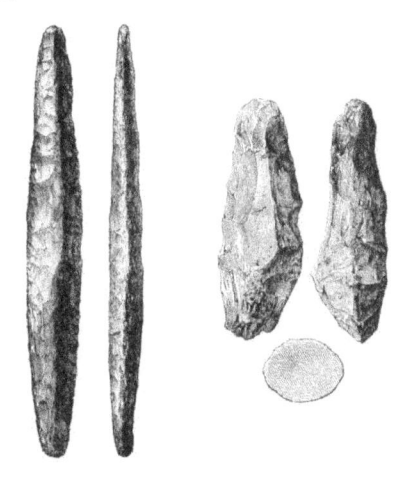

Fig. 346A.—Corennie. 1/1

Fig. 347.—Bridlington. 1/1

The rougher kinds are usually clumsy in their proportions, as if strength were an object, and they not unfrequently show a certain amount of abrasion at each end. An instrument of this coarser description is shown in Fig. 347. It is worn away and rounded, not only at the point, but for a considerable distance along the sides, the abraded surface having a somewhat bruised appearance. It is remarkable that many of the Danish flint knife-daggers, especially those which have been so long in use that their blades have been much diminished in size by having been frequently re-chipped, present at the end and sides of the handles precisely the same kind of worn surface. At one time I thought it possible that constant contact with hard hands, not free from sand and dirt, might have produced this rounding of the angles; but closer examination proves that this cannot have been the only cause of the wear, as it is sometimes the case that at a certain distance from the end of the hilt, the abraded character disappears entirely, and, with the exception of a slight polish, the angles are as fresh as on the day when the daggers were first manufactured. This feature is most observable in the poignards with the beautifully-decorated handles. I possess one of this kind—like Worsaae, No. 52—with the sides near the blade exquisitely ornamented with a delicate wavy edging, and with a line of similar ornament running along the centre of one face of the handle, the butt-end having also been edged in a similar manner; but for an inch and a half from the end the whole of this ornamentation is completely worn away, and the sides are battered and rounded. To such an extent has this part of the handle been used, that one of the projecting points of the original fishtail-like end has entirely disappeared, and the other is completely rounded. The blade is probably now not more than one-third of its original size, so that we may infer that it must have been long in use for its legitimate purposes. But during all this time the hilt must have been made to serve some other and less appropriate purpose than that of a handle, and as a result its original beauty of ornamentation has been entirely destroyed. I think that this purpose must have been the chipping, or rather the re-working, of the edges of other flint instruments.

Whether this was effected by pressure or by slight blows it is hard to say; but it appears probable that the ancient possessor of two such daggers used the hilt of the one for re-chipping the blade of the other, and it may be for re-chipping other implements. An indirect inference deducible from this disfigurement of the beautifully wrought handles, is that they were not originally made by the owners who thus misused them—though they also must have been fairly accomplished workers in flint—but that the daggers were procured by barter of some kind from the cutlers of the period, whose special trade it was to work in flint. For we can hardly conceive that those who had bestowed so much time and skill in the ornamentation of these hilts, should afterwards wantonly disfigure their own artistic productions. In Britain, where the larger forms of finely-wrought instruments are scarcer, it seems most likely that these flakers were principally used in the making of arrow-heads, though probably hard bone or stag's horn was also employed, as already suggested.

Against regarding the ends of these tools as having been worn away in the manufacture of other instruments of flint, it may be urged that the butt-ends of some chisels present a similar appearance, and therefore that the wear may be the result of hammering with some kind of hard mallet. It must, however, be remembered that no hammering at the ends would produce the wearing away apparent on the sides of the tools, and that the chisels which present the worn ends are in form and size much the same as the "flaking tools," and may, like the Danish daggers, have served a double purpose. It is also worthy of notice that these "flaking tools" are most abundant in districts where flint arrow-heads occur in the greatest numbers, as, for instance, on the Yorkshire Wolds. In parts of Suffolk where arrow-heads are common they too are abundantly present. I have also found them in the camp at Maiden Bower, near Dunstable, in company with arrow-heads.

In the case of the straight implements, like Fig. 347, it is by no means impossible that they were used with a mallet as punches or sets, to strike off flakes in the manufacture of arrow-heads and similar articles. As already mentioned, some of the American tribes use a bone punch for this purpose.

Fig. 348.—Sawdon. 1/1

Fig. 349.—Acklam Wold. 1/1

In Figs. 348 and 349 I have engraved two Yorkshire instruments, the one from Sawdon, and the other from Acklam Wold; both from the rich Greenwell Collection. At first sight they seem chisel-like in character, but the edge in both is semicircular, and not ground, but merely chipped. Fig. 348 is worked on both faces, though more convex on one than on the other. Fig. 349 is merely a flake with its edges chipped towards its outer face, so that it resembles a long narrow scraper. The butt-end in that from Sawdon is much worn and rounded, its sides are also worn away for about 3/4 inch at that end; the butt of that from Acklam Wold is also rounded, but principally towards the flat face. The edges of both are sharp and uninjured. It therefore appears probable that these tools were also made with a view to being used at the blunt, and not at the sharp end; and it is possible that the semicircular sharp ends may have been for insertion in some form of wooden handle, in which the instruments were tightly bound, and their projecting ends then used, it may be, for flaking other flints. A flaking-tool from Unstan Cairn, [1972] Orkney, is of the same character as Fig. 349, but longer. What seems to have been a "fabricator" was found at Torre Abbey Sands, [1973] Torbay. On referring to page 38, will be seen some Eskimo arrow-flakers of reindeer horn attached to wooden handles; and the instrument from Acklam Wold seems well adapted for similar attachment, with its flat side towards the wood.

Some bone instruments which have been found in barrows may possibly have served as arrow-flakers. One from Green Low, [1974] Derbyshire, has been figured. An implement of deer's horn, with a small piece of hard bone inserted in the small end, was found in the Broch [1975] of Lingrow, Scapa, Orkney, but seems to belong to the Iron Period. No flint arrow-heads are recorded from the Broch.

I must confess that the suggestions I have offered with regard to the use of these tools are by no means conclusive. I can only hope that future discoveries may throw more light upon the subject.

Canon Greenwell, who has figured a specimen—like Fig. 346—in the *Archæological Journal*, [1976] was inclined to think that the other form of instrument, like Figs. 348 and 349, was "used in dressing hides, the sharp end for removing the loose parts of the skin, the smooth end for rubbing down the seams when the leather was made up into a garment." I do not think that this can really have been their purpose, as for smoothing down the seams a natural pebble would probably be preferable, and for cutting or removing the loose parts a flint flake would answer better. Still, I have seen a somewhat pointed concretionary nodule of stone, the end and point of which were polished from use by a glovemaker, in recent times, in smoothing down the seams of coarse leather gloves. The late Mr. C. Monkman, [1977] like myself, regarded these instruments as punches or fabricators, used for chipping arrows and delicate flint weapons into shape. This is also Canon Greenwell's present opinion. He has figured an example in "British Barrows." [1978] In Yorkshire they are known as "finger-flints."

The worn appearance of the pointed end of some flakes is not improbably due, as has already been observed, to their having been employed in "picking" into shape implements—such as hatchets or axes—formed of greenstone and other rocks of a somewhat softer nature than flint. The ends of the flaking tools, punches, or fabricators are, however, usually far too blunt for them to have been applied to such a purpose.

Another of the causes of the blunted and worn-away appearance of the ends, and even sides, of originally sharp flint flakes and instruments, I have already described when treating of scrapers—namely, the striking off by their means particles from a block of pyrites, with a view of procuring fire.

CHAPTER XVIII.
SLING-STONES AND BALLS.

Passing on from flint arrow-heads and the tools which were probably used in the process of their manufacture, we come to another form of missile weapon—the sling-stone—which also appears to have been in use in Britain. It is needless here to enter into details as to the early use of the sling among the more civilized nations of antiquity, especially as comprehensive articles on the subject have already been published in this country by Mr. Walter Hawkins [1979] and Mr. Syer Cuming. [1980]

A stone thrown by hand doubtless constituted the first missile weapon, and some form of sling must probably have been among the earliest inventions of mankind. What appears to be the simplest kind, and one which, like Nilsson [1981] and Strutt, [1982] I frequently used as a boy, consists of a stick split for a short distance down one end, so as to form a cleft, in which a stone is placed; the elasticity of the two halves of the stick, which are kept asunder by the stone, retaining it there until the proper moment for its discharge. Nilsson cites Lepsius as engraving in his great work on Egypt a representation of a man armed with such a sling, which he appears to use very actively in fight. At his feet there is a heap of small stones in readiness for use. Nilsson [1983] also suggests that it was with such a sling that David was armed when he encountered Goliath, who addresses him: "Am I a dog that thou comest to me with staves?" [1984] that is, with the shepherd's staff and the sling handle. The most ancient form, however, recorded by classical writers is that of the ribbon sling, with a central receptacle for the stone, and with strings on either side. The neatly plaited or knitted cup or strap of a sling, with a portion of its cord, both formed of flax, was among the objects discovered in the Lake-settlement of Cortaillod, [1985] which was remarkably rich in bronze objects. This probably is the most ancient sling now in existence.

The staff-sling reappears in Roman times in a somewhat modified form, with a receptacle for the stone attached to the end of a staff. To this weapon the name of *fustibalus* was given.

The earliest sling-stones were, no doubt, like those used by David against Goliath, the "smooth stones out of the brook;" but in after-times, among the Greeks and the Romans, sling-bullets of an almond or acorn-like form were cast in lead, and flattened ovoid missiles were formed in terra cotta; both kinds, from their uniformity in size, ensuring greater precision of aim than could be secured with stones, however carefully selected, and the former also offering the advantages of less resistance from the air, as well as greater concentration of force when striking the object. Some polished sling-bullets of loadstone or hæmatite are mentioned by Schliemann [1986] as having been found on the presumed site of Troy. The advantages of uniformity of size and form are recognized among some savage tribes, who make use of the sling at the present day; the sling-stones, for instance, of the New Caledonians being carefully shaped out of steatite, and, what is worthy of remark, approximating closely in form to the Roman *glandes*, being fusiform or pointed ovoids. The same form on a larger scale, about 3 inches in diameter and 4 inches long, has been adopted by the natives of Savage Island for missiles thrown by the hand. These are wrought from calc-spar almost as truly as if turned in a lathe.

Nilsson [1987] has engraved a sling-stone of this same form, found in Sweden, where, however, they are by no means common, as he cites but five specimens in the museums at Lund and Stockholm.

Artificially-fashioned sling-stones are not, however, confined to this fusiform shape; those that were in use among the Charruas of Southern America having been of a lenticular form, though slightly flattened at the centre of each face. One in my collection is about 3 inches in diameter and 1 3/8 inches thick in the middle. It has been ground over the whole of both faces, and has the edge at its periphery slightly rounded.

The objects so frequently found in the Swiss Lake-dwellings, and to which the name of sling-stones has been commonly given, were, as Keller [1988] has pointed out, probably intended for some very different purpose. Many of the forms described by Sir William Wilde, [1989] under the name of sling-stones, may also, I think, be more properly placed in some other category. The carefully polished lenticular disc of flint (Wilde, Fig. 9) seems better adapted for a cutting tool; and the flat oval stones, usually with "a slight indentation, such as might be effected by rubbing with a metal tool," were, as I have already observed, more probably used for obtaining fire, like those of the same class belonging to the early Iron Age of Denmark, [1990] which they much resemble in character.

The objects to which in this country the name of sling-stone has been generally applied are more or less roughly-chipped, and approximately lenticular blocks of flint, varying considerably in proportionate thickness, and usually from about 1 1/2 to 3 inches in diameter. An average specimen from the Yorkshire Wolds is shown in Fig. 350. The contour is frequently more truly circular or oval, and the faces somewhat more carefully chipped. They are found in considerable numbers on the Yorkshire Wolds, in Suffolk, Sussex, and other counties where chalk flints are common. Occasionally also they occur in Scotland. [1991] Similar forms are also abundant in the Danish kjökken-möddings and "coast-finds." In this latter case it appears quite as probable that they may have served for net-sinkers as for sling-stones; although, as Sir John Lubbock [1992] has remarked, "that some have really served as sling-stones seems to be indicated by their presence in the peat-mosses, which it is difficult to account for in any other way."

Fig. 350.—Yorkshire Wolds. 1/2

Prof. Nilsson [1993] objects that they are so irregular and sharp-cornered, "that they would soon wear out the sling, even if it were made of leather." He presumes "that these sharp-cornered stone balls were the first hand-missile weapons of the earliest and rudest savages, and used by them to throw at wild animals or enemies." This objection to regard them as sling-stones seems hardly well founded; especially if we consider them to have been in use with a stick-sling, in which case their angularity would have been of some service in retaining them in the cleft, while their lenticular form adapts them well for this kind of sling. A more valid objection raised by Prof. Nilsson is that no one "would give himself all this trouble to fashion sling-stones which were to be thrown away the next moment, when he could find many natural pebbles quite as suitable." But to this it may be replied, that at the present day we do find the New Caledonians, the Tahitians, and other tribes, carefully fashioning their sling-stones; and also that this flat lenticular form is better adapted for the stick-sling than a natural pebble of the usual oval form. As a fact, however, I think it will be found that these flint discs, to which the name of sling-stones is applied, are most abundant in those districts where natural rolled pebbles happen to be scarce. If the case be really so, we can readily understand why the cores, from which flakes had been struck for conversion into arrow-heads and other instruments, should have been themselves utilized as sling-stones. If these missiles were necessary, it would be a question of which would involve the least trouble, whether to chip into the required form a certain number of flints which came readily to hand, at the same time making use of the resulting chips; or to select and bring together, possibly from a distant sea-coast, a bed of a stream, or some uncovered patch of gravel, a number of pebbles of the right size and form for slinging. In the camp at Hod Hill, near Blandford, which, however, probably belongs to the Early Iron Period, the latter course seems to have been adopted, as several heaps of rounded flint-pebbles, either derived from the sea-coast or from some bed of Lower Tertiary Age, have been found there, and in all probability constituted the munition of the slingers of the camp.

The late Mr. C. Monkman [1994] remarked that in Yorkshire he always found the small globular sling-stones most plentiful at a short distance (50 to 200 yards away) from old entrenchments, and he was inclined to class under the head of sling-stones, nodules chipped over their whole surface, varying from an almost globular form to all degrees of flatness, and in size from 1/2 inch to 3 inches in diameter. This is perhaps too wide a definition, as most of the larger globular forms appear to have been destined for hammer-stones; and pebbles but half an inch in diameter would be almost too light for missiles. It is, however, impossible to say with certainty that any given specimen was undoubtedly a sling-stone, as the flatter forms, which were more probably missiles, merge in the form of a roughly-chipped oval celt like Fig. 17 at one end of the series, and in that of a discoidal scraper with a broken edge at the other. Many may be merely cores, from both faces of which flakes have been struck, so that the term "sling-stones," if employed for these roughly-chipped discs, must always be used in a somewhat doubtful sense, and for convenience rather than precision.

In Polynesia, [1995] besides rounded pebbles, sharp, angular, and rugged stones were used for slinging. These were called *Ofai ara*, faced or edged stones.

Another class of objects in stone which may possibly have served for the purposes of the chase or of war, consists of balls with their surface divided into a number of more or less projecting circles, with channels between them. They seem, so far as is known, to be confined to Scotland and Ireland.

Fig. 351.—Dumfriesshire. 1/2

That shown in Fig. 351 was found in Dumfriesshire, [1996] and has been engraved by Sir Daniel Wilson. It presents six circular faces. Others, almost identical in form, have been found at Biggar, [1997] Lanarkshire; Dudwick, [1998] Chapel of Garioch [1999] and Migvie, [2000] Tarland, Aberdeenshire; Kilmarnock, [2001] Ayrshire; and Montblairy, [2002] Banffshire. Another, about 3 inches in diameter, with three faces only, was found on the Tullo of Garvoch, [2003] Kincardineshire; and one, with four faces, in a cairn at East Braikie, Forfarshire. This latter is in the Montrose Museum. [2004] One of greenstone, 2 1/2 inches in diameter, found at Ballater, [2005] Aberdeenshire, has six plain circular discs, with the interspaces partially cut into small knobs or studs, the ornaments being possibly in course of formation. Stone balls, [2006] about 2 1/2 and 3 inches in diameter, covered over the surface with small rounded projections, like enormous petrified mulberries, have been found in the Isle of Skye, in Orkney, and at Garvoch Hill, Kincardineshire. I presume the latter to be a different specimen from that with three faces, previously described. Others are in the Perth Museum. [2007] A series of such balls, some highly ornamented, has been described by Dr. John Alexander Smith. [2008] One formed of hornblende schist, with six strongly projecting circular faces, was found near Ballymena, [2009] co. Antrim, in 1850, and is now in the British Museum.

Fig. 352.—Towie.

Probably the most remarkable of all these balls is that shown in Fig. 352, from a cut kindly lent me by the Society of Antiquaries of Scotland. It was found at Towie, [2010] Aberdeenshire, and is about 2 1/2 inches in diameter, with four rounded projections, three of which are ornamented with different incised patterns, while the fourth is smooth and undecorated. From the character of the patterns, this object would seem to belong to the Bronze Period rather than to that of Stone, if not, indeed, to still later times. In connection with the pattern upon it, attention may, however, be called to the remarkable carved cylinders of chalk found by Canon Greenwell in a barrow on Folkton Wold, [2011] Yorkshire, and now in the British Museum, which are certainly not of later date than the Bronze Age. The ornament on a clay vessel found in Devonshire [2012] may be compared with that of the sides of the cylinders.

These balls appear to me to differ most essentially from the ordinary "sink-stones" found in Denmark and Ireland, [2013] with which they have been compared. It is, however, by no means easy to suggest the purpose for which they were intended. The only suggestions that I have met with are, that they were used in some game or amusement; for defence when slung in a long thong or line [2014]; as mace heads [2015] attached to a handle; or else for purposes of divination. [2016] I must confess that I hardly see in what manner the last purpose can have been served, especially as in most instances all the faces of the ball are alike. Nor do I see in what manner they can have been used in games, though of course it is possible that they were so employed. It seems more probable that they were intended for use in the chase or war, when attached to a thong, which the recesses between the circles seem well adapted to receive. Among savage nations of the present day we find the use of the *bolas*, or stones attached to the ends of thongs, over a great part of the southern continent of America; [2017] while the principle is known to the Eskimos, whose strings of sinew, weighted with bunches of ivory knobs, are arranged to wind themselves round the bird at which they are thrown, in just the same way as the much stouter cords weighted at the ends with two or three heavy stone balls which form the *bolas*, [2018] twist round, and hamper the movements of larger game.

The *bolas* proper, as in use on the Pampas, consist of three balls of stone, nearly the size of the fist, and covered with leather, which are attached to the ends of three thongs, all branching from a common centre. Leaden balls have now almost superseded those of stone.

The hunter gives to the *bolas* a rotary motion, and can then throw them to a great distance, in such a manner that the thongs entwine round the legs, neck, and body of his prey and thus render it helpless, so that it can then be easily despatched. A *bola* of small size, but of lead or copper, with a single thong about 3 feet long, is also used, and forms both the sling and its stone. It likewise serves as a weapon for striking in close encounter. Among the Patagonians [2019] the same two varieties are used, but those for hunting have usually only two stones, and not three. They sometimes throw the single *bola* at the adversary, rope and all, but generally they prefer to strike at his head with it.

Assuming a difficulty in securing a ball of stone in a leather case, and that therefore it would be necessary to fasten it by means of a thong, some channelling of the surface would become a necessity; and the natural tendency of savages to decorate their weapons might lead to regular circular discs being left between the channels on the ball, and even to these discs being engraved in patterns, that next the cord being, as in Fig. 352, left undecorated. In the Christy Collection is a *bola* formed of a polished red spherical stone, mounted in such a manner as to show a considerable portion of its surface, which has evidently been regarded as too handsome to be entirely concealed by the leather. Mr. C. H. Read suggests that these ornamented balls were entirely covered with raw hide, which was allowed to dry, the ends or edges being tightly tied. When dry the circles over the knots were cut out so as to display the ornament and leave a solid binding round the stone to which a thong might be attached.

These *bola* stones are sometimes wrought so as to present a number of rounded protuberances. Of this kind there are specimens in the Christy Collection [2020] and in that of the late Mr. J. Bernhard Smith. Even if the use of the *bolas* or the single *bola* were unknown, there is a form of military flail or "morning star," a sort of modification of the staff-sling, though the stone never quits the cord by which it is attached to the staff, for which such balls as these might serve. A mediæval weapon [2021] of this kind, in the Meyrick Collection, consists of a staff, to which is attached by a chain a ball of wood with numerous projecting iron spikes. The citizens of London will be familiar with the same weapon in the hands of the giant Gog or Magog at Guildhall. The Calmucks, Mongols, and Chinese, [2022] still use a flail of this sort, with an iron perforated ball about two pounds in weight attached to the end of the thong. Substituting one of these stone balls for the spiked morning-star, and a leather thong carefully adjusted in the channels of the stone for the chain, a most effective form of weapon for close encounters would result. Among the North American tribes a somewhat similar weapon was lately in use, and is thus described by Lewis and Clarke, as quoted by Squier and Davies: [2023]—"The Shoshonee Indians use an instrument which was formerly employed among the Chippeways, and called by them *pogamoggon*. [2024] It consists of a handle 22 inches long, made of wood covered with leather, about the size of a whip-handle. At one end is a thong 2 inches in length, which is tied to a stone weighing two pounds, enclosed in a cover of leather; at the other end is a loop of the same material, which is passed around the wrist to secure the implement, with which they strike a powerful blow." Another form of club in use among the Algonquins consisted of a round boulder sewn in a piece of fresh skin and attached to the end of a long handle, to which, by the drying of the skin, it becomes firmly attached. Examples of both of these kinds are in the British Museum. An engraving of a drumstick-like club of this character is given by Schoolcraft. [2025] Unfortunately, however, the existence of such a weapon in early times is not susceptible of proof. Whatever the purpose of these British balls of stone, they seem to belong to a recent period as compared with that to which many other stone antiquities may be assigned.

CHAPTER XIX.
BRACERS, AND ARTICLES OF BONE.

Another object in stone, not unfrequently found in graves, and of which the use is now comparatively certain, is a rectangular plate usually round on one face, and hollow on the other, with perforations at either end. These plates are commonly formed of a close-grained green chlorite slate, are very neatly finished, and vary considerably in length and proportions.

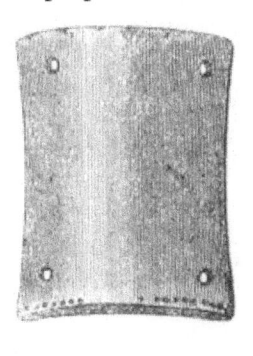

Fig. 353.—Isle of Skye. 1/2

The specimen shown in Fig. 353 is in the National Museum at Edinburgh, and has already been engraved by Sir D. Wilson, [2026] and roughly figured in the *Wiltshire Archæological Magazine*. It was found alongside of a human skeleton, in a rudely-vaulted chamber in a large tumulus on the shore of Broadford Bay, Isle of Skye. It is formed of pale-green stone polished, and has at one end an ornamented border of slightly indented ovals. In the same Museum [2027] is another of longer proportions, being 4 1/2 inches by 1 1/4 inches, formed of fine-grained greenish-coloured stone, and having at each corner a small perforation. It was found, together with an urn and the remains of a skeleton, in a short cist on the farm of Fyrish, Evantown, Ross-shire. It is shown in Fig. 354. There is also, in the same Museum, a fragment of a flatter specimen formed of indurated clay-slate of a lightish green colour, perforated at one end with three small holes. It was found in a stone circle called "The Standing Stones of Rayne." [2028] Another example was found in a grave at Dalmore, [2029] Ross-shire. It is, however, imperfect. In the Arbuthnot Museum, Peterhead, is another object of this class, 4 1/4 inches long, with a hole at each corner, and slightly rounded on one face and hollow on the other. It was found at Cruden, [2030] Aberdeenshire, in a cist surmounted by a small tumulus. In the cist, were the skeletons of an adult and a youth, as well as portions of that of a dog. They were accompanied by two rude urns, several flint arrow-heads, and two flint knives.

The earliest recorded discovery of these objects in England is that which has already been mentioned as having taken place at Tring Grove, Herts, about 1763. [2031] In this case, a skeleton was found in sinking a ditch in level ground; between the legs were some flint arrow-heads, and at the feet "some small slender stones, polished, and of a greenish cast; convex on one side, and concave on the other; the larger were four inches long and one broad; the smaller not quite four inches long nor one inch broad, somewhat narrower in the middle, with two holes at both ends." The interment was accompanied by two urns, and a ring of jet, perforated for suspension at the edge. To judge from the plate and description, the longer of the "slender stones" had not been bored with holes at either end.

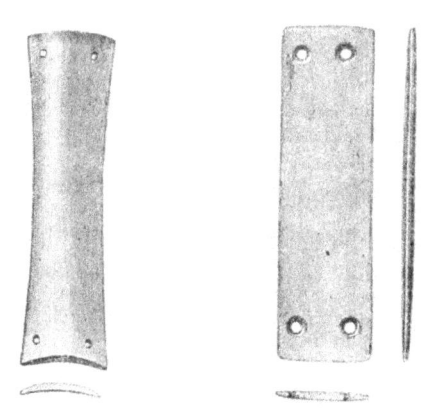

Fig. 354.—Evantown. 1/2

Fig. 355.—Devizes. 1/2

An oblong piece of chlorite slate, 5 3/8 inches long, 1 3/4 inches broad, and 1/4 inch thick, rounded on one face and hollowed on the other, was found in a gravel-pit at Aldington, Worcestershire. [2032] It has four holes through it, one at each corner, just large enough on the rounded face to allow a fine ligament to pass through, and countersunk on the other face. The plate of chlorite slate shown in Fig. 355 is flat, instead of hollowed, and the holes at the corners are countersunk on both faces. It was found in a barrow on Roundway Hill, [2033] near Devizes, in front of the breast of a skeleton, between the bones of the left forearm, and had, when found, a small fragment of bronze, possibly the tang of a knife, much corroded, adhering to it. In the same barrow was a stemmed and barbed flint arrow-head like Fig. 327, and a tanged bronze dagger. This bracer has been kindly lent to me by Mr. Cunnington, of Devizes, who discovered it. Another flat wrist-guard from a barrow at Aldbourne, [2034] Wilts, has only two out of the four holes finished. A third is incomplete. Dr. Thurnam [2035] regards those flat examples as breast-plates or gorgets. One, found with an interment at Calne, Wilts, is in the British Museum. It resembles Fig. 354.

A bracer, formed of a green-coloured stone, was found in a gravel-pit at Lindridge, Worcestershire. [2036] It is about 4 3/4 inches by 1 inch, and 1/4 inch thick; but it has been perforated at one end only, with a countersunk hole in each of the two corners, a third hole between them being only partly drilled. The other end is somewhat sharper and undrilled.

In the Christy Collection, is a plate of pale-green stone 4 1/2 inches long, with both faces somewhat rounded, one of them polished, and the other, which is rather flatter, in places striated transversely by coarse grinding. At each end are three small countersunk perforations in a line with each other. It was found with two small ornamented urns near Brandon, Suffolk. This bracer has been figured [2037] in illustration of some remarks by Sir A. Wollaston Franks.

In a barrow near Sutton, [2038] Sir R. Colt Hoare found, under the right hand and close to the breast of a contracted skeleton, a plate of blue slate, 4 1/2 inches long and 2 3/4 inches wide, with three small countersunk holes arranged in a triangle at either end. Near it were two boar's tusks and a drinking-cup. It has been thought to be too wide for a wrist-guard. A narrower specimen with six holes at each end is also in the Stourhead Collection. [2039]

Another variety has but one hole at each end, and is flat and broadest in the middle. In a cist in a barrow on Mere Down, Wiltshire, [2040] were two skeletons, near the left side of the larger of which was a small bronze dagger, with a tang for insertion in the hilt, and a piece of grey slaty stone about 4 inches long, and 1 1/8 inches broad in the middle, perforated at the ends. There were also present a drinking-cup, and an instrument of bone, as well as two circular ornaments of gold. A similar thin stone, with a hole at either end, was found with part of a bronze spear and other objects, associated with burnt human remains in a barrow at Bulford, Wilts. [2041] One of grey slaty stone with a countersunk hole at each end accompanied an interment at Sittingbourne, [2042] Kent, and is now in the British Museum. Another was found at Lancaster. [2043] I have another from Sandy, Beds, but cannot say whether it accompanied any interment. Another, 3 1/2 inches long, nearly an inch broad in the middle, and only the fifth part of an inch in thickness, was found near the tumulus at Broadford Bay, Isle of Skye, [2044] already mentioned, and is shown in Fig. 356. One (3 1/4 inches) was found in Mull, [2045] two (3 3/8 and 3 inches) came from Fyvie and Ballogie, [2046] Aberdeenshire, and one (2 1/4 inches) from Glenluce. [2047] Another (3 1/2 inches) in the Museum at Edinburgh came from the North of Ireland. [2048]

Fig. 356.—Isle of Skye. 1/2

A few specimens of the same character as Figs. 353 and 356 have been found in Ireland. In that country, also, the same slaty material was used, sometimes green, and sometimes red in colour.

The curious plate of fine soft sandstone, 4 inches long and perforated at each end, found in the Genista Cave, at Gibraltar, [2049] may possibly belong to this class, but it is by no means certain. Some objects of the same kind, with a hole at each end, have been found in the Côtes du Nord. [2050] France. Some early Spanish [2051] whetstones have one and even two perforations at each end.

The material of which this class of objects is formed is not exclusively stone. A plate of bone, now in the Devizes Museum, about 3 1/4 inches by 3/4 inch, bored through at each end from the sides and back, so as not to interfere with the face, was found with a small bronze celt mounted as a chisel in stag's horn, and with bone pins and two whetstones, in a barrow near Everley. [2052] A fragment of another bracer made of bone was found at Scratchbury Camp, Wilts. It is doubtful whether the richly-ornamented flat plate of gold, with a hole at each corner, found with a bronze dagger in a barrow [2053] at Upton Lovel, was destined for the same purpose. It led Sir R. C. Hoare, however, to regard the slate plate from the barrow near Sutton as a mere ornament, "an humble imitation of the golden plate found at Upton Lovel." Others have regarded these stone plates as amulets or charms; [2054] as destined to be affixed to the middle of a bow; [2055] or as personal decorations. [2056] Wilson has called attention to their similarity to the perforated plates of stone, of which such numerous varieties are found in North America. [2057] The holes in these, however, are very rarely more than two in number, and sometimes only one, and these almost always near the middle of the stone; their purpose possibly being to serve as draw-holes for equalizing the size of cords, in the same manner as twine is polished and rendered uniform in size, by being drawn through a circular hole by European manufacturers at the present day. They may, however, have served as ornaments, or even in some cases as wrist-guards. One engraved by Squier [2058] is much like Fig. 356, but thinner, and with the holes rather farther from the ends. Schoolcraft, [2059] suggests their employment to hold the strands or plies apart, in the process of twine or rope making.

The Rev. Canon Ingram, F.G.S., [2060] was the first to suggest that these British plates were bracers or guards, to protect the arm of the wearer against the blow of the string in shooting with the bow, like those in use by archers at the present day. In corroboration of this view, he cites the position of the plate in the Roundway barrow, between the bones of the left forearm, and the fact of so many of them being hollowed in such a manner as to fit the arm; while he argues that the similarity in the character and position of the perforations, in the hollowed and flat varieties, affords presumptive evidence that the use of both kinds of tablets was the same. I am inclined to adopt Canon Ingram's view, though, unless there was some error in observation, plates of this kind have been occasionally found on the right arm. In a barrow at Kelleythorpe, near Driffield, [2061] examined by the late Lord Londesborough in 1851, was a chamber containing a contracted skeleton, the bones of the right arm of which "were laid in a very singular and beautiful armlet, made of some large animal's bone" (actually of stone), [2062] "about 6 inches long, and the extremities, which were a little broader than the middle, neatly squared; in this were two perforations about half an inch from each end, through which were bronze pins or rivets, with gold heads, most probably to attach it to a piece of leather which had passed round the arm and been fastened by a small bronze buckle, which was found underneath the bones." These objects are now in the British Museum. In the cist was also a bronze dagger, with a wooden sheath and handle, some large amber beads, a drinking-cup, and the upper part of the skull of a hawk. Possibly this ancient warrior was left-handed, like the seven hundred chosen men of Benjamin, [2063] every one of whom could yet "sling stones at an hair breadth, and not miss."

It may be observed that left-handedness is thought to have been very prevalent in early times, both in the Old World [2064] and the New. [2065] Certainly this plate strapped upon the arm is curiously similar in character to the bracer in use in England in later times, which, though sometimes of other materials, consisted, according to Paulus Jovius, [2066] of a bone tablet. A bracer of carved ivory, of the sixteenth century, is in the Meyrick Collection, [2067] and Mr. C. J. Longman has a collection of them, many artistically engraved, dating from the 16th and 17th centuries. Among the archers of ancient Egypt, [2068] we find that similar guards were in use for the left arm. These were not only fastened round the wrist, but secured by a thong tied above the elbow. The material of which they were formed appears to be unknown. On a Roman monument [2069] found in the North of England, a soldier is represented with a bow in his hand, and a bracer on his left arm. The Eskimos [2070] of the present day also make use of a guard to save the wrist from the recoil of the bow-string. It is usually composed of three pieces of bone, about 4 inches in length, but sometimes of one only, and is fastened to the wrist by a bone button and loop. An ivory guard, attached by a strap and buckle to the arm, is still worn in India. Whatever was the purpose of those in stone they seem to belong to the latter part of the Stone Period, and to have continued in use in that of Bronze.

These bracers have occasionally been found in Denmark. One of red stone, 4 inches long, and with four holes, was found in a dolmen near Assens. It is ornamented with parallel lines along the ends, and part of the way along the sides. Another, 3 inches long, from a dolmen in Langeland, is of bone, with but two holes, and is ornamented with cross bands of zigzag lines. Both are engraved in the "Guide illustré du Musée des Antiquités du Nord." [2071] What appears to be one of bone, found in a barrow in Denmark, [2072] with two skeletons, but with no other objects, has also been engraved. A second was found under similar circumstances.

One of fine-grained sandstone (4 1/2 inches) with four holes was found near Prenzlow [2073] in North Germany, and another of chocolate-coloured material, probably slaty stone, accompanied an interment at Ochsenfurt, [2074] Lower Franconia.

Although, possibly, not strictly within the scope of the present work, it may be well here to make a few observations relating to the various articles formed of bone which are occasionally found in association with those of stone.

More than three dozen bone instruments were found in the Upton Lovel Barrow, [2075] already frequently mentioned. Most of them were pointed, varying in length from about 3 to 9 inches, and formed apparently from the leg-bones of different mammals. They, for the most part, show a portion of the articular surface at the end which has not been sharpened, at which also they are perforated. Mr. Cunnington, their discoverer, was of opinion that they had been used as arrow-or lance-heads; and possibly some of the larger specimens served as javelin-points, even if the smaller were merely pins to aid in fastening the dress, to which they were secured by a string passed through the hole, so as to prevent their being lost. Numerous other bone instruments from barrows are described and figured by Dr. Thurnam [2076] and Canon Greenwell. I have two that are decidedly lance-heads, about 6 inches long, made from leg-bones, probably of roe-deer, which have been pointed by cutting the bone obliquely through, so as to show a long elliptical section, while the articular end has been excavated into the cavity of the bone, so as to form a socket for the shaft, which was secured in its place by a pin, passing through two small holes drilled through the bone. One was found in Swaffham Fen, and the other at Girton, near Cambridge. Other spear-heads of much the same character, from the same district, from Lincolnshire, [2077] and from the River Thames, are in the British Museum, and some of them have been described and figured by Sir Wollaston Franks.

I have also a bone dagger with the blade about 4 inches long, with a rivet hole through the broad tang. It was found in the Thames near Windsor, and was given to me by Mr. F. Tress Barry, M.P., in 1895. I have also bones worked to a dagger-like form, but without any tang, from the Cambridge Fens.

A pin or awl of bone, [2078] 4 1/2 inches long, made from the *fibula* of some small animal, probably a roe-deer, split, and then rubbed to a point, was among the objects found by the Canon Greenwell, at Grimes's Graves, Norfolk, as well as the rounded piece of bone already mentioned at p. 34.

Bone pins or skewers, closely resembling those from British barrows, are of frequent occurrence on the sites of Roman occupation. In the name of *fibula*, as applied to the small bone of the leg, we have an acknowledgment of its adaptability for making such pins; in the same way as its concomitant *tibia* was the bone best adapted for making into flutes.

Bone pins, perforated at one end, were found in several of the barrows explored by the late Mr. Bateman, [2079] both with burnt and unburnt bodies. Canon Greenwell has also found them in the Yorkshire tumuli: in three instances with burnt bodies. I found one also in a disturbed barrow at Sutton Cheney, Leicestershire, which I opened in 1851. Others without the hole, some of which are termed spear-heads by Mr. Bateman, were found in Derbyshire and Staffordshire barrows, [2080] with burnt and unburnt bodies, associated with instruments and arrow-heads of flint. Another was found with burnt bones in a barrow at Hacpen Hill, [2081] Wilts; and part of one in the Long Barrow at West Kennet. [2082]

It seems probable that many of these pointed instruments may have been used as awls, for making holes in leather and soft materials. Others, as Mr. Bateman and Canon Greenwell suggest, may, with the unburnt bodies, have fastened some kind of shroud; and with the burnt, have served to pin a cloth in which the ashes were placed, after being collected from the funeral pile.

In the Heathery Burn Cave, where so many interesting bronze relics were found, there also occurred a large number of bone pins or awls, a cylindrical bone bead 7/10 inch long, a bone tube 1 1/2 inches long with a small perforation at the side, a pierced disc of bone 1 5/8 inches in diameter and 1/4 inch thick, and a flat bone blade, somewhat resembling in form a modern paper-cutter, 7 3/4 inches long and 1 1/4 inches broad. This same flat form of instrument, about 6 1/2 inches long and 3/4 inch broad, occurred in the Green Low Barrow, [2083] Derbyshire, but then, in company with a fine flint dagger and stemmed and barbed arrow-heads, and with a bone pin. Mr. Bateman [2084] thought that these instruments might have served as modelling tools for making pottery, or as mesh rules for netting. One, 12 inches long, with a drinking-cup and various instruments of flint, accompanied a contracted interment in a rock-grave on Smerrill Moor, [2085] Derbyshire. With a similar interment in a barrow on Haddon Field [2086] was one 6 1/4 inches long, cut from the horn of a red-deer, a flint arrow-head, and a small bronze awl. Two others, cut from the ribs of a large animal, and two barbed flint arrow-heads, were found inside a "drinking-cup" at the head of a contracted skeleton in Mouse Low; [2087] and others, again, with barbed flint arrow-heads, occurred with calcined bones at Ribden Low. [2088] They have also been found in Dorsetshire, perforated. [2089] Whether these instruments really served the purposes suggested by Mr. Bateman it is impossible to determine; but they seem well adapted either for finishing off the surface of clay vessels, or for netting, an art with which the Swiss Lake-dwellers of Robenhausen [2090] were acquainted, though in that settlement but slight traces of a knowledge of metal are exhibited.

Although needles of bone, carefully smoothed all over, and having a neatly-drilled eye, have been found in the cave-deposits both of Britain and France, but few such implements have, as yet, been discovered in these countries associated with objects of the Neolithic and Bronze Periods.

A bodkin or needle of wood, 6 inches long, and of the ordinary form, was, however, found in company with a small bronze dagger-blade, in an urn containing burnt bones near Tomen-y-mur, [2091] Carnarvonshire.

Needles of bone, both with the central hole (like some of those of the Bronze Age) and with the eye at the end (like those of the present day), have also been found in the Swiss Lakes. [2092] One of the latter class was discovered in the Genista Cave at Gibraltar. [2093] It is hard to say to what period it belongs. Needles of both forms have been found with arrow-heads and other articles of flint, in Danish grave-chambers. [2094]

The pins or awls, already described, are so rude and clumsy, and so large at the perforated end, that they could never have been intended for use as needles; and when we consider that the principal material to be sewn must have been the skins of animals, and that, even at the present day, needles are hardly ever employed for sewing leather, but bristles are attached to the end of the thread, and passed through holes prepared by an awl, it seems possible that needles, if ever they were used for this particular purpose, may have been superseded at a very remote period. The small bronze awl, so frequently found in barrows, is singularly like the "cobbler's awl" of the present day, though straight and not curved.

Among the Danish [2095] antiquities of bronze, we find a remarkable form of needle or bodkin, about 2 1/2 or 3 inches long, bluntly pointed at each end, and provided with an oval eye in the centre, so that it could be passed through a hole in either direction. This, with a bronze awl for boring the holes, and a pair of tweezers to assist in drawing the needle through, appears to have constituted the sewing apparatus of that day. I mention this form of needle because in Ribden Low, [2096] Staffordshire, together with a burnt interment, and some barbed arrow-heads of flint, were bone implements "pointed at each end" and "perforated through the middle," which may possibly have served such a purpose. No dimensions are given by Mr. Bateman, but a bodkin of the same kind from a barrow at Stourpaine, Dorset, is 4 inches long. It is in the Durden collection in the British Museum. In a barrow, at Bailey Hill, [2097] some calcined bones were accompanied by a pair of bone tweezers, neatly made and perforated for suspension.

Some of the needles of horn or bone in use among the Indians of North America [2098] were in shape much like miniature elephants' tusks.

Another bone implement appears to have been a chisel, of which a good specimen was found by the Rev. W. C. Lukis, F.S.A., in a chambered barrow at Temple Bottom, [2099] Wilts. It is formed of a portion split from a leg-bone of some mammal, about 3 1/4 inches long, and 5/8 inch wide, sharpened from both faces to a segmental edge at one end. A broader instrument of the same character was found with some long bone pins or awls near Cawdor Castle; [2100] and "a celt-shaped instrument, 5 inches long, with a cutting edge, made from part of the lower jaw of a large quadruped, rubbed down," was found with calcined bones in a barrow near Monsal Dale. [2101]

As has already been mentioned, bone instruments in the shape of a chisel occur in considerable numbers in the Swiss Lake-dwellings and elsewhere, and have been regarded as tools used in making and ornamenting earthen vessels. [2102] That bone chisels are, however, susceptible of more extensive use, is proved by the practice of the Klah-o-quat Indians of Nootka Sound, [2103] who, without the aid of fire, cut down the large cedars for their "dug-out" canoes with chisels formed from the horn of the Wapiti, struck by mallets of stone hafted in withes, or like dumb-bells in shape.

The only other forms of implement I need mention are those of a hammer and a hoe, formed of the lower end of a stag's horn, cut off and perforated. A hammer, or possibly a celt-socket, was found with a skeleton in Cop Head Hill barrow, [2104] near Warminster, together with fragments of flint "polished by use;" another in a barrow at Collingbourn, [2105] Wilts, and a third in a barrow near Biggin, [2106] with a contracted interment, and in company with flint celts, arrow-heads, and knives. Canon Greenwell has likewise found one in a barrow at Cowlam, Yorkshire, with an unburnt body, and together with a stone axe-hammer among burnt bones in a barrow at Lambourn, [2107] Berks. They have also been found in some numbers in the Thames, near Kew.

I have already spoken of the use of stag's horn for pick-axes, and for sockets for stone-hatchets; occasionally, also, the horn itself was sharpened and used as an axe or hoe. [2108] One from the Thames [2109] near Wandsworth, with its wooden handle still preserved, has been recorded by Mr. G. F. Lawrence. Stag's-horn axes occur in various countries on the Continent. They are by no means rare in Scandinavia, except in the case of those having ring and other ornaments engraved upon them. [2110] On an adze of this kind, in the Stockholm Museum, is engraved the spirited representation of a deer. In one instance, [2111] an axe has been made from the *ulna* of a whale. Lindenschmit [2112] has engraved several of stag's horn, principally from Hanover. They occur also in France. [2113] Beads and buttons of bone [2114] have been found with early interments; but the curious bone objects discovered in a pit at Leicester, [2115] and in the caves at Settle, Yorkshire, [2116] belong apparently to too recent a period to be here discussed. A kind of bone chisel has remained in use until recent times for the purpose of removing the bark from oak-trees for the supply of tanners. Some beads and ornaments formed of bone will be mentioned in a subsequent chapter.

CHAPTER XX.
SPINDLE-WHORLS, DISCS, SLICKSTONES, WEIGHTS, AND CUPS.

Besides the weapons and implements used in warfare and the chase, as well as for various constructive purposes, there were in ancient times, as at present, numerous implements and utensils of stone devoted to more purely domestic uses. Some of these, such as corn-crushers, mealing-stones, querns, pestles, and mortars, have been treated of elsewhere in this work, when, from the connection of these instruments with other forms adapted for somewhat different purposes, it appeared appropriate to describe them. There are, however, other classes, connected principally with domestic occupations, such, for instance, as spinning and weaving, about which it will be necessary to say a few words.

At how early a period the introduction of the spinning-wheel superseded to some extent the use of the distaff and spindle, it is difficult to say. It is by no means improbable that it was known in classical times, as Stosch thinks that he has recognized it on antique gems. The distaff and spindle remained, however, in use in many parts of this country until quite recently, and are still commonly employed in some remote parts of Britain, as well as over a great part of Europe. To how early a date this simple method of spinning goes back, we have also no means of judging. We know that it was in use in the earliest times among the Egyptians and Greeks; and we find, moreover, in the lake-habitations of Switzerland [2117]—even in those which apparently belong to a purely stone age—evidence of an acquaintance with the arts both of spinning and weaving, not only in the presence of some of the mechanical appliances for those purposes, but also in the thread and manufactured cloth. The principal fibrous materials in use in the lake-dwellings were bast from the bark of trees (chiefly the lime) and flax. No hemp has as yet been found in any lake-dwelling. It seems probable that the raw materials employed in neolithic times in Britain must have been of the same character; but we have here no such means of judging of the relative antiquity of the textile art, as those at the command of the Swiss antiquaries. Woven tissues have, however, been found with ancient interments, apparently of the Bronze Age, by Canon Greenwell, [2118] and Messrs. Mortimer, but made of wool, and not of vegetable fibre. An article on prehistoric spinning and weaving written by Dr. G. Buschan [2119] is worth consulting, as well as one by Dr. Joseph Anderson, [2120] on these processes in connexion with brochs. Sir Arthur Mitchell [2121] has also written on the subject of the spindle and whorl.

In spinning with the distaff and spindle, the rotatory motion of the latter is maintained by a small fly-wheel or "spindle-whorl," very generally formed of stone, but sometimes of other materials, with a perforation in the centre, in which the wooden or bone spindle was fastened, the part below the whorl tapering to a point so as to be readily twirled between the finger and thumb, and the part above, being also pointed, but longer, so as to admit of the thread when spun being wound round it, the yarn in the act of being spun being attached to the upper point. These spindle-whorls are, as might be anticipated, frequently found in various parts of the country; and though, from the lengthened period during which this mode of spinning was practised, it is impossible under ordinary circumstances to determine the antiquity of any specimen, yet they appear to have been sufficiently long out of use for local superstitions to have attached to them, as in Cornwall they are commonly known by the name of "Pisky grinding-stones," [2122] or "Pixy's grindstones." In North Britain, [2123] they are also familiarly called Pixy-wheels, and in Ireland [2124] "Fairy mill-stones." In Harris, and Lewis, [2125] the distaff and spindle are still in common use, and were so until quite recently on the mainland of Scotland. [2126] For twisting hair-lines or "imps" for fishing, stone, lead, or earthenware whorls with a hook in them are used. They are known by the name of "imp-stones." [2127] Notwithstanding this recent use, the original intention of the stone spindle-whorls, which occur in Scotland, as elsewhere, appears often to be unknown. They are called *clach-nathrach*, adder-stones or snake-stones, and have an origin assigned them much like that of the *ovum anguinum* of Pliny. "When cattle are bitten by snakes, the snake-stone is put into water, with which the affected part is washed, and it is cured forthwith." Glass beads [2128] with spirals on them seem to have been regarded as even more efficacious.

Spindle-whorls vary considerably in size and weight, being usually from an inch to an inch and a half in diameter, but occasionally as much as from two to three inches. They are sometimes flat at the edge or cylindrical, but more frequently rounded. They differ much in the degree of finish, some appearing to have been turned in a lathe, while others are very rough and not truly circular.

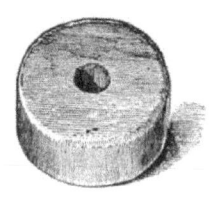

Fig. 357.—Scampston. 1/2

Fig. 358.—Holyhead. 1/1

Fig. 359.—Holyhead. 1/1

Fig. 360.—Holyhead. 1/1

The specimen I have selected for engraving as Fig. 357 is one of the more highly finished class, and rather flatter than usual. It was found in draining, at Scampston, Yorkshire, and is formed of a hard slaty stone. It has been turned in a lathe on one face, and at the edge; the other face is irregular, and seems to have been polished by hand. What was evidently the upper face, is ornamented with two parallel incised circles, and there are two more round the edge. The hole seems to have been drilled, and is quite parallel. One of the cheese-like spindle-whorls, of red sandstone, and another, rounded at the rim, found in hut-circles in Holyhead and Anglesea, [2129] are shown in Figs. 358 and 359. Another, of sandstone, was found in Thor's Cave, [2130] Derbyshire, with various objects, some of them of iron. One of lead, 1 1/8 inches in diameter, convex on one face, was found in the same place. One found at Ty Mawr, Holyhead, [2131] by the late Hon. W. O. Stanley, F.S.A., who kindly lent me this and the preceding blocks, is shown in Fig. 360. Numerous other specimens were discovered in the same place. They are sometimes decorated with incised radial lines and shallow cavities more or less rudely executed. One such, found near Carno, Montgomeryshire, [2132] has been figured. Several others are recorded as having been found in the Principality. [2133] In Cornwall, [2134] they seem to be especially numerous, occasionally occurring in subterranean chambers. They have also been found in considerable numbers in Scotland. [2135] The half of a clay spindle-whorl was found by Canon Greenwell in the material of a barrow at Weaverthorpe. [2136]

Sir Wollaston Franks [2137] has suggested that some of these perforated discs may have been used as dress-fasteners or buttons, and mentions that very similar objects have been found in Mexico, which there is every reason to believe have been used as buttons. He also instances a specimen from South Wales, which has evidently had a cord passed through it, as the edges of the hole in the centre are much worn by friction. Such a view carries much probability with it, so far as it relates to the thin discs of stone with small central holes not parallel, but tapering from both faces; especially if they are in any way ornamented. Some of the rougher kind, however, may have served some such purpose as that of plummets or net-sinkers, as has been suggested by Professor Nilsson. [2138] Perforated [2139] pebbles of much the same form have served as net weights in Scotland, and are still occasionally in use. In Samoa, flat circular discs of stones, about two inches in diameter, with central holes, are used to prevent rats from reaching provisions, which are suspended in baskets by a cord. One of these discs strung on the cord suffices for the purpose. A specimen is in the Christy Collection. Their use is analogous to that of the flat stones on the staddles on which corn-stacks are built in this country, though in that case, the stones are to prevent the ascent and not the descent of the rats.

Judging, however, from all analogy, there can be little doubt that in most cases where the holes are parallel, the perforated discs found in Britain were spindle-whorls. As has been already observed, they are frequently formed of other materials than stone; and both the spindles of wood and the whorls of bone have been found with Roman remains. [2140] They are also frequently formed of lead and earthenware. Spindles of ivory sometimes occur both with Roman and Saxon relics. I have several such, found with whorls of slaty stone in Cambridgeshire. The Saxon whorls are of the same materials and character as those of Roman age. Spindles of wood have been found in the lake-settlements of Savoy. [2141] An interesting and profusely illustrated chapter on spindle-whorls will be found in Hume's "Ancient Meols." [2142] Earthenware whorls, variously decorated, have been found in large numbers on the site of Troy, and with Mycenæan remains.

Allied to the whorls, but evidently destined for some other purpose, is a flat disc of shelly limestone, now in my collection, found at

Barrow, near Bury St. Edmund's. It is 5 1/2 inches in diameter, 3/4 inch thick, ground from both faces to an edge all round, and perforated in the centre with a hole 5/8 inch in diameter, countersunk on each face, so as to leave only a narrow edge in the middle of the hole, which is much polished by friction. The edge of the periphery is also worn smooth. I am at a loss to assign a use to this object. In the Greenwell Collection a similar disc from the North Riding of Yorkshire shows polish on one face. A somewhat similar disc with the hole a little larger, so that it rather resembles a quoit, is in the Norwich Museum. It may be a plaything of no great antiquity. An instrument of similar form, engraved by Lindenschmit, [2143] has a parallel shaft-hole. Among the North American Indians, [2144] perforated discs, but with broad and not sharp peripheries, appear to have been used as a kind of quoits.

Some flat imperforate discs of stone, from two to nine inches in diameter, roughly chipped round the edges, and in one instance oval, were associated with bronze tweezers and articles of iron, in a Pict's house at Kettleburn, Caithness. [2145] Two polished stone discs were found in a crannog near Maybole, [2146] Ayrshire, and a nearly square piece of stone that had been polished on both sides in a crannog at Dowalton, [2147] Sorbie, Wigtownshire. Others of large size occurred in another Pict's house in Orkney, [2148] and were regarded as plates. Six black stone dishes, all about 2 1/2 inches thick, and varying from 1 foot 8 inches to 10 inches long, were found with numerous other objects, among them a copper needle, in a circular building in South Uist. [2149] Other similar dishes have been found near Sand Lodge, in Shetland, [2150] and elsewhere. Possibly such stones may have been used in cooking oatmeal cakes or bannocks—like the stones on which formerly "pikelets" or crumpets were cooked in Leicestershire and other Midland counties, where their modern iron substitutes are still called "pikelet-stones." Ornamented stones for toasting oatmeal cakes in front of a peat fire are or were until lately in use in Scotland. [2151] Cooking slabs of thin stone are used by the natives of Guiana, [2152] for baking cassava bread.

Dr. Joseph Anderson [2153] has suggested that some of the small discs, with the surface highly polished, such as have been found in Scottish brochs of the Iron Age, may have served as mirrors.

Another purpose to which stone implements seem to have been applied, in connection with weaving and the preparation of leather, is that of burnishing or smoothing, somewhat in the same manner as is now effected by the flat-iron. An oval pebble (4 inches) rubbed all along one side was found by General Pitt Rivers in one of the pits at Mount Caburn, [2154] Lewes. Sir W. Wilde, speaking of a quite recent period, observes that "it is well known that weavers in the north of Ireland used a smooth celt, whenever they could find one, for rubbing on the cloth, bit by bit, as they worked it, to close the threads and give a gloss to the surface." [2155] Canon Greenwell had a celt from Yorkshire, which was used by a shoemaker for smoothing down the seams he made in leather. The old English name for the smooth stones used for such purposes is "slickstone." In the "Promptorium Parvulorum," [2156] written in the fifteenth century, a SLEKYSTŌN or SLEKENSTONE is translated, *linitorium*, *lucibriunculum*, *licinitorium*—terms unknown to classical Latinity. Mr. Albert Way, in a note on the word, after giving its various forms as slyke-stone, sleght-stone, sleeke-stone, &c., remarks, "In former times, polished stones, implements in form of a muller, were used to smooth linen, [2157] paper, and the like, and likewise for the operation termed calendering. Gautier de Bibelesworth says,—

"Et priez la dame qe ta koyfe luche (slike)

De sa luchiere (slikingston) sur la huche."

In directions for making buckram, &c., and for starching cloth, (Sloane MS., 3548, f. 102), the finishing process is as follows: '*Cum lapide slycstone levifica*.'" "She that hath no glasse to dresse her head will use a bowle of water, she that wanteth a sleeke stone to smooth her linnen will take a pebble." [2158]

"Slickstones occur in the Tables of Custom-House Rates on Imports, 2 James I., and about that period large stones inscribed with texts of Scripture were occasionally thus used. (See Whitaker, 'Hist. of Craven,' [2159] p. 401, *n*.) There was a specimen in the Leverian Museum. Bishop Kennett, in his 'Glossarial Collections,' *s.v.* 'Slade,' alludes to the use of such an appliance 'to sleek clothes with a sleekstone.'" Cotgrave, in his French Dictionary, translates *calendrine* or *pierre calendrine*, as a sleekstone; and under the word "lisse" makes mention of "a rowler of massive glasse wherewith curriers do sleeke and gloss their leather." This, probably, was a substitute for a more ancient instrument of stone. Sir Thomas Browne mentions slickstones among electric bodies, and implies that in his time they were of glass. "Glass attracts but weakly though clear; some slickstones and thick glasses indifferently." [2160]

I have two or three specimens of glass slickstones, which in form resemble mushrooms. The lenticular part is usually about 5 inches in diameter, and its rounded surface was used for polishing the linen. The handle or stalk is ribbed and about 4 1/2 inches long. They are of both clear and of bottle-green glass. A small slickstone of black glass without a handle was found in a Viking grave of a woman in Islay. [2161] The same form was recently in use in Scotland. A large one is in the Kirkcudbright [2162] Museum. Another [2163] provided with a long smooth handle has likewise been figured.

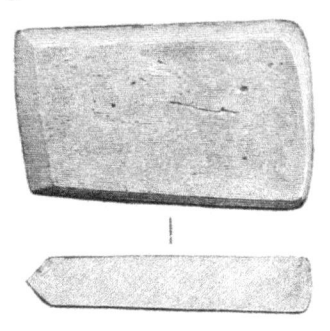

Fig. 361.—Holyhead.

A four-sided implement of stone, fashioned with considerable care, the sides flat and smooth, and with an edge at one end, was found by the late Hon. W. O. Stanley, F.S.A., at Pen-y-Bonc, [2164] and is shown in Fig. 361, kindly lent to me by him. It has been regarded as a burnisher or polishing stone. A similar specimen is in the Blackmore Museum.

Mr. Syer Cuming [2165] mentions the discovery, at Alchester, Oxfordshire, of a flat pyriform piece of red sandstone, 3 1/2 inches long, 3 1/4 inches wide, and 1 inch thick in the middle, with the edges rounded, and the whole surface, with the exception of the obtuse end, polished; and he inclines to the belief that it was employed in smoothing hides and rendering them pliant for clothing. Another "slickstone for tawing or softening hides by friction," formed of quartz, 6 1/8 inches broad by 2 1/2 inches in height, with a depression on either side to admit the finger and thumb, and having the surface rounded and polished by use, was found at a depth of three feet in the ground at Culter, Lanarkshire. [2166] In the Shrewsbury Museum [2167] is a perforated stone in shape like a broad hoe, but with rounded edges; it is thought to be a currier's tool. Three flint pebbles found with late Celtic enamelled bronze horse-trappings at Westhall, Suffolk, [2168] and having one or both of their sides much rubbed down, may possibly belong to this class of objects. Sir R. Colt Hoare [2169] speaks of "the hard flat stones of the pebble kind, such as we frequently find both in the towns as well as in the tumuli of the Britons," but does not suggest a purpose for them. Polished pebbles have not unfrequently been found in tumuli with stone weapons and implements. One tapering toward the ends, which are rubbed flat, was found by Mr. Bateman. [2170] Another was found in a barrow near Ashford-in-the-Water. [2171] It is possible they may, as subsequently suggested, have been ornaments or amulets; but some pebbles, polished on part of their surface, as if by use, have been found in tumuli by Canon Greenwell.

A "smoothing-stone" of hard grey stone, with a short tang apparently for fixing it in a handle, has been engraved by the Rev. Dr. Hume. [2172] He does not, however, state where it was found. A somewhat similar implement is engraved by Schoolcraft, [2173] which he thinks may have been designed for smoothing down seams of buckskin. As stated at page 416, I have seen a stone which had been used for this purpose in England.

Granite and other pebbles are used as ironing-stones in Orkney [2174] and in Scotland. Several have been described by Professor Duns. [2175]

Dr. Keller [2176] has shown that, in connection with what was probably the earliest form of loom, weights were employed to stretch the warp. These, however, in Switzerland, seem to have been for the most part formed of burnt clay, though possibly some of the stones which have been regarded as sink-stones or plummets, were used for this purpose. Some of these have already been described.

Loom weights of burnt clay have been found in Scotland [2177] and of chalk [2178] in Sussex. I have one of burnt clay from Cambridge.

Another domestic use to which stones were applied was as weights for the balance or scales; though we have no evidence at present that in this country, at all events, any weighing apparatus was known so early as the Stone or even the Bronze Period. Among the Jews the same word אֶבֶן (*Eben*) denoted both a stone and a weight; and we have a somewhat similar instance of customs being recorded in language in the case of our own "stone" of eight or fourteen pounds. Discoidal weights formed of stone are not unfrequently found on the sites of Roman occupation.

The moulds in which bronze weapons and tools were cast, were often made of stone, but for any account of them I refer the reader to my book on "Bronze Implements."

Another class of domestic utensils, frequently found in Scotland and the adjacent islands, consists of cup-like vessels formed of stone, of various degrees of hardness, and usually provided with a small projecting handle.

Fig. 362.—Scotland.

Fig. 363.—Sutherlandshire.

Fig. 362, borrowed from the *Proceedings of the Society of Antiquaries of Scotland*, [2179] will serve to show their general character. Of the two cups here engraved, one was found near a megalithic circle at Crookmore, Tullynessle, Aberdeenshire, and the other in another part of Scotland. The material is described as a soft calcareous stone. One of steatite or "pot-stone," with a large unpierced handle, was found in a cairn at Drumkesk, [2180] near Aboyne, Aberdeenshire; and two others, one with the handle projecting from the side, and the other with a long straight handle, at Strathdon [2181] in the same county. Two others, one of them of micaceous sandstone, ornamented with a band of rudely-cut projecting knobs, and the other with incised lines in zigzag herring-bone patterns, were dug out of a large cairn on Knockargity, [2182] and others at Cromar, [2183] also in Aberdeenshire. One ornamented in a similar manner was found at Needless, [2184] Perth. Others have been found in cairns in Banffshire, [2185] Morayshire, [2186] and Sutherlandshire, [2187] the engraving of the last of which is here reproduced as Fig. 363. It is 6 1/2 inches in diameter. They have also been found in brochs, in Caithness, [2188] Shetland, [2189] and in a "fort" in Forfarshire. [2190] They have likewise been discovered under various circumstances in Aberdeenshire, [2191] at Balmoral, [2192] and in Forfarshire, [2193] Perthshire, [2194] and the Isle of

Skye, [2195] as well as in the Isle of Man. [2196] They occur, though rarely, in Ireland. [2197] I have one from Trillick, Tyrone.

In former times these cups were regarded as "Druidical *paterœ*;" but Sir Daniel Wilson [2198] has pointed out that in the Faroe Islands, a similar kind of vessel is still in use as a lamp or as a chafing-dish for carrying live embers. He has engraved one of them in the cut here reproduced. The same kind of rude lamp or cresset is in use in Ceylon. [2199] These Scottish vessels probably belong to no very remote antiquity.

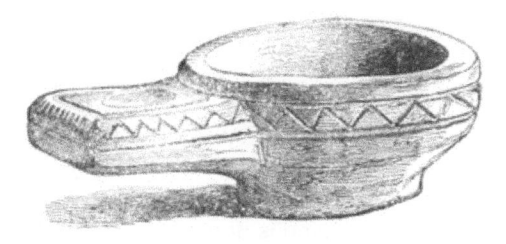

Fig. 364.—Faroe Islands.

A shallow one-handled saucer or stand of Kimmeridge shale was found at Povington, Dorset, [2200] but was probably intended for some other purpose than the Scottish cup. It has been suggested that it was for holding the flakes of flint supposed to have been used for turning the armlets and other objects of Kimmeridge coal, many fragments of which, as well as numerous pieces of flint, were found with it; but it seems more probable that the turning tools were of metal. It may be an unfinished lamp-stand, or possibly a lamp.

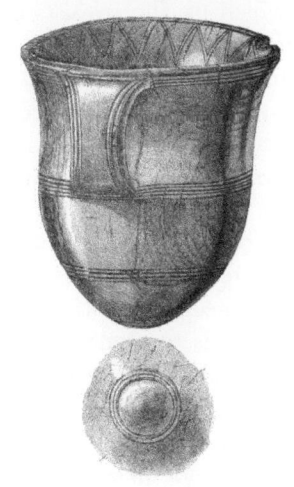

Fig. 365.—Broad Down or Honiton.

Cups, however, formed of shale, and most skilfully made, have occasionally been found in barrows. The most remarkable is that which was discovered in a tumulus at Broad Down, [2201] near Honiton, by the Rev. Richard Kirwan, to whom I am indebted for the loan of the full-sized figure (Fig. 365) on the next page. The woodcut gives so perfect a representation of its form that any detailed description is needless. Its height is 3 5/8 inches, and its greatest diameter, which is at the mouth, 3 inches. Its capacity is about a gill. The material of which it is formed appears in all probability to be Kimmeridge [2202] shale, though it is difficult to pronounce on this point with certainty. In another barrow, also on Broad Down, [2203] Mr. Kirwan came upon a bronze spear-head, or rather dagger, which had been attached to its haft by rivets, lying on a deposit of burnt bones; and at a distance from it of about 3 feet he discovered a drinking-cup of shale, of almost similar form and size to that previously found. It is about 3 1/4 inches high, and 3 inches in diameter at the mouth, and is now preserved in the Albert Museum at Exeter. One very remarkable feature about these cups is that they have been turned in the lathe, and not made by hand; and it has been suggested that by the use of the pole-lathe, the great apparent difficulty of leaving the projection for the handle would be entirely removed. I had already arrived at this conclusion before seeing, in Mr. Kirwan's paper, the views of a "skilful practical turner" on this point; but it may be well to describe the simple instrument known as a pole-lathe, with which most of the constituent parts of a Windsor chair are turned at the present day. [2204]

On the bed of the lathe, which usually consists of two pieces of squared wood nailed to two standards fixed in the ground, are two wooden "heads," both furnished with pointed screws passing through them, to form the centres on which the piece of wood to be turned revolves. This, after having been chopped into an approximately cylindrical form, is placed between the two centres, and above the lathe is fixed a long elastic pole of wood, to the end of which a cord is attached, connecting it to the end of a treadle below the lathe. The cord is hitched round the wood, and adjusted to such a length as to keep the treadle well off the ground when the pole is at rest. When the treadle is pressed down with the foot, it draws down the pole, and the cord in its passage causes the piece of wood to revolve. When the pressure is relieved, the elasticity of the pole draws it back in the opposite direction, so that the workman by treading causes an alternate rotary motion of the wood. He turns this in the ordinary manner, except that his tool can cut only intermittently, that is, at the time when the revolution is towards, and not from him. If now, a projecting stop were attached to the object in the lathe, so as to prevent its making a complete revolution, it is evident that a portion like that forming the handle of the cup might be left unturned. Still, in the case of these cups, something more than the ordinary pole-lathe with two "dead" centres must have been used, as with such a lathe, it would be almost impossible to bore out the hollow of the cup. It appears probable, therefore, that a mandrel-head with a "live" centre, like that of our ordinary lathes, must have been used; though probably the motion was communicated by a pole and treadle, and not, as with modern foot-lathes, by a large pulley on a cranked axle.

We shall subsequently see that the waste pieces of Kimmeridge shale, to which the unwarrantable name of "coal-money" has been applied, testify to the use of such a lathe. Whatever may be the date to which the manufacture of this shale into bracelets and other objects was carried down, it seems probable that, assuming this cup to have been of home manufacture and not imported, the use of the lathe was known in this country in pre-Roman times. In the Broad Down barrow no other object accompanied the burnt bones, and in the trunk-interment in the King Barrow, Stowborough, [2205] near Wareham, cited by Mr. Kirwan, where a somewhat similar cup appears to have been found, there was no weapon nor trace of metal, unless it were what was imagined to be some gold lace. The ornamentation of this cup is different from that of the Devonshire specimen, and the workmanship appears to be ruder. It was described at the time as of wood, but was probably of shale, as has been suggested by Dr. Wake Smart. [2206] Some fragments of cups of shale with flat handles were found in the Romano-British village at Woodcuts. [2207]

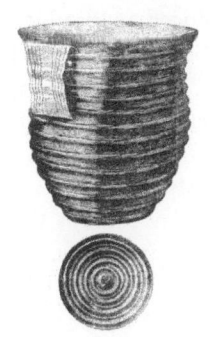

Fig. 366.—Rillaton, height 3 1/4 inches.

It is, however, but right to mention that a *wooden* cup with a handle at the side, and which had been turned in a lathe, was found in a barrow in Schleswig, [2208] in a coffin made from the trunk of an oak, together with a skeleton wrapped in woollen cloth, a bronze dagger, and other objects. Professor Worsaae attributes these objects to the Early Bronze Age. Mr. Kirwan has cited another instance of a somewhat similar cup, found with "coal-money."

It is true that these instances afford no actual guide as to date, but the interments were clearly not Roman. Some clue, however, is afforded by the discovery of the gold cup shown in Fig. 366, not unlike this in form, in a barrow at Rillaton, [2209] Cornwall, accompanied by what appears to have been a bronze dagger; [2210] but the best evidence as to the date to be assigned to this class of cups is probably that of the very remarkable and beautiful specimen formed of amber, and found in a barrow at Hove, [2211] near Brighton.

Fig. 367.—Hove.

In this instance an interment in a rude oaken coffin was accompanied by the amber cup, here, by the kindness of the Sussex Archæological Society, reproduced, a double-edged battle-axe of stone (see Fig. 119, p. 186), a bronze dagger, and a whetstone. This cup is 3 1/2 inches in diameter and 2 1/2 high, about 1/10 inch in thickness, and its capacity rather more than half a pint. It is perfectly smooth inside and out, and, so far as I could judge from seeing it through glass in the Brighton Museum, it was turned in a lathe. It has been suggested by Mr. Barclay Phillips that some process like that of boiling amber in spirits of turpentine may have been known by which it would be rendered plastic; but this seems hardly probable.

It is, of course, possible that such an object as this may have come by commerce into Britain; and, indeed, amber is one of the articles mentioned by Strabo as exported from Celtic Gaul to this country.

In the case of the shale cups, however, the evidence seems in favour of their having been articles of home manufacture, and we shall shortly see to what an extent jet was used here in early times for ornamental purposes.

So far as amber is concerned, it is to be remembered that after storms it occurs in considerable quantities along the eastern coast of England, and on the southern coast at all events to Deal. An important work on the amber ornaments of the Stone Period has been published by Dr. Richard Klebs. [2212]

Fig. 368.—Ty Mawr. 2/3

Vessels without handles were also occasionally formed of stone. Six or seven of these, of various sizes and forms, were discovered in a "kist-vaen" in the Island of Unst, [2213] and are now for the most part in the British Museum. Four of them are of a rude quadrangular form, with flat bottoms, and from 3 1/2 to 7 inches in height. The other three are oval. They are formed of schistose rock, and some of them still bear traces of the action of fire. Sir Wollaston Franks, with reference to these vessels, has stated that stone-vessels of a rude type are still in use in some remote parts of Norway. One is engraved, as ancient, by Nilsson. [2214]

Several were found in the ancient dwelling at Skara, Orkney, [2215] one of which is hexagonal.

A small stone cup, found by the late Hon. W. O. Stanley in an ancient circular habitation at Ty Mawr, Holyhead, is, through his kindness, shown in Fig. 368. [2216] A more oval cup, somewhat broken, was also found.

An oval stone cup (4 1/2 inches long), apparently made out of half of a rounded boulder from the beach, was found in a barrow at Penmaenmawr. [2217]

A circular cup or mortar, barely 4 inches in diameter, from Anglesea, is engraved in the *Archæological Journal*. [2218]

Some small cup-shaped vessels of chalk, probably used as lamps, were found by Canon Greenwell, in the excavations at Grimes' Graves. [2219]

A cylindrical stone vessel, 5 inches high and 6 1/2 inches in diameter, with a cup-shaped cavity above, and a small hole below, as if for fixing it on a stand, was found at Parton, Kircudbrightshire. [2220] Another, found with a polished stone hatchet in a cairn in Caithness, [2221] is of circular form, ribbed externally like a melon.

Cups without handles have been found in Orkney [2222] and Caithness, some with a place for a wick, so as to serve as lamps.

In a cist in a barrow in Orkney [2223] the cinerary urn was formed of "mica stone," about 19 1/2 inches high and 22 1/2 inches in diameter, and covered with a lid of undressed stone. Another of nearly the same size was found in a barrow at Stennis. [2224] Another stone urn and two stone dishes, with handles or ears, were found in a grave in Forfarshire; [2225] and two stone urns, one within the other, were turned up by the plough at Aucorn, [2226] near Wick, Caithness. [2227] One of these was 13 inches high and 21 inches in diameter, with two handles rudely cut in the sides. The other was 8 inches in height and 11 1/2 inches in diameter, and was provided with a stone lid. Long oval vessels from Shetland [2228] probably belong to more recent times. The "mell" [2229] for preparing pot-barley may be still in use.

Stone vessels, one with a movable bottom and partly filled with burnt bones, have been found in the Shetland Isles. [2230]

Stone vessels have also been discovered, though rarely, in barrows in England. One such was found by Mr. Bateman, in company with a small bronze bucket with an iron handle, in a barrow at Wetton. [2231] It is only 4 inches high, and carved in sandstone, with four grooves running round it by way of ornament. It is probably of late date.

A few urns formed of stone have also been found in Ireland.

One of the varieties of steatite has long been in use for the formation of hollow vessels for cooking and other purposes, and is still known by the name of Pot-stone in English. Many of the cooking vessels of the Eskimos are made of this material.

I now pass on to the consideration of personal decorations formed of stone.

CHAPTER XXI.
PERSONAL ORNAMENTS, AMULETS, ETC.

Among all savage tribes the love of ornament and finery is very great; though it cannot well be greater than that exhibited by more highly civilized races. It has, however, to content itself with decorations of a simpler kind, and requiring fewer mechanical appliances in their production; so that shells, feathers, and trophies of the chase, and ornaments wrought from bone and the softer, yet showy, kinds of stone, usually replace the more costly products of the loom and the jeweller's art.

The ornaments commonly found in this country associated with interments belonging to the period when stone implements were in use, are for the most part formed of jet, shale, and amber, and occasionally, as has already been mentioned, of bone, and possibly ivory, and even gold. Nearly all, however, appear to be characteristic of the time when stone was already being superseded by bronze for cutting purposes, and on this account, as well as from their not being implements, but personal decorations, some of them but slightly differing from those in use at the present day, I had at first some scruples in including them in this work. It would, however, appear incomplete, were I not to take a short review of some of the principal discoveries of such objects; and this will also incidentally be illustrative of some of the funeral customs of prehistoric times and of the use of amulets of stone.

The simplest form of ornament, if indeed it can be properly so called, is the button, which not unfrequently accompanies interments of an early date. The usual shape is that of an obtusely conical disc, in the base of which two converging holes are drilled so as to form a V-shaped passage, through which the cord for attachment could be passed. These buttons are formed of different materials, but most commonly of jet or shale.

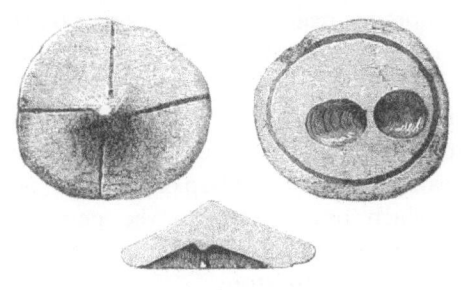

Fig. 369.—Butterwick. 1/1

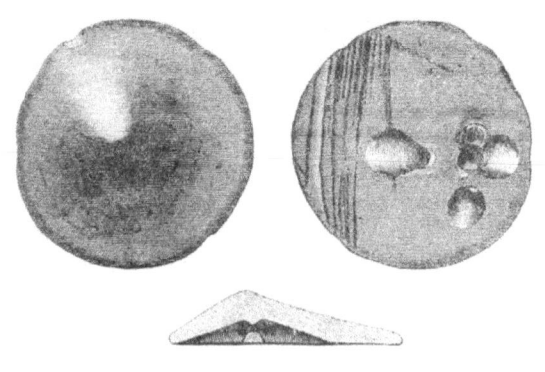

Fig. 370.—Butterwick. 1/1

In Fig. 369 a ruder example than usual is shown, full size. It is formed of a fine grained limestone, and was found by Canon Greenwell, [2232] F.R.S., with a contracted body, in a barrow at Butterwick, Yorkshire, in company with five buttons of jet, from 1 1/4 to 1 3/4 inches in diameter, of which one that is pierced in an unusual manner is engraved as Fig. 370. With the body, were a small dagger-knife, awl, and flat celt of bronze, and a flint flake trimmed along one edge. Another large plain button was found by the same explorer in a cist at Great Tosson, [2233] Northumberland. A jet button nearly square and ornamented with marginal lines was found in a cist on Dundee Law. [2234] The cruciform ornament on the stone stud would at first sight suggest the possibility of its being the Christian symbol. It is, however, so simple a form of ornament, that it may be said to belong to all time. Numerous instances of its occurrence at an early period have been collected by M. de Mortillet. [2235] Another instance of the kind is afforded by two jet studs found in two barrows near Thwing and Rudstone, [2236] Yorkshire, by Canon Greenwell, one of which is engraved as Fig. 371. In one case, the button lay about the middle of the right arm, and with it a highly ornamented ring of jet pierced at the sides. In the other instance, there was a second jet button, as well as a ring of the same character, a bronze dagger-knife, and other objects, some of which have been already described. [2237] One of the rings is shown in Fig. 372. [2238] In both there are two V-shaped perforations close together, and formed in the body of the ring by drilling two converging holes. There can be little doubt that the ring and stud together formed some sort of clasp or fastening, but in what manner the string which passed through the perforation, was managed, it is difficult to say. Another jet ring and a kind of button were also found in a barrow at Rudstone. [2239]

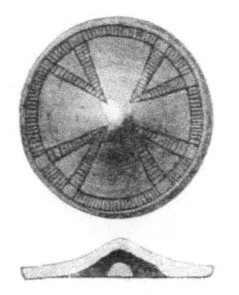

Fig. 371.—Rudstone. 1/1

Fig. 372.—Rudstone. 1/1

A very highly ornamented jet ring of this class, square in section, and with a sort of beading at each angle, the two faces and periphery decorated with fine raised lines, and with three perforations as if for suspension, has been engraved in the "Crania Britannica." [2240] It was found with the skeleton of a man, in a cist in a barrow near Avebury, Wilts, with one small and two large jet studs, the largest almost 3 inches in diameter, a flint flake, and an ovoid implement of serpentine subsequently to be noticed.

Fig. 373.—Crawfurd Moor. 1/2

The specimen engraved as Fig. 373, on the scale of one-half, is of jet, and was found on Crawfurd Moor, Lanarkshire. [2241] It is now in the National Museum at Edinburgh. It shows the most common form of button, and the cut has been made use of frequently. One of the same character, 1 3/4 inches in diameter, and found in a barrow on Lambourn Down, Berkshire, is preserved in the British Museum. It has a rounded projection at the apex of the flat cone. In two of Kimmeridge shale, from Net Low, Alsop Moor, Derbyshire, [2242] there is a similar projection and also a slightly raised beading round the edge. They accompanied a large bronze dagger, which lay close to the right arm of an extended skeleton. A button of jet, 1 3/4 inches in diameter, was found near the shoulder of a contracted skeleton, in a barrow near Castern, Derbyshire. [2243] A small piece of calcined flint lay near.

Several studs or buttons of polished Kimmeridge coal, of the same character, but slightly more conical than Fig. 373, were found by Mr. F. C. Lukis in a barrow near Buxton. [2244] A flint celt accompanied another interment in the same barrow. What appears to be a small stud of jet, but which is described as a cone, was found with a ring, like a pulley, of the same material, and a fine flint dagger and other objects, buried with a skeleton at Durrington Walls, Wilts. [2245] A larger ring and disc, perforated with two holes for suspension, together with some beautifully formed stemmed and barbed flint arrow-heads (see Fig. 320), and a bronze dagger, accompanied a contracted interment in a barrow near Fovant, in the same county. [2246] A button formed of a substance like concrete was found with part of a leaf-shaped arrow-head, some beads, &c., in a barrow at Boscregan, [2247] Cornwall. It is nearly hemispherical in shape. In four cists at Tosson, near Rothbury, Northumberland, [2248] were contracted skeletons, two of them accompanied by an urn. In one of the cists were three of these buttons, 2 inches in diameter, described as of cannel coal; and in another was an iron javelin-head. They are sometimes of much smaller dimensions. One of this character, found in the Calais Wold barrow by Messrs. Mortimer, has been figured full size in the late Mr. Ll. Jewitt's *Reliquary*. [2249] His cut is reproduced as Fig. 374. Twenty small buttons of inferior jet were found by Canon Greenwell in a barrow at Hunmanby, [2250] Yorkshire. Two small buttons of jet were picked up at Glenluce, [2251] Wigtownshire.

Fig. 374.—Calais Wold Barrow. 1/1

Occasionally we find conical studs of this form perforated by two converging holes in the base, forming what were, in some cases, apparently the termination of necklaces or gorgets. It seems possible that these were not made to clasp the whole neck, but were merely attached in some manner between the shoulders in front, as is supposed to have been the case with many of the Anglo-Saxon necklaces. Two of these studs were found with other beads of a necklace in Holyhead Island, [2252] and are mentioned at p. 459. With other necklaces, however, the studs are more numerous, and seem to have been a form of beads.

These studs or buttons are occasionally of amber. In a stone cist in a barrow near Driffield, Yorkshire, [2253] a contracted skeleton was found, and with it, the bracer before described (p. 429), a bronze dagger, and three conical amber studs, about 1 inch in diameter, flat on the under-side, and pierced with two converging holes. Such buttons of amber are found on the Baltic [2254] coast, and even in Northern Russia.

Conical studs or buttons perforated at the base, formed of wood or lignite covered with gold, and of bone or ivory, have been found in the Wiltshire barrows. [2255] The jet studs are sometimes concave at the base, with a knob left in the centre for attachment, instead of being perforated. Five such were found with urns at Stevenston, Ayrshire. [2256] They are about an inch in diameter.

The rings of jet with perforations at the edges, such as have been before mentioned as found in connection with buttons or studs, are sometimes found without them. One such, nearly 2 inches in diameter, perforated in the centre with a hole 3/4 inch in diameter, and with "two deep grooves in the edges, and four holes near together, two communicating with each other and capable of admitting a large packthread," was found with the skeleton at Tring Grove, [2257] Herts, with which had been buried the flint arrowheads and "wrist-guards" before described. [2258] Two rings of jet, one punctured with two holes as if for suspension, the other with one hole only, accompanied an urn and two "spear-heads" of flint in a barrow near Whitby. [2259] A pulley-like ring, described as of cannel coal, with four perforations through the sides at irregular intervals, was found in a cist near Yarrow, Selkirkshire, [2260] and has been engraved. A part of a stone hammer lay in another cist at the same spot. A portion of what appears to be a similar ring was found near Lesmahago, [2261] Lanarkshire.

A jet ring notched on the outside, or ornamented with imperfect circles, was found in the Upton Lovel Barrow, [2262] together with doubly conical and cylindrical beads. There were both stone and bronze objects in the same barrow, many of which have already been mentioned.

A ring of Kimmeridge shale, 1 3/8 inches in diameter, was found with a penannular ring of bronze, flint flakes and arrow-heads, a perforated whetstone, a bead of glass and one of bone, in examining a series of barrows at Afflington, Dorset. [2263]

Another form of ornament, of which numerous examples have been found with ancient interments, is the necklace, consisting of beads, usually of jet, amber, or bone, generally of jet alone, but sometimes of two of these materials together. It is, of course, almost impossible to re-arrange a group of beads, often more than a hundred in number, in the exact order in which they were originally worn; there are, however, frequently several peculiarly formed plates found with the beads, which seem susceptible of being arranged in but one particular order, so that it appears probable that the manner in which some of these necklaces have been reconstructed, as in Fig. 375, is not far from being correct.

The original was found in an urn within a barrow at Assynt, Ross-shire, [2264] and is here represented about one-fourth size, in a cut from Wilson's "Prehistoric Annals of Scotland," kindly lent me by Messrs. Macmillan. The flat beads, which are perforated obliquely from the edges towards the back, have patterns engraved upon them now studded with minute specks of sand, [2265] which resemble gold. Besides those figured, there were present a number of irregularly oval jet beads. Other such necklaces have been found at Torrish, [2266] Sutherlandshire (with flint arrow-heads), at Tayfield, [2267] Fife (in a cist), and at Lunan-head, [2268] near Forfar, in a cairn.

Fig. 375.—Assynt, Ross-shire.

In most cases the flat beads of these necklaces are ornamented by having dotted or striated patterns worked upon them by means of some sharp-pointed instrument. These markings also occur on the bone or ivory portions, when the necklace, as is sometimes the case, is formed of a mixture of bone and jet or Kimmeridge shale.

A necklace ornamented in this manner was found, with a female skeleton, by the late Mr. Bateman, in a barrow near Hargate Wall, Derbyshire. [2269] He describes the flat plates as being of ivory. Two other somewhat similar necklaces were found by the same explorer with a contracted female skeleton in a cist in a barrow at Cow Low, near Buxton; [2270] but the plates in this case are described as of Kimmeridge coal. A most elaborate necklace, consisting of no less than 425 pieces, was found by Mr. Bateman in a barrow near Arbor Low. [2271] They consisted of 348 thin laminæ of jet, fifty-four cylindrical beads, and eighteen conical studs and perforated plates of jet and bone, some ornamented with punctured patterns. Some flat ornamented beads of bone were found in Feltwell Fen [2272] in 1876.

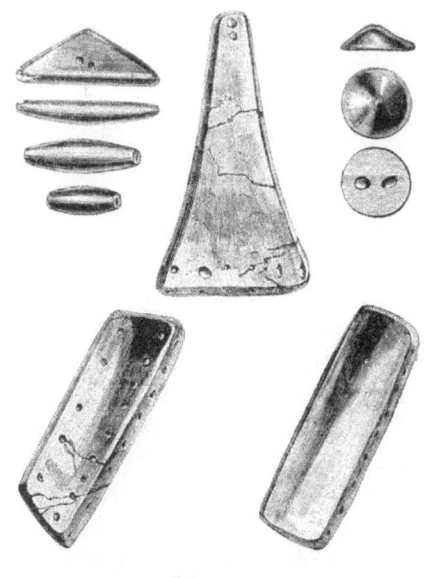

Reverse.

Fig. 376.—Pen-y-Bonc. 1/1

Obverse.

In a barrow, called Grind Low, at Over Haddon, [2273] the ornaments were seventy-three in number, of which twenty-six were cylindrical beads, thirty-nine, conical studs of jet, pierced at the back by two holes meeting at an angle in the centre, and the remaining eight, dividing plates ornamented in front with a punctured chevron pattern superficially drilled. Of these, seven are of jet, laterally perforated with three holes; and the eighth of bone, ornamented in the same style, but with nine holes on one side, diminishing to three on the other by being bored obliquely.

Fig. 377.—Probable arrangement of the jet necklace found at Pen-y-Bonc, Holyhead.

Worked flints accompanied several of these Derbyshire interments. The skeletons are all reported by Mr. Bateman to have been those of females, but possibly he may have erred in some instances. Jet ornaments of a similar character have been found in Yorkshire barrows, near Pickering [2274] and at Egton, [2275] with flint-flakes; and some from Soham Fen are in the British Museum. A very fine set of beads of jet, or possibly cannel coal, found at Pen-y-Bonc near Ty Mawr, Holyhead, [2276] is, through the kindness of the late Hon. W. O. Stanley, shown in Figs. 376 and 377. The flat beads are not engraved with any patterns. Armlets of bronze are said to have been found with them. Some jet beads of the same character have been found near Whitby. [2277] In Scotland several necklaces of this class have been discovered, as, for instance, near Aberlemno, [2278] Forfarshire; at Rothie, [2279] Aberdeenshire, with two beads of amber, fragments of bronze, and burnt bones; at Rafford, [2280] Elginshire; Houstoun, [2281] Renfrewshire; Fordoun House, [2282] Kincardineshire; and Leuchland Toll, near Brechin. Some found at Letham, [2283] Forfarshire, are described as having been strung together with the fibres of animals. A remarkably fine necklace of this kind, consisting of 147 beads in all, was found in a cist at Balcalk, [2284] Tealing, in the same county. Another of over 100 beads was found at Mountstuart, [2285] Bute.

The plates are occasionally of amber; a set of six such, together 7 inches by 2 1/8 inches in extreme length and breadth, perforated and accompanied by upwards of forty amber beads, some of jet, two of horn, and others of "the vitrified sort called pully-beads," representing seven spherical beads joined together, were found with burnt bones in a barrow at Kingston Deverill, [2286] Wilts. Another ornament of the same character, formed of eight tablets, together upwards of 10 inches by 3 inches, with numerous amber beads and some gold studs(?), was found with a skeleton in a barrow near

Lake. [2287] In what was probably another necklace, also from Lake, many of the beads were round pendants, tapering upwards, and slightly conical at the bottom. A necklace composed of small rounded beads, and somewhat similar pendants of amber, was found near the neck of a contracted skeleton at Little Cressingham, Norfolk. [2288] By the side lay a bronze dagger and javelin-head, and on the breast an ornamented oblong gold plate. Near it was part of a gold armilla, one very small gold box, and remains of two others.

In one of the Upton Lovel barrows, examined by Mr. Cunnington, a burnt body was accompanied by somewhat similar little boxes of gold, thirteen drum-like gold beads perforated at two places in the sides, a large plate of thin gold highly ornamented, the conical stud covered with gold already described (p. 456), some large plates of amber like those from Kingston Deverill, and upwards of 1,000 amber beads. A small bronze dagger seems to have belonged to the same deposit. I am inclined to think that the so-called gold boxes may have been merely the coverings of some discs of wood perforated horizontally, and thus forming large flat gold-plated beads. The gold itself is not perforated, but the edges appear in the engraving to be much broken. Possibly the supposed lids and boxes were in both cases the coverings of one face only of a wooden bead. [2289] From the occurrence of weapons in these interments, it seems probable that this class of decoration was not confined to the female sex, but that, like most savages, the men of Ancient Britain were as proud of finery as the women, even if they did not excel them in this particular. A necklace of large spheroidal beads of amber was found at Llangwyllog, [2290] Anglesea.

I am not aware of any of the jet necklaces having occurred on the Continent, but beads and flat plates of amber perforated in several places horizontally have been found in the ancient cemetery at Hallstatt, in the Salzkammergut of the Austrian Tyrol.

Fig. 378.—Fimber.

In several instances, jet necklaces do not comprise any of these flat plates, but consist merely of a number of flat discoidal beads with one larger piece for a pendant. In a barrow at Weaverthorpe Ling, Yorkshire, E.B., Canon Greenwell, F.R.S., discovered a contracted skeleton of a young person buried with a plain urn and a necklace of 122 flat beads of jet, with a flat, spherically triangular pendant, perforated at the middle of one of its sides, a short distance from the edge. The beads vary in size from a little under, to a little over a quarter of an inch in diameter, and the sides of the pendant are about three-quarters of an inch long.

In a barrow near Fimber, [2291] Yorkshire, Messrs. J. R. & R. Mortimer found, with other interments, a female skeleton in a contracted posture, with a small food-vase near the hand, a small bronze awl in a short wooden haft behind the shoulders, and on the neck, a necklace almost identical with that found at Weaverthorpe, of which, by the kindness of the late Mr. Llewellynn Jewitt, F.S.A., I am able to give a representation in Fig. 378. One of the beads, the pendant, and the bronze awl, and part of its wooden handle, are numbered 2, 3, 4, and 5.

Fig. 379.—Yorkshire. 1/1

Another form of jet bead is long, sometimes cylindrical, and sometimes swelling in the middle, and in a few instances almost square in section. Fourteen of those with a round section, and from 1 inch to 1 3/4 inches long, and one of those with the square, had been strewn among the burnt bones, after they were cold, in an interment found by Canon Greenwell, in a barrow near Egton Bridge, Whitby. Two are here reproduced (Fig. 379) from the *Archæological Journal.* [2292] In another Yorkshire barrow the same investigator found, also with burnt bones, a small flake of flint, a portion of a bronze pin, and four jet beads, two of which are barrel-shaped and one oblong, while the fourth is a small stud, like those already described. They are shown full-sized in the annexed cut (Fig. 380), also borrowed from the *Archæological Journal.* [2293]

Fig. 380.—Yorkshire. 1/1

Small barrel-shaped beads, accompanied by smaller disc-shaped beads, and two little studs of jet, were found by the late Mr. Bateman in Hay-Top Barrow, Monsal Dale, [2294] accompanying the skeleton of a woman. With them was a curious bone pendant of semicircular outline, widening out to a rectangular base somewhat like a modern seal.

A necklace of ten barrel-shaped jet beads, and about a hundred thin flat beads of shale, was found with a flint knife in a barrow at Eglingham, [2295] Northumberland, by Canon Greenwell. Some long and short barrel-shaped jet beads accompanied burnt bones in an urn at Fylingdales, [2296] Yorkshire, and a necklace of short barrel-shaped beads, principally of bone, was found in a barrow at Aldbourne, [2297] Wilts.

Jet beads, long and thin, but larger at the middle than at the extremities, and others barrel-shaped, were found with burnt bones in a barrow examined by the late Rev. Greville J. Chester, near Cromer; [2298] and a magnificent necklace of jet beads, ranging from 1 to 5 inches in length, some of them expanding very much in the middle, with a sort of rounded moulding at each end, and having a few rough beads of amber intermingled with them, was found with a polished celt of black flint at Cruden, [2299] Aberdeenshire, in 1812, and is preserved in the Arbuthnot Museum, Peterhead.

Some curious jet beads, one of them in the form of a ring perforated transversely, found with bronze buttons, rings, armlets, &c., in Anglesea, [2300] are now in the British Museum.

A flat circular bead of jet, a flint scraper, and a bronze dagger and celt, were found by the late Mr. Bateman in a barrow near Bakewell. [2301] A large pendant, apparently of jet, pear-shaped, and perforated near the smaller end, was found in a barrow on Stanton Moor, [2302] Derbyshire; and a rudely-made bead of Kimmeridge shale in the long chambered barrow at West Kennet, [2303] Wilts. Another pendant, consisting of a flat pear-shaped piece of shale 2 1/2 inches long and 2 inches broad, and perforated at the narrow end, was found along with querns, stones with concentric circles and cup-shaped indentations worked in them, stone balls, spindle-whorls, and an iron axe-head, in excavating an underground chamber at the Tappock, [2304] Torwood, Stirlingshire. One face of this pendant is covered with scratches in a vandyked pattern. Though of smaller size, this seems to bear some analogy with the flat amulets of schist, of which several have been discovered in Portugal, [2305] with one face ornamented in much the same manner. A barrel-shaped bead of cannel coal (?), 4 1/2 inches long, found near Loch Skene, and a flat eye-shaped one of shale, found near Pencaitland, East Lothian, have been figured. [2306]

Pendants of jet of other forms are also occasionally found with interments. That shown in Fig. 381 was discovered in a barrow at Hungry Bentley, Derbyshire, by the late Mr. J. F. Lucas, who kindly let me engrave it. It lay in company with a globular and a barrel-shaped bead in an urn containing burnt bones. In character this ornament recalls to mind the bronze pendants of which so many occurred in the cemetery at Halstatt, though this is of far simpler design.

Armlets manufactured from a single piece of jet are not uncommon among Roman antiquities. They seem, however, also to have been made in this country in pre-Roman times. Portions of jet or lignite armlets of almost semicircular section, and "evidently turned on the lathe," were found with numerous bronze and bone relics in the Heathery Burn Cave, [2307] Stanhope, Durham. One of these, by permission of the Society of Antiquaries, is shown as Fig. 381A. Another bracelet of jet was found at Glenluce, [2308] Wigtownshire, together with several fragments. In the cromlech of *La Roche qui sonne*, [2309] Guernsey, Mr. F. C. Lukis discovered a remarkable oval armlet of jet ornamented on its outer surface, and with countersunk perforations in several places. With it was found a bronze armlet of whitish colour. By the kindness of the Council of the British Archæological Association, figures of both, on the scale of 1/3, are here reproduced. With them were found pottery and stone instruments, mullers and mills of granite. Armlets of bone [2310] or ivory also accompany ancient burials, but hardly come within my province.

Fig. 381.—Hungry Bentley. 1/1

Fig. 381A.—Heathery Burn Cave. 1/2

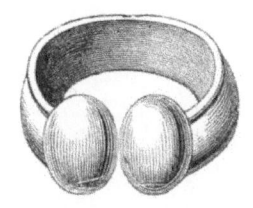

Fig. 382.—Jet.—Guernsey. 1/3

Fig. 383.—Bronze.—Guernsey. 1/3

The use of jet for personal ornaments in pre-Roman times in Britain is quite in accordance with what might be gathered from the testimony of early historians. Solinus (*circ.* A.D. 80) mentions the abundance in this country of jet, which, he relates, burns in water and is extinguished by oil, and which, if excited by friction, becomes electric like amber. His statements are repeated by other authors. The occurrence of amber on our coasts does not appear to have been observed in ancient times, unless possibly by Sotacus. [2311] As already observed, it is occasionally found at the present day on our Eastern coast.

Beads formed of selected pebbles of quartz or other material are rarely found accompanying interments of the Stone Age in Britain. In France [2312] they seem to be more common. Some neatly-pierced pebbles of rose-quartz, bored in the same manner as the perforated stone hammers, were found in the *Allée couverte* of Argenteuil; and pendants of jasper and *callais* in some of the tumuli near Carnac, Brittany.

It is rather doubtful whether the discs of Kimmeridge shale, so abundantly found in Dorsetshire, and to which the absurd name of Kimmeridge coal-money has been given, date back to pre-Roman times. Many of them were found by General Pitt Rivers, [2313] in the Romano-British village at Woodcuts. These discs, as is well known, have on the one face a centre-mark showing where they revolved on the centre of the "back-poppet" in the course of being turned; and on the other face a square recess, [2314] or occasionally two or three smaller round holes, showing the manner by which they were attached to the chuck or mandrel of the lathe. Very rarely they occur with a portion of an armlet, which has broken in the process of turning, still attached to their edges. One such has been engraved in the *Archæological Journal,* [2315] and another is in my own collection. There can, therefore, be no doubt, that instead of their having been expressly made for any purpose, such as for use as money, they are merely the refuse or waste pieces from the lathe. They all appear to me to have been worked with metal tools, and, from a mass of them having been found "conglomerated by the presence of irony matter," [2316] these would appear to have been of iron or steel; at the same time, however, numerous chippings of flint were found, which, if used at all in the turning process, may have served for roughing out the discs. I have, however, not had an opportunity of personally examining these flint chippings. An interesting article on objects made of Kimmeridge shale [2317] has been written by Mr. J. C. Mansel-Pleydell.

Rings of different sizes formed of stone are occasionally found, but their purpose is unknown. In a barrow at Heathwaite, [2318] in Furness, half a stone ring, about a couple of inches in diameter, and apparently of circular section, was found. A ring of diorite, 4 1/4 inches in diameter, with a central hole of 1 1/4 inches, sharp at the edge, but 1 3/8 inches thick at the border of the perforation, and of nearly triangular section, was found at Wolsonbury, Sussex, and was in the collection of the late Mrs. Dickinson of Hurstpierpoint. A somewhat similar ring of serpentine, 5 1/2 inches in diameter, is in the Museum at Clermont Ferrand. Another was found near Dijon. A ring of black stone, found above the stalagmite in Kent's Cavern, is shown in Fig. 384. It is slightly rounded at its edges.

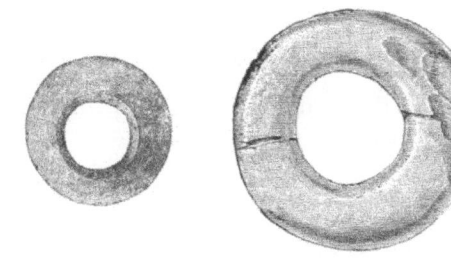

Fig. 384.—Kent's Cavern. 1/1

Fig. 385.—Ty Mawr. 1/1

Five small rings about an inch in diameter, of a brown colour and apparently made of lignite, were found in an urn with burnt bones and a bronze pin in a barrow near Winterbourn Stoke. [2319] One of them was perforated near the edge as if for suspension.

A flat ring, from one of the ancient circular habitations at Ty Mawr, [2320] in Holyhead Island, is shown, full size, in Fig. 385. It was found by the late Hon. W. O. Stanley, F.S.A., who obligingly lent me the cut. It is supposed to have been used as a brooch. There is a slight notch on each side, which might have served to catch the pin.

He subsequently found a ring of the same kind made from a piece of red "Samian" ware. The presumption, therefore, is that the other rings are also Roman or post-Roman. A ring and a pendant of lignite were found with burnt bones in a barrow at Aldbourne, [2321] Wilts. The latter resembles a mediæval finger-ring. A flat, oval, pendant, [2322] of close-grained stone, was found in another barrow at the same place.

In Scotland, a curved pendant of jet was found at Glenluce. [2323] Rings of shale, from Wigtownshire, [2324] have been figured, as also a ring of stone from a crannog at Glenluce. [2325] A peculiar ring of shale, hollowed externally, was found near West Calder. [2326] In Ireland, some rings of shale were found in a cinerary urn at Dundrum, [2327] co. Down.

Another form of personal ornament, or, more probably, amulet or charm, consisted of pebbles, usually selected for their beauty or some singularity of appearance. They are very frequently accompaniments of ancient interments, and are sometimes, though rarely, perforated. In a barrow near Winterbourn Stoke, [2328] there had been deposited near the body, "a perforated pebble-stone, about

2 inches long, and very neatly polished," which Sir R. Colt Hoare thought might have been suspended as an amulet from the neck.

In another barrow, in the same group, [2329] the interment comprised "a pair of petrified fossil cockle-shells, a piece of stalactite, and a hard flat stone of the pebble kind," besides a brass or bronze pin and other objects.

In a third, near Stonehenge, [2330] there was at the left hand of the skeleton a dagger of bronze, and close to the head, a curious pebble described as "of the sardonyx kind, striated transversely with alternate spaces that give it the appearance of belts; besides these *striæ*, it is spotted all over with very small white specks, and, after dipping it in water, it assumes a sea-green colour."

In another barrow near Everley [2331] a heap of burnt bones was surrounded by a circular wreath of horns of the red deer, within which, and amidst the ashes, were five stemmed and barbed flint arrow-heads and a small red pebble.

In a barrow at Upton Lovel, [2332] near the legs of a skeleton, there lay, with a number of other objects, "a handful of small pebbles of different colours, several not to be found in the neighbourhood," and five hollow flints broken in two and forming a rude kind of cup.

In a barrow at Rudstone, [2333] Canon Greenwell found with a skeleton a part of an ammonite which appeared to have been worn as a charm.

A beautiful pink pebble, supposed to have been placed with the body as a token of affection, was found in a sepulchral cist at Breedon, [2334] Leicestershire. Some querns and an iron knife appear to have accompanied the interment, so that it may belong to a comparatively late period. Quartz pebbles are, however, very frequently found with ancient burials, and Mr. Bateman has recorded numerous instances of their occurrence. Three such, one red, the others of a light colour, together with a ball of pyrites, a flat piece of polished iron-ore, a flint celt, and various other instruments of flint, were found with a skeleton in a barrow on Elton Moor. [2335] In opening Carder Low, [2336] near Hartington, about eighty quartz pebbles and several instruments of flint, including a barbed arrow-head, were found; and with the body, a bronze dagger and an axe-hammer of basalt. Mr. Bateman has suggested that the pebbles were possibly cast into the mound during its construction, by mourners and friends of the deceased, as tokens of respect. Numerous quartz pebbles, supposed to be sling-stones, were found in a barrow near

Middleton. [2337] In the same barrow was a porphyry-slate pebble, highly polished, "the sides triangular and tapering towards the ends, which are rubbed flat." A stone from a barrow near Ashford-in-the-Water [2338] is said to have been of the same character.

In a barrow near Avebury, [2339] already mentioned, there were in a cist with a male skeleton, three studs and a ring of jet, a flint knife, and a beautifully veined ovoid implement of serpentine, 4 inches long and 2 broad, the apex at each end ground flat. Dr. Thurnam does not attempt to assign any purpose to this implement, if such it were.

Sometimes the pebble appears to have been actually placed in the hand of the deceased, as was the case in a barrow near Alsop, [2340] where a round quartz pebble was found in the left hand of the skeleton; and in another barrow on Readon Hill, [2341] near Ramshorn, where a small pebble was found at the right hand. A quartz pebble lay among a deposit of burnt bones, accompanied by a bronze pin, in another barrow near Throwley. [2342] In another Derbyshire [2343] barrow a quartz pebble, found near an urn, was regarded as a sling-stone.

In two barrows near Castleton, [2344] opened by Mr. Rooke Pennington, a quartz pebble accompanied the remains of children or young persons.

Pebbles have been found with interments in other parts of the country, as in the long barrow at Rodmarton, [2345] Gloucestershire, where were a small round white pebble and flint arrow-head. An ovoidal stone 4 × 2 1/2 inches occurred in a grave at Athelney; [2346] and one of chert, 8 1/2 × 5 1/2 inches, in a barrow on Petersfield Heath. [2347] Canon Greenwell has also found large pebbles or boulders in some of the Yorkshire barrows. They seem to come under another category than that of the smaller ornamental pebbles.

A small piece of rock crystal, probably an amulet or charm, lay in a small cist at Orem's Fancy, Stronsay, [2348] Orkney, and fragments of quartz and selected pebbles frequently accompany early Irish interments. [2349] At Caer Leb, Anglesea, [2350] two silicious pebbles, one black and the other red, with a band of little pits round it, were found in 1865, and supposed to be amulets.

Mr. Kemble [2351] has observed that in Teutonic tombs stones occur, deposited apparently from some supposed virtue or superstition, and has instanced two egg-shaped objects, apparently of Carrara marble, from Lüneburg tumuli. It has also been stated that in Penmynydd churchyard, [2352] Anglesea, numerous skeletons were found with a white oval pebble, of the size of a hen's egg, near each. It is doubtful whether the bones were of Christians or not; but the Rev. T. J. Williams, in describing the discovery, has suggested that the stones might bear reference to the passage in Revelations (ii. 17):—"To him that overcometh will I give to eat of the hidden manna, and will give him a white stone, and in the stone a new name written, which no man knoweth saving he that receiveth it."

In interments of an earlier date, such instances seem to point to some superstitious custom, possibly like that in India, where "the mystic Salagramma pebble, held in the hand of the dying Hindoo, is a sure preservation against the pains of eternal punishment." [2353] This pebble, however, was black.

Among the Tasmanians [2354] sacred pebbles play a not unimportant part; and crystals, or sometimes white stones, are frequently worn in bags suspended from the neck, and women never allowed to see them.

The symbolism of a white pebble, as representing happiness or a happy day, was widely known. The "calculi candore laudatus dies" [2355] was not confined to the Romans, but known among the Thracians; and the "black balls" at ballots of the present day carry us back to the times when

> "Mos erat antiquus niveis atrisque lapillis
>
> His damnare reos, illis absolvere culpâ." [2356]

Occasionally, fossil *echini* in flint are found buried with bodies. Mr. Worthington Smith found more than a hundred of them in a barrow of the Stone Age on Dunstable Downs. [2357] A pebble of white quartz lay with two skeletons, which were those of a woman and child.

In a tumulus on Ashey Down, [2358] in the Isle of Wight, an "echinite" accompanied an interment of burnt bones, with which was a bronze dagger. Douglas also found one with an amber bead by the side of a Saxon skeleton near Chatham. He regarded it as an amulet, and states that in Scotland the peasants still have a belief in the virtue of these fossils. I have seen *cidares* forming part of Saxon necklaces after having been perforated; and others converted into spindle-whorls.

In fact, the use of stones as amulets still lingers on in the northern parts of this country. There is in the National Museum at Edinburgh [2359] a flat oval pebble, 2 1/2 inches long, which was worn as a charm in a small bag hung by a red string round the neck of a Forfarshire farmer, who died in 1854, æt. 84. The heart-shaped nodule of clay iron-stone in the same Museum, with a copper loop for suspension, and heart-shaped and oblong pendants of copper and silver, mentioned in my former edition, proves to be a forgery.

The custody of charms sometimes became hereditary. Martin [2360] describes a stone in Arran possessed of various miraculous virtues. "The custody of this globe is the peculiar privilege of a little family called Clan Chattons." Other charm-stones and curing-stones have been described in interesting papers by Sir J. Y. Simpson, Bart., [2361] Mr. James M. Gow, [2362] Dr. Alexander Stewart, [2363] and Mr. G. F. Black. [2364]

Among the Scandinavian nations [2365] the possession of certain stones was believed to secure victory in encounters, and the belief is constantly mentioned in ancient poetry.

A confidence in the virtues of "lucky stones," that is to say, pebbles with a hole through them, or with a band around them, is still widely spread, and I well remember the incantation—

"Lucky-stone, lucky-stone, bring me some luck,

To-day, or to-morrow by twelve o'clock."

These perforated stones were also sovereign against the nightmare. "Take a Flynt Stone that hath a hole of hys owne kynde, and hang it ouer hym and wryte in a bill—

'In nomine Patris, &c.

Saint George, our Ladye's Knight,

He walked day, so did he night,

Untill he hir found.

He hir beate and he hir bounde,

Till truely her trouth she him plyght

That she woulde not come within the night,

There as Saint George, our Ladye's Knight,

Named was three tymes Saint George.'

And hang this Scripture ouer him, and let him alone." [2366]

In Bavaria [2367] a *Druten-stein* is a natural pebble with a hole through it, and is a charm against witches.

In Scotland such a stone is often called a witch-stone, [2368] and hung up in the byres as a protection for the cattle. The same is the case in some parts of England. In the Museum at Leicester is a "witch-stone" from Wymeswold, a pebble with a natural hole towards one end, which has been preserved for many generations in one family, and has had great virtues attributed to it. It prevented the entrance of fairies into the dairy; it preserved milk from taint; it kept off diseases, and charmed off warts, and seems to have been valuable alike to man and beast. In the Western Islands [2369] ammonites are held to possess peculiar virtues as "cramp-stones" for curing cramp in cattle.

Stones remarkable either for their colour or shape appear at all times to have attracted the attention of mankind, and frequently to have served as personal ornaments or charms among those to whom the more expensive and civilized representatives of such primitive jewellery, which now rank as precious stones, were either unknown or inaccessible.

Among the cave-dwellers of a remote age, both of France and Belgium, fossil shells appear to have been much in use as ornaments, numbers having been found perforated for suspension. Pendants of stone occur in some abundance with interments in the dolmens of France; [2370] occasionally the living forms of shells also were perforated and worn as ornaments, both in the days when the reindeer formed the principal food of the cave-dwellers, and in more recent yet still remote times. A black polished oval pebble, found in the lake-dwelling of Inkwyl, [2371] has been regarded by De Bonstetten as an amulet.

In Merovingian and Teutonic interments, we find occasionally, pendants of serpentine [2372] and other materials, balls of crystal, and sometimes of iron pyrites. [2373]

A peculiar stone with a groove round it, not unlike in form to the Danish fire-producing stones of the early Iron Age, was in use for divining purposes among the Laplanders, and has been engraved and described by Scheffer. [2374]

What are regarded as ancient amulets of stone, found in Portugal, [2375] are highly decorated.

Numerous amulets, commonly formed of various kinds of stone and teeth of animals, usually perforated for suspension, were worn by the North-American Indians. [2376] Indeed, among almost all savage nations such charms and ornaments abound.

As I am not treating of the hidden virtues of stones and gems, nor of their use as amulets, it is needless to say more in illustration of the causes why selected pebbles may have been placed in ancient graves. Before proceeding, however, to the next part of my subject, which carries me back from recent times to those long anterior, not only to the use of metals, but to that of the various stone implements of which I have been treating, it will be well to say a few words as to the results of the general survey which, so far as regards the antiquities of the Neolithic, or Surface Stone Period, is now complete.

These results, I must acknowledge, are, to my mind, by no means entirely satisfactory. It is true that regarding the various forms of objects described from a technological, or even a collector's, point of view, the series of stone antiquities found in Britain does not contrast unfavourably with that from any other country. We have hatchets, adzes, chisels, borers, scrapers, and tools of various kinds, and know both how they were made and how they were used; we have battle-axes, lances, and arrows for war, or for the chase; we have various implements and utensils adapted for domestic use; we have the personal ornaments of our remote predecessors, and know something of their methods of sepulture, and of their funeral customs. Indeed, so far as external appliances are concerned, they are almost as fully represented as would be those of any existing savage nation by the researches of a most painstaking traveller. And yet when we attempt any chronological arrangement of the various forms we find ourselves almost immediately at fault. From the number of objects found, we may indeed safely infer that they represent the lapse of no inconsiderable interval of time, but how great we know not; nor, in most cases, can we say with any approach to certainty, whether a given object belongs to the commencement, middle, or close, of the Polished Stone Period of Britain.

True it is that there are some forms, which from their association together in graves, we know to have been contemporaneous; and some, which from their occasionally occurring with interments belonging to a time when bronze was beginning to come into use we must assign to the later portion of the Neolithic Period of this country; yet it is impossible to say of these latter forms that they may not have been long in use before bronze was known; nor of the former, that certain kinds were not introduced at a much earlier period than the others, which at a later date became associated with them. The utmost that can with safety be affirmed is, that some forms, such as the perforated battle-axes, the skilfully chipped lance-heads or daggers, the cups fashioned in the lathe, and the ornaments of jet, appear to have been of later introduction than most of the others. Moreover, though we may regard these particular objects as comparatively late, the bulk of the others, such, for instance, as celts, and possibly arrow-heads, were subject to so little modification during the whole of the Neolithic Period, that it is almost impossible, from form only, to assign to individual specimens any chronological position. The light reflected by foreign discoveries, such as those in the Swiss lakes, and by the habits and customs of modern savages, enables us, to some extent, to appreciate the relations and bearings of our native stone antiquities; but the greater part of them have unfortunately been discovered as isolated examples, and without attendant circumstances calculated to furnish data for determining their exact age, or the manners of those who used them.

Enough facts, however, are at our command to show that preceding the use of metal in this country, there was a time when cutting instruments and weapons were made of stone, either chipped or ground to an edge; and to encourage a hope that future discoveries may throw more light on the length of the period through which those who used them lived, and on the stage of culture that they had reached. It will, I trust, be of some service to those who are labouring, and will yet labour, in this field of research, to find in these pages a classification of the forms at present known, a summary account of the discoveries hitherto made, and references to the books from which further details may be gathered.

I now turn to the relics of a still earlier period, when the art of grinding stone to an edge appears to have been unknown, and when man was associated in this country with a group of animals which has now for the most part disappeared, either by migration to other latitudes, or by absolute extinction of the race.

IMPLEMENTS OF THE PALÆOLITHIC PERIOD.

CHAPTER XXII.
CAVE IMPLEMENTS.

In this second division of my subject, I must pass in review a class of implements of stone, which, though belonging to an earlier period than those already described, it appeared to me to be better to take second rather than first in order. My reasons for thus reversing what might seem to be the natural arrangement of my subject, and ascending instead of descending the stream of time, I have already to some extent assigned. I need only now repeat that our sole chronology for measuring the antiquity of such objects is by a retrogressive scale from the present time, and not by a progression of years from any remote given epoch; and that though we have evidence of the vast antiquity of the class of implements which I am about to describe, and may at the present moment regard them as the earliest known works of man, yet we should gravely err, were we for a moment to presume on the impossibility of still earlier relics being discovered. Had they been taken first in order, it might have been thought that some countenance was given to a belief that we had in these implements the first efforts of human skill, and were able to trace the progressive development of the industrial arts from the very cradle of our race. Such is by no means the case. The investigators into the early history of mankind are like explorers in search of the source of one of those mighty rivers which traverse whole continents: we have departed from the homes of modern civilization in ascending the stream, and arrived at a spot where traces of human existence are but few, and animal life has assumed strange and unknown forms; but further progress is for the moment denied, and though we may plainly perceive that we are nearer the source of which we are in search, yet we know not at what distance it may still be from us; nor, indeed, can we be certain in what direction it lies, nor even whether it will ultimately be discovered. Whether or no, traces of human existence will eventually be found in deposits belonging to Miocene, or even earlier, times, I may take this occasion of remarking that the evidence hitherto adduced on this point by continental geologists is, to my mind, after full and careful examination still very far from satisfactory. At the same time, judging from all analogy, there can be but little doubt that the human race will eventually be proved to date back to an earlier period than the Pleistocene or Quaternary, though it will probably not be in Europe that the evidence on this point will be forthcoming.

The instruments of stone, found in ossiferous caves and in ancient alluvial deposits, associated with remains of a fauna now in great part extinct, belong to a period which has been termed by Sir John Lubbock, the Palæolithic, in contradistinction to the Neolithic Period, the relics of which are usually found upon, or near, the surface of the soil. By others, the more familiar, even if less accurately discriminative, terms of Cave Period and River-drift, or even Drift Period, have been adopted.

Though I propose in these pages to treat of the implements from the caves and from the river-gravels separately, it must not be supposed that there exists of necessity any demonstrable difference in the age of the two classes of relics. On the contrary, though there can be but little doubt that the deposition of the implement-bearing beds, both in the one case and the other, extended over a very considerable space of time, and that therefore neither all of the cave-deposits nor all of the river-drifts can be regarded as absolutely contemporaneous; yet there appears every probability that some, at least, of the deposits in each of the two classes synchronize; and that some caves were being partially filled with earth containing relics of human workmanship and animal remains, at the same time that, in certain ancient river-valleys, alluvial drifts were being formed with similar works of man and bones of animals belonging to the same fauna, incorporated in them.

And yet, as a rule, the character of a group of implements collected from the cave-deposits differs in its general *facies* from one obtained from the old River-drifts. This is no doubt mainly due to the different conditions under which the two deposits were formed; for, especially when they were undoubtedly human habitations, the caves seem to have been under more favourable conditions both for the reception and the preservation of a greater proportion of the smaller forms of instruments than the River-drifts; but their comparative scarcity in the collections formed from the latter is also no doubt partly due to the difficulty in finding such minute objects when imbedded in a mass of gravel, even had they remained uninjured in the course of its deposition. On the other hand, the rarity of the larger forms of implements in the cave deposits, appears to be due to these instruments having been mainly used for what may be termed "out of doors" purposes.

Again, though in some instances the River-drift and Cave-deposits belong apparently to the same period, yet in others it seems possible that we have, in the caves, relics derived from a period alike unrepresented in the old alluvia and in the superficial soil; and which may belong to an intermediate age, and thus possibly assist, especially in the case of some caves in the neighbourhood of Mentone, to bridge over the gap that would otherwise intervene between the River-drift and the Surface Period. It is not, indeed, in our English caves, that such good evidence of a sequence in the order of the deposition of their contents can be observed, as in those of the south of France, and of Belgium, in which a sort of chronological succession has been pointed out by M. Gabriel de Mortillet and others, as will subsequently be seen. It will of course be understood that this sequence in no way refers to the occupation of caverns by man in modern, or even Neolithic times. Many caves in this, as in other countries, have been the retreats or dwelling-places of man at various, and often very remote, periods: though subsequent to the time when their earlier contents had been sealed up beneath a layer of stalagmite, itself a work of centuries of slow deposition of carbonate of lime held in solution by water infiltrating from above. It is owing to the occasional admixture of the more recent remains with those of older date, either in the progress of the excavation of the caverns, or by the burrowing of animals, or in some cases possibly by pits having been sunk in the floor of the cave by some of its successive human occupants, that doubt has been thrown in former times on the value of the evidence afforded by cavern-deposits, as to the co-existence of man with animals now extinct, such as the Siberian mammoth and its common associate, the woolly-haired rhinoceros. The more careful researches of modern times have, however, in most cases, removed all sources of error under this head; and the fact of this co-existence being now established, we are to a great extent able to eliminate the doubtful portions of the older-recorded observations, and to give to the residue a value which it did not formerly possess.

Before proceeding, however, to discuss any of the evidence afforded by cavern-deposits on the existence of man and the nature of his tools and implements in those early days, it will be well to say a few words both as to the nature of ossiferous caves in general, and as to the probable manner in which their contents were deposited in the positions in which we now find them. In doing this, I shall be as brief as possible, and will content myself with referring the reader, who is desirous of further details, to works more strictly geological. [2377]

What must strike all observers at the outset is, that caverns vary greatly both in their character and in their dimensions; some being long and sinuous, in places contracting into narrow passages, and then again expanding into halls more or less vast; while others are merely vaulted recesses in the face of a rock, or even long grooves running along the face of some almost perpendicular though inland cliff. Most of the English ossiferous caverns belong to the former class, while the majority of those of the Dordogne and some other parts of the south of France belong to the latter. These recesses and rock-shelters apparently owe their existence to a somewhat different cause from that which produced the long sinuous cavities. They usually occur in cliffs of which the stratification is approximately horizontal, but where the different beds vary much in their degree of hardness and permeability to water. The softer strata, underlying the harder masses, are in consequence more liable to be acted upon by rain, wind, and frost, so that they weather away faster, and leave deep recesses in the face of the cliffs, admirably adapted for conversion, with but little trouble, into dry and commodious shelters from the weather, which have in consequence been seized on for habitation by man from the earliest times to the present day. Caves of this character may possibly in some rare instances have been due to the eroding action of the sea, before the land was elevated to its present level; but in most cases they have originated from the atmospheric agencies that I have mentioned, attacking most destructively the softer portions of the rocks, which are usually of a calcareous nature.

The caverns of the other class also generally occur in limestone districts, and seem in like manner to be mainly due to atmospheric causes, though operating in a different manner. They usually appear to have originated with some small crack or fissure in the rock, along which, water falling on the surface was able to find its way to some vent at a lower level; and this, by its continual passage, was able to enlarge the channel along which it flowed. The mechanically erosive force of pure water in passing over or even falling upon a rock of moderate hardness is indeed but small, though its powers of friction were long since recognized by that most enlightened of ancient geologists, the poet Ovid, [2378] who classes its effects with the wearing away of a ring upon the finger. Nor was Solomon's likening of the contentions of a wife to a continual dropping, without its geological significance. But in the case of water derived from rain falling on the surface, and passing through a fissure in a limestone rock, its first effects are chemical rather than mechanical. [2379]

By contact with decaying vegetable matter the water becomes charged with a certain amount of carbonic acid, and is rendered capable of dissolving a portion of the calcareous rock through which it passes, and thus carries it off in solution, while in so doing it acquires the character known as "hard." Taking the case of water delivered by springs in the chalk, which has but a moderate degree of hardness, it is proved by analysis to contain about seventeen grains of carbonate of lime to the gallon. Now, out of a rainfall of say twenty-six inches annually, it has been found by experiment, that in a chalk district about nine inches would, in average seasons, make their way down to the springs; and it may be readily calculated that at the rate of seventeen grains to the gallon, the amount of dry chalk or carbonate of lime dissolved by this quantity of water, and delivered by the springs, and thus carried away, is, in each square mile of such a district, upwards of one hundred and forty tons in each year, or about a ton to every four and a half acres. This serves to show how great are the solvent powers of water charged with carbonic acid, and the extent to which, in the course of centuries, it might remove the calcareous rocks with which it came in contact. But when once by this action a channel had been excavated sufficiently large to admit of the rapid passage of a stream of water through it, and the circumstances of the case allowed of such a stream, its enlargement would probably become more rapid, as the water would be liable to be charged with sand and small pebbles, the friction of which would materially conduce to the removal of the rock, the varying hardness of which, combined with the intersection of other channels and fissures, would probably lead to the formation of chambers of various sizes along the course of the channel. In some caverns, we find the streams of water, to which probably they owe their existence, still flowing through them; but in others, the external features of the surrounding country have so much changed since their formation, that the gathering grounds for such streams have been removed by denudation, and water now only finds its way into them by slow percolation through the rock which forms their roof and walls.

It is this same process of denudation which, by removing some portion of the rock in which the caverns were originally formed, has brought them in communication with the outer world, and has thus rendered them accessible to man.

Leaving out of the question the blocks and fragments of stone falling in from the ceiling of the caverns, the methods by which the ossiferous deposits in them may have been formed, are various. The bones may be those of animals which have died in the caverns, or they may have been brought there by beasts of prey, or by man, or by running water, or possibly by several of these agencies combined.

In the case of the caves and rock-shelters of the Dordogne, and many of those in Belgium, the deposits are almost exclusively neither more nor less than refuse heaps, containing the bones, fractured and unfractured, of animals which have served for human food, mixed with which are the lost and waste tools, utensils, and weapons, and even the cooking-hearths of the early cave-dwellers; so that in character they closely resemble the kjökken-möddings of the Danish coasts; though, from their position being usually inland, the marine shells in which these latter abound are, for the most part, absent. The object in resorting to the caves was, no doubt, shelter; while the reason for the Danish kjökken-möddings occurring along the coasts is to be found in the fact, that the principal food of those who left these heaps of refuse, was derived from the sea.

In other instances, the tenancy of a cave by man seems to have alternated with that by bears, hyænas, or other predaceous animals; so that the relics left by the two classes of occupants have become more or less mixed, sometimes without the intervention of water, and sometimes by its aid. In such caves, it is commonly the case that the bones are imbedded in a red loamy matrix, to which the name of "cave-earth" has been given, and which appears to consist, in a great measure, of those portions of the limestone-rock that are insoluble in water charged with carbonic acid. [2380] Such red loams are common not only in caves, but on the surface of many calcareous rocks, and would be liable to be brought into any place of resort of man or beast, adhering to the feet and skin, especially in wet weather; though some portion of what is found in the caves may be a kind of *caput mortuum* left in position after dissolution and removal of the calcareous rock; or it may be sediment deposited from turbid water.

Another important feature in caverns is the stalagmitic covering with which the bone deposit is so frequently sealed up or converted into a breccia. Like the stalactites on the ceiling, the stalagmite on the floor is a gradually-formed laminated deposit, composed of thin films of crystalline carbonate of lime, deposited from the water in which it was held in solution as a bicarbonate, by the escape of the excess of carbonic acid which rendered it soluble. I have already cited the action of rain-water falling on a surface of limestone covered with decaying vegetable matter as an agent in forming subterranean channels; but we have here, curiously enough, the reverse action produced of filling them up. For this to take place, contact with the air appears to be necessary; so that at the time when a cavern was completely filled with water, no calcareous spar would be deposited. If partially filled, though stalactites might be formed, stalagmite would not; and it is probably to some alternation of wet and dry conditions that several beds of alluvium [2381] occasionally occur interstratified between successive layers of stalagmite. When, as occasionally happens, the water percolating through the rock finds its way into the cave by the walls rather than the roof, we find stalagmite only, exhibiting its greatest thickness round the edges of the cave and cementing its contents into a breccia. This is the case with some of the caves of the Dordogne and the South of France, and does not seem of necessity to imply any great alteration in the physical conditions of the surrounding country since the caves were formed. It is also possible that the floors of the caves have, by being trodden, become more impervious to water than they originally were, and that a loose mass of porous bones upon them may, by conducing to evaporation, have caused a deposit of carbonate of lime from water which, had the caves remained unoccupied, might have run through or over the floors without forming such a deposit.

With the other class of long and tortuous caves we must, in nearly all cases, recognize, with Sir Charles Lyell, [2382] three successive phases:—1st, the period of the dissolution of the rock to form the channel; 2nd, the time when the channel was traversed and enlarged by subterranean currents of water; and, 3rd, the period when these currents were diverted, and the cave became filled with air instead of water.

The rate of deposit of stalagmitic matter varies so much with different conditions, that its thickness affords no true criterion of the length of time during which it has accumulated. Under ordinary circumstances, however, a thickness of even a few inches requires a long period of years for its formation.

Having made these few preliminary remarks as to the formation of caverns and the deposits occurring in them, I proceed to notice some of their characteristics in connection with the relics of human workmanship found in the deposits, and in doing so cannot restrict myself to British caves, but must refer also to some of those on the Continent, which are more numerous, and have likewise furnished a more extensive and varied series of remains.

It had not escaped the attention of early authors, that in remote times *specus erant pro domibus;* [2383] and, to use the words of Prometheus, [2384] "men lived like little ants beneath the ground in the gloomy recesses of caves." It is, however, strange to find a Roman author recording the occurrence of worked flints in the caves of the Pyrenees; for if we accept the description of the *ceraunia* given by Sotacus, and preserved by Pliny, of which mention has already been made, there can be but little doubt of the term referring either to stone hatchets, worked flints, or arrow-heads, of some such kind as those still known as thunderbolts; and therefore that when Claudian, [2385] early in the fifth century, wrote

"Pyrenæisque sub antris

Ignea flumineæ legere ceraunia nymphæ,"

he must have had in his mind some account of the occurrence of such objects in that district, where so many discoveries of this character have since been made.

The researches of MM. Tournal, de Christol, and Marcel de Serres, now some sixty or seventy years ago, by which the co-existence of man with many of the extinct mammals was rendered probable, if, indeed, not actually proved, were directed to caverns which, though not in the immediate neighbourhood of the Pyrenees, were still in the South of France. These researches are well known to geologists, but the most important discoveries are those made in more modern times, in caverns principally in the Dordogne and other departments of the ancient Province of Aquitaine, by the late Prof. E. Lartet [2386] and Mr. Henry Christy, as well as by M. Alphonse Milne-Edwards, the Marquis de Vibraye, MM. Garrigou, Rames, Brun, Cazalis de Fondouce, Ferry, Gervais, Cartailhac, Piette, Boule, Massénat, Chantre, and numerous other active investigators.

The discoveries made by Dr. Schmerling [2387] in the caves of Belgium, an account of which he published in 1833, showed that human bones, as well as worked flints, and bone instruments were associated with the remains of extinct animals in several instances; and, though not gaining general acceptance at the time, have since been fully borne out by the investigations so ably conducted by Dr. E. Dupont.

The late Prof. E. Lartet [2388] some years ago suggested a classification of the different divisions of Time represented in the French caves containing traces of man associated with various animal bones, under successive heads, as the Ages of the Cave-bear, the Mammoth, the Reindeer, and the Bison, in accordance with the comparative abundance of the remains of each of these animals in the different caves. Had the conditions in all cases been the same, there can be no doubt that any marked variations in the fauna of the same region would afford valuable criteria for determining such a chronological sequence. But such decided differences cannot at present be traced; and inasmuch as the animal remains in the caverns under consideration have, almost without exception, been introduced into the caves by human agency, and been merely the refuse of the spoils of the chase consumed by the old cave-dwellers, we may readily conceive reasons why, without any great natural change in the fauna, the proportionate numbers of the different animals eaten during a certain number of years might vary in different caves. Still the effect of human agency in causing an alteration in the larger mammalian fauna of a district is great, and of this, researches in caverns may probably afford evidence.

Dr. E. Dupont [2389] has adopted a somewhat similar, but more limited, and therefore safer view with regard to the caverns of Belgium, and has moreover correlated the cave-deposits with those of wider range. The rolled pebbles and stratified clay of the river-valleys he regards as synchronous with the deposits in certain caves belonging to what he terms the Mammoth Period; and the angular gravels and brick-earth, of somewhat later date, he connects with the caves of the Reindeer Period.

As will shortly be seen, there appears good reason for regarding the two sets of caverns thus characterized, as belonging to different ages; and if the use of the terms Mammoth and Reindeer Periods be not supposed to limit the duration of the existence of those animals in France and Belgium to so short a space of time, geologically speaking, as that represented by the infilling of each set of caves, no harm can arise from the adoption of the terms.

Under any circumstances, with our present knowledge, there seems a sufficient variation in the proportion of the different animals one to the other, and also in the character of the implements in different caves, to justify the conclusion that the cave-remains of Western Europe are memorials, not of some comparatively short Troglodyte phase of the human race, but of a lengthened chapter in its history. And yet this chapter seems to have been completely closed before the implements belonging to the Neolithic or Surface Stone Period had come into use; for though these also occur in the more superficial cavern-deposits, they are not only stratigraphically more recent than the instruments often found imbedded deep below them, but are also associated with a different and more modern fauna, and even with domesticated animals, of which none are as yet known to have belonged to the Palæolithic Period.

M. Gabriel de Mortillet, [2390] judging rather from the character of the works of man found in the caves, and from what appears to be the order of superposition in certain cases, than from the mammalian fauna, has arranged them in a manner which to some extent coincides with the views of M. Lartet and Dr. Dupont. To each division he has assigned the name of some well-known deposit, such as he regards as being the most characteristic in its contents.

As M. de Mortillet's classification has now been almost universally accepted, it will be well here to adopt it, though in some respects it differs from the arrangement proposed in my first edition. I there attempted to give references to the works in which the different caves in France and other continental countries have been described, but, at the present day, the number of caves explored is so great, and the literature relating to them so extensive, that I must confine myself to British caves, and make but passing reference to some of those in other countries.

I take M. de Mortillet's arrangement in ascending, and not in descending geological order; that is to say, I here describe the older deposits first. Leaving the Age of Chelles, or, as I prefer to call it, of St. Acheul (ACHEULÉEN), which is characterized by the high-level River-gravels, subsequently described, we come to:—

1. AGE OF LE MOUSTIER, [2391] DORDOGNE (MOUSTÉRIEN).—Characteristics—Ovate-lanceolate implements much resembling some of those from the River-gravels; large broad implements and flakes worked on one face only into "choppers" or "side-scrapers," like those from High Lodge, Mildenhall; large subtriangular flakes wrought at the edge into spear-head-like and round-ended forms; rough "sling-stones" and flakes; scrapers not abundant.

An almost entire absence of instruments of bone; and a large proportion of those of flint, of considerable size.

Remains of mammoth and hyæna apparently more abundant than in the following ages. Reindeer less dominant numerically than at Solutré or la Madelaine. Bones comparatively scarce. No remains of birds or fish.

2. AGE OF SOLUTRÉ [2392] (SAÔNE ET LOIRE) (SOLUTRÉEN).—Characteristics—Lance-heads or daggers delicately chipped on both faces; lozenge and leaf-shaped arrow-heads (?) closely resembling some of those of the Neolithic Period. They are all scarce. Sharp knife-like flakes trimmed to a narrow point at one end from a shoulder about midway of the blade; scrapers; borers.

Pointed lance-heads of bone or reindeer horn. Engraved bones, extremely scarce, but a small figure of a reindeer carved in calcareous stone found at Solutré. Some carvings in bone towards the end of the Period. A few marine or fossil shells.

Fauna much as at la Madelaine. Several teeth of mammoth, *felis spelæa* and *cervus megaceros*, found at Laugerie. Horse common; but at Solutré, reindeer the principal food.

3. AGE OF LA MADELAINE, DORDOGNE (MAGDALÉNIEN).—Characteristics—Long and well-shaped flint flakes and neatly-formed cores abundant, as are also scrapers; but side-scrapers extremely rare, and the leaf-shaped lance- and arrow-heads unknown. Pebbles with mortar-like depressions, rounded hammer-stones, grooved sharpening-stones. Scraped hæmatite. Saws of flint in some caves.

Pointed dart-heads, both plain and ornamented on the faces, arrow-heads, of bone split at the base, as well as harpoon-heads formed of reindeer horn or bone, barbed on one or both sides, and adapted to fit in a socket at the end of the shaft. Perforated bone needles, often of minute size.

Works of art, such as engravings on stone, bone, reindeer horn, and ivory; carvings in most of these materials, perforated and carved "bâtons de commandement" of reindeer horn. Ornaments formed of pierced bones and teeth, and of fossil shells.

Fauna much as in other caves, but a larger proportion of reindeer than horse. Mammoth remains scarce. Bones of birds and fish abundant.

In the cave of the Mas d'Azil [2393] was a layer of pebbles with various patterns painted upon them in red. Such pebbles have not as yet been found in any British cave deposits. Some of the designs curiously resemble early alphabetic characters. There is some doubt as to the exact age of the contents of this cave, which not improbably may be Neolithic.

Such is a general summary of what appear to be the characteristics of these three divisions. It must, however, be remembered that, in some caves at all events, there is a probability of the contents belonging to more than one of these periods, where the occupation by man has been of sufficiently extended duration.

M. Philippe Salmon [2394] has united the Palæolithic and Neolithic Ages into one which he regards as continuous, and sub-divides into six stages with transitions between them.

With regard to the fauna of the caves of Britain, I cannot do better than refer to the comprehensive list published by Professor Boyd Dawkins, F.R.S.; [2395] and will merely cite some of the principal animals now either extinct or no longer found living in this country, the remains of which have occurred in association with objects of human manufacture in caverns:—*Spermophilus citillus*, pouched marmot; *Mus lemmus*, lemming; *Lepus diluvianus*, extinct hare; *Lagomys pusillus*, tail-less hare; *Ursus arctos*, brown bear; *Ursus spelæus*, cave-bear; *Ursus ferox*, grizzly bear; *Hyæna crocuta*, var. *spelæa*, cave-hyæna; *Felis leo*, var. *spelæa*, cave-lion; *Felis pardus*, leopard; *Machairodus latidens*, sabre-toothed tiger; *Cervus megaceros*, Irish elk; *Cervus tarandus*, reindeer; *Bos primigenius*, urus; *Bison priscus*, bison or aurochs; *Rhinoceros tichorhinus*, woolly-haired rhinoceros; *Elephas primigenius*, mammoth; *Hippopotamus amphibius*, var. *major*, Hippopotamus. Further details as to the fauna of Kent's Cavern will be found on a subsequent page.

The fauna of the caves is in fact practically identical with that of the River Gravels.

The same author [2396] has pointed out how vast is the difference between the mammalian fauna of the Pleistocene, Quaternary, or Palæolithic Period, and that of the Pre-historic or Neolithic Period. "Out of forty-eight well-ascertained species living in the former, only thirty-one were able to live on into the latter; and out of those thirty-one, all, with the exception of six, are still living in our island. The cave-bear, cave-lion, and cave-hyæna had vanished away, along with a whole group of pachyderms, and of all the extinct animals, but one, the Irish elk, still survived. The reindeer, so enormously abundant during the post-glacial epoch, lived on, greatly reduced in numbers; while the red deer, which was rare, became very numerous, and usurped those feeding grounds which formerly supported vast herds of the reindeer. With this exception, all the Arctic group of mammalia, such as the musk-sheep and the marmots, had retreated northwards; a fact which shows that the climate of Britain during prehistoric times was warmer, or rather less severe than during the former epoch." Only in the Neolithic Period do the goat, sheep, long-faced ox (*Bos longifrons*), and dog, make their appearance in Britain.

This difference in the fauna is of great importance, as affording some guide in judging of the antiquity of human remains when found in caverns without any characteristic weapons or implements; such, for instance, as the human skull cited by Prof. Boyd Dawkins [2397] as having been found in a cave at the head of Cheddar Pass, in Somersetshire. For it must never be forgotten that the occupation of caves by man is not confined to any definite period; and that even in the case of the discovery of objects of human workmanship in direct association with the remains of the Pleistocene extinct mammals, their contemporaneity cannot be proved without careful observation of the circumstances under which they occur, even if then. Another point may also be here mentioned, namely, that where there is evidence of the occupation of a cavern by man, and also by large carnivores, they can hardly have been tenants in common, but the one must have preceded the other, or possibly the occupation by each may have alternated more than once. Bones [2398] that have been gnawed by animals have sometimes the appearance of having been shaped by man. This is especially the case when beavers or porcupines have gnawed the bones. In determining the age of a cave-deposit the greatest circumspection is required, and special evidence is necessary in each individual case. Without, therefore, at present entering on any such questions, I proceed to notice the principal explorations of British caves, which have as yet been made, and the narratives of those who conducted them. In doing this I shall, of course, confine myself to those caverns in which some traces of man or his works have been discovered in connection with the earlier fauna, of which mention has already been made.

First on the list of systematic explorers stands the name of the late Dr. Buckland, subsequently Dean of Westminster, who, upwards of seventy years ago, conducted excavations in most of the ossiferous caves of Britain at that time known; and also made more than one expedition into Germany, with a view of studying analogous caverns in that country. His "Reliquiæ Diluvianæ," published in 1823, and containing, in part, matter already printed in the *Philosophical Transactions* of the previous year, presents an interesting account of his researches. Unfortunately, however, he sought in the phenomena of the caves and the old alluvia evidence of a universal deluge, and not any record of an extended chapter in the world's history; and, though at a later period of his life he renounced these views, yet the effect of his regarding all human relics as post-diluvial, was to give a bias to geological opinion so strongly against the belief in their true association with the remains of the extinct mammals, as to cause some careful inquirers almost to doubt the correctness of their own observations.

Still, so far as the instances cited in the "Reliquiæ Diluvianæ" go, his judgment appears to have been in the main correct. The only case in which there can be much doubt is that of the so-called "red woman of Paviland;" for, as Prof. Boyd Dawkins [2399] has pointed out, there appears to have been in this, as in some other caves, a mixture of remains belonging to two distinct periods. This is proved by the presence of remains of sheep, underneath the bones of elephants and other Pleistocene mammals, as well as by the disturbed state of the cave-earth, so that the skeleton, though of very early date, may not impossibly belong to the Neolithic Period. The discoveries in the caves near Mentone may, however, eventually throw more light upon the question.

In size the skeleton equalled that of the largest male in the Oxford Museum, [2400] so that the name of "red woman" appears misplaced. The most remarkable feature in the case is that with the skeleton were found a number of nearly cylindrical rods and fragments of rings of ivory, which appear to have been made from some of the elephant tusks in the cave. If this were so, the state of preservation of the tusks at the time of their being manufactured must have been better than is usual in caverns, though fossil ivory from Siberia is still employed for making knife-handles and for other purposes; and an elephant's tusk, found in a clay deposit in the Carse of Falkirk, [2401] was sold to an ivory-turner and cut up into pieces for the lathe before it could be rescued. The late Dr. Falconer, [2402] suggested that the ivory articles may have been imported, and have had no connection with the older tusks. Be this as it may, the case is not one on which to insist; and I therefore pass on at once to a consideration of those caves in Britain in which the occurrence of stone instruments of human manufacture, in close association with the relics of extinct animals, and under such circumstances as prove a vast antiquity, are thoroughly well authenticated.

KENT'S CAVERN, TORQUAY.

The notices of this well-known cave by various authors, prior to 1859, have been carefully collected and published by the late Mr. Pengelly, F.R.S., [2403] but of these, it is needless to cite here more than the accounts given by the Rev. J. MacEnery, F.G.S., Mr. R. A. C. Godwin-Austen, F.R.S., and Mr. E. Vivian.

MacEnery, who for many years was chaplain at Tor Abbey, having had his attention first directed to the cave by the discovery in it of fossil bones, during the year 1824–5, by Mr. Northmore and the late Sir W. C. Trevelyan, devoted himself in the most enthusiastic manner to an examination of the contents of the cavern, and with the most successful results. He prepared for the press an account of his "Cavern Researches," for which numerous plates were engraved, apparently by the aid of Dr. Buckland, but he did not live to publish it, and it was first printed in a somewhat abridged form by Mr. Vivian in the year 1859. The whole of what remained of his MS. has, however, since been published *verbatim*, by Mr. Pengelly. [2404] He relates the discovery in the upper deposits of numerous relics, such as flakes and nuclei of flint, polished celts of syenite and greenstone, bone pins, and long comb-like instruments, all belonging to the Neolithic or Surface Stone Period, and in some cases to a later date. But he also describes three [2405] special kinds of flint or chert instruments, to which he calls particular attention. 1st. Flakes pointed at one end. 2nd. Oblong double-edged splinters truncated at each end, which he thinks may "have been employed as knives or chisels for dividing and shaping wood, and which exhibit the marks of wear on their edges;" and 3rd. "Oval-shaped discs chipped round to an edge, from 2 to 3 1/2 inches across, and some of them diminished to a point, like wedges. This part in these specimens was observed to be blunted, apparently from knocking like a hammer against hard bodies, while the sides, which in such an operation would not be used, still remained sharp." The modification in the substance of the flint of which these instruments are composed is noticed, and it is stated that at their transverse fracture many are porous and absorbent, adhering to the tongue, like fossil bones, and so closely that they support their weight.

Though evidently in dread of recording facts not quite in accordance with Dr. Buckland's views, he states distinctly that the true position [2406] of these implements was below the bottom of the stalagmite; and it is not a little remarkable that among the nine specimens selected for engraving by Mr. MacEnery, and given in his Plate T, as knives, arrow-heads, and hatchets of flint and chert found in Kent's Hole, Torquay, three are of a distinctly palæolithic type, and two presumably so, the others being mere flakes, but of a character quite in accordance with their belonging to the same period as the better-defined types.

He further observes that "none of the cavern blades appeared to have been rubbed or polished, but exhibit the rough serrated edge of the original fracture. This difference alone may not be sufficient to authorize us in assigning to the cavern reliques a higher antiquity, but the absence of other Druidical remains at the depth where the flints abound, is a negative confirmation." That one who observed so well should, out of deference to the prejudices of others, have sometimes been doubtful of the evidence of his own eyes, and have been driven to postpone until too late the publication of the records of his observations, must ever be a cause of regret to all lovers of science and of truth.

The next explorer of the cavern was Mr. R. A. C. Godwin-Austen, F.R.S., who in 1840 communicated a paper on the "Bone Caves of Devonshire" [2407] to the Geological Society, and subsequently another memoir on the "Geology of the South-east of Devonshire," in which the former was incorporated. He stated that "works of art, such as arrow-heads and knives of flint, occur in all parts of the cave, and throughout the entire thickness of the clay; and no distinction founded on condition, distribution, or relative position can be observed whereby the human can be separated from the other reliquiæ," among which he mentions teeth and bones of elephant, rhinoceros, ox, deer, horse, bear, hyæna, and of a feline animal of large size.

In 1846 a committee was appointed by the Torquay Natural History Society, to explore a small portion of the cavern, and a paper detailing the results of the investigation was communicated by Mr. E. Vivian to the British Association and to the Geological Society, in which he stated that the important point established was that relics of human art are found beneath the floor of stalagmite, even where its thickness is about three feet. The abstract of this paper, as published in the *Quarterly Journal of the Geological Society*, [2408] seems to show how little such a statement was in accordance with the geological opinion of the day. It runs as follows:—"*On* KENT'S CAVERN, *near* TORQUAY, *by* EDWARD VIVIAN, ESQ. In this paper an account was given of some recent researches in that cavern by a committee of the Torquay Natural History Society, during which the bones of various extinct species of animals were found in several situations."

In 1856, Mr. Vivian again called the attention of the British Association to this cavern, and, in 1859, he published the greater part of Mr. MacEnery's MS., of which mention has already been made. The ossiferous cave at Brixham had been discovered in the previous year, in which also the collection of implements discovered in the river-drift of the Valley of the Somme, formed by M. Boucher de Perthes, had been visited by the late Dr. Falconer—a visit which resulted in that of the late Sir Joseph Prestwich and myself in 1859, and in public interest being excited in these remarkable discoveries, the area of which was soon extended to numerous other valleys, both in France and Britain. Encouraged by the success which had attended the exploration of the old alluvia, the British Association, in 1864, appointed a committee consisting of Sir Charles Lyell, Sir John Lubbock, Professor Phillips, Mr. Vivian, Mr. Pengelly, and myself, to make a systematic exploration of Kent's Cavern, which was placed at our disposal by Sir Lawrence Palk, the proprietor. From that time, until 1880, the exploration was steadily carried on under the immediate and constant superintendence of Mr. Pengelly and Mr. Vivian; and the names of Professor Busk, Professor Boyd Dawkins, and Mr. W. A. Sanford, F.G.S., were added to the list of the committee. Mr. Pengelly, who acted as reporter to the committee, has in successive years rendered sixteen accounts to the Association [2409] of the progress of the researches, which have been printed in their yearly Reports from 1865 to 1880. Mr. Pengelly has also communicated a long series of papers upon the exploration of the Cave [2410] to the Devonshire Association. I have been allowed, for the purposes of this volume, to figure a certain number of the instruments discovered in Kent's Cavern, and for the details I give concerning them, I am indebted partly to the annual reports already mentioned, and partly to the kindness of the late Mr. Pengelly.

The cave is about a mile east of Torquay harbour, and is of a sinuous character, running deeply into a hill of Devonian Limestone, about half a mile distant from the sea. In places, it expands into large chambers, to which various distinctive names have been given.

It is needless for me to enter into any particulars as to the method employed in conducting the explorations, by which the position of each object discovered was accurately determined. I may, however, shortly describe the series of deposits met with in the spacious chamber near the entrance to the cave, which has been the principal scene of the discoveries, and which corresponds in its main features with the other parts of the cave. The deposits are as follows, in descending order:—

- 1. Large blocks of limestone which have fallen from the roof, sometimes cemented together by stalagmite.

- 2. A layer of black, muddy mould, 3 inches to 12 inches in thickness.

- 3. Stalagmite 1 foot to 3 feet thick, almost continuous, and in places containing large fragments of limestone.

- 4. Red cave-earth, varying in thickness, and containing about 50 per cent. of angular fragments of limestone, with numerous bones of extinct animals, and implements fashioned by the hand of man. Above this and below the stalagmite, in one part of the cave there is a black band from 2 inches to 6 inches thick, formed of soil like No. 2, containing charcoal, numerous flint instruments, and bones and teeth of animals.

- 5. At the base of the cave-earth is another floor of stalagmite in places 10 or 12 feet in thickness.

- 6. Below this again a breccia of sub-angular and rounded pieces of dark-red grit, a few quartz pebbles, and angular fragments of limestone, embedded in a sandy paste. This also contained implements, and in places had been broken up and become lodged in the cave-earth.

Above the upper stalagmite, principally in the black mould, have been found a number of relics belonging to different periods, such as socketed celts, and a socketed knife of bronze, some small fragments of roughly-smelted copper, about four hundred flint flakes, cores, and chips, a polishing stone, a ring of stone already described, numerous spindle-whorls, bone instruments terminating in comb-like ends, probably used for weaving, pottery, marine shells, numerous mammalian bones of existing species, and some human bones, on which it has been thought there are traces indicative of cannibalism. Some of the pottery is distinctly Roman in character, but many of the objects belong, no doubt, to pre-Roman times.

It is, however, with the implements found in the beds below, which had already, at least two thousand years ago, been sealed up beneath the thick coating of stalagmite, formed by a deposition of film upon film of calcareous matter once held in solution, that I have here to do.

In some places, it is true that owing to previous excavations, and to the presence of burrowing animals, the remains from above and below the stalagmite have become intermingled; but I shall not cite any objects, about the original position of which there is any doubt.

The principal forms are these: flat ovoid implements with an edge all round; pointed kite-shaped or triangular implements; flakes of flint of various sizes and wrought into different shapes, including the so-called scrapers; the cores from which flakes have been struck, and stones which have been used as hammers or pounders. Besides these, a few pins, harpoons, and needles of bone have been discovered.

Fig. 386.—Kent's Cavern. (1,163) 1/2

Fig. 387.—Kent's Cavern. (286) 1/2

Prominent among the instruments of stone, both as exhibiting a great amount of skill and design in fashioning them, and as being distinct in character from the forms usually found on the surface, are the ovoid discs such as had already attracted the attention of Mr. MacEnery. Of these, specimens are engraved on the scale of one-half linear measure in Figs. 386 and 387. The first (No. 1,163 in Mr. Pengelly's list) is of grey cherty flint, carefully chipped on both faces, one of which is rather more convex than the other. It is wrought to a slightly undulating edge all round, except at one spot on the side, where blows seem to have been given in vain in attempting to remove a flake. The traces upon the edge, of wear or use, are but slight. It was found in January, 1866, in the red cave-earth, four feet below the stalagmite, which was about a foot thick, and continuous for a considerable distance in every direction. The smaller implement

(No. 286) Fig. 387, is of much the same general form, but more sub-triangular in outline. It is brought to an edge all round, but this is not in one plane, and on one of the sides shows a sort of ogival curve. The flint has become nearly white, and has a lustrous surface. A portion of the edge along one of the sides has been sharpened by removing minute chips from one face. It was found in June, 1865, between 3 and 4 feet deep in the cave-earth in the great chamber.

Fig. 388.—Kent's Cavern. (4,155) 1/2

But in addition to these ovoid instruments which have been chipped to a more or less acute edge all round, a thick pointed instrument (No. 4,155) of sub-triangular outline, represented as Fig. 388, has been met with, lying on the surface of the cave-earth in the "Sally-port." It is much altered in structure, but seems to have been formed from a cherty nodule "apparently selected from the supracretaceous gravel so abundant between Torquay and Newton." The butt-end still exhibits the original surface of the nodule, the rounded form of which renders it well adapted for being held in the hand. The point has unfortunately been damaged, so that it is impossible to say whether it exhibited any signs of use. One face of the implement is more convex than the other, and has been chipped in such a manner as to leave a sort of central ridge. This implement may have been derived from the breccia.

During the progress of the explorations [2411] subsequent to the appearance of the former edition of this book, numerous other implements of flint and chert were discovered, closely resembling in form the implements from the river-gravels, and apparently of the age of St. Acheul or Chelles. Mr. Pengelly [2412] has pointed out that these belong to the breccia at the base of the cave-deposits, rather than to the cave-earth above, in which thinner and more delicately-worked forms have been found. He considers that there was a considerable interval of time between the two deposits, and that there was a difference between the fauna of the one and of the other. I have an implement almost the exact counterpart of Fig. 388 from the Thetford gravels.

Fig. 388A.—Kent's Cavern. (6,022) 3/4

Another implement (No. 6022) found on Nov. 27th, 1872, at a depth of 16 inches in the undisturbed breccia, is by the kindness of the Plymouth Institution, shown in Fig. 388A. Its resemblance to Fig. 414 from Biddenham, near Bedford, is striking. The illustration is on the scale of three-fourths linear measure, instead of on the usual scale of one-half. From fifteen to twenty implements were found in the breccia and about seventy worked flints of various forms in the cave-earth.

Several implements, varying in size and slightly in form, but of the same general character as the first two described, have also been discovered in the cave. Some of these present an appearance of having been used for scraping a hard substance, a part of the edge towards the narrower end being worn away, leaving a sort of shoulder near the extremity. The wear on the two sides is from the opposite faces, as if the instrument had been turned over in the hand and used in the same direction, whichever edge was employed. MacEnery, in his Plate T, has engraved three instruments of this class, as Nos. 11, 12, and 13, and has remarked on the pointed ends being blunted, "apparently from knocking like a hammer against hard bodies." The blunting in those which I have seen, does not, however, appear to me to be the result of hammering, but rather of minute splinters breaking off during some scraping process.

Implements much resembling in form these from Kent's Cavern have been found in the Cave of Le Moustier, Dordogne; but these latter are for the most part thicker in proportion to their size, especially towards the base, which is usually rather truncated, instead of being brought to an edge. It is possible that they may have been mounted in some sort of handle for use, but on the whole it appears more probable that they were used unmounted in the hand, as a sort of knives or scraping tools.

A smaller form (No. 1,515) of pointed instrument from the cave-earth, is shown in Fig. 389. Both its faces are equally convex, and are chipped over their whole surface in the same manner as those of larger sizes. In shape, it seems adapted to have formed the point of a lance, but the edges and base are in many parts worn away, as if it had been a sort of scraping tool. It much resembles some of the instruments found in the Wookey Hyæna Den, by Prof. Boyd Dawkins.

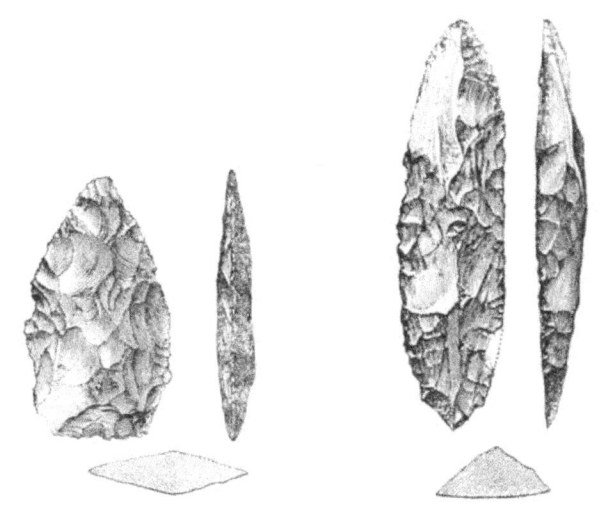

Fig. 389.—Kent's Cavern. (1,515) 1/2

Fig. 390.—Kent's Cavern. (3,922) 1/2

Among the wrought flakes which next demand our attention, the most striking are some finely-pointed lanceolate blades of which one (No. 3,922) is represented in Fig. 390. It has a somewhat rounded point at each end, and has been made from a long flake, the outer face of which has been fashioned by secondary chipping. A part of the inner face at one end has also been re-worked. The edges seem to be slightly worn away, and show, along the greater part of their extent, the minute chipping probably produced by scraping some hard material. The flint is white and porcellanous on the surface, and has become so light and soft in structure, that it can readily be cut with a knife. It was found in the south-west chamber of the cavern, beneath stalagmite not quite a foot thick, but touching the ceiling of the chamber, or nearly so, in company with teeth of hyæna, bear, and fox, and a small quartz crystal.

With regard to this alteration in the colour and structure of the flint, it may be well here to make a few remarks. At first sight, it seems difficult to believe that in a material so hard, and under ordinary circumstances so extremely durable, as flint, so complete a change in colour and texture should have taken place, during any lapse of time, however great. We find, however, that under certain circumstances, even Neolithic implements, which still retain their original black or dark colour in the interior, have on their exterior become completely whitened, and in some cases softened so much that they can be scratched with a knife. The cause, as was first pointed out to me by the late M. Meillet, [2413] of Poitiers, appears to be inherent in the nature of most flints, the silica in which is of two kinds; the one crystallized silica or quartz, with a specific gravity of 2·6, and insoluble in water, the other colloid or glassy silica, known as opal, with a specific gravity of 2·2, which is much more transparent, horny, and soluble; though in their other properties both are chemically the same. It appears, then, that in these whitened flints, the soluble portion has been removed by the passage of infiltrating water through the body of the flint, while the insoluble portion has been left in a finely-divided state, consisting of particles susceptible of disaggregation by moderate force, and is consequently white. This alteration in structure is not confined to artificially-wrought flints, but may take place even in flint pebbles, under certain circumstances, in pervious soils; for I have found Lower Tertiary pebbles in the Woolwich and Reading beds, and also in the resulting conglomerates, which have become sufficiently disintegrated to be cut with a steel knife. When it is considered that these pebbles were originally the hardest part of chalk flints, or at all events those parts which were best able to withstand the rolling and wearing action of the Tertiary sea, the amount of alteration they have since undergone, by the slow dissolution of a portion of their substance, is very striking. The decomposed flint pebbles in the cliff at Southbourne-on-Sea [2414] are well known, and belong to a still more recent geological period. There is some difficulty in ascertaining the exact loss of weight incurred during the process of alteration: but I find that a flake of this porous white flint, which, when dry, weighed one hundred and twenty-nine grains, gained, by immersion for half an hour in water, thirteen grains, so that, taking the specific gravity of flint at about 2·6, and assuming that the flake was originally perfectly non-absorbent, the loss would appear to have been about one-fifth of the original weight.

But to return from this digression to the subject of the instruments, of which several belonging to the same class as Fig. 390 have been found in Kent's Cavern. Some of them are pointed at only one extremity, and that usually the point of the original flake, the bulb-end being left more or less obtuse.

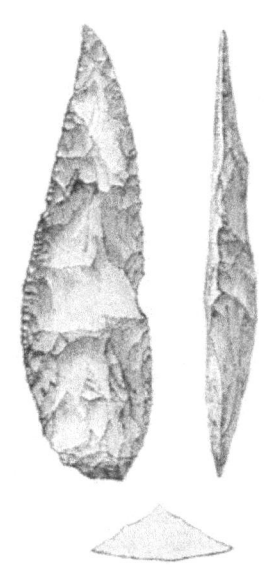

Fig. 391.—Kent's Cavern. (3,869) 1/2

A remarkably elegant instrument of this class (No. 3,869) is shown in Fig. 391. It has been made from a ridged or carinated flake, though having three facets at the butt-end, and a little secondary working on one side; and at the butt this external face has been left in its original condition. The inner face of the flake, however, which is shown in the figure, has been almost entirely removed by secondary working, extending from the edges to the middle of the blade, while the edges have again been re-touched, so as to make them even and sharp. At the butt-end it is chisel-like in form. It was found, on July 4th, 1868, at a depth of 2 feet in the cave-earth, beneath stalagmite 2 feet 8 inches thick. Several other instruments of the same kind have been found in the cavern. Some of them are even longer than those figured.

These instruments so closely resemble in character the long flakes of obsidian and other silicious stones in use, as javelin heads, among the Admiralty Islanders and other savage tribes until the present day, that one is tempted to assign to them a similar purpose. [2415] It is possible that they may have been merely knives, or they may have served for both purposes, like the arrow-heads of the inhabitants of Tierra del Fuego. These English specimens may be compared with some of the lance-heads from the cave of Laugerie Haute, belonging to the Age of Solutré, but they are not quite so dexterously chipped.

Another form of implement which is shown in Fig. 392 (No. 117) was found in 1865, in the second foot in depth, in the cave-earth of the great chamber. It appears best adapted for being held in the hand and used as a scraping tool, possibly in the preparation of skins for clothing; and has been formed from a triangular flake, the ridge of which is slightly curved, and runs obliquely along the instrument. It has been trimmed by blows administered on the flat face, into a pointed oval form with a bevelled edge all round, and this edge towards the middle of one side of the blade is rounded and worn away by use. It is well adapted for being held in the hand as a side-scraper, and it is precisely that part of the edge which would be most exposed to wear, if thus held, that is actually worn. This instrument is not unlike some of the boat-shaped implements of the Surface Period, but is broader and thinner in its proportions. Almost identical forms have occurred in the Brixham Cave, and in that of Aurignac, explored by M. Lartet. Some of the trimmed flakes from the cave of Le Moustier are of much the same character, but the edges are perhaps sharper, and the butt-end of the flake is left of a more rounded form. I have an instrument of much the same general character, from the gravel of the valley of the Lark, at Icklingham, Suffolk, but it is not so neatly or symmetrically finished, and the inner face of the flake is somewhat convex, instead of being concave.

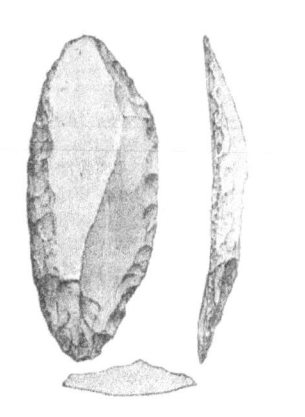

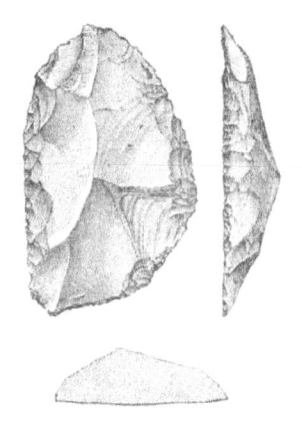

Fig. 392.—Kent's Cavern. (117) 1/2

Fig. 393.—Kent's Cavern. (3,918) 1/2

Another instrument, of nearly the same nature, is shown in Fig. 393 (No. 3,918); one of its sides is, however, much straighter than the other. The edge of this also is somewhat abraded by use. It is formed of flint, which has become white, porcellanous, and light. It was found in the south-west chamber, as was also that shown in Fig. 394 (No. 1/3912). This is a broad flat flake, the side edges of which appear to have been trimmed by secondary chipping, and subsequently to have been somewhat worn away by use, whether as a saw or a scraping tool it is difficult to say. The material is black flint, now weathered grey, and is much heavier than the white flint, and apparently more cherty. Other examples of semilunar implements were also found.

Some of the large flakes found in the cavern appear to have been utilized with very little secondary trimming. That shown in Fig. 395 (No. 56) is of cherty flint, with a sharp edge along one side, while the other side is blunt for half its length from the butt-end, where it is half an inch thick and nearly square with the face, something like the back of the blade of a knife. The edge on the left side of the figure has been trimmed by secondary chipping, mainly on the outer face of the flake, except for about an inch near the butt, where the trimming has been on the inner face, the evident object having been to bring the edge into one plane. The tool is well adapted for being held in the hand, with the thick side resting against the forefinger, leaving the straight edge free for cutting or sawing along its entire length. Part of the right edge near the point seems to have been used for scraping some hard substance, such as bone. It was found in 1865, between one and two feet deep in the cave-earth in the entrance chamber. There is considerable analogy between these large boldly chipped flakes trimmed at the edge, and some of those found in the River-drifts and in the cave of Le Moustier.

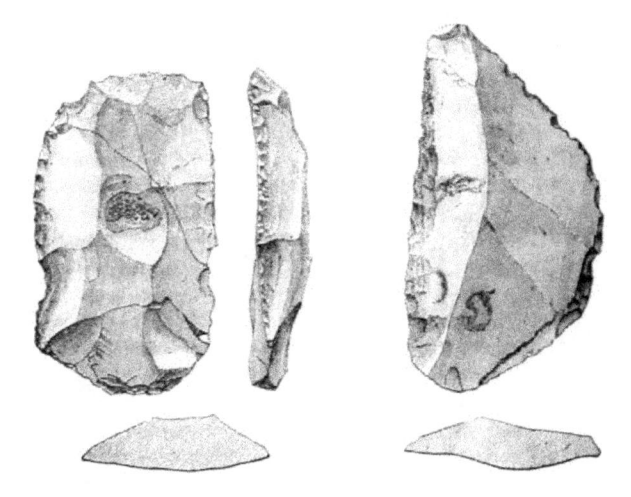

Fig. 394.—Kent's Cavern. (1/3912) 1/2

Fig. 395.—Kent's Cavern. (56) 1/2

A few of the round-ended instruments, to which the name of scraper has been given, were also found in the cave-earth. One of these (No. 2,183) is shown, full size, in Fig. 396. It has been formed from an external flake, struck off a flint from the chalk, the end and one of the sides of which have been re-chipped to a bevelled edge. This, however, at the side becomes nearly at right angles to the face. The butt-end has been also chipped almost to a point. The edge shows symptoms of wear in several places. It was found in the fourth foot in depth, in the cave-earth; but the ground at the spot had been previously broken, so that its position cannot be regarded as certain.

Another instrument of the same class (No. 1,822) is shown, full size, in Fig. 397. It has been formed from a ridged flake, and exhibits marks of having been in use as a scraping tool, not only at one end but at the sides. The inner face is beautifully smooth and flat. Some of these scraper-like tools are more square at the end, and chipped and worn along both sides, having evidently seen much service. So far as form is concerned, there is little or nothing to distinguish them from the analogous instruments of the Neolithic Period. Such scrapers also occur in most of the caves which have furnished implements in France and Belgium, and usually in much greater proportional abundance than has been the case in Kent's Cavern. In some caves, however, as for instance in that of Le Moustier, instruments of this character are extremely scarce. They appear to me to have served for other purposes besides that of dressing skins—one of the uses to which such instruments are applied by the Eskimos of the present day. There is great probability of some of them having been used for striking fire by means of pyrites, as the French and Belgian caves have yielded specimens of that mineral. In the Trou de Chaleux [2416] a block of pyrites was found deeply scored at one end, as if by constant scraping blows with flint; and another block from Les Eyzies, with the end worn, is in the Christy Collection.

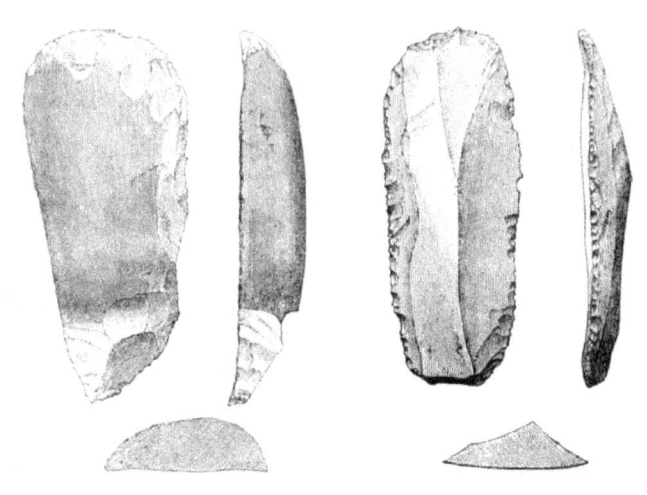

Fig. 396.—Kent's Cavern. (2,183) 1/1

Fig. 397.—Kent's Cavern. (1,822) 1/1

Several examples of another form of tool, manufactured from simple triangular or polygonal flakes, have occurred in Kent's Cavern. In these, one end of the flake has been worked to an oblique straight scraping edge, forming an obtuse angle with one side of the flake, and an acute angle with the other; the point being sometimes on the right, and sometimes on the left side of the flake. Specimens of each variety, Nos. 1/1963 and 2/1963, which were found together, are engraved as Figs. 398 and 399. The long side of the flake is usually but little worn, but the short side and the oblique end are always minutely chipped, and sometimes have the edge quite rounded by wear. This is particularly the case in Fig. 398, of which the long side also has been used for scraping. This flake is considerably curved longitudinally, and its point has much the appearance of having been used as a sort of drill. It seems probable that the obliquity of the edge at the end of the tool is connected with the manner in which it was held in the hand.

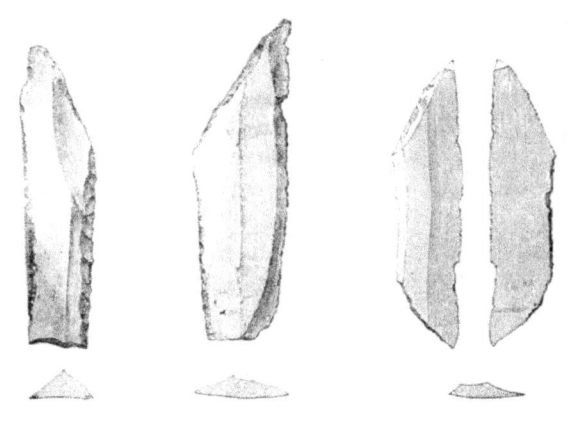

Fig. 398.—Kent's Cavern. (1/1963) 1/1

Fig. 399.—Kent's Cavern. (2/1963) 1/1

Fig. 400.—Kent's Cavern. (2,253) 1/1

The perfectly sharp condition of one edge of the flake, while the other is chipped away and worn, is probably due to its having been protected by some sort of wooden handle. We have already seen how in the Swiss Lake-dwellings flakes of flint were mounted; and though probably for these small flakes, such highly-finished handles were not prepared, yet the insertion of one edge of a flake of flint into a piece of split stick involves no great trouble, while it would shield the fingers from being cut, and would tend to strengthen the flint. In several of the French caves, extremely slender flakes have been found, with one edge quite worn away and the other untouched, a condition for which it is difficult to account on any other hypothesis than that of their having been inserted longitudinally into some sort of back or handle, probably of wood.

At least two specimens of another form have occurred in which both ends, instead of only one, have been slanted off. One of these (No. 2,253) is shown in Fig. 400. The other is of precisely the same size and shape. In both, the two sloping ends and the short side are worn by use, while the long side is unscathed except by accidental breakage. In the instrument not figured, the scraping edge, both at the side and ends, has been on the flat face of the flake. In the other, this has been the case at the ends only, while at the side the scraping edge has been on one of the facets. I am not aware of this form of instrument having as yet been elsewhere noticed, nor indeed, to my knowledge, has observation been called to those like Fig. 399, found in the French caves. One or two specimens, of much the same character as Fig. 399, were, however, found at La Madelaine, and are in the Christy Collection. These bevel-ended flakes also occur in Neolithic times. [2417]

Fig. 401.—Kent's Cavern. (1,970) 1/2

As might be expected, the bulk of the worked flints found in Kent's Cavern are flakes and spalls, more or less perfect, and a very large proportion of them show, on some part of their edges, traces of use. It seems needless to engrave any of these simple forms, as they present no characteristics different from those of the flakes and splinters of any other age. Many of them have been made from rolled pebbles, no doubt derived from the adjacent beach. Some of the cores from which they have been struck have occurred in the cave, of which one (No. 1,970) is represented, on the scale of one-half, in Fig. 401.

Curiously enough, among the animal remains is a portion of a large canine tooth of a bear, with the edges chipped away, so as much to resemble a worked flake.

Fig. 402.—Kent's Cavern. (597) 1/2

Of the stone implements not consisting of flint or chert, perhaps the most remarkable is the hammer-stone (No. 597), shown on the scale of one-half, in Fig. 402. It is formed from a pebble of coarse, hard, red sandstone, the outer surface of which is still retained on the two flatter faces of the stone; but all round, with the exception of a small patch, the edge of the original pebble has been battered away by hammering, until the whole has been brought into an almost cheese-like form. It was found in 1865, between one and two feet deep in the red cave-earth, over which lay an enormous block of limestone, but no stalagmite. MacEnery mentions, among the objects which he discovered, a ball of granite, which was probably of the same class as this. Many such hammer-stones have been found in the French caves. I have one, formed from a micaceous quartzose pebble, which I found in the cave of La Madelaine, explored by Messrs. Lartet and Christy, which almost matches this from Kent's Cavern in size and shape. It seems possible that their use was for pounding some substances, either animal or vegetable, for food. It is, however, hardly probable that any cereals were cultivated by those who handled them. They may have been used in breaking open the bones for the marrow, which seems, from the fractured condition of all bones that contained it, to have been a favourite food among the French cave-dwellers. Wexovius, quoted by Scheffer, [2418] says: "The marrow of raindeer is of a delicious taste, which they value in Lapland, just as we do oisters or some other outlandish dainties."

Another object which has to be mentioned is a sort of whetstone of purplish-grey grit. It is a nearly square prism, 4 3/4 inches long, and with the sides rather less than 1 inch wide. It was found in a recess beneath a projecting bed of limestone, *in situ*, but sealed in beneath a thick mass of stalagmitic breccia. A fragment of another, of finer grained greenish grit, has also been found beneath stalagmite, 26 inches thick. This latter, according to Sir Wollaston Franks, closely resembles some stones found in the Bruniquel caves, both in form and material.

It will naturally be inquired, for what purpose were these whetstones required, and what is the meaning of all these marks of wear on the edges of the flint tools, as if they had been used for scraping some hard substance? Fortunately the answer is not far to seek. The latter were used not only as weapons of the chase, and in cutting and preparing food, but also in the manufacture of various implements of bone, and possibly of ivory, such as harpoon-heads, pins, and even needles, as well as other instruments of unknown use. The wearing away of the edges of many of the flint-flakes is precisely of that character which I find by experiment to result from scraping bone; while it seems probable that the use of the whetstones was for putting the final polish on the bone instruments, and sharpening their points, for either of which purposes, mere scraping-tools like those of flint would be but inefficient.

It is not, of course, to be expected, that these instruments and weapons of bone should occur in anything approaching to the same numbers as the simple instruments of flint. The latter were readily made, and therefore of little value. They were also soon worn out and thrown aside; but the former required considerable time and skill in their preparation, and would not be discarded unless broken; and if accidentally lost, would be worth the trouble of being sought for. In some of the French caves, however, in which the deposits, unlike those in Kent's Cavern, are strictly of a refuse character, like the shell-mounds of Denmark, a larger proportion of them has occurred than here.

The principal objects of the kind, discovered below the stalagmite in Kent's Cavern, are portions of harpoon-heads, a pin, awl, and a needle, which it will be well to describe, as they afford links of connection between the relics of this and other caves.

The harpoon-heads are of two kinds, some being barbed on both sides, others on one only. Of the former kind, but one example (No. 2,282) has been found, which is shown in Fig. 403. It lay in the second foot in depth, in the red cave-earth in the vestibule. Above this was the black band 3 inches thick, containing flint-flakes and remains of extinct mammals; and above this again, the stalagmite floor 18 inches in thickness. It is as usual imperfect, but the 2 1/4 inches which remain, show the tapering-point and four barbs on either side, which are opposite to each other and not alternate. It is precisely of the same character as some of the harpoon-heads from the cave of La Madelaine, which are usually formed of reindeer horn. The material in this instance is I believe the same. The striated marks of the tool by which it was scraped into form are still distinctly visible in places. Such harpoon-heads have been regarded as characteristic of the latest division in the sequence of this class of caverns, and have been found in numerous localities on the Continent. A doubly-barbed harpoon-head of bone, belonging to a much more recent period, was found in the Victoria Cave, [2419] at Settle.

Fig. 403.—Kent's Cavern. (2,282) 1/1

Fig. 404.—Kent's Cavern. (2,206) 1/1

Fig. 405.—Kent's Cavern. (1,970) 1/1

Of the other kind, which have the barbs along one side only of the blade, two examples have been found. One of these (No. 2,206), though in two pieces, is otherwise nearly perfect, and is shown in Fig. 404. It also has its analogues among the harpoon-heads found in the cave of La Madelaine and elsewhere, especially at Bruniquel. Its stem shows the projection for retaining the loop of cord by which it was connected with the shaft, though it was probably still susceptible of being detached from immediate contact with it. In this respect, as indeed in general character, these early weapons seem closely to resemble those of the Eskimos of the present day. A good series of modern and ancient instruments of this class is engraved in the "Reliquiæ Aquitanicæ." [2420] An article on the distribution of harpoons in the caverns of the Pyrenees, from the pen of M. Ed. Piette, [2421] may be consulted with advantage. The other instrument of this kind (No. 1,970), shown in Fig. 405, is the terminal portion of a similar point, but with the barbs all broken off at the base. It is about 3 3/4 inches long, and was found in the black band.

The pin (No. 1,929), already mentioned, is shown in Fig. 406, and was found in the fourth foot in depth, in the cave-earth below the stalagmite in the vestibule, which there attained a thickness of 20 inches. It lay with an unworn molar of *Rhinoceros tichorhinus*. In the black band above the cave-earth, but below the stalagmite, were remains of the hyæna and other cave-mammals. The pin is 3 1/4 inches long, nearly circular in section, expanding into a head much like that of a common screw, and tapering off to a sharp point. It bears a high polish as if from constant use, and was probably employed as a fastener of the dress, itself most likely made of skin.

Fig. 406.—Kent's Cavern. (1,929) 1/1

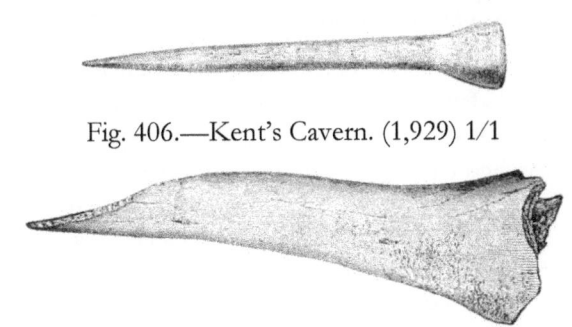

Fig. 407.—Kent's Cavern. (1,835) 1/1

A kind of awl made of bone (No. 1,835), about 3 3/4 inches long, and sharply pointed at one end, was also found beneath stalagmite 16 inches thick. It is shown full size in Fig. 407. The marks of the tool by which it was scraped into form may be distinctly seen upon it.

A lance-shaped bone tool (No. 3,428) 2·7 inches long, flat on one face and convex on the other, was also found in the cave-earth.

Fig. 408.—Kent's Cavern.

But perhaps the most interesting of all the objects discovered in the cavern, is the small bone needle found in 1866 in the black band below the stalagmite, but not recognized until 1868, in consequence of its having been enveloped in a stalagmitic covering, which then fell off, and displayed the true character of the object it contained. The needle has unfortunately lost its point, but what remains is nearly 7/8 of an inch long, as will be seen from Fig. 408. It tapers slightly, and is somewhat elliptical in section, the greatest diameter at the larger end being barely 8/100 of an inch, and at the smaller end 3/100. It has a neatly-drilled circular eye capable of receiving a thread about 3/80 of an inch in diameter, or about the thickness of fine twine. The surface of the shaft shows numerous fine longitudinal *striæ*, as if it had been scraped into shape.

Such needles have been found in considerable numbers in the caves of the age of La Madelaine, such as Les Eyzies, Laugerie Basse, Bruniquel, and the lower cave of Massat, always associated with harpoons of the barbed type. They vary in length from 3 1/4 inches to 1 inch, and some have been found which show that, after they had been accidentally broken through the eye, a fresh eye was drilled. That this could readily be effected by means of a pointed flint was proved, as before observed, by the late Mons. E. Lartet, who both made bone needles and bored eyes in them by means of flint tools alone. An excellent and exhaustive essay on the employment of sewing-needles in ancient times, more especially in connection with those from the French caves, has been communicated by M. E. Lartet to the "Reliquiæ Aquitanicæ," [2422] to which the reader is referred for further particulars. As with the Lapps, it seems probable that the thread in use with these needles was made from reindeer sinews; that animal, at all events in the Dordogne, having formed a principal article of food at the period of the occupation of the caves.

Such are the principal works of human art which have been discovered in this most interesting cavern, in the researches conducted under the superintendence of the late Mr. Pengelly, and mainly through grants made by the British Association for the Advancement of Science. A series of them is exhibited in the British Museum.

Before attempting to account for their presence in the cave-deposits, or to ascertain what that betokens, it will be well to take a cursory glance at the animal remains with which they were found associated. For this purpose I take the list prepared by Prof. Boyd Dawkins and Mr. W. A. Sanford, and published in the Report of the British Association for 1869. It embodies, however, the result of an examination of less than one-tenth part of the whole number of specimens obtained, though that tenth exceeded 4,000 in number. The following list comprises nearly all the mammals, bones of which undoubtedly belong to the cave-earth, and omits all species the determination of which is at all uncertain, as well as birds and fishes:—

Lepus timidus (var. *diluvianus?*), Hare	Rare.
Lagomys pusillus, Tail-less hare	Very rare.
Felis leo, var. *spelæa*, Cave-Lion	Abundant.
Hyæna crocuta, var. *spelæa*, Cave-Hyæna	Very abundant.
Gulo luscus, Glutton	Very rare.
Ursus spelæus, Cave-Bear	Abundant.
Ursus priscus = *ferox*, Grizzly Bear	Abundant.
Ursus arctos, Brown Bear	Scarce.
Canis lupus, Wolf	Rare.
Canis vulpes, var. *spelæus*, large Fox	Rare.

Elephas primigenius, Mammoth	Not very common.
Rhinoceros tichorhinus, Woolly Rhinoceros	Abundant.
Equus caballus, Horse	Very abundant.
Bos primigenius, Urus	Scarce.
Bison priscus, Bison	Abundant.
Cervus megaceros, Irish Elk	Not uncommon.
Cervus elaphus (*Strongyloceros spelæus*, Owen), Stag	Abundant.
Cervus tarandus, Reindeer	Abundant.
Arvicola amphibius, Water-vole	Rare.
A. agrestis, Field-vole	Rare.
A. pratensis, Bank-vole	Very rare.
Castor fiber, Beaver	Scarce.

In the breccia the hyæna appears to be absent, while remains of bear occur in great abundance.

The list published by Prof. Boyd Dawkins in his "Cave-hunting" [2423] adds a few mammals of minor importance, but also the *Machairodus latidens*, of which an incisor was found in the cave-earth in 1872. [2424] Of this "sabre-toothed tiger" five canine teeth and one if not two incisors were found in the cavern by MacEnery, but doubts had been thrown upon his accuracy. The discovery of 1872 justified the Committee in reporting that *Machairodus latidens* and Man had been contemporaries in Britain.

In the black mould above the stalagmite, where polished stone and bronze instruments have occurred, a different fauna is present. We there meet with the dog, short-horn ox (*Bos longifrons*), roe-deer, sheep, goat, pig, and rabbit, of which no remains are found in the cave-earth. In that deposit, on the contrary, by far the greater number of the remains are of mammals now either entirely extinct, or no longer to be found in Britain.

The mineral condition of the bones in the cave-earth, it is but right to say, varies considerably; so much so, as to lead to the conclusion that some of the bones, especially of bear, are derived from an earlier deposit of the same character. These more ancient remains are, according to Prof. Boyd Dawkins, much more crystalline, much heavier, and of a darker colour than the ordinary teeth and bones. Still, nearly the whole of the bones in the cave-earth beneath the stalagmite appear beyond doubt to belong to one and the same period, though that period may have been of long duration, and the breccia which contained implements of River-drift types is of still earlier date. These bones have for the most part been broken into fragments, sometimes split longitudinally, and vast numbers of them have been gnawed, apparently by hyænas. In what manner are we to account for the presence of the works of man among them, and are they of the same age as the animal remains with which they are associated?

In considering this question, I do not take into account those portions of the cave in which there are variations from what may be regarded as the typical section, these being mainly due to accidental and local causes, such as the breaking up of beds of stalagmite of earlier date than those above the cave-earth, but restrict myself to the main features of the case.

There can be little doubt that, as has been pointed out by Mr. Pengelly, the accumulation of the cave-earth containing these remains took place slowly and gradually; large blocks of limestone and films of stalagmite encrusting stones and bones, or cementing them into a firm concrete, running at all levels and in all parts of the principal chamber. So that, without entering into any discussion as to the manner in which the red earth and pebbles of the deposit were introduced into the cavern, which would be here somewhat out of place, we may safely assume that the bones and teeth, whatever may have been their antiquity at the time of their introduction into the cave-earth, were deposited in the positions in which they are now found, at the same time as the implements with which they are associated. We can, however, readily conceive circumstances under which old deposits, containing relics of extinct animals, might be disturbed from their position in a cave, and re-deposited with objects of human workmanship belonging to a far more recent period. In fact, among the bones themselves there are some which, as has already been pointed out, have belonged to an earlier deposit than that in which they are now found. Let us, therefore, examine into the possibility of these instruments of flint and bone belonging to a different period from that of the animals with the remains of which they now occur. One thing, of course, is evident, that whether there has been a mixture in the cave-earth of objects belonging to various ages or no, such a mixture could only have taken place before the thick coating of stalagmite which now overlies them had even begun to accumulate. The amount of time represented by such a coating, it is, of course, impossible to calculate; but, even under the most favourable circumstances, it must have been the work of hundreds, or more probably thousands of years; and yet its deposit had been completed before the introduction of the overlying black mould, which has proved to contain objects to which an antiquity of at least two thousand years may safely be assigned.

But what do the presence and condition of these instruments denote? The flint flakes occur in great numbers, and have mostly been used; the blocks from which they were struck are present; there are traces of fire on some of the bones; there are hammer-stones, whetstones, weapons of the chase, and the needle of the housewife; all prove that during the accumulation of the cave-earth, the cavern was, at all events from time to time, the habitation of man. How far this human occupancy may have alternated with that of predaceous animals may be a matter of question; but of man's sojourn in Kent's Cavern for a lengthened period in all, before the deposition of the upper stalagmite, there can be no doubt. But in all cases of human occupancy of caves we find, and it could not well be otherwise, the refuse of man's food, in the shape of the bones of the animals whose flesh he consumed, or the shells of the edible molluscs with which his meals were varied. We have seen that in the black mould above the stalagmite, the implements of bronze and stone are associated with a fauna essentially the same as that of the present day. But the bulk of the mammals which are found above the stalagmite do not occur below it; and assuming, as we must do, that the earlier occupants of the cave subsisted on animal food, and were unable to eat the whole of the bones as well as the flesh, some portion of the bones below the stalagmite must be the refuse from their meals. Without insisting on the perfect contemporaneity of all the animal remains found together in the cave-earth, we may therefore safely affirm that we have here relics of man associated with a fauna from which the ordinary forms of ox, sheep, goat, pig, and dog are entirely absent, and of which the majority of forms are now either totally or locally extinct.

That the fauna represented in the cave-earth is, however, to be regarded as all belonging to one and the same period—unless possibly the *Machairodus* is to be excepted—is shown, as will subsequently be seen, by the occurrence of the remains of, at all events, all the larger mammals, associated together in the old River-drifts.

Comparing this result with that obtained from an examination of the French caves, the rock-shelters in which almost the whole accumulation is a kind of refuse heap, we find it fully confirmed, so far as the animals best adapted for human food are concerned. The rarity of the remains of the other animals in these rock-shelters is probably to be accounted for by the fact that the sole occupants were human; and that either their tenancy was continuous, or that during their absence these rock-shelters were not the haunts of predaceous animals, for which indeed they are far less well adapted than the sinuous caves.

In attempting to correlate the works of man from Kent's Cavern with those from the French caves, we find in the first place that implements of the types usually characteristic of the River-gravels have been found in about a dozen French caves, of which a list has been given by M. E. D'Acy, [2425] and, secondly, that the harpoons and needle belong to the age of La Madelaine, though bones engraved with pictorial designs—which are also characteristic of that period—are wanting. Some of the flint implements, however, approximate more closely in character with those of the age of Le Moustier; while the age of Solutré is not so decidedly represented by any of its peculiar forms. If any value attaches to these analogies, there would seem to be reason, on these grounds also, for supposing that the infilling of the cave with the red earth, to say nothing of the breccia at a lower level, was the work of an immensely long lapse of time. The black band, which in part of the cave lay beneath the stalagmite, and contained numerous pieces of charcoal, seems to indicate some more continuous occupancy of the cave by man, than at the time when the red earth was accumulating. Then comes the stalagmite, in which but few remains whether human or otherwise have been found, and these for the most part may have fallen in from higher levels. It seems to indicate a vast period of time, during which the cavern was entirely unfrequented by man or beast, and during which the fauna of the country was undergoing those changes—by the extinction or migration of some forms of mammalian life, and the incoming of others—which is so strongly marked by the difference in the contents of the beds above and below the stalagmite. As concerns this long chapter in the history of human existence the records of the cavern are a blank.

It is, moreover, to be observed that though in Kent's Cavern we have evidence of its occupation by Man more or less continuously from the Acheuléen down to the Magdalénien Age, a space of time embracing nearly all the phases of the Palæolithic Period, there is no sign of any transition to the Neolithic Period, the remains of which first make their appearance after the deposit of the stalagmite.

BRIXHAM CAVE, TORQUAY.

The ossiferous cave of Brixham, near Torquay, was discovered in the year 1858, and was almost immediately brought under the notice of the Geological and Royal Societies by the late Dr. Hugh Falconer. [2426] The latter society, acting on the recommendation of the council of the former, made a grant towards the exploration of the cave in the manner suggested by the late Mr. Pengelly, who was also assisted with money by the Baroness Burdett Coutts, Sir J. K. Shuttleworth, and the late Mr. R. Arthington of Leeds. With Dr. Falconer was associated a committee of distinguished geologists, including Mr. Pengelly, under whose immediate superintendence the works were carried on. Owing to various delays, the final report of this committee, drawn up by the late Sir Joseph Prestwich, was not presented to the Royal Society until 1872, though some accounts of the progress of the explorations [2427] had from time to time been made public.

The Report will be found in the *Philosophical Transactions* for 1873 [2428] and comprises a memorandum of my own on the objects of human industry discovered in the cave.

Accounts of the cave have also been given by Mr. Pengelly [2429] and Prof. Boyd Dawkins. [2430]

The cave itself is in Devonian Limestone, and consists of three principal galleries, in plan not unlike the letter Z, with various diverging tunnel-shaped passages, and a chamber at the right-hand lower corner of the Z, the two entrances being at the extreme points on the opposite side. The gallery represented by the middle limb of the letter, known as the Flint Knife Gallery, bears the most distinct marks of having been hollowed out by the long-protracted action of running water, and the deposit in it was nearly free from stalagmite. In the others, which are known as the Reindeer and Pen Galleries, and which have more the character of fissures, stalagmite abounded.

Where all the deposits of the cave were present, [2431] the following was the section in descending order.

- 1. Irregular layer of stalagmite, 1 to 15 inches thick.
- 2. Ochreous red cave-earth, with angular stones and some pebbles, 2 to 13 feet.
- 3. Gravel, with many rounded pebbles in it.

In and on the stalagmite, were found antlers of reindeer, and a humerus of bear, and in the cave-earth, numerous mammalian remains. Among them, in one place, were nearly all the bones of the left hind-leg of a bear, still preserving their true anatomical position, [2432] though with one of the bones of the fore-leg lying with them. In close proximity lay one of the worked flints, of which several were found in this bed. A few occurred in the gravel. The fauna appears to be nearly identical with that of Kent's Cavern, though the *Machairodus* is absent. We have, therefore, here another instance of the association of these works of man with the remains of the extinct mammals, in a cave-deposit beneath a thick layer of stalagmite, which, in this case, had been for the most part deposited before the reindeer had quitted the south of England, and while a large bear, probably *Ursus spelæus*, was still living in Britain. An interesting feature in the case has been pointed out by Mr. Pengelly, [2433] who, from the nature and origin of some of the pebbles in the cave-earth, argues that to allow of their having been brought into the cave by means of water—which in this instance, for various reasons, seems to have been the transporting agent—the configuration of the surface of the land in the neighbourhood must have been very different from what it is at present; and that a valley, 75 feet in depth, which now runs in front of the cave, could not then have existed, but must have been subsequently excavated.

The fragments of flint of various sizes discovered in the cave, and showing in a greater or less degree traces of human workmanship upon them, were upwards of thirty in number. Like those from Kent's Cavern, they have, for the most part, undergone much alteration in structure, having become white, absorbent, and brittle to a greater or less depth from their surface, which in some instances still retains a bright porcellanous glaze. The flint appears to have been derived originally from the chalk, though in some cases it had, before being utilized, been rolled into pebbles on the beach.

The following are some of the most remarkable specimens:—

Fig. 409.—Brixham Cave. 1/2

A round-pointed lanceolate implement, shown on the scale of 1/2 in. Fig. 409. The point is symmetrically chipped, but the original surface of the flint has been left untouched over the greater part of the butt-end, which is roughly cylindrical, and more truncated than is usual with chalk flints, but is well adapted for being held in the hand. This implement has had the pointed end broken off by an irregularly diagonal fracture rather more than half way along it, and the butt-end has subsequently split up lengthways with what may be termed a "faulted" line of fracture; and about a quarter of it has been lost. The fractures are evidently of very ancient date; but what is most remarkable is that the butt-end was found in August, 1858, 3 feet deep in the cave-earth in the Flint Knife Gallery, and the point was not found until nearly a month afterwards, a long distance away in the Pen Gallery, at a depth of 3 feet 6 inches in the same bed. It was not until some time afterwards that it was discovered that the two fragments fitted each other, or that the true character of the implement was seen. In general form it closely resembles one type of the pointed instruments from the Valley-gravels. In fact, it is in all essential points identical with them, and agrees in character with many of the implements from the breccia of Kent's Cavern—especially with one (No. 7,328) which might have been made by the same hand—while it differs materially in form from the flat ovoid implements from the cave-earth, such as Fig. 386, which, however, also find their analogues in the River-Drift.

Another instrument, of an elongated-oval form, has been made from a large flake, or splinter, of flint with an approximately flat inner face, showing strongly the curved and waved lines of conchoidal fracture. It has been shaped by a succession of blows given in such a manner as not to injure the flat face, but to produce a more or less bevelled scraping or cutting edge all round, some parts of which present appearances of wear by use. It is shown in Fig. 410, and, as will be seen, is of much the same character as the implement from Kent's Cavern, Fig. 392, in the description of which the analogy of this type with that of some of the French cave-implements is pointed out.

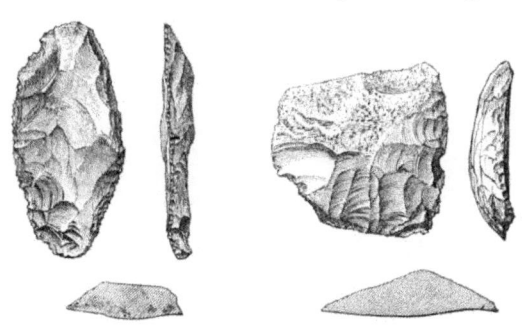

Fig. 410.—Brixham Cave. 1/2

Fig. 411.—Brixham Cave. 1/2

In Fig. 411 is represented an instrument found in the gravel in a fissure in the West Chamber of the cave. It is a fragment of a large broad flake, showing on its convex face a portion of the original crust of the flint. It seems to have been at first of an approximately oval form, but has lost one of its ends by a straight fracture. This end appears to have been broken off in ancient times, after the rest of the instrument had been chipped into shape. A portion of the other end is also wanting, but the fracture in this case must have existed before the completion of the implement, as several flakes have been removed from its convex face, by blows administered on the fractured surface. One side of the flake has been trimmed by chipping, at first boldly and then more minutely, to a segmental bevelled edge, much resembling in character that of some of the large "side-scrapers" from the cave of Le Moustier [2434] in the Dordogne. Instruments of the same character occur occasionally, though rarely, in the ancient River-deposits. There are some traces of use on the edge of this specimen.

A remarkably symmetrical scraper was also thought to have come from the Brixham Cave, and is shown full size in Fig. 412. I remarked in publishing it that it closely resembled the scrapers found on the surface of the soil, and that it was exceptionally short for a cave-specimen. A little time after the first edition of this book had appeared, I discovered that this scraper had been found on the surface near the top of Windmill Hill, and had been included with the other specimens by mistake. [2435] It is undoubtedly neolithic.

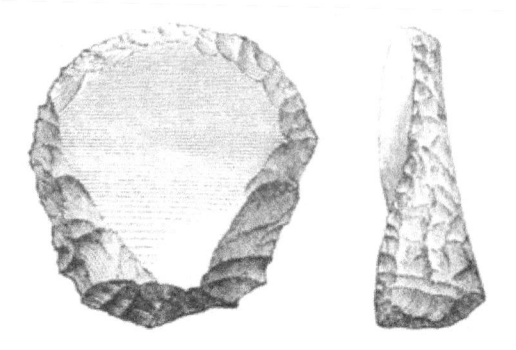

Fig. 412.—Brixham Cave. 1/1

The other implements from the Brixham Cave consist for the most part of flakes and splinters of flint of different sizes, and more or less chipped. One of these, 2 3/4 inches long, has been chipped or jagged along one edge, apparently by use, while the broad round end is so much worn away as to almost assume the appearance of a "scraper." Most of them bear decided marks, either on their sides or ends, of having been in use as scraping tools. About half way along one of them is a rounded notch, apparently produced by scraping some cylindrical object; and in connection with this it may be mentioned that a portion of a cylindrical pin, or rod, of ivory was found in the cave, being the only object wrought from an animal substance. A cylindrical piece of ivory about 3/8 inch in diameter was found in the Gorge d'Enfer cavern, and is in the Christy Collection. Some of the splinters of flint are very small, and yet one of them only 3/4 inch by 5/8 inch shows the worn edge resulting from use. An irregular subangular flint pebble somewhat pear-shaped in form has some of its angles much battered, as if by hammering, and has probably served as a hammer-stone, simply held in the hand. Pebbles similarly bruised at the more salient parts have frequently been found in the French caves.

The Brixham Cave specimens are now in the British Museum, and the general result of the examination of them, is that they are found to present analogous, and in some cases almost identical, forms with those discovered in other caves, and in the ancient river-gravels, associated with the remains of animals now for the most part extinct; and that most of the implements prove not only to have been made by man, but to have been actually in use before becoming imbedded in the cave-loam; while from the whole of the flints discovered presenting these signs of human workmanship or use upon them, it is evident that their presence in the cave must in some measure be due to human agency, though it was probably by means of water that they were deposited in the positions in which they were found.

THE TOR BRYAN CAVES.

These caves, rock-shelters, or fissures are situated near Denbury, Devon, and were explored by Mr. J. L. Widger, with results recorded by the late Mr. J. E. Lee. [2436] In them were found numerous mammalian remains, including teeth of rhinoceros, hyæna, and bear, and several worked flints. One of these, described as a "Flint Implement of the older type," [2437] was found beneath two thick stalagmite floors. Many of the implements from these caves are now in the British Museum.

In the Happaway Cavern, [2438] Torquay, teeth of the same mammals were found, together with human bones and apparently a flint flake as well as many splinters of flint. Human remains were also found with those of hyæna in a cave at Cattedown, [2439] Plymouth.

THE WOOKEY HYÆNA DEN.

The so-called Hyæna Den at Wookey Hole, near Wells, Somerset, has been explored at different times between 1859 and 1863 by Prof. Boyd Hawkins, F.R.S., assisted by the Rev. J. Williamson, F.G.S., Mr. James Parker, F.G.S., and Mr. Henry Willett, F.G.S., and accounts of the exploration have been published in the *Quarterly Journal of the Geological Society*. [2440]

The cave is situated no great distance from the mouth of the large and well-known cavern of Wookey Hole, and pierces the Dolomitic Conglomerate. It was first discovered about the year 1849, in cutting a mill-race along the edge of the rock, and consists of a principal chamber, or *antrum*, connected with a bifurcated tunnel narrowing as it recedes from the chamber, and with one branch terminating in a vertical passage. At the time of the discovery, both the chamber and the passage were for the greater part filled with red earth, stones, and animal remains quite up to the roof, and in other parts to within a few inches of it. In a few places only was there any deposit of stalagmite. In the *antrum*, both the upper and lower part of the red earth which filled the cave contained but few organic remains, though they were abundant towards the middle of the deposit. In part of the passage, however, there was an enormous accumulation of animal remains, forming a bone-bed at the top of the cave-earth. The evidences of human occupation were all found in the principal chamber.

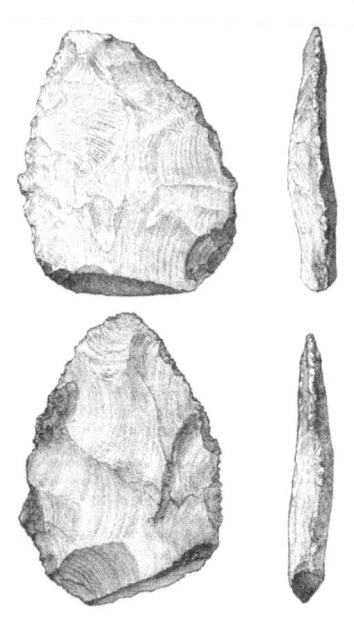

Fig. 413.—Wookey Hyæna Den. (Four views of implement.) 1/1

They consisted of bone-ashes, and some instruments of stone and bone. The bone objects are described as two rudely fashioned arrow-heads of the shape of an equilateral triangle, with the angles at the base bevelled off. They have, however, both been lost, so that I am unable to speak more positively as to their character. The stone objects are still forthcoming, and some of them are preserved in the Museums at Brighton and Oxford. One of the finest is shown in full size in four views as Fig. 413, having been engraved for the *Quarterly Journal of the Geological Society.* [2441] It lay at a depth of 4 feet from the roof, and at a distance of 12 feet from the present entrance. It is described as having lain with some other implements in contact with teeth of hyæna, between dark bands of manganese full of bony splinters, which may have been old floors [2442] of the cave; so that the occupation by the hyæna seems to have succeeded, or alternated with, that by man. It is of white flint, and closely resembles in form some of the smaller implements from the River-drift. It is of less size than the ovoid instruments from Kent's Cavern, and is not so neatly made as some of them. A smaller instrument from the Wookey Hyæna Den is of much the same form, but still less artistically worked. It is 2 3/8 inches long and 1 3/4 inches broad, and may be compared with that from Kent's Cavern shown in Fig. 389. Other specimens were more of the "sling-stone" form; in addition to which there were numerous flakes and splinters of flint and chert. One flake, which, though it has lost its point, is still 2 3/4 inches long, has been trimmed by secondary chipping on the flat face, slightly so along one side, but on the other, over half the surface of the flake, which is 1 1/4 inches wide near the base. When perfect this instrument was probably much like that from Kent's Cavern, Fig. 391. Both its edges show considerable signs of wear by use. Another form described by Prof. Boyd Dawkins is roughly pyramidal, with a smooth and flat base, and a cutting edge all round, much like an instrument found in the cave of Aurignac by M. Lartet. Of this form there were two examples, both made of chert from the Upper Greensand.

The fauna of the cave, so far as the larger animals are concerned, is the same as that of Kent's Cavern, with the addition of *Rhinoceros hemitœchus*, and of a lemming, and with the exception of *Machairodus*. The exact method of accumulation of the deposits in this cave it is very difficult to explain. Prof. Boyd Dawkins has suggested that during its occupation by hyænas, and perhaps for some time afterwards, it was subject to floods similar to those which now from time to time take place in the caverns in the neighbourhood. One thing appears certain, that previously to the filling up of the principal chamber it must, for a longer or shorter period, have been occupied by man; who here also again appears to have been associated with that same fauna, now either totally or locally extinct, with which traces of his handiwork have been discovered intermingled in so many other deposits of a similar character, both on the Continent and in Britain. With regard to the physical features of the country, Sir Charles Lyell [2443] observes, "When I examined the spot in 1860, after I had been shown some remains of the hyæna collected there, I felt convinced that a complete revolution must have taken place in the topography of the district since the time of the extinct quadrupeds. I was not aware at the time, that flint tools had been met with in the same bone-deposit."

LONG HOLE, GOWER, AND OTHER CAVES.

The next British cavern which I have to mention is one of the series in the Peninsula of Gower, in Glamorganshire, explored by Colonel Wood and the late Dr. Hugh Falconer, F.R.S. The cave in question was discovered in 1861, and is known as Long Hole. [2444] It is about one mile east of the well-known Paviland Caves, and is about 130 feet above ordinary high-water mark. It penetrates the limestone rock to a distance of about 44 feet, and when discovered did not exceed in its greatest dimensions 12 feet in width, and 7 feet in height.

There was a deposit of about 7 feet of ferruginous, unctuous cave-earth, mixed with angular fragments of limestone rock, forming the floor, which was in part, if not wholly, of stalagmite. The fossil remains found in the cave included *Ursus spelæus*, *Hyæna spelæa*, *Felis spelæa*, *Rhinoceros hemitœchus* and *tichorhinus*, *Elephas antiquus* and *primigenius*, *Bison priscus* and *Cervus tarandus*. Flint implements, unquestionably of human manufacture, were found along with these remains; and one very fine flint "arrow-head," as termed by Dr. Falconer, [2445] was found at a depth of 4 1/2 feet in the cave-earth, contiguous to a detached shell of a milk molar of *Rhinoceros hemitœchus*, and at the same depth. Other flint implements were found at a depth of 3 feet below the stalagmite, associated with remains of *Cervus Guettardi*, a variety of reindeer. Sir Charles Lyell [2446] has remarked that this is the first well-authenticated example of the occurrence of *Rhinoceros hemitœchus* in connection with human implements. Dr. Falconer has also recognized the same species, in the fragment of an upper milk molar, discovered in the Wookey Hole Hyæna Den by Prof. Boyd Dawkins.

I have had an opportunity of examining casts of the worked flints from Long Hole, in the Christy Collection, and find them to consist exclusively of flakes, some of them well and symmetrically formed, and exhibiting on their edges the marks arising from use.

In some of the other caverns in the same district, Prof. Boyd Dawkins has also discovered flint flakes associated with the remains of a similar group of animals. The Oyle Cave, [2447] Tenby, and Hoyle's Mouth, [2448] have also afforded flint flakes associated with the remains of a nearly similar fauna.

In the Coygan Cave, [2449] Carmarthenshire, Mr. Laws, of Tenby, found two flint flakes with remains of mammoth and rhinoceros below a foot of stalagmite. In the Ffynnon Beunos Cave, [2450] Dr. H. Hicks, F.R.S., found several worked flints (one like Fig. 390) with bones of Pleistocene animals below a stalagmite breccia, and in the Cae Gwyn Cave [2451] a long scraper with bones of rhinoceros. A flint flake [2452] was found under Drift outside the covered entrance to the cave. Dr. Hicks regards these caves as Pre-Glacial, a view in which I cannot agree.

In the Pont Newydd Cave [2453] near Cefn, Prof. T. McK. Hughes, F.R.S., found, with plentiful remains of the Pleistocene fauna, including *Rhinoceros hemitœchus*, a number of implements of distinctly palæolithic forms made of felstone and chert, as well as one of flint. This cave can be proved to be Post-Glacial.

Another cave which may be mentioned is that known as King Arthur's Cave, near Whitchurch, Ross, which was explored by the late Rev. W. S. Symonds, F.G.S., of Pendock. [2454] In this instance flint flakes, and cores formed of chert were found in the cave-earth, with bones and teeth of the usual mammals, in one part of the cavern; while in another, beneath a thick layer of stalagmite, itself covered by what appeared to be a portion of an old river-bed, flint flakes were found associated with the same fauna. Mr. Symonds assigns these fluviatile deposits to an ancient river now represented by the Wye, which flows 300 feet below the level of the cave. If this view be correct, there can, as he observes, hardly be better authenticated evidence of the antiquity of man in the records of cave-history, than that afforded by this old river-bed overlying the thick stalagmite, beneath which the human relics were sealed up.

Since this book first appeared several important and interesting discoveries have been made in British Caves between Chesterfield and Worksop. Perhaps the most remarkable are those made in Creswell Crags on the north-eastern border of Derbyshire, by the Rev. J. Magens Mello, [2455] and Prof. Boyd Dawkins, F.R.S., [2456] who commenced their labours in the year 1875. The ossiferous deposits, in which also traces of man were found, lay both in fissures and in caves in the Lower Magnesian Limestone. Those which yielded the most important stone implements were the Robin Hood and the Church Hole Caves, though Mother Grundy's Parlour also contributed a few. In the Robin Hood Cave a stalagmitic breccia lay above the cave-earth. In this were found implements of quartzite and iron-stone, eighty-six in number, ruder than those of flint in the breccia. By the kindness of the Council of the Geological Society I am able to give a few representations of those of both classes. Fig. 413A shows an implement formed from a quartzite pebble worked at the point and side and of a distinctly Palæolithic type. It is much like the specimen from Saltley, Fig. 450B, and some made of similar material found in the neighbourhood of Toulouse.

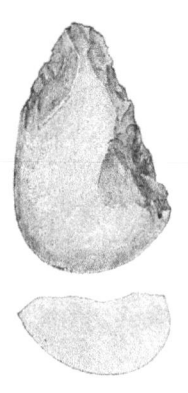

Fig. 413A.—Robin Hood Cave. 1/2

Fig. 413B is of iron-stone, and so far as form is concerned might well have been found in a bed of old River-drift. Some hammerstones and a side chopper of quartzite, in form like Fig. 443, were also found in the cave-earth. Some flint tools from the breccia are shown in the next three figures. Fig. 413C recalls one of the blades from Kent's Cavern, Fig. 390, though of smaller dimensions. Fig. 413D is almost identical with Fig. 399, while the borer, Fig. 413E, resembles those of the Neolithic Period. In all, there were found in the Robin Hood Cave no less than 1040 pieces of stone and bone showing traces of human workmanship. Among the bone objects were an awl and numerous pointed antler-tips, but the most remarkable is a smooth and rounded fragment of a rib having the head and forepart of a horse incised upon it. It is shown in Fig. 413F. In the Church Hole Cave 213 relics of human workmanship were found, principally flakes of flint, splinters, and quartzite stones. Two of the flakes, one of which is shown in Fig. 413G, are worn away on one edge only, as if the other edge had been protected by a wooden handle as suggested in the sketch.

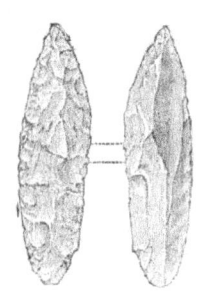

Fig. 413B.—Robin Hood Cave. 1/2

Fig. 413C.—Robin Hood Cave. 1/2

Fig. 413D.—Robin Hood Cave. 1/1

Fig. 413E.—Robin Hood Cave.

Among the bone objects was an oval plate notched at the sides and a bone needle, Fig. 413H. It is of larger size than is usual in caves of this period.

The fauna comprised cave-lion, hyæna, bear, Irish elk, woolly rhinoceros, and mammoth. A fine upper canine of *Machairodus* was also found. Most of the objects described are now in the British Museum. We have here another instance of quartzite implements of Palæolithic type, being found well to the north of the area in which drift-implements are usually discovered.

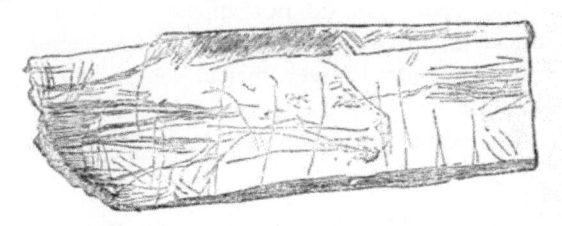

Fig. 413F. Robin Hood Cave. 1/1

The relics found in the Victoria Cave [2457] at Settle belong to a later period than that of which I am treating.

A cave at Ballynamintra, [2458] Co. Waterford, is Neolithic.

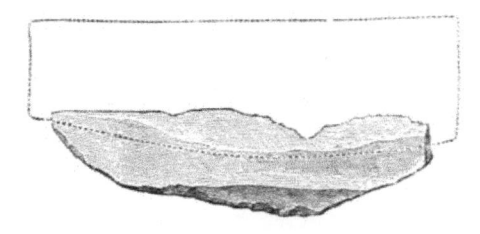

Fig. 413G.—Church Hole Cave. 1/1

The Mentone caves would open so large a field for discussion that I content myself with a passing reference to them.

Fig. 413H.—Church Hole Cave. 1/1

Were no other evidence forthcoming, the results of an examination of the British caves already described would justify us in concluding that in this country man co-existed with a number of the larger mammals now for the most part absolutely extinct, while others have long since disappeared from this portion of the globe. The association, under slightly differing circumstances, and in several distinct cases, of objects of human industry with the remains of this extinct fauna, in which so many of the animals characteristic of the existing fauna are "conspicuous by their absence," in undisturbed beds, and for the most part beneath a thick coating of stalagmite, leads of necessity to this conclusion. This becomes, if possible, more secure when the results of the exploration of other caves on the Continent of Western Europe are taken into account. How long a period may have intervened between the extinction, or migration, of these animals and the present time is, of course, another question; but such changes in the animal world as had already taken place at least three thousand years ago, do not appear to occur either suddenly or even with great rapidity; and, leaving the stalagmite out of consideration, we have already seen that in some instances the physical configuration of the country in the immediate neighbourhood of the caves seems to have been greatly changed since the period of their infilling.

These changes are perhaps more conclusively illustrated in the case of the old river deposits, in which the remains of the same extinct fauna as that of the caves occur associated with implements manufactured by the hand of man, to which we must now direct our attention.

CHAPTER XXIII.
IMPLEMENTS OF THE RIVER-DRIFT PERIOD.

In treating of the implements belonging to the Palæolithic Period, and found in the ancient freshwater or river drifts in Britain, I propose first to give a slight sketch of the nature of the discoveries which have been made in this particular field of archæology; then to furnish some details concerning the localities where implements have been found, and the character of the containing beds; next, to offer a few remarks on the shape and possible uses of the various forms of implements; and, finally, to consider the evidence of their antiquity.

So much has already been written in England, [2459] as well as on the Continent, as to the history of these most curious discoveries, that a very succinct account of them will here suffice. It was in the year 1847, that M. Boucher de Perthes, of Abbeville, called attention to the finding of flint instruments fashioned by the hand of man, in the pits worked for sand and gravel, in the neighbourhood of that town. They occurred in such positions, and at such a depth below the surface, as to force upon him the conclusion that they were of the same date as the containing beds, which he regarded as of diluvial origin, or as monuments of a universal Deluge. In 1855, Dr. Rigollot, [2460] of Amiens, also published an account of the discovery of flint implements at St. Acheul, near Amiens, in a drift enclosing the remains of extinct animals, and at a depth of 10 feet or more from the surface. From causes into which it is not necessary to enter, these discoveries were regarded with distrust in France, and were very far from being generally accepted by the geologists and antiquaries of that country.

In the autumn of 1858, however, that distinguished palæontologist, the late Dr. Hugh Falconer, F.R.S., visited Abbeville, [2461] in order to see M. Boucher de Perthes's collection, and became "satisfied that there was a great deal of fair presumptive evidence in favour of many of his speculations regarding the remote antiquity of these industrial objects, and their association with animals now extinct." Acting on Dr. Falconer's suggestion, the late Sir Joseph Prestwich, F.R.S., whose extensive and accurate researches had placed him in the first rank of English geologists, visited Abbeville and Amiens, in April, 1859; where I, on his invitation, had the good fortune to join him. We examined the local collections of flint implements and the beds in which they were said to have been found; and, in addition to being perfectly satisfied with the evidence adduced as to the nature of the discoveries, we had the crowning satisfaction of seeing one of the worked flints still *in situ*, in its undisturbed matrix of gravel, at a depth of 17 feet from the original surface of the ground.

I may add that on March 26th, 1875, I dug out from the gravel, in a pit close to the seminary at Saint Acheul, a pointed implement at a depth of 10 feet 10 inches from the surface.

From the day on which Sir Joseph Prestwich gave an account to the Royal Society, of the results of his visit to the Valley of the Somme, the authenticity of the discoveries of M. Boucher de Perthes and Dr. Rigollot was established; and they were almost immediately followed by numerous others of the same character, both in France and England.

Before proceeding to describe the discoveries made in this country, it will be well to say a few words as to some others of those which have been made on the continent of Europe. In France such discoveries have been so abundant that it would be an almost hopeless task to enumerate the whole of them, I must, therefore, content myself by calling attention to a few only; and, moreover, shall not overburden my pages with references. One of the earliest discoveries was made by M. Vincent at Troyes [2462] (Aube), where, in 1850, at a depth of 3 metres, he found an ovoid implement, but most of the recent finds date subsequently to 1859. Those made at Chelles [2463] (Seine et Marne) deserve especial mention, inasmuch as M. Gabriel de Mortillet, regarding the deposits at that place as being more of one and the same age than those at St. Acheul, has termed his oldest stage of the Palæolithic Period *Chelléen* rather than *Acheuléen*. He places the *Moustérien* next, but in some respects the subdivision is unsatisfactory. The *Elephas antiquus* occurs at Chelles, but at Tilloux [2464] (Charente) *E. meridionalis*, *E. antiquus*, and *E. primigenius* all occur together with well-marked palæolithic implements of usual types. At Paris itself, in the gravels of the valley of the Seine, numerous implements have been found, as well as lower down the valley at Sotteville, near Rouen. At Argues, [2465] near Dieppe, Saint Saen, and Bully, [2466] near Neufchâtel, they have also occurred. At Grand Morin [2467] (Seine et Marne) and Quiévy, [2468] (Nord), fine specimens have been found. At the Bois du Rocher, [2469] near Dinan, in the Côtes du Nord, numerous implements, mostly small and of fine-grained quartzite occur—I found eight there myself in 1876—and near Toulouse [2470] many larger and coarser examples chipped out of quartzite pebbles. I have also implements from Chelles made of a kind of quartzite. Of other localities in the north of France I may mention Guînes and Sangatte, near Calais; Montguillain and other spots near Beauvais; Thenay and Thézy, near Amiens, and Vaudricourt, near Béthune. In the district of the Loire I have found implements in the gravels of Marboué, near Châteaudun, and at Vendôme. Further south in Poitou they are abundant on the surface at Coussay-les-Bois and other places near Leugny. They have also been found in some abundance near Sens (Yonne), and occur in Dordogne, the Mâconnais and Champagne, the departments of Corrèze, Indre et Loire, Nièvre, and indeed over the greater part of France.

In Belgium several discoveries have been made, notably at Curange [2471] and Mesvin. [2472]

To the east, in Germany, [2473] Austria, [2474] Hungary, [2475] and Russia, [2476] such discoveries, though rare, seem to be not entirely unknown. Further evidence, however, is desirable.

In Italy [2477] various implements, presumed to be of Palæolithic age, have been found in the gravels of the Tiber, but they are nearly all rude flakes. One, however, of ovate form, has been found near Gabbiano, [2478] in the Abruzzo.

Other well-defined implements have been found near Perugia, [2479] in the Imolese, [2480] Ceppagna [2481] (Molise), and elsewhere.

In the gravels of the valley of the Manzanares, at San Isidro, near Madrid, palæolithic implements of the usual types have been found, as well as some of a wedge shape, unlike the ordinary European types, but similar to one of the Madras forms. They are associated with the remains of an elephant, probably *E. antiquus*. The Quaternary beds at San Isidro are nearly 200 feet above the level of the existing river, and the implements that they contain are varied in character, some chipped out of porphyry and other old rocks, being very rude in fabric, while others of flint are as dexterously made as any of the ordinary specimens from St. Acheul. The first discovery made there was by M. Louis Lartet. [2482] I have on several occasions visited the spot. Diagrammatic sections of the valley have been given by Prof. A. Gaudry [2483] and M. E. Cartailhac. [2484] Messrs. Siret [2485] mention several other localities in Spain that have yielded palæolithic implements.

In Portugal [2486] also, both in gravels and in caves, such implements have been found, and a good ovate specimen, made of quartz, from Leiria, near Lisbon, has been figured by [2487]Cartailhac.

In Greece some almond-shaped implements, of the true palæolithic type, are said to have been discovered in beds of sand near Megalopolis, [2488] with bones of the great pachyderms.

Returning to this country and to the year 1859, I may observe that it turned out on examination that more than one such discovery as those of Abbeville and Amiens had already been recorded, and that flint implements of similar types to the French had been found in the gravels of London at the close of the seventeenth century, and in the brick-earth of Hoxne, in Suffolk, at the close of the eighteenth, and were still preserved in the British Museum, and in that of the Society of Antiquaries.

During the thirty-eight years that have elapsed since renewed and careful attention was called to these implements, numerous other discoveries have taken place in various parts of England of instruments of analogous forms in beds of gravel, sand, and clay, for the most part on the slopes of our existing river valleys, though in some instances at considerable distances from any stream of water, and occasionally not thus embedded, but lying on the surface of the ground. Several of these discoveries have been made in localities where, from the nature of the deposits, it had already been suggested by the late Sir Joseph Prestwich and myself that implements would probably be found; and others have resulted from workmen, who had been trained to search for the implements in gravel, having migrated to new pits, where also their search has proved successful. In not a few instances the researches for such evidence of the antiquity of man have been carried on by fully qualified observers. It is, however, needless here to trace the causes and order of the discoveries, and I therefore propose to treat them in geographical, and not chronological, sequence. In so doing it will be most convenient to arrange them in accordance with the river systems in connection with which the gravels were deposited, wherein for the most part the implements have been found.

The district of which, following the order formerly adopted, it seems convenient first to treat, is the basin of the river Ouse and its tributaries, comprising, according to the Ordnance Survey, [2489] an area of 2,607 square miles. Beginning in the west of this district, I may mention the finding by Mr. Worthington G. Smith, F.L.S., of several implements near one of the sources of the Ouse, a little to the north of Leighton Buzzard. Through his kindness I possess a pointed, thick and deeply-stained implement, found at Bossington, about a mile north of Leighton. A more important scene of discoveries of this kind is the neighbourhood of Bedford, where the late Mr. James Wyatt, F.G.S., obtained specimens so early as April, 1861, since which time considerable numbers have been found. The pit in which they first occurred is one near Biddenham, in which I had, some few years before, discovered freshwater and land shells, [2490] and which I had, previously to Mr. Wyatt's discovery, already visited with him in the expectation of finding flint implements in the gravel. The other localities in the immediate neighbourhood of Bedford where palæolithic implements have been found, are Harrowden, [2491] Cardington, Kempston, Summerhouse Hill, and Honey Hill, all within a radius of four miles.

The Ouse near Bedford winds considerably in its course, which has in all probability much changed at different periods, the valley through which the river now passes being of great width. As instances of its changes even within historical times, it may be mentioned that the chapel in which Offa, [2492] King of Mercia, was interred, is said to have been washed away by the Ouse; and in the time of Richard II. [2493] its course was so much altered, near Harrold, that the river is recorded to have ceased flowing, and its channel to have remained dry, for three miles.

At Biddenham, the beds of Drift-gravel form a capping to a low hill about two miles in length, and about three quarters of a mile in width, which is nearly encircled by one of the windings of the river. Judging from the section given by Sir Joseph Prestwich, [2494] the highest point which the gravel attains is about 59 feet above the river, and its surface in the pit, where the implements are found, is 40 feet above it. The gravel rests upon the Cornbrash, or upper member of the Lower Oolite; but the valley itself, though partly in the limestone rock, has been cut through a considerable thickness of Oxford Clay and of Boulder Clay, which here overlies it. The gravel consists of subangular stones in an ochreous matrix, interspersed with irregular seams of sand and clay. [2495] It is principally composed of fragments of flint, local Oolitic *débris*, pebbles of quartz and of sandstones from the New Red Sandstone conglomerates, with fragments of various old rocks. All these latter have no doubt been derived from the washing away of the Boulder Clay or of other Glacial beds. The thickness of the gravel, in the pit where the implements have been principally found, is about 13 feet, and detailed sections of it have been given by Sir Joseph Prestwich and by Mr. Wyatt. Dispersed throughout, from a depth of about 5 feet from the surface down to the base, are to be found land and freshwater shells, mostly in fragments, but occasionally perfect. Their character has been determined by the late Mr. Gwyn Jeffreys,

F.R.S.; [2496] and they consist—including some specimens from Harrowden and Summerhouse Hill—of various species of *Sphærium*, or *Cyclas*, *Pisidium*, *Bythinia*, *Valvata*, *Hydrobia*, *Succinea*, *Helix*, *Pupa*, *Planorbis*, *Limnæa*, *Ancylus*, *Zua*, and *Unio*. Of these the *Hydrobia* (*marginata*) has never been found alive in this country.

Fig. 414.—Biddenham, Bedford. 1/1

Mammalian remains also occur in the gravel, principally towards its base. Including other localities in the neighbourhood of Bedford, besides those already mentioned, but where the gravel is of the same character, remains of the following animals have been found: [2497] *Ursus spelæus*, *Cervus tarandus*, *Cervus elaphus*, *Bos primigenius*, *Bison priscus*, *Hippopotamus major*, *Rhinoceros tichorhinus*, *Rhinoceros megarhinus*, *Elephas antiquus*, *Elephas primigenius*, *Equus*, and *Hyæna spelæa*.

Fig. 415.—Biddenham, Bedford. 1/1

I have already given in the *Archæologia* [2498] full-size figures of two of the implements from the Biddenham pit, which are here reproduced.

Fig. 416.—Biddenham, Bedford. 1/2

Fig. 417.—Biddenham, Bedford. 1/2

Fig. 414, though worked to a wedge-like point, is very massive, weighing something over 1 1/2 lb. The butt-end has been roughly chipped into form, and has some sharp projections left upon it, so that it can hardly have been intended to be simply held in the hand when used, but was either mounted in some manner, or else some means were adopted for protecting the hand against its asperities. I have already called attention to its resemblance to an implement from Kent's Cavern, Fig. 388A.

The second specimen, Fig. 415, still shows the natural crust of the flint at its truncated end, and is well adapted for being held in the hand when used.

Other specimens from the Biddenham Pit are engraved on the scale of one-half linear measure in Figs. 416 to 418.

The whole, with the exception of Fig. 417, were in the collection of the late Mr. Wyatt.

Fig. 416 is of ochreous cherty flint, symmetrically chipped, and showing a portion of the original crust of the flint at the base. Its angles are sharp, and not water-worn. In character it much resembles many of the implements from the valley of the Little Ouse, and from St. Acheul, near Amiens.

The original of Fig. 417 is in my own collection, having been kindly presented to me by Mr. Wyatt. As will be seen, it is remarkably thick at the butt, which is somewhat battered, almost as if the instrument had been used as a wedge. On a part of the butt is a portion of the white crust of the flint, which is somewhat striated, and suggestive of the block of flint from which the implement was fashioned having been derived from some Glacial deposit.

Fig. 418 represents a very curious form of implement made from a part of a sub-cylindrical nodule of flint, and chipped to a rounded point at one end, and truncated at the other, where the original fractured surface of the flint is left intact. The angles at the pointed end are but little worn.

Implements of various other forms and sizes have been found in the gravels near Bedford, but in character they so closely correspond with those found in other parts of England, and in France, that it seems needless to particularize them. One of them, however, in my own collection, 10 1/4 inches long by 4 1/4 inches wide, tongue-like in character, but of a long ovate shape, deserves special mention. It was found at Biddenham. The flat ovate, or oval type, is there of extremely rare occurrence.

Fig. 418.—Biddenham, Bedford. 1/2

I have numerous other specimens from the Bedford gravels, principally from Kempston, and others exist in various public and private collections. Like the mammalian remains, they occur for the most part towards the base of the gravel, but occasionally at higher levels in the beds. Besides the more highly wrought instruments, knife-like flakes of flint have been found, some of them presenting evidence of use upon their edges. A few flakes trimmed at the end into scraper-like form have also been discovered.

At Tempsford, some seven or eight miles below Bedford, the river Ouse is joined by the small river Ivel, a branch of which, the Hiz, rises from the Chalk escarpment near Hitchin, and joins the Ivel at Langford. About two miles south of the junction of these two streams, near Henlow, Bedfordshire, Mr. F. J. Bennett, of the Geological Survey, found in 1868 a flint implement of palæolithic type, not indeed in gravel, but lying on the surface. It is 4 inches long and 2 1/2 broad, and of the same general character as that from Icklingham, Fig. 420, but rather more acutely pointed at each end. It is ochreous on one face, and grey black on the other, and not improbably may have been derived from some gravelly bed. I remarked in 1872 that this discovery seemed to place the Ivel and Hiz among the rivers, in the valley-gravels of which, farther search would probably be rewarded.

Since then at Ickleford, [2499] near Hitchin, numerous implements, some of them much water-worn, have been found by Mr. Frank Latchmore and others in gravels lying in the valley of the Hiz. I have also an acutely-pointed specimen from Bearton Green, [2500] a little to the north of Hitchin, in an angle between the rivers Oughton and Hiz.

But the most important discoveries are those which have been made a short distance to the south of the town of Hitchin. There, near the summit of a hill cut off by valleys on three sides from higher land, a brickfield has been worked for some years by Mr. A. Ransom. Although attention was called to the discovery in 1877, [2501] the whole circumstances of the case are only now being thoroughly worked out. At that time the section exposed was about 20 feet in depth, of reddish brick-earth with numerous small angular fragments of flint throughout. In places there were seams in which flints were more abundant. With them were a few quartz and quartzite pebbles. Above one seam, about 9 feet from the surface, was a layer of carbonaceous matter. The implements, [2502] which are of various forms, both ovate, like Pl. II., No. 17–19, and pointed, like Pl. I., No. 5–7, are said to occur in the brick-earth, but not in the alluvial beds below. They are mostly ochreous, but some are white. I have a hammer-stone found with them which is made of an almost cylindrical portion of a nodule of flint about 4 1/4 inches long, truncated at each end; the edges round both ends are much battered. It was probably used in the manufacture of the other implements; a hammer of the same kind was found at Little Thurrock. [2503] In October, 1877, a well was sunk at the bottom of the pit showing—

	ft.	in.
(*a*) Red loam with a few quartz pebbles and flints, about	4	0
(*b*) White very sandy loam with freshwater shells about	5	6
(*c*) Dark greenish-brown loam with numerous shells and vegetable remains, among them *Bythinia*, *Planorbis* and *Limnæa*, also elytra of beetles, about	10	6
	20	0

Mammalian remains are reported to have been found in the argillaceous beds at Hitchin, [2504] including bear, elephant, and rhinoceros.

In Fig. 418A is shown a small shoe-shaped implement from the brick-earth at Hitchin, on which a considerable amount of the crust of the original nodule of flint from which it was made still remains.

At the Folly Pit, about half a mile south and at a lower level, a section was shown in 1877 of about 18 feet of Glacial Drift, with large rounded pebbles of different rocks, false-bedded sands, &c. On an eroded surface of sands and gravels of the Glacial Series was brick-earth extending in the direction of Mr. Ransom's pit. At one spot white marly sand-like beds, full of freshwater shells, were visible. The brick-earth at Hitchin, like that at Hoxne, seems to have been deposited in what were locally Post-Glacial times.

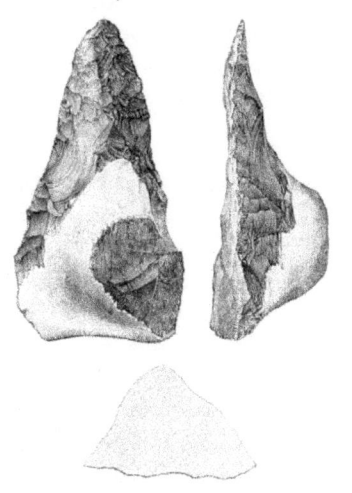

Fig. 418A.—Hitchin. 1/2

A detailed examination of the spot has recently been carried out by Mr. Clement Reid, F.G.S., who finds that the alluvial deposits beneath the palæolithic brick-earth fill a deep channel and contain a temperate flora, including such trees as the oak, ash, cornel, elder, and alder. Towards the margin of the channel, in at least one place, the Chalky Boulder Clay occurs beneath the ancient alluvial and palæolithic strata. The succession corresponds closely with that found at Hoxne. [2505]

At Biggleswade, farther down the valley of the Ivel, a few palæolithic implements have been procured from the railway ballast-pit.

Northwards of Hitchin a flint flake has been found in the gravel of the Ouse at Hartford, [2506] near Huntingdon, together with remains of *Elephas primigenius* and *Rhinoceros tichorhinus*. I have also a well-shaped ochreous pointed implement (5 inches) found at Abbot's Ripton, 3 1/2 miles north of Huntingdon, in 1896, as well as one like Fig. 457 (5 3/4 inches) from gravel at Chatteris, Cambs.

Proceeding eastward, the next important affluent of the Ouse which is met with, is the Cam, the gravels along the valley of which present in various places characters analogous with those near Bedford. Numerous mammalian remains of the same Quaternary fauna have been found along its course, especially at Barnwell and Chesterton, [2507] near Cambridge, where also land and freshwater shells occur in abundance. I have also found them in a pit near Littlebury, a few miles from Saffron Walden.

From Quendon, Essex, about 5 miles south of Saffron Walden, and in the valley of the Cam, Mr. C. K. Probert, of Newport, Bishop Stortford, obtained a magnificent sharp-pointed implement with the sides curved outwards, 8 inches in length. It lay in sandy drift in a pit about 12 feet deep.

In the publications of the Cambridge Antiquarian Society [2508] is a paper by the late Prof. Chas. C. Babington, F.R.S., "On a flint hammer found near Burwell." It is described as a pointed implement, very similar to those found at Hoxne and Amiens, as represented in Phil. Trans., 1860, Pl. XIV., 6 and 8. It was not found *in situ*, nor in gravel, but is said to have come from a mill used for cleaning coprolites, where it had been well washed with them. If it be the specimen that I have seen in the museum of the Cambridge Antiquarian Society, I fear it is a forgery. Another worked flint, also of rather uncertain origin, but perfectly genuine, and having all the characteristics of belonging to the River-drift, was found in 1862 on a heap of gravel, near Cambridge, by Mr. W. Whitaker, F.R.S., who kindly placed it in my collection. It is a thick polygonal flake, about 3 inches long and 1 inch broad at the base, tapering to the point, which is broken off. Its surface is stained all over of a deep ochreous colour, its angles are slightly water-worn, and the edges worn away, either by friction among other stones in the gravel, or by use. In the Woodwardian Museum is another flake, apparently of palæolithic date, which was found in gravel near the Cambridge Observatory. The Rev. Osmond Fisher, F.G.S., possesses an implement in form and character much like Fig. 470, from Highfield, Salisbury, which was found on a heap of gravel brought from Chesterton. Other discoveries have confirmed this evidence of the presence of palæolithic implements in the gravels of the valley of the Cam.

Mr. A. F. Griffith [2509] in 1878 described a fine implement from the Barnwell gravels (6 3/4 inches) in form and size almost identical with Fig. 414. Others have been found in gravel from the Observatory Hill, Cambridge, and from Chesterton. Another tongue-shaped implement from the plateau near Upper Hare Park, [2510] Cambridge, has been found by Mr. M. C. Hughes.

I may add that in the gravel at Barnwell, at a depth of 12 feet, and associated with remains of elephant, rhinoceros, and hippopotamus, was found in 1862, a portion of a rib-bone like that of an elephant, showing at one end "numerous cut surfaces, evidently made with some sharp instrument used by a powerful hand." I have not seen the specimen, but Mr. H. Seeley, F.R.S., [2511] who records the fact, has "no doubt that the whittling is as old as the bone." The *Corbicula fluminalis*, *Hydrobia marginata*, and *Unio rhomboideus* are among the shells which are found in the River-drift of Barnwell, but are no longer living in England.

I have a number of implements, principally of ovate form, which are said to have been found in the neighbourhood of Bottisham, but I am not sure as to the exact locality. I believe them to have come from gravel-pits about a mile to the north of Six Mile Bottom Station.

In gravel at Kennett Station, [2512] about 5 miles north-east by east of Newmarket, but still in Cambridgeshire, several specimens have been found by Mr. Arthur G. Wright and others.

I have a much-worn flat ovate specimen from Herringswell, three miles to the north of Kentford Station.

Implements occur, though rarely, at the base of the peat in the Fen country, below Cambridge. I have a small ovate specimen (3 1/4 inches) from Swaffham Fen. It is of black flint with the surface eroded as if a portion of its substance had been dissolved away. A much larger implement (6 inches) from Soham Fen is also black, but its surface is uninjured.

The valley of the Lark, the next river which empties itself into the Ouse, has been much more prolific of implements in its gravels, than that of the Cam. The fact of their occurrence in this valley was first observed by myself, in 1860, in consequence of my finding among the stone antiquities in the collection of a local antiquary—the late Mr. Joseph Warren, of Ixworth—two specimens, which I at once recognized as being of palæolithic types. On inquiry, it appeared that one had been found by a workman in digging gravel at Rampart Hill, Icklingham; and the other by Mr. Warren himself on a heap of gravel by the roadside, which had been dug in the same neighbourhood. The late Sir Joseph Prestwich [2513] and I at once visited Icklingham, and though our search was at the time unsuccessful, yet the instructions given to the workmen soon resulted in their finding numerous implements. The examination of the gravel was at the same time taken up by the late Mr. Henry Prigg (subsequently Trigg), of Bury St. Edmunds, to whose discrimination and energy the discovery of implements in various other localities in Suffolk is due.

He brought together a large collection of antiquities, of which the greater part, after his decease, came into my hands.

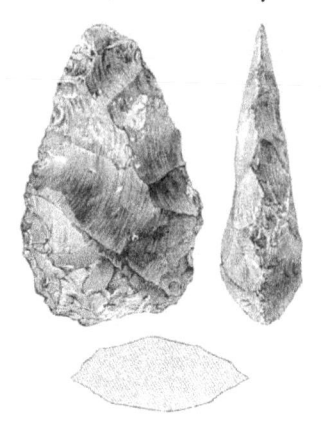

Fig. 419.—Maynewater Lane, Bury St. Edmunds. 1/2

The principal places in the valley of the Lark, where palæolithic implements have been found, are in the neighbourhood of Bury St. Edmunds, Icklingham, and Mildenhall. The first specimen from the River-drift at Bury St. Edmunds was obtained by Mr. Trigg in gravel at a low level, near the ruined Gatehouse of St Saviour's Hospital, in October, 1862; [2514] since which time numerous other specimens have been discovered, principally through his agency. Several were found in the excavations made for the drainage of the southern part of the town in 1864—one elongated oval implement having been discovered in Botolph's Lane; and three others, varying in form, in Maynewater Lane, where also a flake was found. That here engraved as Fig. 419 is from this latter locality, and was found at a depth of 14 feet in a bed of loamy, sub-angular gravel, underlying a deposit of fine grey loam 6 feet thick, containing scales of fish, and abundant remains of *Anodonta* and *Bythinia*. It is now deposited in the Blackmore Museum at Salisbury. Its edges are sharp and unworn, and its colour black, with ochreous spots. Others, since discovered, are of even finer workmanship. One in my collection is a much ruder specimen, though of nearly similar general form, which was found in the South Gate in 1869. Several have been found in Westgate and St. Andrew's Streets, and in Newton Road. The greatest number of implements found at Bury have, however, come from what is known as the Grindle Pit, a short distance to the south-east of the town, and on the summit and western slope of a tongue of land between the Linnet and the Lark. Some of them occurred in a dark, stiff, rather argillaceous gravel, composed mainly of sub-angular flints, but also containing a small proportion of the pebbles of the older rocks, derived from Glacial deposits. This gravel is from 2 to 3 feet in thickness, and underlies a stratum of red brick-earth from 2 to 6 feet thick, which is again, in places, surmounted by sands and clay with angular flints about 4 feet in thickness, on which the surface soil reposes. This was the section exhibited in 1865, but the beds are very irregular, and the character of the section exposed in the pit varies considerably from time to time, as material is removed. In places the Drift-beds are faulted, as if by the giving way of the subjacent beds.

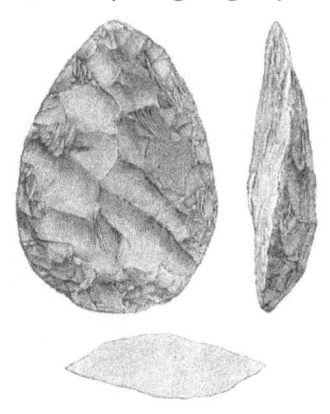

Fig. 419A.—Grindle Pit, Bury St. Edmunds. 1/2

A beautiful and absolutely perfect specimen from this pit is shown in Fig. 419A. It was found in a black vein in the lower loamy bed, on February 4th, 1870. Though the implement has been most skilfully chipped, the edge is not in one plane, but when looked at sideways, shows an ogival curve. The regular contour is partly due to secondary working, but the edge is as sharp as on the day when the instrument was made. Several others of almost the same form, though not quite so delicately fashioned, came from the same pit, and may have been made by the same hands.

I have a fine pointed implement, (5 1/2 inches), also from the Grindle Pit. Another, ovate, is 7 inches in length.

A remarkably fine palæolithic flake from Thingoe Hill, [2515] Bury St. Edmunds, is shown in Fig. 419B. It is water-worn, and much resembles some from the low-level gravels at Montiers, near Amiens, and Montguillain, near Beauvais. It belongs, of course, to a much earlier period than the mound in, on, or near which it was found.

As already observed, remains of shells, and some scales of fish, were found in the Drift-beds during the drainage works, as also some mammalian remains. They were, however, scarce. Higher up the valley by about three miles, there have been found in a pit at Sicklesmere, remains of *Rhinoceros tichorhinus* and *Elephas primigenius*; and, in another pit, elephant remains; specimens of all of which are now preserved in the Bury Museum. Mr. Trigg obtained several well-wrought implements from the brick-earth of Sicklesmere, near Nowton, which there overlies the Boulder Clay; and has also found examples in the gravels of the valley of the Kent, another small affluent of the Ouse.

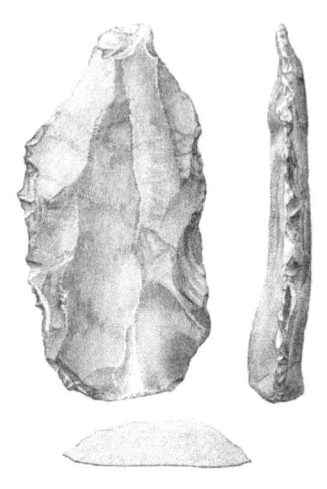

Fig. 419B.—Bury St. Edmunds. 1/2

One of these Nowton specimens is shown in Fig. 419C. It is broad and kite-shaped in form and has weathered to a creamy white. In type it approaches Fig. 435, from Santon Downham. Some remarkably fine implements, principally ovate, have been found at Westley, about two miles west of Bury, and at Fornham All Saints, two miles to the north; and I have a pointed one from the Beeches Pit, West Stow, five miles to the north-west, and nearer Icklingham. It was in one of the pits at Westley, eroded in the old chalk surface and filled with loam, that Mr. Trigg discovered portions of a human skull which he described to the Anthropological Institute. [2516] In other pits at the same spot were molars of *Elephas primigenius*, and the chopper-like instrument shown in Fig. 419D.

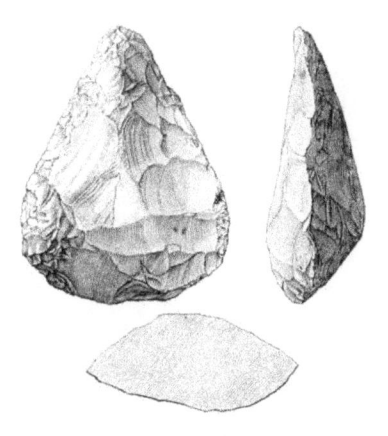

Fig. 419C.—Nowton, near Bury St. Edmunds. 1/2

In the valley of the Lark, about seven miles down from Bury, lies the village of Icklingham, in the neighbourhood of which numerous remains belonging to the Roman and Saxon Periods have been found, but where also relics belonging to both the Neolithic and Palæolithic Periods abound. Many of the latter have been discovered in the gravel of Rampart Hill, about a mile to the south-east of Icklingham, and nearer to Bury; but still more numerous specimens have now for many years also been found in the gravel at Warren Hill—sometimes termed the Three Hills—about two miles on the other side of Icklingham, and midway between that place and Mildenhall. A section across the valley of the Lark, near Icklingham, has been given by Sir Joseph Prestwich. [2517] The valley, which is excavated in the chalk, is in its lower part covered by recent alluvial deposits, but on the slopes of its northern side, the chalk is covered with sands and gravels belonging to the Glacial Series, which are again overlain by the Boulder Clay. The gravel both at Rampart Hill and Warren Hill is of a different character from that belonging to the Glacial Series, though of course containing a number of the silicious pebbles from the conglomerate beds of the New Red Sandstone, and other pebbles of the older rocks derived from the Glacial Drift. It is for the most part composed of sub-angular flints in an ochreous sandy matrix, and is spread out in irregular beds interstratified with seams of sand. At Warren Hill there are great numbers of quartzite pebbles, as well as very many formed from rolled chalk, mixed with the other constituents. These are less abundant in the upper part of the deposit, which is there of considerable thickness. I am not aware of the exact levels having been taken at either place, but the surface of the ground is probably from 40 to 50 feet above the level of the river. The gravel beds are in places as much as 14 or 15 feet in thickness. Mammalian remains are scarce, but teeth and portions of tusk of *Elephas primigenius* have been found at Rampart Hill, and the core of the horn of an ox, and teeth of horse, and bones and teeth of elephant, at Warren Hill.

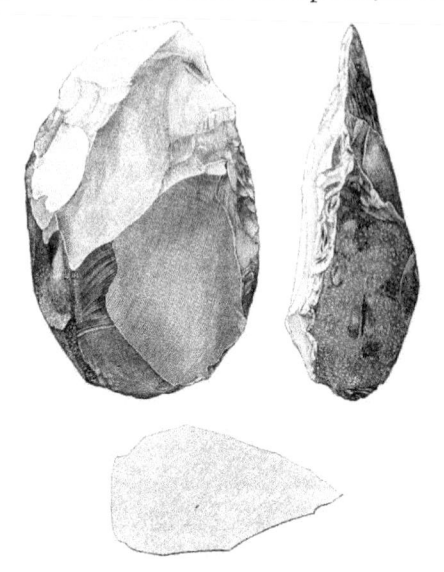

Fig. 419D.—Westley, near Bury St. Edmunds. 1/2

Up to the present time the search for remains of testacea in these beds has proved unsuccessful.

Not only have the worked flints been discovered in considerable numbers, but Canon Greenwell, F.R.S., has found in the gravel at Warren Hill, several quartzite pebbles bearing evident marks of abrasion and bruising at the ends, such as may have resulted from their having been in use as hammer-stones, either for chipping out the flint implements or for other purposes. He also obtained an ovate lanceolate implement from this spot, 4 3/4 inches in length, and formed from a quartzite pebble, the original surface of which is still preserved over nearly the whole extent of one of the faces.

Examples of the Icklingham implements are given in Figs. 420 to 424.

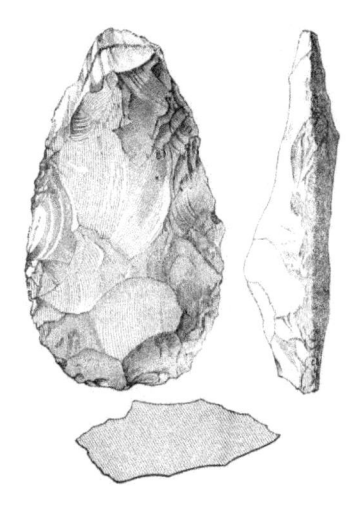

Fig. 420.—Rampart Hill, Icklingham. 1/2

The finer of the two, of which mention has already been made as having formed part of the collection of the late Mr. Warren, of Ixworth, is now in my own, and is shown in Fig. 420. It is more convex on one face than the other, and a portion of the butt presents an almost scraper-like appearance. The angles formed by the facets are slightly worn, and the surface of the flint has been much altered in character, having become nearly white, and quite lustrous. This alteration in structure is almost universal with the Icklingham implements, though in many cases they are ochreous instead of white, and not unfrequently the discoloration is only partial, giving them a dappled appearance. In many specimens the angles are much water-worn.

The original of Fig. 421 is in the Blackmore Museum, and is of dark brown lustrous flint, almost equally convex on both faces, and of very regular elliptical form. In most cases the outline approximates more to that of Fig. 467. These thin, flattened, oval, and almond-shaped, or ovate, implements seem, as Mr. Trigg has pointed out, to predominate at Icklingham. Those of oval form are especially abundant at Warren Hill.

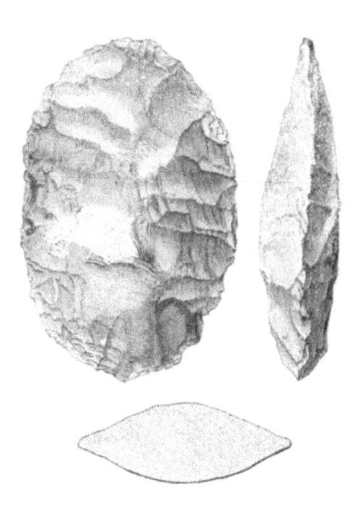

Fig. 421.—Icklingham. 1/2

Many of ruder character, however, also occur, one of which, in my own collection, is shown in Fig. 422. It approaches more nearly in form to some of the roughly chipped instruments of the Surface period, such as Fig. 16, than do most of the implements from the River-drift.

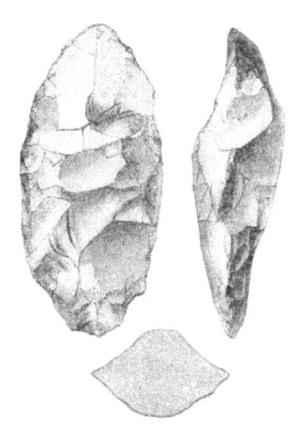

Fig. 422.—Icklingham. 1/2

One of the finest specimens hitherto found in this country is that shown in Fig. 423, from the original in the Blackmore Museum. It is of dark ochreous flint, with the surface considerably decomposed, and the angles but little worn. In the same collection is another Icklingham specimen, in form like that from Thetford, Fig. 427, but 9 inches long and 4 1/2 wide.

Besides the more finished implements, a few flakes occur in the Icklingham gravels. Some of these have been chipped all round the periphery by blows administered on the flat face, thus producing a bevelled edge. One such, from Warren Hill, in my own collection, somewhat resembles the implement from Reculver, Fig. 461. It is, however, narrower in its proportions, being 4 1/2 inches long and 2 3/8 broad. It has been formed from an external flake, and has been carefully trimmed all round into an almost perfect oval form, the butt alone having been left untrimmed for about half-an-inch in width. A small part of the other rounded and scraper-like end has been broken off in ancient times. Others are wider in their proportions though not so symmetrically worked. The trimmed flake, shown in Fig. 424, is in my own collection, and at its rounded end is very scraper-like in character. A very large flake, rounded into a broad scraper, and about 5 inches in diameter, was found by myself at Warren Hill, and is now in the Christy Collection.

Fig. 423.—Icklingham.

Three-quarters of a mile to the north of the Warren Hill pits, and on the same ridge, but at a rather higher level, is High or Warren Lodge, distant about two miles from Mildenhall. To the south of this house, and by the side of the Thetford road, is a small pit on the slope of the hill, where, in the process of digging clay for brick-making, a considerable number of worked flints have been obtained, many of which passed into the collection formed by Canon Greenwell, who has furnished me with particulars of the discovery. I have also visited the spot. The clay or brick-earth is of a reddish hue, and rests upon a chalky Boulder Clay, which is exposed farther up the hill. It ranges in thickness from about 4 to 6 feet; and above it are sands and gravel, the latter varying in thickness from about 2 to 6 feet, and of much the same character as that of the Warren Hill pits, but containing far less chalk. The sand occasionally comes down in pipes or pockets into the clay, and some of the worked flints occur in it, as well as in the clay. Many of these are merely roughly-chipped splinters, but several well-wrought forms have also been found.

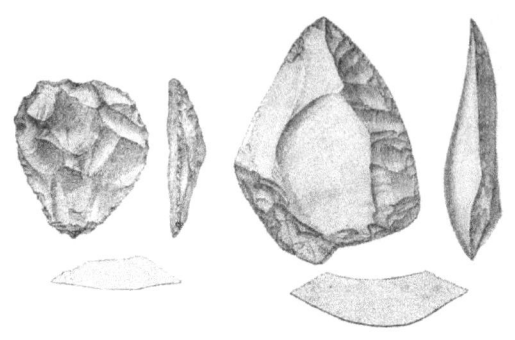

Fig. 424.—Icklingham. 1/2

Fig. 425.—High Lodge. 1/2

Among them is an oval implement of a common River-drift type, 4 1/2 inches long, which, with three or four others of the same kind, was found in the upper sands and gravel. From the clay itself are several large side-scrapers, or choppers, made from broad flakes, 4 or 5 inches long, and in form similar to the specimen from Santon Downham, Fig. 437, and of the same character as the implements from the cave of Le Moustier. [2518] Besides these, there are several other large flakes worked along the edge into side-scrapers, and presenting a Le Moustier form. [2519] Another is like that from Thetford, Fig. 431, and worked along both edges. Even external flakes have been utilized; one of these, 4 inches long, having been neatly worked at one end into a segmental edge. Another large implement, 5 1/2 inches long and 3 inches broad, is ovate-lanceolate in form, flat on one face, and worked to a sharp edge all round. Several others have been found of the same type. I have a considerable number from the Trigg collection.

One of the most beautifully formed of these implements from High Lodge Hill is shown in Fig. 425. It has been made from a broad, flat truncated flake, with a well-marked cone of percussion. The two sides have been carefully trimmed to a curved edge, by secondary chipping, and the edge itself has been finished by a subsequent process of finer chipping. The angles where the truncated chisel-like end joins the sides have also been retouched, but a portion of the sharp edge is left in its original condition. The edge formed by the outer face of the flake with its flat butt-end has also been re-chipped, and in one place appears to have been bruised by an unskilful blow. The workmanship generally is of a finer and neater character than is usual on the implements found in the river gravels. In form and character this instrument is remarkably similar to some of those found in the cave of Le Moustier in the Dordogne.

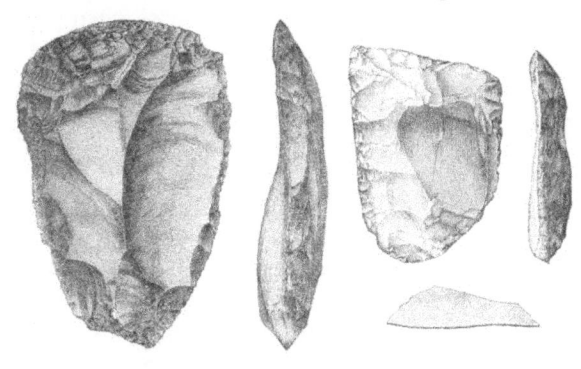

Fig. 426.—High Lodge. 1/1

Fig. 426A.—High Lodge. 1/2

Others, again, resemble the scrapers from the surface and the caves. One of these is engraved full size in Fig. 426. The edge is more acute than usual with scrapers, perhaps in consequence of the curvature of the inner face of the flake from which it was made.

Another example with a straight terminal edge at an angle of 80° to the side is shown on the scale of one half in Fig. 426A.

The flint of the High Lodge implements is but little altered in character, but has either remained black or has been stained of a deep brown; the angles and edges being still as sharp as the day when they were formed. In this respect they resemble the worked flints from the brick-earth of Hoxne. Those from the brick-earth of the valley of the Somme are usually quite white and porcellanous.

I have seen fragments of a molar of *Elephas*, probably *primigenius*, from the clay at this spot, and also a bone of a ruminant, probably *Cervus megaceros*.

As will subsequently be seen, there appears some reason for believing that at a remote period, the River Lark took a northerly, instead of a north-westerly, course from the neighbourhood of Mildenhall, and thus joined the Little Ouse instead of the Ouse itself;

so that this pit may possibly be connected with the old channel of the stream. On the slope of the hill to the east of Eriswell is gravel of much the same character as that at Warren Hill, but in which as yet few implements have been found. I have, however, one of ovate form from Holywell Row, near Eriswell, and another, not unlike Fig. 471, from the surface at Cardwell, about three miles farther north. To the east of Lakenheath, still farther to the north, is an isolated hill, near Maid's Cross, capped with gravel, in which flint implements have been found. It will be best to describe this spot when treating of the discoveries that have been made in the valley of the Little Ouse.

The source of this stream and that of the Waveney may be regarded as one, inasmuch as both take their rise in a fen crossed by the road at Lopham Ford; the one river running east, and the other west, of the road. By the time it reaches Thetford, however, a distance of about 12 miles, the Little Ouse has been joined by the Ixworth stream and the Thet, so that the area of ground drained by it is considerably more than would at first sight appear probable, being upwards of 200 square miles. With the exception of a broad flint flake, found by Mr. Trigg at Santon Downham, [2520] the first discovery of flint implements in the gravels of the Little Ouse was made in 1865 at Redhill, near Thetford, by a labourer from Icklingham, who had been trained to search for implements in the gravel pits in his own parish. These specimens he brought to Mr. Trigg, who subsequently obtained others at Whitehill, farther down the valley on the same—or Norfolk—side of the river; and on my visiting the spot with him in December, 1865, Mr. Trigg found in my presence a well-formed pointed implement in some gravel at Santon Downham, on the opposite—or Suffolk—side. Since then the discoveries have extended farther down the valley, and numerous implements have been found at several localities in the neighbourhood of Brandon, and at Shrub Hill, in the parish of Feltwell, Norfolk.

In June, 1866, [2521] the late Mr. J. W. Flower, F.G.S., who had long carried on investigations in the district, communicated a paper to the Geological Society on the subject of the discoveries at Thetford, and again in April, 1869, [2522] a second paper on the discoveries of flint implements in Norfolk and Suffolk, with some observations on the theories accounting for their distribution, on which I shall have to make some comments hereafter.

The highest point up the valley of the Little Ouse at which, up to the present time, flint implements have been discovered in the gravel on its slopes, is Redhill, on the Norfolk side of the river, about a mile north-west of Thetford. The gravel at this place is coarse in character, and consists principally of sub-angular flints, some of large size, mixed with a few pebbles derived from beds of the Glacial series, and deposited in a red sandy matrix. It forms a terrace running nearly parallel with the present stream, and ranging from about 12 feet to nearly 40 feet above its level. In places, the gravel is from 12 to 16 feet in thickness, [2523] the largest stones, as usual, occurring towards its base, in which part of the gravel the greater number, but by no means all, of the flint implements occur, as some are dispersed throughout the whole thickness of the mass. Occasionally they have been found in pipes of gravel, let down into the chalk by means of water charged with carbonic acid eroding its upper surface. Sandy seams [2524] are, as usual, interbedded with the gravel; and in one of these, about 10 feet below the surface, I found shells of *Helix, Bythinia, Cyclas, Pisidium, Ancylus,* and *Succinea*. Of mammalian remains, those of *Elephas primigenius,* ox, horse, and stag have occurred.

A very large number of implements have been found in the gravel at Redhill, of which specimens exist in the Christy Collection, the Blackmore Museum, and in numerous private collections. [2525] Those selected for engraving here, are all in my own possession.

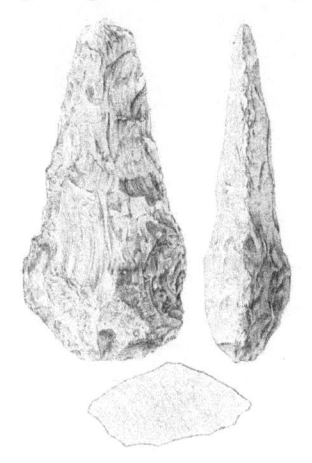

Fig. 427.—Redhill, Thetford. 1/2

Fig. 427 shows a remarkably fine specimen, stained all over of a deep ochreous red, though slightly mottled, owing to the original structure of the flint from which it was chipped. The angles are to a small extent waterworn. On what is in the figure the left side of the base, a portion of the original crust of the flint has been left, so as to form a protuberance at that part, instead of the edge being continued all round the instrument. This protuberance is well adapted to fit into the hand, like that of the Picts' knife, described at page 345, so that this may have been a cutting tool intended to be grasped. I have another specimen of nearly the same size, and with the same protuberance, from Santon Downham, and one of the implements from Southampton presents the same feature, which, indeed, is not unusual. A flat surface is frequently left on the sides of the ovate implements in or about the same position. This flat space has been referred to by the late Mr. Flower, [2526] who considered it intended to receive the thumb of the right hand, and not to go against the palm or the fore-finger, as suggested by myself long ago. [2527]

Fig. 428.—Redhill, Thetford. 1/2

Fig. 428 represents another singularly fine specimen of a very uncommon form, it being much more acutely pointed than usual. It is stained all over of a deep ochreous colour, and its angles are still sharp. It has been boldly but symmetrically chipped, and has a thick, heavy butt, well adapted for being held in the hand. As is the case with almost all these implements, an analogous form has been found in the gravels of the valley of the Somme. The magnificent implement from the gravel of Vaudricourt, near Béthune, which was exhibited at Paris in 1867, was also much of this type. Its length is 10 1/4 inches; that of the Thetford specimen being 8 1/2 inches. It would be an endless task to attempt to engrave all the varieties of form found at this place, but Mr. Trigg is correct in his remark as to the comparative absence of the flat oval form with a cutting edge all round. The most common type here is the ovate-lanceolate, like Pl. I., Fig. 5, rather thick towards the butt-end. Mr. Flower has figured a fine lanceolate specimen, and one of more ovate form from this place. [2528]

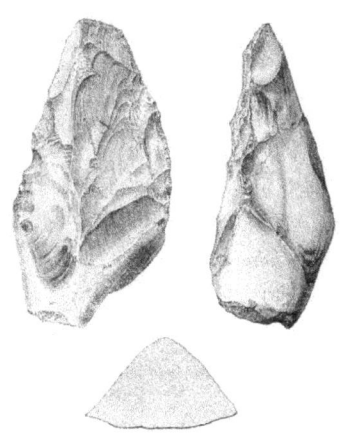

Fig. 429.—Redhill, Thetford. 1/2

The finely-wrought symmetrical specimens are rarer at Redhill than at Santon Downham; but here, as elsewhere in this district, implements are occasionally found of what has been aptly termed the shoe-shaped type, of which an example is shown in Fig. 429. The form is flat on one face, the other being brought to a central ridge rising towards the butt, which is usually rounded and obtusely truncated. In this specimen the greater part of the butt-end or heel of the shoe exhibits the original crust of the nodule of flint from which the implement was formed. The point, which is usually brought to a semicircular sharp edge, has been broken in old times either by use or by attrition in the gravel. Most of these shoe-shaped instruments have been formed from large spalls of flint, so that the flat face has been the result of a single blow, though occasionally retouched by subsequent chipping.

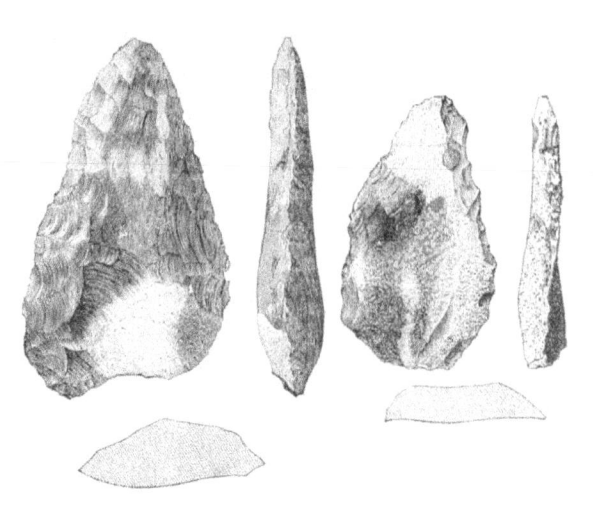

Fig. 430.—Redhill, Thetford. 1/2

Fig. 431.—Redhill, Thetford. 1/2

The implement shown in Fig. 430 is of this character, but is too thin, in proportion to its size, to represent the typical shoe-shape. It has been formed from a large external flake, the bulb of percussion being at the lower left-hand corner of the figure, but on the opposite face to that shown. The flake has been trimmed into shape by chipping along the edges on both faces, so that not above half of the original inner face remains free from secondary working. The surface is, as usual, stained of a rich ochreous brown.

A considerable number of flint flakes of various sizes and shapes have been found at Redhill, many of them showing signs of use and wear on their edges, and some being worked to a quadrant of a circle or more, at the point, so as to make them almost assume the form of scrapers. I have one external flake in which is worked a curved recess, as if by scraping some hard cylindrical object, such as a round bone. The flake engraved as Fig. 431 was found by myself in December, 1865, and has had both its edges retouched by secondary chipping. The edge thus produced seems to have been worn away by use. I have a rather larger flake, presenting precisely the same characteristics, from the valley gravel of the Somme, at Porte Marcadé, Abbeville.

A little lower down the river, and on the same side as Redhill, is the spot to which the name of Whitehall has been given by Mr. Trigg. The gravel is composed of similar materials to that at Redhill, of which it may be said to form a continuation, except that the matrix is whiter. Mr. Trigg has informed me that beneath the gravel are beds of red sand, and that at one time, a section was exposed of 26 feet in depth. Of late, the gravel at this spot has been but little worked, and but few implements have been found in it.

Mr. Trigg [2529] records having obtained three flint implements from this place, one of which, at present in the Blackmore Museum at Salisbury, is engraved as Fig. 432. Its surface has become white and decomposed, and is partially covered by an incrustation of carbonate of lime. A part of the edge, towards the point, on the right side of the figure, appears to be worn away by use.

Fig. 432.—Whitehill, Thetford. 1/2

Remains of *Elephas primigenius* and horse have been found here, but no land or freshwater shells.

Between Whitehill and Santon Downham, but on the Suffolk slope of the valley, a considerable quantity of gravel has been dug on Thetford Warren. Though the gravel is of much the same character as at Redhill, no implements appear to have been found in it.

About three miles north-west of Thetford, and also on the Suffolk side of the Little Ouse, is Santon Downham Warren, on the slope of which towards the river, is a considerable expanse of gravelly beds, which have been largely excavated for road-making purposes. On the sketch map given by Mr. Flower, [2530] this place is erroneously called Whitehill. As has been already stated, the first implement from this spot was discovered by Mr. Trigg, when in my company, in 1865. Since that time, it has produced, at a moderate estimate, several hundred specimens, some of them affording the finest instances of the skill of the Palæolithic Period which have been found in Britain, or indeed elsewhere. The gravel is at a somewhat higher level above the river than that at Redhill, but resembles it in character. It contains, besides flints, a few of the quartzite pebbles of the New Red conglomerate, which have been derived from the Glacial beds and Boulder Clay which cap the chalk hills on either side of the river. The gravel is of considerable thickness, so much so that in places, caves of sufficient magnitude to allow of a man standing inside, have been formed within it, in consequence of the lower beds being let down into the chalk, through its erosion by water charged with carbonic acid. The same phenomenon has been observed at Bromehill, the spot next to be mentioned; and some connection was at one time supposed to exist between these cavities and the implements often found in and near them. I think, however, that the explanation [2531] that I have elsewhere given of their origin will be deemed satisfactory. No testaceous remains have been found here, and mammalian remains are very scarce.

Among the implements from Santon Downham, the almond-shaped [2532] type seems to predominate, though other forms are also found.

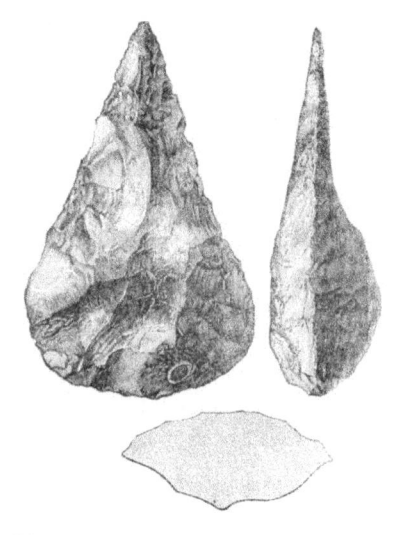

Fig. 433.—Santon Downham. 1/2

A very elegant pointed specimen, in my own collection, is shown in Fig. 433. It is chipped with great skill, and brought to a fine point, the butt-end being comparatively blunt, so that it may have been used in the hand without being in any way hafted. At the shoulder, shown in the side-view, a part of the original crust of the flint is left, and small portions are also left on the other face. In form, this implement curiously resembles some of those from Hoxne, and that from Gray's Inn Lane (Fig. 451). Like many of the implements from the gravel, it is cracked in various directions, apparently from inward expansion, and would break up into fragments with a slight blow. A very sharp point, such as that presented by this specimen, is not uncommonly met with in implements found at Santon Downham.

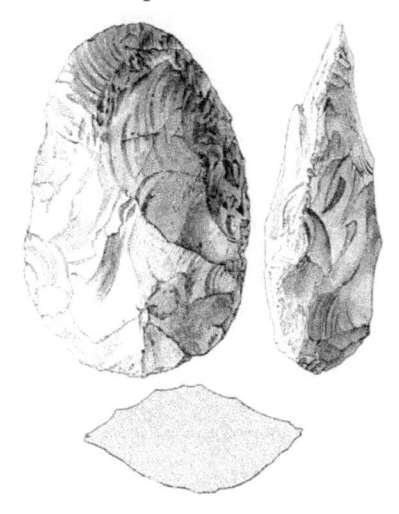

Fig. 434.—Santon Downham. 1/2

The original of Fig. 434 is also in my own collection, and is cracked in a similar manner. It is uniformly stained of a light buff colour, as are many of the implements from this spot, and has dendritic markings upon it, and in places, particles of ferruginous sand adhering to the surface. It is fairly symmetrical in contour, with an edge all round, which is somewhat blunted at what is the base in the figure. This edge, however, is not in one plane, but considerably curved, so that when seen sideways it forms an ogee sweep, even more distinctly than appears from the figure. I have other implements of the same and of more pointed forms, with similarly curved edges, both from France, and other parts of England, but whether this curvature was intentional, it is impossible to say. In some cases it is so marked that it can hardly be the result of accident, and the curve is so far as I have observed, almost without exception ℇ, and not S. If not intentional, the form may be the result of all the blows by which the implement was finally chipped out, having been given on the one face, on one side, and on the opposite face on the other.

Fig. 435 represents an implement of porcellanous, slightly ochreous flint, found at that place, and now in the Fitch collection at Norwich. The late Mr. Robert Fitch, F.S.A., kindly allowed me to engrave it, as well as the specimen next to be described. Implements of this broad, ovate-lanceolate form are extremely uncommon, and this is a remarkably symmetrical specimen, of good workmanship, and almost equally convex on the two faces. A few implements, almost circular in outline, have been found at this spot.

Another specimen from Nowton, Fig. 419C, shows almost the same form. In the Toulouse Museum is an implement (5 inches) in flint from Clermont, about 18 miles south of that town, found with remains of mammoth and reindeer.

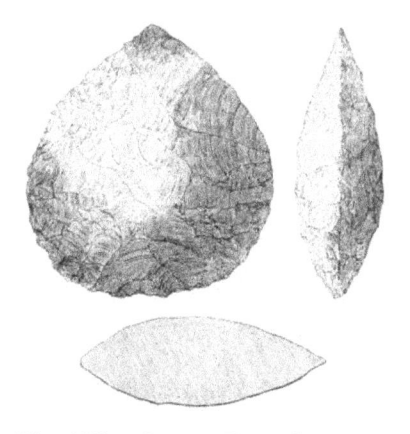

Fig. 435.—Santon Downham. 1/2

The original of Fig. 436 presents an example of another rare form, almost crescent-like in character. There is frequently a slight want of symmetry between the two sides of the ordinary ovate implements, which gives them a tendency to assume this form, but I have never seen it so fully developed as in some of the implements from Santon Downham.

Another somewhat uncommon form is shown in Fig. 437, the original of which, with several others, was presented to the Christy Collection by the late Rev. W. W. Poley. It has been formed from a large broad flake, the flat face of which is not shown in the figure, and has been chipped to a bevelled segmental edge, so that it assumes the form of a 'broad' or 'side' scraper, resembling in character some of the implements from the cave of Le Moustier in the Dordogne.

In the Greenwell Collection is a thick flake from Santon Downham, 4 1/4 inches long and 2 1/4 inches wide, trimmed at the butt-end to a semicircular scraper-like edge.

Viewed as a whole, the implements from Santon Downham present a higher degree of finish, and a greater skill in chipping the required forms out of flint, than those found in the gravels of any other part of the valley of the Little Ouse, or, it may perhaps be added, of England or France.

Following the course of the river, the next spot at which flint implements have been found in the gravel, is a pit known as the Bromehill or Broomhill Pit, in the parish of Weeting, and on the Norfolk side of the Little Ouse, about a mile and a quarter east of Brandon. The gravel here is at a lower level than that at Santon Downham, or even Redhill, its base not being more than six or eight feet above the river, to which it is close.

Fig. 436.—Santon Downham. 1/2

The late Mr. Flower [2533] has described the spot, but his description of the section, and of the position in which the implements are found, does not completely coincide with mine. On the occasion of one of my visits to this pit, in July, [2534] 1868, in company with him, the section exposed was 24 feet in height, from the chalk at its base to the superficial soil at the summit. The upper part of the section showed sand, with a few gravelly seams, and from 8 to 10 feet in thickness; at the base of this, a dark ferruginous band, a few inches in thickness; then some 8 or 9 feet of ochreous gravel, with a red sandy matrix, which was separated by a band of grey sand from the lower beds of gravel, which contained a very large percentage of rolled chalk and seams of chalky sand. Below the chalky gravel, ferruginous beds also sometimes occur, containing large blocks of flint. In the chalky gravel (the base of which is but a few feet above the level of the river) implements are rarely found, but what there are, are usually black. In the upper gravel they are more abundant, and ochreous in tint. It was in this gravel that I had the opportunity of examining one of the cavities already mentioned; and in the pipe formed through the more chalky gravel into which a part of the upper bed had been let down. I witnessed the finding of a pointed flint implement. In character, the implements found at this spot much resemble those from Redhill. They are, however, usually more rolled and waterworn. There are but few pebbles from the Glacial Beds in the gravel, but among these Canon Greenwell has found one of quartzite, with the ends battered as if from its having been used as a hammer-stone.

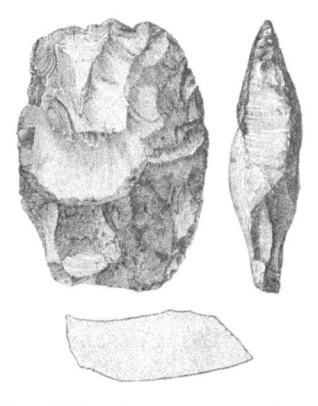

Fig. 437.—Santon Downham.

Remains of *Elephas primigenius*, and of horse, have been found here, but as yet no land or freshwater shells.

The only specimen from this spot which I have thought it worth while to engrave, is shown in Fig. 438. It presents a much narrower form than is usual among the River-drift implements, and in outline closely approximates to some of the neolithic rough-hewn celts. It is, however, much more convex on one face than on the other, and presents what are apparently signs of wear along both the sides and the ends, the broader of which is somewhat gouge-like in character.

Fig. 438.—Bromehill, Brandon. 1/2

In addition to the pit in the bluff facing the river, there is another in the same gravel, but on the other side of the railway, which has been here cut through the Drift deposits. In this also implements have been found.

The next locality to be mentioned is on the Suffolk side of the river, about two miles S.W. of Brandon Station. This spot has already been described by Mr. Flower, [2535] under the name of Gravel Hill, Brandon; it is also known as Brandon Down, or Brandon Field; and from the contiguity of one of the pits to Brick-kiln Farm, Wangford, some specimens from this place have been labelled as found at Wangford.

The gravel is worked on both sides of the point of a high ridge of land, nearly at right angles to the course of the river, and about a mile distant from it. The summit of the ridge between two of the pits was found by Mr. Flower to be 91 feet above the level of the river at its nearest point. The surface of the ground where gravel has been dug is lower only by a few feet, and the beds possibly extend through the ridge. Between the ridge and the higher land to the S.W. a valley intervenes, along which the road to Mildenhall passes, so that the hill on which the gravel reposes is isolated. The gravel is usually not more than 10 feet in thickness, but often less, and it rests in some places immediately on the chalk. It contains a very large proportion of quartzite pebbles from the New Red Conglomerate, in some spots more than 50 per cent. of the whole, as well as fragments of jasper, clay-slate, quartz, greenstone and limestone; all derived from Glacial Beds, from which also many of the flints appear to have come. The matrix is of coarse red sand, and there is usually some thickness of sand above the gravel. In some few places there are beds formed almost exclusively of the quartzite pebbles; but Mr. Flower's estimate of their forming three fourths of the whole mass of gravel is, I believe, very far in excess.

Flint implements have been found here in considerable numbers—at all events, many hundreds. I have myself found several, and many flakes, but all in gravel already dug and not *in situ*. They appear to occur at all depths; but, as usual, for the most part, near the base, and occasionally resting on the chalk. A large proportion of them are very rude, though they were evidently chipped into shape for some particular purpose, and approximate to the more symmetrical specimens in general form. It seems hardly worth while to figure any of these roughly chipped implements, the character of which was no doubt in some measure determined by the shape of the original blocks of flint from which they were fashioned.

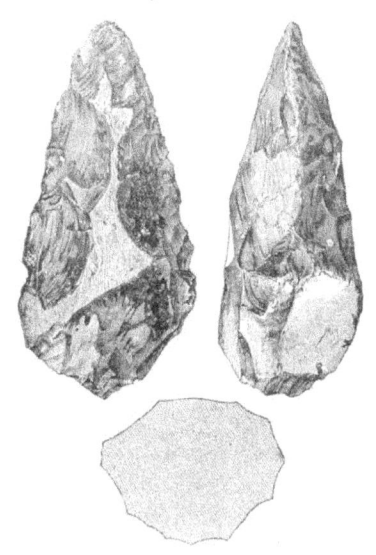

Fig. 439.—Gravel Hill, Brandon. 1/2

Mixed with these ruder tools or weapons, are some of much higher design and finish. Mr. Flower had some remarkably beautiful specimens, in form much like Fig. 472, from Milford Hill, two of which he bequeathed to me. One of these is rather more than 9 inches long and 4 1/2 inches broad. Some of the flattened oval implements, such as are common at Icklingham, occur also at Gravel Hill. I have one approaching the circular form, the length being 3 1/4 inches and the breadth 3 1/8. Those which I have selected for engraving are for the most part in my own collection. Fig. 439 shows an unusually thick pointed specimen of dark flint, with ochreous stains in places. This implement has been dexterously made from a nodule of flint, the original outer skin of which is visible along the greater part of the ridge of one of the faces. It has also been left on part of the butt, which, though presenting some rather sharp angles, may have been intended to be held in the hand.

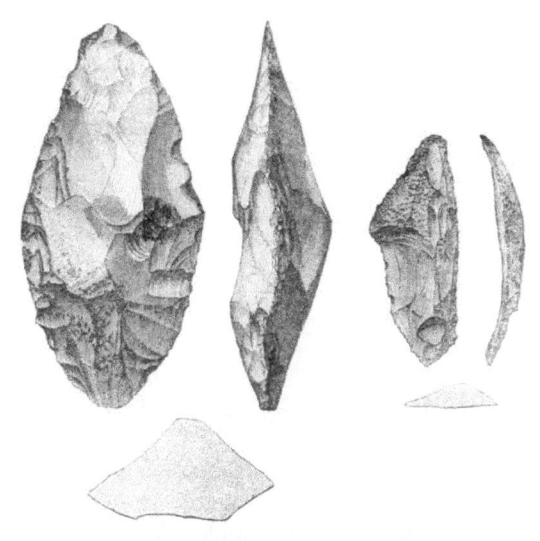

Fig. 440.—Gravel Hill, Brandon. 1/2

Fig. 441.—Gravel Hill, Brandon. 1/2

I am not quite sure as to the locality along the course of the Little Ouse from which the implement shown in Fig. 440 was obtained by Mr. Flower, to whom it belonged, but it probably came from Gravel Hill. It presents the peculiarity of being almost as much pointed at one end as at the other. The depression in the centre is the result of a large flake having been removed, and is probably accidental. Though pointed at both ends, it seems probable that only one was intended for use, as a small flat surface has been left at the other end, which unfits it for cutting or piercing.

Flakes and spalls of flint are abundant in the gravel, though not often noticed by the workmen. That shown in Fig. 441 was found by myself near Brick-kiln Farm. Except that the surface has undergone more decomposition than is usual with flakes of the Neolithic Period, and that it bears upon it some of those bright shining specks, so common on flints from the gravel, there is nothing to distinguish it from one of much more modern date. These bright or polished spots, which are very minute, seem to indicate points of contact with other stones, and the lustre upon them is probably due in part to pressure and in part to friction. They are most apparent on dark-coloured flint, and afford one of the tests of the authenticity of a worked flint professing to belong to the River-drift Period.

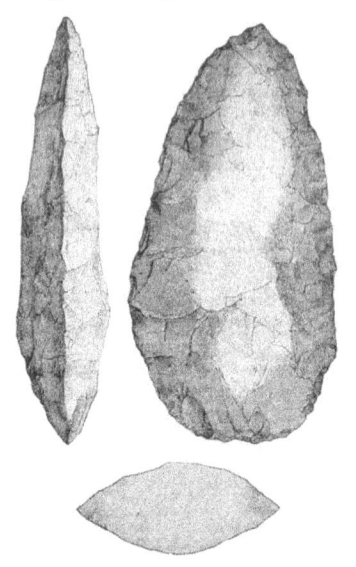

Fig. 442.—Gravel Hill, Brandon. 1/2

One of the most interesting features at Gravel Hill is that there, for the first time, were found cutting stone implements of the Palæolithic Period formed of other materials than flint, chert, or quartzite. That shown in Fig. 442, though so identical in form with many of the implements of flint, is formed of felstone, no doubt derived either from the Boulder Clay or from some other of the Glacial Beds. One face appears to show a considerable portion of the original surface of the block of stone from which the instrument was fashioned, but the whole surface is now somewhat decomposed, so much so, that it is difficult to determine with certainty the nature of the material, which by some has been regarded as diorite rather than felstone. One face has been carefully chipped, the flakes having been removed in much the same manner as if the substance wrought had been flint. At one part of the other face there is a considerable shoulder between the central ridge and the edge near the butt, where, owing to the 'grain' of the stone, the flakes have run in and not come off kindly. The angles and edges are slightly rounded.

Fig. 443.—Gravel Hill, Brandon. 1/2

Even the quartzite pebbles so abundant in this neighbourhood, were occasionally utilized instead of flint. Mr. Flower obtained two pointed instruments manufactured from such pebbles, one of which he bequeathed to me. Lord Northesk had another well-formed ovate specimen. Another has already been mentioned as having been found near Icklingham. Another instrument, of a different form, was found by myself in the gravel near Brick-kiln Farm, and is represented in Fig. 443. It is a broad flake, having a well-marked cone of percussion on the flat face. The other face shows, over nearly its whole extent, the original surface of the quartzite pebble from which it has been formed. It has, however, had a portion removed on one side of the cone, apparently to produce a symmetrical form; and the whole of the edge at the broad end of the flake has been trimmed by chipping from the flat face, so as to produce a bevelled edge, which is now somewhat rounded, either by wear in the gravel or by use. In character this implement is like those from Santon Downham and Highbury (Figs. 437 and 453), or the side-scrapers from the cave of Le Moustier.

On the opposite side of Wangford Fen, rather more than 2 1/2 miles S.W. of Gravel Hill, and 3/4 mile E. of Lakenheath, close to Maid's Cross, is an isolated hill, about three miles distant from the Little Ouse, locally known as the Broom, but distinguished on the old Ordnance Map by the words, "The Old Churchyard." The spot has been described by Mr. Flower, [2536] with whom I have examined it. The greater part of the hill is capped with gravel, in places from 8 to 10 feet thick, and of much the same character as that at Gravel

Hill, but less ferruginous, and not containing so many quartzite pebbles. The beds here have not been excavated to the same extent as those near Brandon, the gravel being only dug for the repairs of the parish roads; but several well-fashioned implements have been found in them, mostly of pointed form.

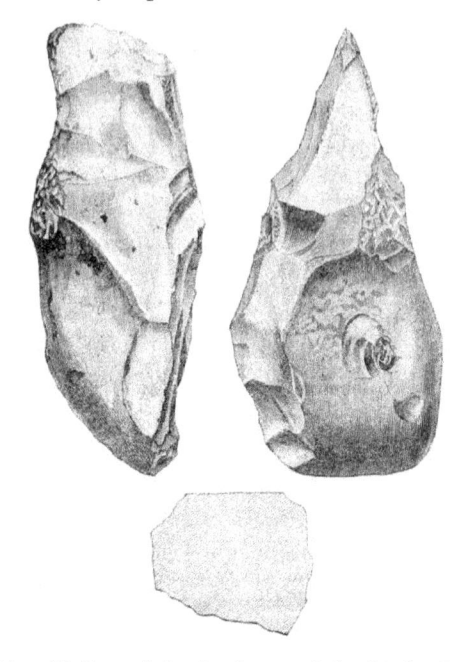

Fig. 444.—Valley of the Lark, or of the Little Ouse. 1/2

Some implements have also been found at a lower level in the gravel on the slope of the hill towards the Fens, and close to the main street of Lakenheath; amongst them one of ovate form most skilfully chipped into shape.

The curious implement shown in Fig. 444, which was presented to me by Canon Greenwell, F.R.S., was procured from a Lakenheath workman, but it is not certain whether it was found in the gravel near that place, or in one of the pits near Brandon. It differs from all other implements that I have seen from the River-drift, in having an oblique hatchet-like edge at the end, so that the side-view somewhat resembles that of the iron *Francisca*, of Saxon times. A considerable portion of the original crust of the flint remains at the butt-end. Until other specimens of the same form are discovered, it is hardly safe to regard this as furnishing an example of a new type of implement; yet its symmetry and character seem to prove that it was designedly chipped into this form, to fulfil some special purpose.

It will be best to postpone any remarks as to the probable connection of the beds near Lakenheath with the ancient course of the Lark and Little Ouse, until I come to consider the geological aspects of the whole case.

It was from a place called Botany Bay, near Brandon, that Mr. S. B. J. Skertchly, F.G.S., of the Geological Survey, first obtained evidence on which he founded the existence of the beds that he termed Brandon Beds, which though containing palæolithic implements he regarded as occurring below the Chalky Boulder-clay, and as, therefore, of Interglacial date. The evidence that the implement-bearing beds are, at all events in the Eastern Counties, later than the Boulder Clay is now beyond all cavil, and, so far as I could judge, the supposed Boulder Clay lying above the implement bed at Botany Bay was not in its original position, but was either *remanié* or had slipped down from a higher level. It is, however, but fair to state that the Rev. O. Fisher, [2537] F.G.S., has accepted Mr. Skertchly's views, at all events with regard to some of the localities, as to there having been three successive Palæolithic Periods in Britain, each preceded and succeeded by a Glacial Period. [2538] I can only say that I am not prepared to accept such a view.

I must now proceed to describe another of the River-drift deposits in the more immediate neighbourhood of the Little Ouse, and lower down its course, at Shrub Hill, in the parish of Feltwell, Norfolk.

This too has been described by Mr. Flower in the paper to which I have already so frequently referred. It has also been described by Mr. H. Trigg, [2539] to whom flakes from this deposit were brought, so early as 1865. It caps a low-lying hill in the middle of the Fens, about 8 miles nearly due W. of Brandon, and 1 mile N. of the present course of the Little Ouse, and just to the N. of Fodder Fen Drove on the old Ordnance Map. Mr. Flower states that the gravel here is about 12 feet in thickness, but that at the surface it is only 6 feet above the river. Of course, however, the thickness varies, being often less than 8 feet; and I am inclined to think that the elevation above the river is somewhat underestimated. The gravel consists mainly of subangular flints, mixed with some rolled chalk, a considerable number of quartzite pebbles, and rolled fragments of other old rocks, derived from the Glacial Beds higher up the river. It is in a very sandy matrix, more or less ochreous at different spots. In places, the sand predominates.

The Drift-beds rest upon the Gault clay, and not, as in most of the cases already described, upon the Chalk. The implements found here occur usually towards the base of the gravel, and as a rule are rolled and waterworn. They have been found in considerable numbers, and of various types, including many flakes. It will be remembered that a barbed arrow-head and a partially polished stone celt were also found here; from which it seems probable that in Neolithic times, Shrub Hill formed a habitable spot in the midst of the Fens, or possibly of the watery waste since choked up by vegetation. Teeth of *Elephas primigenius*, [2540] and fragments of the horns of deer, and teeth of some ruminant—probably deer also—and of a small horse, have been found at Shrub Hill in the gravel, but I have searched in vain for testaceous remains.

Among the implements found at Shrub Hill is one which is probably the largest of its class as yet discovered in England or France, and which was presented by the late Mr. Flower to the Christy Collection. It is fully 11 1/2 inches long and 5 1/4 inches broad near the base. Its greatest thickness is 3 inches. One face is much more highly ridged than the other, and it has been boldly chipped with large facets. In general form it resembles Fig. 445 from the same locality, but is somewhat thicker and more elongated in its proportions, and is, as nearly as may be, six times the length of the figure. It weighs 5 lbs. 7 oz.

An interesting account of large and heavy examples of palæolithic implements has been compiled by Mr. Worthington Smith. [2541] The heaviest is one formed of quartzite in the Central Museum at Madras. It is 9 3/4 inches long and 5 3/4 wide with a weight of 6 1/4 lbs.

The small specimen here shown as Fig. 445 was found in 1866, and is less waterworn than is usual with Shrub-Hill implements, though its surface is beautifully sand-polished. It is of dark brown flint, in places mottled with a fine amber colour. It shows a part of the original crust of the flint at its base.

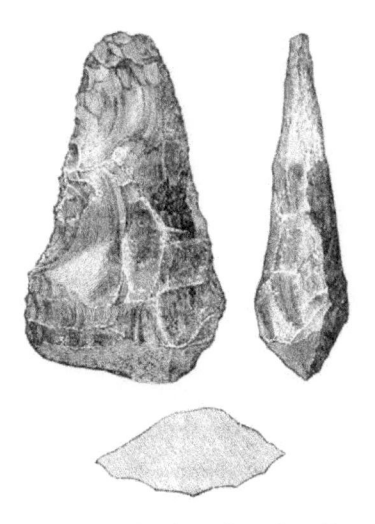

Fig. 445.—Shrub Hill, Feltwell. 1/2

The same is the case with the implement shown in Fig. 446, which also is in my own collection. It is a specimen of a thin broad type occasionally met with. Towards the point the edge bears all the appearance of having been worn away by use as a scraping tool.

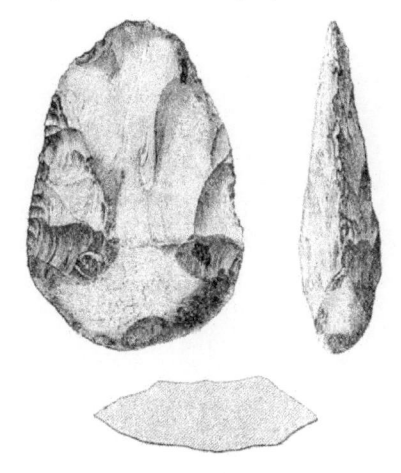

Fig. 446.—Shrub Hill, Feltwell. 1/2

Another implement of somewhat the same character, but thicker at the butt, and having the sides rather straighter, so as to be more acutely pointed, is shown in Fig. 447. The angles are much waterworn, and the greater part of the base shows the natural crust of the flint.

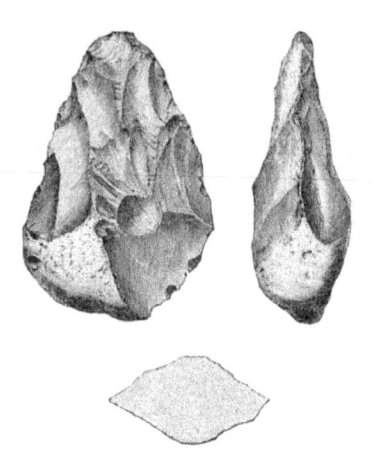

Fig. 447.—Shrub Hill, Feltwell. 1/2

The only other specimen which I have thought it worth while to engrave from this locality (Fig. 448), shows a considerably smaller example of the crescent-like implements, such as that already figured from Santon Downham. It is, however, of coarser workmanship, and not so broad in proportion to its length.

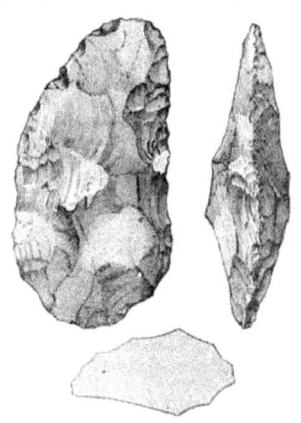

Fig. 448.—Shrub Hill, Feltwell. 1/2

Most of the forms which are found higher up the valley of the Little Ouse occur also at Shrub Hill, and include some of the flattened oval type. But as a rule, the general *facies* of the implements is more like that of Redhill and Bromehill than that of either Santon Downham or of Gravel Hill, Brandon.

The Little Ouse joins the main river about 4 miles N.W. of Shrub Hill; and 5 miles N. of the junction the Ouse receives another affluent—the Wissey or Stoke River, draining 243 square miles—

along the course of which, however, no palæolithic implements have as yet been found. The same is the case with the valley of the Nar or Setchy, a river which joins the Ouse just above King's Lynn, a few miles before it discharges into the Wash, and which drains an area of 131 square miles.

Along a great portion of its lower course the Ouse runs through a Fen country, where, of course, no gravel is to be seen; but at Ash Wicken and Leziate, a few miles E. of King's Lynn, and at South Wootton, about 2 miles to its N., the late Rev. John Gunn, F.G.S., found Drift-beds of apparently fluviatile character. In the gravels in a side valley leading into the marshes, near the School at South Wootton, Mr. W. H. Houghton, having been set upon the search for flint instruments by Mr. Gunn, found, in 1884, a tongue-shaped specimen, 5 1/4 inches long, in form much like that from Shrub Hill (Fig. 447), but having the whole surface worked, and having the flatter face slightly concave longitudinally. It is stained all over of an ochreous colour, and shows signs of use near the point, a part of which has been broken off. The angles, though not sharp, are not waterworn. The late Mr. James Wyatt, F.G.S., of Bedford, also found, in the year 1870, in gravel in a pit near Lynn—the base of which is seldom reached on account of its lying below the level of the water—an oval flint implement, well formed and deeply stained, and another of rude workmanship.

Many miles to the east, but still in Norfolk, there is seen in the cliff at West Runton, [2542] near Cromer, what appears to be the channel of an old river, filled up with gravelly deposits. In these, at a depth of 12 feet from the surface, and above a black freshwater bed, Mr. A. C. Savin, of Cromer, in 1878, found *in situ* a fine well-wrought ovate implement of flint 4 3/4 inches long. A few years later I found on the sea-shore below, a large ochreous flake, apparently palæolithic, which I gave to Mr. Savin.

About 3 miles S.W. of Runton, near Gallows or Gibbet Corner, in Aylmerton parish, Mr. F. C. J. Spurrell found, in 1882, an ochreous implement from the gravels capping the hill, not far from Sherringham Heath. At East Runton, [2543] in the pre-glacial "Forest Bed," Mr. W. J. Lewis Abbott thinks that he has found worked flints. I fail, however, to see any distinct marks of human workmanship upon his specimens.

With these discoveries in Norfolk and those near the mouth of the river, my account of the basin of the Ouse ceases, but before proceeding southwards I must record some others of the same kind.

Yorkshire lies far away from the usual scenes of palæolithic discoveries, but I have seen a pointed implement (3 3/4 inches), in form like Fig. 419, that was found on the surface at Huntow, near Bridlington. There is no record of its having been associated with any remains of the Quaternary fauna.

In the first edition of this book I recorded my finding an implement in form like Fig. 434, on a heap of stones near King's Langley, within a short distance of the railway. As the staining and incrustation upon it were unlike those on the stones of the local gravel, and corresponded with those on the flints in the ballast of the railway, I was inclined to refer the implement to that source, and to believe that it had been brought from Oundle with the gravel, at that time used for ballast. A visit to the pit proved unfruitful, but I suggested that in all probability a prolonged search might result in adding the valley of the Nene to those in which palæolithic implements have been found. My suggestion has now been justified. In 1882 Mr. T. George, F.G.S., found in a ballast pit at Elton, about 5 miles N. of Oundle, an ochreous pointed implement, in colour and appearance identical with mine from Langley, and kindly added it to my collection.

At Overton Longville, or Little Orton, two miles S.W. of Peterborough, a spot visited by Sir Joseph Prestwich and myself in search of palæolithic implements about 1861, some were found a few years ago by the late Dowager Marchioness of Huntly. [2544]

The next valley to be considered is that of the Waveney, a river which, after a circuitous course of 53 miles, joins the Yare a few miles S.W. of Yarmouth, and passes through Breydon Water to the sea. It takes its rise, as has already been stated, at Lopham Ford, close by the source of the Little Ouse.

Up to the present time there is but one locality known in its valley, where palæolithic flint implements have been found; but this is of peculiar interest, on account of the discoveries having been observed and recorded before the close of the last century, and, therefore, at a time when speculations as to the great antiquity of the human race can hardly be said to have commenced. And yet Mr. John Frere, F.R.S., [2545] in the concise and able account which he gives of the discovery, shows himself to have been so much struck by the situation in which the implements were found as to be tempted to refer them "to a very remote period, indeed, even beyond that of the present world." Mr. Frere states that the implements or weapons, as he terms them, lay in great numbers at the depth of about 12 feet, in a stratified soil, which was dug into for the purpose of raising clay for bricks; and he gives a section of the strata. He states that shells, which he erroneously regarded as marine, occurred in sand at a depth of 9 feet, together with bones of great size, and that below this, in a gravelly soil, the flints were found. His account is illustrated by excellent engravings of two of the implements, which I was enabled to reproduce in illustration of my first Essay on Flint Implements from the Drift, in 1859, and which have since been copied, on a smaller scale in Lubbock's "Prehistoric Times." [2546] Mr. Frere presented some specimens of the Hoxne implements to the Society of Antiquaries, which are still preserved in their museum; and it was my seeing these, on my return from Amiens and Abbeville, in 1859, that again directed attention to this most interesting discovery.

Sir Joseph Prestwich, F.R.S., in his admirable Papers on Flint Implements and their containing Beds, published in the *Philosophical Transactions* [2547] for 1860 and 1864, has given full details of the contour of the surrounding country, and of the section at that time exposed in the brick-field visited by Mr. Frere more than sixty years before, which is still in operation. It is situated to the S.W. of the village of Hoxne, in Suffolk, and close to Fairstead Farm; Hoxne itself being about 4 miles to the east and slightly to the south of the market town of Diss, which is on the other, or Norfolk, side of the Waveney.

> The Drift deposits rest in a kind of trough, in the Boulder Clay [2548] which caps all the neighbouring hills, and forms a sort of table-land through which the small valleys are cut. The top of the freshwater beds reaches within 6 or 8 feet of the summit of the hill of which they form an unbroken and uniform part. Their upper surface is about 40 feet above the neighbouring Goldstream, from which they are not more than 200 yards distant, and 50 feet above the Waveney, of which the Goldstream is a tributary, and which flows within about a mile of the spot. The present configuration of the surface is totally unconnected with these beds of Drift, and must have been produced after they were deposited.

The part of the pit which was being worked in 1859 exhibited the following section:—

1. Surface soil, with a few flints	2 feet.
2. Brick-earth, consisting of a light-brown sandy clay, divided by an irregular layer of carbonaceous clay	12 feet.
3. Yellow sub-angular gravel	6 in. to 1 foot.
4. Grey clay, in places peaty, and containing bones, wood, and freshwater and land shells	2 to 4 feet.
5. Sub-angular flint gravel	2 feet.
6. Blue clay, containing freshwater shells	10 feet.
7. Peaty clay, with much woody matter	6 feet.
8. Hard clay	1 foot.

The thickness of these lower beds was ascertained by Sir Joseph Prestwich and myself by boring, as the pit was not worked below the bed of clay, No. 4. In another part of the pit we had a trench dug, which exhibited the following section:-

1. Ochreous sand and gravel, passing down into white sand	4 ft. 9 in.
2. Seams of white and ochreous gravel	1 ft. 8 in.
3. Light grey sandy clay	0 ft. 8 in.
4. Coarse yellow gravel	1 ft. 0 in.
5. Grey and brown clay, with abundance of *Bythinia*	2 ft. 4 in.
6. Boulder Clay	1 ft. 0 in.

In the gravel thrown out from Bed No. 4, I found an implement in form like Fig. 433, but which had lost its point through having been struck by the pick of the workman.

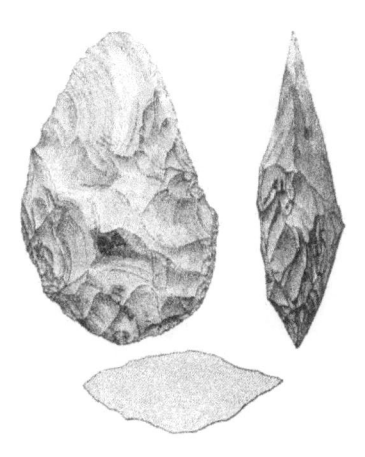

Fig. 449.—Hoxne. 1/2

The mammalian remains, which had then recently been found in this pit, consisted of those of deer, horse, and elephant. The shells comprised *Cyclas*, *Pisidium*, *Unio*, *Bythinia*, *Helix*, *Limnæa*, *Planorbis*, *Succinea*, and *Valvata*. Among the remains of trees, those of oak, yew, and fir had been recognized.

Implements [2549] still continue to be found from time to time in this pit. Several of those found long since are also extant, in addition to those already mentioned. One of pointed form was in the Meyrick [2550] Collection of Armour, and is stated to have been found 12 feet below the surface of the ground, and to have once been in the Leverian Museum. I have another of much the same character, which was sold by auction in London as an ancient British spear-head, but which I at once recognized as Palæolithic, and after purchasing it, found my opinion confirmed by the word *Hoxne* being written on its base.

In the account given by Mr. Frere, it is stated that the implements had been found in such quantities that they had been thrown into the ruts of the adjoining road, and it therefore appeared probable that in the disturbed upper soil of the worked-out parts of the pit, some implements still existed. I accordingly made search for them, and succeeded in discovering, besides several flakes—one of which is 5 inches long and 2 inches broad—three implements, of which one is engraved in Fig. 449. It will be observed that a flat place has been left on one of the side edges of this instrument, probably to allow of its being held comfortably in the hand, so as to serve for a rude kind of knife.

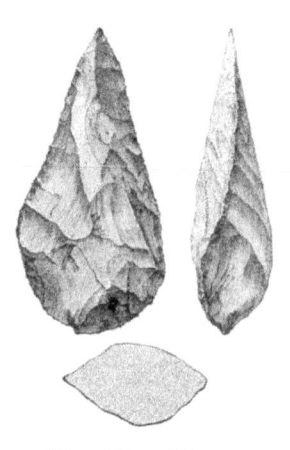

Fig. 450.—Hoxne.

Two remarkably fine specimens—one of them much like that from Reculver, Fig. 459, and the other somewhat more irregular in form but also round-pointed—were likewise found in the disturbed soil by Mr. Charles M. Doughty, of Caius College, Cambridge, and are now in the Woodwardian Museum. There are other specimens in the Christy Collection. A pointed implement from this place has been figured by Prestwich. [2551]

Another of these very acutely pointed implements is shown in Fig. 450, the original of which is in my own collection. It presents the peculiarity, which is by no means uncommon in ovate implements, of having the side edges not in one plane but forming a sort of ogee curve like that of Fig. 434. In this instance, the blade is twisted to such an extent that a line, drawn through the two edges near the point, is at an angle of at least 45° to a line through the edges at the broadest part of the implement. I think, however, that this twisting of the edges was not in this case intended to serve any particular purpose, but was rather the accidental result of the method pursued in chipping the flint into its present form. Curiously enough, one of the specimens presented by Mr. Frere [2552] to the Society of Antiquaries exhibits the same peculiarity, and, indeed, so closely resembles mine, that they might have been both made by the same hand. An essay on the Hoxne deposits by the late Mr. Thomas Belt, F.G.S., will be found in the *Quarterly Journal of Science.* [2553]

I have left my original account of this locality almost unaltered, but the whole circumstances of the deposit have now been most thoroughly and satisfactorily investigated. In 1888 Mr. Clement Reid, F.G.S., and Mr. H. N. Ridley, F.L.S., communicated a paper to the British Association, [2554] calling attention to the presence of fossil

Arctic plants in the lacustrine deposits at Hoxne. This was followed, in 1895, by some further [2555] notes on the deposits by the same authors, with the result that a small committee, of which I was chairman, was appointed by the Association, [2556] "to ascertain by excavations at Hoxne, the relation of the Palæolithic deposits to the Boulder Clay, and to the deposits with Arctic and Temperate plants." A sum of money, subsequently supplemented by a grant from the Royal Society, enabled Mr. Clement Reid, Messrs. E. P. and H. N. Ridley, to carry out the necessary borings and excavations, while Miss Morse aided in washing out specimens, and Mr. Mitten in determining the species of the mosses. I cannot here enter into the details of the case, but must refer the reader to the "Report of the Committee" [2557] for them. The general results of the examination are as follows.

The deposits lie in a valley excavated in the Chalky Boulder Clay of the district, through which a stream ran, probably connected with the valley of the Waveney. By subsidence the channel of the stream was converted into the bed of a freshwater lake which gradually silted up, and its site became covered with a dense thicket of alders. From some cause or other, lacustrine conditions reappeared and 20 feet more of freshwater strata were deposited, but the climate had become Arctic or sub-Arctic. Then followed floods which deposited the implement-bearing beds, and finally the strata became sandy. During the formation and the silting up of the channel, the climatic conditions seem to have changed at least twice, having been at one time mild and then again Arctic. To use the words of the report: "The Palæolithic deposits at Hoxne are therefore not only later than the latest Boulder Clay of East Anglia, but are separated from it by two climatic waves, with corresponding changes of the flora. Such sweeping changes cannot have been local. They must have affected wide areas."

Subsequently, however, to the Palæolithic beds being deposited, all traces of the shores of the old lake have disappeared, and but for artificial excavations the surface of the ground would give no indication either of a stream or lake having existed at the spot.

Though terraces of gravel are found at various places along the course of the Waveney, and apparently of the same age as those of the Little Ouse valley, yet up to the present time no discoveries of implements in them have been recorded, although it seems improbable that it is at Hoxne alone that implements exist.

In the gravels of the valleys of the Gipping, and other small streams between the Waveney and the Stour, no works of man have as yet been discovered; but in a pit worked for ballast, near Melford Junction, on the Great Eastern Railway, and at no great distance from the Stour, the late Mr. Henry Trigg discovered one or two implements of flint, and a portion of a tooth of *Elephas primigenius*. Some worked flints have also been found in the gravel at Sudbury, Suffolk, and some palæolithic implements in the valley of the Stour, north of Colchester. In the cliff at Stutton, opposite Manningtree, is a freshwater deposit containing many shells of *Corbicula fluminalis*. Numbers of these washed out from the cliff are lying on the shore, and among them I found, in 1883, a broad flake about 3 inches long, which has all the appearance of being palæolithic. At Lexden Park, [2558] near Colchester, Mr. Edward Laver has found a small ovate implement with a cutting edge all round, ogival in character. Some other specimens have been discovered to the north of Colchester. On the banks of the Ter, a tributary of the Chelmer, Mr. J. French [2559] has found two palæolithic implements near Felstead; and in 1883, at North End Place, 1 1/2 miles south of Felstead, the Rev. A. L. Rowe, F.G.S., picked up a rudely chipped heavy oval implement of quartzite (6 inches) which he has kindly added to my collection.

The valleys of the small rivers between the Stour and the Thames, the Colne, the Blackwater, and the Crouch, have up to the present time produced no relics of human workmanship, though I have seen a rudely worked flint, apparently from gravel, which was found on the sea-shore by Mr. W. Whitaker, F.R.S., a little to the north of the mouth of the Colne.

Before proceeding to discuss the discoveries that have been made within the basin of the Thames and in the Southern counties, I must call attention to one that was made in 1890 in the Midland Counties, not far from Birmingham.

The old gravels of the river Rea at Saltley, Warwickshire, have for a long time been subjected to a careful examination by Mr. Joseph Landon, F.G.S., of Saltley College, in the hope of finding in them some relics of human workmanship; and his search has been rewarded by the discovery of the undoubted palæolithic implement, which through his kindness I am able to exhibit in Fig. 450A. It is 4 inches in length and has been formed from a brown quartzite pebble which, by dexterous chipping, has been brought into a nearly symmetrical form with a sharp point and edge. It much resembles one from the Robin Hood Cave, Creswell Crags, Fig. 413A.

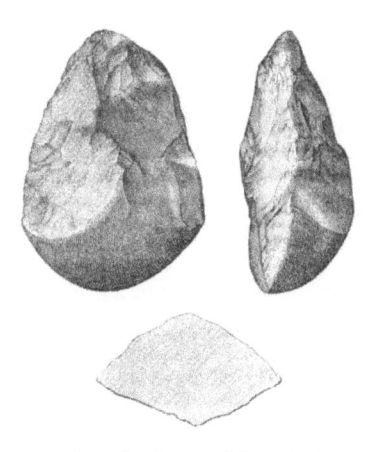

Fig. 450A.—Saltley. 1/2

The valley of the river Rea runs at Saltley in a more or less N.N.E. direction, and is about a mile in width. Several stretches of gravel are found at different heights on both sides of the valley, but especially on the southern side. The highest and oldest gravels on this side are exposed in a clay-pit just in front of Saltley College, and are about 3 feet in thickness. They consist in the main of small quartzite pebbles in a light-brown sandy matrix, though some large pebbles and a few broken foreign flints also occur, and below the sandy beds is a layer, 3 or 4 feet thick, of Glacial clay and sand, with pebbles and boulders (Arenig felsite, &c.), and below this again come the Keuper marls, which are used for brick-making. The level of the top of the gravels is 395 feet above Ordnance Datum and that of the river is about 315 feet, so that the valley must have been excavated to the depth of at least 80 feet since the gravels were deposited.

The implement was found at the base of the sandy gravel at a distance of about 60 yards from the front of Saltley College. In the same beds and in a small area, some 10 yards square, were found a number of fractured quartzite pebbles, which though not presenting such distinct signs of design may possibly owe their forms to human workmanship. Some of the chipped pieces of quartzite in the caves of Creswell Crags are rude in the extreme. The discovery of this well-fashioned specimen suggests some interesting considerations.

It has been held that the absence of palæolithic implements in Britain north of an imaginary line drawn from about the mouth of the Severn to the Wash, is due to glacial conditions having prevailed in the north-west part of England and in Scotland at the time when the makers of these early tools or weapons occupied the southern and eastern parts of this country, which, however, in those days was not an island but was still connected with the Continent.

The question now arises whether the assumed absence of palæolithic implements over this area may not be due to their not having as yet been found, and not to their non-existence.

It must be remembered:—

- 1st. That flint is extremely scarce over a great part of the area, and therefore that any implements would almost of necessity have to be formed from some other material, such as quartzite or one of the older rocks.

- 2nd. That in the case of implements made of such materials, the evidences of human workmanship are not so conspicuous or so easily recognized as on those formed of flint.

- 3rd. That owing to the nature of the rocks over which the ancient rivers flowed, the alluvial deposits within the area in question are of quite a different character from those formed in districts where flint abounds.

- 4th. That such alluvial deposits are not so constantly being excavated for economic purposes, and consequently not so open to examination as ordinary flint gravels, and that implements made from such materials as quartzite being probably more difficult to make, they would be fewer in number over a given area and also more highly treasured.

Even in the case of cave-deposits we have seen how, in those of Creswell Crags, a locality which lies within the presumed non-implementiferous district, all the larger implements were made from quartzite, some of the tools being so rude that human workmanship can hardly be recognized upon them. I therefore venture to think that if competent observers like Mr. Landon will devote their attention to the ancient gravel-like alluvial deposits of our northern rivers, and seek for implements not formed of flint but of quartzite or some other of the older rocks, their search will be rewarded. In some of the Welsh caves the implements were for the most part made of felstone and chert.

The finding in the neighbourhood of Bridlington of a flint implement of a distinctly palæolithic type, seems to afford corroborative evidence in favour of extending the area of such discoveries, though it must be admitted that so far as at present known it was not lying in association with any remains of the pleistocene fauna.

It may be incidentally mentioned that palæolithic implements of quartzite, and even of Tertiary sandstones, occur though rarely in districts in which flint abounds. Possibly it was found that this material was tougher and less brittle than flint, and therefore better adapted for certain uses when the sharpness of the edge was not of primary importance. Most of the implements from India are formed of a quartzite which is more easily chipped into form than that of our English pebbles.

I now come to the important district drained by the Thames and its affluents, which comprises an area of upwards of 5,000 square miles. The number of localities within this area, where discoveries have been made in the ancient River-drift, has greatly increased since 1872, and at some of them palæolithic implements have been found in abundance.

Fig. 451.—Gray's Inn Lane. 1/1

The Thames valley may moreover lay claim to the first recorded discovery of any flint implement in the Quaternary gravels, whether in this or any other country. An implement is preserved in the British Museum to which my attention was first directed by Sir A. Wollaston Franks, and which is thus described in the Sloane Catalogue:—"No. 246. A British weapon found, with elephant's tooth, opposite to black Mary's, near Grayes Inn Lane. *Conyers.* It is a large black flint shaped into the figure of a spear's point. K." This K. signifies that it formed a portion of Kemp's collection. It appears to have been found at the close of the seventeenth century, and a rude engraving of it illustrates a letter on the antiquities of London, by Mr. Bagford, dated in 1715, and printed in Hearne's edition of Leland's "Collectanea." [2560] From his account it would seem that a skeleton of an elephant was found not far from Battlebridge by Mr. Conyers, and that near the place where it was found, "a British weapon made of a flint lance, like unto the head of a spear, was dug up."

A full-sized engraving of this implement illustrated my first notice of these discoveries, in the *Archæologia*, [2561] and is here reproduced as Fig. 451. As will be seen, it is remarkably similar in form to that from Santon Downham, Fig. 433, though rather larger in size. During some excavations in Gray's Inn Lane [2562] in 1883 and 1884, several palæolithic implements of different forms were found; but none I think so fine as that described by Leland. One found in Clerkenwell Road in 1883 by Mr. G. F. Lawrence, [2563] was, however, slightly larger. Another implement was found in Drury Lane, [2564] and others from Jermyn Street and Prince's Street, Oxford Street, are in the Museum of Economic Geology.

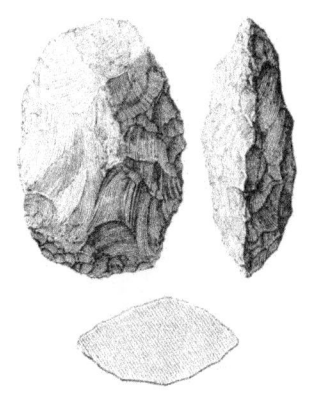

Fig. 452.—Hackney Down. 1/2

Before describing the recent discoveries which have been made higher up the valleys of the Thames and its affluents, it will be well to discuss the various localities in the immediate neighbourhood of London, so as not to disturb the sequence of the Figures which is necessarily that of my first edition. It will be needless to do this at any great length, as the principal investigator of the gravels around London, to whom indeed the greater part of the discoveries are due—Mr. Worthington G. Smith—has given full particulars in his excellent book, "Man, the Primeval Savage." [2565]

In the British Museum is an oval implement, formerly in the collection of the late Rev. Dr. Sparrow Simpson, F.S.A., shown in Fig. 452, and found by Mr. G. H. Gaviller in gravel dug at Hackney Down, to the north-east of London, and not far from Shacklewell. It is of ochreous flint, slightly rolled, and in form remarkably like that from Bournemouth, Fig. 476. Though the exact place whence it came is unknown, there can be no doubt of its belonging to the Hackney Down gravels, which may be regarded as identical in age and character with those of Shacklewell, which have been described by Sir Joseph Prestwich. [2566] The surface of the ground at Hackney Down [2567] is 70 feet above Ordnance Datum, and in 1866 a shaft was there sunk through gravel and sand, to a depth of 22 feet. In the sandy beds at the base Mr. G. J. Smith [2568] discovered numerous land and freshwater shells, and among them the *Hydrobia marginata*—already mentioned as having been found in the Bedford Drift, and as being no longer an inhabitant of Britain—and the *Corbicula fluminalis*, which has already been cited as occurring near Cambridge, and of which more will be said immediately. The Shacklewell gravel mainly consists of subangular broken flints, some large flints but little worn, Lower Tertiary pebbles, a few quartz and sandstone pebbles, and some rolled blocks of hard Tertiary sandstone. In the pit described by Sir Joseph Prestwich there is, at a depth of about 8 feet, a bed of sandy clay intercalated in the gravel, and containing mammalian remains, numerous land and freshwater shells, and remains of oak, elm, alder, and hazel. The group of shells procured here resembles that of the Salisbury Drift, of which mention will be made hereafter.

Since 1854, when his paper was read, numerous specimens of the *Corbicula fluminalis*, or, as it was formerly called, the *Cyrena consobrina*, have been found here by Sir Joseph Prestwich, Sir Charles Lyell, [2569] and others, including myself. This shell, of a mollusc no longer living in Europe, though still found in the Nile and in several Asiatic rivers, has also been found in the Drift deposits of the Somme at Menchecourt, near Abbeville, associated with flint implements; and is likewise to be met with in the drift deposits of the Thames at Gray's Thurrock, Ilford, Erith, and Crayford, in several of which implements have now been found. The beds at these places have by some geologists been regarded as belonging to an older and Pre-glacial period; but the discovery of an implement at Hackney Down raises a presumption that the gravel there is, like other flint implement-bearing gravels, Post-glacial; and the discovery of an implement in beds of fluviatile origin at a still higher level than those of Hackney Down corroborates this view, as the lower bed is probably the more modern.

The fluviatile beds in question were exposed in two brick-pits at Highbury New Park, near Stoke Newington, and attention was first called to them in August, 1868, [2570] by the late Mr. Alfred Tylor, F.G.S. The surface of the ground at the more eastern of these two pits is, according to Mr. Tylor, 102 feet above Ordnance Datum; and 22 feet below the surface there is a bed of clay 2 feet thick, full of land and freshwater shells, accompanied by much wood. There are also shells in the lower part of the reddish loam or brick-earth immediately above the clay. The shells are said to consist of *Helix, Zua, Clausilia, Succinea, Carychium, Limnæa, Planorbis, Valvata, Pisidium,* and *Cyclas*; to which Mr. J. Wood Mason, F.G.S., [2571] added *Achatina, Bythinia, Pupa,* and *Velletia*.

On reading the account of this discovery, I was at once impressed with the possibility of the occurrence of palæolithic implements in the deposit; and accordingly in September, 1868, I visited the pit with the view of searching for them, taking with me my youngest son, Norman, who had a quick eye, and an almost instinctive power of recognizing a worked flint. Our search was soon rewarded, for immediately on descending into the lower part of the pit, where the shell-bearing beds were exposed, my son picked up the remarkably well-formed implement shown in Fig. 453. It was not *in situ*, but was lying in the bottom of the pit; and judging from the staining upon a portion of its surface, it appears to have been derived from the brick-earth, rather than from the more shelly beds below.

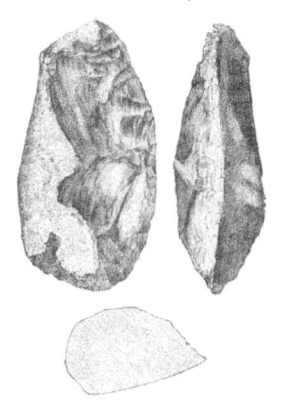

Fig. 453.—Highbury New Park. 1/2

It is well adapted for being held in the hand as a sort of knife or chopper, having a thick rounded back formed of the natural crust of the nodule of flint from which it was formed. One face of it has been the result of a single blow, and its surface is that of a portion of a what irregular cone, at the apex of which the blow was struck, by which it was produced. The other face, as will be seen by the figure, has been fashioned by first roughly chipping the implement to a curved edge, by blows administered on the flatter face, and then neatly trimming this edge to a regular sweep by secondary chipping. The ends have also been trimmed into shape. At the upper end, as shown in the figure, a small piece has been broken off, but otherwise the edge is uninjured. In character it is identical with the implement from the Santon Downham gravel, Fig. 437, and it closely resembles some of the large trimmed flakes from High Lodge, near Mildenhall, and the "choppers" from the cave of Le Moustier. The surface of the flint is stained ochreous in places, and presents much the same appearance as do some of the implements from the brick-earth at Hoxne.

It was in consequence of my publication of these discoveries that the attention of Mr. Worthington Smith was directed to the gravels of North-Eastern London, among which his labours have been crowned with such marked success. Not only has he found palæolithic implements in the City, [2572] Gray's Inn Lane, Clerkenwell, London Fields, Dalston, Kingsland, Homerton, Hackney, Lower Clapton, Upper Clapton, Stamford Hill, Mildmay Park, South Hornsey, Abney Park Cemetery, Stoke Newington, and Shacklewell, but he has been able to identify the old surface of the ground, which was occupied by the early men who chipped out the implements. To this old land-surface he has given the name of the "Palæolithic floor," and he has been able to trace its existence over a considerable area of ground on the western as well as the eastern side of the river Lea. [2573] It consists of a stratum of five or six inches of subangular ochreous gravel, in some places, however, only one or two inches in thickness, or only visible as a tone of colour. On, and imbedded in this floor among rolled and waterworn stones and bones, black, sharp and unabraded implements of flint occur, together with flakes which, in some instances, have been susceptible of being replaced in their original juxtaposition. Below the floor are usually thin beds of sand containing shells of land and freshwater mollusca, and beds of gravel, sometimes as much as 12 feet thick, containing palæolithic implements more or less abraded. The sand is not always present. Above the floor are usually contorted loamy beds of "warp and trail," generally 4 to 6 feet thick, including the superficial humus. These seem to be of subaërial origin and may be due to a lengthened prevalence of a cold and rainy climate. The fauna of the gravels is described as including *Felis spelæa*, *Hyæna*, *Elephas primigenius*, *E. antiquus*, *Rhinoceros megarhinus*, *R. leptorhinus*, and *R. tichorhinus*, *Cervus tarandus*, and *Megaceros hibernicus*. Remains of *Antilope Saïga* have, I believe, been also found. Among the testaceous remains *Corbicula fluminalis* and *Hydrobia marginata* have already been noted.

Another diligent investigator of the gravels of North-East London, who has also treated of the Palæolithic floor, is Mr. J. E. Greenhill. [2574] He has given some interesting sections, showing how the waterworn, abraded implements underlie those of the Palæolithic floor which are quite unworn. [2575] Professor Rupert Jones, F.R.S., has also written on the subject. The best geological account is that given by Mr. W. Whitaker, F.R.S. [2576]

By the kindness of Mr. Worthington Smith most of the important specimens that he has found are now in my collection. I am further indebted to him for the use of the blocks illustrating some of the implements. [2577] Fig. 453A exhibits a finely pointed implement from Lower Clapton. Its surface is lustrous and it shows at its butt part of the original crust of the nodule of flint out of which it was chipped.

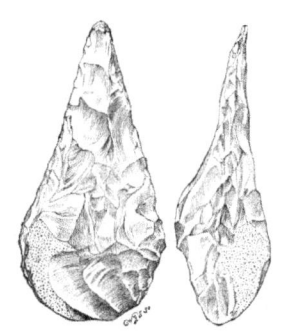

Fig. 453A.—Lower Clapton. 1/2

The fine ovate implement, [2578] Fig. 453B, came from the 12 feet stratum at Stamford Hill. It is of dark colour, lustrous, and has the angles slightly abraded.

A small example from the Palæolithic floor at Stoke Newington is shown in Fig. 453C. [2579] The edges are still quite sharp, and at one place there appear to be traces of use. A quartzite [2580] implement from the same locality is shown in Fig. 453D.

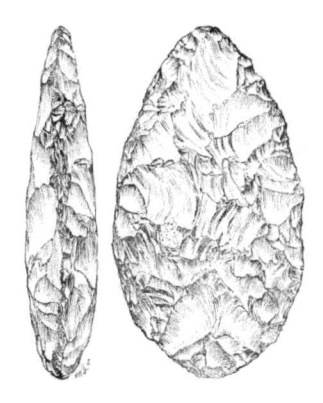

Fig. 453B.—Stamford Hill. 1/2

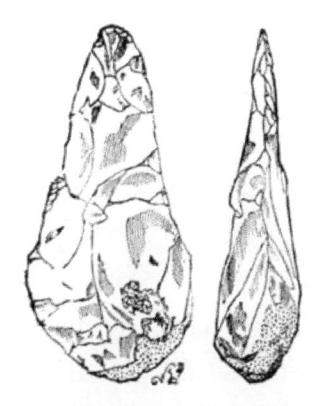

Fig. 453C.—Stoke Newington Common. 1/2

Implements presumably of Palæolithic Age have been found in the bed of the Thames. One from Battersea is of peculiar form, with a truncated butt, and has been presented to the Christy Collection by Sir A. Wollaston Franks, F.R.S. Another from Hammersmith is in the same collection, having been formerly in that of the late Rev. Dr. Sparrow Simpson, F.S.A. It is 8 1/4 inches long, and much resembles that from Reculver, Fig. 458, though somewhat longer in its proportions and thicker in the butt. It is much rolled and water-worn, so that it has probably belonged to a bed of gravel at a much higher level than that from which it was dredged up. Another (5 5/16 inches) from the bed of the Thames at the Chelsea Suspension Bridge was found by Mr. Lambton Young, C.E., in 1854, before general attention had been directed to such relics. Mr. G. F. Lawrence, of Wandsworth, has ovate specimens from the Thames, at Wandsworth, Battersea, Putney, and Richmond, all but the latter much rolled.

It will be most convenient to reserve the discoveries in the South of London and in the valley of the Lea for future pages, and to proceed up the Thames valley towards its sources.

Nearly ten miles to the west of London, and on the northern side of the Thames, the careful researches of General Pitt Rivers, F.R.S., have been amply rewarded, he having found several implements of well-marked palæolithic types, and numerous flakes, in the gravels of Ealing Dean and Acton. [2581] He has fully described the localities and given sections of the beds in a communication to the Geological Society. [2582]

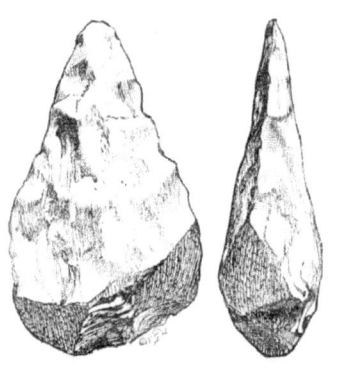

Fig. 453D.—Stoke Newington Common. 1/2

At the former spot, the surface of the ground is 92 feet above Ordnance Datum, and here several implements have been found. At Acton the surface is from 60 to 80 feet above high-water mark, and here an implement of oval form was found beneath 7 feet of stratified sand and gravel, and resting on the clay beneath; another, of pointed form, was found in the middle of the gravel, about 10 feet from the surface, and beneath beds of sand 8 feet in thickness. Others were found in gravel from the same spot, and from Mill Hill, half-a-mile to the westward, which had been spread on the roads. One of the pointed implements from Ealing Dean is shown in Fig. 454. In form it much resembles that from Reculver, Fig. 458, though smaller in size. Like all the other implements from these two spots, it is stained of the ochreous colour of the gravel, and has had its angles worn away by being rolled in water along with the other constituents of the gravel. The flakes, which are comparatively abundant, are for the most part large and rude, but many appear to have had their edges chipped by use. Some have been wrought into the scraper form. Cores or blocks of flint from which flakes have been struck have also been found.

In May, 1871, an implement, 8 inches long, and of rather less tapering form than that from Ealing, Fig. 454, was found at Acton, beneath 13 feet of sand and gravel, at a spot where the surface is 70 feet above high-water mark. General Pitt Rivers has also seven or eight flakes of flint, one of them 5 1/2 inches long and 1 inch wide, which were found together, beneath 9 feet of brick-earth and gravel, in excavating for the foundations of a house at Acton. Their edges are sharp and unworn, so that they must have been deposited where they were found, prior to the accumulation of the 9 feet of drifted beds above them. They lay in a bed of ochreous sandy clay, about 1 foot in thickness, which reposed immediately on the blue London Clay.

Fig. 454.—Ealing Dean. 1/2

In Acton village, the beds of Drift which constitute the first patch of gravel occurring at so high a level as we go westward from London, and which form a sort of terrace overlooking the broad valley of the Thames, attain a thickness of 18 feet, and consist of layers of sub-angular gravel, mixed with yellow and white sand, very irregularly stratified. The gravel consists principally of flints and Tertiary pebbles, with some of quartz and quartzite. A few mammalian remains, including a tooth of *Elephas primigenius*, have been found in these beds, and south of Ealing Park [2583] land and freshwater shells. At a lower level, and cut off from the upper gravels by an outcrop of London Clay, is a wide terrace of alluvial deposits at an average height of about 20 feet above high-water mark, and a lower terrace still is to be found in the immediate neighbourhood of the river. General Pitt Rivers's researches in the mid-terrace beds of gravel and brick-earth have not produced any implements of the River-drift types, but he has obtained animal remains which were identified by the late Mr. G. Busk, F.R.S., as those of *Elephas primigenius, Rhinoceros hemitœchus, Hippopotamus major, Bos primigenius, Bison priscus, Cervus tarandus*, and other species of deer. They occur invariably at the base of the gravel 12 or 13 feet from the surface. The late Mr. Thomas Belt, F.G.S., [2584] has speculated on the age and character of the Acton deposits.

Mr. J. Allen Brown, F.G.S., [2585] has diligently continued these researches, and in laminated clay, 200 feet above O.D. at the Mount, Ealing, has found an ochreous flake trimmed at the edge. At Creffield Road, Acton, [2586] Middlesex, he has discovered another "Palæolithic floor," having found more than 600 flakes and implements in an area of not more than 40 feet square. Besides implements from Acton and Ealing up to 130 feet above O.D. he has described specimens from East Sheen, on the other side of the Thames, and Hanwell, [2587] Iver, Gunnersbury, Kew, Turnham Green, and Dawley, near West Drayton. An ovate implement from Dawley is of felsite. He has also described implements found at Southall [2588] associated with remains of *Elephas primigenius*. A pointed specimen from Southall is made of quartzite. At Hounslow [2589] also implements have been found. It is possible that the gravels at West Drayton belong to the valley of the Colne rather than to that of the Thames, as also those at Hillingdon, where in the Town-pit, 180 feet above O.D., Mr. Brown has found palæolithic implements.

Farther west, at Langley and at Burnham, implements have been found in the gravels. One from Burnham was given to me by Mr. E. Sawyer. He has also found a broad-pointed implement at Cookham, near Maidenhead. They have likewise been discovered at Ruscombe, [2590] Taplow, [2591] Maidenhead, and Marlow. A very broad-pointed implement (5 1/2 inches) found in high-level gravel at Cookham, Maidenhead, has been shown to me by Mr. E. Sawyer. In my own collection are specimens from the majority of the other localities here enumerated. In form and character they approximate so closely to those from similar deposits elsewhere that it seems needless to figure any of them.

Higher up the river Thames, the next important discoveries to recite are those which have been made in and near Reading by Dr. Joseph Stevens. At Grovelands, [2592] about 80 feet above the level of the river, near the junction of the Kennet and the Thames, the Drift deposits are ferruginous and about 15 feet thick. In them were found a tooth of a mammoth and numerous implements, principally of ovate forms and made of flint, but among them one made of quartzite. At Redlands, at a lower level, about 40 feet above the river, mammoth remains occur, as also at the Kennet Mouth Pit, Newtown, where a kite-shaped implement was found. The geological position and structure of the Redlands beds have been described by Prof. Poulton, F.R.S. [2593] In 1882 I found in the gravel at Pig's Green, near Reading, the butt-end of a pointed implement, which had been originally about 4 1/2 inches long and had lost its point before being deposited in the Drift. The gravel was subangular and ochreous, and contained from 15 to 20 per cent. of quartzite pebbles. Flint flakes were fairly abundant, but finished implements, scarce. On the other side of the river, at Caversham, Dr. Stevens has found implements in gravel 120 feet above the level of the Thames. I have myself found an acutely-pointed implement (4 inches) in the same beds.

These Caversham Beds have been well described by Mr. O. A. Shrubsole. [2594] At Toots Farm the implements are usually pointed, as also at Shiplake, at a distance of about three miles and at a slightly lower level. At Henley Road, Caversham, about 59 feet above the Thames, he obtained a flat ovoid implement of flint. A molar of *Elephas primigenius* was found at this spot. South of the Thames, besides the pits mentioned by Dr. Stevens, Mr. Shrubsole enumerates the following localities: a cutting of the South Western Railway at Earley, one of the Great Western Railway at Sonning, a gravel-pit at Charvil Hill, Sonning, and a brick-yard at Ruscombe, near Twyford. In the last-mentioned place several implements of various types have been found. Some extremely doubtful specimens, probably of purely natural origin, have been found on Finchampstead Ridges, [2595] but in gravel at Wokingham [2596] a large highly finished pointed implement has been obtained by Mr. P. Sale.

Some more or less worked flints from the Reading [2597] gravels have been described and figured by Mr. O. A. Shrubsole, who has assigned uses to what he terms "the less familiar forms of Palæolithic Flint Implements."

Still higher up the Thames, near Wallingford, there is a considerable spread of gravel, some of it at a distance of two miles or more from the existing streams. In this gravel implements have been found, though up to the present time in no great abundance. I have a fine kite-shaped specimen of the type of Plate I., No. 6 (5 1/2 inches), that was found at Gould's Heath, East of Wallingford, and two from Turner's Court, [2598] rather nearer the town. In all three cases the flint has become more or less whitened. I have another large flat ovate implement more like Plate I., No. 16, that was found at Cholsey, on the other side of the river. It is more lustrous and not so much whitened. Another was found on the surface at Ipsden, [2599] 3 miles S.E. of Wallingford.

In the neighbourhood of Oxford a fair number of palæolithic implements have been found, some of which are in the University Museum. The first of these was a fine specimen with a heavy butt and pointed tip (broken off), procured, in 1874, by Sir Joseph Prestwich from gravel on the left bank of the Cherwell, at Marston Ferry, not more than from 4 to 5 feet from the surface. Another, ovate (3 3/4 inches), was obtained by the late Professor Rolleston from the foundations of the New Schools in the High Street, in 1878, and two more of ruder workmanship came from the site of the Girls' High School in the Banbury Road, in 1880. Yet another was found below Oxford by the side of Bagley Wood, opposite Iffley. The principal discoveries have, however, been made at Wolvercote, about 1 1/2 miles north of Oxford, whence many have been collected by Mr. A. M. Bell, [2600] from whose account of the discoveries I have been quoting. Among the specimens in his and other collections are pointed and ovate implements, a fine example of the shoe-shaped type, like Fig. 429 (8 1/2 inches), trimmed flakes and a hammer-stone. One of Mr. Bell's pointed implements has been chipped out of quartzite. The brick-earth and gravel deposits lie in what appears to be an old river-channel, which has been cut into the Oxford clay and the superimposed Northern Drift to a depth of about 17 feet from the surface. It is at the base of this channel that the implements are found. In the sand near the base nine or ten species of land and freshwater shells occur, and in a peaty bed immediately above the sand and gravel the remains of various plants; but both the testaceous and vegetable remains belong to species still found in the neighbourhood. Mammoth, rhinoceros, and hippopotamus as well as *Corbicula fluminalis* have, however, been found in the Oxford gravels. The beds at Wolvercote above the peat consist of clay and sand deposited evenly in successive layers, but towards the surface they are traversed by an irregular line of "trail," such as is often seen above palæolithic deposits and for which it is so difficult to account.

Mr. Percy Manning, F.S.A., possesses several palæolithic implements found near Oxford. Among eleven specimens from Wolvercote, mostly tongue-shaped, is one of brown flint 9 1/2 inches long and 4 1/2 inches broad, sharply pointed with a truncated butt and the sides curving outwards somewhat like Fig. 475. Another fine implement from the same place has straighter sides and is 6 3/4 inches long. The others are smaller, but among them is one of pointed form rather rudely chipped from a quartzite pebble.

Mr. Manning has also three implements dredged from a backwater of the Thames between Oxford and North Hinksey, one of them (4 3/4 inches) like Fig. 422, but more roughly chipped and much waterworn. Another (4 inches) is like Fig. 436, but more pointed. The third (5 1/8 inches), is a remarkably symmetrical ovate-lanceolate implement, in outline like Plate II., No. 11, made out of a pebble of quartzite, or possibly of chert. This also is waterworn.

At Broadwell, Oxon, on the borders of Gloucestershire, Mr. Manning found an implement (4 1/4 inches) resembling Fig. 459, apparently from gravel dug upon the spot. The village of Broadwell lies about 3 miles to the north of the Thames.

In my former edition I called attention to the discovery in the valley of the Wey, at Peasemarsh, between Guildford and Godalming, by the late Mr. Whitbourn, F.S.A., [2601] some sixty years ago, of the implement shown in Fig. 455, which is now in my own collection. It was found embedded in the gravel in a layer of sand about 4 or 5 feet from the surface, in apparently undisturbed ground. Mr. Whitbourn had heard of remains of large animals having been discovered in the same beds, but not in very close proximity to the spot where the implement was found. It is, as will be seen by the figure, of a different shape from the majority of the implements found in the River-drift, being very broad at the base and short in proportion to its width. The flint of which it consists is grey and slightly ochreous. At the base is a considerable portion of the original crust of the flint, which is stained of a dull red. The gravel beds, in which it was found, have been described by Mr. R. A. C. Godwin-Austen, F.R.S. [2602] They rest on Wealden Clay, and in places, on beds of the Lower Greensand. The material principally consists of sub-angular chalk flints, and in it have been found numerous remains of *Elephas primigenius*. In places, the gravel overlies what appears to have been an old land-surface, in the mould of which fragments of branches of trees, and bones of ox and elephant, have been found uninjured and lying together. Mr. Godwin-Austen does not record the discovery of any land or freshwater shells in the gravels, nor on visiting the spot was I able to find any, or any more worked flints. In the Woodwardian Museum, at Cambridge, is an implement of palæolithic type, and of the ovate form, found higher up the valley of the Wey, near Alton, but on the surface, and not in gravel.

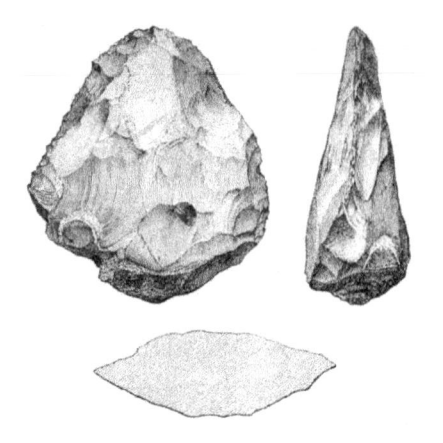

Fig. 455.—Peasemarsh, Godalming. 1/2

At Farnham, between Alton and Godalming, many palæolithic implements have been secured from the gravels of the valley of the Wey, principally through the intelligent care of Mr. Frank Lasham, of Guildford, and Mr. H. A. Mangles, F.G.S., of Littleworth Cross, Tongham. The former has contributed a paper on "Palæolithic Man" to the Surrey Archæological Society, [2603] and has kindly given me much information on the subject. The beds of gravel are from 10 to 40 feet deep, and lie upon the Lower Greensand. They attain an elevation of 364 feet [2604] above the mean sea-level, or about 150 feet above the present bed of the river, and are principally dug in pits on the southern or right side of the Wey towards Wracklesham, pits which have furnished several hundreds of palæolithic implements of various forms and sizes. The oval and ovate seem to predominate, but there have been found not a few fine pointed implements. Associated with the more sharply preserved specimens, are many of dark ochreous colour, with their angles much abraded, which in all probability have been brought down by the old river from beds higher up its valley. Remains of mammoth occur occasionally in the gravels. Some specimens of the implements are preserved in the Charterhouse School Museum. Mr. Lasham informs me of an implement having been found in gravel at Peperharow, of a part of one near Farley Heath, and of one found at Frimley, [2605] in the valley of the Blackwater.

The discoveries of palæolithic implements in the valley of the Colne near its junction with the Thames, have already been recorded. In the valley of the Misbourne, an affluent of the Colne, an implement was found in 1891 in digging the foundations of the bridge over the Metropolitan Extension Railway, just north of Great Missenden. It is of a thick ovate form, made of grey flint, rather narrower than Pl. II., No. 18, and with small flat surfaces of the original crust of the flint left about the middle of each side. The specimen is in my own collection.

In the valley of the Gade, in Hertfordshire, a few have been found by myself. The first of these was lying on the surface of a ploughed field near Bedmond, [2606] in the parish of Abbot's Langley, at a spot which, though probably 160 feet above the level of the nearest part of the stream, is towards the bottom of one of the lateral valleys leading into the main valley of the Gade, between Boxmoor and Watford. The implement, which has unfortunately lost its point, is remarkably similar in form and size to that from Gray's Inn Lane, Fig. 451. The flint of which it is made has become nearly white and porcellanous on both faces, though more so on one than on the other. In places it has been so much altered in structure that it can be cut with a knife. I have noticed this feature in flints which have lain long in pervious red brick-earth, and this leads me to suppose that the implement may have been derived from some beds of that character at the spot where it was found, though on this point I have no direct evidence. In 1892 [2607] I found another small implement (4 inches) of rude ovate form, among some stones recently placed in a rut at Bedmond Hill. Here, again, there is no evidence as to the exact geological position. Nor is there with regard to two other implements, both of which I found in 1868, in gravel laid on the towing-path of the Grand Junction Canal, which is there united with the Gade, between Apsley and Nash Mills, about two miles south of Hemel Hempstead. There is, however, no doubt of the gravel in which they lay having been dredged or dug from the bottom of the valley in the immediate neighbourhood. One of them, of grey flint, is a neatly-chipped, flat implement, of ovate outline, about 4 inches long, in form much like Fig. 468, from Lake. The other is imperfect, but appears to have been originally of much the same character, though flatter on one face. It is deeply stained of an ochreous colour, and its angles are considerably waterworn. I have searched in the gravels of the neighbourhood for other specimens, but as yet in vain. I may add that during the formation of this part of the canal, some eighty years ago, an elephant's tooth was found in the gravel, within about 200 yards of the spot where I discovered one of the implements.

Other specimens are reported to have been found near the head of the tributary valley of the Bulbourne, at Wigginton, near Tring.

At Watford, Herts, on the left bank of the Colne, in gravel near Bushey Park, at a height of about 40 feet above the level of the existing river, Mr. Clouston has found several implements of ochreous flint of various types. He has kindly given me a square-ended flake, much like Fig. 426A, from High Lodge, Mildenhall.

Some of the discoveries made by Mr. Worthington G. Smith were in localities within the valley of the Ver, an affluent of the Colne, rather than in that of the Lea, but inasmuch as many of the beds which contained the implements found by him seem to bear but little relation to existing watersheds, and are at no great distance from the Lea, I shall at once proceed to the discussion of the remarkable series of facts which he has brought to light. All details must, however, be sought for in Mr. W. G. Smith's own book, "Man, the Primeval Savage." [2608]

The main source of the Lea is at Leagrave Marsh, about 3 miles N.W. of Luton, and 376 feet above Ordnance datum. On the surface near this place, Mr. Smith [2609] found a flat ovate implement, in form much like those from Warren Hill or that from near Dunstable, Fig. 17. He says that it may be neolithic, but that he has found palæolithic flakes, both ochreous and grey, *in situ* in gravel at Leagrave. At Houghton Regis, [2610] 1 1/2 miles north of Dunstable, Mr. Smith found a fragment of an ovate implement on the surface. Another implement, found so long ago as 1830 by Mr. William Gutteridge, at Dallow, [2611] or Dollar farm, 3/4 of a mile west of Luton, is distinctly palæolithic in form.

The most interesting of Mr. Worthington Smith's discoveries have, however, been made on or near the summit of a hill, a good 2 miles from the Lea, and somewhat nearer the Ver. At and around the village of Caddington there are several brickfields, some of them no longer worked. The original surface of the ground in some of these is as much as 550 [2612] to 595 feet above the Ordnance Datum. The brick-earth is of great thickness, in places fully 50 feet, and overlies the Chalk. The upper portion of the beds is much contorted, and has in it occasional seams of flint gravel or tenacious clay, in which cream-coloured or brownish palæolithic implements occur. In the gravel, brown, ochreous, slightly abraded implements and flakes are found, and at the base in many cases is the old land-surface or "Palæolithic floor" resting on and surmounted by brick-earth. In one pit were three heaps of flints brought by hand in Palæolithic times from flint-bearing beds either above or in the Chalk. On the Palæolithic floor were numerous sharp-edged flakes, which had hardly been moved from the original place at which they were struck off. Mr. Smith has replaced more than 500 flakes either on to other flakes or on to implements and cores from the same floor.

One old land-surface was full of narrow vertical fissures, due perhaps to the heat of a burning summer sun. While they were still open 18 inches of watery brick-earth, perhaps brought down by a heavy storm of rain, filled up the fissures, covered up the old surface and formed a new surface at a higher level. The upper deposits often resemble contorted masses of half-frozen mud and stone pushed over an old water-laid and perhaps frozen surface of brick-earth. Mr. Smith's view is that Palæolithic man lived here by the side of one or more small freshwater lakes, and manufactured his implements upon the spot which eventually, by successive storms and flooding, became buried beneath accumulations of mud. The neighbouring valley on the west was not at that time excavated to its present depth. He considers that the ochreous implements found at Caddington are of earlier date than those of lighter colour found on the Palæolithic floor, and points out that there is, moreover, a difference in the nature of the tools, inasmuch as some well-formed scrapers occur in the brick-earth of the Palæolithic floor, while they are never found amongst the ochreous tools. The difference seems consistent with the probability that the tools for domestic use would be more abundant on the spot where the men of the period were at home than elsewhere. One of the most interesting features of the case is the number of instances in which Mr. Smith has been able to bring together the fragments of implements broken in Palæolithic times, [2613] and to replace upon them the flakes removed during the process of their manufacture. Of these he has given a long series of illustrations in his book; [2614] those relating to one instance are here by his kindness reproduced as Figs. 455A, B, and C.

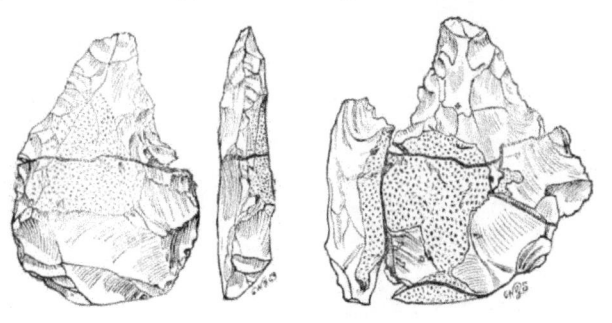

Fig. 455A.—Caddington. 1/2

Fig. 455B.—Caddington. 1/2

In Fig. 455A is shown a finished implement broken in Palæolithic times, both pieces found separately and now conjoined. Fig. 455B shows the other side of the implement, with three of the flakes struck off during its manufacture replaced, and Fig. 455C reproduces the first view, but shows a fourth flake replaced.

A good series of these reconstructed implements is in the British Museum.

Fig. 455C.—Caddington. 1/2

Fig. 455D shows an ovate implement from the brown stony clay at Caddington. Fig. 455E represents a scraper, and Fig. 455F a pointed tool from the Palæolithic floor, and an ivory-white sharp-edged implement from the same source is illustrated in Fig. 455G. For all these figures, [2615] I am indebted to Mr. Worthington Smith, as well as for very many acts of kindness.

Fig. 455D.—Caddington. 1/2

A paper by Mr. Smith on Neolithic and Palæolithic scrapers, replaced and re-worked, will be found in the *Essex Naturalist*. [2616]

At Mount Pleasant, [2617] Kensworth, to the west, on the other side of the extension northwards of the valley, and at a height of 760 feet above Ordnance datum, or nearly 200 feet higher than the Caddington deposits, Mr. Worthington Smith has found some ochreous flint flakes, apparently of Palæolithic age, one of them trimmed.

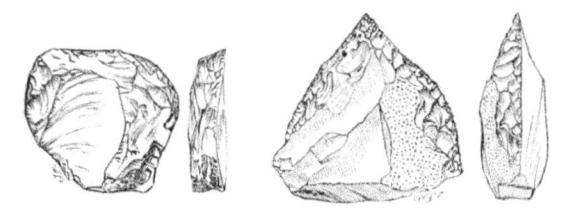

Fig. 455E.—Caddington. 1/2

Fig. 455F.—Caddington. 1/2

At Harpenden, 8 1/2 miles from the source of the Lea, and not far from the stream, he has obtained a few ochreous palæolithic flakes. At Wheathampstead, a few miles further down the Lea, he also met with a few ochreous flakes in gravel near the railway station.

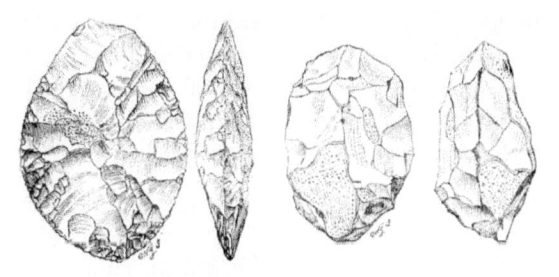

Fig. 455G.—Caddington. 1/2

Fig. 455H.—Wheathampstead. 1/2

In gravel brought from No Man's Land, a common about a mile south of Wheathampstead, the late Rev. Dr. Griffiths, of Sandridge, found two small ovate implements of whitened flint, [2618] one of which he presented to my collection. Mr. Worthington Smith, on visiting the spot in 1886, discovered a rude implement of nearly the same character *in situ* in the gravel, and has lent me the block, [2619] Fig. 455H, on which it is represented. He subsequently found an implement with only one edge and the point chipped into shape, also *in situ*. He likewise discovered a third implement and a well-formed scraper in the beds. The gravel at No Man's Land is in a valley along which in former times the Lea or a branch of its stream may have taken its course. Near Ayot St. Peter [2620] and Welwyn, in the valley of the Maran, Mr. Worthington Smith has found flakes only. I have recorded the finding of an implement at North Mimms, [2621] south of Hatfield.

At and near Hertford and Ware, the Lea receives several other affluents coming from the north. Among these is the Beane, the present source of which is near Stevenage. At Fisher's Green, [2622] a little to the north of that town, pointed ochreous implements have been found in the brick-earth by Mr. Frank Latchmore and myself. I have also a rough ovate specimen made from a large broad flake, and found in a brick-field south of Stevenage. Further south, in gravels exposed in a cutting of the Great Northern Railway near Knebworth, [2623] some well-formed implements, both pointed and ovate, were found in 1887. I have several specimens, as well as an ovate implement found on the surface in 1890. Still farther south, in a clay-pipe near Welwyn Tunnel, a pointed ochreous implement (4 inches) was obtained in 1896, which Mr. Frank Latchmore has kindly added to my collection.

Palæolithic implements have been found by Mr. Worthington Smith in the gravels of the Lea [2624] and Beane at Hertford and Ware, one of them at Bengeo. They are of pointed forms, fairly well made, and much water-worn. He has recorded other implement-bearing gravels a mile north-west of Ware and at Amwell. General Pitt Rivers has a remarkably fine palæolithic implement, which is said to have been found at Bayford, a mile or so south-west of Hertford.

In the valley of the Stort, which joins the Lea near Hoddesdon, two palæolithic implements have been found by Mr. W. H. Penning, F.G.S., in the neighbourhood of Bishop's Stortford. Though in both instances lying on the surface, yet the condition of the implements is such that there can be no doubt as to their having been but recently dug out of the soil; the colour of both is a dark brown, ochreous in places, and the general appearance much like that of the implements found in the brick-earth at Hoxne. One of them was found at a short distance from the river, by the side of a ditch cut in a thin deposit of valley brick-earth, about a mile north of Bishop's Stortford, and probably had been thrown out with the soil from the ditch. It is 5 1/2 inches long and 3 3/4 inches broad, and in form it much resembles Fig. 421. The other is of the same character, but is somewhat broader, and is squarer at the base. It was found farther north, on the sandy surface of a ploughed field, close to Pesterford Bridge.

In 1872 Mr. Penning also found, near Stocking Pelham, five miles north of Bishop's Stortford, an ochreous, somewhat water-worn, oval implement 5 inches in length.

At Flamstead End, [2625] one mile west of Cheshunt, and on the right side of the Lea, Mr. Worthington Smith has obtained several implements in the gravels, some of which he has kindly added to my collection. He has also found specimens at Bush Hill Park and Forty Hill, near Enfield; Rowan Tree Farm, Lower Edmonton, and between Edmonton and Winchmore Hill. For his discoveries on the east or left side of the Lea I must refer the reader to Mr. Smith's book, "Man, the Primeval Savage." Suffice it to say that he has found implements in Drift deposits at Plaistow, [2626] Stratford, Leyton, Leytonstone, Wanstead, Walthamstow, Higham Hill, West Ham, Forest Gate, and Upton. In the valley of the Roding he has added Barking, East Ham, and Ilford, and farther east again Rainham, Gray's Thurrock, Little Thurrock, Tilbury, Mucking, Orsett, and Southend.

Mr. Hazzeldine Warren, of the Cedars, Waltham Cross, has obtained several palæolithic implements from gravels at Bull's Cross and Bush Hill Park, Enfield, and a few at Hoddesdon. A fine pointed specimen (7 inches) from Bull's Cross is rather like Fig. 459, but is battered at the butt.

From gravel at Grove Green Lane, Leyton, [2627] some good pointed implements have been obtained by Mr. A. P. Wire. One of them is 6 inches long.

A thin ovate implement made from a piece of tabular flint was found in gravel at Lake's Farm, [2628] Cannhall Lane, Wanstead.

A sub-triangular implement with a heavy butt was found in gravel of the Roding Valley at St. Swithin's Farm, [2629] Barking Side, and two others at Wallend, one mile west of Barking town. Mr. G. F. Lawrence found an oval implement *in situ* at Stratford. [2630] I have a rude specimen found at Shoeburyness by Mr. B. Harrison.

Returning to London we must notice some discoveries on the southern side of the Thames.

In 1872 [2631] General Pitt Rivers recorded the finding of a palæolithic implement and a flake in gravel on Battersea Rise, at the junction of Grayshot Road and the Wandsworth Road; and in an excavation for a new house on Battersea Rise, [2632] near Clapham Common, on one of the higher gravel-terraces of the Thames, Mr. Worthington Smith picked up a palæolithic implement in 1882.

Mr. G. F. Lawrence has also found two or three implements in gravel at East and West Hill, Wandsworth, on each side of the Wandle, as well as at Earlsfield. One from the latter place, now broken, must originally have been of very large size. This and another are pointed. He has also found one at Lavender Hill, and a small ovate specimen at Roehampton.

At Lewisham also an implement has been discovered. One of ovate form (4 inches) was found in 1874 in gravel on Wickham Road by Mr. A. L. Lewis, and by him liberally added to my collection.

Further south, in a branch of the valley of the Ravensbourne, on a patch of gravel upwards of 300 feet above Ordnance Datum, Mr. George Clinch, [2633] in 1880, found several ovate palæolithic implements, and in subsequent years many more; in all some fifty [2634] in number.

About four miles farther east, at Green Street Green, [2635] about 250 feet above Ordnance Datum, Mr. H. G. Norman found two palæolithic implements, on the surface of what is now a dry part of the valley of the river Cray, about two miles above its present source. They are both of ovate form, one much like Fig. 420, the other like Fig. 468. Each is about 5 1/2 inches in length. "The gravel at this spot has afforded remains not only of the mammoth, but also of the musk-ox."

Mr. de B. Crawshay [2636] has also found about 40 ovoid and pointed palæolithic implements near Green Street Green.

The valley may be traced upwards for nearly five miles, in a south-easterly direction, to Currie Wood, between Knockholt and Shoreham; and on the border of this wood, not far from Currie Farm, I found on the surface of the ground, in 1869, a well-marked flint implement, in character and size closely resembling that from Swalecliffe, Fig. 462, and stained of a rich ochreous colour. In places there are some ferruginous concretions adhering to the surface, and it has all the appearance of having been derived from the gravel which here not unusually forms the superficial deposit. A part of one of the faces has been lost owing to a recent fracture, and it can be seen that the implement has been formed of what is now a light buff, somewhat chalcedonic, flint, similar in character to that of most of the pebbles in the gravel at Well Hill, near Chelsfield, about midway between Currie Wood and Green Street Green. A subsequent search on the spot, in company with Sir John Lubbock, Sir Joseph Prestwich, General Pitt Rivers, and Sir Wollaston Franks, was unproductive of any more specimens. The remarkable feature in the case is the elevation at which this implement was found, the level of the ground being probably 300 feet above the neighbouring valley of the Darent, and upwards of 500 feet above the sea. Regarding the gravel, however, as connected with the valley of the Cray, and not with that of the Darent, its elevation above the head of the valley is but slight. In 1872 I remarked that it was "necessary that further discoveries should be made in this district, before it will be safe to speculate on the origin of these gravels, and their relation to the superficial configuration of the neighbourhood." Since then, as will be seen in subsequent pages, these discoveries have been made.

Farther down the valley of the Cray than Green Street Green, near Dartford Heath, about half a mile to the south of Crayford Station, Mr. Flaxman C. J. Spurrell, F.G.S., has been so fortunate as to discover, *in situ*, the beautifully symmetrical implement which, through his kindness, I am enabled to engrave as Fig. 456.

It is of dark, brownish grey flint, in places mottled with white. It is worked to an edge all round, but is less sharp towards the base than towards the point. On one side, near the point, the edge has been worn away by use into a curved notch. On the opposite side is a more modern break. It is almost equally convex on the two faces.

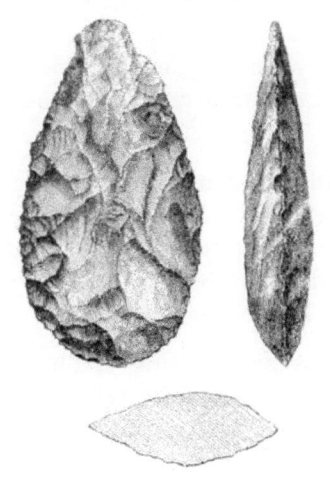

Fig. 456.—Dartford Heath. 1/2

Mr. Spurrell informs me that he found this implement lying on its face, at a depth of 8 feet below the surface of the gravel, which is that of the upper level of Dartford Heath, and appears to belong to the valley of the Thames, and not to that of either the Cray or the Dart.

Another implement has been found near the same spot by Mr. C. C. S. Fooks. [2637] A little to the north of Crayford, in the brick-earth below an old cliff of chalk and Thanet sands, Mr. Spurrell has found a number of flakes of flint associated with remains of the Pleistocene fauna. He has, indeed, discovered a "Palæolithic floor" on which the ancient workmen lived while they fashioned their tools. Not many of the larger implements were found, but many of the flakes after having been struck off the nucleus had been trimmed at the butt-end. By patience and skill Mr. Spurrell was able to bring many of the flakes together into their original positions, and thus to reconstitute the blocks of flint from which they had been manufactured. [2638] In one instance he was able to build up around an implement—broken in old times—the various flakes struck off during its manufacture, and thus to reproduce the block of flint originally taken in hand by the workman. Two hammer-stones were present, made from cylindrical nodules of flint.

It is to be remembered that in April, [2639] 1872, the Rev. O. Fisher, F.G.S., found a worked flint, or flake, in Slade's Green Pit, Crayford, beneath a sandy stratum containing among other shells those of *Corbicula fluminalis*. In 1875 a large broad flake (5 1/2 inches) was picked up by Dr. J. H. Gladstone, F.R.S., [2640] in a brick-earth pit at Erith. It is figured and described in the *Argonaut*. [2641] Another flake found in 1876 in the same stratum as that in which ten years earlier a skull of a musk ox occurred, has been figured by Professor Boyd Dawkins. [2642]

The fauna of the Crayford beds is remarkable, and comprises two Arctic forms, *Oribos moschatus* and a *Spermophilus*, as well as *Megaceros hibernicus*, *Rhinoceros megarhinus*, *tichorhinus* and *leptorhinus*, *Elephas primigenius* and *antiquus*, lion, hyæna, bear, and bison. Professor Boyd Dawkins regards it as Mid-Pleistocene. [2643]

Before proceeding to discuss the discoveries that have been made in and near the valley of the Darent, it will be well to follow the course of the Thames a little farther eastward, and record those that have been made in the neighbourhood of Northfleet, opposite Gray's Thurrock. At several places within about a mile of Northfleet Station, and to the west of it, especially at Swanscombe, Milton Street, and Galley Hill, gravel has been dug in considerable quantities, and has proved to contain a very large number of palæolithic implements of various forms, among which the pointed type is most abundant. At Milton Street [2644] the surface level is about 100 feet above the Thames, and at Galley Hill [2645] about 90 feet. It was in this pit, apparently at a depth of about 8 feet from the top of the gravel, that a human skull, or to judge from the presence of both *tibiæ*, a whole skeleton, was discovered in September, 1888. No formal account of the discovery was given until nearly seven years afterwards, when Mr. E. T. Newton, F.R.S., communicated a detailed notice of the skull and limb-bones to the Geological Society. [2646] I was present at the meeting, but it appeared to me that the evidence as to the contemporaneity of the bones with the containing beds was hardly convincing, and I ventured to assume an attitude of doubt with regard to the discovery which I still maintain. There can, however, be no question as to the true palæolithic character of the implements found in the gravels, of which a few are figured in illustration of Mr. Newton's paper. [2647]

Leaving the Thames we come to the valley of the Darent, in which, about a mile E.S.E. [2648] of Horton Kirby, Mr. W. Whitaker, F.R.S., in 1861, found upon the surface, on the top of a hill, a small ovate implement about 3 1/2 inches long, and in form much like Fig. 468.

At Lullingstone, [2649] at an elevation of 400 feet, another implement has been found, and a pointed specimen of the Amiens type was picked up by Miss H. Waring on Cockerhurst Farm, [2650] near Shoreham, at the level of about 430 feet.

I now come to the numerous and important discoveries made during the last thirty years by Mr. Benjamin Harrison, [2651] of Ightham, which, aided by Sir Joseph Prestwich's interpretation of them, have done much to revolutionize our ideas as to the age and character of the Drift deposits capping the Chalk Downs in Western Kent, north of the escarpment facing the Weald.

All around Ightham, at different elevations above the bottom of the neighbouring valley of the Shode, Mr. Harrison has succeeded in discovering palæolithic implements of flint, for the most part of oval or ovate forms, but not unfrequently pointed. Fane Hill, Bewley, Chart Farm, Stone Pit Farm, Stone Street, Seal and Ash to the North may be mentioned among the localities where his search was successful. He has also found nearly fifty implements in the talus of Oldbury Hill. [2652]

Some of those from Seal occurred at a height of 420 feet above Ordnance Datum, and on what appeared to be the watershed between the Medway and the Darent. An almost circular specimen formed of ochreous flint and found at Bewley, Ightham, is shown in Fig. 456A.

For full particulars of the localities and their relative levels, the reader must be referred to Sir Joseph Prestwich's comprehensive paper [2653] on the occurrence of palæolithic flint implements in the neighbourhood of Ightham, Kent, in which about forty places are mentioned. Since that paper was published, Mr. Harrison, aided by Mr. de B. Crawshay, has extended his researches with the result that many more implements have been found at high elevations to the north of the escarpment of the chalk. These discoveries enabled Sir Joseph Prestwich in another paper [2654] on the Age, Formation and successive Drift-stages of the valley of the Darent, and on the origin of its chalk escarpment, still farther to extend his interesting speculations. It is true that he accepts as being of human manufacture, flints with bruised and battered edges, which I and some others venture to regard as owing their shape to purely natural causes. But fortunately this does not invalidate his arguments, as in most cases where the so-called "Plateau types" have been found, more or less well-finished palæolithic implements of recognized form, though much abraded and deeply stained, have also been discovered. The evidence of such witnesses is not impaired by calling in that of others of more doubtful character.

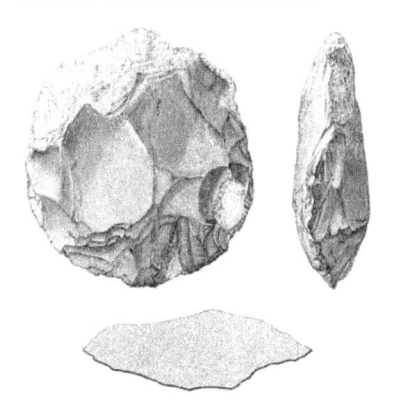

Fig. 456A.—Bewley, Ightham. 1/2

The continuous slope now extending from the neighbourhood of the Thames to the summit of the Chalk escarpment, and in many places capped with implementiferous drift, appears to have been continued southward within the human period over a part of what is now the Lower Greensand area, if not, indeed, into that of the Weald; and subsequently the great valley that now intervenes between the Lower Greensand escarpment and the North Downs must have been excavated.

Whatever causes we may assign for the changes in the surface-configuration of the district, it must be borne in on all that the time required to effect them is beyond all ordinary means of calculation.

West of Ightham, at the head of the present valley of the Darent, is Limpsfield, [2655] the scene of some interesting discoveries made by Mr. A. Montgomerie Bell. These, also, have been discussed by Sir Joseph Prestwich in his paper on the Drift-stages of the Darent valley, already mentioned; but for the following account of the locality I am in the main indebted to Mr. Bell. Palæolithic implements have been found by him and others in the parish of Limpsfield, Surrey, from the year 1883 up to the present time. They are of the usual forms, both pointed and oval, symmetrical and well made, though rarely exceeding 4 1/2 inches in length. Many of them have been found on the surface of the ground; but in a gravel-pit on the water-shed between the Darent and the Medway, at an elevation of 500 feet above the sea, Mr. Bell has succeeded in obtaining several implements out of the solid bed of gravel, at depths of from 3 to 7 feet from the surface. The gravel is about 8 feet in thickness and covers a considerable area. The late Mr. Topley [2656] has pointed out that it presents some features that are unusual in river gravels, and Mr. Bell is inclined to invoke some kind of ice-action in its formation. I content myself with recording these opinions.

Besides the gravel there is a second implementiferous deposit at Limpsfield, on the slope of the Lower Greensand escarpment. Here more than three hundred implements have been found, at elevations of from 450 to 570 feet above the sea, principally on the surface, but also in the brick-earth at a depth of from 3 1/2 to 5 feet. They have been most frequent on Ridland's Farm, and comprise all the forms that are usually obtained.

Eastward of Ightham, within the watershed of the Medway, implements from the gravels have been obtained at West Malling. [2657]

Dr. C. Le Neve Foster, F.R.S., in 1865, picked up a broken ovate implement about a quarter of a mile S.W. of Marden Church, on the edge of the valley of the Teise, an affluent of the Medway. Though found on the surface, it is of an ochreous colour, and apparently has been derived from some bed of gravel. In the same year, in the valley of the Medway itself, at Sandling, he found a rude, almost circular, implement, which, though on the surface, was also ochreous.

The most important discoveries, however, have been made in the well-known pits near Aylesford, in which some very fine implements have been found. I have several, one of which, of pointed form, with a heavy butt, must originally have been 9 inches long. It has, however, had the end broken off. Mr. B. Harrison has given me another thinner and more perfect pointed specimen made from a flat block of flint. Numerous remains of the pleistocene fauna have been found in the gravels.

In 1862, Prof. T. McK. Hughes, F.R.S., found a rude palæolithic implement near Otterham Quay, Chatham, and another at Gillingham, in the same neighbourhood. He also picked up a small oval implement at Tweedale, half-way between Chatham and Upchurch; and one of larger size, 5 inches long, with a rounded point and truncated base, on the railway, west of Newington Station. Prof. Hughes likewise found a rudely-chipped implement in gravel said to have been brought from a pit near the railway-cutting at Hartlip. There may be some question whether the gravels at these latter places would be more properly classed as belonging to the valley of the Thames, or to that of the Medway. On the north of the Medway, at St. Mary, in the hundred of Hoo, Mr. W. Whitaker, F.R.S., found a small, neatly-chipped, pointed implement; and another at Stoke, in the same district, with rounded point, and sub-triangular in form. They are both ochreous in colour, and have their angles much abraded. To the south of Gravesend, at some distance from either the Medway or the Thames, near Meopham, Nursted, and Cobham, he has also found broken implements of palæolithic types.

In the Christy Collection is an ovate implement, 4 1/4 inches long, in form like Fig. 462, which was discovered by Mr. E. A. Bernays on a heap of gravel at Chatham.

I have also an ovate implement found in gravel at the Engineering School, Chatham, in 1882, by Prof. J. W. Judd, F.R.S., who presented it to me; as well as a good pointed implement found at Chatham by Mr. Worthington Smith.

Farther east, Prof. Hughes found a large implement, which, though wanting its point, is 8 inches long, in gravel said to have been brought from a pit on the hill north of the railway, and half a mile east of Teynham Station; and at Ospringe, near Faversham, Prof. W. Boyd Dawkins found, in 1865, not in gravel, but on the surface, a small, neatly-chipped, ovate implement. In form it resembles Fig. 467, from the Isle of Wight, but is white and porcellanous. I have another fine specimen, from the brick-earth at Faversham, which was given to me by Mr. J. W. Morris of that town. It is 5 inches long, in form much like Fig. 456, but thinner, and it has weathered to a porcellanous white on one face, and to a light grey on the other. South of Faversham, at Moldash, Mr. C. E. Hawkins, of the Geological Survey, in 1872 came across a smaller and thicker porcellanous ovate implement lying on the surface of the ground. In the same district, 1 1/2 miles south of Selling Church, Mr. W. Whitaker, F.R.S., has found another small pointed implement of palæolithic character.

Fig. 457.—Reculver. 1/1

It is, however, in the neighbourhood of Herne Bay and Reculver, that palæolithic implements have been found in the greatest number. The first discoveries in that locality were made in the autumn of 1860 by Mr. Thomas Leech, [2658] who had studied in the School of Mines, in Jermyn Street, and who, while searching for fossil remains at the base of the cliff between Herne Bay and Reculver, picked up a flint implement which he at once recognized as analogous in form with some of those from the River-drift of the valley of the Somme. Continuing his search, he found six implements in all, which he placed in the Museum of Economic Geology, in Jermyn Street. One of those is shown full size in Fig. 457, from a block which has already been used in the *Archæologia*. It is of considerable interest, as having been formed from a Lower Tertiary flint pebble, and not from a flint derived directly from the chalk. The rounded end of the pebble, which forms the butt of the instrument, is admirably adapted for being held in the hand. It is singularly like the implement from St. Acheul, shown in Pl. I., Fig. 9.

On being informed of this discovery, the late Sir Joseph Prestwich and I at once visited the locality. I have also been there on many subsequent occasions. The implements in this case have not been found in their original matrix, but exposed upon the sea-shore at the base of the cliff, between Herne Bay and Reculver, and for the most part at a short distance from the Bishopstone Coast-guard Station. In all, there must have been upwards of a hundred discovered. I have myself found at various times eight specimens. Sir Joseph Prestwich, [2659] Mr. James Wyatt, Mr. Whitaker, and others, have also found some. The greatest number, however, have either been found by or passed into the hands of the late Mr. John Brent, [2660] F.S.A., of Canterbury, who has supplied a series of twelve or fourteen to the Christy Collection.

A magnificent implement was found near Bishopstone about 1891, and has been brought under my notice by Col. A. J. Copeland, F.S.A. It is rather more pointed than Fig. 472, and is 11 inches long and nearly 6 inches wide towards the base. It rivals in size that from Shrub Hill, mentioned on p. 569.

Fig. 458.—Near Reculver. 1/1

The majority of the specimens seem to be of the pointed form, of which the implement engraved full size in Fig. 458 offers a fine example. It was found by myself in 1861, and has already been figured in the *Archæologia*, [2661] as has also Fig. 459, the original of which was found by Sir Joseph Prestwich.

Fig. 459.—Near Reculver. 1/1

A small, but rather curious implement from Mr. Brent's collection is shown in Fig. 460. It is slightly curved in the direction of its length, and has a remarkably thick butt. The original of Fig. 461 is in the Christy Collection, and has been made from a broad flake, which has subsequently been chipped into an oval form. Its surface is much altered in structure, and has become mottled and ochreous. In general character this instrument much resembles the large broad flakes from the gravel at Montiers, near Amiens, but it has been chipped to a more symmetrical outline than that which they usually present. Another, of much the same form, has been found by Mr. Brent, in the gravel at Canterbury. An engraving of another pointed implement from Reculver is given in *Once a Week*. [2662] A few specimens have been found of oval or ovate, and of sub-triangular form, and equally convex on both faces.

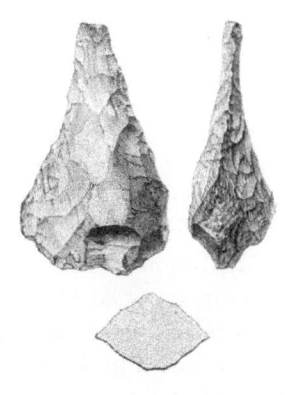

Fig. 460.—Reculver. 1/2

Thanks to Mr. F. Rutley, F.G.S., I have a small ochreous oval implement, which he found on the shore 1 1/2 miles west of Reculver.

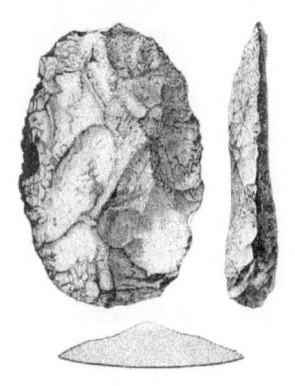

Fig. 461.—Reculver. 1/2

Though the implements are usually found on the sea-shore at the foot of the cliff, there can be no doubt of their being derived from the gravels at its summit. They are generally somewhat worn by the action of the waves, but occasionally they have preserved their edges quite sharp, and their angles unabraded, so that they could not have been many days upon the shore, and must have been quite recently derived from the cliff. I have, indeed, been informed by a coastguard-man that in 1884 he found an implement *in situ* in the gravel on the cliff somewhat west of Old Haven Gap. Many of them are stained of the same ochreous colour as the other flints in the gravel, and I have, moreover, in one instance, found the point of an implement on the surface a short distance inland. Dr. G. D. Gibb, F.G.S., [2663] also records finding a broken implement on the top of the cliff, half-way between Herne Bay and Reculver. The late Mr. Brent, F.S.A., had a long flake stained of an ochreous colour, and apparently derived from the gravel, which also came from the top of the cliff.

The lower part of the cliff, of which a section has been published by Sir Joseph Prestwich, [2664] consists of Thanet Sands and the sandy beds of the Woolwich Series, above which is a local pebbly clay deposit of small extent, and about 8 feet thick, to which he is inclined to refer the flint implements. Its height is about 50 feet above the sea. At a higher level farther west, near Old Haven Gap, are other gravel beds, which he presumes to be of older date. Into this question I need not enter, but for further geological details will refer the reader to my account of this discovery in the *Archæologia*. [2665]

There are pits, in which gravel is dug, near Chislet, where not improbably similar implements will eventually be discovered. I may add that it is difficult to form an idea of the position of the coast-line at the time when these gravels, which appear to be of freshwater origin, were deposited; as, owing to the soft nature of the base of the cliffs, the gain of the sea upon the land has been very rapid in this district, for even since Leland's time—say three and a half centuries ago—it has encroached nearly a mile, [2666] but to this subject I shall have to recur.

To the west of Herne Bay, and about midway between that place and Whitstable, is another cliff, near Studhill, where, in the gravel which caps it, 50 feet above the sea, I have found a portion of a molar of *Elephas primigenius*, and at the foot of the cliff, rather farther to the west, the implement shown full size in Fig. 462. [2667] It is stained of an ochreous colour to some depth, and its surface is much altered in structure. Sir Joseph Prestwich [2668] seems inclined to refer this implement to a stratum of clay and gravelly sand at a lower level, but its colour is more in accordance with the higher beds. I subsequently picked up another implement of sub-triangular form, deeply stained, and much waterworn at the edges, at the foot of the same cliff. Tusks and bones of *Elephas primigenius*, [2669] are stated to be found near this spot when the cliff falls, as is frequently the case, from its being undermined by the sea. Elephants' teeth are occasionally dredged up off the shore, and I have seen one which was found on the shore at Reculver.

At Swalecliffe, nearer Whitstable, where, in the shingle, an ochreously-stained flint flake was found by my son, and again, nearer Herne Bay, at Hampton, there are more argillaceous freshwater beds at a lower level, and containing land and marsh shells; but these seem to be comparatively modern, and connected with small lateral valleys rather than with the main valley of the Thames, or of any other ancient river.

Fig. 462.—Studhill. 1/1

Immediately east of Reculver lies the marshy valley which separates the Isle of Thanet from the rest of Kent, a valley which is traversed by the river Stour, the principal stream of which passes by Sandwich, eastward, while a smaller channel connects it with a small stream rising to the west of Chislet, and conducts part of its waters northward to Northmouth sluice. The Stour and its tributaries drain an area of upwards of 300 square miles, and not far from its source at Rowton Chapel, near Lenham, Mr. G. Bunyard, of Maidstone, found in 1885 a good ovate palæolithic implement of flint, while near Canterbury, flint implements have been found in considerable numbers in the gravels in the neighbourhood of the river.

Fig. 463.—Thanington. 1/2

Their discovery is due to the late Mr. John Brent, F.S.A., of Canterbury, with whom I have visited the neighbourhood, and who has most kindly furnished me with all the information at his command, including some particulars of the levels, and has allowed me to engrave some of his specimens. One of the finest of these is shown in Fig. 463. The flint of which it is composed has become porcellanous, and nearly white. Small portions of the original crust are left at the base, and on one of the faces; the point has been broken off in ancient times. It was found in Thanington parish, on the surface, and not in the gravel, from which, however, it was undoubtedly derived. Several other specimens have been found in the same manner, among stones gathered from the surface of the slope of the southern side of the valley of the Stour, between Thanington and Canterbury. I have a pointed implement, but unfortunately broken, which was found by the late Mr. Frederick Pratt Barlow, on a heap of stones, when he visited the spot with me in 1868. The gravel beds near Thanington, out of which the implements appear to have come, must be from 80 to 100 feet above the river. Nearer Canterbury, at the back of Wincheap, between the waterworks and the gasometer, pits have been sunk in the gravel, at a lower level, where the surface of the ground is about 29 feet above the river, from which the pits are distant about 600 yards; and from this spot Mr. Brent has procured several well-wrought implements of various forms. One of these is shown in Fig. 464. [2670] Its surface is lustrous, and of an ochreous colour, and the central ridge is waterworn.

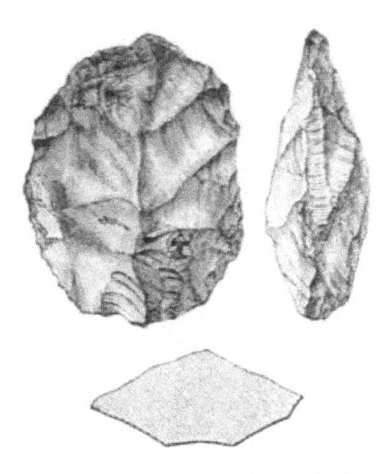

Fig. 464.—Canterbury. 1/2

The gravel, which is about 12 feet in thickness, and rests on the chalk, is coarse, and consists principally of sub-angular flints, with an admixture of rounded chalk, sandstone and iron-stone pebbles, with some fragments of fossil wood apparently from the Thanet Sands. The matrix is sandy, and there are some sandy veins. In parts of the pit there is a great thickness of brick-earth or loam. No land or freshwater shells have as yet been found, but some mammalian remains have occurred, among which is a molar of *Elephas primigenius*. At a lower level, in the gravel exposed by drainage works along Wincheap, I found several flakes; and more recently, in 1870, Mr. Brent has kindly sent me two pointed implements found in gravel in a pit near the new gasometer, where the surface is lower than that near the waterworks by 5 or 6 feet. One is of much the same type as the Reculver specimen, Fig. 458, but of coarser workmanship, and about 6 inches long. The other is less symmetrical, and only 4 1/2 inches in length. The surface of each is very much bruised and waterworn, and deeply stained of a dark ochreous colour.

There are in my collection numerous other specimens from Canterbury, both pointed and ovate. Many of them are deeply stained and much waterworn. One of these, by the kindness of Mr. Worthington Smith, is shown in Fig. 464A. [2671] The white patches marked A show where chips that have been detached before the implement was left in its final position in the gravel have left an unabraded surface. Mr. Smith regards this implement as one of the oldest class, and certainly it appears to have met with many vicissitudes and to have travelled a long way down the valley of the Stour before attaining its last resting-place. Another specimen, from the New Cemetery, is sharp and unabraded, and almost black and unstained. A fine pointed implement 7 inches long, has become white and porcellanous.

Higher up the valley, an implement has been found on the surface near Chilham, by Mr. John Marten, formerly of Easinge. It was at a distance of a quarter of a mile from the river, and at a height of about 100 feet above it.

Lower down, near Wear Farm, between Chislet and Reculver, on the western bank of the North Channel of the Stour, is a pit with sand and loam above the chalk, which has been described by Prestwich. [2672] In the lower beds of sand, at a height of but a few feet above the sea, he found freshwater shells (including the *Corbicula fluminalis*), mammalian remains, and valves of the marine shell *Balanus*, as well as *Entomostraca* and *Foraminifera*, characteristic of brackish water conditions. It would appear that we have here another instance of the occurrence of beds with the *Corbicula*, at no great distance from those productive of flint implements, but at a lower level. From a pit of the same character, on the opposite side of the road, I have seen elephant remains in the possession of Mr. Slater, of Grays, near Chislet.

Fig. 464A.—Canterbury. 1/2

Another palæolithic implement of ovate form was discovered in 1865, on a heap of stones, about 3 miles north of Folkestone, by Mr. W. Topley, F.R.S., of the Geological Survey. It is of course impossible to say from what source it was derived; but it may be mentioned that at Folkestone itself, at the top of the West Cliff, near the Battery, at the height of 110 feet above low-water mark, are some beds of Drift of much the same character as those in which flint implements have occurred in other localities, containing remains of

Elephas primigenius, *Hippopotamus major*, and other mammals, and shells of *Helix*.

Since this passage was written, a remarkably well-shaped ovate implement has been found in St. John's Road (Radnor Park end), Folkestone, by Mr. Richard Kerr, F.G.S., in August, 1893. It lay in brick-earth at a comparatively low level, and is of flint partially whitened. With it was found a molar tooth of *Rhinoceros tichorhinus*. It is now, through Mr. Kerr's kindness, in my collection, and is represented in Fig. 464B.

Proceeding along the southern coast, the next discoveries that have to be recorded are those made to the west of Eastbourne by Mr. R. Hilton. At Bell's Field, Friston, he has found ovate implements, both ochreous and white and porcellanous, and he has given me a pointed implement from Crow Link Gap, East Dean. Although found on the surface and not in gravel or brick-earth, the implements present types which seem to justify their being regarded as of Palæolithic age.

Farther west, in the so-called Elephant bed at Brighton, a bed apparently of subaërial origin, and containing numerous mammalian remains of the Pleistocene period, Mr. Ernest Willett, in 1876, found a well-marked ovate implement, 5 1/2 inches long, of the type shown in Plate II., No. 11.

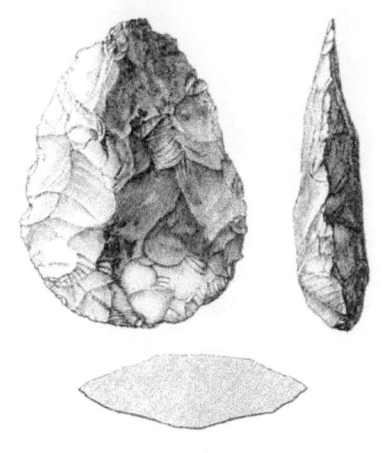

Fig. 464B.—Folkestone. 1/2

With these exceptions, if such they be, the valleys of the smaller rivers along the southern coast of England have as yet been barren of discoveries of implements in their gravels, until we come to the Itchen and the Test, which unite below Southampton, and now discharge into Southampton Water. As will be subsequently seen, there is good reason for believing that at the time when these implements were in use, a portion of the ground now covered by this estuary formed the bed of a river, itself a branch of a larger stream, only a small part of the course of which now remains, and that in a greatly altered condition, having been widened out into the Solent and Spithead.

The localities at which palæolithic implements have been found in the neighbourhood of the Itchen and Test are as yet mainly confined to the lower part of their course, namely, near the town of Southampton and along the shore of Southampton Water. The first discoveries in the district were made in 1863, [2673] by Mr. James Brown, of Salisbury, who found several implements in the neighbourhood of Hill Head, about nine miles S.E. of Southampton; while the earliest discoveries near the latter place are of somewhat more recent date, and due to Mr. W. Read, C.E., until lately a resident of Southampton.

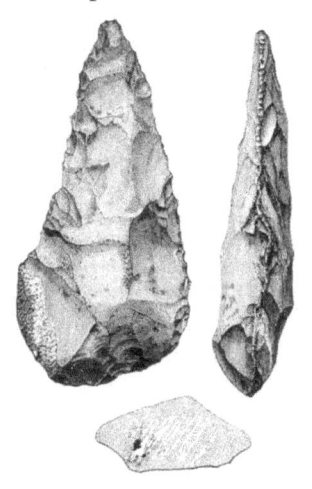

Fig. 465.—Southampton. 1/2

I take the Southampton discoveries first, as being nearer the sources of the rivers. The implements obtained by Mr. Read have come from four different excavations in the gravel, at some distance from each other, three of them on Southampton Common, all of which I have, through his courtesy, had the opportunity of examining in his company, and the other at Freemantle, to the west of the town, about 60 feet above mean-tide level. The first of those on the Common was on the southern side, close by the road leading to the cemetery, where a section of gravel about 6 feet in thickness was exposed. This consisted principally of sub-angular flints and Lower

Tertiary flint-pebbles mixed with a few of quartz, in a loose sandy matrix, and with some sandy and marly seams in places. At the base of the gravel was found the pointed implement shown in Fig. 465. It is stained of an ochreous colour, and has a projection on one side, towards the base, like that on the implement from Thetford, Fig. 427. One face is more carefully chipped than the other, and the edges and angles are slightly water-worn. The elevation of the ground, at the spot where it was found, is estimated to be 86 feet above the mean sea-level. [2674]

In another small pit, at a rather higher level, and close to the N.E. corner of the cemetery, at a depth of 5 feet from the surface, an oval implement was found by Mr. Read, *in situ*, in the gravel, which here attains a thickness of about 8 feet. In this, as also in the preceding case, a bed of brick-earth or loess has been removed from above the gravel. The surface of this implement is ochreous and polished, and its angles are waterworn. The periphery is much twisted, like that of Fig. 434 from Santon Downham.

At the N.W. corner of the Common, fully half a mile from the first pit, and at a higher level still, where the surface of the ground is stated to be more than 160 feet above the mean sea-level, was the extensive excavation known as the Town Pit. The gravel here retains the same character, but is perhaps rather less coarse; and above it is a thin bed of marl, which separates it from the loess or brick-earth, which in most places has been removed for use. The gravel itself attains a thickness of from 8 to 15 feet, and from "a fall," at about 6 feet from the surface, was picked out an ovate implement 4 1/2 inches in length, and in form like Fig. 419 from Bury St. Edmunds. Its edges are sharp, and its surface lustrous and stained of an ochreous tint, though on one face the flint has become partially whitened.

Another and still more interesting specimen (5 1/2 inches), which, like that last described, is now, by the kindness of Mr. Read, in my own collection, has also been found in this pit. It is irregularly oval in form, being somewhat truncated at one end, but bearing a strong general resemblance to that from Hill Head, Fig. 466. Its surface is lustrous and deeply stained all over of a bright ochreous colour, and its angles and edges are much waterworn. The significance of this fact, in the case of an implement found in gravel capping a gently sloping tongue of land, between two rivers, the levels of which are now 160 feet below it, will be considered hereafter. Numerous other implements have been found near Southampton, and extensive collections of them are in the possession of Mr. W. E. Darwin and

Mr. W. Dale. There is also a series in the Hartley Institution at Southampton. Higher up the valleys of the Itchen or the Test, none of the more highly-wrought implements have as yet been found in the gravels, although it seems probable that they may eventually be discovered, especially if the drift-beds at some considerable height above the present river levels be excavated. I have, however, seen a flake with one face artificial, and with signs of use or wear at the edge, which was found in a gravel-pit near the Fleming Arms, Swathling, a few miles north of Southampton, by Mr. Spencer G. Perceval. In the gravel near this place a molar of *Elephas primigenius* is recorded to have been found. [2675]

I have also a deeply-stained ovate implement from Redbridge, close to Southampton, found by Mr. Worthington G. Smith.

I have already, in 1864, described elsewhere [2676] the discoveries which have been made in the gravels on the eastern shore of Southampton Water, in the neighbourhood of Hill Head. Since that time a considerable number of flint instruments have been found in this locality, principally by Mr. James Brown, the original discoverer, and his friends.

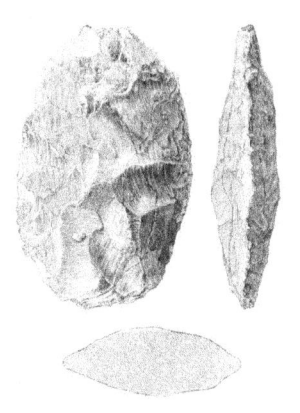

Fig. 466.—Hill Head.

A large number of specimens from this district are preserved in the Blackmore Museum at Salisbury. Among them is at least one of chert. Of those found near Hill Head, a large proportion are flat, oval, and ovate specimens, one of which is engraved as Fig. 466. It was found by Mr. James Brown, in 1863, on the shore between Brunage and Hill Head. It is ochreous, and has its angles slightly waterworn, possibly in modern times, by the action of the pebbles on the shore. Some of the specimens have suffered considerably from this cause; but that the implements are derived from the gravel is proved by the fact of one having been discovered by Mr. James Brown, [2677] in a mass which had fallen from the cliff. Some of the implements are of the pointed form with straight sides, and a few have the rounded butt of the flint left untouched, apparently by way of handle. One or two well-chipped broad flakes have also been found. The discoveries have extended over about 9 miles of the coast between Warsash and Gosport. Along a great part of this distance there is a low cliff, ranging in height from about 20 to 38 feet [2678] above the mean sea-level, and consisting of sands belonging to the Bracklesham series, capped by gravelly beds, in many places 10 to 12 feet thick, and in some, as much as 15 or 16 feet. These beds are almost continuous, and rest on a nearly horizontal base, except where the cliff is intersected by transverse valleys. The gravel consists almost entirely of chalk flints, mostly subangular, among which are some of considerable size, and some quite fresh and unrolled. There are also a few quartz and chert pebbles in the mass, and some large blocks of sandstone of Tertiary origin. Some loamy and sandy beds occur at intervals, but no mammalian remains or land or freshwater shells have, I believe, as yet been found in these beds of Drift. The gravels extend eastward a considerable distance, as may be seen on the excellent map [2679] given by Mr. Codrington in illustration of his paper on the Superficial Deposits of this District, as well as on the new Geological Survey Map. Since his paper was written Mr. Codrington has found *in situ*, in a gravel-pit at Warsash, a mile to the north of Hook a well-wrought, long, pointed implement, at a height of about 46 feet above the mean sea-level. Two implements, one of them much like Fig. 468, found on Southsea Common to the east of Portsmouth, by Lieut. Oliver, R.E., and Mr. G. Smith, are now in the Blackmore Museum.

During building operations at Lee on the Solent, [2680] numerous palæolithic implements have been found and preserved by Sir J. C. Robinson, F.S.A., to whom I am indebted for several specimens.

On the other side of Spithead, at the Foreland or most eastern point of the Isle of Wight, the cliff-section shows a bed of shingly gravel, apparently a beach-deposit, according to Mr. Codrington, and between 30 and 40 feet thick, resting in a deep valley in the Bembridge marl. Towards the edge, where the gravel would abut against the marl, it is cut off by a trough filled with brick-earth 36 feet thick, with a few seams of small angular flints. This brick-earth appears to extend some distance upwards over the slope of the marl as well as over the shingly gravel; and among some flints derived from it, at a height of about 80 feet above the mean sea-level, Mr.

Codrington found the neatly-chipped ovate implement shown in Fig. 467. Its surface is lustrous and in part whitened, and its angles and edges are sharp and unworn. The possible connection of the bed containing this instrument with others in this district is a matter for future consideration.

The discovery is not, however, the only one that has been made in the Isle of Wight. I have two ovate water-worn specimens, found on the shore at Bembridge, and a thick, pointed implement, found on the beach between the flag-staff at Bembridge Point and the ferry. Prof. E. B. Poulton, F.R.S., has also found two implements on the shore at Seaview between Ryde and Bembridge.

I now turn to the discoveries made in the valleys of the Avon and its affluents, which drain an area of about 670 square miles. The first of these took place in the River-drift beds, in the neighbourhood of Salisbury; beds which were pointed out by Sir Joseph Prestwich in 1859 [2681] as likely to contain implements of the same class as those from the valley of the Somme. This prognostication was made in ignorance of the fact that, already in 1846, a palæolithic implement had been found near Salisbury, and had come into the possession of the late Dr. S. P. Woodward, of the British Museum, who at that time put it aside, as having little reference to his own special studies.

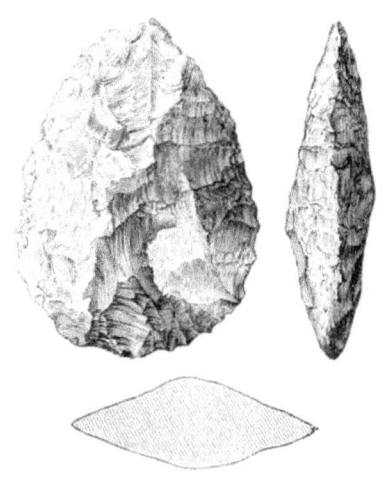

Fig. 467.—The Foreland, Isle of Wight. 1/2

In 1863, however, Dr. Humphrey P. Blackmore, of Salisbury, discovered a flint implement in the gravel at Bemerton, near that town; and since that time numerous other discoveries have been made by him in the district, and also by the late Mr. E. T. Stevens, Mr. James Brown, and other explorers resident at Salisbury, the results of whose zealous researches may be seen in the admirable Blackmore Museum. These discoveries have been made in the valleys of the Avon and the Wiley, and also on the spur of land separating those streams, and on that between the Avon and the Bourne. In the valley of the Avon, implements have been found at Lake, about 6 miles above Salisbury; and also at Ashford, near Fordingbridge, about 12 miles below its junction with the Wiley and Nadder at that city. As Lake is the highest point in the Valley of the Avon proper at which, up to the present time, such discoveries have been made in the River-drift, it will be well to notice it first, though it must be mentioned that Mr. F. J. Bennett, of the Geological Survey, has found a good palæolithic implement farther north, near Pewsey Station.

Implements were found at this spot, in 1865, by Mr. Tiffin, jun., of Salisbury, [2682] but only a few have since been discovered, as the gravel is little, if at all, worked; and it is therefore only on the slope of the hill where the beds have been cut through by the deepening of the valley that they occur. That shown in Fig. 468 is preserved in the Blackmore Museum. It is stained of an ochreous tint, and is worn at its edges. Others of similar form, but white, have also been found, as well as some large broad flakes. It is needless to discuss the character of the gravel, as so many discoveries, of which the circumstances can be better ascertained, have been made in the same neighbourhood. In the valley of the Wiley, at South Newton, about 5 miles above Salisbury, an isolated specimen of a flat ovate implement has also been found.

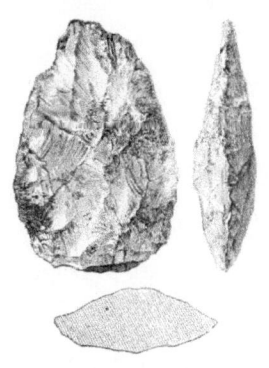

Fig. 468.—Lake. 1/2

Nearer Salisbury, at Bemerton and Fisherton, the discoveries have been of more interest and importance. They have already, to some extent, been described by myself, [2683] principally from information given me by Dr. Humphrey P. Blackmore. The beds of

Drift at these two places are at different levels on the slope of the north side of the valley of the Wiley, and of different characters; that at Bemerton being at the higher level, and principally gravel, and that at Fisherton lower, and principally consisting of brick-earth, with a few gravelly seams.

The pit at Bemerton, in which most of the implements have been found, is about a mile west of Salisbury, nearly opposite the new church, and close to the lane connecting the roads to Wilton and Devizes, and nearly midway between them. The gravel consists mainly of subangular flints, with a few Upper Greensand pebbles and Tertiary sandstone blocks in a red clayey matrix. It is 10 to 12 feet in thickness, and attains a height of at least 100 feet above the river, though in this particular pit it is only about 80 feet above it. The gravel caps the hill, instead of lying merely in a trough along its side, so that in this particular, the section I have elsewhere given is incorrect. The chalk comes nearly to the surface, lower down the slope, and divides the gravel from a brick-earth deposit continuous with that of Fisherton, farther down the valley.

Fig. 469.—Bemerton. 1/2

Fig. 470.—Highfield. 1/2

The implements found at Bemerton are principally oval, ovate, and ovate-lanceolate. They are for the most part considerably altered in texture at the surface, and many of them are much rolled and waterworn. A few flakes and spalls of flint have also been found. The original of Fig. 469 is in the Blackmore Museum, and is of grey flint, not waterworn. It shows some marks of use on the edge, towards the point, and a portion of the natural crust of the flint remains at the base. In all, upwards of twenty specimens have been found in this gravel, one of them as high as the cemetery. Several others have also been found between that place and Highfield, which is about a quarter of a mile nearer Salisbury than the Bemerton Pit; and in gravel which there caps the hill between the Wiley and the Avon, implements have also been found.

A remarkably small specimen from this place is shown in Fig. 470. It is of grey flint, slightly ochreous, and with its angles somewhat worn. The original is in the Blackmore Museum.

I am not aware of any organic remains having as yet been found in these upper gravels, though they are abundant in the brick-earth at a lower level, at Fisherton Anger, where, however, flint implements are so scarce that only few have been found; two of these are in the Blackmore Museum. One of them, obtained beneath remains of the mammoth, in 1874, [2684] is shown in Fig. 471. The flint of which it is made has become white and porcellanous, its angles are sharp, but along the edges of both sides towards the base there are marks of wearing away by use. The other specimen is only fragmentary, but the flint has assumed the same characters. The edge is like that of Fig. 437; one face of the implement having been flat and the section wedge-shaped.

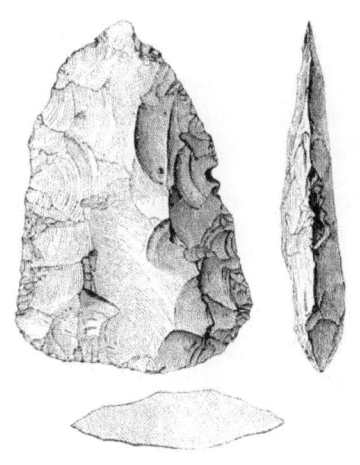

Fig. 471.—Fisherton. 1/2

The Drift deposits at Fisherton have long been known to geologists, and have been described by Sir Charles Lyell, [2685] Sir Joseph Prestwich, [2686] and others. They present a great similarity to the implement-bearing beds at Menchecourt, near Abbeville, as has been pointed out by Sir Joseph Prestwich; [2687] and this circumstance led us to visit the spot in 1859, with a view of discovering works of man in the beds, though at that time our search was unrewarded.

It is needless for me here to describe the beds in detail: suffice it to say, that resting on a more highly inclined surface of chalk is a deposit, the upper portion of which forms the surface of the present slope on the northern side of the valley of the united Wiley and Nadder. It is in some places nearly 30 feet in thickness, but thins out towards the bottom of the valley. This deposit, [2688] leaving the superficial soil out of the question, has usually in its upper part a rubbly gravel, with angular and subangular flints, fragments of chert, iron-stone, and chalk, mixed with clay and brick-earth, to a thickness of 4 or 5 feet; below that is from 10 to 18 feet of brick-earth mixed with variable masses of flint and chalk rubble, and containing bones and shells, principally in its lower part; below this again, from 1 to 2 feet of fine marl, full of well-preserved shells and a few bones; and at the base, flint and chalk rubble, with sand and clay.

The following species are recorded by Dr. Blackmore as having occurred in these beds:—*Canis lupus*, *Canis vulpes*, *Hyæna spelæa*, *Felis spelæa*, *Bison minor*, [2689] *Bos primigenius*, *Ovibos moschatus*, *Cervus tarandus*, *Cervus (Guettardi?)*, *Cervus elaphus*, *Equus* (four varieties), *Rhinoceros tichorinus*, *Elephas primigenius*, *Spermophilus* (*superciliosus?*), *Lemmus torquatus*, *Lemmus* (*norvegicus?*), *Arvicola* (*sp. nov.?*) and *Lepus timidus*.

Of birds, some bones of the wild goose, *Anser segetum*, have been found, and portions of the shells of eggs corresponding to those of the same bird, and of the wild duck, *Anas boscas*.

The land and freshwater shells consist of *Ancylus*, *Limnæa*, *Planorbis*, *Bythinia*, *Valvata*, *Pisidium*, *Acme*, *Carychium*, *Succinea*, *Helix*, *Limax*, *Pupa*, *Zonites*, and *Zua*.

It is worthy of notice in passing, that the presence of the musk ox, the marmot, and the lemming, to say nothing of the reindeer, seems to point to a colder climate having prevailed at the time of the deposit of these beds, than now. The egg of the wild goose, if such it be, is also suggestive of a more arctic climate; as the breeding-place of this bird is presumably in the far north. This question of climate will come under consideration farther on.

The discoveries at Milford Hill have already been placed on record by Dr. H. P. Blackmore. [2690] This hill, the name of which has on the old Ordnance Map been by error assigned to Cricket Down, forms a spur between the valleys of the Avon and the Bourne, and is in fact a continuation of Mizmaze Hill, from which, however, it is cut off by a transverse valley about 30 feet in depth. The summit of the hill rises to an elevation of about 100 feet above the waters of the Avon and the Bourne, which flow on either side of it, and unite below the point of the spur. At the summit of the hill the gravel attains its greatest thickness, which is about 12 feet. It rests on an irregular surface of chalk, occasionally running down into pipes, and thins out towards the sides, ceasing altogether rather more than half way down the hill. In places, there is chalk rubble or gravel in a chalky matrix at the base. The gravel consists principally of subangular flints, a few Tertiary pebbles, and blocks of sandstone, and contains a larger proportion of Upper Greensand chert than the Bemerton gravel—the whole mixed with a variable proportion of sand and stiff clay, and for the most part deeply stained by iron. Many of the large flints are said to present no signs of wearing by water transport. On the slope of the hill, near the base of the gravel, a narrow seam of sand was found to contain some land shells of the genera *Helix, Pupa,* and *Zua.* No mammalian remains, with the exception of a tooth of horse, have been found in the gravel.

Flint implements have been discovered here in considerable numbers, mostly of the pointed lanceolate form; some of ovate, and other forms, including a scraper, have also occurred. Most of them are now in the Blackmore Museum. More than one specimen is of chert. In about 150 yards of gravel, excavated to form a cellar at Elm Grove, Milford Hill, no less than twenty implements of different forms were found, principally by Mr. James Brown. Dr. Blackmore observes that the implements on the side of the hill are relatively only half as numerous as on the top, and that the condition of their surface varies considerably, the majority being waterworn, but others having their edges and angles as sharp as if they had been made yesterday. The degree of staining also varies, and is not always due to their present position in the gravel, some deeply stained having been dug out of the chalk rubble at the base, where they lay side by side with fragments of flint, which retained their original colour; and, on the other hand, perfectly unstained specimens having been obtained from the ochreous gravel. Several implements were observed, *in situ,* by Mr. Wheaton, Mr. James Brown, and others; and they were found scattered unevenly through the deposit, but the majority low down and towards the base. Many of them are extremely rude; in fact, as a whole, "ruder and less skilfully made than most of the specimens from the valley of the Somme." Flakes and spalls were found in considerable numbers, and also a few remarkably well-made implements, of which a magnificent specimen is shown in Fig. 472. It is of light-grey flint, with the natural crust on part of the base. The face not shown is roughly chipped, but it has been neatly wrought at the edge to a symmetrical form. Its angles are but slightly rounded. A detailed account of the discoveries at Bemerton [2691] and Milford Hill, with maps and figures of several implements, has been given by Mr. C. J. Read, of Salisbury.

A scraper-like implement from Britford, a short distance below Salisbury, is in the Blackmore Museum.

About 6 miles below Salisbury, in gravel, near Downton, [2692] and at an elevation of about 150 feet above the river Avon, Sir Joseph Prestwich picked up a small ovate implement, in form like Fig. 456, but more sharply pointed and only 3 inches in length. Between the pit, in which it was found, and the river, two gravel-terraces occur, one 80 to 110 feet, and the other 40 to 60 feet, above its level. At Breamore, farther south, a well-shaped pointed implement of chert was found by Mr. E. Westlake in 1888, in gravels 100 feet above the Avon.

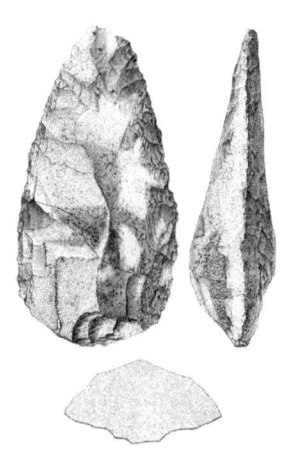

Fig. 472.—Milford Hill, Salisbury. 1/2

A few miles farther down the valley, and about half a mile S.W. of Fordingbridge, at Ashford [2693] railway station, is a gravel-pit, which was largely worked for the purpose of ballasting the railway, and in this gravel also, implements have been found; first by Mr. Toomer, of Salisbury, in 1866, and subsequently by Mr. James Brown, myself, and others. Several specimens are preserved in the Blackmore Museum, one of which is shown in Fig. 473. It is of ochreous flint, with the angles slightly waterworn. Some of the implements found in this gravel have been much rolled. Mr. J. W. Brooke, of Marlborough, has in his collection a series of about forty implements and flakes from Fordingbridge, many of them waterworn.

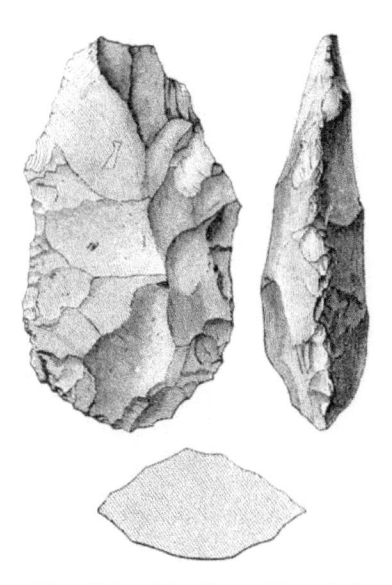

Fig. 473.—Fordingbridge. 1/2

The gravel here rests upon Tertiary beds, and consists principally of subangular flints, with many Lower Tertiary pebbles, a few pieces of greensand iron-stone, and more rarely quartz pebbles among them. The beds are about 10 feet thick, and their height above the river about 40 feet. Remains of mammoth [2694] have been found in them.

Farther down the course of the Avon, palæolithic implements have not as yet been found; and in the basin of the Stour, which joins the Avon at Christchurch, but one discovery has been made. This was of a small brown ochreous implement, made from a large external flake, trimmed into a somewhat kidney-shaped outline, and having its edges worn round, and its angles waterworn. It was found at Wimborne Minster, by Mr. W. F. Tiffin, of Salisbury, in gravel brought from a pit in the neighbourhood, and not *in situ*. I have searched for implements, but in vain, in some of the pits near Wimborne, though the gravel, especially at Oakley, has all the characters of a deposit likely to contain them.

Though the united Avon and Stour now find their way into the sea near Christchurch, it seems probable, as will subsequently be shown, that they were in remote times affluents of a river running from west to east, and that a portion of this river, now widened out by the sea, has become the Solent between the Isle of Wight and the mainland. The course of this ancient river appears to have been a little to the south and seaward of the present line of the coast at Bournemouth;

and some of the gravels which formerly lined its valley now cap the cliffs for some distance between Poole Harbour and Hengistbury Head, and thence on in the direction of Portsmouth.

In these gravels, a very large number of palæolithic implements has been found. The first discovery at Bournemouth was made in 1866, [2695] by Mr. Alfred H. Stevens, of Salisbury, and in immediately subsequent years they were principally due to Dr. H. P. Blackmore, my son, P. Norman Evans, Mr. Albert Way, and others. The first implements were found in the gravel, after it had been dug and spread upon the roads; but Dr. Blackmore found an implement *in situ*, and two or three rough flakes, close to Boscombe Mouth, at almost the highest point of the cliff, more than 100 feet above the sea-level.

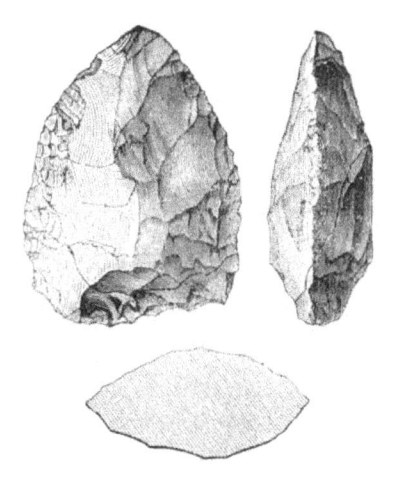

Fig. 474.—Boscombe, Bournemouth. 1/2

This implement, which is nearly white and unworn, is preserved in the Blackmore Museum, and is represented in Fig. 474. Numerous implements of other forms have since been found in the gravel dug in the neighbourhood of Boscombe. Among them is a side-scraper 3 1/2 inches long and of the same type as that from Santon Downham, Fig. 437. It was found by Mrs. E. Sandars, of Bournemouth, who has kindly added it to my collection. A rude chopper-like implement was also found there. One of the finest, however, of all the early Boscombe implements is that shown in Fig. 475, which was found by my son Norman in 1868. It has unfortunately lost a portion near the base, through a crack in the stone, but is otherwise perfect. The material is not, as usual, flint from the Chalk, but chert from the Upper Greensand. The surface is slightly ochreous, and to some extent lustrous. I have another implement of chert, but of ovate form, found at Boscombe, as well as some good pointed implements of flint. In the railway-cutting east of Boscombe, I, some years ago, found a flake of flint. Other implements have been found in gravel which is believed to have been dug to the west of Bournemouth, near the Bourne Valley Pottery and the turnpike on the Poole road. That shown in Fig. 476 was found by Miss Way, and kindly communicated to me by her father, the late Mr. Albert Way, F.S.A. It is of flint, now of a milky-white colour. Mr. Way has found three or four other specimens of much the same character. I have two large, rather coarsely chipped, irregularly oval specimens from the same gravels, both found by my son Norman.

Fig. 475.—Boscombe, Bournemouth. 1/2

The beds near the turnpike are from about 6 to 8 feet thick, and rest on a slightly irregular surface of Bagshot Sands. The gravel consists principally of subangular and rolled flints, a few Tertiary flint-pebbles, a considerable proportion of small quartz pebbles, and a few fragments of old rocks and Upper Greensand chert; the whole in a sandy matrix, and having in places some sandy seams. I am not aware of any mammalian or molluscan remains having been found in them. They are nearly, if not quite, on the summit of table-land, slightly inclining seawards, and with the valley of the Bourne to the north, with higher ground beyond it and also to the west. The surface near the turnpike is about 130 feet above the mean sea-level.

Following the presumed course of the ancient river Solent for about ten miles eastward, along what is now the coast, we come to Barton. For the whole distance the land to the north is thickly capped with gravel; and at Barton, on the slope of the cliff, a flat, oval implement, 6 inches long, and in form much like that from Hill Head, Fig. 466, was found by an officer of the Coast Guard, about 1868, and was subsequently presented to the Christy Collection by Mr. Albert Way, F.S.A.

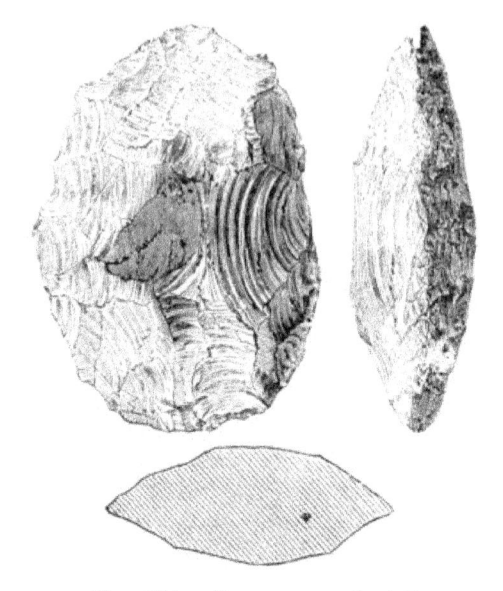

Fig. 476.—Bournemouth. 1/2

Since that time an astonishing number of palæolithic implements has been found in the district extending from Chuton Bunny by Barton and Hordwell to Milford. I have about sixty specimens from this district in my own collection, many of them very perfect of their kind. For the most part they have been picked up on the shore and on the talus of the gravel-capped cliff, but they have occasionally been found in the gravel itself. A few have been made of Upper Greensand chert, but the majority are of flint. Nearly all the usual types are represented, several by large examples. I have pointed, oval, and ovate specimens, as much as 8 and 8 1/2 inches in length. Those from the gravel are as a rule sharp and but little abraded, while the condition of those found on the shore depends upon the length of time that they have been exposed to the rolling action of the sea since their fall from the cliff.

A palæolithic flake has been found still farther east, at Stone, [2696] between Exbury and Calshot Castle.

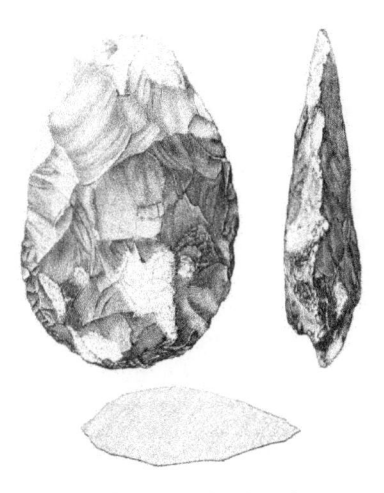

Fig. 477.—Broom Pit, Axminster. 1/2

Assuming the existence of an ancient river Solent flowing at an elevation of upwards of 100 feet above the present level of the sea at Bournemouth, its western sources must have drained much the same basin as that of the rivers now discharging into Poole Harbour; but without at present entering into that question, I may mention the discovery of a palæolithic implement at Dewlish, about 3 miles N. of Piddletown, Dorsetshire, by Mr. James Brown, of Salisbury. It is very neatly chipped, but slightly unsymmetrical in form, one side being straight and the other curved; but in general character it resembles Fig. 430 from Thetford, having been made from a large flake, and showing the original crust of the flint at its base. It was found on the surface, at the top of a high hill, at no great distance from the branch of the Trent or Piddle, which flows past Dewlish. Elephant [2697] remains have been found near the same place, which have, however, been assigned to *Elephas meridionalis*.

In the Blackmore Museum there were in 1872 four implements of chert, of oval and tongue-shaped types, found during the erection of the telegraph posts between Chard and Axminster. There was also another thin oval implement of ochreous flint, 7 1/2 inches long and 3 1/2 broad, which was found near Colyton, Devon. The exact locality where those first mentioned were found, is unknown; but it appears probable that the gravel, like that at Colyton, belongs to the valley of the Axe, in which I suggested in 1872 that further search should be made.

Such a search has long since been rewarded. In 1877 [2698] I recorded some discoveries at Broom, near Axminster, and in 1878 the late Mr. W. S. M. D'Urban [2699] gave an account of the ballast pit at Broom, in the parish of Hawkchurch, near Axminster, and close to the river Axe. It was worked in a low hill consisting of chert gravel intermingled with seams of ferruginous and sandy clay, and a section was exposed about 40 feet deep, the base being about 150 feet above the level of the sea, which comes within a distance of about six miles. At that time numerous palæolithic implements of various types had been found in the pit. They were formed of dark Upper Greensand chert, and some were much water-worn, while others were quite sharp and uninjured. Since then very many more have been collected, and a fine series of them is preserved in the Albert Memorial Museum at Exeter. There are also some good specimens in the Horniman Museum [2700] at Forest Hill, S.E. I have engraved a typical example of the ovate form in my own collection as Fig. 477.

Some implements from Broom are of large size. I have a very rude specimen that I found among the ballast on the South Western Railway in August, 1877. It is 8 1/2 inches long and 6 inches wide. Other specimens are small. The ovate type seems to predominate, but the pointed forms are not scarce. A few broad flakes trimmed at the edges, of the so-called Le Moustier type, occur with the other forms.

In the valley of the Culm, at Kentisbeare, near Cullompton, Mr. W. Downes, [2701] in 1879, found a chert implement in form like Plate II., Fig. 17.

With the exception of those from the bone-caves of Devonshire, no palæolithic implements have as yet been found farther west in Britain.

CHAPTER XXIV.
FORMS AND CHARACTERISTICS OF IMPLEMENTS FROM THE RIVER-DRIFT.

Having now briefly described the circumstances of the discovery of these palæolithic implements in various localities in England, and given illustrations showing their usual forms, it will be well to say a few words as to their character and probable uses. The general resemblance in form between the series of implements found in the River-drift of England and in that of France, is obvious to all who have had the opportunity of examining collections formed in the two countries; while the character of the deposits and of the associated mammalian and molluscan remains being also the same, the implements in each may be regarded as being practically of the same age, and formed by the same race of men. In my former attempt at classifying them, I therefore took my characteristic specimens indifferently from either side of the Channel; more especially, as in 1861, when I drew the plate [2702] illustrative of the different types, but few discoveries had been made in England. As this plate has been considered useful as affording a convenient conspectus of the prevailing forms found in the River-drift, I make no apology for here reproducing it in a somewhat modified form, though many of the specimens engraved are of French and not of British origin. In conjunction with the woodcuts given in the text, the two plates into which it is now divided will give a fairly complete idea of most of the forms of palæolithic implements.

In first writing on this subject in 1859, [2703] I divided these implements generally into three classes, as follows:—

- 1. Flint-flakes apparently intended for arrow-heads or knives.

- 2. Pointed weapons analogous to lance or spear-heads.

- 3. Oval or almond-shaped implements presenting a cutting edge all round.

I stated at the same time that of the second class there were two varieties, the one with a rounded cutting point, and the other acutely pointed; and that there was also so much diversity in their forms, that the classes, especially the second and third, might be said to blend, or run one into the other. In reconsidering the question in 1861, [2704] I saw but little to alter in the proposed classification, and even now find no cause for suggesting any material modification, though there are certainly some additional types to be added to those with which I was then acquainted.

The late Mr. E. T. Stevens, [2705] who had as much experience as any one in classifying these implements, suggested a somewhat different arrangement of the forms, dividing them under seven heads; and in the following remarks I shall adopt some of his terminology, though slightly departing from his order of sequence.

FLAKES.

These may be divided in the same manner as those belonging to the Surface or Neolithic period, into external, ridged, flat, and polygonal. They are either simple or unworked; or wrought into form along the whole or part of the edge.

- 1. External flakes, or those first struck off a block of flint, the crust of which forms their convex face, are of common occurrence in the River-drift, but they are not often noticed or preserved by the workmen. Many of them are probably mere spalls resulting from the manufacture of the more highly-wrought implements. Some few, however, appear to have been utilized as tools, apparently for scraping.

- 2. Ridged flakes, or those of triangular section with a single ridge formed by two facets on the convex face, are extremely rare in the gravel-deposits, though occasionally found. Indeed, the art of making long narrow flakes, such as abounded in Denmark in Neolithic times, and are not uncommon in Britain, seems to have been almost unknown to the men whose relics we find in the River-drift; unless, perhaps, their absence in the gravel may be accounted for in some other way than by their non-existence. It is indeed possible that the implements found in the River-gravels were those for out-door, and not for domestic, use; and certainly, in some of the cave-deposits, where the large implements are extremely scarce, these skilfully-formed long flakes occur in considerable numbers. Generally speaking, the proportion of flakes to the more highly-wrought implements appears also to be far greater in the caves than that in the gravels. This apparent greater abundance may, however, to some extent be due to the flakes in the gravel escaping the notice of the workmen, or to their having been broken to pieces during the formation of the gravel.

- 3. Flat flakes are more common, but these are usually shorter, thicker, and broader than those of the Surface Period. They frequently exhibit that minute chipping at the edge, which is probably the result of wear from scraping some hard substance, such as bone or even wood. Occasionally a notch has been worn in the edge of the flake, as if the object scraped had been cylindrical.

- 4. Polygonal flakes are those most abundant in the River-drift; but the large, broad flakes of this character, such as are common in the valley of the Somme, and especially in its lower deposits, as at Montiers, near Amiens, are much rarer in England. Fig. 461, from Reculver, is a flake of this character, but I am not sure whether it does not, more properly speaking, come under the head of a wrought flake, as it appears to have been somewhat trimmed at the edges. It is worth while remarking, that many of the French specimens have the edge worn away by use, just on one side of the bulb of percussion, at a place where there is generally a clean sharp edge in a newly-made flake of this form. Occasionally similar marks of use are apparent on English specimens of the same character.

Taken as a whole, the simple flakes of the River-drift Period may be described as larger, coarser, thicker, and broader than those of the Surface Period, or of caves of later date than Le Moustier. Their use appears to have been for cutting and scraping whatever required to be cut or scraped.

I formerly regarded some of them as having possibly been arrow-heads, but the extreme rarity of any light, sharp-pointed flakes, and the absence of any evidence that those who fashioned them were acquainted with the use of the bow, render this assumption almost untenable. It is, however, barely possible that some may have served to tip spears or lances.

TRIMMED FLAKES.

One of the commonest forms into which flint flakes were fashioned in Neolithic times, is that produced by trimming the end of the flake to a semicircular bevelled edge. To this form the name of "scraper" has been applied, from its still being used in that capacity by the Eskimos and some North American tribes. The same, or nearly the same, form occurs among the instruments belonging to the Palæolithic Period. Such scrapers are very abundant in many of the French caves, and, as has already been seen, are not entirely wanting in Kent's Cavern and in other British caves. They are, however, of very rare occurrence in the River-drift, and when found, are hardly ever trimmed to so regular and neatly-chipped a segmental edge, as those either from the surface or from the caves.

Occasionally the end of a flake has been worked to a quadrantal edge, so that one of the straight sides is much longer than the other. In some cases the end of the flake appears to have become rounded by wear rather than by trimming.

The implement from Icklingham, Fig. 424, formed from a polygonal flake, is very scraper-like in character. Its convex face shows a great many more facets than is usual with the scrapers of the Neolithic Period. A more characteristic scraper is that from High-Lodge Hill, Fig. 426. It is mainly among the implements found in a matrix of clay, or on a "Palæolithic floor," that these more delicate forms occur. They are not only more likely to have been injured by rolling, but when they form constituent parts of beds of gravel are also less liable to attract observation than are the larger implements.

There is another form which, when of large size, seems almost peculiar to the caves and the River-drift, and to which the term "side-scraper" may be applied. The instruments of this kind are made from broad flakes, usually about twice as broad as they are long. The butt-end of the flake—that at which the blow was administered to strike it off from the parent block—is either left blunt, or trimmed into such a form as may conveniently be held in the hand; the other end, which, owing to the great breadth of the flake, forms the side of the implement, is trimmed to a segmental edge by blows given on the flat inner face of the flake which is left as originally produced. Figs. 437 and 453 show implements of the side-scraper form in flint, and Fig. 443 one less carefully finished in quartzite. The edge is in some instances much more acute than in others. They appear to have been held in the hand, and used in some cases for cutting or chopping, and in others for scraping. The flints of what have been termed the "Plateau types" have their edges much more obtuse and rounded, and their chipping and wear seem to me due to natural causes and not to human workmanship. There are some implements which have been made from broad flakes, but which have both faces more or less trimmed, so as to come perhaps more properly under another category. Another form of trimmed flake is that in which the side-edges have received their outline by secondary chipping, as in Fig. 431. Occasionally they are worked to a sharp point, like the Le Moustier type of Mortillet; and when large, and boldly re-chipped on the convex face, merge in what has been termed the shoe-shaped type.

POINTED IMPLEMENTS.

These are very various in form, and present great difficulties in any attempt to classify them. There are, however, some characteristic types, to attain which would seem to have been the aim of those who made the implements, though they were not always successful; and an innumerable variety of intermediate forms has been the result. To one of these types Mr. Stevens has applied the term "pear-shaped," but though the outline may be that of a pear, the section is so different, that the term seems open to objection. I would rather follow the nomenclature of the French quarry-men, who have given the name *langues-de-chat* to these implements; and term them "tongue-shaped." They are indeed as varied in their forms as the tongues of the different members of the higher orders of the animal creation, including both birds and beasts, and range as widely in their proportions, but they still retain a general resemblance to a tongue. They are either acute, or round, at the point, and the side-edges are usually sharp; but the characteristics of the form are that the greatest thickness of the implement is far nearer to the butt than to the point, and that the butt is more or less truncated. Fig. 428 gives a typical example of a long, narrow, acutely-pointed, tongue-shaped implement, equally convex on both faces, with straight side-edges, and thick truncated butt trimmed into form. Fig. 417, though so different in proportions, is a short implement of the same character. Fig. 427 affords an example of a broader variety, with a rounded point, and Fig. 447 of one broader still.

Figs. 458 and 463 may be described as tongue-shaped implements, with incurved sides; Fig. 433 as kite-like; Figs. 420 and 472 as ovate; and Fig. 423 as sub-triangular; but the general form of the implements is still, in each instance, tongue-shaped. It is frequently the case that one face of these implements is more convex than the other.

Another variety shows upon the rounded butt some considerable portion of the outer surface of the original pebble or flint from which the implement was made, as in Fig. 457. All such seem to belong to the tongue-shaped class, the character of the butt proving beyond all doubt that it was the pointed end that was used for cutting or piercing, while the butt-end, as is almost universally the case with the tongue-shaped implements, is adapted for being held in the hand.

I was at one time inclined to think that a considerable proportion of these instruments might have been attached to shafts, so as to serve for spear or javelin-heads; but so few of them are so roughly chipped at the butt-end as to render them really inconvenient to be held in the hand, that their use as spear-heads is very doubtful. A specimen from Bedford [2706] is said to have had the appearance of having had the butt-end wrapped round with grass so that it might be the more conveniently held in the hand. It is true that the acutely-pointed instruments appear to be rather weapons of offence than mere tools or implements, and not improbably to have been used in the chase; while those with rounded points seem to have been more adapted for the ordinary purposes of life. Some of them show marks of wear at the end, as if they had been used for chopping; and others, at each side, as if produced by boring some hard substance. They may have been used for digging in the ground for esculent roots; for cutting holes through ice, for fishing purposes, as suggested by Sir Joseph Prestwich; or even for tilling the soil, were those who fashioned them acquainted with agriculture, which I must confess appears to me improbable.

Another form of pointed implement is flat on one face, and convex on the other. The flat face has frequently been produced by a single blow, so that the form might be regarded as a variety of trimmed flake. The convex face has, however, in general been fashioned by bold strokes, in the same manner as the more common forms of large implements. In typical specimens the butt is thick, and the whole form is so like that of a shoe, that the term "shoe-shaped" has been applied to it. For the thinner specimens, I would suggest the term "flat-faced." Specimens of the shoe-shaped and flat-faced types are given in Figs. 418A, 429, and 430. It is hard to say what particular purpose such instruments were intended to serve.

Another form of pointed implement has a sharp edge along one side and at the point only, the other side being left thick, and occasionally with the natural crust of the flint upon it. Such thick-backed single-edged implements appear to have served as knives of the rudest kind. Fig. 10 in Plate I. shows a specimen of this character. Others, like Fig. 419D, present a more chopper-like form, and were probably used as hatchets held in the hand without hafts. The form is not uncommon in the Le Moustier cave.

In other cases, the end of a long nodule of flint has been chipped to a pointed form, as in Fig. 418; or a flint has been converted by half a dozen blows into a rude pointed implement, probably to serve some temporary purpose. If, after being used, such tools were thrown away, as not being worth preserving, their abundance in some gravels is the less remarkable.

There is yet another large subdivision of the pointed implements, in which the butt is chipped to a sharper edge than in those to which the name of tongue-shaped more properly applies. They pass imperceptibly from the tongue-shaped at one end of the series into the oval or almond-shaped implements, presenting a cutting edge all round, at the other. For these latter I would propose the name of

SHARP-RIMMED IMPLEMENTS.

These are usually almost equally convex on the two faces, but vary in form, being most frequently ovate—that is to say, rounded at both ends, but having one end broader than the other—oval, with the two ends similar or nearly so, and almond-shaped, or ovate-lanceolate, with one end pointed. Rarer forms of the same character are heart-shaped, sub-triangular, lozenge-shaped, and lunate. To these must be added the form to which the term "perch-backed" has been given, from its resemblance to that fish; and that to which Mr. Stevens has applied the term discoidal.

The ovate sharp-rimmed implements vary considerably in size and also in general proportions. Specimens of the type may be seen in Figs. 456 and 467.

In some of these ovate specimens a flat place has been intentionally left on one of the sides towards the broad end, apparently to facilitate its being held in the hand and used as a knife. In some of the implements, which, like several of those from Hoxne, and that from Bury St. Edmunds, Fig. 419A, have lain in brick-earth instead of gravel, so that the edges are uninjured, minute marks of wear, as if from scraping or cutting, may be seen on the edges, principally opposite to this flat spot.

Both these and the oval sharp-rimmed implements are, as a rule, thin in proportion to their size. Specimens of the latter form are shown in Figs. 421 and 466.

The typical almond-shaped implements are scarcer than either of the foregoing. They also occasionally exhibit the flat spot already described, on one of their sides. A remarkably symmetrical and short example of this form is shown in Fig. 435.

The heart-shaped sharp-rimmed implements are rare, and resemble the sub-triangular, with the exception of their having a slight curvature inwards at the base. One of these is shown in Fig. 432. Mr. Stevens considers, that if any of the drift implements were used as spear-heads, they were of this form.

The sub-triangular sharp-rimmed implements are much rarer than those of the tongue-shaped character, in which the base of the triangle is blunt. Fig. 471, however, belongs to this class, though it is much rounded at the point. Some of the cave-implements, like Fig. 386, are intermediate between this and the ovate form. Among the curious implements, apparently of Palæolithic age, which have been found in some abundance in parts of Poitou, the sharp-rimmed sub-triangular type is common. The form has also been found in the Department of the Aisne, [2707] and in the cave of Hydrequent, in the Pas-de-Calais.

The lozenge-shaped implements of this class are pointed at each end, but the sides are never straight. Fig. 440 shows a thick specimen of this form. Some of the large flat implements from the valley of the Somme are more of the pointed oval or *vesica piscis* form, than lozenge-shaped.

The lunate and perch-backed implements having one side considerably more curved than the other are very scarce, but more have been found at Santon Downham than elsewhere. One of these is shown in Fig. 436, and another from Shrub Hill in Fig. 448. I have also met with the form among the implements from Barton Cliff, Hants. They are possibly mere accidental varieties of the oval or ovate form; and indeed it seems doubtful whether it is worth while to insist much on these subdivisions of form, many of which must, necessarily, have resulted from the manner in which the flint happened to break during the process of manufacture. Though, therefore, I have here attempted a somewhat detailed classification, it must not be supposed that I consider each form of implement to have been specially made to serve some special requirement, as is the case with many of the tools and weapons of the present day. I am far more ready to think that only two main divisions can be established, though even these may be said to shade off into each other; I mean pointed implements for piercing, digging, or boring, and sharp-edged implements for cutting or scraping.

The discoidal implements are described by Mr. Stevens [2708] as very coarsely worked; in typical specimens, nearly circular, very thick in the centre, and brought to an edge all round. He thinks they may have been used as missiles. The same may be said of polygonal blocks of flint, from the whole surface of which broad flakes have been dislodged by blows given in various directions. They may, however, possibly be only cores. In form they much resemble the blocks or "knuder" from the Danish kjökken-möddings.

I have never seen any of the long prismatic cores from the River-drift, though some are of rather regular form. A few hammer-stones, such as must have been used in fashioning the flint implements, have been found, and some have been already mentioned. It is, however, difficult, among a mass of rolled and waterworn pebbles, to recognize with certainty such as have served as hammers.

If, to the more regular types embraced in the foregoing classification, we add a considerable number of roughly-chipped, unsymmetrical, but, generally speaking, pointed forms of implements, and a few abnormal shapes, as, for instance, that shown in Fig. 444, we shall have a good idea of the character of the stone implements hitherto discovered in the River-drift, whether of England or the Continent.

A glance at the figures will at once show how different in character they are, as a whole, from those of the Surface or Neolithic Period, excepting, of course, mere flakes, and implements made from them, and simple blocks and hammer-stones. So far as we at present know, not a single implement from the River-drift has been sharpened by grinding or polishing, though, of course, it would be unsafe to affirm that such a process was unknown at the time when they were in use. With the unpolished implements of the Neolithic Period, which most nearly approach those of the Palæolithic in form, it will as a rule be found that the former are intended for cutting at the broader end, and the latter at the narrower or more pointed end. Even in the character of the chipping, a practised observer will, in most instances, discern a difference.

Thirty-eight years ago, when first treating of the character of these instruments, [2709] I pointed out these differences between the implements of the two periods, as being marked and distinct; and though since that time, from our knowledge of the form and character of the stone implements of both periods having been much enlarged, some few exceptions may be made to a too sweeping assertion of these differences, yet on the whole, I think, they have been fully sustained.

Unground flint implements, with a sharp point, and a thick truncated butt, and, in fact, what I have termed tongue-shaped in form, are, for instance, no longer confined to the Drift, but have been found by myself, with polished implements, on the shores of Lough Neagh, [2710] in Ireland; and yet, though analogous in form, they differ in the character of the workmanship, and in their proportions, from those from the gravel. The difference is such, that though possibly a single specimen might pass muster as of Palæolithic form, yet a group of three or four would at once strike an experienced eye as presenting other characteristics.

In the same manner, some of the roughly-chipped specimens from Cissbury and elsewhere, such, for instance, as that shown in Fig. 28, appear to be of the tongue-shaped type, or of some other River-drift forms. These are, however, exceptional in character; and as their finding appears to be confined to the sites of manufactories of flint implements, where a very large proportion of the specimens found are merely "wasters" produced in the manufacture, it is doubtful how far they are to be regarded as finished tools.

On this subject of the difference in character between the Palæolithic and Neolithic forms, I have been severely taken to task by M. Zinck, [2711] who has figured several Danish Neolithic specimens in juxtaposition with some of my own figures of implements from the Drift. In many cases, however, the comparison is made between implements of very different dimensions, though, by being drawn to different scales, they are made to appear of the same size in the figures; and, in other cases, the specimens engraved are apparently unfinished, or merely wasters thrown away.

But even granting that these exceptional instances of resemblance can be found, there is no one who can deny that the general *facies* of a collection of implements from the River-drift, and that of one from the Surface is absolutely distinct. With regard to the Scandinavian stone antiquities, I possess perhaps as extensive a collection of them as any one out of that country; and further, I have more than once examined the collections, both public and private, at Copenhagen, as well as at Christiania, Stockholm, and Lund, and yet I do not remember to have seen any specimen—unless, possibly, a mere flake or rough block—which, if placed before me without comment, I should have taken to be Palæolithic.

In most cases, even if a similarity of form should be found to exist, there will be a difference in the character of the surface of the material; the deep staining, more especially, and the glossy surface so common on the implements from the gravel, being but rarely met with on those from the surface soil.

But though, on the whole, so widely differing from the implements of the Neolithic Period, those belonging to Palæolithic times show a marvellous correspondence with each other, in whatever part of England they are found; and this correspondence extends, in an equal degree, to the implements found in the River-gravels of France and of other Continental countries. In illustration of this, Mr. Flower has engraved, [2712] side by side, two implements from Thetford, and two from St. Acheul, each pair being almost identical both in shape and size. But what is more remarkable still, this resemblance in form prevails not only with the implements from the River-gravels of Western Europe, but with those from the lateritic beds of Southern India. It is true that the material is somewhat different, the Indian implements being formed of compact quartzite instead of flint, and that this circumstance somewhat affects the character of the fracture and facets; but so far as general form is concerned, they may be said to be identical with those from the European River-drifts.

The original discoverer of these implements (in 1863), Mr. R. Bruce Foote, [2713] has described them on more than one occasion, and it would be out of place here to enter into details concerning them. Suffice it to say, that they have been found in the Madras Presidency by Mr. Bruce Foote, Mr. King, and others, *in situ*, in beds to which, whether correctly or not I will not attempt to determine, the name of "lateritic" has been given, and at an elevation of 300 feet and upwards, above the sea in the neighbourhood of which they often lie. These lateritic beds consist principally of a red ferruginous clay, more or less sandy, and occasionally contain, or pass into, gravelly beds. Those fringing the coast have been regarded as of marine origin, but as they contain no marine organisms, and as in some of their characters they closely resemble undoubtedly fluviatile deposits, it is possible that this view may be incorrect, and that they originally covered one of the slopes of a valley connected with a large river, the other slope of which has now disappeared in consequence of the encroachment of the sea. However this may be, in several valleys, at a higher level above the sea than the beds in which most of the specimens were found, "chipped quartzite implements were obtained from unquestionable river-gravels." [2714]

They have also been found in the South Mahratta country, especially in the Malprabba [2715] valley. In 1873 Mr. Hacket [2716] found an ovate implement of quartzite (5 inches), *in situ*, in clay, in the Narbadá valley, eight miles north of Gadarwara, below a bed of ossiferous gravel, apparently of Pleistocene age. Mr. W. T. Blanford has found them in Hyderabad, Mr. V. Ball in Orissa, and Mr. J. Cockburn [2717] in South Mirzapore. Mr. Bruce Foote [2718] has recorded a large number of other Palæolithic finds in Southern India, between 10° and 16° of N. latitude and 76° to 80° E. longitude, mostly in connection with existing river-valleys.

The curious flint or chert implements found at Abu Shahrein, [2719] in Southern Babylonia, which much resemble those of the Palæolithic age in form, seem more probably to be Neolithic. The broad end appears to have been that intended for cutting, the point being left blunt.

An implement of more truly palæolithic character, found on the surface of a bed of gravel between Mount Tabor and the Lake of Tiberias, was exhibited by the Abbé Richard [2720] at the meeting of the British Association at Edinburgh in 1871.

Another implement of palæolithic type was obtained by M. de Vogué at Bethsaour, [2721] near Bethlehem. Others, both of quartzite and flint, have been found by Mr. Frank Calvert on a ridge of hills near the Dardanelles. [2722] Mr. H. Stopes, F.G.S., also found such an implement near Jerusalem [2723] in 1880.

In Algeria implements of undoubted palæolithic forms have occurred at Ousidan [2724] and at Palikao, [2725] in the province of Oran. Sir John Lubbock has also found a specimen made of flint at Kolea, [2726] Algeria. What may be instruments of the same age have been found in gravel at Gafsa, [2727] in Tunis. In Egypt several well-marked palæolithic implements have been found. That picked up near Thebes in 1872 by the late Mr. Ouvry [2728] I then regarded as Neolithic, but it may be of earlier date. Those described by Sir John Lubbock [2729] in 1873, and Professor Henry W. Haynes, of Boston, Mass., in 1881, have many of them greater claims to be regarded as palæolithic. But the discovery of flint flakes by General Pitt Rivers [2730] in the stratified gravel in which the Tombs of the Kings, near Thebes, are hewn, placed their great antiquity beyond doubt. Mr. H. Stopes also found an implement of palæolithic type half a mile from the spring of Moses, near Cairo, [2731] in 1880. More recent discoveries of well-marked palæolithic implements at high levels above the valley of the Nile, such as have been made by Professor Flinders Petrie [2732] and Mr. H. W. Seton-Karr, show that what is now Egypt was occupied by man in Palæolithic times. Numerous other discoveries in Egypt of implements of well-marked palæolithic forms have been recorded by M. J. de Morgan. [2733] More remarkable still is the discovery by Mr. Seton-Karr of implements of most of the well-known palæolithic forms at high levels in Somaliland, [2734] in positions apparently connected with existing river-courses, such as that of the Issutugan.

In the southernmost part of Africa, in the Cape Colony, [2735] and in Natal, stone implements have been discovered which, from their shape, if that alone were sufficient, may be classed as Palæolithic. They are chipped out of various silicious rocks, and are for the most part found upon the surface, though occasionally at considerable depths below it. They have been described by Mr. W. D. Gooch, [2736] Mr. W. H. Penning, [2737] Mr. J. C. Rickard, [2738] and others. Mr. Rickard describes four series from the Junction, Port Elizabeth, East London, and the Diamond Fields. He has presented me with several specimens, mostly in quartz. Mr. E. J. Dunn has given me a remarkably symmetrical ovate implement (6 inches), made of some metamorphic schist, and found under nine feet of stratified beds at Process-fontein, Victoria West, in 1873, and Mr. J. B. Taylor has presented to me ovate implements of quartzite from the valley of the Embabaan, Swaziland.

I have elsewhere, [2739] when calling attention to the discoveries of Mr. Seton-Karr in Somaliland, remarked that their great interest consists in the identity in form of the implements with those found in the Pleistocene deposits of North-Western Europe and elsewhere. Any one comparing the implements from such widely separated localities, the one with the other, must feel that if they have not been actually made by the same race of men, there must have been some contact of the closest kind between the races who manufactured implements of such identical forms. Those from Somaliland occur in both flint (much whitened and decomposed by exposure) and in quartzite, but the implements made from the two materials are almost indistinguishable in form. Those of lanceolate shape are most abundant, but the usual ovate and other forms are present in considerable numbers.

Turning westward from Somaliland we meet with flint implements of the same character found by Professor Flinders Petrie at a height of many hundred feet above the valley of the Nile. A few have been discovered in Northern Africa; they recur in the valley of the Manzanares in Spain, in some districts in Central Italy, and abound in the river-valleys of France and England. Turning eastward we encounter implements of analogous forms, one found by M. Chantre in the valley of the Euphrates, and many made of quartzite in the lateritic deposits of India; while in Southern Africa almost similar types occur, though their age is somewhat uncertain.

That the cradle of the human family must have been situated in some part of the world where the climate was genial, and the means of subsistence readily obtained, seems almost self-evident; and that these discoveries in Somaliland may serve to elucidate the course by which human civilization, such as it was, if not indeed the human race, proceeded westward from its early home in the East is a fair subject for speculation. But, under any circumstances, this discovery aids in bridging over the interval between Palæolithic man in Britain and in India, and adds another link to the chain of evidence by which the original cradle of the human family may eventually be identified, and tends to prove the unity of race between the inhabitants of Asia, Africa, and Europe, in Palæolithic times.

With regard to the reputed discoveries of palæolithic implements at Trenton, [2740] New Jersey, and elsewhere in the United States of America, I venture to reserve my judgment. Opinion in America [2741] is divided, one antiquary recording that in a quarry, the antiquity of which does not exceed two hundred years, and from which the Indians obtained chert from which they chipped out their implements, forms which exactly resemble the "turtle-backs" of Trenton occur; while other writers carry back the beds and the implements they contain so far as to Glacial times. Recent excavations seem to give evidence of, at all events, a high antiquity.

To return to the purposes of the implements themselves. With regard to their general uses, many opinions have been expressed. Sir Joseph Prestwich [2742] has suggested that some of them may have been used as ice-chisels, for cutting holes in ice, to obtain water and to be enabled to fish during continued frosts, as is practised by many occupants of northern regions at the present day. Such a use is of course possible; but the occurrence of implements of similar forms in Madras, Somaliland, Northern and Southern Africa, seems to militate against this view, unless we are to suppose that at some remote time a glacial climate may have prevailed in those parts of the world also, as we believe it to have done here.

M. Boucher de Perthes thought that some of the pointed forms might have been used as wedges for splitting wood or grubbing for esculent roots, or possibly for tilling the ground. Some of the sharp-rimmed implements he regarded as hatchets. He has pointed out various methods in which they might have been hafted and used. [2743] Some of the smaller size, I have suggested, may have been missiles. On the whole, however, although I have pointed out the manner in which some of the implements appear to have been held, and have called attention to the marks of wear on their edges, I revert to my old opinion, [2744] "that it is nearly useless to speculate on the purposes to which they were applied."

To use the words of Sir John Lubbock, [2745] "Almost as well might we ask to what would they not be applied. Infinite as are our instruments, who would attempt even at present to say what was the use of a knife? But the primitive savage had no such choice of tools; we see before us, perhaps, the whole contents of his workshop; and with these weapons, rude as they seem to us, he may have cut down trees, scooped them out into canoes, grubbed up roots, killed animals and enemies, cut up his food, made holes in winter through the ice, prepared firewood, built huts, and in some cases at least, they may have served as sling-stones." To these possible uses I may add that of fashioning other instruments of wood and bone, such as may yet be eventually discovered with them in the same beds of drift, as has already been the case in caves, with regard to those of bone or stag's horn.

Considering the number of the stone implements which have been collected, it seems at first sight singular that no other relics of those who made them have as yet been discovered. For, nothing of moment in the shape of implements, utensils, or appliances, made of other materials than stone, have as yet been found, nor with but few exceptions, any portions of the human skeleton. It must, however, be remembered how imperishable in their nature are flint and the other silicious stones used for these ancient implements, as compared with the other materials which, among a savage people, come readily to hand, such as wood, bone, horn, or hide; and, moreover, that even the flint implements, in many cases testify to the rough usage they have undergone by water transport, before being finally laid in their resting-place in the gravel. Lighter objects, such as those of wood and other organic materials, would, if exposed to the action of a stream, in many cases have been washed right away to the sea; or, if accidentally lodged, would have perished by the ordinary processes of decay. It is only in the case of bone implements that we can hope that future discoveries may bring them to light; but even this contingency depends mainly on their attracting the eye of some intelligent gravel-digger; since, for one yard of gravel examined by a scientific observer, it is probable that thousands pass through the hands of ordinary labourers, who require some instruction before they can be brought to recognize even the best-wrought forms of flint implements. Some few objects both of wood and bone, showing traces of having been cut by Palæolithic man, have been found near London by Mr. Worthington Smith, [2746] but these traces are but slight.

The comparative absence of human bones in these beds seems to be partly dependent on the same cause of deficient observation; but portions of a human skeleton, apparently contemporary with the beds in which they lay, and in which also palæolithic implements occurred, have been found in the neighbourhood of Paris, and a human skull near Bury St. Edmunds. [2747] The Galley Hill [2748] skeleton affords but a doubtful instance.

Living, as in all probability man must have done, by the chase, his numbers must necessarily have been small, as compared with those of the animals on which he subsisted. Sir John Lubbock has calculated that among the North American Indians the proportion is about 1 to 750: and as man is in all probability at least four times as long-lived as most of these animals, the proportion might be increased to 1 to 3,000. If this were so, and all the bones were preserved, it would follow that about 3,000 bones of the different animals of the chase would be found to one of human origin. But here again the fact comes in, which is also pointed out by Sir John Lubbock, that in most of the beds of gravel no trace has as yet been found of any animal so small as man. Other possible causes for this scarcity of human remains in the River-drift will be mentioned at a subsequent page. Even in sepulchres of the Neolithic [2749] period the bones of those buried have not unfrequently entirely disappeared.

Of what was the condition and stage of civilization of the men of that time, it is probable that the implements by themselves afford but insufficient means for judging. Many of them, though rude, may be matched in that respect by stone implements in use among the Australian savages of the present century; while others again show great dexterity in working so intractable a material as flint, though in no way approaching that attained by some of the flint-workers in Neolithic times. Comparing the implements of the two periods together, the main differences are that the forms are fewer, and, as a rule, larger and more rudely chipped in the earlier period; and, beyond this, that the art of grinding to an edge appears to have been unknown. If we regard, as probably we safely may do, the remains of human art found in caves like Kent's Cavern, associated with bones of animals belonging to the same fauna as that of the River-Drift, as being attributable to the same age and probably to the same race of people, we get some further insight into their habits and conditions of life. The evidence seems to justify us in regarding these River-drift or Cave folk as hunters, and probably nomads, subsisting to a great extent on the produce of the chase; living where possible under natural shelters, to which they brought either the whole or portions of the slaughtered animals, the bones of which, fractured for the purpose of extracting the marrow, we find accumulated in the caves: during the latter part of their occupation of this country acquainted with the art of spearing fish by means of barbed harpoons; and able to sew, though probably not to spin or to weave. This last supposition, like some others, rests on negative evidence only, but is still justified by the absence of spindle-whorls. Their thread, like that of the Eskimos, would seem to have been formed of animal sinew or intestine, and to have been used for joining together skins, in which the holes, for the needle to pass through, were made by awls of pointed bone.

Some knowledge of drawing and engraving is evinced by our own Cave-dwellers, as well as by those of France. These latter had personal ornaments in the shape of perforated shells and teeth, and if the view could be supported that the perforated fossil *Coscinopora globularis* [2750] was in use for beads of necklaces, we should have evidence of a similar use of personal ornaments among the River-drift folk.

A want of acquaintance with cereals is suggested by the absence of mealing-stones or corn-crushers. The pounding-stones, such as have been found, would seem to have been used for crushing some other sort of food, possibly roots.

The art of pottery also appears to have been unknown, so far as this country is concerned, but it is said to have been practised in Belgium.

Slight as was the knowledge of the useful arts exhibited by the River-drift men, it will I think be clear to the dispassionate observer, that we cannot regard their implements, however ancient they may be, as the earliest productions of the human race; on the contrary, we must conclude that man had already existed for an extended period upon the earth, before these relics were imbedded in the gravels. The mere identity in shape of various classes of implements occurring in distant localities, seems to afford sufficient evidence of a long lapse of time, during which it was discovered that certain forms were best adapted for certain purposes, and the custom of thus fashioning them became established, and, as it were, hereditary over a large area. Still, though eventually works of man will, in all probability, be discovered in older beds than these Quaternary gravels, I must repeat that I cannot at present accept the views of the Abbé Bourgeois [2751] and others as to their occurring in the Pliocene beds of St. Prest, near Chartres, and in the Miocene beds at Thenay, near Pontlevoy; nor can I regard the so-called Plateau [2752] types as being of necessity of human workmanship, and still less as being the precursors of the Palæolithic forms. To judge from the figures, the so-called Pliocene flake from Burma is not artificial, as it has no flat face. An article on the fractured flints found on the sea-shore, and their resemblance to so-called Tertiary implements, has been published by M. Michel Hardy. [2753]

Leaving these older deposits out of the question, I must now pass on to a consideration of the degree of antiquity which must be assigned to the Quaternary beds of River-drift; but before doing so, it will perhaps be well to say a few words as to the characteristics of authenticity presented by these implements; for, as is so universally the case, where the demand for an article has exceeded the supply, spurious imitations of them have been fabricated, and in some cases successfully passed off upon avid but unwary collectors. In England, indeed, this has perhaps not been the case to the same extent as in France; but I have seen a few fabrications of Palæolithic forms, produced both by the notorious "Flint Jack" and by more humble practitioners in Suffolk. More skilful, however, have been some forgers in the North-East of London, [2754] whose productions can with difficulty be distinguished from the genuine articles.

As a rule, however, unless the forged implement has been put through some process, for the purpose of altering the character of its surface (which it is hardly ever worth the while of the ordinary forger to do, even supposing him to be acquainted with means for so doing), its surface can always be restored to its original condition, assuming it to have been smeared over with some substance in order to give it an appearance of antiquity, by thoroughly washing it in hot water. The surface of a newly-chipped flint can then in almost all cases be at once recognized by its peculiar dull lustreless appearance, especially if it be black flint, such as is best adapted for being chipped into form. Not unfrequently the metallic marks of the iron hammer with which it has been chipped out are visible, the angles are sharp and harsh, or, if smooth, show traces of having been ground, and the character of the chipping is usually different from that of genuine implements, as is also often the form.

The genuine specimens from the beds of River-drift, with but very few exceptions, present some one or more of the following characteristics; [2755]—glossiness of surface, dendritic markings, calcareous incrustations, and discoloration, varying, of course, with the nature of the beds in which they have lain. The angles are often somewhat smoothed, even if not distinctly waterworn; and when, as happens in some rare cases, the flint has remained unaltered in colour, and without presenting in a marked manner any of the characteristics above specified, its surface will, on close examination, be found dotted over at intervals with bright glossy spots, probably those at which for ages it has been in contact with other stones. [2756] The glossiness of surface so frequent on these implements appears to be partly due to mechanical, and partly to chemical causes. The polishing effect of the friction of sand on flints in the bed of a river, or even when lying on the surface of the ground, is well known; and the brilliantly-polished flakes not unfrequently found in the bed of the Seine at Paris, and those from the sandy heaths of Norfolk and Suffolk, afford examples of the results of this friction since Neolithic times. In the Palæolithic implements, however, the gloss which so frequently accompanies a structural alteration in the surface of the flint, seems due to the same chemical cause which has produced the alteration in the structure; and this cause, as I have already remarked, appears to be the infiltration of water partially dissolving the body of the flint.

An interesting paper by M. E. d'Acy, [2757] on the patination of the worked flints of St. Acheul, was communicated to the Anthropological Congress at Paris in 1878.

The dendritic markings are more common on the implements from some localities, as, for instance, Santon Downham, than from others, and are due to the crystallization of peroxide of manganese upon their surface. Although these moss-like forms do not of necessity take any great length of time for their production, as is proved by their occasional occurrence in paper of recent manufacture, in which particles of manganese have been accidentally present, yet to superinduce them on a forged flint would pass the ordinary fabricator's skill, and their presence may safely be regarded as an indication of an old surface. The same may be said of the calcareous incrustations, which also are by no means of universal occurrence. The safest and indeed the most common indication of an implement being really genuine is the alteration in the structure of the flint which has taken place over the greater part, if not the whole, of its surface, and the discoloration it has undergone. In ochreous beds of gravel the specimens are frequently much stained of a yellow, buff, or brown colour; where less iron is present they become grey, especially at the angles, and often more so on one face than the other. In red or brown marl, and in places where they lie at no great depth from the surface, or where there is a free passage for water charged with carbonic acid, they frequently become white; whereas, in more impervious clay, they are often stained brown, or even remain black, though the surface is rendered glossy. In beds where much chalk is present they seem to have a tendency to retain their original colour. The discoloration of the surface is not always attended by the glossy appearance already mentioned, but this depends in a great measure on the character of the flint originally employed.

It sometimes happens that the upper side of an implement has been whitened during its sojourn in the earth, while its lower side has remained almost unaltered.

The recognition of these marks of authenticity has in some cases induced forgers to re-work, and according to their view, improve, genuine but imperfect ancient implements; but the newly-chipped surfaces can always be recognized on washing the specimens. In France some attempts have been made to discolour the surface of flints by chemical means, but in the instances which have come under my notice, the process has not been very successful; for though the surface of a dark flint has been whitened, it has become rough and somewhat pitted. A more deceptive discoloration has sometimes been produced by leaving the forged implements for many months in a kitchen boiler, the hot water in which gradually dissolves away a small portion of the surface of the flint and thus changes its colour. In such cases the form will often reveal the hand of the forger. It may, however, be thought that, by dwelling too much on this subject, suggestions will be offered, of which the fraudulent skill of some future forger will avail himself; and I therefore return from this digression to the consideration of the antiquity of the flint implements from the River-drift.

CHAPTER XXV.
ANTIQUITY OF THE RIVER-DRIFT.

In order to discuss this subject, it will be necessary to enter into some geological details; as it is evident that the least antiquity that can be assigned to the implements is that of the beds of gravel, sand, and clay in which they occur, and of which, in fact, they may be regarded as constituent portions. Whether they may not in some instances have been derived from beds of even greater antiquity than those in which they are found, is another question, which will subsequently be dealt with; but any one examining the condition of the beds in which the implements occur, will have no difficulty in seeing that they have not been disturbed since their deposit; while in most cases, the colouring of the worked and of the unworked flints they contain is similar, and affords proof of their having long lain together under the same conditions.

That the containing beds have, at all events in most cases, been deposited by fresh water, and not by the sea, is proved by the occasional abundance in them of land and freshwater shells, and the absence of those of marine origin; while their general analogy with the flood deposits of existing rivers, and their almost universal contiguity to them, raises the strongest possible presumption of their existence being due to river action. At the risk of being thought to have prejudged the question, I have, therefore, made no scruple in treating them hitherto as being River-drift. To show that for the most part they are so in reality, and to enable the reader to form some opinion of the manner in which deposits originally formed in and about the beds of streams or lakes, now in some cases occupy the tops of hills, and cover the slopes of valleys, far above the level of any existing neighbouring river, or even at a considerable distance from any stream, it will, I think, be well to state a hypothetical case; and then to compare the actual phenomena with it, and see how far they correspond.

Should it appear that with a certain given configuration of the land surface, a certain character of rock, a certain climate, and a certain number of years, certain effects must, judging from all analogy, have been produced; and should we in the case of these ancient Drifts find some of the conditions to have existed, and all the phenomena to be in accordance with the hypothesis, we may with some confidence assume that the other original conditions existed also; and build up a connected theory which will account for the whole of the observed results, and will also throw light on their causes, as well as on the duration of time necessary for their operation to have produced such effects. In stating the case, I lay no claim to originality, and do little more than follow in the steps of Sir Charles Lyell, Sir Joseph Prestwich, and others who have made a study of the character and effects of fluviatile action.

As it is in the gravels of Chalk districts that Palæolithic implements have been chiefly, though by no means exclusively, found, let us base the hypothesis on the assumption that an extensive and almost horizontal area of Upper Chalk, covered for the most part with beds of marine clay and shingle, gradually rose from beneath the sea, to an elevation of 200 feet above its level. Let us also assume that the land was elevated at a rate far in excess of that at which any subaërial action, such as rain, frost, or snow, would enable a river flowing over it to excavate its valley to the depth of 200 feet in the space of time required for its elevation to that height. Let us further assume, that the winter climate was somewhat more rigorous than that which at present prevails in this country, and that there was a considerably greater annual rainfall. We may also, for the purposes of the argument, take the position of the coast-line as permanent, instead of its constantly receding in consequence of the eroding power of the sea upon the cliffs.

Let us now see what would theoretically be the effect produced by subaërial causes on the river-valleys in this area during an indefinite number of centuries.

Under ordinary circumstances, and with our present amount of rainfall, there is no geological formation less liable to floods than the Chalk, or at all events, its upper portion. It is of so absorbent a nature that it is only in the extraordinary event of the ground being hard frozen at the time of a heavy fall of rain, or of a rapid thaw of snow; or of some inches of rain falling in the course of a few hours, that the soil is unable to absorb the water as fast as it is delivered upon it. The moisture when once in the soil is either carried off again by evaporation and vegetation, or descends to a point at which the chalk is saturated with water, which is, however, constantly being drained off by springs along the valleys. This body of water has been termed "the subterranean reservoir" in the Chalk. The consequence of this absorbent power of the soil is that the streams and rivers in a Chalk country are not liable to floods, and moreover that their flow is but little affected at the time by rain; they being almost entirely dependent on perennial springs, which, during the driest of summers, still continue to deliver the water that in the course of the preceding winter, or even previously, has accumulated in the body of the Chalk.

The surface of the "subterranean reservoir" in the Chalk is by no means level, but always presents a gradient towards the point at which the springs are delivering its contents, so that within a chalk-hill forming a watershed between two streams there is what may be termed a hill of subterranean water, the summit of which need not, and often does not, correspond with the apparent watershed on the surface. The angle of the water-surface gradient depends principally on two factors, the degree of friction in passing through the chalk, and the amount of rain that finds its way down from the surface.

The height of saturation varies much in different seasons, as is evinced by the intermitting streams, often known as bournes, [2758] which perhaps only flow for a few months once in every six or seven years. Near the Chalk escarpment in Hertfordshire, at a spot several miles distant from any stream, I have known this height of saturation, as shown by the level of water in a deep well, to vary as much as 70 feet in the course of a single year. But with a greater rainfall than at present, the Chalk might at all times be in a state of saturation up to within a few feet of the surface; and this would be materially assisted, were there no deep valleys in existence into which the subterranean water could be delivered; as, of course, if the outfall were raised, the level of permanent saturation would be raised also. Were the Chalk in a less porous condition than at present, of course also its absorbent powers would not be so great. Under the circumstances, therefore, which have been supposed, the river-and spring-water from a Chalk district would be delivered in a manner very materially differing from that which at present prevails. The delivery of water by springs would be but small in shallow valleys; and, indeed, the only important springs would be those along the sea-shore; while irrespective of this, the greater rainfall would keep the soil so saturated, that floods would be as readily produced by heavy storms of rain as if the soil were the most unabsorbent of rocks. If after some lapse of time the rainfall diminished, and the valleys were deepened, so that the outlets for the springs were at a considerably lower level than that of the principal area of the country, the case would be altered, and the tendency to floods would be immediately reduced.

At the commencement of the state of things supposed in our hypothesis, these outlets, with the exception of those on the sea-shore, would be but little lower than the general surface of the country, which, however, would not be perfectly plane. For it seems probable that the waters of the retreating sea would, during the elevation of the tract of land, form shallow channels, cutting down some little distance into the clay or chalk; and thus, as it were, mark out a course along which streams or rivers would flow, after the land was completely free from the sea. In some places, perhaps, shallow lakes might be left, but these also would have channels draining off their waters when they rose above a certain elevation.

With a bare surface, such as a newly-elevated tract would expose, there can be no doubt that the eroding power of heavy rains would be highly effective; as may be seen at the present day in the far greater effects of heavy showers on bare soil than on that which is protected by turf and vegetation. At the same time, with a rigorous climate, such as that supposed, the winter accumulation of snow and ice would be great, and its thawing during the summer months would add enormously and rapidly to the streams draining the area, which would in consequence have great power to deepen and widen their channels. The outflows from the lakes, if any such existed, would also be enlarged, while their upper portions would be filled with material brought down by the streams, and eventually they would be drained, with the exception of some channels in their beds through which the streams would pass.

We may therefore readily suppose that in the course of no very great interval of time, geologically speaking, a river-system for carrying off the waters falling from the heavens, analogous in character to those of the present day, but with shallower valleys, would be formed on the surface of the elevated tract. Let us suppose that while this, as it may be termed, preliminary configuration of the surface has been taking place, the land has become tenanted by various trees, shrubs, and plants affording means of subsistence to different forms of animal life; while the streams also have been occupied by colonies of freshwater *testacea*; and let us now trace what would be the action of the rivers. To use the words of Sir Charles Lyell, [2759] "when we are speculating on the excavating force which a river may have exerted in any particular valley, the most important question is, not the volume of the existing stream nor the present levels of its channel, nor even the nature of the rocks; but the probability of a succession of floods at some period since the time when the valley may have been first elevated above the sea."

Now in the first place, all rivers whose banks are not artificially protected, and whose channels are not kept clear, are of necessity more liable to floods than those in civilized countries, which bear much the same relation to rivers flowing through uncultivated lands, as domesticated animals do to wild. We have, moreover, *ex hypothesi*, a fruitful source of floods in a greater rainfall and in a more rigorous winter climate. The marvellous effects of such floods in excavating channels, and in transporting materials, can only be estimated by those who have seen their results, or have studied the accounts given of them. When we read of a small rivulet on the Cheviots, [2760] swollen by heavy rain, having transported several thousand tons of gravel and sand into the neighbouring plain, and having carried blocks of stone, weighing upwards of half a ton, two miles down its course, while another block weighing nearly two tons was transported the distance of a quarter of a mile, we may form some conception of the effects of even a flooded brook. The blocking of a stream by ice or fallen trees, so as to keep back its waters, and thus form a lake, which is suddenly drained by the breaking of the barrier; a heavy fall of rain; or a rapid fall of snow on ground hard frozen, and therefore impervious, are common causes of floods; and such as we may presume to have prevailed in our hypothetical case. What, therefore, would be the effect of such floods?

The first effect would no doubt be to cause the streams to overflow their banks, and spread over the bottom of the valleys in which they usually flowed. The shallower the valley the greater probably would be the sinuosities of the stream, and the wider would its waters spread. The greater also would be the probability of the stream, on the cessation of the flood, not returning to its original channel, which might have become obliterated or filled up, but of its flowing along some new course, it may be miles away from its former channel. Even when not flooded so as to overflow their banks, rivers along which a larger body of water flowed than there does at present, would, so long as they were not confined within deep valleys, have a tendency to wander over a much wider tract of country than that now occupied by their valleys. The tendency of all rivers to produce sinuosities in their course is well known; but Mr. Fergusson, in his excellent paper on recent changes in the Delta of the Ganges, [2761] has called attention to the fact that all rivers oscillate in curves, the extent of which is directly proportionate to the quantity of water flowing through them.

But rivers in a state of flood, or passing even at a moderate speed over soft or incoherent soil, are always turbid, owing to the presence in their waters of earthy matter which they are transporting towards the sea. The character of the solid matter thus transported by water in motion is entirely dependent on its velocity. A velocity of 300 yards per hour is sufficient to tear up fine clay; of 600 yards, fine sand; of 1,200 yards, fine gravel; and of a little over two miles per hour, to transport shivery angular stones of the size of an egg. [2762] Considering the small velocity requisite to remove the finer particles of the soil, and to retain them in suspension, a river such as has been supposed, must have been excessively turbid, so long as any fine earthy particles were accessible to its waters, or to those of the streamlets delivering into it.

The amount of solid matter suspended in turbid water is greater than might be imagined. Mr. A. Tylor has calculated that the detritus carried down by the Ganges is equivalent to what would result from the removal of soil a foot in depth over the whole of the area which it drains in 1,791 years, [2763] and that brought down by the Mississippi to one foot in 9,000 years. Other estimates fix this at one foot in 6,000 years, while the sediment contained in its stream has been estimated at from 1/1245 to 1/1500 of the weight of the water. [2764] Taking this latter proportion, an inch of rain falling on a square mile of ground, and flowing off it in a turbid state, would carry with it at least forty-three tons of sediment; and were we to assume an annual rainfall of fifty-four inches—which, though exceptional, is by no means unknown even in the British Isles—about 2,300 tons of fine earthy matter would be removed from a square mile of country in a single year. Taking a cubic yard of solid ground as equal to a ton in weight, this would involve the removal of one foot in depth from the surface in about 450 years. If, however, a portion of the rainfall were delivered by springs, or fell on hard or rocky ground, so as not to be rendered turbid, of course the effect would be proportionally diminished. Sir Archibald Geikie [2765] has estimated that practically, at the present day, the Thames (apart from about 450,000 tons of chalk and other matter carried away annually in solution), lowers its basin at the rate of one foot in 11,740 years; the Boyne, one foot in 6,700 years; the Forth, one foot in 3,111 years; and the Tay, one foot in 1,482 years. It is, however, with water moving with far greater velocity than that merely sufficient to keep fine sediment in suspension, that we have to deal in this hypothetical case; and we may readily suppose the streams, at more or less regular intervals, liable to violent floods, eroding the chalk and the superimposed clays and gravels, and carrying with them not only the finer particles and sand, but the pebbles, large and small, of the gravel, and the flints washed out of the chalk.

Let us now consider what would be the condition of the surface of a broad shallow valley, on the cessation of a flood such as that which has been supposed. In certain parts removed from the main current, and where the water had been nearly stationary, we should find deposits of fine mud or clay; in others, where the water had still moved with sufficient velocity to retain the clay and fine silt in suspension, the heavier particles of sand would have accumulated; in others, again, the smaller stones and pebbles; while near the main current, especially on the inner side of any curves which it had made, and where of course its velocity had been diminished, we should find the larger flints and pebbles, probably to some extent intermixed with part of the finer materials. In the beds of mud and sand, we should probably find the shells of some of the molluscs inhabiting the waters, and also those of terrestrial species, washed in from the inundated land surface, or brought down from the banks of the tributary rivulets; while mixed among the larger pebbles we might expect to find any animal bones that had been lying on the land contiguous to the stream, or any of the larger and heavier objects of human workmanship, that would have been carried off by such an inundation, had mankind been living on the banks of the river.

Were men, or any of the larger animals overwhelmed and drowned by the flood, it seems probable that, owing to the slight difference between their specific gravity and that of water, they would eventually have been carried down to the sea, unless by some means accidentally arrested in their course, or carried into the more stagnant waters. In either case, they would, on the waters subsiding, probably be exposed on or near the surface, and not be imbedded in any of the deposits of the stream. Assuming the existence at that time of a respect for the dead, such as may be regarded as almost instinctive in man, any human remains would be buried or otherwise disposed of, while the bones of the other carcases would be left within reach of the waters, should another flood occur.

At the mouth of the river, where it joined the sea, its excavating power would be considerably greater than farther inland; for at first, on account of the land having—as was presumed, in this hypothetical case—risen faster than the river could excavate its valley, the stream must have fallen as a cascade into the sea. This, by the cutting back of the lip in such a soft rock as the Chalk, would soon be converted into a rapid, where the greater velocity of the water would much add to its erosive power; and, ere long, a mouth to the river would be formed, which would soon become tidal. Before tracing the results that would be due to this greater declivity of the river-bed in the immediate neighbourhood of the sea, it will be well to consider what would be the results of successively recurring floods, in the less inclined broad shallow valley, on which we have been speculating.

There can be no doubt that with each succeeding flood the valley would be deepened; and the fact of its being thus deepened would tend to make it narrower, by restricting the windings of the river. We can, however, hardly imagine that in this deepening process the whole of the deposits spread by the former floods over the bottom and slopes of the valley would be removed, but must acknowledge the extreme probability of some portions of them having remained intact, especially those which were left at the greatest distance from the course eventually taken by the river during its period of flood. When once they had been thus left, the chances of their being again assailed by the stream would become more and more remote with each successive flood; and though the waters might reach some deposit of the larger pebbles formerly carried down by the main stream, but now at a distance from it, yet they would only belong to the more sluggish portions of the flood, and at first might envelope them in beds of sand; and subsequently, when they were only accessible to the more stagnant turbid waters, leave layer upon layer of muddy silt or clay upon them. In forming the more loess-like beds the action of the wind in transporting sand and dust might also assist. In some cases, and especially at the extremity of curves, and at the end of the tongue between two streams, the accumulation of one period, though at a lower level than that of earlier date, might abut upon it, or even become mingled with it, so that an almost continuous coating of Drift-deposits might extend from the highest level to the lowest.

The bulk, however, of the deposits of one inundation would be moved by the next, or by one of those which subsequently recurred; and stones, and pebbles, and other objects might thus be transported down stream, from place to place, an indefinite number of times, and form constituent parts of an indefinite number of gravelly beds along the bottom of the flooded stream. They might, under some circumstances, lie for a long period of years in some particular bed, in which they would become stained by salts of iron or otherwise, and subsequently be transported and re-deposited among unstained, or differently stained pebbles. The angles of any flints thus transported from place to place would also become rolled, as would, in like manner, those of bones or teeth. In the same way, assuming, as we have done, that the surface of the Chalk in the district was in part, or wholly, covered with beds of marine clay and shingle, it is evident that in the earlier deposits, when the river flowed at the higher level, and was, as it were, commencing to excavate its valley, the proportion of the pebbles derived from these beds to the flints washed out from the Chalk, would be much greater than at a later period. For in the course of time the river would have worked its way below the level of these upper beds, and many of the pebbles at first deposited in its gravels would have been disturbed, again and again, in their beds; on each disturbance carried farther down the stream, and eventually so far as the sea or the tidal portion of the river. At the same time the river itself would be principally excavating the Chalk which had been freed from the marine shingle, and would therefore be forming the gravel in its bed, for the most part, from flints derived from the Chalk.

In the same manner, pebbles brought from a distant part of the country, and higher up the river, would eventually become more abundant in the deposits near its mouth, than they were at the first. Still no amount of transport of this kind could bring any pebbles into the bed of the river, which did not, in some form or other, exist within its drainage area.

Besides the transporting power of water, which by itself is, under favourable circumstances, capable of producing considerable excavations in a comparatively short period, there is another force at work, where, as has been supposed in this case, the climate is severe, which not only aids in the transport of pebbles and blocks of stone from one part of the bed of a river to another, but is a fertile source of floods. This is the formation of ground-ice. Sir Joseph Prestwich, [2766] in his second "Memoir on the Flint Implement-bearing Beds," has given numerous instances of the transporting power of this agent, and shown the method of its occurrence in running streams, when the cold suffices to reduce the temperature of the water, and of the bed of the river itself, to the freezing point. Under such circumstances a gravelly river bed—and on mud alone, ice rarely forms—may become coated with ice, which being lighter than water will, on acquiring certain dimensions, overcome the forces which keep it at the bottom, and rise to the surface, carrying with it all the loose materials to which it adhered.

M. Engelhardt, [2767] director of the forges at Niederbronn, in the Vosges, has, perhaps, more minutely than any one else investigated the causes of the formation of ground-ice; and to prevent its effects in causing floods, actually removed each year from the bed of the stream supplying the motive power to his works, the stones and other extraneous bodies round which it was likely to form. His account of the effects of ground-ice in causing floods in the upper part of the Rhine and the Danube is worth transcribing. These two rivers having "a rapid current, do not freeze, like the Seine, by being covered with a plane and uniform stratum; they bear along large blocks of ice, which cross and impinge upon one another, and becoming thus heaped together, finally barricade the river. It is a grand spectacle, when the Rhine is thus charged, to see these countless drifts adjust themselves in their relative position, where they unite by congelation, and convey the idea of the fall of some mountain which has covered the plain with rocks of every dimension. But it is not this accumulation of ice-drifts in the Rhine which is of itself the cause of danger; it is, on the contrary, the *débâcle*, or breaking-up, which is often productive of calamitous consequences. When this *débâcle* commences in the upper part of the river, above the point where the latter is completely frozen, the masses of ice, drifting with the current and unable to pass, are hurled upon those already soldered together; thus an enormous barrier is formed, which the water, arrested in its course, cannot pass over, and hence overflows to the right and left, breaking the dykes, inundating the plains, and spreading devastation and suffering, far and near. The disasters caused by the *débâcles* of the Rhine have taught the riparian inhabitants to observe attentively the facts which may serve them as a prognostic, and put them on their guard against the irruption of the ice. It is thus that they have been led to observe the *grund-eis*—that is to say, the ice formed at the bottom of the rivers—for it is this ice which, in becoming detached from the bottom and rising towards the surface, unites itself to the under surface of the masses already in place, and by further embarrassing the discharge, exposes the country to inundation."

Another most effective agent in transporting the pebbles and larger blocks of stone along the course of rivers is shore-ice. During a severe winter masses of thick ice are formed which enclose the larger stones on the bottom of the river towards its edge; these masses are dislodged and carried away by subsequent floods, whether arising from rapid thaws or from rain higher up the river, or from accumulations of ice, such as those described, having formed a temporary barrier across the stream through which the pent-up water eventually burst and carried all before it. The lateral pressure of such dams of ice, with a large body of water behind, must be enormous; and we can readily conceive their crumbling-up any beds of gravel on the banks of the rivers against which they might happen to abut.

But there is still another way in which a severe climate, such as has been supposed, would act upon the rocks, namely, by their being rent and disintegrated by frost. This has been well pointed out by Sir Joseph Prestwich, [2768] who has cited numerous instances of its effects, and mentions having seen a low cliff of chalk, 15 feet high, form a talus or heap of fragments at its foot, 6 feet broad and 4 feet high, in the course of an ordinary winter.

As I am by no means attempting an exhaustive geological essay on this subject, which is indeed hardly needed, I think that enough has been said to show that under conditions such as have been supposed in this hypothetical case, the great subaërial agents—rain and snow, ice and frost—would, in the course of time, enable rivers to excavate their valleys to an almost indefinite extent. Indeed, one can conceive the process being carried on, until what had been rivers became estuaries or arms of the sea; or, until a large island once traversed by rivers became converted into several smaller islands, by the cutting back, and subsequent junction, of its various river-valleys.

Without, however, carrying the excavatory process to such an extreme, let us now consider what would be the condition of our hypothetical river-valley when excavated to a depth of say 100 feet, at a point about midway between its source and the sea. We have already seen that at an earlier period—when the river ran at a higher level by 100 feet than that it is now supposed to occupy—its valley must have been broader, and its bottom strewn with detritus of various kinds, in the shape of gravel, sand, and clay, and, it may be, some larger blocks of stone. In the further process of excavating by agents such as have been described, it has also been seen, that it is in the highest degree improbable that the succeeding floods and other transporting agents should have entirely removed and obliterated the deposits left by those of earlier date. We should, therefore, expect to find, at various heights on the slope of the valley, remains of such beds of detritus, and especially at points such as the junctions of affluents with the river, and the inner side of the bends it makes in its course, which would naturally be the least exposed to the violent invasion of the stream. In these beds we might reasonably search for the remains of the surface and freshwater life of the period; and had there been any amelioration of climate during the process of excavation, a larger proportion of silt and clay, and less of coarse gravel, in the lower and more recent deposits, would testify to the fact. Looking also at the power possessed by rivers of levelling the bottoms of their valleys, during their successive changes of course, we might expect to find in places, tracts of these old valley-bottoms left as terraces on the slopes of the more deeply excavated valleys. The upper surface of any such relics of a former condition of things would, of course, be covered with *débris* and rain-washed clay, brought down from a higher level on the slopes, but on digging into them their true nature might be recognized.

Nearer the sea, and farther up the valleys, the state of things would be somewhat different. At the mouth of the river, as has already been pointed out, the declivity of the stream would have been greater, and its excavating power therefore increased. If, as originally assumed, the bed of the river, when the land was first elevated, was, at a mile distant from the sea, 200 feet above its level, the declivity would be 200 feet to the mile; when the 200 feet level was 4 miles from the sea, the slope would still be 50 feet to the mile; at 10 miles distance it would still be 20 feet, and it would not be until the 200 feet level was 15 miles from the sea that the ordinary slope of the bottom of the Chalk valleys of Hertfordshire, which is about 13 feet 6 inches to the mile, would be attained. In the meantime, however, if the sea were encroaching on the shore, or were, owing to the nature of the rocks, widening and extending that portion of the river subject to tidal influences, the actual point of contact with the sea would be carried far inland, and—assuming the rock traversed to be of one uniform nature and hardness—it would be long before the river towards its mouth ceased to have a greater declivity than nearer its source. We see, then, that the amount of excavation effected by the river, during the time necessary for the deepening of the valley by 100 feet, at a point midway in its course, would, near the sea, have been twice as great, or 200 feet. We should, therefore, expect to find beds of the same age as those which, at the middle of its course, were 100 feet above the river, at relatively twice that elevation near the mouth; and any intermediate beds would also be proportionally higher above the then existing stream, than contemporary beds farther up the valley.

At the heads of the valleys, the excavation would, on the contrary, have been less than towards the middle of the course of the river; partly owing to there always being less water present, partly to the reduced liability to floods, and partly to other causes. The heads of the valleys would, however, be constantly receding in all cases, and their retrogression would in most instances be aided by springs issuing from them. In cases where, from some geological cause, the heads of two valleys running in opposite directions receded in the same line, we can readily imagine their meeting eventually at the watershed, and cutting through it so as to form apparently but a single valley, though on either side of the highest portion of its bottom, the waters flowed in opposite directions.

The mention of springs recalls another denuding agent, which has been already discussed in connection with caverns, and seems to have assisted in moulding the surface of the country and in excavating the valleys. It is well known that the water flowing in the streams of a chalk-country contains, in solution, a considerable amount of chalk, or rather, of bi-carbonate of lime; the water on entering the ground deriving a certain amount of carbonic acid from the decaying vegetable matter contained in the soil, and when thus charged, becoming capable of dissolving a corresponding quantity of the chalk. The amount is usually 17 or 18 grains in the gallon; and even in the Thames at London, not a purely chalk-stream, there are about 14 grains. Taking the proportion of 17 grains to the gallon, it will be found by calculation that every inch of rain which falls over a square mile of chalk-country, and passes off by springs, carries with it, in solution, and without in the slightest degree interfering with its brightness, no less than from 15 to 16 tons of solid chalk. The quantity of rain which thus finds its way to the springs has, as already stated, been ascertained by experiment to be as much as 9 inches per annum in average seasons, giving an amount of about 140 tons of chalk thus annually carried away from each square mile of country at the present day; so that the loss is still going on at the rate of 140,000 tons of dry chalk to each square mile in every ten centuries.

The lowering of level from this cause is probably not uniform over the whole surface. For the acidulated water sinking into the chalk on the top of a hill, and descending one or two hundred feet before reaching the surface of "the subterranean reservoir," [2769] might, in its almost vertical passage, become saturated with carbonate of lime, and only render the chalk through which it passed somewhat more porous, without materially affecting the level of its surface. On the other hand, that absorbed in a valley would probably, to some extent, acquire the chalk which it eventually held in solution during its almost horizontal passage to the point of its delivery by springs; and as this would be at no great depth, the abstraction of solid matter would become more perceptible on the surface, so that the level of the valley would be lowered more rapidly than that of the hill. With an increased rainfall, such as we have supposed, this removal of solid matter by solution must have been considerable; but still nothing in comparison with that effected by the other denuding agencies which have been mentioned. It is, moreover, to be borne in mind that, as will shortly be seen, until the valleys had been excavated to a considerable depth, the amount of water delivered by the springs would, with the same rainfall, have been far less than at present. The springs would also, to some extent, have been affected by the chalk being in a less porous condition than it now is, owing to its not having lost so much of its substance by the chemical action which has just been described.

Before comparing the actual phenomena with the results of the conditions which have been assumed, it will be well to say a few words as to the probable effects of an amelioration of climate, and a diminution in the rainfall, upon a valley already excavated to an average depth of 100 feet, such as has already been described. It is evident that any transport of materials due to the action of ice, by floating loose stones and pebbles from one part of the bed of the stream to another, would be materially diminished; as would also the number of floods resulting from the thawing of the winter accumulation of ice and snow, and from rain falling on frozen ground. The only remaining principal cause for floods would be the heavy fall of rain during storms or wet seasons; but here, a comparatively slight alteration in the conditions will have made a vast difference in the results. When the valleys were once excavated to a certain depth, the level of the springs or outfalls carrying off the accumulation of water in the absorbent soil, would be proportionally reduced, as would also be the line of permanent saturation in the chalk. The effect of this would be that during any dry interval, the water contained in the upper part of the chalk would gravitate downwards, until it reached the subterranean reservoir of water saturating the chalk; and thus leave the surface soil in the same absorbent condition as it is at present, and capable of receiving a much greater amount of rain than formerly, before any would flow from off its surface.

Even with a constant and excessive rainfall, the result of the continued deepening of the valleys would be to cause more and more to flow off by the springs, and less from the surface; but with the valleys once deepened, a small diminution in the rainfall, or its more even distribution over the whole year, might cause the flow from the surface almost entirely to cease, and allow the whole to be carried off by the springs. Whenever this was the case, any great and rapid excavation of the valleys from rain alone would be rendered almost impossible; and with no extreme reduction in the total amount of annual flow of the rivers, yet by their originating in perennial springs subject to but slight variations, and from their being no longer to any extent immediately connected with the surface drainage, there would cease to be that immense difference between their maximum and minimum volume, which must have formerly existed. The result of this comparatively uniform flow would be a great diminution in the tendency of any river to change its bed, and even if it occasionally received a great accession of water, it would find relief by overflowing into the wide valley due to its former more violent action. In the less inclined portions of its valley, the parts now almost deserted by the stream would be favourable for vegetation, such as would result in the formation of peat, and any occasional overflowing of the banks might, owing to the less torrential character of the inundations, have a tendency to fill up and level these marginal spaces rather than to excavate them deeper. The deposits of gravel, sand, and clay at the low levels would also be more continuous than those at the higher.

In tracing the effects of subaërial action in forming valleys, I have assumed the subsoil or rock in which they were formed to have been chalk, as it is principally in valleys in the Chalk that the gravels containing Palæolithic implements are known to occur. This is probably on account of the greater natural abundance of flints in such valleys, which of course led to implements being there chipped out in greater numbers, as well as to their being less cared for, from their being more easily replaced than they would be where flint was scarce. The effects on other soft and absorbent soils would not materially differ from those on chalk. On clay, the general amount of denudation would perhaps be greater, but the valleys broader, and with less inclined slopes on their sides. In a clay country we might, I think, expect to find the old river-gravels not unfrequently at greater distances from the existing streams than in a chalk-district.

It must, however, be borne in mind that in such a country the materials from which river-gravels can be formed are usually absent, and can only have been derived from older superficial beds, or brought from Chalk higher up the valley. In some valleys, partly or almost entirely excavated in Pre-Glacial times, gravels belonging to the Glacial Period exist, and tend to complicate the question of the more recent River-drifts.

Any theory of the valleys having been excavated at some remote period in some unknown manner, and then having been filled with gravels derived from an unknown source, and again re-excavated, presents such difficulties that, to my mind, it cannot well be entertained. If, however, such a view be accepted, it seems to add to the time necessary for the excavation of the valleys; as much of the rainfall might find a subterranean vent at a low level through the gravel lining the bottom of the filled-up valleys, and thus keep the upper soil in a more absorbent condition and therefore less liable to erosion.

I must not, however, dwell too long upon this hypothetical case, which perhaps is such as may not have found an absolutely exact analogue in nature, but which may yet, I think, be accepted as a fair typical example of the results which, under the supposed conditions, must, judging from what we know of the action of subaërial causes, in all probability have ensued.

Let us now compare the phenomena as we find them in the gravel-beds of our present river-valleys, with those of the hypothetical case, and we shall, I think, find them coincide in a remarkable manner.

In the first place, the constituent parts of the gravels of the beds of Drift containing Palæolithic implements are always, petrologically, such as are to be found in the existing river-basins, as they must also of necessity have been in the hypothetical case. This fact, which holds good both in France and England, has been insisted on by Sir Joseph Prestwich, and such insistency cannot be too often reiterated. Where old superficial marine deposits of the Glacial or any other period, consisting of pebbles of various ages and origins, exist within a river-basin, there also will such pebbles be found in its gravels, but the originally derivative character of the pebbles prevents any strong argument being founded upon their presence. Where, however, no such beds exist, the case can clearly be made out. Unless a river traverses a granite or slate country, no granite or slate is found in the Quaternary gravels of its valley: unless it passes over Oolite, Purbeck, or Greensand, no blocks or pebbles of these rocks occur. This fact suffices to prove that the gravels are due to some local cause, such as river-action, and not to any general submergence or supposed "wave of translation," which would of necessity bring in materials not to be found in the existing basins.

That the various deposits resulting from a flooded river, should contain some of the land and freshwater shells, and animal bones of the period, is, as has been shown, most natural. Such shells and remains are of constant occurrence in the Quaternary gravels. If they prove nothing else, their evidence as to the freshwater origin of the beds must be accepted as conclusive. It is true that in all cases such land and freshwater remains have not as yet been found; but if in a dozen instances we find beds of a certain character containing these remains, and also flint instruments wrought by the hand of man; and in a dozen other instances, similar beds in analogous positions, also containing implements of the same kind, but, so far as is known, no such organic remains; we are justified in regarding both sets of beds as due to the same original cause, and in believing that the organic remains, if actually absent, are so from some accidental circumstance. We may indeed accept the implements as being truly characteristic fossils of a certain class of deposits. The character of the beds, consisting as they do, of gravel, sand, and fine silt, brick-earth or loess, and their manner of deposition, are also absolutely in accordance with the river-hypothesis.

On the higher levels above but near the valleys, we frequently find these beds at a considerable distance from the existing stream; we find them at all levels on the flanks of the valleys, and occasionally almost at their bottom, or even below it. In these lower beds, the implements, if of the same form and character as those in the upper beds nearer the source, are, in accordance with what would be the case under the hypothesis, very frequently much rolled and water-worn. The beds at the low level are also usually, so far as the gravel is concerned, of a finer character than those at the high level, and present a greater abundance of sand and brick-earth. They seem, in fact, indicative of some such amelioration of climate as that supposed.

Looking again at the position of the deposits with regard to the neighbouring rivers, we find them, as a rule, exactly in such positions as might have been expected, had their presence been due to the action of a stream in the process of excavating its valley, in such a manner as that described. So constantly is this the case, that a practised geologist, from a mere inspection of the Ordnance map, could with almost certainty predict where deposits of River-drift would occur, of such an age and character as to be likely to contain Palæolithic implements. In more than one instance, indeed, as has already been mentioned, the probability of certain gravels containing these relics of human art, was pointed out before their actual discovery.

These are some, but by no means all, of the points in which the actual phenomena agree with those which must have resulted from river-action such as suggested in the hypothesis, and they are alone sufficient to raise the strongest presumption that the phenomena are due to such action, and that the theory that would account for them in this manner, cannot be far from the truth.

I will, however, now pass in review some of the principal localities where Palæolithic implements have been found in Drift-deposits, and see what other points of accordance, and what difficulties, if any, they present.

Taking first the basin of the Ouse and its tributaries, we find at Biddenham, near Bedford, one of the principal localities for Drift-implements, the gravel on the inner side of a bold sweep made by the river, and from forty to fifty feet above it. Its constituent stones are all derived either from the rocks in the neighbourhood, or from the Glacial beds which cap them, and which have evidently been cut through by the river. Throughout the beds are seams containing numerous freshwater shells, mixed with some derived from the land and from marshy places; numerous bones of terrestrial mammals also occur. In the valley of the Lark remains of such shells occur at Bury St. Edmunds, in the same beds as the implements. Farther down, at Icklingham, the beds at Rampart Field cap a rounded knoll on the inner side of a curve of the river, which appears, however, to have somewhat straightened its course since they were deposited. Below Icklingham, the whole surface of the country, and its drainage, have been so much modified by the invasion of the sea, which produced the wide level of the Fens, that we should expect to find any deposits of an ancient river, which existed before that great planing down of the adjacent country, in somewhat anomalous positions.

I need not here enter into the history of the origin of the Fens; it is enough to say that the subsoil of almost the whole district consists of clays, belonging either to the Oolitic or Cretaceous series, and unprotected by any rocks of a more durable nature towards the sea, which has thus been enabled to invade it. The presence of the sea is attested in various localities by marine remains. *Buccinum, Trophon, Littorina, Cardium,* and *Ostrea* are abundant in the gravel at March. [2770] In the valley of the Nene, near Peterborough, oysters and other marine shells occur, mixed with those of land and freshwater origin. In Whittlesea Mere, remains of walrus and seal, and sea shells are found; while so far south as Waterbeach, less than ten miles from Cambridge, remains of whale have been discovered.

The old land-surface having been thus destroyed, we cannot with certainty trace the course of the ancient representative of the river Lark, below Mildenhall; it seems, however, to have proceeded northwards by Eriswell and Lakenheath, to join the Little Ouse. At Eriswell, a gravel of the same character as that near Mildenhall, occurs on the slope of the hill towards the Fen; but in it, as yet, few implements are recorded to have been found. At Lakenheath, however, they occur in the gravel now capping the hill overlooking the Fen, as well as on the slope.

Owing to the distance of these beds from any existing rivers, the late Mr. Flower [2771] found great difficulty in reconciling them with any theory which would account for their presence by the action of rivers. If, however, we regard the great denudation of the Fen country as subsequent in date to the deposit of the gravels, it appears to me that any difficulty on this point vanishes. That this denudation was in fact, at all events in part, subsequent to the deposit of the gravels, is proved by the position of the beds at Shrub Hill, which there cap a small area of Gault, and which, being above the general level of the Fens, can hardly have been deposited in the position they now occupy, when the configuration of the country was at all like what it now is. Such beds must, on the contrary, have been deposited in the bottom of a valley; and it appears as if in this case, by their superior hardness to the clay around them, or from some other accidental cause, they had protected this small spot from tidal action, which in the adjacent river, previously to the construction of Denver Sluice, extended nearly as far as Brandon.

The rolled condition of so many of the implements found at Shrub Hill, proves that they must have been transported some distance by water, from beds of a higher level.

Turning now to the existing valley of the Little Ouse, we find, at Brandon Down, the gravel occupying the summit of a high ridge of land almost at right angles to the present course of the river. It is difficult to account for its occurring in this position, unless we are to suppose that at an early period before the complete denudation of the Fen country, and while the Boulder Clay still covered the surface of the Chalk, and the level of saturation was higher in the latter than at present, a tributary stream, possibly the old representative of the Lark, flowed into the Little Ouse near this spot, and the gravel was deposited on the tongue of land near the confluence. The country drained by the Little Ouse seems at one time to have been almost covered by Glacial deposits, including beds of shingle, composed for the greater part of quartzite pebbles. The beds at Brandon Down are nearer the sea than any analogous beds towards the source of the stream, and occupy a higher position relatively to the existing river, being 90 feet above it. If they resulted from river-action, they would, in accordance with the hypothesis, be among the oldest of the river-deposits; and would, as indeed they do, consequently contain a far larger proportion of the quartzite pebbles than those of somewhat later age and farther up the valley.

At Bromehill, where the drift is but a few feet higher than the present level of the stream, and would, in accordance with the hypothesis, belong to a later period, there are but few of these quartzite pebbles, but the gravel contains a very large proportion of rolled fragments of chalk, which, so far as I have observed, are absent in the probably older beds, at Brandon Down; the implements also are frequently much rolled and water-worn. This fact is also in accordance with the hypothesis, for the river at the time of the formation of these lower beds would, in the lower part of its course, have completely cut through the Glacial deposits above the Chalk, and would have been attacking the Chalk itself. There is also an abundance of rolled chalk in the Shrub Hill beds, which seem to be of much the same age. In the valley of the Lark, the rolled chalk pebbles occur in gravels at a somewhat greater elevation. Higher up the Little Ouse, the gravel at Santon Downham occupies the slope of a hill on the inner side of a great sweep of the river, while at Thetford, the beds form a long terrace by the side of the stream, with a rather abrupt slope towards it. Here also, land and freshwater shells have been found in the gravel, but neither these nor implements have as yet been observed in the gravels of the valley of the Little Ouse, or of its tributaries, above Thetford.

Tracing the main stream back to its source, we find that both the Little Ouse and the Waveney, the one flowing westward, and the other eastward, take their rise in the same valley, and within a few hundred yards of each other, at Lopham Ford. With regard to the elevation of this spot above the sea-level, there has been some diversity of opinion. On the Greenough map, published by the Geological Society, it is erroneously stated at 15 feet; and Mr. Flower, [2772] in arguing in favour of his views, that the beds at Brandon are not connected with any river-action, assigns it a height of only 23 feet above high-water mark. That this also is erroneous can be readily shown, for Sir Joseph Prestwich [2773] has recorded the level of the Waveney at Moor Bridge, near Hoxne, ten miles below its source, as being 59 feet 9 inches above high-water mark at Yarmouth. Mr. Alger, of Diss, who has surveyed the district, informs me that the level at Lopham Ford is 75 feet 3 inches above high-water mark; and as by actual survey he found the fall, from the head of the Waveney to Hoxne Mill, to be upwards of 15 feet, there can be little doubt of this level being approximately correct. Still, the gravel beds at Brandon being upwards of 90 feet above high-water mark, there can be no doubt of their being at an elevation actually above the source of the present stream; and at first sight, this fact appears difficult of reconciliation with the view that they are due to fluviatile action. Without, however, calling to aid any possible oscillations in the level of the land, varying in amount at different parts of the course of the stream, an examination of the local geological conditions suffices to throw light on the causes, why the erosion of the land at the sources of the Little Ouse and Waveney has been abnormally great; so that not only have the streams excavated back the heads of their respective valleys until they have met, but their inclination at the upper part of their course, instead of being as usual in chalk countries at the rate of 12 to 18 feet in a mile, is only about 18 inches.

The general level of the country for some distance around Lopham Ford is at least 100 feet above it, and the Chalk and the superimposed beds are for the most part covered with a deposit of impervious Boulder Clay, through which the valleys of the Little Ouse and of the Waveney have been cut. But, at the time of the last emergence of this district of country from beneath the sea, this clay must have been continuous across the tract since excavated, so that at that time the sources of the streams flowing in either direction must have been at least 100 feet above their present level, and 80 feet above the gravels at Brandon Down, and probably at some distance apart. That the heads of the two streams should have cut back their valleys, and at last have met, appears to be due to the fact that, previously to the covering of Boulder Clay being deposited, there existed an old depression in the Chalk, which had been filled with laminated sandy clays, either Glacial or belonging to what is known by geologists as the Chillesford series. These being more easily acted on than the chalk by running water, led the streams to follow the course of the old depression which they filled, and it is to their presence that the small inclination of the upper part of the valley of the Waveney appears to be mainly due. Another cause is to be found in the country near Lopham Ford being coated with clay, so that the streams, even at the present day, exhibit the remarkable phenomenon of being liable to floods at their source. An isolated hill, about 30 feet high, formed of the laminated beds, and with a slight capping of gravel, still remains in the valley of the Waveney, near Redgrave, to show the nature of the beds which have been removed.

The only spot in the valley of the Waveney, where as yet Palæolithic implements have been found, is at Hoxne, where the summit of the beds is about 111 feet above high-water mark at Yarmouth, and though at a higher level than the existing source of the Waveney, probably much below the level of its earlier source. Since the beds were deposited, the surface of the ground in the neighbourhood has been completely remodelled by subaërial denudation, and they now lie in a trough on the summit of a hill, [2774] both sides of which slope down to small streams which are tributary to the Waveney, and are still at work cutting out their valleys in the Boulder Clay. The beds in which the implements occur are beyond all doubt of freshwater origin, being full of freshwater shells. The trough in which they lie, has much the appearance of the deserted bed of a river, silted up under more lacustrine conditions. Such a change in the position of a river-bed, and its subsequent infilling, is quite in accordance with the hypothetical case of river-action, especially when, as here, its eventual valley had not been distinctly carved out.

The phenomena at Hoxne have lately been more fully examined by Mr. Clement Reid, [2775] by means of grants from the British Association and the Royal Society; and the views that I expressed in 1872 have been in the main corroborated. The deposits are proved to be distinctly more recent than the Chalky Boulder Clay of the district, and there is evidence of oscillations in climate since the valley was formed in which the lacustrine beds were laid down, and before any Palæolithic implements or the brick-earth containing them had been deposited.

The beds at High Lodge, near Mildenhall, are of somewhat similar character to those at Hoxne, though occupying a depression on the slope of a hill, instead of a trough on the summit; and were probably deposited under nearly the same circumstances, though as yet no testaceous remains have been found in them.

Turning south, to the valley of the Thames, we find the gravel-beds at Acton and Ealing, though occasionally at a higher level, forming a terrace 80 or 90 feet above Ordnance Datum, along the side of the broad valley, at a height of some 50 feet above the general surface of the valley. In the bottom of this are spread out other beds of gravel, sand, and brick-earth, exactly as might be expected on the river-hypothesis; while at Highbury New Park, and Hackney Down, we have beds of the same character, which contain land and freshwater shells and flint implements, at a height, in some cases, of 100 feet above Ordnance Datum. The presence of these beds in such a position, consisting, as they do at Highbury, of sand and brick-earth, such as can only have been deposited in comparatively tranquil water, involves the necessity either of a large lake having existed at the spot, or of its having been within access of the flood-waters of the river. But either of these conditions is impossible, unless we are to suppose that the lower part of valley of the Thames, in which

London now stands, was at that time non-existent. It must, therefore, have been subsequently excavated. But again, at lower levels at Hackney Down, and in Gray's Inn Lane, we have gravels of a more distinctly fluviatile character, and also containing palæolithic implements. The existence, character, and position of all these beds is, therefore, perfectly in accordance with the theory of the excavation of the valley by the river, and it is extremely difficult, if not impossible, to account for them satisfactorily in any other manner.

At Hitchin beds of much the same character occur, which there also are newer than the Boulder Clay of the district.

At Caddington the discoveries are quite consistent with the hypothesis, but point to a period when the excavations of the existent valleys had made but little progress.

Higher up the Thames valley at Reading and at Oxford the phenomena are all in accordance with the hypothesis; at the former place the river has deepened its valley to the extent of at least 100 feet.

The discoveries in the gravels capping the North Downs and those made near Ightham and Limpsfield in the transverse valley at the foot of the Downs, seem at first sight difficult to reconcile with any river-theory. But assuming that the beds capping the hills were at one time continuous with others in the Wealden area, and that the transverse valley was produced by denudation at a later date, the difficulties disappear, though the time requisite to effect such superficial changes may seem to be immense.

Passing by other localities where implements have been found in the valley of the Thames, such as Swanscombe and Northfleet, though it may be observed that the gravels in which they have occurred are, on the river-theory, exactly where they might have been expected to be present, we come to the beds near Reculver, where they have been found in large numbers. Looking, however, at the enormous encroachment of the sea, even within the last few centuries, upon the soft cliffs of sand and clay at that spot, it is difficult to form any satisfactory idea of the conditions under which a river may have flowed near the spot at a remote period, or of the position of the coast at the time. Where, however, as is here the case, a large tract of land has been washed away, which must of necessity have had its system of superficial drainage by streams, and may possibly have had rivers passing through it, which now, owing to the altered conditions, find their way into the sea at a point much nearer their source than formerly, we should expect to find on the top of the cliffs traces of the former state of things; and where any portion of the slope of an old valley remained, to see its gravels, though now so close to the sea, at a height far above its level. Still, it is hard to say whether the implement-bearing beds at Reculver are connected with the old valley of the Thames, or with that of some other stream which has now disappeared, but of which the upper portion is to be traced in the Swale, which now separates the Isle of Sheppey from Kent, and which appears to afford, in its junction with the West Swale and Long Reach, an instance of two valleys being gradually eroded inland until they met. The beds may even be connected with the valley of the Stour; for it is by no means impossible that the present second and northward mouth of that stream may run along the valley of an old river, which originally flowed southward past Reculver, and joined the old representative of the Stour, somewhere to the south of where is now the village of Sarre.

The great tract of gravel which at some little distance inland fringes the East Essex coast, between Shoeburyness [2776] and the Blackwater estuary, may also be connected with some old river; but as yet no well-defined implements or freshwater shells have been found in it, though Mr. Whitaker has discovered shells near Southend. The fluvio-marine deposits at a lower level at Clacton, just north of the Blackwater, like those at Chislet, in Kent, seem to belong to a somewhat later period, when the rivers had so far deepened their beds as to have become tidal.

Though no land or freshwater shells have as yet been found in the gravel beds near Canterbury, yet their position is quite in accordance with the theory of the excavation of the valley by river-action; and here as elsewhere the implements from the lower beds are often much water-worn.

The superficial deposits of the south of Hampshire and the Isle of Wight, and in a lesser degree those of the neighbouring counties, have been fully discussed in an able paper by Mr. T. Codrington, F.G.S., [2777] though since it was published a large number of implements has been found near Bournemouth, Barton, and Hordwell. He has pointed out that the whole of the New Forest, between Poole and Southampton Water, appears at one time to have been an extensive plain, with a gradual slope to the south, very generally covered with gravel and brick-earth. This has since been in great part cut up, and over large areas entirely removed by the action of the streams and rivers, which latter flow in well-defined valleys.

The formation of this table-land and the overlying deposit of gravel which, in places far inland, is found at a height of more than 420 feet above the present sea-level, appears to be due to marine action, though as yet no marine remains have been discovered in it. Sea-shells have, however, been found by Sir Joseph Prestwich [2778] in an old sea-beach at Waterbeach, near Goodwood, and similar beds, at Avisford Bridge, near Arundel, occur at a height of 80 or 100 feet above the sea. We seem, then, here to have evidence of a considerable elevation of the land from beneath the sea; and as the gravel in places overlies late Tertiary beds, this must have taken place at a comparatively late geological epoch. When rivers run through a tract of country covered with a marine gravel of this kind, itself apparently deposited in a somewhat contracted area, it is, in the absence of organic remains, difficult to distinguish the reconstructed gravels resulting from fluviatile action, from the older beds. Any one, however, who is acquainted with the country, or who will examine Mr. Codrington's map, will see what an enormous denudation has been effected in this great sheet of gravel, by rivers and streams, and by subäerial action. When once the protecting gravel has been cut through, and the soft Tertiary beds of sand and clay below have been reached, the process seems to go on with great rapidity. A large tract of land west of Southampton appears to have been in this way almost cleared of its gravel, of which but patches are left. Even the principal portion of the old table-land which has survived, that to the east and south-east of Fordingbridge, is deeply cut into by numerous valleys, many of a depth of 200 feet. The existence of these valleys is clearly in accordance with the river theory.

Let us now examine the discoveries in the valleys of the Test and of the Itchen from this point of view. Looking at the numerous instances of the finding of flint implements in gravels containing terrestrial and freshwater remains, and looking at the improbability of their occurring in a purely marine deposit, I venture to regard them as being equally characteristic of freshwater deposits as any organic fossils, and to claim the beds in which they occur as being of freshwater origin.

At Southampton several implements have been found in the pits upon the Common at heights ranging from 80 to 150 feet above the sea-level. The gravel there slopes at a considerably greater inclination than that of the table-land nearer Chilworth, with which it is continuous, and from which it would appear to have been in part derived. It occupies a tongue of land between the valley of the Itchen and that of the Test, now widened out by tidal action. It is in places covered by brick-earth, and its position and character are quite in accordance with a fluviatile origin. If, from their proximity to the apparently marine gravels, we assume these beds to belong to an early period in the history of the excavation of the valley, their high position above the present tidal stream is such as, according to the hypothesis, was to be expected.

The gravels found lower down the course of the river, at Hill Head, Brown Down, and Lee on the Solent, appear to belong to a somewhat later period; and to bear much the same relation to those of Southampton Common, as do the beds at Shrub Hill to those of Brandon Down. As I pointed out long ago, "There can be but little doubt that these gravel beds are merely an extension of the valley-gravels of the rivers Test, Itchen, Hamble, and other streams, which at the time they were deposited, flowed at this spot in one united broad stream, at an elevation of some forty feet above the existing level of their outfall, over a country which has since, by erosive action, been in part converted into the Southampton Water." [2779] We shall shortly have to revert to this circumstance; but before returning to the coast, we must take a short glance at the features of the discoveries near Salisbury.

In the neighbourhood of this city there can be no doubt of the deposits being thoroughly in accordance with the river theory. The Fisherton and Milford Hill beds occupy points or spurs of land, in the forks above the junction of streams, or precisely those spots in which their presence was to be expected. There are the usual beds of gravel, sand, and clay, the usual bones of the Quaternary fauna, some representing what are now Arctic species, and therefore presumably indicative of a severer climate than at present; and the usual land and freshwater shells. Though the valleys, being confluent, are excavated to the same depth, yet, on examination, their sectional areas will be found to be approximately proportional to the extent of country drained by the rivers still flowing through them. At Milford Hill, the deposit is cut off from the main spur of land by a kind of transverse valley, about thirty feet in depth, besides having on either side a valley some 100 feet deep. On any hypothesis of the beds having been deposited by aqueous action—and no other can for a moment be entertained—these valleys must have been mainly excavated since the deposition of the gravels. For had the valleys at that time existed, we can conceive of no conditions under which a body of water sufficient to fill the valleys to their summit, and able to carry along detrital matter with it, would leave its heavy contents at the top of the hills instead of at the bottom. The old fluviatile beds occur also at various levels on the slopes, in complete accordance with the theory of gradual excavation; and farther down the valley, at Fordingbridge, we find them again occurring with remains of *Elephas primigenius* at about forty feet above the river.

The circumstances of the discoveries at Bournemouth seem at first sight almost irreconcilable with any river-hypothesis; as it is difficult to conceive how gravels capping the cliffs along the sea-shore for miles, and at an elevation of from 130 to 90 feet above its level, can have been deposited in such a position by the agency of a stream. And yet on a closer examination of the case, all such difficulties vanish, and the ancient existence of a river at such an elevation, and running in such a direction that it would leave these gravels to testify to its former course, seems absolutely demonstrable. Without being aware of the results at which others had arrived, I came, after due consideration of the facts of the case, to the conclusion that, as has already been mentioned in an earlier page, there must in ancient times have existed a river draining an extensive tract of country along the southern coast, and flowing in an easterly direction; and that of this river a portion still survives in an altered and enlarged condition as the Solent Sea, which separates the Isle of Wight from the mainland. Mr. Codrington, whose paper I have already so often quoted, arrived on independent grounds at substantially the same conclusion. But at an earlier epoch still—in 1862—before any flint implements had been found at Bournemouth, or indeed in any of the gravels of the South of England, the late Rev. W. Fox, [2780] of Brixton, in the Isle of Wight, published nearly similar views as to the origin of the Solent. As his opinions cannot by any possibility be supposed to have been influenced by preconceived views as to the antiquity of man, I prefer stating the case, in the first instance, in his words rather than in my own:—"The severance of this island (the Isle of Wight) from the mainland, it appears to me, was effected under very unusual circumstances, and at a very distant period. The present channel of the Solent, being pretty nearly equally deep and equally broad throughout its entire length of twelve or fourteen miles, proves at once that it was not formed in the usual way of island-severing channels, that is, by gradual encroachments of the sea on the two opposite sides of a narrow neck of land" . . . "it is to be accounted for, therefore, not by the excavations of a gradually approaching sea, but, as I shall hereafter have to attempt to show, by its being originally the trunk or outlet of a very considerable river." . . . "Whoever, as a geologist, examines the vertical strata of the Chalk at the Needles, nay, and throughout the whole length of the Isle of Wight, and the strata of the same rock in exactly the same unusual position on the bold white cliff on the Dorsetshire coast some twenty miles westward of the Needles, will not doubt but that the two promontories were once united, forming a rocky neck of land from Dorset to the Needles. This chain of chalk might, or might not, be so cleft in twain as to allow the rivers of Dorset and Wilts to find a passage through them to the main ocean. My opinion, however, is that they had no such outlet, but that at that far distant period, the entire drainage of more than two counties, embracing the rivers that join the sea at Poole and Christchurch, flowed through what is now called Christchurch Bay, down the Solent, and joined the sea at Spithead."

"According to this theory, the Solent was at that time an estuary somewhat like the Southampton Water, having but one opening to the British Channel, but of so much more importance than the latter as it was fed by a vastly greater flow of fresh water." "Of course, according to this view, the sea would lose its original condition as an estuary at the time when the British Channel had so far made a breach through the chain of rocks connecting the Isle of Wight with Dorsetshire as to give an opening into itself for the Dorsetshire rivers, somewhere opposite to the town of Christchurch. From that time forth the Solent would become what it is at present, losing its character as an estuary, and assuming that of a long narrow sea." . . . "The distant period at which such changes took place it would be hopeless to guess at, amid the dimness of the data on which calculations could be founded. It could not be less, however, than many thousands of years, seeing that since that time, the British Channel has not only made a broad breach of twenty miles through a chain of slowly yielding rocks, but has also pushed its way gradually across the broad extent of the Poole and Christchurch Bays."

Such is the theory of Mr. Fox, which places the probable course of events fully and fairly before our view. I see in it but little on which to comment, except that it does not appear to have sufficiently taken into account the widening of the Solent subsequently to the time of its becoming a channel of the sea; and that in a passage, which I have not quoted, Mr. Fox estimates the drainage area of the ancient river as but little inferior to that of the Thames or Humber. Taking the basins of all the streams discharging into the sea between Ballard Down, near Poole, on the west, and Calshot Castle and the Medina on the east, but not including the latter river, I find that, according to the Ordnance Map, [2781] the present land area which would have drained into an ancient river such as that supposed, is 1,617 square miles. To this may be added another 100 square miles, representing the area included between the present coast and an extension of the chalk downs from Ballard Down to the Needles, the whole of which has been washed away; though within this large area, the present depth of the sea attains in but very few places to ten fathoms. The drainage area of the ancient river Solent can therefore have been but about one-third of that of the Thames and its affluents, unless we are to suppose that, as is the case in the neighbourhood of Carisbrooke Castle and with the Medina, a portion of land to the south of the old chalk downs drained northward through some gap in the range of hills. That such land existed seems probable, from the occurrence of gravels with elephant remains along the south-west coast of the Isle of Wight at an elevation of 80 feet and upwards above the sea, which, Mr. Codrington has suggested, may have been deposited by tributary streams of a river flowing northwards through the chalk range to the Solent. But even with any such addition the area drained by the old River Solent can hardly have been half that of the basin of the Thames.

With regard, however, to the former existence of this range of chalk hills and the land to the north of them, Mr. Codrington has shown, in the paper already so often quoted, that the spreading out of the marine gravel, and the levelling of the table-lands was probably effected in an inlet of the sea, shut in on the southern side by land which connected the Isle of Wight with the mainland, and opening to the eastward. Assuming, then, the existence of this ridge of high land, it is evident, as Mr. Fox has pointed out, that the only outlet for the rivers now represented by the Frome, the Trent or Piddle, the Stour, Blackwater, Avon, and other streams now discharging into the sea, must have been by an eastward channel, in fact, a continuation of the rivers now discharging through Poole Harbour. The course of such a river would naturally be guided, in the first instance, by the configuration of the surface of the old marine gravels of the sloping table-land. This, as has been shown, slopes upward from the present coast northward, and attains its highest level inland; but traces of the same gravel occur also in the Isle of Wight, though it there slopes upward in a southerly direction, attaining a height of 368 feet at St. George's Down, but being only from 100 to 160 feet above the sea in various places along the northern shore of the island, at a distance of about a mile inland. It appears, therefore, that there must originally have been a valley running east and west in the old marine gravel, forming a natural course for the drainage of the country, and probably finding its way towards the sea, somewhere within the space now occupied by the

Solent and Spithead, though not actually discharging into the sea until it had attained some distance eastward.

Evidence as to the highest level at which freshwater action removed and re-deposited the marine gravel on the southern slope of the valley is at present wanting; but, judging from a section across the Isle of Wight from St. George's Down to Norris Castle, given by Mr. Codrington, the declivity is so much more rapid below the 160 feet level than above it, that the ancient river may have commenced its action at about that level. How far eastward the Isle of Wight may have extended at that time it is difficult to say; but from the enormous denudation of land to the west, and the range of the ten-fathom line, there may probably have been land at all events as far east as opposite to Selsey, the extensive estuarine beds at which place, containing remains of *Elephas primigenius*, [2782] are possibly connected with this old river.

The precise manner in which the Foreland gravels and brick-earth, in which Mr. Codrington found a palæolithic implement at 85 feet above the sea-level, were connected with the old river-deposits, is difficult to determine. Mr. Codrington is inclined to think that a rise of land to the extent of 70 or 80 feet must have taken place since the deposition of the brick-earth in which the flint implement was embedded, but this to me seems unnecessary. It is, however, unsafe to speculate on a single specimen found in such a position. The implements found at Seaview and Bembridge may have been washed out of gravel-beds at a lower level than those of the Foreland, or even have been transported for some distance by marine currents.

Turning to Bournemouth, where so many more have been found, the highest and most westerly point at which implements have occurred appears to be about 130 feet above the sea. [2783] Farther east, near Boscombe, the level is about 120 feet; midway between that spot and Hengistbury Head, the height of the gravel is 90 feet; at High Cliff, 84 feet; at Hordwell, where implements abound, a short distance inland, 60 feet; and about midway along the northern shore of the Solent, 50 feet. The surface of the ground is, of course, much cut up by the numerous streams coming in from the north; but the general fall of the gravel from west to east is perfectly in accordance with its having been deposited in the valley of an ancient river running in this direction, the whole of the southern side of which has since been carried away by the sea. Whether the old river had become tidal so far west as Hurst Castle, when first it was intercepted by the sea to the south, does not appear to me to be a matter of importance, inasmuch as no doubt a valley was already formed, along the course of which the encroachments of the sea would be more rapid than where the cliffs were higher, and more solid matter had to be removed. That the valley, in which is now Southampton Water, was also originally, for the most part, scooped out by the rivers coming from the north, which in remote times flowed into the old River Solent, is, I think, beyond all reasonable doubt. The increased volume of the ancient river, after receiving so important an affluent, is evinced by the widening of the channel, from Calshot Castle eastward by Spithead, to a full third more than it is to the west, along what is now the Solent Sea.

As to the character of the gravels at Bournemouth, it is, as already observed, hard to distinguish those presumably of fluviatile origin from the older and probably marine beds. In the railway-cutting between Bournemouth and Christchurch, I thought, however, that in places I could trace the superposition of the one upon the other. The more recent deposits contain water-worn fragments of quartz, granite, and porphyry, as was noticed long ago by Mr. Godwin-Austen, [2784] who, from this circumstance, saw reason for connecting them with the gravels capping the tabular hills of Devon and Dorset to the west.

It is, of course, evident that at the period when the river ran at this high level, past the spot where now is Bournemouth, all the land to the immediate west must have been far higher than it is at present, and that Poole Harbour could not have existed. In attempting to reconstruct the map of a country, the shores of which have been much wasted by the sea, in order to show what must have been at some remote period the old coast-line, the task is rendered difficult and within certain limits impossible by the absence of any evidence as to the elevation above the sea of the land removed, and as to the channels along which the sea could work. In this case, however, there is a strong presumption as to the unbroken continuity of the chalk-range, and of its elevation having been much the same throughout, as it now is at both ends of the breach. The general character of the beds above the Chalk, so far as their power of resistance to water-action goes, seems also much the same at either extremity; though perhaps the beds at the Isle of Wight end of the breach are somewhat the harder. Assuming nearly equal conditions, and looking at the form of the present coast-line, which is indented by two distinct broad bays, it seems probable that the old course of the river may have been intercepted by the sea at two several points, the one nearer Poole and the other nearer Lymington. Directly this closer communication with the sea was formed for the Dorsetshire rivers, they would, of course, owing to the more rapid fall, excavate their valleys with greater speed at their mouth, and directly they became tidal, the sea would make rapid inroads on the soft sand and clay exposed to its action. So effective is this action, that at Hordwell Cliff the waste of the shore is said to be now going on at the rate of about a yard per annum, [2785] or upwards of half a mile every thousand years, though perhaps this is somewhat exaggerated.

In discussing this question, I have purposely avoided complicating the subject with the effects of any general lowering of the surface of the ground by erosion either chemical or mechanical; or of upheavals and depressions of the land during the period of the formation of the valleys, though no doubt this also has taken place, especially along the southern coast of Britain. I must, however, mention the existence of a submerged forest, occasionally visible at low water, at the foot of the cliffs at Bournemouth, which seems to show that there as elsewhere a depression of a former land surface has taken place. The late Mr. Albert Way, F. S. A., who had the opportunity of examining some of the stumps of trees exposed at rare intervals at low water, informed me that they appeared to be those of the true Scotch fir; and also that local tradition speaks of an impassable morass having, so late as the commencement of the present century, intervened between the line of cliffs and the sea. On the occasion of one of my visits to Bournemouth, some of these stumps were fortunately visible, and were pointed out to me by Mr. Way at a spot but a few yards to the west of the pier, and between high and low water-mark. They appear to be of no very remote antiquity, geologically speaking, and to be connected rather with the present valley of the Bourne than with the valley of the old river Solent, as the trees, some of which were fully a hundred years old, grew on the surface of a thick bed of hard peat. Under any circumstances, however, the presence of such remains at the foot of the cliff does not tend to diminish our estimate of the antiquity of the freshwater beds containing the works of man, which we find occupying their summit.

In passing the deposits containing flint implements in different parts of this country under review, enough has, I think, now been said to show that in position, in character, and in the nature of their organic contents, they are perfectly in accordance with what might have been expected from river-action under certain circumstances. The case might indeed have been made much stronger had deposits in other places, in all respects similar, except that the presence of flint implements has not as yet been observed in them, been brought into account; and it must not be forgotten that this might, with perfect propriety, have been done, as there can be no possible doubt that a certain series of gravels, sands, and clays, containing organic remains and flint implements in extremely variable quantity, all belong to one geological period, and owe their existence to similar causes.

But though on no other hypothesis than that of river-action can the phenomena be accounted for, yet, as has already been seen, it is necessary, in order that river-action should have produced such effects, that the streams, during some portion of the year at all events, should have been more torrential in character than they are at the present day. If, however, we see satisfactory grounds for attributing these beds containing land and freshwater shells and remains of terrestrial animals, to rivers formerly flowing at much higher levels than at present, which have since excavated their valleys—and it seems impossible to do otherwise—then we must also accept as a fact that the climatal conditions were such as would enable the rivers to perform the work. It is, as Sir Joseph Prestwich [2786] has shown, quite out of the question to suppose that with the valleys excavated to the present depth, any meteorological causes could fill them to their summits; or even if they could and did, that they would leave such deposits as we find at high elevations on their slopes, or even on detached eminences. It will, however, be well to examine briefly any corroborative evidence that may be forthcoming, as to the probability either of a severer climate involving a greater accumulation of winter snows, or of a greater rainfall, or of both. The one, indeed, seems hardly probable without the other, as a cold land surface "presented to vapour-laden sea-winds, as in the mountainous districts of the north-west of Spain, in our own lake districts, and in Scandinavia," [2787] involves of necessity a heavy rainfall.

With regard to climate, we may take into account that which prevailed at a somewhat earlier date; for there appears no doubt that the flint implement-bearing gravels are all of later date than the Chalky Boulder Clay of the Eastern Counties, a deposit which belongs to the so-called Glacial Period, during a portion of which a great part of England and Scotland was submerged beneath the sea, and became coated with masses of Boulder Clay and other deposits, derived for the most part from the moraines of glaciers, sometimes at no great distance, and possibly in the main transported and dropped in their present positions by means of icebergs and coast ice. That they are of later date is proved by more than one of the implement-bearing beds reposing in valleys either in, or cut through, this Chalky Boulder Clay; and at Hoxne the interval between the Glacial deposits and the Palæolithic beds is marked by two sets of lacustrine strata, the lower and earlier with a flora characteristic of a mild climate, and the upper by one which points to the recurrence of Arctic conditions. Prof. Boyd Dawkins [2788] has suggested the probability of the higher ground of North Wales and the northern part of England having been still enveloped in an ice-mantle at the time that the mammoth, reindeer, and other post-glacial mammals were living in the lower and less inclement districts. But this view is to some extent founded on negative evidence, and on the assumption that palæolithic implements do not exist in this northern area. I have already commented [2789] on the possibility of implements being eventually found in it.

The crumpling and contortion of some of the beds of River-drift, especially at high levels, has been regarded by Sir Joseph Prestwich [2790] as possibly resulting from the lateral pressure produced by packing and jamming together of blocks of ice, such as may now be witnessed in rivers like the Danube and the Rhine. The "trail and warp" of Mr. Trimmer, those superficial deposits so common over a large portion of this country, which, indeed, constitute so large a portion of the arable soil, seem also, as the Rev. Osmond Fisher [2791] has pointed out, to be significant of a severer climate than at present prevails. The "Palæolithic floors," both near London and at Caddington, are buried under a considerable thickness of this "trail." There is moreover a high probability that, at the time of the deposit of the gravels, Britain was still united to the continent; so that, apart from other causes, there was a tendency for the climate to partake more of a continental character than at present, and to induce greater cold in winter and greater heat in summer.

That the existence of enormous glaciers is as indicative of the action of heat, in order to convert the water of the ocean into vapour, as of cold to condense it, has been insisted on by Professor Tyndall, [2792] and even more strongly by Professor Frankland. If at the time of the rivers flowing at the high level, Britain was still connected with the continent, it is by no means impossible that the temperature of the seas on either side of the connecting isthmus may have been different. That connected more immediately with the Southern Ocean would have been the warmer of the two, from which a copious supply of vapour would be carried by the southerly winds, and be condensed as rain in its passage northward.

Mr. Alfred Tylor, F.G.S., [2793] in his profusely illustrated papers on the Amiens gravel, and on Quaternary gravels, contends for the existence of a "Pluvial period" subsequent to the Glacial, in which the rainfall was far greater than at present, and such a view has much to commend it for acceptance. But when he proceeds to assert that the surface of the Chalk in the valley of the Somme, and in all other valleys of the same character, had assumed its present form prior to the deposition of any of the gravel or loess now to be seen there, and to argue that the whole of the gravels at all levels on the slopes are of one age, and due to floods extending to a height of at least 80 feet above the level of the rivers, we may well hesitate before we give in our adhesion to such views. In the first place, it is, to say the least of it, unphilosophical to rely too much on a single example, such as that of the valley of the Somme; and to account for its phenomena by causes which are evidently incapable of producing the effects observable in other localities, as, for instance, at Southampton, close to the sea, and 160 feet above its level. But what shall we say to floods raising the levels of rivers upwards of 80 feet, yet having no erosive power, and the waters of which, regardless of the laws of gravity, tranquilly deposited their solid contents evenly over the slopes, or often in the greatest thickness on their higher part, and in some cases on almost isolated hills, instead of principally on the bottom of the river-valley? Whence all the materials for the gravels are to be derived, how they are to be reduced to a subangular condition by water-wear, especially in the case of the flint implements occurring in the gravels, are points on which further information will have to be supplied, before any such views can be seriously entertained.

I have up to this point almost left out of view any distinctive differences between the deposits at a high level and those at a low level in the river-valleys. That such, however, exist has been pointed out by Sir Joseph Prestwich; [2794] and judging from the northern range of the group of shells found in the high-level beds, the absence of southern species, the character of the mammalian and vegetable remains, the transport of large blocks such as could only be effected by ice and the other physical features of the case, he is inclined to assign a winter temperature to the period of their deposit from 19° to 29° Fahr. below that which now obtains in these regions. From a consideration of the features of the low-level deposits he considers that at the time of their deposit, the climate was rather less severe, by about 5°. The presence of the mammoth and woolly-haired rhinoceros, animals specially adapted for cold climates; of the musk-ox, the reindeer, the lemming, and marmot, corroborates the same view; while the hippopotamus, which seems characteristic of the low-level deposits, is suggestive of a somewhat warmer climate. Like the mammoth and rhinoceros, its structure may, however, have been somewhat modified, so as to enable it to occupy colder regions than at present, or it may have been merely a summer visitor ranging northwards before the separation of Britain from the continent. Under any circumstances its presence seems to indicate that the volume of the rivers was probably in excess of what it is at the present time. But whatever may have been the degree of winter cold, or the amount of the snow and rainfall, the one was not so extreme as to prevent there being an abundance of animal life, nor the other so great as to interfere with the growth of a sufficient supply of vegetable food on which it might subsist.

It has, indeed, been supposed by some that the remains of the early mammals occurring in the gravels are derived from older beds, and that their presence in association with flint implements no more proves the contemporaneity of the men who made those implements with the old Quaternary fauna, than their association with Chalk fossils proves that mankind were originally inhabitants of the bed of the Cretaceous ocean. Did the gravels only occur at such levels as are within reach of existing streams, there might be some reason in such a view, which is, moreover, in certain cases and within certain limits, probably correct. For we have seen how in the course of the excavation of a valley, the beds deposited at one time are liable to be disturbed at another, and re-deposited in a fresh place; which could hardly happen without an admixture of fresh materials, some probably of a more recent date. In the process of transport, however, not only the implements but the still softer bones are liable to wear and abrasion of the angles, and it is impossible to conceive that, assuming the Quaternary fauna to have disappeared from this region before the valleys were excavated, and the implement-bearing beds deposited, their bones could still exist in such numbers, and so often in an unrolled condition in the low-level beds.

Had this older fauna disappeared, it is evident that man could not have subsisted here alone, unaccompanied by other animals to furnish him with food; and if these animals belonged to the later or "prehistoric" fauna, where, as Sir John Lubbock pertinently asks, are their bones? If, however, we acknowledge that the pleistocene mammals still occupied this country at the time of the low-level beds being formed, and if we find their remains also in those at a high level, and at all intermediate heights, it is evident that they must have persisted here during the whole period of the excavation of the valleys; while, if we find also flint implements in an unrolled and unworn condition at all heights, it is evident that those who made them must also have been co-occupants of the region during the same period. If, indeed, as appears to be in some valleys the case, the unworn implements occur only in the high-level deposits, while in the lower they are either absent or in a much worn condition, the inference is, that in those particular valleys the occupation by man, though for some time contemporaneous with that of the mammoth and his congeners, ceased before the extinction or emigration of the old fauna. In some cases, however, as at Fisherton, [2795] the worked flints have been found below the remains of mammoth; while in the beds at Menchecourt, near Abbeville, [2796] in which the implements occur, were found the bones of a hind leg of rhinoceros still in their natural position, so that they must have retained their ligaments when deposited, and could not since have been disturbed. With regard to the amelioration of climatal conditions which led to the cessation of the excavation of the valleys, it may not impossibly have been connected with the insulation of the country, when the isthmus connecting it with the continent was cut through by the sea. But this is hardly the place for such speculations. If, however, we may regard the estuarine deposits at Selsey, in which almost entire skeletons of mammoth occur, as belonging to the period when the deposit of the low-level gravels was ceasing, it would appear from the associated molluscan forms, as interpreted by Mr. Godwin-Austen, that the temperature of the waters of the English Channel was at that time such as may now be met with twelve degrees farther south.

If there was a difference in the climatal conditions of the high and low-level deposits, it might have produced some effect on the method of living, and on the implements of the men of the two periods. At one time I thought it probable that a marked distinction might eventually be drawn between the high-and low-level implements, but so far as Britain is concerned, this can hardly be done. Still the *facies* of a collection from two different spots is rarely quite the same, and I think there is generally a preponderance of the ruder pointed implements in the high-level gravels, and of the flat ovate sharp-rimmed implements in the low-level. In the valley of the Somme, the broad polygonal flakes are certainly most abundant in the lower beds, as at Montiers, near Amiens.

I would, however, deprecate the introduction of such terms as "Eolithic" and "Mesolithic" in order to distinguish two phases in the Stone Period as being both unfounded and misleading. We know not where or when the dawn of human civilization arose, but it was probably long before the date of our earliest River-Gravels and in some part of the world more favoured by climate than Britain. Why then should we speak of British implements as Eolithic? And how can we apply the term Mesolithic to a period intervening between the Palæolithic and Neolithic Ages, when we know neither when the one ended nor when the other began?

Enough has now been said with regard to the manner in which these beds of River-drift were probably deposited; and the irresistible conclusion is, that, owing to the wasting agency of rain, frost, and rivers, there must have been a vast change in the superficial features of the country, since the time when those who fashioned the flint implements found in the high-level gravels were joint occupants of the land with the mammoth and rhinoceros and the other departed members of the Quaternary fauna. A similar change in the surface of the country has also taken place in the neighbourhood of the caves in which the remains of this same fauna occur, associated also with similar relics of human workmanship.

What length of time it must have taken for such changes to be effected, is a question we must now approach; but before doing so it will be well to say a few more words, in addition to what has already been said, on the almost entire absence of human bones in the beds containing those of the associated mammalia.

In the first place, it is well to repeat that whatever may be the case in the brick-earth, or loess, there have not, as has been pointed out by Sir John Lubbock, [2797] been found in the gravel up to the present time any remains of animals so small as man, who, as the same author observes, must of necessity have been few in number in comparison with the animals by the chase of which he must have subsisted. Another cause appears also to have been at work; for however barbarous we may suppose the human race to have been at that remote period, we can hardly believe them to have been so destitute of all natural affection as to deny some rites of sepulture to friends or relatives removed by death. There would, therefore, in all probability, be but few or no human bones exposed on the surface in such a manner as to be carried off by the flooded streams, and imbedded in their gravels; while, in case of any human beings perishing by drowning, their bodies, as I have already shown, would probably either be carried to sea, or left in such a position as to allow of their recovery, at all events before they became disarticulated.

This is, however, a matter of but small importance, as there will be but little difficulty in conceding that an implement fashioned by human agency—and on this point there can be no question, unless we are to assume in ancient times the existence of some other now extinct race of intelligent beings—is as good an evidence of the existence of man, as would be any or all of his bones. Moreover, human bones are reported to have been discovered in these Quaternary beds, both in this country and in France. In England, I have already mentioned a human skull found near Bury St. Edmunds by Mr. Trigg, and the more doubtful skeleton found near Northfleet. I will not, however, insist upon either discovery being beyond all cavil.

Nor will I do more than allude to the too celebrated Moulin Quignon jaw, over which I have already pronounced a *Requiescat in pace*, [2798] but the discovery of portions of the human skeleton by M. Bertrand, and M. Reboux, in the valley of the Seine, at Clichy [2799] and elsewhere near Paris, in the same beds in which implements of true Palæolithic types have been found, seems better substantiated.

Whether the *Pithecanthropus erectus* of Dr. Dubois was human or simian, and what is the date of the beds in which his remains were found, and whether there is evidence of the existence of Miocene or Pliocene Man [2800] in Burma, Portugal, France, Italy, or California, are questions which want of space compels me to leave on one side. I have, however, more than once elsewhere expressed my opinion on the subject of Tertiary Man. [2801]

I need hardly again repeat that according to my view it is not in Britain, but in some part of the world more favoured by climate that the cradle of the human race is to be sought. And yet the antiquity of Man in Britain seems to extend far beyond any of our ordinary methods of computation. In attempting to estimate it, however vaguely, I must at the outset observe that with our present amount of knowledge, it is hopeless to expect that it can be determined with anything approaching to precision. Not only have we no trustworthy measure of the rate of excavation of the valleys, which might give us an approximate date for the higher deposits in them, but we are at a loss to know at what epoch their excavation in the lower part of their course ceased, and what may be termed the modern alluvial deposits, which to some extent have partially refilled the old channels, began to accumulate.

That the general configuration of the surface of the country, in Neolithic times, when the ordinary forms of polished stone implements were in use, was much the same as it is at present, is proved by the fact of such implements being frequently found in recent superficial deposits. Were we, in defiance of probability, to assume that the use of these polished implements did not date farther back than two thousand years from the period when we are first made acquainted with this country by history, this would give an additional four thousand years beyond the period necessary for the excavation of the valleys for the date of the older River-drift implements. Such a period as two thousand years is in all probability almost ridiculously small to assign for the duration of the Neolithic and Bronze Periods; but however this may be, there appears, in this country at all events, to be a complete gap [2802] between the River-drift and Surface Stone Periods, so far as any intermediate forms of implements are concerned; and here at least the race of men who fabricated the latest of the palæolithic implements may have, and in all probability had, disappeared at an epoch remote from that when the country was again occupied by those who not only chipped out but polished their flint tools, and who were, moreover, associated with a mammalian fauna far nearer resembling that of the present day than that of Quaternary times.

So different, indeed, are the two groups of animals that, as has already been observed, Prof. Boyd Dawkins [2803] has shown that out of forty-eight well-ascertained species living in the Post-glacial or River-drift Period, only thirty-one were able to live on into the Prehistoric or Surface Stone Period. Such a change as this in the fauna of a country can hardly have been the work of a few years, or even of a few centuries; and yet we must intercalate a period of time sufficient for its accomplishment between the remotest date to which we can carry back the Neolithic Period, and the close of the Palæolithic Period as indicated by the low-level gravels. The antiquity, then, that must be assigned to the implements in the highest beds of River-drift may be represented (1) by the period requisite for the excavation of the valleys to their present depth; plus (2), the period necessary for the dying out and immigration of a large part of the Quaternary or Post-Glacial fauna and the coming in of the Prehistoric; plus (3), the Polished Stone Period; plus (4), the Bronze, Iron, and Historic Periods, which three latter in this country occupy a space of probably not less than three thousand years.

A single equation, involving so many unknown quantities, is, as already observed, not susceptible of solution; but various attempts have been made to arrive at some approximate idea of the amount of time it represents. One method has been that of assigning a date for the Glacial Period, deduced from astronomical causes, mainly in connection with the eccentricity of the earth's orbit, as pointed out by M. Adhémar and Mr. Croll. From data thus obtained, Sir Charles Lyell [2804] inclines to place it at a period of extreme cold about 800,000 years ago, though Sir John Lubbock [2805] would rather accept an epoch of somewhat less severity about 200,000 years removed from our time.

Another and more direct method suggested by Sir Archibald Geikie, [2806] following in Mr. A. Tylor's track, is that of estimating the time required for the excavation of the valleys by the amount of solid matter carried down in suspension by various rivers at the present day. He estimates that this amount, if spread over the whole area drained by the rivers, represents, on an average, an annual loss of about 1/6000 of a foot; but inasmuch as the erosion of the slopes and watercourses is very much greater than that of the more level grounds, the excavation of the valleys must proceed at a more rapid rate, which he assumes to be about 1/1200 part of a foot per annum, or one foot in 1,200 years. Such a calculation is, of course, open to various objections, as we may readily conceive the bottom and slopes of a valley to have been so far washed that, under ordinary circumstances, they afford little or no fine earthy matter to be taken up by the rain falling on their surface; and in such a case, the rivers, if turbid, would derive their turbidity from the water delivered from the higher and comparatively unwashed table lands. Or again, the soil may, like the Chalk under ordinary circumstances, be so absorbent that but little of the rainfall flows off from its surface. The calculation has already been made, that a rainfall of 54 inches annually, supposing the whole of it flowed off the land into the sea in a turbid state, containing, like the Mississippi, 1/1500 part of its weight of solid matter, would lower the surface a foot in 450 years; but as has already been observed, we cannot conceive it possible that with such soils as we have here to do with, the constant turbidity should have been anything like so great. And, in fact, the whole system of calculation is one which may be regarded rather as proving the necessity of valleys being in course of time formed by subaërial action, than as giving any definite guide by which to calculate the period requisite for their formation. There can, indeed, be no doubt that the denuding power of the falling rain is greater on the slopes than on the level surfaces; but it seems impossible to assign any proportions to the effects on land lying at different inclinations, of different characters, and under different circumstances as to any vegetable covering. Were the action uniform over the whole surface exposed, of course no alteration beyond a general lowering of the land-surface would result from this cause, and the valleys would remain of precisely the same depth with regard to the adjacent land as they did at remote epochs. Looking at the quantity of brick-earth still left on the slopes of many of our valleys, I am inclined to think that the lowering of the surface has been more general than has been supposed by Sir Archibald Geikie. The presence of these soft and easily denuded beds is also an argument against the excavation of the valleys having progressed in a uniform manner, by heavy rains falling during the period of the year when such beds were soft and unfrozen; and seems rather significant of the excavation of the valley by floods principally occurring at a time when the upper part of the soil was in a frozen condition.

Certainly the whole character of the deposits is more in accordance with their resulting from the occasional flooding of the streams than from any other cause. If this be so, who shall tell at what intervals such floods occurred, and what was the average effect of each in deepening the valleys? That they were of comparatively rare occurrence, and not so frequent that they were foreseen by the men of those days, seems deducible from the number of their implements found in the gravels. For there is much probability that these must have been washed in from settlements on the banks of the rivers, which, notwithstanding previous catastrophes of the same kind, were constantly placed within reach of the stream when flooded.

Sir Joseph Prestwich [2807] has suggested as a possible gauge of the antiquity of the deposits, the natural funnels eaten into the chalk by the action of water charged with carbonic acid, and has cited one at Drucat, near Abbeville, which has been formed since the deposit of the gravel containing flint implements, and is upwards of 20 feet in diameter at top, and probably 100 feet in depth; but here also it seems impossible to introduce a factor by which the time represented can be ascertained. There are, however, features in connection with this case which can only be reconciled with the former high level of the bottom of the adjacent valley, and with its gradual excavation. It will be remembered that similar pipes of erosion, leading in some cases to caverns above them, occur in the Drift-beds of the valley of the Little Ouse.

There is yet another means at our command for forming, at all events, an approximate idea of the time that has elapsed since the deposit of the beds containing the remains of the old Quaternary fauna, inasmuch as at the time of their introduction into this country, if not for a lengthened period afterwards, Britain had apparently not become an island, but was still connected by an isthmus of greater or less width with the Continent. To estimate the time, however, that would be required for cutting through this isthmus and widening the Channel to its present dimensions, is a work from which the mind almost recoils. Even the wearing away of that tract of land to the south of the present Hampshire coast, which must almost of necessity have existed at the time when the Bournemouth flint implement-bearing gravels were deposited, taking the present rapid inroad of the sea on the unusually soft cliffs at Hordwell as a guide, would seem to involve a period of not less than 10,000 years; but inasmuch as the cliffs during a considerable portion of the time must have been of chalk instead of sand and clay, and as a chalk cliff 500 feet high, instead of being worn away at the rate of a yard each year, is said only to recede at the rate of an inch in a century, [2808] the actual period necessary for the removal of this tract must probably have been many times 10,000 years, and can with certainty be regarded as having been immensely in excess of such a lapse of time.

On the whole, it would seem that for the present, at least, we must judge of the antiquity of these deposits rather from the general effect produced upon our minds by the vastness of the changes which have taken place, both in the external configuration of the country and its extent seaward, since the time of their formation, than by any actual admeasurement of years or of centuries. To realize the full meaning of these changes, almost transcends the powers of the imagination. Who, for instance, standing on the edge of the lofty cliff at Bournemouth, and gazing over the wide expanse of waters between the present shore and a line connecting the Needles on the one hand, and the Ballard Down Foreland on the other, can fully comprehend how immensely remote was the epoch, when what is now that vast bay was high and dry land, and a long range of chalk downs, 600 feet above the sea, bounded the horizon on the south? And yet this must have been the sight that met the eyes of those primeval men who frequented the banks of that ancient river which buried their handiworks in gravels that now cap the cliffs, and of the course of which so strange but indubitable a memorial subsists in what has now become the Solent Sea.

Or again, taking our stand at Ealing, or Acton, or Highbury, and looking over a broad valley fully four miles in width, with the river flowing through it at a depth of 100 feet below its former bed, in which, beneath our feet, are relics of human art deposited at the same time as the gravels; which of us can picture to himself the lapse of time represented by the excavation of a valley on such a scale, by a river larger, it may be, in volume than the Thames, but still draining only the same tract of country? But when, to this long period we mentally add that during which the old fauna, with the mammoth and rhinoceros, and other to us strange and unaccustomed forms, was becoming extinct, so far as Britain was concerned; and also that other, we know not how lengthened period, when our barbarous predecessors sometimes polished their stone implements, but were still unacquainted with metallic tools; and then beyond this, add the many centuries when bronze was in use for cutting purposes; and after all this, further remember that the ancient and mighty city now extending across the valley does not, with all its historical associations, carry us back to the times even of the bronze-using people, the mind is almost lost in amazement at the vista displayed.

So fully must this be felt, that we are half inclined to sympathize with those who, from sheer inability to carry their vision so far back into the dim past, and from unconsciousness of the cogency of other and distinct evidence as to the remoteness of the origin of the human race, are unwilling to believe in so vast an antiquity for man as must of necessity be conceded by those, who however feebly they may make their thoughts known to others, have fully and fairly weighed the facts which modern discoveries have unrolled before their eyes.

FINIS.

DESCRIPTION OF THE PLATES.

PLATE I.

1. Simple ridged flake. *Porte Marcadé, Abbeville.*

2. Sharp-pointed flake, with several facets on its convex side. *Montiers, near Amiens.*

3. Chisel-pointed flake. *Ibid.*

4. Large polygonal flake. *Ibid.*

5. Round-pointed, tongue-shaped, sub-triangular implement. *Biddenham, near Bedford.*

6. Acutely pointed, kite-shaped ditto. *St. Acheul, near Amiens.*

7. Sub-triangular ditto, with truncated butt. *Ibid.*

8. Ditto, with incurved sides, and butt formed of the natural surface of the flint. *Ibid.*

9. Ditto, made from a round-ended nodule of flint. *Ibid.*

10. Thick-backed, single-edged implement of wedge-shaped section. *Ibid.*

PLATE II.

11. Ovate tongue-shaped implement. *St. Acheul, near Amiens.*

12. Ovate-lanceolate ditto, with rough butt. *Ibid.*

13. Ditto, with truncated butt. *(Brick-earth), St. Acheul, Amiens.*

14. Rough, wedge-shaped implement. *St. Acheul, Amiens.*

15. Round-pointed implement with untrimmed butt. *Ibid.*

16. Ditto, with naturally rounded butt and side. *Ibid.*

17. Thin, ovate, tongue-shaped implement. *Champ de Mars, Abbeville.*

18. Ovate implement of intermediate form between the tongue-shaped and sharp-rimmed. *St. Acheul, Amiens.*

19. Ovate, thin, sharp-rimmed implement. *Menchecourt, Abbeville.*

20. Irregularly ovate ditto. *Moulin Quignon, Abbeville.*

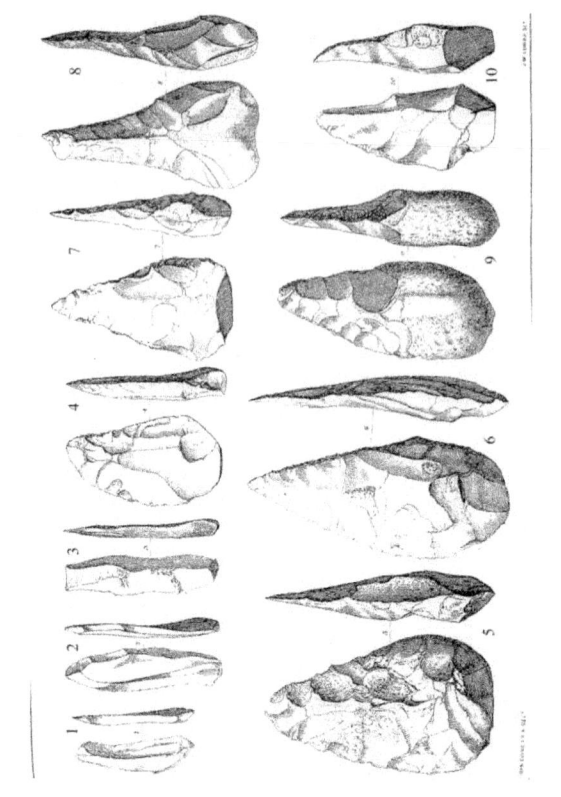

Plate I. IMPLEMENTS FROM THE RIVER-DRIFT.

Scale six inches to the foot or half linear measure.

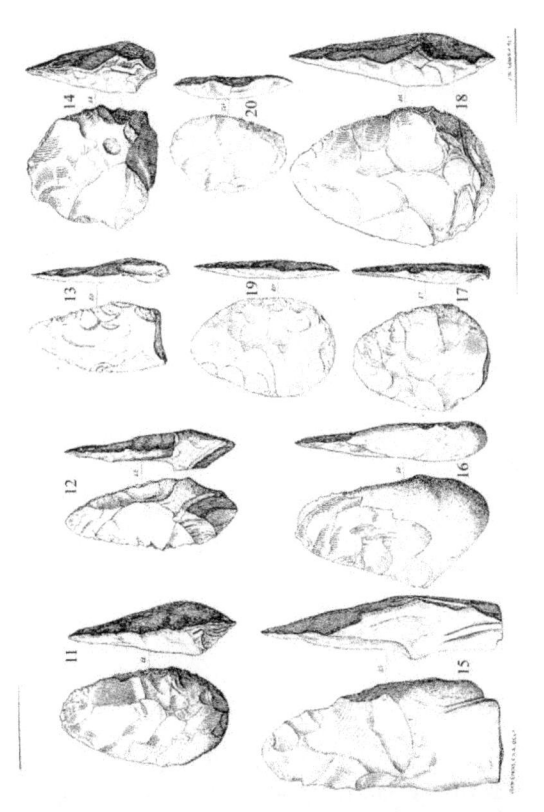

Plate II. IMPLEMENTS FROM THE RIVER-DRIFT.

Scale six inches to the foot or half linear measure.

NOTES—CHAPTER I.

1

Some interesting remarks on the succession of the three periods and the possibility of abnormal variations from it will be found in a lecture to the Archæological Institute delivered by the late Mr. E. T. Stevens in 1872. (*Arch. Journ.*, vol. xxix., p. 393.)

2

1872, p. 11, *et seqq.*

3

Mém., vol. xii., 163.

4

Archæologia, vol. ii. p. 118.

5

p. 778.

6

I would especially refer to an excellent article by the Rev. John Hodgson in Vol. I. of the *Archæologia Æliana* (A.D. 1816), entitled "An inquiry into the æra when brass was used in purposes to which iron is now applied."

7

"Op. et Di.," I., 150.

8

"De Rerum Nat.," v. 1282.

9

Suetonius, Vit. Aug., cap. lxxii. M. Salomon Reinach has disputed my views as to the meaning of this passage, but I see no reason for changing my opinion as to the "arma heroum" referring to "res vetustate notabiles." (See *Mém. de l'Acad. des Inscr.*, 14th Dec., 1888.)

10

"Laconica," cap. 3.

11

Op., ed. 1624, vol. i., p. 17.

12

Wilkinson, "Anc. Egypt.," vol. iii. p. 241.

13

Æn., 1. vii. 743.

14

Χαλκεύειν δὲ καὶ τὸ σιδηρεύειν ἔλεγον, καὶ χαλκεάς τοὺς τὸν σίδηρον ἐργαζομένους, Jul. Pollux, "Onomasticon," lib. vii. cap. 24.

15

Macrobius, "Saturnal.," v. 19. Rhodiginus, "Antiq. Lect.," xix. c. 10.

16

Met., lib. vii. 228.

17

Homer, Il., xxiii. 826.

18

Zeitsch. f. Ægypt. Sprache, &c. 1870, p. 114.

19

Cong. Préh. Bruxelles, 1872, p. 242.

20

See a valuable paper by Dr. L. Beck, *Arch. f. Anth.*, vol. xii. (1880) p. 293.

21

See De Rougemont, "L'Age du Bronze," p. 159.

22

See Percy's "Metallurgy," vol. i. p. 873.

23

De Rougemont, *op. cit.*, p. 158. See "Ancient Bronze Imps.," p. 6, *seqq.*

24

Photii "Bibliotheca," *ed.* 1653, col. 1343.

25

Jour. Anth. Inst., vol. xx. p. 330.

26

Lib. i. c. 21.

27

"Das Grabfeld von Hallstatt und dessen Alterthümer." Vienna, 1868.

28

London, 1881.

29

De Nat. Deor., Lib. ii. c. 28.

30

Lib. iv. c. 28.

31

Lib. i. v. 66.

32

"Early History of Mankind," p. 218; 2nd edit. p. 221, *q. v.*

33

Lib. ii. 86.

34

Lib. i. 91.

35

Trans. Ethn. Soc., N. S., vol. vii. 112.

36

Exod. iv. 25.

37

Josh. v. 2.

38

Ib. xxiv. 30.

39

See also Tylor's "Early History of Mankind," 2nd ed., p. 217. The entire chapter on the Stone Age, Past and Present, is well worthy of careful perusal, and enters more fully into the whole question of the Stone Age throughout the world than comes within my province.

40

C. R. du Cong. Int. des Sc. Anth. 1878. Paris 1880, p. 280. *Comptes Rendus de l'Acad. des Sciences*, vol. lxiii, August 28, 1871.

41

Comptes Rendus, 1871, vol. lxxiii. p. 540.

42

Livy, lib. i. c. 24.

43

Rapt. Proserp. I. 201.

44

"Horæ Ferales," p. 136. *Arch. Journ.*, vol. xi. p. 169.

45

Arch. für Anthropol., vol. iii. 16.

46

"Coins of the Ancient Britons," pp. 42, 263, *et alibi*.

47

Herodian, lib. iii. c. 14.

48

"Cat. of Stone Ant. in R. I. A. Mus.," p. 81.

49

Wood's "Nat. Hist. of Man," i. p. 97.

50

Klemm, "Allgemeine Culturwissenschaft," part i. p. 86. *Proc. Soc. Ant. Scot.*, vol. x. 360.

51

Mitchell's "Past in the Present," p. 10, 44. *Proc. Soc. Ant. Scot.*, vol. xix. p. 385, xx. p. 146, xxiii. p. 16.

52

Phil. Trans., 1860, p. 311. *Archæologia*, vol. xxxviii. p. 293.

53

"Prehistoric Times," (1865), p. 60.

NOTES—CHAPTER II.

54

This chapter was for the most part written in 1868, and communicated to the International Congress of Prehistoric Archæology held at Norwich in that year. See *Trans. Preh. Cong.*, 1868, p. 191, where a short abstract is given.

55

N. and Q. 7th S., vol. x. p. 172.

56

Mat. 3me S., vol. ii. (1885) p. 61.

57

Op. cit., p. 38.

58

Spec. Naturæ, lib. ix. sect. 13.

59

Morlot in *Rec. Arch.*, vol. v. (1862), p. 216. *Geologist*, vol. v. p. 192. Engelhardt found several similar pieces of pyrites at Thorsbjerg, with iron and other antiquities of about the fourth century of our era. He says that steels for striking fire are not at present known as belonging to the Early Iron Age of Denmark. This late use of pyrites affords strong evidence of iron and steel having been unknown to the makers of flint implements, for had they made use of iron hammers, the superior fire-giving properties of flint and iron would at once have been evident, and pyrites would probably soon have been superseded, at all events in countries where flint abounded.— Engelhardt, "Thorsbjerg Mosefund," p. 60; p. 65 in the English edit. The quartz pebbles with grooves in them which belong to the Iron Age seem, however, to have been used for producing fire by means of a pointed steel.

60

Weddell, "Voyage towards the South Pole," p. 167; Tylor, "Early History of Mankind," 2nd edit., p. 249. Wood's "Nat. Hist. of Man," vol. ii. p. 522.

61

Hist. Nat., lib. xxxvi. cap. 19.

62

Lib. vii. cap. 56.

63

II. Macc. x. 3.

64

Æneid, i. v. 174.

65

Æneid, vi. v. 6. See also (Georg. I. 135)—"Ut silicis venis abstrusum excuderet ignem." On this passage Fosbroke remarks (Enc. Ant. i. 307), "A stone with a vein was chosen as now."

66

Eidyllia, v. 42.

67

Keller, "Lake-dwellings," p. 119.

68

Vol. ii. p. 536. Bohn's edit., 1846.

69

An interesting paper on tinder-boxes will be found in *The Reliquary*, vii. p. 65. See also Mitchell's "Past in the Present," p. 100, and *Arch. Camb.*, 5th s., vol. vii. p. 294.

70

Stevens'. "Flint Chips," p. 588.

71

Op. cit., vol. ii., p. 537.

72

"Classe Mathématique et Physique," t. 3, an. ix. An abstract of this account is given in Rees' Encyclop., *s. v.* Gun-flint.

73

"Physische und technische Beschreibung der Flintensteine," &c., von Hacquet. Wien, 1792, 8vo. A nearly similar account is given in Winckell's "Handbuch für Juger," &c., 1822, Theil iii. p. 546.

74

Skertchly, *op. cit.*, p. 78.

75

Mat., 3me, s. ii., 1885, p. 61.

76

An account of the process of making gun-flints, written by the late Mr. James Wyatt, F.G.S., has been published in Stevens' "Flint Chips," p. 578. A set of gun-flint makers' tools is in the Musée de St. Germain, and the process of manufacture has been described by M. G. de Mortillet ("Promenades," p. 69). An account of a visit to Brandon is given by Mr. E. Lovett in *Proc. Soc. Ant. Scot.*, xxi p. 206, and an article on "Flint-Knapping," by Mr. H. F. Wilson, is in the *Magazine of Art*, 1887, p. 404.

77

See *postea* p. 273.

78

Petrie, "Medum," 1892, Pl. xxix., p. 18, 34.

79

Nature, vol. xxv. p. 8.

80

P. 52.

81

"Bosnia and Herzegovina," 2nd ed. (1877), p. 153, *B.A. Rep.* 1885, p. 1216.

82

"Stone Age," p. 6.

83

"Lake-dwellings," p. 36.

84

l. c. pp. 86 and 97.

85

Comptes Rendus, 1867, vol. lxv. p. 640.

86

Troyon, "Mon. de l'Antiquité," p. 52.

87

Proc. Soc. Ant. Scot., vol. iv. p. 385.

88

Proc. Soc. Ant., 2nd series, vol. iii. p. 38.

89

Geol. Mag., vol. iii. (1866) p. 433.

90

"Monarquia Indiana," lib. xvii. cap. 1, Seville, 1615, translated by E. B. Tylor, "Anahuac," p. 331. See a correction of Mr. Tylor's translation in the *Comptes Rendus*, vol. lxvii. p. 1296.

91

Tylor's "Anahuac," p. 332.

92

P. 871.

93

Trans. Roy. Soc. Canada, 1889, p. 59.

94

Tylor's "Anahuac," p. 99.

95

"Last Rambles amongst the Indians," 1868, p. 188. The whole passage is reprinted in "Flint Chips," p. 82.

96

B. B. Redding in *Am. Naturalist*, Nov., 1880. *Nature*, vol. xxi. p. 613.

97

Transactions of the Ethnological Society, N. S., vol. iv. p. 242.

98

Op. cit., N. S., vol. i. p. 138.

99

"Völkerkunde," vol. ii. (1888), p. 748.

100

Zeitsch. f. Ethnol., vol. xvi. p. 222.

101

Rep. of U.S. Nat. Mus., 1888, Niblack, Pl. xxii.

102

Rep. of Bureau of Ethn., 1887–8, p. 95.

103

Anthrop. Rev., vol. iv. p. civ. Mr. Baines has also communicated an interesting letter on this subject, with illustrations, to Mackie's "Geol. Repertory," vol. i. p. 258.

104

Archæologia, vol. xl. p. 381. See also Prof. Steenstrup and Sir John Lubbock in the *Trans. Ethnol. Soc.*, N. S., vol. v. p. 221.

105

Arch., vol. xlii. p. 68. *Arch. Jour.*, vol. xxv. p. 88. *Suss. Arch. Coll.*, vol. xxiv. p. 145. *Jour. Anth. Inst.*, vol. v. p. 357; vi. p. 263, 430; vii. p. 413.

106

Journ. Ethnol. Soc., N. S., vol. ii. p. 419. See also *Proc. Soc. Ant. Scot.*, vol. viii. p. 419.

107

Journ. Anth. Inst., vol. i. p. 73.

108

Pennant describes a flint axe as having been found stuck in a vein of coal exposed to the day in Craig y Parc, Monmouthshire.

109

"Rapport sur les Découvertes Géologiques et Archéologiques faites à Spiennes en 1867." Par A. Briart, F. Cornet, et A. Houzeau de Lehaie. Mons, 1868. Malaise, *Bull. de l'Ac. Roy. de Belg.*, 2° S. vols. xxi. and xxv., and *Geol. Mag.*, vol. iii. p. 310. See also *Cong. Préh. Bruxelles*, 1872, p. 279; *l'Anthropologie*, vol. ii. p. 326. *Mat.* 3me s. vol. i. (1884), p. 65, likewise *Bull. de la Soc. d'Anthrop. de Bruxelles*, tom. viii. 1889–

90, Pl I. C. Engelhardt has described Spiennes and Grime's Graves in the *Aarb. for Oldkynd.*, 1871, p. 327. What appears to have been a neolithic flint mine at Crayford, Kent, has been described by Mr. Spurrell, *Arch. Journ.*, vol. xxxvii. p. 332. The Deneholes were probably dug for the extraction of chalk and not of flint.

110

l'Anthropologie, vol. ii. (1891) 445.

111

Mat., 3me s. vol. iv. (1887) p. 1.

112

Arch. Assoc. Journ., vol. xxviii. 220.

113

Cochet, "Seine Inf.," pp. 16. 528. *Archivio per l'Antropol., &c.*, vol. i. p. 489.

114

Proc. Soc. Ant. Scot., vol. xxx. (1896) p. 346.

115

Mat., vol. x. (1875) p. 521.

116

Lartet and Christy's Rel. Aquit., p. 13.

117

Trans. Ethnol. Soc., N.S., vol. i. p. 139. See also *Rev. Arch.*, vol. iii. (1861) p. 341.

118

"Rel. Aquit.," p. 18. For the loan of this cut I am indebted to the executors of the late Henry Christy. The same specimen has been engraved by the Rev. J. G. Wood. "Nat. Hist. of Man," vol. ii. p. 717. Another example from Greenland is figured in *Mat.*, vol. vi. p. 140.

119

Gastaldi's "Lake Habitations of Northern and Central Italy," translated and edited by C. H. Chambers, M.A. (Anth. Soc., 1865), p. 106.

120

Mortillet, *Mat. pour l'Hist. de l'Homme*, vol. ii. p. 517.

121

"Flint Chips," p. 78.

122

Arch. f. Anth., vol. vii, p. 263. *Bull. U.S. Geol. and Geog. Survey*, vol. iii. p. 547.

123

Nat., vol. xxi. p. 615.

124

Nat., vol. xxii. p. 97.

125

Amer. Anthrop., 1895, p. 307. *Nat.*, vol. xx. p. 483.

126

Trans. Ethnol. Soc., N. S., vol. iii. p. 365. "Rel. Aquit.," p. 17.

127

"Articles on Anth. Sub.," 1882, p. 9.

128

Schoolcraft, "Ind. Tribes," vol. i. p. 212.

129

Sixth voyage, "Pinkerton's Travels," vol. xiii. p. 36, quoted also in "Flint Chips," p. 79.

130

Bracer, a girdle or bandage.

131

Schoolcraft, "Indian Tribes," vol. iii. p. 81; see also 467.

132

Arch. Journ., vol. liii. 1896, p. 51.

133

P. 46.

134

Mortillet, *Matériaux*, vol. ii. p. 353.

135

"Pfahlbauten, 1ter Bericht," p. 71. "Lake-dwellings," pp. 18, 125. See also Lindenschmit, "Hohenz. Samml.," taf. xxvii.

136

Proc. Ethnol. Soc., N. S., vol. vii. p. 47.

137

Anzeiger für Schweiz. Alterth., 1870, p. 123.

138

"Habit. Lacust.," p. 19.

139

See *Comptes Rendus*, vol. lxvii. p. 1292, where a suggestion is made of some stone implements from Java having been sawn in this manner.

140

An article by Dr. Rudolf Much on the preparation of Stone Implements is in the *Mitth. d. Auth. Ges. in Wien*, 2d. S., vol. ii. (1883), p. 82; and one by Mr. J. D. McGuire, in the *Amer. Anthrop.*, vol. v., 1892, p. 165. He has also written on the Evolution of the Art of Working in Stone, in a manner that has called forth a reply from Mr. C. H. Read, F.S.A., *Amer. Anthrop.*, 1893, p. 307; 1894. p. 997.

141

"Illahun, Kahun, and Gurob," 1891, p. 51.

142

Fischer in *Arch. f. Anth.*, vol. xv., 1884, p. 463.

143

The Reliquary, vol. viii. p. 184.

144

Matériaux, vol. iv. p. 293.

145

"Prehist. Ann. of Scotland." 2nd edit., vol. i. p. 193.

146

"Cat. Stone Ant. Mus. R. I. A.," p. 78.

147

P. 26.

148

Matériaux, vol. i. p. 463; vol. iii. p. 307.

149

Anz. f. Schweiz. Alt., 1870, pl. xii. 18–20.

150

Archivio per l'Ant. e la Etn., vol. xx. 1890, p. 378.

151

"Primeval Ants. of Denmark." p. 16.

152

P. 392. *Archiv für Anthrop.*, vol. iii. p. 187.

153

Schoolcraft, "Ind. Tribes," vol. iii. pp. 228, 466.

154

Tylor, "Early Hist, of Mankind," p. 248.

155

Wilkinson, "Anc. Egyptians," vol. ii. pp. 180, 181; vol. iii. pp. 144, 172.

156

Odyss., ix. 384.

157

2nd ed., pp. 341 *et seqq.*; see also "Flint Chips," p. 96.

158

Rep. U. S. Nat. Mus. for 1894, p. 623.

159

"Guide ill. du Mus. des Ant. du Nord," 2nd edit. p. 8.

160

Anzeiger f. Schweiz. Alt., 1870, pl. xii. 24. Munro's "Lake Dw.," fig. 24, No. 12.

161

Keller's "Lake-dwellings," p. 22. 1ter Bericht, p. 74. See also *Anzeiger für Schweiz. Alterth.*, 1870, p. 139.

162

Aarsb. Soc. Nor. Ant., 1877, pl. i. 5. Montelius, "Ant. Suéd.," 1874, fig. 34.

163

Morgenblatt, No. 253.

164

"Allgemeine Culturwissenschaft," vol. i. p. 80. See also Preusker, "Blicke in die Vaterländische Vorzeit," vol. i. p. 173.

165

Mém. de la Soc. des Ant. du Nord, 1863, p. 149.

166

"Heidnische Alterthümer," p. 66.

167

"Alterthümer. u. h. V.," vol. i. Heft viii. Taf. i.

168

"Frederico-Franciscum," p. 111.

169

Journal of the Anthrop. Soc., vol. vi. p. xlii.

170

"Archæol. Undersögelser," 1884.

171

"Smithson. Report," 1868, p. 399. "Drilling in Stone without Metal."

172

Schoolcraft, "Indian Tribes," vol. i. p. 93.

173

Anzeiger f. Schweiz. Alt., 1870, p. 143.

174

Mitth. d. Anth. Ges. in Wien, vol. vii. (1878), p. 96.

175

"Habitations Lacustres," p. 66. *Rev. Arch.*, 1860, vol. i. p. 39.

176

Matériaux, vol. iii. p. 264.

177

Ibid., vol. iii. p. 294.

178

"Les Palafittes," p. 19.

179

Keller, "Lake Dwellings," xxv. 1. 7, p. 91.

180

Op. cit., xxvii. 11, 24, p. 110.

181

Brit. Assoc. Rep., 1881, p. 698.

182

"Thor's Donnerkeil," p. 13.

183

"Stone Age," p. 79. The boring-tool is, in the English edition, mistakenly called a centre-bit.

184

"Stone Age," p. 80.

185

Wood, "Nat. Hist. of Man," vol. ii. p. 157.

186

"Mœurs des Sauv. Amér.," 1724, vol. ii. p. 110. "Flint Chips," p. 525.

187

Tylor, "Early Hist. of Mankind," 2nd edit., p. 191. Wallace, "Travels on the Amazon and Rio Negro," p. 278.

188

C. C. Abbott in *Nature*, vol. xiv. p. 154.

NOTES—CHAPTER III.

189

Cap. xix. v. 24. It also occurs in a quotation of the passage by St. Jerome, in his "Epist. ad Pammachium." See *Athenæum*, June 11, 1870.

190

P. 329, 1. 23.

191

Vol. iii. p. 418.

192

Proc. Soc. Ant., 2nd S. vol. vii. p. 395.

193

N. and Q., 5th S. vol. ix. p. 463.

194

Op. cit., x. p. 73.

195

Mitth. d. Anth. Ges. in Wien, vol. xxiv. (1894) p. 84.

196

Arch. f. Anth., vol. x. (1876) p. 140.

197

Barnes, "Notes on Ancient Britain," 1858, p. 15.

198

Tylor, "Early Hist. of Man.," 2nd ed. p. 226, which also see for many of the facts here quoted. See also Tylor's "Prim. Culture," vol. ii. p. 237, &c.

199

Halliwell, "Rambles in West Cornwall," 1861, p. 205. *Rev. Celt.*, 1870, p. 6. Polwhele's "Traditions, &c.," 1826, vol. ii. p. 607. *Folk-lore Journ.*, vol. i. p. 191.

200

Sibbald mentions two perforated *cerauniæ* found in Scotland. "Prod. Nat. Hist. Scot.," ii. lib. iv. p. 49. See also *Proc. Soc. Ant. Scot.*, vol. xxiv. p. 379.

201

Comptes Rendus, 1864, vol. lix. p. 713. Cochet, "Seine Inf.," p. 15. B. de Perthes, "Ant. Celt, et Antéd.," vol. i. p. 522, &c.

202

F. C. Lukis, F.S.A., in *Reliquary*, viii. p. 208.

203

Bull., Soc. de Borda, Dax, 1894, p. 159. See also De Nadaillac, "Les Premiers Hommes," vol. i. p. 12; Cartailhac, "La France préh.," p. 4.

204

Ibid.

205

Nilsson, "Stone Age," pp. 199–201.

206

"Mus. Wormianum," p. 74.

207

Preusker, "Blicke in die Vaterländische Vorzeit," vol. i. p. 170.

208

"Old Northern Runic Monuments," p. 205. *Ant. Tidsskr.*, 1852–54, p. 258. Sjöborg, "Samlingar för Nordens Förnälskara," vol. iii. p. 163.

209

Ant. Tidsskr., 1852–54, p. 8. *Mém. de la Soc. des Ant. du Nord*, 1850–60, p. 28.

210

Arch. Journ., vol. xxv. p. 116.

211

"Preh. Man," vol. ii. p. 185.

212

Jahrb. d. V. v. Alth. am Rheinl., Heft lxxvii. 1884, p. 216, lxxix. 1885, p. 280.

213

Arch. f. Anth., vol. xxii. 1894, Corr. Bl. p. 102.

214

Mitth. d. Anth. Ges. in Wien, 1882, p. 159. *Zeitsch. f. Eth.*, vol. xii. 1880, p. 252.

215

Notes and Queries, 2nd S., vol. viii. p. 92.

216

Tylor, "Early Hist. of Man.," p. 227.

217

Ann. for Nord. Oldk., 1838, p. 159. Klemm., "C. G.," vol. i. p. 268. Prinz Neuwied, ii. p. 35.

218

Nicolucci, "di Alcune Armi, &c., in Pietra," 1863, p. 2.

219

"Mus. Mosc.," 1672, p. 144.

220

Rev. Arch., vol. xv. p. 358; xvi. p. 145. Finlay, "Προϊστ. Ἀρχάιολ.," p. 5.

221

Alexius, Lib. iii. p. 93, *et seqq.*, quoted by Gibbon, "Dec. and Fall," c. 56.

222

Cartailhac, p. 4.

223

"Early Hist. of Mankind," p. 211. Klemm, "Cultur-Geschichte," vol. vi. p. 467.

224

Tylor, *op. cit.* 214.

225

Franks, *Trans. Preh. Cong.*, 1868, p. 260.

226

Rev. Arch., vol. xxvii. 1895, p. 326.

227

Notes and Queries, 2nd S., vol. viii. p. 92. *Arch. Journ.*, vol. xi. p. 121.

228

Arch. für Anthrop., vol. iv. *Corr. Blatt*, p. 48. Rumphius, "Curios. Amboin.," p. 215.

229

Proc. Soc. Ant., 2d S., vol. iii. p. 97.

230

Proc. Ethnol. Soc., 1870, p. lxii. *Jour. Anth. Inst.*, vol. i. p. lxi.

231

Proc. As. Soc. Beng., July, 1869. *Nature*, vol. ii. p. 104.

232

Noulet, "L'âge de la pierre en Cambodge," Toulouse, 1877.

233

Morlot, *Actes de la Soc. jurass. d'Emul.*, 1863. Earl, "Native Races of the Indian Archip.," vol. v. p. 84.—Von Siebold, *Nature*, vol. xxxiv. 1886, p. 52.

234

Nature, vol. xxxii. 1885, p. 626.

235

Proc. As. Soc. Bengal, 1861, p. 81. Do., 1862, p. 325.

236

"Ausland," 1874, p. 82.

237

Rev. T. J. Bowen, "Gram. and Dict. of Yoruba Language." "Smithsonian Contr.," vol. i. p. xvi., quoted by Dr. E. B. Tylor, *Trans. Preh. Cong.*, 1868, p. 14.

238

Jour. Anth. Inst., vol. xii. p. 450.

239

Arch. per l'Ant. e la Etn., vol. xiv. (1884), p. 371.

240

1882, p. 111.

241

Vol. iii. 1868, p. 1.

242

Arch. Journ., vol. xxv. p. 151.

243

Ibid. p. 103.

244

Matériaux, vol. iv. p. 9.

245

Mat., vol. xi. p. 538.

246

Mat., vol. xiv. p. 274. *Bull. della Comm. Arch. Comunal. di Roma*, 1870.

247

"Quæst. Græc.," ed. 1624, p. 301.

248

Congrès Intern. d'Anth. et d'Arch. Préh., 1867, pp. 39, 40.

249

Kruse. "Necroliv.," Nachtrag, p. 21. *Journ. As. Soc. Beng.*, vol. v. p. 34.

250

See also Tylor, *l. c.*, p. 228.

251

"Metallotheca Vaticana," p. 242. De Rossi, "Scoperte Paleoetnol.," 1867, p. 11. *Mat.*, vol. x. p. 49.

252

"Lithographia Angerburgica," cited in *Mat.*, vol. x. 297.

253

"Hist. et Mém.," vol. xii. p. 163. *Mat.*, vol. x. 146.

254

P. 397.

255

No. 201.

256

Aldrovandus, "Mus. Met.," 1648, p. 607–611. Gesner, "de Fig. Lapid.," p. 62–64. Boethius, "Hist. Gem.," lib. ii. c. 261. Besler, "Gazophyl. Rer. Nat.," tab. 34. Wormius, "Musæum," lib. i. sec. 2, c. 12, p. 75. Moscardi, "Musæo," 1672, p. 148. Lachmund, "de foss. Hildeshem.," p. 23. Tollius "Gemm. et lapid. Historia," Leiden, 1647, p. 480. De Laet, "de Gemm. et lapid.," Leiden, 1647, p. 155.

257

Gesner, "de Fossilibus," p. 62 *verso*.

258

"De re metallicâ," Basel, 1657, pp. 609, 610.

259

"Marbodæi Galli Cænomanensis de gemmarum lapidumque pretiosorum formis, &c." (Cologne, 1539), p. 48.

260

"Hist. Nat.," lib. xxxvii. c. 9. For a series of interesting Papers on "La Foudre, &c., dans l'Antiquité," see M. Henri Martin in the *Rev. Arch.*, vol. xii. *et seqq.*

261

An interesting paper on "Bætuli" by Mr. G. F. Hill, is in the *Reliquary and Illustrated Archæologist*, vol. ii. 1896, p. 23.

262

Geason, Scarce. "Scant and geason." Harrison's "England."—Halliwell, *Dict. of Archaic Words*, s. v.

263

"Nec multo post in Cantabriæ lacum fulmen decidit, repertæque sunt duodecim secures, haud ambiguum summi imperii signum," Galba, viii. c. 4.

264

See *Arch. Assoc. Journ.*, vol. iii. p. 127, and Wilde's "Cat. R. I. A.," p. 72.

265

Comptes Rendus de l'Ac. des Sci., 1865, vol. lxi. pp. 313, 357; 1866, lxiii. p. 1038.

NOTES—CHAPTER IV.

266

Madsen, "Afbild.," pl. iii. 1 to 3. *Kgl. Danske Vidensk. Selskabs Forhand.*, 1861, Fig. 1.

267

De Baye, "l'Arch. préhist.," p. 55.

268

Lubbock, Preh. Times, 4th ed., p. 100.

269

Kgl. Danske Vidensk. Selskabs Forh., 1861, p. 342.

270

Aarb. for. Nord. Oldk., 1891, p. 383. See also S. Müller, *Mém. des Ant. du Nord*, 1884–89, p. 371; *Aarb.*, 1888, p. 238.

271

"Archæol. Undersögelser," 1884, p. 3.

272

Jour. Anth. Inst., vol. ii., p. 368, pl. xxi.

273

Smithsonian Report, 1863, p. 379; 1868, p. 401. "Flint Chips," 445.

274

Proc. Soc. Ant., 2nd S., vol. v., p. 331.

275

Vol. xix., 53; xxxii., 173.

276

"Nænia Cornubiæ," p. 194.

277

The discoveries of Mr. Worthington Smith at Caddington, a few miles from Dunstable, suggest the possibility of this specimen being, after all, palæolithic.

278

Jour. Eth. Soc., N. S., vol. ii., pl. xxviii. 7.

279

Arch., vol. xlii., pl. viii. 10, 11.

280

Arch. Assoc. Jour., vol. xlv., p. 114.

281

Arch., vol. xlii., pl. viii. 17.

282

Arch. Jour., vol. xxxi., p. 301.

283

"Exc. on Cranborne Chase," vol. ii., pl. xc.

284

See also Chichester vol. of Arch. Inst., p. 61.

285

Proc. Soc. Ant., 2nd S., vol. x., p. 34.

286

Rev. W. W. Gill, LL.D., *Rep. Austral. Assoc. for the Adv. of Science*, vol. iv., 1892, p. 613.

287

Low's Tour., quoted in *Folklore Jour.*, vol. i., p. 191.

288

Aarb. f. Nord. Oldk., 1886, p. 200; *Mèm. Soc. R. des Ant. du Nord*, 1886–91, p. 227; *Mat.*, 3rd. S., vol. v., 1888, p. 105.

289

Proc. Soc. Ant., 2nd S., vol. iv., p. 521.

290

Vol. vi., p. iii.

291

Jour. Eth. Soc., vol. ii., pl. xxviii. 4, 5.

292

Watelet, "Age de Pierre du Dép. de l'Aisne," &c.

293

"Restes de l'Ind., &c.," pl. xiii. 1.

294

Trans. Herts Nat. Hist. Soc., vol. viii., 1896, pl. xi. 1.

295

See *Proc. Soc. Ant.*, 2nd S., vol. v., p. 113; *Arch. Jour.*, vol. xxx., p. 28.

296

Zeitsch. f. Eth., vol. xii., p. 237.

297

Cong. Préh. Moscou, 1893, p. 249.

298

Proc. Soc. Ant., 2nd S., vol. v., p. 94; *Arch. Jour.*, vol. xxx., p. 35.

299

Suss. Arch. Coll., vol. ii., p. 268.

300

Vol. xlii., p. 53; xlv., p. 337.

301

Arch., vol. xlii., pl. viii. 1.

302

"Reliq. Aquit.," A., pl. v.

303

Jour. Anth. Soc., 1869, p. cxii.

304

Trans. Ethnol. Soc., N. S., vol. iii., p. 269.

305

Smiths. Inst. Rep., 1894.

306

Vol. xlii., pl. viii. 18.

307

"Horæ Ferales," pl. ii. 36.

308

Arch., vol. xlii. pl. viii. 21.

309

Trans. Norf. and Norw. Naturalists' Soc., vol. v., 1891, p. 250.

310

Vol. xv., p. 122, pl. ii., iii., iv., v.

311

"South Wilts," p. 75, pl. v., vi., vii.

NOTES—CHAPTER V.

312

Arch., vol. xv., pl. iv. 1. Hoare's "South Wiltshire," pl. v. 1. "Cat. Devizes Mus.," No. 9*b*.

313

Arch. Assoc. Jour., vol. xxxvii., 1881, p. 214.

314

Arch. Jour., vol. xxxi., pp. 296, 301.

315

Proc. Soc. Ant. Scot., vol. xiv., p. 265; xxiv., p. 6.

316

Proc. Soc. Ant. Scot., vol. ix., p. 258.

317

Proc. Soc. Ant. Scot., vol. xi., p. 24.

318

"Vest. Ant. Derb." p. 43. Cat., p. 31.

319

Proc. Soc. Ant. Scot., vol. vi., p. 178.

320

See *Cambridge Antiq. Comms.*, vol. ii, 285, where there is a woodcut of the skull, and *Geol. Mag.*, Dec. II., vol. i. p. 494.

321

Journ. Ethnol. Soc., 1869, vol. ii., pl. xv., fig. 11.

322

Proc. Soc. Ant., Scot., vol. xiv., p. 265.

323

Proc. Soc. Ant., 2nd S., vol. iii. p. 406.

324

Journ. Ethnol. Soc., 1869, vol. ii., fig. 7.

325

A large celt formed of "indurated clay-stone with garnets," is mentioned by Mr. F. C. Lukis, F.S.A., as having been found in the Channel Islands (*Arch. Assoc. Journ.*, vol. iii. 128).

326

Proc. Soc. Ant. Scot., vol. vii. p. 101.

327

P. S. A. S., vol. vii. 213.

328

Proc. Ethnol. Soc., 1870, p. xxxix.

NOTES—CHAPTER VI.

329

"Man the Primeval Savage," p. 310.

330

See "Horæ Ferales," pl. ii. 8.

331

Vol. xvii., pl. xiv. "Horæ Ferales," pl. ii. 10.

332

Arch. Journ., vol. xxviii., p. 242.

333

Surr. Arch. Coll., vol. xi. pp. 247, 248.

334

Arch. Journ., vol. ix. p. 194. "Salisbury vol.," p. 112.

335

Arch. Æliana, vol. v. p. 102.

336

Arch. Journ., vol. xx. p. 192.

337

Proc. Soc. Ant., 2nd S. vol. ix. p. 71.

338

Arch. Journ., vol. xxx. p. 284.

339

Anderson's "Croydon: Preh. and Present," pl. ii.

340

Proc. Soc. Ant. Scot., vol. xvi. 437.

341

L. Simonin, "La Vie Souterraine," &c., 1867. Mortillet, *Mat.*, vol. iii. p. 101.

342

Arch. Journ., vol. xxvii., pl. x. 1, p. 164.

343

Arch. Journ., vol. xlviii. p. 436.

344

Pp. 577, 578.

345

Proc. Soc. Ant., 2nd S., vol. v., p. 34.

346

Arch. Journ. vol. xxvii. p. 238.

347

Proc. Soc. Ant., 2nd S., vol. ix. p. 71.

348

Arch., vol. xliii. p. 406.

349

Arch., vol. xii. pl. ii. 1.

350

Arch., vol. vii. p. 414; *Proc. Soc. Ant.*, 2nd S., vol. vi. 37.

351

Proc. Soc. Ant. Scot., vol. xxvi. p. 175; xxviii. p. 322.

352

P. S. A. S., vol. xvii. p. 382; xxviii. p. 329.

353

Op. cit., vol. x. p. 600; xvii. p. 383.

354

Op. cit., vol. ix. p. 346; xvii. p. 384.

355

Op. cit., vol. xxiii. p. 272.

356

Ibid.

357

Bonstetten, "Supp. au Rec. d'Ant. Suisses," pl. ii. 1.

358

Proc. Ethnol. Soc., 1870, p. cxxxvii.

359

Mortillet, "Promenades," p. 145; "Mus. Préh.," No. 459.

360

See the account of the discovery, *Rev. Arch.*, 3rd S., vol. xxiv. (1894), p. 260.

361

"L'homme Fossile," 2nd Ed., p. 147.

362

Van Overloop. Pl. ix. and x.

363

Lindenschmit, "Alt. u. H. V.," vol. i., Heft. vol. ii., Taf. i. 19, &c.

364

Voss. "Phot. Album," vol. vi., sec. vi.

365

Jahrb. d. V. v. Alt. im Rh., L. p. 290.

366

xix. p. 119. See also, for the origin of Jade, Fischer's "Jadeit und Nephrit," Westropp in *Journ. Anth. Inst.*, vol. x. p. 359, and Rudler in *Brit. Assoc. Rep.*, 1890, p. 971.

367

Mitth. d. Ant. Ges. in Wien, N. S., vol. iii. 1883, p. 213–216.

368

Op. cit., N. S., vol. v. 1885, p. 1.

369

Journ. Anth. Inst., vol. x., p. 359; xx. p. 332; xxi., pp. 319, 493; *Aarbög. f. Oldkynd.*, 1889, p. 149.

370

Calcutta, 1871.

371

Vol. xvi., pl. lii. p. 361.

372

Canon Greenwell, F.R.S.

373

Mr. James Brown.

374

Mr. Frank Buckland, F.Z.S.

375

Rev. S. Banks.

376

Proc. Soc. Ant. Scot., vol[1] xvi. p. 408.

377

"Stone Age," p. 63.

378

Vol. iv. p. 2.

379

Proc. Soc. Ant. Scot., vol. iii. p. 486.

380

Proc. Soc. Ant. Scot., vol. xiii. p. 306.

381

Z. f. Eth., 1878. Supp. pl. iii.

382

"Horæ Ferales," pl. ii. 14.

383

Nature, vol. xxx. p. 515. See also *Archiv. f. Anth.*, vol. xvi. p. 241, and *Proc. Soc. Ant.*, 2nd S., vol. ix. p. 211.

384

Journ. Anth. Inst., vol. xvii. p. 66.

385

Proc. As. Soc. Beng., Sept., 1870. *Proc. Ethnol. Soc.*, 1870, p. lxii.

386

Kanda's, "Stone Implements of Japan," *Nature*, vol. xxxi. p. 538; *Cong. Préh. Bruxelles*, 1872, p. 337.

387

Proc. Soc. Ant. Scot., vol. xxvi., p. 404.

388

Tr. Dev. Assoc., vol. xix. p. 56.

389

See "Acct. of Soc. Ant. of Scot.," p. 55.

390

"Horæ Ferales," pl. ii. 11.

391

"Horæ Ferales," pl. ii. 13. *Arch. Journ.*, vol. xv. p. 178.

392

"Horæ Ferales," pl. ii. 7.

393

Arch. Journ., vol. vii. p. 389.

394

Arch. Assoc. Journ., vol. xv., p. 232.

395

Proc. Soc. Ant., vol. iii. p. 225.

396

Proc. Soc. Ant. Scot., vol. ix. p. 174.

397

Journ. Ethn. Soc., vol. ii. p. 165.

398

Journ. Ethn. Soc., vol. ii. p. 165.

399

Mem. Accad. R. di Torino, Ser. 2, vol. xxvi., Tav. iv. 4.

400

Schoolcraft, "Ind. Tribes," vol. i., pl. xi. 3; xiv. 2.

401

Arch. Assoc. Journ., vol. x. p. 105.

402

"Horæ Ferales," pl. ii. 5.

403

Proc. Soc. Ant. Scot., vol. xvii. pp. 14, 15, 18, 19.

404

Proc. Soc. Ant., 2nd S., vol. vi. p. 235.

405

Journ. Ethnol. Soc., vol. ii. pl. xxx. 3.

406

Dawkins' "Cave-hunting," p. 157. *Arch. Camb.*, 4th S., vol. iii., 1872, p. 30.

407

See Schliemann's "Mycenæ," p. 76; "Troy," p. 71; *Rev. Arch.*, vol. xxxiv. p. 163, &c., &c.

408

Schoolcraft, "Ind. Tribes," vol. i. p. 91. Other North American celts are engraved in the "Anc. Mon. of the Miss. Valley," pp. 217, 218; Squier, "Abor. Mon. of New York," p. 77.

409

Journ. Anth. Inst., vol. i. p. xcvi., pl. ii. *Brit. Assoc. Rep.*, 1870, p. 154.

410

Journ. Anth. Inst., vol. xii. p. 449, pl. xiii.

411

"Anc. Mon. of Miss. Val.," p. 215, fig. 106.

412

Proc. Soc. Ant. Scot., vol. xv. p. 245.

413

P. S. A. S., vol. xxvii. p. 370.

414

Wilson's "Preh. Man," vol. i. p. 154. See *postea*, p. 150.

415

Vol. xvii. p. 222.

416

Proc. Soc. Ant., 2nd S., vol. v. pp. 300, 442.

417

Arch. Assoc. Journ., vol. xxix. p. 343. Cumming's "Churches and Ants. of Cury and Gunwalloe," 1875, p. 66.

418

Proc. Soc. Ant. Scot., vol. iv. p. 62: xi. p. 514.

419

P. S. A. S., vol. xi. p. 514.

420

P. S. A. S., vol. xii. p. 207.

421

P. S. A. S., vol. xvii. p. 16.

422

"Acct. of Soc. Ant. of Scot.," 1782, p. 91.

423

Proc. Soc. Ant. Scot., vol. xvii. p. 15.

424

Vol. vi., 1865.

425

Arch., vol. xliv. p. 281.

426

Proc. Soc. Ant., 2nd S., vol. vi. p. 438.

427

Proc. Soc. Ant. Scot., vol. ix. p. 174.

428

"Etudes Paléoethnol.," pl. viii. 5.

429

Trans. Ethnol. Soc., N. S., vol. vii. p. 46.

430

Proc. Soc. Ant. Scot., vol. vi. p. 179.

431

Proc. Soc. Ant. Scot., vol. xvii. p. 14.

432

Proc. Soc. Ant. Scot., vol. xii. p. 119; xxiii. p. 201.

433

Mat. vol. xiii. p. 135; xv. p. 462. "Mus. préh.," No. 463.

434

Jan. 7, 1868. See also *Reliquary*, vol. viii. p. 184.

435

"Mus. préh.," No. 430.

436

Schoolcraft, "Ind. Tribes," vol. ii., pl. xliv.

437

"Anc. Mon. of Miss. Valley," p. 218.

438

Lubbock "Preh. Times," 4th ed. p. 513, figs. 215, 216.

439

Arch. Journ., vol. viii. p. 422.

440

Proc. Soc. Ant. Scot., vol. x. p. 509. Dalgarno, "Notes on Slains, &c.," 1876, p. 6.

441

P.S.A.S., vol. xviii. p. 77.

442

Lubbock, *op. cit.*, p. 102, fig. 111–113.

443

"Vestiges of the Ants. of Derb.," p. 53.

444

Mat. vol. xvi. p. 464.

445

Im Thurn, "Among the Indians of Guiana," 1883, pl. x. 4.

446

Chantre, "Le Caucase," 1885, pl. ii. 9.

447

"Indicateur Arch. de Civrui," 1865, p. 271.

448

Mat. 3rd S., vol. i., 1884, p. 243.

449

Proc. Soc. Ant., 2nd S., vol. i., p. 281.

450

Bonstetten, "Supp. au Rec. d'Ant. Suisses," pl. ii., 1.

451

Arch. Camb., 3rd S., vol. vi., p. 303. Watelet, "Age de Pierre dans le Dépt. de l'Aisne," pl. v. 9. "Ep. Antéd. et Celt. de Poitou," pl. x. 7.

Rev. Arch., vol xii., pl. xv., i.; *op. cit.*, vol. xv., pl. viii. and x. Lindenschmit, "Hohenz. Samml.," Taf. xliii., No. 12. I have an example that I bought in Florence.

452

Wilde, "Cat. Mus. R. I. Ac.," p. 44.

453

"Vest. Ant. Derb.," p. 6.

454

Journ. Ethn. Soc., vol. ii. p. 157.

455

Arch. Assoc. Journ., vol. xxxix. p. 344.

456

"South Wilts," p. 75. *Arch.*, vol. xv. p. 122.

457

Arch. Assoc. Journ., vol. vi. p. 3.

458

Arch. Journ., vol. x. p. 161.

459

Proc. Soc. Ant. Scot., vol. iv. p. 396.

460

Proc. Soc. Ant. Scot., vol. vi. 48.

461

Arch. Journ., vol. vi. p. 17; xvii. 170.

462

Arch. Assoc. Journ., vol. xii. p. 177.

463

Sussex Arch. Coll., vol. ii. p. 258.

464

Arch., vol. xix. p. 183.

465

Surrey Arch. Coll., 1868, pl. iii. 6.

466

"Exc. on Cranborne Chase," vol. i. pl. lvii.

467

"Durobrivæ," pl. xxix. 4.

468

Proc. Soc. Ant., 2nd S., vol. i. p. 249.

469

Douglas, "Nænia," p. 92.

470

Rev. Arch., vol. xx. p. 322.

471

Rev. Arch., vol. iv. p. 484.

472

Ann. for Nordisk Oldkynd., 1838–9, p. 176.

473

Cong. Intern. d'Anth. et d'Arch. Préh., 1867, p. 119.

474

Kirchner has collected a number of cases.—"Thor's Donner-Keil," p. 27.

475

"Dictionarium Saxonico-et Gothico-Latinum," *s. v.*

476

"Twybyl, a wryhtys instrument," is in the "Promptorium Parvulorum" translated *bisacuta* or *biceps*, and "Twybyl or mattoke," *Marra*, or *ligo*.

477

1855, vol. ii. p. 811.

478

Vol. xi., 1876, p. 385.

479

Mitth. d. Anth. Gesellsch. in Wien, vol. vii., 1878, p. 7.

480

O'Curry, "Mann. and Cust. of the Anc. Irish," vol. i. p. cccclviii.

481

Wright's "The Celt, the Roman, and the Saxon," p. 72.

482

"Stone Age," p. 73.

483

"Georg.," lib. i. 62.

484

See p. 105 *supra*.

485

A woodcut of these is given in the *Arch. Assoc. Journ.*, vol. iv. p. 105. The objects are now in the British Museum.

486

"South Wilts," p. 85.

487

"Ten Years' Diggings," p. 221.

488

Ibid., p. 222.

489

"Vestiges of the Ant. of Derbyshire," p. 53.

490

Ibid., p. 42.

491

"Vestiges of the Ant. of Derbyshire," p. 49.

492

"Ten Years' Diggings," p. 216.

493

Vol. viii. p. 86.

494

Suss. Arch. Coll. vol. xxxii. p. 175.

495

P. 112 *supra*.

496

P. 135. See *Proc. Soc. Ant. Scot.*, vol. vi. p. 179.

497

"Cat. Arch. Inst. Mus. at Edinburgh," p. 8.

498

Arch. Journ., vol. viii. p. 422.

499

"Cat. A. I. Mus. at Edin.," p. 10.

500

Proc. Soc. Ant., 2nd S., vol. i. p. 82.

501

Journ. Ethnol. Soc., vol. ii. p. 159.

502

Vol. i. p. 53. See p. 129, *supra*. *Proc. Soc. Ant. Scot.*, vol. i. p. 44.

503

Arch., vol. xli. p. 405.

504

"Horæ Fer.," p. 134. *Trans. Hist. Soc. Lanc. and Chesh.*, vol. xiv. pl. ii. 3.

505

Vol. iv. 112.

506
"Stone Age," Eng. ed., p. 65.

507
Vol. xliv., pl. viii. fig. 3.

508
Rev. Arch., vol. xviii. p. 268. Mus. Préh. No. 442.

509
Cartailhac, "La France préh.," p. 237.

510
Suss. Arch. Coll., vol. xxxix. p. 97.

511
Lit. Gaz., 1822, p. 605, quoted in *N. and Q.*, 2nd S., vol. vi. p. 32.

512
Proc. Soc. Ant. Scot., vol. ix. p. 460.

513
Op. cit., vol. xxx. p. 6.

514
"La Suède préhist.," 1874, p. 21.

515
"Musée préhist.," 1881, No. 428.

516
Wilde, "Cat. Mus. R. I. A.," p. 46.

517
Arch. Journ., vol. iv. p. 3.

518
Wood Martin's "Lake-dw. of Irel.," 1886, p. 59, pl. vi. 7.

519
Keller's "Lake-Dwellings," Eng. ed., pl. x. 14.

520

Ibid., pl. xi. 1.

521

Wood, "Nat. Hist. of Man," vol. i. pp. 321, 404.

522

Squier, "Abor. Mon. of New York," p. 180.

523

Mitth. d. Ant. Ges. in Wien, vol. ix., 1880, p. 135, pl. i.

524

"Aventures du Sieur C. le Beau," Amsterdam, 1738, p. 235. Quoted in *Arch. per l'Ant. e la Et.*, vol. xiv. p. 372.

525

Quoted in "Anc. Mon. of Miss. Valley," p. 198.

526

Zeitsch. f. Eth., vol. xxiv., 1892, p. (229), pl. v. 2.

527

Ratzel, "Völkerk," vol. ii. p. 246.

528

Intern. Arch. f. Eth., vol. ii. p. 272. *Arch. per l'Ant. e la Etn.*, vol. xx. p. 65.

529

2nd S., vol. i. p. 102. See also Ratzel, "Völkerk.," vol. ii. p. 582.

530

Int. Arch. f. Ethn., vol. iii. p. 195.

531

"Musæum Metallicum," p. 158.

532

It has also been figured by Klemm, "Cult.-Wiss.," vol. i. fig. 136.

533

"Cult.-Gesch.," vol. ii. Taf. vi. a.b.

534

See *Int. Arch. f. Eth.*, Bd. ix., Supp. pl. iii.

535

Klemm's "Allgemeine Cultur-Wiss.," vol. i. p. 71, whence I have copied the figure. See also "Cult.-Gesch.," vol. ii., p. 352.

536

Skelton's "Meyrick's Armour," pl., cl. 1.

537

"Lake-Dwellings," pl. x. 7; 5ter "Bericht," pl. x. 17. Another from St. Aubin is engraved by Chantre, "Etudes Paléoethn.," pl. xi. Keller has published several others. See also "Ant. Lac. du Mus. de Lausanne," 1896, pl. iii.

538

"Palafittes," fig. 17. See also Troyon, "Habit. Lacust."; but some of his engravings, like those of Meillet in the "Epoques Antédil. et Celtique de Poitou," appear to have been made from modern fabrications.

539

Keller, "Lake-Dwellings," pl. xxii. 7. "Mus. de Lausanne," 1896, pl. iii.

540

Wilde's "Cat. Mus. R.I.A.," p. 251; Lindenschmit, "Sigmaringen," pl. xxix. 7; Keller, "Lake-Dwellings," pl. ii.

541

Ibid., pl. xxii. 12.

542

"Note sur un Foyer, &c.," Châlon, 1870. pl. iv.

543

Cochet, "Seine Inf.," 2nd ed., p. 16.

544

Rev. Arch., vol. xv. p. 364, pl. viii.; Mortillet, "Promenades," p. 123.

545

Matériaux, vol. v. p. 96.

546

Vol. xxi. p. 54. See also vol. xiv. p. 82.

547

Hoare's "South Wilts." pl. xxi.

548

Arch. Journ., vol. xxi. p. 54.

549

B. de Perthes' "Antiquités Celtiques, &c.," vol. i. p. 282, pl. i., ii.

550

Rev. Arch., vol. xxxv. p. 307, whence the cut is copied on a reduced scale.

551

Arch. Préh., 1880, p. 99, pl. i. and v. *Mat.*, vol. xvi. p. 298.

552

Arch. Assoc. Journ., vol. iv. p. 105. *Supra*, p. 148.

553

"Palafittes," fig. 18.

554

"L'Homme Fossile," 2nd ed. p. 149.

555

"L'Homme pend. les Ages de la Pierre." p. 214.

556

"Les Ages de la Pierre en Belgique," pl. ix.

557

L'Anthropologie, vol. i. p. 385.

558

Proc. Soc. Ant. Scot., vol. xviii. p. 365.

559

Ratzel, "Völkerk," vol. ii. 245, 247, &c.

560

"Les armes et les outils préh. réconst.," Paris, 1872.

561

"Lake-Dwellings," Eng. ed., p. 110. See also pl. x. 16, xi. 2, and xxviii. 24; and Lindenschmit, "Hohenz. Samml.," pl. xxix. 4.

562

"Cultur-Wiss.," fig. 127, p. 70.

563

"Alt. u. H. V.," vol. ii. Heft viii. Taf. i. 7; *Archiv. für Anthropol.*, vol. iii. p. 105. *Jahrb. d. Ver. f. Alt. im Rhein.*, lxi. (1877) p. 156.

564

Bericht Nat. Hist. Verein, Bremen, 1879.

565

Zeitsch. f. Ethn., vol. xi. p. (162).

566

"Reliq. Aquit.," fig. 12.

567

Vol. iv. p. 297.

568

"Etudes Paléoeth.," pl. xii. See also Worsaae, "Primev. Ants. of Denmark," p. 12; "Dänemark's Vorz.," p. 10; and "Danmark's Tidligste Bebyggelse," 1861, p. 17.

569

1868, vol. lxvii. p. 1285.

570

"Cultur-Wiss.," p. 70.

571

Proc. S. A. S., vol. ii. pp. 423, 424; Wilson's "Preh. Man," vol. i. p. 156.

572

"Nat. Hist. of Man," vol. ii. p. 32.

573

Op. cit., vol. ii. p. 201.

574

Op. cit., vol. ii. pp. 369, 373.

575

Int. Arch. f. Ethn., vol. iii. p. 181, pl. xv. 1, 2.

576

Rev. Arch., vol. xviii. p. 266.

577

Vol. xxxiv. p. 172.

578

P. S. A. S., vol. x. p. 263. See also "Notes on some Australian and other Stone Implements," by Prof. Liversidge, F.R.S. (*Journ. R. S. of New South Wales*, vol. xxviii., 1894), and Mr. E. J. Hardman's account of some West Australian implements (Wood Martin's "Rude St. Mons. of Ireland," 1888, p. 115).

579

"Journ. of Voy. to N. S. Wales," p. 293; Klemm, "Cult.-Gesch.," vol. i. p. 308.

580

"Nat. Hist. of Man," vol. ii. p. 32. *Conf.* Worsaae, "Dänemark's Vorz.," p. 10.

581

Vol. xxxi. p. 452.

582

See Jones's "Hist. of Ojibway Indians."

583

"Nat. Hist. of Man," vol. ii. p. 652. *Conf.* Catlin, "N. A. Ind.," vol. i. pl. xcix. *f.*

584

Col. A. Lane-Fox, "Prim. Warf.," part ii. p. 17.

585

"Ind. Tribes," vol. i. pl. xv. 1, p. 285.

586

Proc. Soc. Ant. Scot., vol. xxvii. p. 49.

587

Vol. xxiv. p. 80.

588

"Arch. of Mersey District," 1867, p. 15.

589

Arch., vol. xxxii. p. 400; *Proc. Soc. Ant.*, 1st s. vol. i. p. 131.

590

Worsaae's "Nordiske Oldsager," fig. 14.

591

Chantre, "Le Caucase," 1855, vol. i. p. 50, pl. ii.

592

Schoolcraft, "Ind. Tribes," vol. ii. pl. 73; Klemm, "Cult.-Gesch.," vol. ii. p. 62.

593

Proc. Soc. Ant. Scot., vol. v. p. 287.

594

Journ. Anth. Inst., vol. xi. p. 448.

595

Int. Arch. f. Eth., vol. v., Supp. pl. i.

596

"Illahun" (1891), p. 55.

597

"Kahun," pl. xvi. "Illahun." pl. vii.

598

"Medum" (1892), Frontisp. 14, p. 31.

599

Vol. xxxiv. p. 172. See also Wood, "Nat. Hist. of Man," vol. ii. p. 32.

600

Bonwick's "Daily Life of the Tasmanians," p. 44; *Trans. Ethnol. Soc.*, N. S., vol. iii. p. 267. Several specimens are figured in Ratzel, "Völkerk," vol. ii. p. 46.

601

See *Arch. per l'Anth. e la Etn.*, vol. xxv., 1895, p. 283.

602

Proc. Soc. Ant., 1st s. vol. ii. p. 305.

603

Quoted by Klemm, "C. G.," vol. i. p. 268.

604

Journ. Eth. Soc., vol. ii. p. 109, fig. 7.

605

Nat. vol. x. p. 173.

606

"Smithsonian Contributions," 1876, p. 46.

607

(London, 1872) pl. ii. p. 66.

608

Proc. Soc. Ant. Scot., vol. v. p. 327. See also R. Brough Smyth, "Aborig. of Victoria," vol. i. p. 357.

609

It is, however, to be observed that among the North American Indians fire was the great agent employed in felling trees and in excavating canoes, the stone hatchet being called in aid principally to remove the charred wood.—Schoolcraft, "Ind. Tribes," vol. i. p. 75.

NOTES—CHAPTER VII.

610

Arch. Journ., vol. xvii. p. 170.

611

Wilde, "Cat. Mus. R. I. A.," p. 27.

612

Archæologia, vol. xli. p. 402, pl. xviii. 7.

613

"Brit. Barrows," pp. 225, 396.

614

"Le Camp de Catenoy," N. Ponthieux, Beauvais, 1872, pl. v. i.

615

Parenteau, "Invent. Archéol.," 1878, pl. i. 2.

616

"Flint Chips," p. 76.

617

Proc. Suff. Inst. Arch., vol. vii. p. 209.

618

"Seine Inf.," 2nd ed., p. 528.

619

"Cat. Mus. R. I. A.," p. 27.

620

Worsaae, "Nord. Olds." Nos. 20, 22; Nilsson, "Stone Age," pl. vi. 127.

621

"Hohenz. Samml.," Taf. xliii. 5.

622

"Etude Préhist. sur la Savoie," 1869, pl. ii. 4.

623

Desor, "Palafittes," p. 23, fig. 19.

624

Wood, "Nat. Hist. of Man," vol. ii. p. 201.

625

Nilsson, "Stone Age," pl. vi. 129, p. 54.

626

Int. Arch. f. Ethn., vol. ii. p. 273.

627

"Brit. Barrows," p. 181.

628

Arch., vol. xli. pl. xviii. 10.

629

Mém. Soc. R. des Ant. du Nord, 1872–77, p. 105. Zeitsch. f. Eth. vol. xix. p. 413.

630

Cartailhac, "Ages préh. de l'Esp. et du Port.," p. 91.

631

Trans. Ethn. Soc., N. S., vol. vii. p. 47.

632

Trans. Preh. Cong., 1868, p. 130.

633

Schoolcraft, "Indian Tribes," vol. iv. p. 175.

634

Sproat, "Scenes and Studies of Savage Life," p. 316.

NOTES—CHAPTER VIII.

635

Wilson, "Preh. Ann. of Scot.," vol. i. p. 191; *Arch. Scot.*, vol. i. p. 291.

636

"Itin. Curios.," 2nd ed., vol. i. p. 57.

637

P. 58.

638

"Necrolivonica," Beil. C., p. 23; and Nachtrag, p. 20.

639

"Stone Age," p. 71.

640

Proc. Soc. Ant. Scot., vol. xviii. p. 310.

641

P. S. A. S., vol. xxiv. p. 277.

642

"Heidnische Alterthümer," 1846, pl. vi. 16.

643

Vol. ii. fig. 144.

644

Vol. ix. p. 120. See *Arch. Journ.*, vol. xiii. p. 184, and vol. xv. p. 90.

645

Greenwell, in *Arch.*, vol. lii. p. 60.

646

Hoare's "South Wilts," p. 174.

647

Arch. Assoc. Journ., vol. xx. pl. vii. 1.

648

"Ten Years' Diggings," p. 155.

649

"Vest. of Ants. of Derbyshire," p. 7.

650

"Ants. of Worcestershire," pl. iv. 8 and 9.

651

P. 108, No. 4.

652

Arch. Journ., vol. vii. p. 399.

653

Pl. iii. 9.

654

Aspelin, "Ant. du Nord Finno-Ougrien," No. 78.

655

"Mém. sur les Restes d'Indust.," &c., 1866, pl. x. 12.

656

Mortillet, "Promenades," p. 146.

657

Cong. préh. Bologne, 1871, p. 101. *Do. Buda-Pest*, 1876, p. 87. "Mus. Préh.," No. 500.

658

Rev. Arch., 3rd S., vol. vii. p. 66.

659

Arch. Journ., vol. iii. p. 67.

660

P. 17, pl. ii. 3.

661

"Preh. Ann. of Scot.," vol. i. p. 193.

662

Simony, "Alt. von Hallstatt," p. 9; Taf. vi. 3.

663

Vol. iii. p. 128.

664

Trans. Herts. Nat. Hist. Soc., vol. viii., 1896, p. 176.

665

Journ. Ethnol. Soc., vol. ii. pl. xvi. 14.

666

"Nordiske Oldsager," No. 50.

667

"Alterthümer," vol. i. Heft ii. Taf. i. 10 and 12.

668

Smithsonian Report, 1863, p. 379.

669

Anz. f. Schw. Alt., 1870, p. 141.

670

Mitth. Auth. Ges. in Wien, vol. xxv. (1895) p. 39.

671

Tr. Dev. Assoc., vol. xxii. p. 44.

672

Proc. Soc. Ant., 2nd. S., vol. iv. p. 339. *Arch.*, vol. xliii. p. 410. A. C. Smith's "Ant. of North Wilts.," p. 168. "Salisbury Vol. Arch. Inst.," 1849, p. 110; *Arch. Journ.*, vol. xxiv. p. 29.

673

Arch. Assoc. Journ., vol. xxv. p. 272.

674

Pr. Lanc. and Ch. Arch. Soc., vol. xi. p. 172.

675

"Essai sur les Dolmens," pl. iv. 1.

676

P. S. A. S., vol. viii. p. 264.

677

P. S. A. S., vol. xxiii. p. 208.

678

Wilde, "Cat. Mus. R. I. A.," p. 79.

679

"Alt. u. H. V.," vol. i. Heft i. Taf. i. 18.

680

Matériaux, vol. i. p. 462.

681

"Brit. Barrows," p. 158.

682

"Vest. Ant. Derb.," p. 63. Cat., p. 6, No. 49.

683

Skelton's "Meyrick's Armour," pl. xlvi. 3.

684

Proc. Soc. Ant. Scot., vol. xxix. p. 6.

685

"Brit. Barrows," p. 266.

686

Trans. E. R. Ant. Soc., vol. ii. 1894, p. 21.

687

"Horæ Ferales," pl. iii. 4.

688

Proc. Soc. Ant., 2nd S., vol. ii. p. 295.

689

"Vestiges of Ants. of Derbyshire," p. 7; Cat., No. 36; Brigg's "History of Melbourne," p. 15; Wright's "Celt, Roman, and Saxon," p. 69.

690

"Ten Years' Diggings," p. 227. Cat., p. 25, No. 256.

691

Worsaae, "Nord. Olds.," No. 109; Lindenschmit, "Alt. u. H. V.," vol. i. Heft iv. Taf. i. 5, 6.

692

Zeitsch. f. Ethn., vol. xxiv., 1892, p. (178).

693

Lindenschmit, *op. cit.*, vol. i. Heft i. Taf. i. 8, 9, and 10.

694

Proc. Soc. Ant. Scot., vol. ii. p. 306; xviii. p. 319; "Cat. Arch. Inst. Mus. Ed.," p. 19; "Horæ Ferales," pl. iii. 20; "Sculpt. Stones of Scot.," vol. i. p. xx.; Wilson, "Preh. Ann. of Scot.," vol. i. pl. iii.

695

P. S. A. S., vol. ix. p. 383, pl. xxii.

696

P. S. A. S., vol. xxi. p. 264.

697

Arch. Journ., vol. xii. p. 277.

698

Vol. iii. p. 234.

699

Arch. Camb., 5th S., vol. v. p. 170.

700

Montg. Coll., vol. xiv. p. 271.

701

Arch. Journ., vol. xxxi. p. 302.

702

Vol. viii. p. 421.

703

"Cat. Arch. Inst., Mus., Ed." p. 6.

704

Ibid., p. 45.

705

Arch. Scot., vol. iii., App., p. 121.

706

Proc. Soc. Ant. Scot., vol. vii. p. 478.

707

Ibid., vol. iv. p. 55.

708

Ibid., vol. vi. p. 86.

709

Ibid., vol. iv. p. 379.

710

Pl. xlviii. 1.

711

See *P. S. A. S.*, vol. xii. p. 568; xiv. p. 126; xv. p. 266; xvi. p. 76; xxiii. p. 205, 210; and Smith's "Preh. Man in Ayrshire," 1895, p. 39.

712

Arch. Assoc. Journ., vol. xv., p. 232.

713

Geologist, vol. vii. p. 56.

714

Arch. Ael., vol. xii. p. 118.

715

"Cat. Arch. Inst. Mus., Ed.," p. 38.

716

Arch. Journ., vol. x. p. 65.

717

Arch., vol. xliv. p. 284.

718

Proc. Soc. Ant., 2nd S., vol. viii. p. 489.

719

Tr. Lanc. and Chesh. Ant. Soc., vol. v. p. 327. See also xi. p. 171.

720

Tr. Dev. Assoc., vol. xxvi. p. 51.

721

Tr. Dev. Assoc., vol. xxii. p. 208.

722

Rep. Leic. Lit. and Phil. Soc., 1887–8, pl. iii.

723

Mem. Real. Acc. delle Scienze, &c., di Torino, Ser. II., vol. xxvi. Ta. i. 1. See also for Italy, *Bull. di Pal. Ital.*, 1882, p. 1.

724

Vol. xvii. p. 20.

725

Vol. ii. p. 125.

726

Vol. xxxi. p. 452.

727

Arch., vol. ii. p. 118.

728

Arch., vol. xxx. p. 459.

729

P. S. A. S., vol. xiii. p. 334; xxii. p. 384.

730

"Horæ Ferales," pl. iii. 3.

731

Allies' "Ants. of Worc.," p. 150, pl. iv. 10.

732

P. 111.

733

Proc. Soc. Ant., 2nd S., vol. iv. p. 349.

734

Arch., vol. ii. p. 127.

735

"Stone Age," p. 73.

736

L'Anth., vol. vi., 1895, p. 10.

737

"Abitaz. lac. di Fimon," 1876, p. 150, pl. xiv.

738

"Cat. of Objects found in Greece," fig. 3.

739

Pl. iii. 24.

740

Schliemann's "Troy," 1875, p. 94. Atlas, pl. xxii. 610.

741

Proc. Soc. Ant., 2nd S., vol. iv. p. 61. "Brit. Barrows," p. 222.

742

Proc. Soc. Ant., 2nd S., vol. iv. p. 60. "Brit. Barrows," p. 224.

743

Proc. Soc. Ant. Scot., vol. xxix., 1895, p. 66.

744

Thoresby's Cat. in Whitaker's ed. of "Ducatus Leod.," p. 114.

745

Leland's "Coll.," vol. iv. vi.

746

P. S. A. S., vol. xxvii., 1893, p. 56.

747

Montg. Coll., vol. xiv. p. 276.

748

"Celtic Tumuli of Dorset," p. 63.

749

Arch., vol. xliv. p. 427.

750

Arch. Journ., vol. vi. p. 74.

751

"South Wilts," Tumuli, pl. viii. "Cat. Devizes Mus.," Nos. 15, 17.

752

"Ants. of Worcestershire," pl. iv. 5, p. 146.

753

"Celt, Roman, and Saxon," p. 70.

754

"Horæ Ferales," pl. iii. 15.

755

P.S.A.S., vol. xxiii. p. 8.

756

"South Wilts," Tumuli, pl. i. "Cat. Devizes Mus.," No. 283.

757

Arch., vol. lii. p. 70.

758

Archæol. Journ., vol. xviii. p. 158. *Arch. Assoc. Journ.*, vol. xvi. p. 295, pl. xxv. 8; *Trans. Hist. Soc. Lanc. and Chesh.*, vol. xii. p. 189.

759

"Guide des Touristes, &c., dans le Morbihan," 1854, p. 43.

760

P. S. A. S., vol. xxviii. p. 241.

761

"South Wilts," Tumuli, pl. v.; "Cat. Devizes Mus.," No. 8; Arch., vol. xv. pl. v. 1.

762

Supra, p. 83.

763

Hoare's "South Wilts," p. 209; Arch., vol. xliii. p. 411; A. C. Smith's "Ants. of North Wilts," p. 19.

764

27th Report Roy. Inst. of Cornw., 1846, p. 35. I am indebted to the Secretaries of this Institution for permission to engrave the specimen. It is also figured in Borlase's "Nænia Cornubiæ," p. 191.

765

Proc. Soc. Ant. Scot., vol. xiii. p. 347; xxvi. p. 398.

766

"Ten Years' Diggings," p. 24.

767

"Crania Brit.," vol. ii. xviii. pl. 2.

768

"Vest. Ant. Derb.," p. 29. Smith, "Coll. Ant.," vol. i. pl. xx. 3.

769

Mém. Soc. R. des Ant. du Nord, 1872–77, p. 107. Aarbög. for Oldk., 1872, d. 309–342. Cong. préh. Stockholm, 1874, p. 290. Aspelin, "Ant. du Nord. Finno-Ougrien," No. 71–76.

770

"Indian Tribes," vol. iv. p. 174.

771

Op. cit., vol. i. p. 92; vol. ii. pl. 48.

772

Op. cit., vol. iv. p. 167.

773

"Mus. préh.," No. 449. *Mat.*, vol. xvii. p. 284.

774

Ratzel, "Völkerk.," vol. ii. p. 247. *Mitth. d. Anth. Ges. in Wien*, vol. ix. (1880) pl. ii.

NOTES—CHAPTER IX.

775

Arch. Assoc. Journ., vol. xx. p. 102.

776

Stevens, "Flint Chips," p. 499.

777

Vol. vii. p. 385.

778

"Indian Tribes," vol. iv. p. 168.

779

P. S. A. S., vol. xvi. p. 57.

780

Bellucci, "Mat. Paletn. dell' Umbria," Tav. xi. fig. 3.

781

Proc. Soc. Ant. Scot., vol. vi. p. 327.

782

Proc. Soc. Ant. Scot., vol. vii. p. 499.

783

Ant. Tidsk., 1858–60, p. 277.

784

Vol. xxx. p. 461.

785

"Cat. Mus. R. I. A.," p. 80.

786

P. 94. See also *Arch. Journ.*, vol. iii. p. 94; and Worsaae's "Prim. Ants. of Den.," p. 15.

787

Proc. Soc. Ant., 2nd S. vol. vii., p. 268.

788

P. S. A. S., vol. ix. p. 155.

789

Proc. Soc. Ant. Scot., vol. ix. p. 39; xvii. p. 453.

790

P. S. A. S., vol. xvi. p. 171.

791

Vol. xxvii. p. 142.

792

Montg. Coll., vol. xiv p. 275.

793

Proc. Soc. Ant. Scot., vol. v. p. 240.

794

Trans. Devon. Assoc., vol. iii. p. 497.

795

"Ant. Celt. et Antéd.," vol. i. pl. xiii. 9, p. 327.

796

Arch. Jour., vol. xix. p. 92. *Arch. Camb.*, 3rd S., vol. vi. p. 307.

797

Proc. Soc. Ant. Scot., vol. vi. p. 43. See also *Arch. Camb.*, 4th S., vol. vii. p. 183.

798

Proc. Soc. Ant. Scot., vol. ix. p. 259.

799

Proc. Soc. Ant., 2nd S., vol. xv. p. 349.

800

"South Wilts," p. 204. "Cat. Devizes Mus., No. 150."

801

Supra, p. 128.

802

Surr. Arch. Coll., vol. xi. p. 248–9.

803

Archæologia, vol. xiv. p. 281, pl. lv.; Cat., p. 14.

804

Arch. Journ., vol. ix. p. 297.

805

Arch. Journ., vol. x. p. 72.

806

Archæologia, vol. xxxi. p. 452.

807

Sussex Arch. Coll., vol. ix. p. 118.

808

Sussex Arch. Coll., vol. xxvii. p. 181.

809

Arch., vol. xlvi. p. 492, pl. xxiv. 22.

810

Proc. Soc. Ant., 2nd S., vol. iii. p. 406.

811

Vol. xxvi. p. 190.

812

Essex Nat., vol. viii. p. 164.

813

Arch. Assoc. Journ., vol. xxix. p. 77.

814

Proc. Soc. Ant., 2nd S., vol. ii. p. 400.

815

"Brit. Barrows," p. 248.

816

Arch. Journ., vol. xxv. p. 250.

817

Rep. Leic. Lit. and Phil. Soc., 1878, pl. iii.

818

Arch. Assoc. Journ., vol. xxix. p. 305.

819

Tr. Cumb. and West. Ant. Soc., vol. ix. p. 203.

820

Tr. Lanc. and Ch. Ant. Soc., vol. ii. pl. i.

821

Arch. Camb., 5th S., vol. xii. p. 247.

822

Op. cit., p. 249.

823

Arch. Camb., 5th S., vol. v. p. 315.

824

P. S. A. S., vol. xx. p. 105.

825

P. S. A. S., vol. xii. p. 183.

826

Arch. Assoc. Journ., vol. xxii. p. 314. *Arch. Camb.*, 3rd S., vol. xii. p. 212.

827

Arch. Journ., vol. xxvi. p. 321; vol. xxvii. p. 147.

828

Surrey Arch. Coll., vol. iv. p. 237; 1868, p. 24.

829

Arch. Assoc. Journ., vol. xv. p. 233.

830

Arch. Assoc. Journ., vol. xvii. pl. iv. p. 5.

831

Proc. Soc. Ant. Scot., vol. vi. p. 41.

832

Ibid., vol. iii. p. 437.

833

Ibid., vol. iv. p. 55.

834

P. S. A. S., vol. xii. 568.

835

Op. cit., p. 610.

836

Rev. d'Ant. 1st S., vol. iv. p. 255.

837

"Seine Inf.," 2nd ed., p. 313.

838

Wood, "Nat. Hist. of Man." vol. i. p. 254. *Proc. Soc. Ant. Scot.*, vol. xi. p. 140.

839

P. S. A. S., vol. xiv. p. 173.

840

Rau. "Smithson. Arch. Coll.," p. 31.

841

Sir J. Lubbock, in *Journ. Anth. Inst.*, vol. i. p. xcv.

842

Journ. Anthrop. Inst., vol. i. p. 198.

843

Sup., p. 64.

844

"Stone Age," pl. i. 12.

845

"Alt. u. h. V.," vol. i. Heft i. Taf. i. 4.

846

Op. cit., vol. i. Heft viii. Taf. i. 6.

847

"Or. de la Navig., &c.," fig. 20.

848

Trans. preh. Cong., 1868, p. 236.

849

Proc. As. Soc. Beng., 1866, p. 135.

850

Proc. As. Soc. Beng., Mar., 1874.

851

Zeitsch. f. A. and E., vol. viii., 1876, pl. xxv.

852

Arch. Journ., vol. vii. p. 68; *Gent.'s Mag.*, 1819, p. 130.

853

Arch. Assoc. Journ., vol. xv. p. 234.

854

Arch. Journ., vol. vii. p. 69.

855

Arch. Camb., 2nd S., vol. i. p. 331.

856

Arch. Camb., 4th S., vol. v. p. 181.

857

Arch. Journ., vol. xvii. p. 66.

858

Vol xxvi. p. 320, figs. 10 and 11.

859

Arch. Journ., vol. xxvii. p. 161.

860

Lib. Cit., p. 164.

861

Journ. Anth. Inst., vol. v. p. 2.

862

Cat., p. 28, No. 293.

863

P. S. A. S., vol. xxiii. p. 213.

864

"Cat. Mus. R. I. A." p. 85. The chisel-edged specimens there described are not improbably American.

865

P. 557.

866

Mortillet, "*Matériaux.*" vol. iii. p. 98; vol. iv. p. 234. Tubino, "Estudios Prehistoricós." p. 100. Cartailhac, p. 202.

867

Rev. Arch., vol. xiii. p. 137.

868

Jorn. de Sci. Math. Phys. y Natur., 1868, pl. viii.

869

Simony, "Alt. von Hallstatt." Taf. vi. 5.

870

"Präh. Atlas." Wien, 1889, Taf. xix.

871

Perrin, "Et. Préhist. sur la Savoie," pl. xv. 17.

872

Quart. Journ. Geol. Soc., 1869, vol. xxv. p. 34.

873

"Troy and its Remains," p. 97.

874

Schoolcraft, "Indian Tribes," vol. i. p. 96; Squier's "Ab. Mon. of New York," p. 184; Lapham, "Ants. of Wisconsin," p. 74.

875

"Prehist. Man," vol. i. pp. 246, 253.

876

Comptes Rendus, 1866, vol. lxii. p. 470; *Geol. Mag.*, vol. iii. p. 214; Mortillet, "*Mat.*," vol. ii. pp. 331, 401; vol. iii. p. 99.

877

Brit. Assoc. Report, 1870, p. 158.

878

Brit. Barrows, p. 239.

879

Vol. x. p. 64.

880

Arch. Journ., vol. xxvii. p. 164, pl. xi. 5.

881

Arch. Camb., 4th S., vol. v. p. 181; ix. p. 34.

882

Proc. Soc. Ant. Scot., vol. vi. p. 209.

883

P. S. A. S., vol. ix. p. 382; xii. p. 266. Mitchell, "Past in the Present," p. 124.

884

Mem. Anthrop. Soc. Lond. vol. iii. p. 261.

885

"Ind. Tribes," vol. ii. pl. 39.

886

Op. cit., vol. ii. p. 90.

887

1884, p. 156 *seqq.*, also *Arch. f. Anth.*, vol. v. p. 262.

888

"Cat. Mus. R. I. A.," p. 95, fig. 77.

889

"Nord. Oldsag.," fig. 88; Nilsson, "Stone Age," pl. ii. p. 34.

890

Arch. Assoc. Journ., vol. xiv. p. 327.

891

Proc. Soc. Ant. Scot., vol. iv. p. 489.

892

Arch. Assoc. Journ., vol. xvii. p. 19.

893

See a paper on "Antike Gewicht-steine," by Prof. Ritschl, in the *Jahrb. d. Ver. v. Alterthums-fr. im Rheinl.*, Heft. xli. 9; also xliii. 209.

NOTES—CHAPTER X.

894

Proc. Soc. Ant., 2nd S., vol. ii. p. 274.

895

Mem. Geol. Surv. Ind., vol. iv. pl. i. p. 203. *Trans. Preh. Cong.*, 1868, p. 238.

896

Journ. Ethnol. Soc., vol. ii. p. 263, pl. xxi. 7.

897

Catlin's "Last Rambles," p. 188.

898

Arch. Camb., 5th. S., vol. i. p. 307.

899

Tr. Dev. Assoc., vol. xii. p. 71.

900

Montg. Coll., vol. xiv. p. 273.

901

Proc. Soc. Ant. Scot., vol. iv. p. 440; xiv. p. 127; xv. p. 108.

902

P. S. A. S., vol. xi. p. 583, Munro "Lake-dw.," p. 448.

903

P. S. A. S., vol. xiv. 127; xv. 267; xxiii. p. 211.

904

Kindly lent by the Society of Antiquaries of Scotland.

905

P. S. A. S., vol. xxii. p. 62.

906

P. S. A. S., vol. xii. p. 688.

907

Worsaae's "Nord. Oldsager," No. 32, 33. Nilsson's "Stone Age," pl. i. 14. A Lüneburg specimen, with deep conical depressions, is given by Lindenschmit. "Alt. u. h. V.," vol. i. Heft viii. Taf. i. 4.

908

Wilde's "Cat. Mus. R. I. A.," fig. 75.

909

"Ind. Tribes," vol. iv. p. 165.

910

"Stone Age," p. 12, pl. i. 2, 3.

911

"Prim. Industry," p. 425, *et. seqq.*

912

Arch. f. Anth., vol. v. p. 263.

913

Vol. ix. p. 118.

914

Arch. Assoc. Journ., vol. xxix. p. 344. Cumming's "Churches and Ants. of Cury and Dunwalloe," 1873, p. 69.

915

P. S. A. S., vol. x. p. 634. Mitchell, "Past in the Present," p. 126.

916

Journ. Anth. Inst., vol. iv. p. 139.

917

Anz. f. Schw. Alt., 1876, Taf. viii.

918

"Cat. Arch. Inst. Mus., Edin.," p. 12.

919

"Naukratis," 1886, pl. i. p. 42.

920

"Brit. Barrows," p. 200.

921

Pr. Lanc. and Ch. Arch. Soc., vol. xi. p. 172.

922

"Naukratis," pl. i. 1886, p. 42.

923

Journ. Anth. Inst., vol. vi. pp. 41, 195.

924

Proc. Soc. Ant., 2nd S., vol. i. p. 71.

925

Arch. Journ., vol. xvii. p. 171.

926

Amer. Anthropologist, vol. iv., 1891, p. 301.

927

"South Wilts," Tumuli, pl. vi. "Cat. Devizes Mus.," No. 3.

928

See *Arch.*, vol. xliii. p. 408.

929

Arch. Journ., vol. xxvi. p. 320, figs. 14, 15. *Arch. Camb.*, 4th S., vol. v. p. 181.

930

Proc. Soc. Ant., 2nd S., vol. iii. p. 396.

931

Arch. Journ., vol. x. pp. 64, 160.

932

Proc. Soc. Ant. Scot., vol. vi. p. 208.

933

Greenwell, "Brit. Par.," pp. 200, 239, 242.

934

Arch. Journ., vol. xxviii. p. 148.

935

P. S. A. S., vol. xxviii. p. 341.

936

"Etudes Paléoéthnol.," 1867, pl. iv. 1.

937

Squier and Davis, "Anct. Mon. of Mississ. Valley," p. 222.

938

P. S. A. S., vol. xiv. p. 314, xxi. p. 135.

939

"Mus. préh.," fig. 592.

940

See Sir J. Y. Simpson, *Proc. Soc. Ant. Scot.*, vol. vi. App.

941

"Brit. Barrows," 341, *et seqq.*

942

See "Reliquiæ Aquit.," p. 60.

943

"Rel. Aquit.," p. 108.

944

Arch. Assoc. Journ., vol. vii. p. 84. See Eyre's "Central Australia," vol. ii. pl. iv. p. 14.

945

Keller's "Lake-dwellings," p. 137. Lindenschmit, "Hohenz. Samml.," pl. xxvii. 8.

946

"Hab. Lac. de la Savoie," 1st Mem. pl. xi. 2.

947

Rev. Arch., 3rd S., vol. vii. p. 68.

948

"Brit. Barrows," p. 193.

949

Trans. Ethnol. Soc., N. S., vol. iv. p. 242.

950

Journ. Ethnol. Soc., vol. ii. p. 413.

951

Arch. Camb., 4th S., vol. v. p. 184.

952

P. S. A. S., vol. xiii. p. 204, Munro, "Lake-dw.," p. 102.

953

P. S. A. S., vol. xxiii. p. 214.

954

Journ. Anth. Soc., 1869, p. cxvii.

955

The burnishing stones in use among pewterers are, when dismounted from their setting, curiously like these blunt-ended celt-like instruments. They have no ridge, however, at the truncated end. Some of the stone burnishers used by bookbinders are also in form like celts, but have a flattened edge.

956

Arch. Journ., vol. xxvii. p. 161.

957

Trans. Ethn. Soc., N. S., vol. vii. p. 48.

958

De Gongora, "Ant. Preh. de Andalusia," p. 108.

959

Zeitsch. f. Ethn., vol. xx. p. (365).

960

Vol. xxiv. p. 251.

961

Vol. xxvi. p. 320; xxvii. 147.

962

Arch., vol. xxxviii. p. 416.

963

"Cran. Brit.," vol. ii. pl. 58, p. 2.

964

Trans. Preh. Cong., 1868, p. 70.

965

P. S. A. S., vol. xxv. p. 496.

966

Vol. xxvii. pl. xi. 2, 3.

967

Suss. Arch. Coll., vol. xxxii. p. 174.

968

Arch., vol. xlvi. p. 492, pl. xxiv. 26.

969

Miln's "Excav. at Carnac," 1881, pl. xv.

970

Arch. Journ., vol. xxv. p. 47.

971

Proc. Soc. Ant., 2nd S., vol. ii. p. 265.

972

Arch. Assoc. Journ., vol. xviii. p. 393.

973

Ibid., vol. xxiii. p. 391.

974

Arch. vol. xxxviii. p. 416.

975

Arch. Assoc. Journ., vol. xxiii. p. 391.

976

"Ten Years' Diggings," p. 223.

977

Trans. Ethn. Soc., N. S., vol. iii. p. 278.

978

Sproat's "Scenes and Studies of Savage Life," p. 55.

979

Wood, "Nat. Hist. of Man," vol. i. p. 152. Ratzel, "Völkerk.," vol. i., 1887, p. 216.

980

"Nile Tributaries of Abyssinia," Baker, p. 78. See also "The Albert Nyanza," vol. i. p. 65. Klemm's "Cult.-Wiss.," p. 88.

981

Rev. Dr. Hume, "Illust. of Brit. Ants. from Objects found in S. Amer.," p. 69.

982

See *Arch. Journ.*, vol. xxiv. p. 244, where much information is given concerning such stones.

983

Arch. Journ., vol. xxvii. p. 160, &c. *Arch. Camb.*, 2nd S., vol. iii. p. 210; 3rd S., vi. 376; vii. 40; viii. 157; 4th S., xii. p. 32.

984

Arch., vol. xlvi. p. 285.

985

Arch. Camb., 3rd S., vol. vii. p. 245.

986

Wilde's "Cat. Mus. R. I. A." p. 104.

987

"Itinerary," 1617, pt. iii. p. 161.

988

"Flint Chips," p. 62.

989

Proc. Soc. Ant. Scot., vol. ii. p. 377.

990

P. S. A. S., vol. vii. p. 9.

991

P. S. A. S., vol. xi. p. 176.

992

Garrigon et Filhol, "Age de la Pierre polie," &c., p. 27. *Arch. Camb.*, 4th S., vol. i. p. 292.

993

"Mus. Préh.," No. 587.

994

Trans. Preh. Cong., 1868, p. 155.

995

"Alt. u. h. V.," vol. ii. Heft viii. Taf. i. 16.

996

"Cult.-Wiss.," p. 88.

997

Arch. Camb., 3rd S., vol. iii. p. 356.

998

Proc. Soc. Ant. Scot., vol. iv. p. 117.

999

Arch. Journ., vol. xxvii. p. 160, pl. ii. 1.

1000

A. J., vol. xxiv. p. 247.

1001

Atkinson's "Cleveland," p. 40.

1002

"Nænia Cornub.," p. 221.

1003

Wood-Martin "Lake-dw. of Ireland," 1886, p. 85.

1004

Kirchner, "Thor's Donnerkeil," 1853, p. 97.

1005

"Ten Years' Diggings," p. 172.

1006

Ibid., p. 177.

1007

Ibid., pp. 213, 224, 226.

1008

"Vestiges Ant. Derb.," p. 99.

1009

Arch. Journ., vol. vii. p. 190.

1010

Arch. Journ., vol. xxiv. p. 81.

1011

"Troy," 1875, pp. 151, 163.

1012

British Med. Journ., April 2nd, 1887, quoted in *Essex Naturalist*, vol. i. p. 92.

1013

Arch. Journ., vol. xxiv. p. 252.

1014

Arch. Journ., vol. xiv. p. 357; xvii. 170.

1015

Suss. Arch. Coll., vol. ix. p. 117. "Chich. Vol. Arch. Inst.," p. 63. This cut has been kindly lent me by the Sussex Arch. Society.

1016

Essex Naturalist, vol. ii. p. 4.

1017

Arch. vol. xliii. p. 408. A. C. Smith, "Ants. of N. Wilts," p. 14.

1018

See *Proc. Soc. Ant. Scot.*, vol. vi. p. 179, where the measurements hardly agree with mine.

1019

Arch. Journ., vol. xxiv. p. 253.

1020

Sitzungsb. der K. Akad. der Wiss. in Wien, vol. lv. p. 528.

1021

Trans. Ethn. Soc., N. S., vol. vii. p. 49.

1022

See Laing's "Prehistoric Remains of Caithness," 1866. *Proc. Soc. Ant. Scot.*, vol. vii. *Passim*; viii. 64. pl. vi. *Mem. Anthrop. Soc. Lond.*, vol. ii. p. 294; iii. 216. I am indebted to the Society of Antiquaries of Scotland for the loan of Figs. 174 to 179. See also *P. S. A. S.*, vol. viii. pl. vi.; xi. p. 173; xii. p. 271; and Mitchell's "Past in the Present," p. 140.

1023

Proc. Soc. Ant. Scot., vol. vii. p. 136.

1024

P. S. A. S., vol. vii. pp. 358, 400.

1025

P. S. A. S., vol. vii. p. 125.

1026

P. S. A. S., vol. vii. p. 127.

1027

P. S. A. S., vol. xxiii. p. 219.

1028

See Whitaker's "Hist. of Craven.," 2nd ed., p. 468.

1029

Wright's "Prov. Dict.," *s.v.* Cotgrave translates the word *Baton* "a laundress's batting-staff."

1030

Arch. Assoc. Journ., vol. xxiv. p. 65.

1031

Op. cit., vol. xv. p. 232.

1032

3rd S., vol. iii. p. 358.

1033

Schoolcraft, "Ind. Tribes," vol. i. p. 80.

1034

"Anct. Mon. of Mississ. Val.," p. 220.

1035

Schoolcraft, "Ind. Tribes," vol. i. p. 90.

1036

Op. cit., vol. ii. p. 89.

1037

Op. cit., vol. iv. p. 175.

1038

Cuming in *Arch. Assoc. Journ.*, vol. vii. p. 83, where some interesting information relating to mortars will be found. Ratzel, "Völkerk.," vol. ii. p. 179.

1039

Vol. iv. p. 136. See also a paper by Mr. R. N. Worth, on the progress of mining skill in Devon and Cornwall, in the *Trans. Cornw. Polyt. Soc.*

1040

Arch. Journ., vol. vii. 393.

1041

Vol. ii. p. 323.

1042

"Die Burg Tannenberg," &c., *Arch. Journ.*, vol. vii. p. 404.

1043

Vol. iii. p. 130.

1044

"Gesta. Abb. Mon. S. Alb.," vol. ii. p. 249.

1045

Arch. Assoc. Journ., vol. vii. p. 175.

1046

Proc. Soc. Ant. Scot., vol iii. p. 203.

1047

Arch. Assoc. Journ., vol. xv. p. 335.

1048

"Ten Years' Dig.," p. 99.

1049

Arch. Assoc. Journ., vol. xiii. 227.

1050

Ibid., vol. xv. p. 337.

1051

Arch. Journ., vol. v. p. 329.

1052

Smith's "Coll. Ant.," vol. i. p. 112. *Arch.*, vol. xviii. p. 435; xix. 183; xxx. 128. *Proc. Bury and W. Suff. Arch. I.*, vol. i. p. 230, &c. *Proc. Soc. Ant.*, 2nd S., vol. iii. p. 259.

1053

Arch., vol. xliv. p. 285.

1054

Arch., vol. xlv. p. 366.

1055

Arch. Camb., 5th S., vol. viii. p. 320.

1056

Arch. Camb., 2nd S., vol. iii. p. 240.

1057

Lee's "Isca Silurum," p. 114.

1058

Proc. Soc. Ant. Scot., vol. i. p. 267.

1059

P. S. A. S., vol. ii. p. 97. See also vol. v. p. 30.

1060

Preh. Annals of Scot., vol. i. p. 214.

1061

P. S. A. S., vol. xii. p. 261. Mitchell's "The Past in the Present," p. 34.

1062

P. S. A. S., vol. iv. p. 417.

1063

P. S. A. S., vol. xiii. p. 178.

1064

P. S. A. S., vol. xxi. p. 162.

1065

Arch. Camb., 3rd S., vol. vii. p. 38.

1066

"South Wilts," p. 36.

1067

"Vest. Ant. Derb.," 127.

1068

Arch., vol. xxxv. p. 246.

1069

2nd S., vol. ii. p. 89.

NOTES—CHAPTER XI.

1070

"Nord. Olds.," Nos. 35 and 36.

1071

Tidskrift for Oldkyndighed, vol. i. pl. ii. p. 423.

1072

"Stone Age," p. 16.

1073

"Ant. Suéd."

1074

Keller's "Lake-dwell.," p. 24.

1075

Keller, "Pfahlbauten," 1ter Bericht, Taf. iii. 19; 3ter Ber., Taf. ii. 2.

1076

"Les Polissoirs préh. de la Charente," G. Chauvet, Angoulême, 1883.

1077

"Les Polissoirs néol. du Dép. delà Dordogne," Testut. *Mat.*, 3rd S., vol. iii. (1886) p. 65.

1078

"Notice sur deux Instruments," &c., p. 4. Mortillet, *Matériaux*, vol. ii. p. 420.

1079

See "Ant. Celt et Antéd, de Poitou," pl. xxx.

1080

Ann. Soc. Arch. de Bruxelles, vol. x., 1896, p. 109.

1081

B. de Perthes, "Ant. Celt et Antéd.," vol. ii. p. 165. Mortillet, "Prom. au Mus. St. Germain," p. 148.

1082

De Gongora y Martinez, "Ant. Preh. de Andalusia," p. 34, fig. 19.

1083

Journ. Anth. Inst., vol. xvi. p. 73.

1084

See *Arch. Journ.*, vol. xxi. p. 170.

1085

"Brit. Barrows," p. 168.

1086

"Brit. Barrows," p. 220.

1087

Arch., vol. xxxviii. p. 417.

1088

"Cook's Voyages," quoted by Tylor, "Early Hist. of Mank.," 2nd ed., p. 201.

1089

P. S. A. S., vol. xv. p. 263.

1090

"Ten Years' Dig.," p. 169.

1091

Arch. Scot., vol. iii. p. 43.

1092

Arch. Journ., vol. xxv. p. 295.

1093

Arch. Journ., vol. xxvii. p. 161.

1094

Proc. Soc. Ant. Scot., vol. vii. p. 219.

1095

See Lyell, "Ant. of Man," 3rd ed. p. 189.

1096

Worsaae, fig. 36. Nilsson, "Stone Age," pl. ii. 15.

1097

Proc. Soc. Ant. Scot., vol. xv. p. 74.

1098

Arch., vol. xliv. p. 286.

1099

Malton Messenger, Nov. 12, 1870. "Brit. Barrows," p. 263.

1100

Trans. Dev. Assoc., vol. v. p. 551.

1101

Arch., vol. xliii. p. 426.

1102

"South Wilts.," p. 118, pl. xiv.

1103

P. 43.

1104

Proc. Soc. Ant., 2nd S., vol. vi. p. 399.

1105

Proc. Soc. Ant. Scot., vol. xv. p. 264.

1106

"Brit. Barrows," p. 173.

1107

Hoare's "South Wilts," p. 75. *Arch.*, vol. xv. p. 125. "Cat. Devizes Mus.," No. 2.

1108

Hoare, "South Wilts," p. 182. "Cat. Dev. Mus.," No. 97.

1109

"S. W." p. 209.

1110

Arch., vol. xliii. p. 423. A. C. Smith, "Ants. of N. Wilts," p. 68. "Cat. Devizes Mus.," No. 172A.

1111

Arch., vol. xlvi. p. 435, pl. xxiv. 20.

1112

Reliquary, N. S., vol. v., 1891, p. 47.

1113

Arch. f. Anth., vol. ix. p. 249.

1114

13th Rep. Bureau of Ethn., 1896, p. 126.

1115

"Musée préh.," No. 593.

1116

Lindenschmit, "A. u. h. V.," vol. ii. Heft viii. Taf. i. 2. *Zeitsch. des Vereins für Rhein. Geschichte, &c., in Mainz*, vol. iii. *Archiv für Anthrop.*, vol. iii. Taf. ii. *Rev. Arch.*, vol. xix. pl. x. 2.

1117

Sophus Müller, "Stenalderen," fig. 196.

1118

Zeitsch. f. Eth., 1891, p. 89.

1119

Trans. Ethnol. Soc., N. S., vol. vii. p. 49.

1120

Sussex Arch. Coll., vol. ix., p. 120, whence the cut is borrowed. *Arch. Journ.*, vol. xiii. p. 184; xv. 90.

1121

Arch. Journ., vol. x. p. 356. "Chichester Vol.," p. 52.

1122

Thoresby's Cat. in Whitaker's "Duc. Leod.," p. 114.

1123

Hoare's "South Wilts," p. 194.

1124

Ibid., p. 199.

1125

Ibid., p. 209.

1126

Ibid., p. 211.

1127

Ibid., p. 172.

1128

Ibid., p. 164. "Cat. Devizes Mus.," No. 85.

1129

Arch., vol. xliii. p. 424.

1130

Arch., vol. xlix. p. 194.

1131

"Nænia Cornubiæ," 1872, p. 212.

1132

Arch. Journ., vol. xxviii. p. 247.

1133

Arch. Journ., vol. xxxi. p. 302.

1134

Arch. Journ., vol. xxi. p. 101.

1135

Proc. Soc. Ant. Scot., vol. iv. p. 490.

1136

Arch. Journ., vol. xviii. p. 71. Lee's "Isca Silurum," pl. xlii. p. 108.

1137

Arch. Assoc. Journ., vol. iv. p. 105.

1138

P. S. A. S., vol. xii. p. 120; xxiii. p. 219; xxviii. p. 230.

1139

P. S. A. S., vol. xiv. p. 221.

1140

P. S. A. S., vol. xxii. p. 67.

1141

"Preh. Ann. of Scot.," vol. i. p. 188.

1142

Wilde's "Cat. Mus. R. I. A." p. 87.

1143

Perrin, "Et. Préhist. sur la Savoie," pl. xv. 12.

1144

Von Sacken, "Grabf. von Hallstatt," Taf. xix. Simony, "Alt. von Hallstatt," Taf. vi. 6, 7.

1145

Arch. Journ., vol. xxvii. pl. iii. 1.

1146

Arch. Journ., vol. xxvi. p. 321, figs. 18, 19.

1147

"Cat. Mus. R. I. A.," p. 75.

1148

P. S. A. S., vol. ix. p. 358.

1149

P. S. A. S., vol. x. pl. xviii. 115.

1150

P. S. A. S., vol. xxiii. p. 234.

1151

P. S. A. S., vol. xiv. p. 276.

1152

"Nord. Olds.," fig. 343.

1153

Pl. i.

1154

Engelhardt, "Thorsbjerg Mosefund," p. 51, pl. xii. 12.

1155

See *Brit. Assoc. Rep.*, 1881, p. 692.

1156

Jahrb. d. Ver. v. Alt. fr. im Rheinl., Heft xliv. p. 139, Taf. vi. 21.

1157

Notes and Queries, 2nd S., vol. viii. p. 92.

NOTES—CHAPTER XII.

1158

"Cat. Mus. R. I. A.," p. 7.

1159

"Preh. Times," 4th ed., p. 87.

1160

"Geol. and Nat. Hist. Rep.," vol. i. p. 208.

1161

"G. and N. H. Rep.," vol. ii. p. 128; *Proc. Soc. Ant.*, 2nd S., vol. iv. p. 95.

1162

I first learnt the art of producing these cones from the late Rev. J. S. Henslow, F.R.S., and have since then instructed many others in the process, among them the late Dr. Hugh Falconer, F.R.S., whose account of the manufacture of flakes ("Palæont. Mem.," vol. ii. p. 605) is, I find, curiously like what I have written above. He insists rather more strongly on the different characteristics of "iron-struck" and "stone-struck" facets than I should be inclined to do. There is, however, in all probability a difference in the fracture resulting from hammers of different degrees of hardness and elasticity. The mechanics of the fracture of flint have also been studied by the late M. Jules Thore, of Dax. (*Bull. de la Soc. de Borda*, Dax, 1878.)

1163

Archæologia, vol. xxxix. p. 76.

1164

"Spalls or broken pieces of stones that come off in hewing and graving." — "Nomenclator," p. 411, quoted in Halliwell's "Dict. of Archaic Words, &c." "Spalle, or chyppe, *quisquilia, assula*." — "Promptorium Parvulorum," p. 467.

1165

Proc. Soc. Ant., 2nd S., vol. iii. p. 38. *Proc. As. Soc. Beng.*, 1867, p. 137.

1166

Dr. Gillespie, in *Journ. Anth. Inst.*, vol. vi. p. 260.

1167

Wood, "Nat. Hist. of Man," vol. ii. pp. 36–38.

1168

Proc. Soc. Ant., 2nd S., vol. i. p. 73.

1169

Trans. Ethn. Soc., N. S., vol. iv. p. 241.

1170

Arch. Journ., vol. xvii. p. 170.

1171

Journ. Ethnol. Soc. Lond., vol. ii. p. 430.

1172

For neolithic implements from this place, see *Trans. Berks. Archæol. and Archit. Soc.*, 1879–80, p. 49.

1173

"Manx Note Book," vol. i. (1885) p. 71.

1174

Mem. Anthrop. Soc. Lond., vol. i. p. 142.

1175

See Worsaae "Nord. Olds.," No. 60; "Guide to North. Arch.," p. 39; and the authors already cited at p. 272.

1176

"Mus. préh.," pl. xxxiii.

1177

Mém. Soc. R. des Ant. du Nord., 1872–7, p. 103.

1178

Zeitsch. f. Ethn., vol. xvii. p. (133).

1179

P. 23. See also Tylor, "Anahuac.," p. 96.

1180

Geol. Mag., vol. iii. p. 433; iv. 43.

1181

"Objects Found in Greece," G. Finlay, 1869. *Zeitsch. f. Ethn.*, vol. v. p. (110).

1182

Proc. Soc. Ant., 2nd S., vol. i. p. 69. See also *Arch. Journ.*, vol. xvii. p. 171.

1183

Proc. Soc. Ant., 2nd S., vol. v. p. 438.

1184

Tr. Dev. Assoc., vol. xvii. p. 70; xviii. p. 74. *Arch. Assoc. Journ.*, vol. xxviii. p. 220.

1185

Journ. Anth. Inst., vol. v. p. 30. *Notes and Queries*, 5th S., vol. vii. p. 447.

1186

"Flint Impts., &c., found at St. Mary Bourne," Jos. Stevens, 1867.

1187

Journ. Anth. Inst., vol. xiii. p. 137.

1188

Tr. Lanc. and Chesh. Arch. Soc., vol. ii. pl. i. iv. p. 305.

1189

Journ. R. Inst. Cornwall, Oct., 1864.

1190

Proc. Soc. Ant., 2nd S., vol. iii. p. 22.

1191

Trans. Preh. Cong., 1868, p. 89. *Tr. Devon. Assoc.*, vol. i.; pt. v. p. 80.

1192

Op. cit., p. 128.

1193

"Ten Years' Dig.," p. 226.

1194

Arch. Journ., vol. viii. p. 343.

1195

Arch. Assoc. Journ., vol. xxii. p. 241.

1196

Proc. Soc. Ant., 2nd S., vol. vi. p. 48.

1197

Arch., vol. xxxvi. p. 176.

1198

Arch. Journ., vol. xviii. p. 71.

1199

Reliquary, vol. vi. p. 4.

1200

Arch. Journ., vol xii. p. 189.

1201

Arch. Camb., 2nd S., vol. i. p. 331; ii. 222.

1202

Arch. Assoc. Journ., vol. xviii. p. 58.

1203

Tr. Devon. Assoc., vol. vi. p. 272, fig. 2.

1204

Reliquary, vol. iii. p. 162.

1205

Arch. Journ., vol. ix. p. 92.

1206

Arch. Camb., 2nd S., vol. iii. p. 102.

1207

Journ. Ethnol. Soc., vol. ii. p. 306.

1208
Arch. Journ., vol. xiv. p. 281.
1209
Arch., vol. xxxiv. p. 252.
1210
"Cran. Brit.," vol. ii. pl. 1, p. 2.
1211
"Cr. Br.," vol. ii. pl. 24, p. 3.
1212
Mem. Anthrop. Soc. Lond., vol. i. p. 142.
1213
Arch., vol. lii. p. 12, and "British Barrows," *passim*.
1214
Arch. Assoc. Journ., vol. xvii. p. 73.
1215
Arch., vol. xxxviii. p. 416.
1216
Proc. Soc. Ant., 2nd S., vol. ii. p. 278.
1217
Arch. Journ., vol. xi. p. 322.
1218
Wiltsh. Mag., vol. iii. p. 170.
1219
"South Wilts," p. 193.
1220
"South Wilts," p. 195.
1221
Arch. Journ., vol. xxi. p. 172.

1222

"Cat. Arch. Inst. Mus. Edin.," p. 20.

1223

Proc. Soc. Ant. Scot., vol. iv. p. 507.

1224

Op. cit., vol. iv. p. 385, and vi. 234, 240. *Quart. Journ. Geol. Soc.*, 1865, vol. xxi. p. 1.

1225

P. S. A. S., vol. vi. p. 251, and v. 61.

1226

Arch. Journ., vol. xx. p. 35.

1227

Anthrop. Rev., vol. ii.; lxiv.

1228

Wilson, "Preh. Ann. of Scot.," vol. i. p. 177.

1229

Ibid., p. 178.

1230

Proc. Soc. Ant. Scot., vol. v. p. 13.

1231

Arch. Scot., vol. iii. p. 46.

1232

Arch., vol. xlii. p. 64.

1233

Arch. Journ., vol. xx. p. 198.

1234

"Salisb. Vol. Arch. Inst.," p. 106.

1235

Journ. Ethn. Soc., vol. i. p. 10.

1236

Arch. Journ., vol. xxiii. p. 300; vol. xxv. p. 155.

1237

Geol. Mag., vol. vii. 443.

1238

Arch. Journ., vol. xxii. p. 68.

1239

Suss. Arch. Coll., vol. xix. p. 53.

1240

Arch. Assoc. Journ., vol. xxiv. p. 182, &c.

1241

Journ. Ethn. Soc., vol. ii. p. 421.

1242

"Flint Impts.," Jos. Stevens, 1867.

1243

Arch. Journ., vol. xxi. p. 168.

1244

3rd S., vol. iii. p. 304.

1245

Journ. Ethn. Soc., vol. ii. p. 141.

1246

"Prehist. Rem. of Caithness," *Proc. Soc. Ant. Scot.*, vol. vii. p. 37.

1247

P. S. A. S., vol. vii. p. 73.

1248

P. S. A. S., vol. i. p. 101.

1249

Arch. Assoc. Journ., vol. ii. p. 203.

1250

Arch. Assoc. Journ., vol. xiii. p. 319.

1251

Garrigou et Filhol, "Age de la Pierre polie." &c., pl. vii. and viii.

1252

De Bonstetten, "2nd Supp. au Rec. d'Ant. Suisses," pl. i.

1253

On this custom see *Trans. Lanc. and Chesh. Arch. Soc.*, vol. vi. p. 58; viii. p. 63; xi. p. 27.

1254

Arch. Journ., vol. xxii. p. 116.

1255

Proc. Soc. Ant. Scot., vol. i. p. 210.

1256

Arch. Assoc. Journ., vol. xii. p. 299.

1257

See *Arch. Journ.*, vol. xi. p. 211, and xx. 189; Wright, "Rems. of a Prim. Peop. in Yorksh.," p. 10.

1258

See Cochet, "Normandie Souterr.," p. 258; Baudot, "Sép. des Barbares," p. 76; Troyon, "Tombeaux de Bel-Air"; Lindenschmit, "Todtenlager bei Selzen," p. 13.

1259

Arch., vol. xxxv. p. 267.

1260

"Hist. of Lapland," Ed., 1704, p. 313; Keysler, "Ant. Sept.," p. 173.

1261

Sussex Arch. Coll. vol. xvi. p. 63.

1262

Arch. Camb., 2nd S., vol. i. p. 88.

1263

Isaiah, chap. xli. ver. 15.

1264

"De re Rust.," lib. i. cap. 52.

1265

Smith's "Dict. of Gk. and Rom. Ant.," *s.v.* Tribulum. Wilkinson's "Anc. Egyptians," vol. ii. p. 190; iv. 94. *"Arch, per l'Ant. e la Etn.,"* vol. xxiii. 57; vol. xxvi. p. 53. Fellows, "Journ. in Asia Minor," 1838, p. 70. Paul Lucas, "Voyage en Asie," Paris, 1712, p. 231. *N. and Q.,* 7th S., vol. vii. p. 36.

1266

For the use of this cut I am indebted to Sir A. Wollaston Franks, F.R.S.

1267

Proc. Soc. Ant. Scot., vol. vi. p. 253.

1268

Journ. Anth. Inst., vol. x. p. 150.

1269

Arch., vol. xli. p. 404. See also Wilde, "Cat. Mus. R. I. A.," p. 10.

1270

See Lubbock, "Preh. Times," 4th ed., p. 94.

1271

Mém. Soc. R. des Ant. du Nord., 1886–91, p. 232. *Aarb. f. Oldkynd,* 1886, p. 227.

1272

"Alt. u. h. V.," vol. ii. Heft. viii. Taf. i. 4.

1273

Tom. vi. 1865.

1274

Ponthieux, pl. xxvi.

1275

Chantre, "Etudes Paléoéthnol.," 1867. Watelet, "L'Age de Pierre dans le Dép. de l'Aisne," 1866. De Ferry, "Anc. de l'Homme dans le Mâconnais," 1867.

1276

"L'Homme Fossile," 2nd ed., p. 150.

1277

Comptes Rendus, 1866, vol. lxii. p. 347; 1867, vol. lxv. p. 116.

1278

De Gongora, "Ant. Preh. de Andalusia," p. 49, fig. 60.

1279

Trans. Preh. Cong., 1868, pl. viii. 3.

1280

"Ant. do Algarve;" da Veiga, 1886, vol. ii. p. 162, pl. viii.

1281

"Di alcuni armi ed Utensili in Pietra," 1863, Tav. ii.

1282

Keller, "Pfahlbauten," 6ter Ber., p. 272.

1283

"Supp. au Rec. d'Ant. Suisses," pl. i. 5.

1284

Zeitsch. f. Ethn., vol. xvi. p. (105), pl. iii.

1285

Rev. Arch., vol. xx. p. 441. *Matériaux*, vol. v. p. 399 bis; *Comptes Rendus*, 1869, vol. lxix. p. 1312. Arcelin, "Ind. prim. en. Egypte et en Syrie," 1870.

1286

Zeitschrift für Ægypt. Sprache, &c., Juli 1870.

1287

Journ. Anth. Inst., vol. iv. p. 215 (Lubbock): vii. p. 290. *Zeitsch. f. Ethn.*, vol. xxi. pl. iv. v. "Die Stein-zeit Afrika's," R. Andrée. *Intern. Archiv*, vol. iii. p. 81. "Ægypten's vor-metallische Zeit." Much, Würzburg, 1880. *Nature*, vol. xxxii. p. 161: xxxiii. 311 (Wady Halfa).

1288

Tr. Cong. Préh. Stockholm, 1874, p. 76.

1289

Comptes Rendus, 1869, vol. lxviii. pp. 196, 345.

1290

Journ. Anth. Inst., vol. i. pp. 337, 442.

1291

Quart. St. Palest. Expl. Fund, 1874, p. 158.

1292

Trans. Cong. Preh. Arch., 1868, p. 69. *Geol. Mag.*, vol. v. p. 532. *Journ. Anth. Inst.*, vol. xi. p. 124. *Camb. Ant. Comm.*, vol. v. p. 67.

1293

Proc. Soc. Ant., 2nd S., vol. iii. p. 38. *Journ. of Ant. Soc. of Cent. Prov.*, vol. i. p. 21. *Journ. Ethn. Soc.*, N. S., vol. i. p. 175.

1294

"Anct. Mon. of Mississ. Vall.," p. 215.

1295

Lib. iii. c. 15.

1296

Wood, "Nat. Hist. of Man," vol. ii. p. 38.

1297

Journ. Anth. Inst., vol. vi. p. 409, pl. xx.

1298

For the use of this block I am indebted to the executors of the late Mr. Henry Christy. See also Lubbock, "Preh. Times," 4th Ed., p. 93.

1299

"Mus. Metall," p. 157.

1300

Two are figured in *Proc. Soc. Ant. Scot.*, vol. viii. p. 321. See also Ratzel, "Völkerk," vol. ii., 1888, p. 151.

1301

Comptes Rendus, 1868, vol. lxvii. p. 1296.

1302

Arch. Assoc. Journ., vol. iv., 1848, p. 105.

1303

Arch., vol. xxxviii. p. 417.

1304

"Anc. Wilts," p. 195. "Cat. Devizes Mus.," No. 124A.

1305

"Ten Years' Dig.," p. 230.

1306

"T. Y. D.," p. 224.

1307

P. S. A. S., vol. vii. p. 320.

1308

Op. cit., vol. vii. p. 499.

1309

Arch., vol. xli. p. 404.

1310

Others are engraved in Keller's "Pfahlbaut.," 1ter Bericht, Taf. iii. 8. Lindenschmit, "Alt. u. h. V.," vol. i., Heft. xii. Taf. i. 15. "Hohenzollernsch. Samml.," Taf. xxvii. 18. Mackie, "Nat. Hist. Rep.," vol. i. p. 139. Le Hon, "L'homme Foss.," 2nd ed., p. 175. "Ant. Lac. du Mus. de Lausanne," 1896. Pl. x.

1311

"Mus. préh.," Nos. 276, 277. "Ant. Lac. du Mus. de Lausanne," 1896. Pl. x., 10, 11.

1312

Zeitsch. f. Ethn., vol. xiv. p. (531).

1313

Keller's "Lake-Dw.," pl. iii. 1; xxi. 10; xxviii. 9, 10. Troyon, "Hab. Lac.," pl. v. 11. "Pfahlbauten," 2ter Ber. Taf. iii. pl. 40. Desor, "Palafittes," fig. 12. Rau's "Preh. Fishing," 1884, p. 186.

1314

"Stone Age," pl. v. 86.

1315

P. S. A. S., vol. x. p. 263.

1316

Tr. Lanc. and Chesh. Arch. Soc., vol. iv. p. 377.

1317

Ibid.

1318

Zeitsch. f. Ethn., vol., xiv. p. 28.

1319

"Illahun, &c.," 1891, p. 13, pl. xiii.

1320

"Nat. Hist. of Man," vol. ii. p. 32.

1321

See *Archiv. f. Anth.*, vol. v. p. 234.

1322

Worsaae, "Prim. Ants. of Den.," p. 17. Nilsson, "Stone Age," pl. vi. 125, 126. Madsen, "Afb.," pl. xl.

1323

Wilson's "Preh. Man," vol. i. p. 225. "Anct. Mon. of Missis. Valley," p. 211. Squier, "Abor. Mon. of New York," p. 180.

1324

"Cultur-wiss.," vol. i. p. 61.

1325

"Stone Age," pl. ii. pp. 28, 29.

1326

"Remains of a Primitive People, &c., in Yorkshire."

1327

Proc. Soc. Ant., 2nd S., vol. iv. 233.

1328

Arch., vol. xxxviii. p. 417.

1329

Arch. Journ., vol. xxvii. p. 74.

1330

Arch. Journ., vol. xxix. p. 284.

1331

Antiq., vol. xv., 1887, pp. 237–8.

1332

Suss. Arch. Coll., vol. xxxii. p. 175.

1333

Suss. Arch. Coll., vol. xxvii. p. 177.

1334

Wilts Arch. Mag., vol. xx. p. 346.

1335

"Brit. Barr.," pp. 251, 262.

1336

"Vest. Ant. Derb.," p. 43.

1337

P. S. A. S., vol. xxv. p. 497.

1338

P. S. A. S., vol. xi. p. 584.

1339

P. S. A. S., vol. xii. p. 208.

1340

P. S. A. S., vol. xxviii. p. 337.

1341

Bull. de la Soc. des Ant. de l'Ouest, 4 Trim., 1863, fig. 18.

1342

"Mus. Préh.," pl. xxxiv., xxxv.

1343

Madsen, "Afbildninger," pl. i. 15.

1344

Zeits. f. Ethn., vol. xxviii., p. 348.

1345

H. and L. Siret, "Les premiers Ages du Métal," pl. xiii., xvi. Capelle, "L'Esp. centr.," 1895, p. 70, pl. vi.

1346

Zeitsch. f. Ethn., vol. xvii. p. 93.

1347

Zeitsch. f. Ethn., vol. xiv. p. (483); xv. p. (116).

1348

"Stone Age," p. 80, pl. v. 93.

1349

"Nord. Olds.," No. 56.

1350

"Nord. Olds.," No. 58.

1351

Lubbock, "Preh. Times," 4th ed., p. 102. "Flint Chips," p. 74.

1352

Nordisk Tidskrift for Oldk., 1832, p. 429.

1353

"Stone Age," p. 42.

1354

Franks, "Horæ Ferales," p. 137. Lisch, "Frederico-Francisc.," p. 145.

1355

"Celt, Roman, and Saxon," p. 70.

1356

"Kahun," 1890, p. 29, pl. ix. "Illahun, &c.," 1891, p. 50 *seqq*. "Medum," 1892, p. 31 *seqq*.

1357

"Troy," 1875, p. 94. Atlas, pl. xxv.

1358

Zeitsch. f. Ethn., vol. xvii. p. (303).

1359

Arch. Journ., vol. xlix. p. 53.

1360

Arch. Journ., vol. xlix. p. 164.

NOTES—CHAPTER XIII.

1361

Pt. ii. p. 14. One from Alaska of this form and another with a long handle are figured in *Zeitsch. f. Ethn.*, vol. xvi. p. (222).

1362

"Prehist. Times," 4th ed., p. 513, figs. 214–6.

1363

"Nat. Hist. of Man," vol. ii. p. 699.

1364

"Rel. Aquit.," p. 13.

1365

Proc. Ethn. Soc., N. S., vol. i. p. 137. See *Rep. Bureau of Ethn.*, 1887–8, p. 294.

1366

P. S. A. S., vol. xxiv. p. 142.

1367

Rep. of U. S. Nat. Mus., Washington, 1891, p. 553.

1368

Schoolcraft, "Ind. Tribes," vol. iv. p. 175.

1369

Intern. Archiv., vol. ii. p. 212.

1370

Arch. per l'Ant. e la Etn., vol. xxiv., 1894, p. 245.

1371

Bull. Soc. d'Anth. de Paris, 4th S. vol. vii., 1896, p. 374.

1372

P. 319.

1373

"Cat. Mus. R. I. A.," fig. 8.

1374

"Nord. Olds.," No. 29.

1375

"South Wilts," p. 172, pl. xix.

1376

Arch., vol. xliii. pp. 420, 421.

1377

"Salisb. Vol. Arch. Inst.," p. 106.

1378

Proc. Soc. Ant., 2nd S., vol. xii. p. 239.

1379

Arch. Assoc. Journ., vol. xxii. p. 450. *Arch.*, vol. xliii. p. 420.

1380

Suss. Arch. Coll., vol. xxxii. p. 174. *Journ. Anth. Inst.*, vol. vi. p. 287.

1381

Proc. Soc. Ant., 2nd. S., vol. x. p. 18.

1382

Trans. Dev. Assoc., vol. xii. p. 140.

1383

"Cran. Brit.," vol. ii, pl. 50, p. 2. *Arch.*, vol. xxxviii. p. 416.

1384

Reliq., vol. xxxii., 1896, p. 109.

1385

Arch. Journ., vol. xiv. p. 83; xxii. 116, 245, 251; xxvii. 71. *Reliquary*, vol. ix. p. 69. "Ten Years' Dig.," pp. 205, 208. "Brit. Bar." pp. 251, 348, and *passim*.

1386

"T. Y. D.," p. 56.

1387

"Vest. Ant. Derb.," p. 92.

1388

"T. Y. D.," p. 78.

1389

"T. Y. D.," p. 35. *Arch. Assoc. Journ.*, vol. vii. p. 217.

1390

Pitt Rivers, "Exc. on Cranb. Chase," vol. ii. pl. lxvi. and lxxxix.

1391

Proc. Soc. Ant., 2nd S., vol. iii. p. 76.

1392

Sussex Arch. Coll., vol. xix. p. 53.

1393

Journ. Ethn. Soc., vol. i. pl. i.

1394

Arch. Journ., vol. xxv. p. 155.

1395

Journ. Ethn. Soc., vol. i. p. 4.

1396

Arch. Camb., 4th S., vol. ix. p. 37.

1397

Arch. Journ., vol. xxxi. pp. 297, 301.

1398

Proc. Soc. Ant., 2nd S., vol. viii. p. 385.

1399

Arch. Cant., vol. xiii. p. 124. "Coll. Cant.," p. 4.

1400

Arch. Cant., vol. xiv. p. 88.

1401

Essex Nat., vol. ii. p. 67.

1402

Essex Nat., vol. iii. p. 159.

1403

A considerable number of them are in the Lewes Museum. *Sass. Ant. Coll.*, vol. xxxviii. p. 226; xxxix. p. 97.

1404

Proc. Soc. Ant. Scot., vol. xv. p. 109. Munro's "Lake-dw.," pp. 109, 174.

1405

P. S. A. S., vol. ix. p. 461; vol. xix. p. 250.

1406

P. S. A. S., vol. xviii. p. 249.

1407

Journ. Anth. Inst., vol. vii. p. 202; ix. pp. 167, 320.

1408

Zeitsch. f. Ethn., vol. xvi. p. (356).

1409

Journ. Anth. Inst., vol. x. p. 352.

1410

"Preh. Times," 4th ed. p. 110.

1411

Trans. Preh. Cong., 1868, p. 69. *Journ. Ethnol. Soc.*, vol. i. p. 52.

1412

Journ. Anth. Inst., vol. v. p. 239, pl. xi., 4.

1413

Arch. Journ., vol. xxii. p. 101.

1414

As another purpose to which these instruments may have been applied, Dr. Keller ("Lake-Dwellings," pp. 34, 97) has suggested that some of the scrapers found in the Swiss Lake-dwellings may have been in use for scaling fish.

1415

P. 16.

1416

P. 15.

1417

"Vest. Ant. Derb.," p. 53.

1418

Op. cit., p. 59. *Reliq.*, vol. iii. p. 176. "Cran. Brit.," vol. ii. pl. xli.

1419

"Vest. Ant. Derb.," p. 96.

1420

"Nænia Cornub.," p. 227.

1421

"South Wilts," p. 195. *Arch.*, vol. xliii. p. 422.

1422

Reliquary, vol. xxiv. p. 128.

1423

Arch. Journ., vol. xxv. p. 295.

1424

Cong. Préh. Lisbonne, 1880, p. 387.

1425

"Normandie Souterraine," p. 258.

1426

Arch. vol. liv. p. 375.

1427

"British Barrows," p. 266.

1428

"Brit. Barr.," pp. 266, 390.

1429

Wood, "Nat. Hist. of Man," vol. ii. p. 522.

1430

Hough, "Fire Making Apparatus" in *Rep. of U. S. Nat. Mus.*, Washington, 1888, p. 573.

1431

Figured in *Arch.*, vol. xliii. p. 422.

1432

Proc. Soc. Ant. Scot., vol. xix. p. 356.

1433

P. S. A. S., vol. viii. p. 137.

1434

"Expl. des Dolmens," Vannes, 1882, I. p. 6.

1435

C. R. de l'Assoc., fr. pour l'av. des Sciences, Grenoble, 1885.

1436

"Les Cav. de la Belgique," vol. ii. pl. ix. 2. "L'homme pendant les Ages de la Pierre," 1871, p. 74.

1437

Proc. Soc. Ant. Scot., vol. xxv. p. 499.

1438

Proc. Soc. Ant. Scot., vol. xxv. p. 497.

1439

P. S. A. S., vol. xi. p. 512.

1440

Dr. J. S. Houlder, *Journ. Anth. Inst.*, vol. iii. p. 338; iv. p. 19. See also *Journ. R. H. and Arch. Assoc. of Irel.*, 4th S., vol. v. p. 124.

1441

Journ. Anth. Inst., vol. xi. pl. xxx.

NOTES—CHAPTER XIV.

1442

Lubbock, "Preh. Times," 4th ed., p. 103. Monkman, *Yorks. Arch. and Top. Journ.*, 1868.

1443

Journ. Ethnol. Soc., vol. ii. pl. xxviii. 2, 3.

1444

Arch. Journ., vol. xxix. p. 284.

1445

See *Arch.*, vol. xli. pl. xviii. 5.

1446

Proc. Soc. Ant. Scot., vol. xi. p. 546; xxv. p. 498.

1447

P. S. A. S., vol. xv. p. 265.

1448

Aarböger f. Nord. Oldk., 1866, p. 311.

1449

P. S. A. S., vol. xiii. p. 106. *Journ. Anth. Inst.*, vol. iv. p. 311.

1450

Journ. Anth. Inst., vol. viii. p. 15.

1451

"Lake-Dwellings," p. 25. "Pfahlbauten," 1ter Bericht, p. 76.

1452

Proc. Soc. Ant. Scot., vol. xxvii. p. 361; vol. xxviii. p. 338.

1453

Proc. Soc. Ant. Scot., vol. xxv. p. 498.

1454

Perrault, "Note sur an Foyer, &c.," pl. ii. 15.

1455

Science Gossip, vol. ii. (1895) p. 36.

1456

Journ. Anth. Inst., vol. xxv. pp. 122, 137.

1457

Bull. de Palet. It., vol. i. (1875) pp. 2, 17, 141; vol. ii. (1876) *passim*.

1458

Proc. Soc. Ant. Scot., vol. xxvi. p. 409. The cut is kindly lent by the Society. *Journ. Anth. Inst.*, vol. xviii. p. 134. *Proc. Vict. Inst.*, March, 1889.

1459

Proc. Soc. Ant., 2nd S., vol. vii. p. 229. *P. S. A. S.*, vol. xii. p. 614. *Journ. Anth. Inst.*, vol. vii. p. 396. De Morgan, "Rech. sur les Orig. de l'Egypte," 1896, p. 130. He regards the crescents as arrow-heads, but I cannot agree with him.

1460

Pierpont, *Bull. de la Soc. Arch. de Brux.*, 1894–5.

NOTES—CHAPTER XV.

1461

Rev. Arch., N. S., vol. ii. p. 129.

1462

Marchant, "Notice sur divers insts.," 1866, pl. i. Parenteau, "Inv. Arch." 1878, pl. ii.

1463

"Ant. Celt. et Antéd.," vol. i. p. 379.

1464

Cazalis de Fondouce, "La grotte sép. de St. J. d'Alcas," pl. i. 1.

1465

Rev. Arch., N. S., vol. xv. pl. ix. 26.

1466

Mortillet, *Matériaux*, vol. v. p. 321.

1467

Rev. de la Soc. Lit. de l'Eure, 3rd S., vol. v.

1468

"Coll. Caranda," Moreau, 1877, pl. iii.

1469

"L'anc. de l'homme dans le Vivarais," De Marichaud, 1870, pl. xi. 5.

1470

Mat., vol. ix. p. 162.

1471

"Ant. Lac. du Mus. de Lausanne," 1896, pl. ix.

1472

"Horæ Ferales," p. 137, pl. ii. 32.

1473

"Arch. Inst. Salisb. Vol.," p. 105.

1474

Arch., vol. xxx. p. 333.

1475

Arch., vol. xxxiv. p. 253.

1476

Proc. Soc. Ant. Scot., vol. xvii. p. 72.

1477

Arch., vol. xli. pl. xviii. 6.

1478

"Reliq. Aquit.," p. 18.

1479

"Brit. Barrows," p. 380, where it is figured full size. See also pp. 196, 270, &c.

1480

"Ten Years' Dig.," p. 151. See also p. 227, and "Vest. Ant. Derb.," p. 105.

1481

Proc. Soc. Ant., 2nd S., vol. xi. p. 188. *P. S. A. Newc.-on-Tyne*, N. S., vol. ii. p. 171.

1482

"Hist. of Berwicksh. Nat. Club, 1863–68," pl. xiii. 4. "Brit. Bar.," p. 407.

1483

"Brit. Barrows," p. 153.

1484

Op. cit., p. 285.

1485

By permission of the delegates of the Clarendon Press.

1486

Arch., vol. lii. p. 31.

1487

Reliq. and Ill. Archæologist, vol. ii. p. 46.

1488

Trans. Devon. Assoc., vol. xii. p. 367.

1489

Arch. Cant., vol. xiii. p. 124.

1490

Proc. Soc. Ant. Scot., vol. xiii. p. 254.

1491

P. S. A. S., vol. xxii. p. 25.

1492

"Brit. Barr.," p. 198.

1493

Journ. Ethn. Soc., vol. i. pl. i. 14.

1494

P. S. A. S., vol. xix. p. 10; vol. xxv. p. 498.

1495

Arch. Journ., vol. xxii. p. 243. "Brit. Barr.," p. 359.

1496

Trans. E. R. Ant. Soc., vol. i., 1893, p. 49.

1497

"The Bone Caves of Ojcow," 1884, pl. i. 7.

1498

"Cran. Brit.," vol. ii. pl. 58, p. 2.

1499

"Brit. Barr.," p. 158, and 41, where it is figured full size.

1500

Arch. Journ., vol. viii. 344.

1501

Journ. Ethnol. Soc., vol. ii. p. 414.

1502

Arch. Journ., vol. xxii. p. 243.

1503

Proc. Soc. Ant. Scot., vol. xiv. p. 221.

1504

"Brit. Barr.," p. 153, fig. 98.

1505

Proc. Soc. Ant. Scot., vol. vii. p. 102.

1506

Mat. vol. xvi. p. 239.

1507

Mem. Acc. R. delle Sc. di Turino, vol. xxvi. Tav. v. 1.

1508

Op. cit., Tav. viii. 20.

1509

Le Hon, "L'Homme foss.," 2nd ed., p. 184.

1510

De Gongora, "Ant. Preh. de And.," p. 78, fig. 92.

1511

"Brit. Barr.," p. 410.

1512

Nilsson. "Stone Age," p. 44. See Col. A. Lane-Fox, "Prim. Warfare," pt. II. p. 11.

1513

Arch. Cant., vol. xiv. p. 87. *Antiquary*, vol. xv. p. 234.

1514

Reliq. and Ill. Arch., vol. ii. p. 46.

1515

Yorks. Arch. and Top. Journ., 1869, figs. 12, 13, 16. *Journ. Ethn. Soc.*, vol. ii. p. 159.

1516

Journ. Ethn. Soc., vol. i. pl. i. 15, 17.

1517

Yorksh. Arch. and Top. Journ., 1868, fig. 46.

1518

Proc. Soc. Ant. Scot., vol. xxviii. p. 339.

1519

"Mém. sur les Restes d'Indust.," &c., pl. x. 6.

1520

Matériaux, vol. v. p. 249.

1521

Kindly communicated to me by the late Mr. Joseph Clarke, F.S.A.

1522

"Nuovi Cenni, &c.," Torino, 1862, pl. vi. 16.

1523

Rev. Arch., vol. xv. p. 17.

1524

"Anc. Mon. of Mississ. Vall.," p. 211, fig. 3.

1525

Proc. Soc. Ant., 2nd S., vol. vi. p. 34. *Arch. Journ.*, vol. xl. p. 323; xli. p. 50. *Journ. Anth. Inst.*, vol. vi. p. 37.

1526

Jones, "Ants. of Tenn." (Smithson. Coll.), p. 58.

1527

Journ. Anth. Inst., vol. i. p. xcvi. pl. i.; vol. xiii. p. 162.

1528

Matériaux, vol. v. p. 249.

1529

P. S. A. S., vol. ix. p. 239.

1530

Mem. Anthrop. Soc., vol. ii. p. 248. *P. S. A. S.*, vol. vi. p. 450.

1531

P. S. A. S., vol. ix. p. 239.

1532

Proc. Soc. Ant. Scot., vol. xxviii. p. 324.

1533

P. S. A. S., vol. xxiii. p. 204.

1534

P. S. A. S., vol. xxv. p. 499.

1535

"Stone Age," pl. x. 205.

1536

Arch. Journ., vol. xii. p. 285.

1537

Arch. Journ., vol. xi. p. 414; xvii. p. 171.

1538

"Cat.," p. 66, No. 18.

1539

Bateman, "Cat.," p. 66.

1540

Arch. Journ., vol. xi. p. 414; xvii. p. 171.

1541

Arch. Camb., 3rd. S., vol. vi. p. 138.

1542

"Flint Chips," p. 75.

1543

Proc. Soc. Ant., 2nd S., vol. v. p. 95.

1544

Proc. Soc. Ant., 2nd S., vol. v. p. 441. *Montg. Coll.*, vol. v. p. xxvi.; vi. p. 215; xii. p. 26; xiv. p. 278.

1545

Rooke Pennington, "Barrows and Bone-caves of Derbyshire," 1877, p. 62.

1546

P. S. A. S., vol. xi. p. 576.

1547

P. S. A. S., vol. xii p. 207.

1548

Arch. Journ., vol. xxix. p. 285.

1549

Otis Mason, *Rep. of U. S. Nat. Mus.* for 1890, Washington, 1892.

1550

P. 341.

1551

P. 299.

1552

"Cat. Ant. Soc. Ant.," p. 14. "Cat. A. I. Mus. Ed.," p. 7.

1553

Pl. ii. 15.

1554

Proc. Soc. Ant. Scot., vol. iii. p. 437; iv. p. 52.

1555

P. S. A. S., vol. xii. p. 271; xxix. p. 54.

1556

P. S. A. S., vol. xii. p. 270.

1557

Smith's "Preh. Man in Ayrshire," 1895, p. 45.

1558

"Preh. Ann.," vol. i. p. 184.

1559

"Statist. Account of Zetland," 1841, p. 112, *et seqq.*, quoted at length in *Mem. Anthrop. Soc. Lond.*, vol. ii. p. 315. The late Dr. Hunt appears to have thought that the passage referred to rude pestle-like stone implements such as he found in Orkney, and not to these knives.

1560

"Cat. Arch. Inst. Mus. Ed.," p. 7.

1561

See *P. S. A. S.*, vol. xi. p. 579.

1562

N. and Q., 4th. S., vol. xi. p. 302.

1563

Cong. préh. Stockholm, 1874, p. 177, *et seqq.*

1564

De Bonstetten, "Supp. au Rec. d'Ant. Suisses," pl. i. 1.

1565

Schoolcraft, "Ind. Tribes," vol. ii. pl. xlv. 1.

1566

Arch. Journ., vol. viii. p. 329. "Brist. Vol. Arch. Inst.," p. lix. *Proc. R. I. A.*, vol. v. p. 176.

1567

"Hor. Fer." p. 137.

1568

"Stone Age," p. 38, pl. iii. 65.

1569

Arch., vol. xliii. p. 413.

1570

"Hor. Fer.," pl. ii. 27.

1571

Arch. Journ., vol. xvii. p. 170.

1572

Proc. Soc. Ant., 2nd S., vol. vi. p. 73.

1573

Arch. Assoc. Journ., vol. vi. p. 441.

1574

Skelton's "Meyrick's Armour," vol. i. pl. xlvi. 5.

1575

Lond. and Midd. Notebook, vol. i. (1891), p. 21.

1576

Arch. Journ., vol. xvii. p. 170.

1577

Mat., vol. xi. p. 87.

1578

Jewitt's "Grave Mounds," fig. 155, where it is shown full size.

1579

"South Wilts," p. 172, pl. xix. "Cat. Devizes Mus.," No. 85B.

1580

"South Wilts," p. 164, pl. xvii. "Cat. Devizes Mus.," No. 84.

1581

"Vest. Ant. Derb.," p. 59. "Cran. Brit." pl. 41, p. 3. *Reliq.*, vol. iii. p. 177.

1582

"Ten Years' Dig.," p. 52.

1583

Ibid., p. 167. Bateman, "Cat.," p. 38.

1584

"Vest. Ant. Derb.," p. 5.

1585

"Ten Years' Dig.," p. 228. Bateman, "Cat.," p. 43.

1586

Arch. Assoc. Journ., vol. x. p. 177.

1587

Arch. Camb., 4th S., vol. ii. p. 327.

1588

March, 1797, p. 200.

1589

"Preh. Ann. of Scot.," vol. i. p. 182.

1590

P. S. A. S., vol. xxiii. p. 18.

1591

Smith, "Preh. Man in Ayrshire," 1895, p. 184.

1592

Wilde's "Cat. Mus. R. I. A.," p. 34.

1593

P. S. A. S., vol. xi. p. 170.

1594

Cazalis de Fondouce, "La Gr. sép. de St. J. d'Alcas," 1867, pl. i.

1595

Matériaux, vol. v. p. 321; viii. p. 39.

1596

Matériaux, vol. v. p. 538.

1597

Cong. Préh. Bruxelles, 1872, pl. 67, 3. Van Overloop, "Les Ages de la Pierre," pl. viii.

1598

Cong. Préh. Moscou, 1892, ii. p. 241.

1599

Mem. R. Acc. delle Sc. di Torino, xxvi. Tav. viii. 24. See also *Bull. di Pal. Ital.*, 1881, pl. vii.

1600

Arch. Journ. vol. liii. p. 46. See also *Mat.*, vol. ix. p. 24, and De Morgan, "Rech. sur les Or. de l'Égypte," 1896, p. 121.

1601

Zeitschr. für Ægypt. Sprache, &c., July, 1870. Wilkinson, "Anc. Egyptians," vol. iii. p. 262.

1602

P. S. A. S., vol. xxvi. p. 399.

1603

Zeitschr. für Æg. Sp., ibid.

1604

Journ. Anth. Inst., vol. xi. pl. xxxiii. See also vol. xiv. p. 56; *Proc. Soc. Ant.*, 2nd S., vol. vi., p. 21: and Petrie's "Hawara," 1889, pl. xxviii.

1605

Zeitsch. f. Ethn., vol. xxii., 1890, p. (516).

1606

Journ. Anth. Inst., vol. i. p. xcvi. pl. i. 3.

1607

See Fig. 1 p. 8.

1608

Archæologia, vol. liv. 391.

1609

"Musæum Metallicum," p. 156.

1610

Aarb. f. Oldk., 1879, p. 290.

1611

Proc. Soc. Ant., 2nd S., vol. vii. p. 328.

1612

Mat., vol. ix. p. 401, pl. vii. 9.

1613

Nature, vol. xii. p. 368.

1614

"Madsen," pl. xxxvi. 8.

1615

"Nord. Olds.," Fig. 51. *Mém. de la Soc. des Ants. du Nord.*, 1845–49, p. 139.

1616

Vol. xxii. p. 75.

1617

2nd S., vol. iii. p. 19, where it is erroneously stated to be only 5 inches in length.

1618

Proc. Soc. Ant., 2nd S., vol. iii. p. 210.

1619

Arch. Cant., vol. xiii. p. 124, xi. Payne's "Coll. Cant.," 1893, p. 3.

1620

P. S. A. S., vol. xxiii. p. 18.

1621

Keller, "Pfahlbauten," 6ter Ber., Taf. vii. 32.

1622

"Präh. Atlas," Wien, 1889, Taf. xiii.

1623

Cartailhac, "Mon. prim. des Iles Baléares," 1892, p. 54.

1624

Cong. Préh. Moscou, 1892, ii. p. 243.

1625

L'Anthrop., vol. vi., 1893, p. 12. De Baye, "C. R. du neuv. Congrès russe d'Arch.," 1893, p. 54.

1626

Arch. Journ., vol. liii. 1896 p. 46. See also *Zeitsch. f. Ethn.*, vol. xx., 1888, p. (209), (344); vol. xxiii., 1891, (p. 474), pl. vii. viii.

1627

"Naquada and Ballas," 1896, p. 60.

1628

J. De Morgan, "Recherches sur les Origines de l'Égypte. L'âge de la pierre et Les métaux," 1896, p. 115.

NOTES—CHAPTER XVI.

1629

Trans. Ethn. Soc., N. S., vol. iii. p. 266.

1630

See Lubbock, "Preh. Times," 4th ed., p. 478.

1631

Pliny, "Nat. Hist.," lib. vii. cap. 56.

1632

Herodotus, lib. iv. cap. 132; v. 49; vii. 61.

1633

"Sola in sagittis spes, quas inopiâ ferri ossibus asperant."—"Germ.," cap. 46.

1634

Smith's "Dict. of Ant." *s. v.*, Sagitta.

1635

Homer, "Il.," viii. 296.

1636

P. 396.

1637

"Prod. Nat. Hist. Scotiæ," pt. 2, lib. iv. c. vii.

1638

"Mus. Met.," lib. iv. c. xvii.

1639

P. 49.

1640

"Mus. Wormianum" (1655), p. 39.

1641

L. c. 85.

1642

"Mus. Met.," p. 604.

1643

"Nat. Hist.," xxxvii. c. 10.

1644

London, 1681.

1645

"Mus.," lib. i., sect. 3, c. xiii.

1646

"Mus. Mosc.," lib. ii. c. 1.

1647

Mus. Mosc. (1672), p. 148. See *Mat.*, vol. xi. p. 1.

1648

Proc. Soc. Ant. Scot., vol. iv. p. 66. In the *Theatrum Scotiæ* of Blaeuw's "Atlas," is a plate of arrow-heads found in Aberdeenshire. This has been pointed out to me by the late Dr. J. Hill Burton. See his "Hist. of Scot.," vol. i. p. 136 *n*.

1649

Reliquary, vol. viii. p. 207.

1650

"Cat.," pp. 8 and 127.

1651

"Nænia," pl. xxxiii. 6, p. 154. See Vallancey, "Coll. de Reb. Hibern.," N. xiii. pl. xi.

1652

Pt. iv. pl. iv. fig. 11.

1653

Vol. iv. p. 232, pl. xviii.

1654

"Cat. Mus. R. I. A.," p. 19. See also *Arch. Assoc. Journ.*, vol. xxi. p. 323, and xxii. p. 316.

1655

Journ. R. S. A. of Irel., 5th S., vol. v. p. 61.

1656

Folklore Record, vol. iv. p. 112. *Journ.*, vol. ii. p. 260. See also "Folklore of the Northern Counties," p. 185.

1657

Pennant's "Tour," vol. i. p. 115. "Stat. Account of Scotland," vol. x. p. 15; xxi. 148. Collins' "Ode on Pop. Superst. of the Highlands." "Allan Ramsay's Poems," ed. 1721, p. 224. Brand's "Pop. Ant.," 1841, vol. ii. p. 285.

1658

Reliquary, vol. viii. p. 207.

1659

"Itin. Cur.," (ed. 1776), vol. ii. p. 28.

1660

"Preh. Ann. of Scot.," vol. i. p. 178, *et seqq*.

1661

Pepys' "Diary and Cor." (ed. 1849), vol. v. p. 366.

1662

See Nilsson's "Stone Age," p. 197. Wilson's "Preh. Ann. of Scot.," vol. i. p. 180.

1663

Mat., vol. xi. p. 540.

1664

Gastaldi, "Lake Habitations of Northern and Central Italy," Chambers's transl., p. 6.

1665

Nicolucci, "Di Alcune Armi ed Utensili in Pietra," 1863, p. 2.

1666

Mortillet, *Mat.*, vol. iii. p. 319.

1667

Archivio per l'Antropologia, vol. i. pl. xv. 8.

1668

"L'âge de Pierre dans les Souvenirs et superstitions populaires," Paris, 1877.

1669

Bull. di Paletn. It., 1876, pl. iv. 7.

1670

A. J. Evans, "Bosnia and Herzegovina," 1876, p. 289; 1877, p. 291.

1671

2nd Ann. Rep. of Bur. of Ethn., 1880–1. *Mat.*, 3rd S., ii., 1885, p. 532.

1672

Rev. Arch., vol. xv. p. 145. Leake, "Demi of Attica," p. 100. Dodwell's "Class. Tour," vol. ii. p. 159. *Arch. Journ.*, vol. vii. p. 86.

1673

See Smith's "Geog. Dict.," vol. ii. p. 268.

1674

Lib. vii. cap. 69.

1675

"II.," xiii. 650.

1676

"II.," v. 393.

1677

IV. 81.

1678

See De Morgan, *op. cit.* p. 121.

1679

Academy, Oct. 27, 1894.

1680

Archæologia Scotica, vol. i. p. 389.

1681

This word, still in use in Scotland for the barbs of a fishing-spear or hook, is a good old English term derived from the Saxon piðer. Withther-hooked = barbed:—

"This dragoun hadde a long taile

That was withther-hooked saun faile."

"Arthour and Merlin," p. 210.

Halliwell, "Dict. of Arch. and Prov. Words," *s. v.*

1682

Journ. R. U. Serv. Inst.

1683

Journ. Anth. Inst., vol. vi. p. 482.

1684

Journ. R. S. A. of Irel., 5th S., vol. v. p. 41.

1685

Schoolcraft, "Ind. Tribes," vol. i. p. 212.

1686

Wood's "Nat. Hist. of Man," vol. i. p. 284.

1687

Proc. Soc. Ant., 2nd S., vol. ii. p. 429.

1688

Proc. Soc. Ant., 2nd S., vol. iii. p. 324. *Reliquary*, vol. vi. p. 185.

1689

Arch. Assoc. Journ., vol. iv. p. 103.

1690

Reliq., N. S., vol. iii. pl. iv. 8.

1691

Op. cit., p. 224.

1692

Proc. Soc. Ant. Scot., vol. xix. p. 350.

1693

P. S. S. A., vol. xxv. p. 499.

1694

See Wakeman, "Arch. Hib.," p. 270.

1695

Cong. Préh. Moscou, 1892, vol. ii. p. 240.

1696

Schoolcraft, "Ind. Tribes," vol. i. pl. xxvi. 4.

1697

Arch. Journ., vol. xvii. p. 261.

1698

Arch. Journ., vol. xxv. p. 156.

1699

Vol. vi. pl. xvi. 5.

1700

Journ. Ethnol. Soc., vol. i. p. 5.

1701

P. S. A. S., vol. vii. p. 500.

1702

P. S. A. S., vol. ix. p. 246.

1703

P. S. A. S., vol. xi. p. 586.

1704

Proc. Soc. Ant., 2nd S., vol. iii. p. 170.

1705

A. C. Smith, "Ants. of N. Wilts," p. 182.

1706

Proc. Soc. Ant., 2nd S., vol. ii. p. 278; iii. p. 168.

1707

Reliquary, vol. v. p. 28.

1708

Wilts Arch. Mag., vol. xix. p. 71. A. C. Smith's "Ants. of N. Wilts," p. 197.

1709

Reliquary, vol. vi. p. 185.

1710

Warne's "Celtic Tum. of Dorset," *Errata*, pp. 15 and 27.

1711

"Ten Years' Dig.," p. 148.

1712

See *Proc. Soc. Ant.*, 2nd S., vol. i. p. 20. *Arch. Journ.*, vol. x. p. 362. *Proc. Soc. Ant. Scot.*, vol. iii. p. 362; iv. 54, 377, 553; v. 13, 185; vi. 41, 208, 234; vii. 500; viii. 10.

1713

P. S. A. S., vol. xiv. pp. 111, 129.

1714

P. S. A. S., vol. xxv. p. 499.

1715

P. S. A. S., vol. xix. p. 251.

1716

Arch. Cant., vol. xiii. p. 124.

1717

Proc. Soc. Ant., 2nd S., vol. i. p. 74. *Arch. Journ.*, vol. xvii. p. 171.

1718

Proc. Soc. Ant. Scot., vol. xix. p. 251.

1719

Tr. Lanc. and Chesh. Arch. Soc., vol. iv. p. 306.

1720

Arch. Journ., vol. xviii. p. 75.

1721

"Manx Note-book," vol. i. (1885) p. 72.

1722

Trans. Biol. Soc., L'pool., vol. viii., 1894, pl. xii.

1723

Mortillet, *Mat.*, vol. ii. p. 89.

1724

Arch. Assoc. Journ., vol. iv. p. 103.

1725

Arch. Journ., vol. xii. p. 285. "Cat. Mus. Arch. Inst. at Ed.," p. 40.

1726

Trans. Lanc. and Chesh. Arch. Soc., vol. iv. p. 306.

1727

Trans. Herts Nat. Hist. Soc., vol. viii., 1896, pl. xii. 1.

1728

Arch., vol. viii. p. 429, pl. xxx.

1729

Arch. Camb., 2nd S., vol. ii. p. 292.

1730

P. 579.

1731

Arch. Journ., vol. xvii. p. 60.

1732

Miller and Skertchly, "Fenland," p. 579.

1733

"South Wilts," pl. xxii. p. 183. "Cat. Devizes Mus.," No. 105.

1734

"The Barrow Diggers," p. 75, pl. ii. 7.

1735

"South Wilts," pl. xxxiv.

1736

"The Barrow Diggers," pl. ii. p. 6.

1737

Ib., pl. xxxiv. "Cat. Devizes Mus.," No. 203.

1738

"Salisb. Vol. of Arch. Inst.," p. 94.

1739

Proc. Soc. Ant., 2nd S., vol. vi. p. 398.

1740

Assoc. franç. pour l'avancem. des Sciences, Nancy, 1881, 16 août.

1741

Wilson's "Preh. Ann. of Scot.," p. 127 (2nd ed. p. 182. pl. ii. 15). "Cat. Mus. Arch. Inst. Ed.," p. 6, Fig. 9. For the loan of this block I am indebted to Messrs. Macmillan and Co.

1742

P. S. A. S., vol. ix. pp. 240, 262.

1743

P. S. A. S., vol. xix. p. 251.

1744

P. S. A. S., vol. xxiii. p. 93.

1745

P. S. A. S., vol. xxvii. p. 355.

1746

Smith, "Preh. Man in Ayrsh." (1895), p. 105.

1747

"Preh. Ann. of Scot.," vol. i. pl. ii. 14.

1748

"Preh. Ann. of Scot.," p. 182.

1749

"Acc. of Inst., &c., of S. A. Scot.," p. 389.

1750

P. S. A. S., vol. xii. p. 183.

1751

"Tour. in Scot.," vol. i. p. 156, pl. xxi.

1752

Vol. xvii. p. 19.

1753

Proc. Soc. Ant. Scot., vol. xii. p. 62.

1754

Proc. Soc. Ant., 2nd S., vol. ii. p. 294.

1755

P. S. A. S., vol. vi. p. 208.

1756

Ib., vol. vi. p. 234.

1757

Ib., vol. iv. p. 54; vii. 105.

1758

Ib., vol. viii. p. 10.

1759

Ib., vol. vi. p. 89.

1760

Ib., vol. iv. p. 54; v. 185.

1761

P. S. A., 2nd S., vol. iii. p. 19.

1762

Ib., 2nd S., vol. i. p. 20.

1763

P. S. A. S., vol. iv. p. 54; v. 13.

1764

Arch. Journ., vol. x. p. 362.

1765

Proc. Soc. Ant., 2nd S., vol. i. p. 20.

1766

P. S. A. S., vol. vi. pp. 41, 234.

1767

Ib., vol. iii. p. 362.

1768

Ib., vol. v. p. 326; iii. 438; viii. 50; xiv. 267; xxiv. 13.

1769

P. S. A. S., vol. xxvii. p. 360. See also "Smith's Preh. Man in Ayrshire," (1895).

1770

Arch. Scot., vol. iii. App. 135. *P. S. A. S.*, vol. xii. p. 270.

1771

P. S. A. S., vol. iv. p. 55.

1772

Ib., vol. iv. pp. 67, 377.

1773

Wilson's "Preh. Ann. of Scot.," vol. i. p. 182.

1774

P. S. A. S., vol. xxi. p. 133.

1775

P. S. A. S., vol. xiv. p. 267; vol. xxiv. p. 13. For a list of Kincardineshire arrow-heads see vol. ix. pp. 461, 499; xi. p. 26.

1776

P. S. A. S., vol. xi. p. 585.

1777

P. S. A. S., vol. xxviii. p. 341.

1778

"Cat. Arch. Inst. Mus. Ed.," pp. 11, 12, 14, 16, 17, 20.

1779

P. S. A., 1st S., vol. iii. p. 224.

1780

P. S. A. S., vol. iii. p. 490.

1781

Geologist, vol. i. p. 162.

1782

P. S. A. S., vol. i. p. 42; vol. xix. p. 11; xxv. 500.

1783

Ib., vol. i. pp. 67, 190.

1784

Arch. Journ., vol. xvii. p. 60.

1785

Arch., vol. xxxi. p. 304. "York Vol. of Arch. Inst.," p. 1.

1786

Hoare's "South Wilts," pl. xxx.

1787

Reliquary, vol. iii. p. 177. "Cran. Brit.," vol. ii. pl. 41, p. 3.

1788

Suss. Arch. Coll., vol. xiii. p. 309.

1789

Tr. Hist. Soc. Lanc. and Chesh., N. S., vol. viii. p. 131.

1790

Arch. Camb., 3rd. S., vol. iii. p. 303.

1791

Hoare's "South Wilts," the "Barrow Diggers," Bateman's "Vestiges," *Arch.*, vol. xxx. p. 333; vol. xliii. pp. 418, 420; vol. lii. pp. 48, 53, 61. *Wilts Arch. Mag.*, vol. vi. p. 319.

1792

Vol. xiv. pl. iii.

1793

Tr. Lanc. and Chesh. Arch. Soc., vol. ii. pl. i. *Trans. Manch. Geol. Soc.*, vol. xiii. p. 141; xiv. p. 284.

1794

Op. cit., viii. p. 127. *Trans. Manch. Geol. Soc.*, vol. xvi. p. 287.

1795

For Yorkshire arrow-heads see *Yorksh. Arch. and Top. Journ.*, vol. i. (1870), p. 4.

1796

Proc. Soc. Ant., 2nd S., vol. i. p. 64.

1797

Arch., vol. xxxvii. 369.

1798

Surr. Arch. Coll., vol. xi.

1799

Suss. Arch. Coll., vol. xxvii. p. 177.

1800

Tr. Dev. Assoc., vol. xx. p. 44.

1801

Op. cit., xxvi. p. 53.

1802

Arch. Journ., vol. xx. p. 372.

1803

Bateman's "Cat.," 47, *et seqq.* See also the York, Norwich, and Lincoln Volumes of the Arch. Inst.

1804

Harrison's "Geol. of Leic. and Rutl.," p. 49.

1805

Rel. and Ill. Archæol., vol. ii. p. 45. *Journ. Roy. Inst. of Cornw.* vol. xiii. p. 92.

1806

Arch. Journ., vol. x. p. 354.

1807

Op. cit., vol. xiv. p. 79.

1808

Op. cit., vol. xvi. p. 151.

1809

Arch. Assoc. Journ., vol. i. p. 309.

1810

"Trans. Arch. Assoc. at Glouc.," p. 94.

1811

A. A. J., vol. iv. p. 152.

1812

Op. cit., vol. xviii. p. 272.

1813

Op. cit., vol. iv., p. 396.

1814

Arch., vol. ix. p. 100.

1815

Yorksh. Arch. and Top. Journ., 1868, fig. 5.

1816

P. S. A. S., vol. xiv. p. 267; xxiv. p. 13.

1817

P. S. A. S., vol. xi. p. 585.

1818

Arch., vol. lii. p. 63.

1819

"Kahun, &c." (1890), p. 21, pl. xvi.

1820

Bull. di Pal. Ital., 1877. pl. v. 25.

1821

Wilde, "Cat. Mus. R. I. A.," p. 15, fig. 7.

1822

Proc. Cotteswold Nat. Field Club, vol. x., 1889–90, p. 22, pl. i.

1823

Proc Soc. Ant., March 10, 1897.

1824

P. S. A. S., vol. vii. p. 500.

1825

P. S. A. S., vol. xxi. p. 201; xxii. p. 51. *Journ. R. Hist. and Arch. Assoc. of Ireland*, 4th S., vol. viii., 1887–88, p. 241.

1826

Archivio per l'Anthrop., &c., vol. i. pl. xii. 16.

1827

Wood, "Nat. Hist. of Man," vol. i. p. 679.

1828

Ann. de la Soc. Arch. de Namur, 1859, pl. ii. 9.

1829

Arch. Journ., vol. liii., 1896, p. 46, pl. iv. 3, 4. De Morgan, *op. cit.*, p. 124.

1830

Op. cit., pl. vi. 11.

1831

P. S. A. S., vol. ix. pp. 240, 262; xi. p. 510.

1832

Rev. Arch., vol. xv. p. 367.

1833

"L'Arch. Préh.," p. 191, ed. 1888, p. 253. *Rev. Arch.*, vol. xxvii., 1874, pl. xi. p. 401. *Mat.*, vol. viii. pl. ii. *Bull. Soc. Anthrop.*, 19 Dec., 1889.

1834

Bull. Soc. Ant. de Bruxelles, vol. vi. pl. i.

1835

"Afbild.," pl. xxii. 18, 19. See also *Aarb. f. Oldk.*, 1890, p. 325, 329.

1836

"Stone Age," pl. ii. 36, 37.

1837

"Antiq. Tidskr. för Sverige," vol. iii. fig. 3.

1838

"Mat. paletnol. dell' Umbria," pl. ix.

1839

Zeitsch. f. Ethn., vol. xv. p. 361; xvi. p. (118).

1840

Siret, p. 10.

1841

Cartailhac, pp. 53, 173.

1842

Riv. Arch. della Prov. di Como, Dec. 1879.

1843

Arch. per l'Ant. e al Etn., vol. xiii. (1883), Tav. i.

1844

Arch. Journ., vol. ix. p. 118. Lee's "Isca Silurum," p. 112.

1845

Herodian, lib. i. c. 15.

1846

Arch. Journ., vol. x. p. 247.

1847

Arch. Journ., vol. x. p. 69.

1848

Arch. Assoc. Journ., vol. xvii. p. 19.

1849

Ann. de la Soc. Arch. de Namur, 1859, p. 361.

1850

Rev. Arch., vol. xxxiv. p. 183.

1851

Cong. Préh. Lisbonne, 1880, p. 372.

1852

See also *Nature*, vol. xxiii. p. 218.

1853

Berliner Blätter, vol. iii. p. 172.

1854

Num. Chron., N. S., vol. iii. p. 54.

1855

"South Wilts," p. 239.

1856

Vol. xxx. p. 460.

1857

See "Cran. Brit.," pl. 52, p. 9.

1858

"Vest. of the Ant. of Derbysh.," p. 48.

1859

"Cran. Brit.," vol. ii. pl. xlii. p. 3. *Wilts Arch. and N. H. Mag.*, vol. iii. p. 185.

1860

Arch., vol. viii. p. 429; *supra*, p. 383.

1861

"Cat. Arch. Inst. Mus. Ed.," p. 11. Wilson, "Preh. Ann.," vol. i. p. 224.

1862

Arch., vol. xxxvii. p. 369.

1863

Arch. Journ., vol. xvi. p. 151; xxii. p. 249. "Ten Years' Diggings," pp. 60, 95, 96, 116, 127, 167, 178, &c. *Arch. Assoc. Journ.*, vol. iv. p. 103; vii. 215. *Arch.*, vol. xxxi. p. 304. "Salisb. Vol. Arch. Inst.," pp. 25–105. Hoare's "South Wilts," pp. 182–211. Greenwell's "British Barrows," *passim*.

1864

"Ten Years' Dig.," p. 223. *Arch. Assoc. Journ.*, vol. iv. p. 103.

1865

"Vest. Ant. Derb.," p. 59. "Cran. Brit.," vol. ii. pl. 41, p. 3.

1866

A. A. J., vol. iv. p. 105.

1867

"T. Y. D.," p. 116. *A. A. J.*, vol. vii. p. 215.

1868

For a comparison of arrow-heads from different countries see also Westropp's "Prehistoric Phases," pl. i.

1869

Nature, vol. xxiii. p. 218.

1870

Dr. Mantell, however, found a flint arrow-head in a barrow near Lewes.—"York Vol. of Arch. Inst.," p. 1.

1871

"Cat. Mus. R. I. A.," p. 19 *seqq.*

1872

"Archæol. Hibern." (1891), p. 269 *seqq.*

1873

Arch. Assoc. Journ., vol. xxiv. p. 40.

1874

Rev. Arch., 3rd S., vol. xvi. pl. xvii. p. 304.

1875

Cochet, "Seine Inférieure," 2nd ed., p. 528.

1876

"Epoques Antédil. et Celt. du Poitou," p. 102, pl. iv. *bis.* 3, 4, 5.

1877

De Rochebrune, "Mém. sur les Restes d'Industrie, &c.," pl. x. 8, 9.

1878

Chantre, "Etudes Paléoéthn.," pl. xiii. 7.

1879

Watelet, "L'Age de Pierre, &c.," pl. iv. 2. Coll. Caranda, Moreau, 1877.

1880

Perrault, "Note sur un Foyer, &c.," Châlons, 1870, pl. ii.

1881

Rev. d'Anthrop., vol. iv. p. 258.

1882

Matériaux, vol. xi. p. 207.

1883

De Baye, "Arch. préh.," 1888, pp. 225, 255, 291, 292.

1884

Bull. de la Soc. d'Etude des sc. nat. de Nîmes, 1894.

1885

Mortillet, "Mus. préh.," pl. xliii. *et seqq.*

1886

Journ. Anth. Inst., vol. ii. p. 68.

1887

Rev. Arch., vol. xx. p. 359.

1888

De Rochebrune, pl. xiii. 2.

1889

Cazalis de Fondouce, "La Pierre polie dans l'Aveyron," pl. i. 9 and 10; pl. iv. 2, 3, &c. *Trans. Preh. Cong.*, 1867, p. 189; 1868, p. 351. Mortillet, *Matériaux*, vol. ii. p. 146; vol. iii. p. 231.

1890

Rev. Arch., vol. xv. p. 364.

1891

Cazalis de Fondouce, "All. couv. de la Provence," 2nd Mém. pl. ii. 18. *Mat.*, vol. xii. p. 452, pl. xii. 18.

1892

Matériaux, vol. v. p. 395. Perrault, *op. cit.*

1893

Watelet, "Age de Pierre dans le Dépt. de l'Aisne," pl. iv. 4.

1894

Matériaux, vol. v. p. 249.

1895

In the Wessenbergische Sammlung, Constance.

1896

Keller's "Pfahlbauten," and "Lake-dwellings," *passim.* Desor's "Palafittes," p. 17. Troyon, "Hab. Lac.," pl. v. Ant. Lac. du Mus. de Lausanne, pl. ix.

1897

"Les âges de la pierre," pl. vi. and vii.

1898

Keller, *op. cit.*, 4ter Ber. Taf. i. and ii. Strobel, "Avanzi Preromani," Parma, 1863, 1864.

1899

"Di Aleune armi ed utensile in pietra." *Atti della R. Accad. delle Scienze*, Napoli, 1863 and 1867.

1900

Gastaldi, "Lake Habs. in Italy," p. 7. "Nuovi Cenni, &c.," Torino, 1862, p. 10. *Mem. Acc. R. di Sc. di Torino*, vol. xxvi. (1869).

1901

Archivio per l'Antropol, &c., vol. i. p. 457.

1902

Mortillet, *Matériaux*, vol. ii. p. 87. "Promenades," p. 152. A. Angelucci, "Le Palafitte del Lago di Varese" (1871); and Ragazzoni, "Uomo preh. di Como" (1878).

1903

Mortillet, *Matériaux*, p. 89.

1904

"Alterth. uns. heid. Vorz.," vol. i., Heft vi. pl. i. 9. "Hohenz. Samml.," Taf. xliii.

1905

Mortillet, *Mat.*, vol. iii. p. 319.

1906

Archivio per l'Ant. e la Etn., vol. ix. p. 289. See also Marinoni, "Abit. lacust. in Lombardia," Milan (1868), p. 20.

1907

Dodwell, "Class. Tour in Greece," vol. ii. p. 159. Leake, "Demi of Attica," p. 100.

1908

F. Lenormant in *Rev. Arch.*, vol. xv. p. 146.

1909

Schliemann, "Tiryns," (1886), pp. 78, 174.

1910

"Mycenae," (Murray, 1878), p. 272. See also pp. 76 and 158.

1911

"Antigüedades Prehistóricas de Andalusia," p. 104.

1912

"Les premiers Ages du Métal, &c.," Anvers, 1887.

1913

"Ant. de Algarve," 1886. Cartailhac, p. 88, 159, 170.

1914

"Alterth. u. h. Vorzeit," vol. i. Heft vi. pl. i. "Hohenz. Samml.," Taf. xliii. 17.

1915

"Hohenz. Samml.," Taf. xliii. 25.

1916

"Frederico-Francisceum," 1837, Tab. xxvii.

1917

Von Sacken, "Grabfeld von Hallstatt," p. 38.

1918

Kenner, "Arch. Funde, i. d. Oesterr. Mon.," 1867, p. 41.

1919

O. Rygh, "Norske Oldsager," (1881), No. 76.

1920

Conf. Madsen's "Afbildninger," pl. xxxvii. and xxxix. Worsaae, "Nord. Oldsager," fig. 68 *et seqq.* Nilsson's "Stone Age," pl. iii. and v. *Antiq. Tidskrift för Sverige*, 1864, pl. xxiii.

1921

Foreningen tal Norske Fortidsmindesmerkers Bevaring, Aarsber., 1867, pl. i.; 1868, pl. iii. 8.

1922

Nilsson, "Stone Age," pl. iii. 59.

1923

P. S. A. S., vol. xxx., 1896, p. 291.

1924

L'Anthropologie, vol. vi. (1895), p. 14.

1925

Bonstetten, "Essai sur les dolmens," pl. iv. *Zeitsch. f. Ethn.*, vol. xvii. p. (93).

1926

L'Anthropologie, vol. v. (1894), p. 538.

1927

Rev. Arch., vol. xlii. pl. x. p. 1.

1928

Arch. Soc. Journ., vol. xvii. p. 74.

1929

Journ. As. Soc. Bengal, vol. lvii. 1889, p. 392, pl. iv. 6, 7.

1930

Quart. Journ. Geol. Soc., vol. xxv. p. 35.

1931

Proc. Soc. Ant., 2nd S., vol. i. p. 322.

1932

Schoolcraft, "Ind. Tribes," vol. i. pl. xvii. 9.

1933

Rev. Arch., vol. xxii. p. 378. *Brit. Assoc. Rep.*, 1871.

1934

Proc. Soc. Ant., 2nd S., vol. v. p. 330.

1935

La Nature, 25 juillet, 1896. *L'Anthrop.*, vol. vii., 1896, p. 571.

1936

Chantre, "Le Caucase," (1885), pl. i. *Zeitsch. f. Ethn.*, 1885, Supp., pl. viii.

1937

Journ. R. As. S., 1876, p. 425. *Mitth. Anth. Ges. in Wien*, 1884, N. S., vol. iv. p. (28).

1938

Trans. Preh. Congress, 1868, p. 266. See also *Bull. de la Soc. Roy. des Ant. du Nord*, 1843–45, p. 26. *Journ. Anth. Inst.*, vol. x. p. 395, pl. xviii. *Proc. Soc. Ant.*, 2nd S., vol. vi. p. 15. *Zeitsch. f. Ethn.*, vol. xxiv., 1892, p. (432). *Matériaux*, vol. viii. p. 92; xiv., p. 32. T. Kanda, "Anc. St. Impts. of Japan," (Tokio, 1884).

1939

Journ. Anth. Inst., vol. v. p. 241, pl. xi.

1940

Douglas, "Nænia Brit.," pl. xxxiii. 8. See Squier and Davis, "Anc. Mon. of Miss. Valley," p. 212. Schoolcraft, "Ind. Tribes," vol. i. pl. xvii., xviii.; vol. ii. pl. xxxix.

1941

Schoolcraft, *op. cit.*, vol. i. p. 77. Catlin, "N. A. Ind.," vol. i. pl. xii. See also *Nature*, vol. vi. pp. 392, 413, 515; xi. pp. 90, 215. Gerard Fowke, "Stone Art," *13th Ann. Rep. Bureau of Ethn.* (1891–2), 1896. *P. S. A. S.*, vol. xxiv. p. 396. Abbott's "Primitive Industry," (Salem, Mass., 1881).

1942

"Conquista de Mejico," bk. iii. chap. 14.

1943

Lubbock, "Preh. Times," 4th ed. p. 107. Douglas, "Nænia Brit.," pl. xxxiii. 9, 10.

1944

Strobel, "Mat. di Paletnologia comparata," Parma, 1868. *Journ. Anth. Inst.*, vol. iv. p. 311, pl. xxiii. Nadailhac, "l'Amér. préh." (1863), pp. 27, 57.

1945

"Idle Days in Patagonia," 1893, p. 39.

1946

Arch. Journ., vol. xxxviii. p. 429.

1947

"Ill. of Brit. Ant. from objects found in South America, 1869," p. 89.

1948

See also *Mat.*, vol. xiv. p. 382.

1949

Camb. Ant. Comm., vol. iv. p. 13.

1950

"Method of Fossils" (1728), p. 43.

1951

"Cat. Mus. R. I. A.," p. 254, fig. 164.

1952

Journ. R. H. and A. A. of Ireland, 4th S. vol. vii., 1885, p. 126.

1953

P. S. A. S., vol. xi. p. 509.

1954

"Pfahlbauten," 2ter Ber. Taf. i. 5. "Lake-dwellings," pl. xxxix. 15. It is curiously like an arrow of the Zoreisch Indians, figured *Mitth. d. Ant. Gesells. in Wien*, 1893, p. 119.

1955

Mortillet, *Mat.*, vol. ii. p. 512. Mackie, "Nat. Hist. Rep.," vol. i. p. 137. "Mus. Préh.," fig. 406.

1956

Le Hon, "L'homme foss.," 2nd ed., p. 184.

1957

"Afbildninger," pl. xxii. 19.

1958

See p. 369.

1959

Proc., vol. iv. p. 298.

1960

"Preh. Times," 4th ed., p. 107. "Nat. Hist. of Man," vol. ii. p. 648.

1961

Wood, "Nat. Hist. of Man," vol. i. p. 103.

1962

Ib., vol. i. p. 284.

1963

One is figured in *Trans. Lanc. and Chesh. Arch. Soc.*, vol. iv. p. 369.

1964

"Mus. Wormianum," 1655, p. 350.

1965

"Scut. Herculis," v. 134.

1966

"Iliad," v. 171.

1967

Smith's "Dict. of Ant.," p. 1002.

1968

Lib. vii. cap. 92.

1969

Proc. Soc. Ant. Scot., vol. i. p. 85. *Nature*, vol. x. p. 245.

NOTES—CHAPTER XVII.

1970

P. S. A. S., vol. xv. p. 5.

1971

P. S. A. S., vol. xi. p. 25.

1972

P. S. A. S., vol. xix. p. 351.

1973

Tr. Dev. Assoc., vol. xv. p. 138.

1974

Arch., xliii. p. 437, fig. 136.

1975

Proc. Soc. Ant. Scot., vol. ix. p. 356.

1976

Vol. xxii. p. 246, 101 *note*.

1977

Yorksh. Arch. and Top. Journ., 1868.

1978

P. 40, fig. 24.

NOTES—CHAPTER XVIII.

1979

Arch., vol. xxxii. p. 96. *Proc. Soc. Ant.*, vol. i. p. 157.

1980

Arch. Assoc. Journ., vol. xx. p. 73. See also "Flint Chips," p. 302.

1981

"Stone Age," p. 49.

1982

"Sports and Pastimes," ed. 1845, p. 74.

1983

"Stone Age," p. 49.

1984

1 Sam. xvii. 43.

1985

Keller's "Lake-dwellings," pl. lxxxvi. 2.

1986

"Troy and its Remains," (1878), p. 101.

1987

"Stone Age," pl. v. 115.

1988

"Lake-dwellings," p. 135.

1989

"Cat. Mus. R. I. A.," pp. 18, 74.

1990

Engelhardt, "Nydam Mosefundet," pl. xiii. 65.

1991

Wilson, "Preh. Ann. of Scot.," vol. i. p. 197.

1992

"Preh. Times," 4th ed., p. 105.

1993

"Stone Age," p. 51.

1994

Yorksh. Arch. and Top. Journ., 1868.

1995

Ellis, "Polyn. Researches," vol. i. p. 291.

1996

"Preh. Ann. of Scot.," vol. i. p. 195. I am indebted to Messrs. Macmillan & Co. for the loan of this cut.

1997

Arch. Assoc. Journ., vol. xvii. p. 20.

1998

Proc. Soc. Ant. Scot., vol. vii. p. 102.

1999

Trans. Lanc. and Chesh. A. A., vol. iii. p. 255.

2000

P. S. A. S., vol. ix. p. 393.

2001

Smith's "Preh. Man in Ayrshire," 1895, p. 105.

2002

Proc. Soc. Ant. Scot., vol. vi. p. 11.

2003

"Cat. Arch. Inst. Mus. Ed.," p. 14.

2004

Report Montrose Nat. Hist. and Ant. Soc., 1868.

2005

Proc. Soc. Ant. Scot., vol. v. p. 340.

2006

Ib., vol. iv. pp. 186, 292; vii. p. 209.

2007

Wilson, "Preh. Ann. Scot.," vol. i. p. 195.

2008

P. S. A. S., vol. xi. pp. 29, 313.

2009

Arch. Journ., vol. xi. p. 58.

2010

Proc. Soc. Ant. Scot., vol. iii. p. 439. Wilson, "Preh. Ann. of Scot.," vol. i. pl. iii. Photographs of three of the faces are given in the *Reliquary and Illust. Archæol.*, vol. iii. (1897) p. 103, *q.v.*

2011

Arch., vol. lii. p. 14, pl. i. and ii.

2012

Trans. Dev. Assoc., vol. xii. p. 124.

2013

Worsaae, "Nord. Olds.," fig. 87, 88.

2014

Report Montrose N. H. and Ant. Soc., 1868.

2015

P. S. A. S., vol. xi. p. 56.

2016

Arch. Assoc. Journ., vol. xvii. p. 20.

2017

Tylor, "Early Hist. of Mank.," p. 179.

2018

Klemm, "Cultur-Gesch.," vol. ii. p. 17. "Azara," vol. ii. p. 46. Catlin's "Last Rambles," p. 265. "Cult.-Wiss.," vol. i. p. 55.

2019

Lubbock, "Preh. Times," 4th ed., p. 547. Falkner's "Patagonia," p. 130. A set of these Patagonian *bolas* is engraved by the Rev. J. G. Wood, "Nat. Hist. of Man," vol. ii. p. 529.

2020

See Ratzel, "Völkerk.," vol. ii. (1888), p. 664.

2021

Skelton's "Meyrick's Arm.," pl. xciii. 1.

2022

Klemm's "Cultur-Wiss.," vol. i. p. 129. "Cult.-Gesch.," vol. x. pl. iii. 4.

2023

"Anc. Mon. Mississ. Valley," p. 219.

2024

The same name, *pogamagan*, is applied by the Indians of the Mackenzie River to a different form. See "Reliq. Aquit.," p. 52.

2025

"Ind. Tribes," vol. i. pl. xv.

NOTES—CHAPTER XIX.

2026

"Preh. Ann. of Scot.," vol. i. p. 223.

2027

Proc. Soc. Ant. Scot., vol. vi. p. 233. The Evantown bracer is shown on a larger scale in *P. S. A. S.*, vol. xvii. p. 454; and Anderson's "Scotl. in Pagan Times," p. 15.

2028

Proc. Soc. Ant. Scot., vol. ii. p. 429. "Cat. Mus. Arch. Inst. Ed.," p. 20.

2029

P. S. A. S., vol. xiii. p. 255.

2030

Wilson, "P. A. of S.," vol. i. p. 76. "Cat. Mus. A. I. Ed.," p. 11.

2031

Arch., vol. viii. p. 429, pl. xxx.

2032

Wiltshire Arch. Mag., vol. x. (1867), pl. vi.

2033

Wiltsh. Arch. Mag., vol. iii. p. 186. "Cran. Brit.," vol. ii. pl. 42, p. 3. *Arch.*, vol. xliii. p. 429, fig. 120.

2034

Arch., vol. lii. p. 56.

2035

Arch., vol. xliii. p. 428.

2036

Arch. Journ., vol. vi. p. 409. Allies' "Worcestersh.," p. 142. *Arch. Journ.*, vol. xviii. p. 160.

2037

Proc. Soc. Ant., 2nd S., vol. v. p. 272. *Arch.*, vol. xliii. p. 429, fig. 122.

2038

"South Wilts," p. 103. *Arch.*, vol. xliii. p. 429, fig. 121. "Cat. Devizes Mus.," No. 63.

2039

"Cat. Devizes Mus.," No. 232.

2040

Hoare's "South Wilts," p. 44.

2041

Arch. Journ., vol. vi. p. 319.

2042

Proc. Soc. Ant., 2nd S., vol. x. p. 29. Payne's "Coll. Cant.," p. 12.

2043

Arch. Assoc. Journ., vol. xxxiii. p. 126.

2044

Wilson, "P. A. of S.," vol. i. p. 223. I am indebted to Messrs. Macmillan & Co. for the use of this cut.

2045

P. S. A. S., vol. ix. p. 537. Anderson, "Scotl. in Pagan Times," p. 15.

2046

P. S. A. S., vol. xxvii. p. 11.

2047

P. S. A. S., vol. xi. p. 586.

2048

P. S. A. S., vol. xiii. p. 73.

2049

Trans. Preh. Cong., 1868, pl. viii. 2.

2050

P. Salmon, "L'homme," 1886, p. 279.

2051

Siret's "Album," *passim*.

2052

Hoare's "South Wilts," p. 182. "Cat. Devizes Mus.," No. 96, 19A.

2053

Hoare's "South Wilts," p. 99. "Cat. Devizes Mus.," No. 53.

2054

Arch. Journ., vol. vi. p. 319. "Cran. Brit.," vol. i. p. 80.

2055

"Cat. Mus. Arch. Inst. Ed.," p. 11.

2056

Wilson, "P. A. of S.," vol. i. p. 224.

2057

"Anc. Mon. Mississ. Valley," p. 237.

2058

"Abor. Mon. of New York," p. 79.

2059

"Ind. Tribes," vol. i. p. 89.

2060

Wilts Arch. Mag., vol. x. (1867), p. 109.

2061

Arch., vol. xxxiv. p. 254. Since this was written I have had an opportunity of examining this bracer, and find that it is of the same green kind of stone as the others. It is figured by Greenwell, "British Barrows," fig. 32, p. 36.

2062

Proc. Soc. Ant., 2nd S., vol. v. p. 289. *Arch.*, vol. xliii. p. 427.

2063

Judges, ch. xx. 16.

2064

Mortillet, *Bull. Soc. Anth. de Paris*, 3 July, 1890.

2065

Dr. D. G. Brinton, *Amer. Anthrop.*, vol. ix. 1896, p. 175. Sir Daniel Wilson, "Lefthandedness," 1891. Mr. O. T. Mason reduces the proportion to 3 per cent. only. *Amer. Anthrop.*, vol. ix. (1896) p. 226.

2066

"Desc. Angl.," ap. Bale, Ed. Oporin, vol. ii. p. 21.

2067

Skelton's "Meyrick's Armour," pl. xxxiv.

2068

Wilkinson's "Anc. Eg.," vol. i. p. 306.

2069

Bruce, "Roman Wall," 3rd ed., p. 97.

2070

Wood, "Nat. Hist. of Man," vol. ii. p. 710.

2071

2nd ed., 1870, p. 7. *Aarbög. for Nord. Oldk.*, 1868, p. 100.

2072

Ann. for Nord. Oldk., 1840–1, p. 166. Madsen, "Afbild.," pl. xxv. 16.

2073

Zeitsch. f. Ethn., vol. xi. p. 24.

2074

Arch. f. Anth., vol. xxiv., 1896, corr. Blatt., p. 59.

2075

Arch., xv. p. 122. Hoare's "South Wilts," p. 75.

2076

Arch., vol. xliii. p. 431; lii. p. 5. "British Barrows," *passim.*

2077

Proc. Soc. Ant., 2nd S., i. p. 162.

2078

Journ. Ethn. Soc., ii. p. 429.

2079

"Ten Years' Diggings," pp. 75, 114. "Cran. Brit.," vol. ii. pl. 60, p. 2.

2080

"Ten Years' Dig.," pp. 44, 77, 83, 112.

2081

"Salisb. Vol. Arch. Inst.," p. 91.

2082

Arch., xxxviii. p. 413.

2083

"Cran. Brit.," vol. ii. pl. 41, p. 3. "Vest. Ant. Derb.," p. 60.

2084

Catalogue, p. 5.

2085

"Ten Years' Dig." p. 103.

2086

Op. cit., p. 107.

2087

Op. cit., p. 116. *Arch. Assoc. Journ.*, vii. p. 215.

2088

Op. cit., p. 127.

2089

Arch. Journ., v. p. 352.

2090

Keller, "Lake-dwellings," p. 328.

2091

Arch. Journ., vol. xxiv. p. 17.

2092

Le Hon, "L'homme foss.," 2nd ed., p. 186.

2093

Trans. Preh. Cong., 1868, pl. ix. p. 126.

2094

Madsen, "Afbild.," pl. xvii.

2095

Worsaae, "Nord. Olds.," No. 275.

2096

"Ten Years' Dig.," p. 127.

2097

Ib., p. 169.

2098

Schoolcraft, "Ind. Tribes," vol. i. pl. xxxvii. "Anc. Mon. of Miss. Vall.," p. 220.

2099

Proc. Soc. Ant., 2nd S., vol. iii. p. 215.

2100

Proc. Soc. Ant., 2nd S., vol. i. p. 395.

2101

"Ten Years' Dig.," p. 77.

2102

Keller, "Lake-dw.," 2nd S., p. 26.

2103

Catlin's "Last Rambles," p. 101.

2104

Hoare's "South Wilts," p. 68. "Cat. Devizes Mus.," No. 224*a*.

2105

Arch., vol. xliii. p. 438.

2106

"Vest. Ant. Derb.," p. 42.

2107

Arch., vol. lii. p. 60, fig. 27.

2108

Sproat, "Scenes and Studies of Savage Life, 1868," p. 86. *Trans. Ethn. Soc.*, N. S., vol. v. p. 250.

2109

Daily Graphic, Dec. 28, 1896.

2110

Ant. Tidsk., 1852–54, p. 9. *Mém. de la Soc. des Ant. du Nord*, 1850–60, p. 29. Madsen, "Afb.," pl. xxv.

2111

Mém. de la Soc. des Ant. du N., 1845–49, p. 168.

2112

"Alterth. u. heid. Vorz.," vol. i. Heft v. Taf. 1. See also "Horæ Ferales," pl. i.

2113

Boucher de Perthes, "Ant. Celt. et Antéd.," vol. i. pl. ii. 5, 7.

2114

Arch., vol. xxx. p. 330. Hoare's "South Wilts," p. 103. "Cat. Devizes Mus.," No. 10, 49*b*, 224, 302.

2115

Proc. Soc. Ant., 2nd S., vol. i. p. 246.

2116

Smith's "Coll. Ant.," vol. i. p. 69.

NOTES—CHAPTER XX.

2117

Keller, "Lake-dwellings," p. 326. Desor, "Les Palafittes," p. 30.

2118

Arch. Journ., vol. xxii. p. 253. "Brit. Barrows," pp. 32, 376.

2119

Arch. f. Anthr., vol. xviii. (1889), p. 235. See also *Zeitsch. f. Ethn.*, vol. xxviii. (1896) p. 473.

2120

Proc. S. A. Scot., vol. ix. p. 548.

2121

"The Past in the Present," (1880), p. 1.

2122

Arch. Journ., vol. xxvi. p. 184.

2123

Ib. xxvi. p. 184.

2124

Wilde, "Cat. Mus. R. I. A.," p. 116.

2125

Proc. S. A. Scot., vol. iv. pp. 72, 119–286.

2126

Proc. S. A. S., vol. iv. p. 259.

2127

Proc. S. A. S., vol. xv. pp. 149, 156.

2128

Proc. S. A. S., vol. v. p. 313.

2129

A. J., vol. xxiv. p. 250; xxvii. p. 160. For others from Anglesea see *Arch. Camb.*, 5th S., vol. ix. p. 242.

2130

Reliquary, vol. vi. pp. 207, 211.

2131

Arch. Journ., vol. xxvi. p. 304.

2132

Arch. Camb., 3rd S., vol. iii. p. 305.

2133

A. J., vol. viii. p. 427. *Arch. Camb.*, 2nd S., vol. iii. p. 223; 3rd S., vi. p. 376.

2134

Proc. Soc. Ant., 2nd S., vol. iv. p. 170. *Journ. R. I. Corn.*, vol. ii. p. 280.

2135

Proc. S. A. Scot., vol. iv. p. 54; v. pp. 15, 82; vi. p. 208. *A. J.*, vol. x. p. 219.

2136

"Brit. Barrows," pp. 116, 196.

2137

Arch. Journ., vol. ix. p. 11; xxiv. p. 250.

2138

"Stone Age," p. 81.

2139

Proc. S. A. S., vol. xxiii. p. 213.

2140

C. R. Smith's "Cat. Lond. Ant.," p. 70. Lee's "Isca Silurum," p. 47.

2141

Rabut, "Hab. Lac. de la Sav.," 2me Mém., pl. vii. 1.

2142

1863, p. 151.

2143

"Alt. u. h. V.," vol. i. Heft ii. Taf. 1, fig. 1.

2144

Schoolcraft, "Ind. Tribes," vol. i. p. 83.

2145

Proc. Soc. Ant. Scot., vol. i. p. 268. *Arch. Journ.*, vol. x. p. 219.

2146

Proc. S. A. S., vol. xv. p. 108.

2147

Proc. S. A. S., vol. xxiii. p. 217.

2148

Arch., vol. xxxiv. p. 135.

2149

Proc. Soc. Ant. Scot., vol. iii. p. 125.

2150

Proc. S. A. S., vol. xxiii. p. 216.

2151

Proc. S. A. S., vol. xi. p. 351. Sir A. Mitchell, "The Past in the Present," p. 239 *et seqq.*

2152

Im Thurn, "Among the Indians of Guiana," 1883, p. 427.

2153

Proc. S. A. S., vol. x. p. 717.

2154

Arch., vol. xlvi. p. 430, pl. xxiv. 21.

2155

"Cat. Mus. R. I. A.," p. 45.

2156

Camd. Soc. Ed., p. 458.

2157

A polished flint is still used for producing a brilliant surface on some kinds of coloured papers which are known as "flint-glazed." See "Flint Chips," p. 101.

2158

Lilly's "Euphues and his England," ed. 1617.

2159

2nd ed., p. 468.

2160

"Vulg. Errors," ii. c. 4.

2161

Proc. S. A. S., vol. xiv. p. 64.

2162

Proc. S. A. S., vol. xv. p. 192.

2163

Trans. Lanc. and Chesh. Arch. Soc., vol. iii. p. 256.

2164

Arch. Journ., vol. xxvi., p. 321.

2165

Arch. Assoc. Journ., vol. xii. p. 177.

2166

Arch. Assoc. Journ., vol. xvii. p. 20, pl. v. 1.

2167

Arch. Camb., 4th S., vol. xiii. p. 224.

2168

Arch., vol. xxxvi. p. 456.

2169

"South Wilts," p. 124.

2170

"Vest. Ant. Derb.," p. 29.

2171

Arch., vol. xii. p. 327.

2172

"Ancient Meols," p. 314.

2173

"Ind. Tribes," vol. ii. pl. 50.

2174

Mitchell's "Past in the Present," pp. 122, 128–132. *Proc. S. A. S.*, vol. xii. p. 268.

2175

Proc. S. A. S., vol. xiii. p. 279.

2176

"Lake-dwellings," p. 331.

2177

Proc. S. A. S., vol. ix. pp. 154, 174, 557.

2178

Arch., vol. xlvi. pp. 468, 493.

2179

Vol. i. p. 117. Wilson's "Preh. Ann. of Scot.," vol. i. p. 207.

2180

Proc. Soc. Ant., 2nd S., vol. iii. p. 266.

2181

Proc. Soc. Ant. Scot., vol. v. pp. 30, 83.

2182

P. S. A. S., vol. vi. p. 89.

2183

"Cat. Arch. Inst. Mus. Ed.," p. 20.

2184

Proc. S. A. S., vol. xxii. p. 111.

2185

P. S. A. S., vol. i. p. 138.

2186

"Cat. A. I. Mus. Ed.," p. 18. *P. S. A. S.*, vol. i. p. 267.

2187

Arch. Journ., vol. xxvi. p. 186.

2188

Arch. Scot., vol. iii. app. 50.

2189

Arch. Scot., vol. iii. app. 89.

2190

P. S. A. S., vol. ii. pp. 64, 71.

2191

P. S. A. S., vol. vii. p. 320.

2192

Ibid., vol. v. p. 82.

2193

Ibid.

2194

Ibid., vol. vi. p. 12.

2195

Ibid., vol. i. p. 180.

2196

Arch. Journ., vol. xiii. p. 104. "Cat. A. I. Mus. Ed.," p. 47. *P. S. A. S.*, vol. ii. p. 330. *Arch. Camb.*, 3rd S., vol. xi. p. 429.

2197

Wilde, "Cat. Mus. R. I. A.," p. 114.

2198

P. S. A. S., vol. i. p. 118. "Preh. Ann. of Scot.," vol. i. p. 208.

2199

Arch. Journ., vol. xiii. p. 104.

2200

Engraved in *Arch. Journ.*, vol. xvi. p. 299.

2201

Arch. Journ., vol. xxv. p. 290. *Trans. Preh. Cong.*, 1868, p. 363. *Trans. Devon. Assoc.*, vol. ii. p. 619; xii. p. 124.

2202

See Pengelly in *Tr. Dev. Assoc.*, vol. iv. p. 105.

2203

Trans. Devon. Assoc., vol. iv. p. 302, pl. iv. 2.

2204

The pole-lathe is also still in use in the manufacture of metallic cocks in which the revolution of the barrel being turned has to be stopped before the complete circle has been gone through.—See Timmins's "Birmingham and Mid. Hardware District," (1866), p. 291.

2205

Hutchins' "Dorset," vol. i. p. 38. Gough's "Camden's Brit.," vol. i. p. 70, pl. ii. Warne's "Celtic Tumuli," § 3, p. 4.

2206

Warne, *l. c.*

2207

"Exc. on Cranborne Chase," vol. i. pl. xlviii.

2208

Arch. Journ., vol. xxiii. p. 35.

2209

Arch. Journ., vol. xxiv. p. 189, whence the cut is borrowed.

2210

Erroneously called a celt by Mr. Kirwan.

2211

Arch. Journ., vol. xiii. p. 183; xv. 90. *Sussex Arch. Coll.*, vol. ix. p. 120.

2212

"Der Bernstein-schmuck der Steinzeit," Königsberg in Pr., 1882.

2213

Mem. Anthrop. Soc. Lond., vol. i. p. 296, pl. i. *Proc. Soc. Ant.*, 2nd S., vol. iii. p. 51.

2214

"Stone Age," pl. x. 210.

2215

Proc. Soc. Ant. Scot., vol. viii. p. 213.

2216

Arch. Journ., vol. xxvii. p. 160, pl. ii. 2.

2217

Arch. Camb., 5th S., vol. viii. p. 56.

2218

Vol. xxvi. p. 288.

2219

Journ. Eth. Soc., vol. ii. p. 430.

2220

P. S. A. S., vol. vii. p. 478.

2221

P. S. A. S., vol. vii. p. 502, fig. vii.; viii. p. 232; xxix. p. 6.

2222

Proc. S. A. S., vol. xi. pp. 82, 83.

2223

Proc. Soc. Ant. Scot., vol. ii. pp. 4, 59; vol. x. p. 539.

2224

Proc. S. A. S., vol. x. p. 539.

2225

P. S. A. S., vol. ii. p. 191.

2226

Proc. S. A. S., vol. x. p. 538.

2227

Ibid., vol. i. p. 149.

2228

Proc. S. A. S., vol. x. p. 548.

2229

P. S. A. S., vol. xii. p. 263.

2230

Wilson's "Preh. Ann. of Scot.," vol. i. p. 206. Hibbert's "Shetland," p. 412. "Cat. Mus. Soc. Ant. L.," p. 18.

2231

"Ten Years' Dig.," p. 173.

NOTES—CHAPTER XXI.

2232

"Brit. Barrows," pp. 33, 187, 188.

2233

"Brit. Barrows," p. 431. "Cran. Brit.," pl. 54.

2234

Proc. S. A. S., vol. xiv. p. 266; xxiv. p. 10.

2235

"Le Signe de la Croix avant le Christianisme," 1866.

2236

"Brit. Barrows," p. 264.

2237

Antea, p. 265.

2238

"Brit. Barrows," p. 263.

2239

"Brit. Barrows," p. 230.

2240

Vol. ii. pl. 58, 2. See also "Cat. Devizes Mus.," No. 184A and No. 74.

2241

Wilson's "Preh. Ann. of Scot.," vol. i. p. 442. *Proc. Soc. Ant. Scot.*, vol. ii. p. 307. "Cat. A. I. M. Ed.," p. 22.

2242

"Vest. Ant. Derb.," p. 68.

2243

"Ten Years' Diggings," p. 152.

2244

Reliq., vol. viii. p. 86.

2245

Hoare's "South Wilts," p. 172.

2246

L. c., p. 239.

2247

Arch., vol. xlix. p. 189.

2248

Proc. Soc. Ant. Scot., vol. iv. p. 60. "Cran. Brit.," vol. ii. 54, 2.

2249

Vol. vi. p. 188.

2250

Arch., vol. lii. p. 19.

2251

Proc. S. A. S., vol. xv. p. 269.

2252

Arch. Journ., vol. xxiv. p. 257.

2253

Arch., vol. xxxiv. p. 256. They seem to be incorrectly represented in pl. xx.

2254

Klebs, "Der Bernstein-schmuck der Stein-zeit." Königsberg, 1882.

2255

Hoare's "South Wilts," pl. x. and xii. *Arch.*, vol. xv. pl. vii. "Cat. Devizes Mus.," No. 54.

2256

Wilson's "Preh. Ann. of Scotland," vol. i. p. 441.

2257

Arch., vol. viii. p. 429.

2258

P. 426.

2259

Proc. Soc. Ant., vol. iii. p. 58.

2260

Proc. Soc. Ant. Scot., vol. ii. p. 484; vi. 62.

2261

Arch. Assoc. Journ., vol. xx. p. 304.

2262

Arch., vol. xv. p. 122. Hoare's "South Wilts," pl. vii.

2263

"Cran. Brit.," vol. ii. pl. 45, 3.

2264

Wilson, "P. A. of S.," vol. i. p. 435. *Arch. Scot.*, vol. iii. p. 49, pl. v. *Proc. S. A. S.*, vol. iii. p. 47. "Cat. A. I. Mus. Ed.," p. 15.

2265

Arch., vol. xliii. p. 515.

2266

Proc. S. A. S., vol. viii. p. 409.

2267

Proc. S. A. S., vol. viii. p. 412.

2268

Proc. S. A. S., vol. xii. p. 294.

2269

"Vest. Ant. Derb.," p. 89. *Arch. Assoc. Journ.*, vol. ii. p. 234.

2270

"Vest. Ant. Derb.," p. 92. *Arch. Assoc. Journ.*, vol. ii. p. 235.

2271

"Ten Years' Dig.," p. 25. *A. A. J.*, vol. vii. p. 216. "Cran. Brit.," vol. ii. pl. 35, 2.

2272

"Norfolk Arch.," vol. viii. p. 319.

2273

"T. Y. D.," p. 46. "Cran. Brit.," vol. ii. pl. 35, 3.

2274

"Ten Years' Dig.," p. 228.

2275

Arch. Assoc. Journ., vol. vi. p. 4; xx. 104.

2276

Arch. Journ., vol. xxiv. p. 257. See also *Proc. Soc. Ant.*, vol. i. p. 34.

2277

Arch. Journ., vol. xxix. p. 283.

2278

P. S. A. S., vol. iii. p. 78.

2279

Ib., vol. vi. p. 203.

2280

Wilson, "P. A. of S.," vol. i. p. 434. "Cat. A. I. Mus. Ed.," p. 17.

2281

Wilson, "P. A. of S.," vol. i. p. 435.

2282

"Cat. A. I. Mus. Ed.," p. 15.

2283

Wilson, "P. A. of S.," vol. i. p. 436.

2284

Proc. S. A. S., vol. xiv. p. 261; xxv. p. 65.

2285

Proc. S. A. S., vol. xxvi. p. 6.

2286

Hoare, "South Wilts," p. 46. See also "Cat. Devizes Mus.," No. 173A.

2287

A. C. Smith, "Ants. of N. Wilts," pp. 18, 19. *Wilts Arch. Mag.*, vol. xvi. pp. 179, 181. (These objects are now in the British Museum.)

2288

"Norfolk Archæology," vol. iii. p. 1.

2289

"Cat. Devizes Mus.," Nos. 56, 57. In the *Archæologia*, vol. xv. pl. vii., the rim and the top or bottom of the box are shown as quite distinct. Mr. Cunnington thought they might have covered the ends of staves.

2290

Arch. Camb., 3rd. S., vol. xii. p. 110.

2291

Reliquary, vol. ix. p. 67.

2292

Vol. xxii. p. 112. "Brit. Barrows," p. 334.

2293

Vol. xxii. p. 245. "Brit. Barrows," p. 366.

2294

"Ten Years' Dig.," p. 74. "Cran. Brit.," vol. ii. pl. 60, 2.

2295

"Brit. Barrows," p. 420, fig. 159.

2296

Arch., vol. lii. p. 41.

2297

Arch., vol. lii. p. 57.

2298

Arch. Journ., vol. vii. p. 190.

2299

"Cat. A. I. Mus. Ed.," p. 10.

2300

Arch. Journ., vol. xxii. p. 74. *Arch. Camb.*, 3rd S., vol. xii. p. 97.

2301

Arch. Assoc. J., vol. vii. p. 217.

2302

Arch., vol. viii. p. 59.

2303

Arch., vol. xxxviii. p. 413.

2304

P. S. A. S., vol. vi. p. 112. App. p. 42.

2305

Trans. Ethn. Soc., vol. vii. p. 50.

2306

P. S. A. S., vol. xiii. p. 127.

2307

Proc. Soc. Ant., 2nd S., vol. ii. p. 131. *Arch.*, vol. liv. p. 106.

2308

Proc. S. A. S., vol. xv. p. 268.

2309

Arch. Assoc. Journ., vol. iii. p. 344. *Arch.*, vol. xxxv. p. 247.

2310

Hoare, "South Wilts," p. 124.

2311

Plin., "Nat. Hist.," lib. xxxvii. c. 2.

2312

Rev. Arch., vol. xv. p. 364.

2313

"Exc. on Cranborne Chase," vol. i. pl. xlix.

2314

See *Arch. Assoc. Journ.*, vol. i. p. 325.

2315

Vol. xvi. p. 299.

2316

Ibid., p. 300.

2317

Proc. Dorset Nat. Hist. and Ant. Field Club, vol. xiii., 1892, p. 178.

2318

Arch., vol. xxxi. p. 452.

2319

Hoare's "South Wilts," p. 114, pl. xiii.

2320

Arch. Journ., vol. xxvi. p. 304.

2321

Arch., vol. lii. p. 52.

2322

Op. cit., p. 56.

2323

Proc. S. A. S., vol. xv. p. 269.

2324

Proc. S. A. S., vol. xxiii. p. 219.

2325

Proc. S. A. S., vol. xv. p. 268. Munro, "Lake-dw.," p. 50.

2326

Proc. S. A. S., vol. ix. p. 538.

2327

Wood-Martin, "Rude Stone Mon. of Ireland," 1888, p. 60.

2328

Hoare, "South Wilts," p. 124.

2329

Ibid.

2330

Op. cit., p. 165.

2331

Op. cit., p. 183, pl. xxii.

2332

Hoare, "South Wilts," p. 75. *Arch.*, vol. lii. p. 430.

2333

"Brit. Barrows," p. 249.

2334

Arch. Assoc. Journ., vol. xv. p. 337.

2335

"Vest. Ant. Derb.," p. 53.

2336

Op. cit., p. 63.

2337

Op. cit., p. 29. C. R. Smith, "Coll. Ant.," vol. i. p. 55.

2338

Arch., xii. p. 327.

2339

"Cran. Brit.," vol. ii. pl. 58, 2.

2340

"Vest. Ant. Derb.," p. 67.

2341

"Ten Years' Dig.," p. 123.

2342

"Ten Years' Dig.," p. 130.

2343

Reliquary, vol. iii. p. 206.

2344

Reliquary, vol. xiv. p. 88.

2345

Proc. Soc. Ant., 2nd S., vol. ii. p. 278.

2346

Arch. Journ., vol. xvi. p. 90.

2347

A. J., vol. xiii. p. 412.

2348

Proc. S. A. S., vol. viii. p. 350.

2349

Wood-Martin, "Rude Stone Mon. of Ireland," 1888, p. 86. *Journ. R. Hist. and Arch. Assoc. of Ireland*, 4th S., vol. v. p. 107.

2350

Arch. Assoc. Journ., vol. xxii. p. 314.

2351

A. J., vol. xiii. p. 412.

2352

Arch. Camb., 3rd S., vol. vii. p. 91. *Arch. Assoc. Journ.*, vol. xvi. p. 326.

2353

Bonwick, "Daily Life of the Tasmanians," p. 194.

2354

Bonwick, *op. cit.*, pp. 193–201.

2355

Plin., "Nat. Hist.," lib. vii. cap. 40.

2356

Ovid, "Met.," lib. xv. v. 41.

2357

"Man the Prim. Savage," p. 338.

2358

Arch. Assoc. Journ., vol. x. p. 164.

2359

Proc. Soc. Ant. Scot., vol. v. p. 327.

2360

"Desc. of West. Isl. of Scot., 1703," p. 226, quoted by Stuart, "Sculpt. St. of Scot.," vol. ii. p. lv.

2361

P. S. A. S., vol. iv. pp. 211, 279.

2362

P. S. A. S., vol. xxii. p. 63.

2363

P. S. A. S., vol. xxiv. p. 157.

2364

P. S. A. S., vol. xxvii. p. 433.

2365

De Bonstetten, "Rec. d'Ant. Suisses," p. 8. Nilsson, "Stone Age," p. 215.

2366

Blundevill's "Fower chiefest Offices belonging to Horsemanship," quoted in N. and Q., 6th S., vol. i. p. 54.

2367

Arch. f. Anth., vol. xxii. (1894), "Corr. Blatt.," p. 101.

2368

P. S. A. S., vol. v. p. 128. *Anthrop. Rev.*, vol. iv. p. 401. See also *Journ. Anth. Inst.*, vol. xvii. p. 135, and "The Denham Tracts," vol. ii., Folklore Soc., 1895.

2369

Proc. Soc. Ant. Scot., vol. v. p. 315.

2370

Arch. Assoc. Journ., vol. xxiv. p. 40. *Matériaux*, vol. v. p. 118, 249, &c.

2371

"Supp. au Rec. d'Ant. Suisses," pl. i. 2.

2372

Baudot, "Sép. des Barb.," p. 78.

2373

Lindenschmidt, "A. u. h. V.," vol. ii. Heft xii. Taf. vi. 12.

2374

"Lapland," ed. 1704, p. 277.

2375

"*Cong. Préh. Lisbonne*," 1880, pl. v. Da Veiga, "Ant. de Algarve," 1856. Cartailhac, p. 92.

2376

Schoolcraft, "Ind. Tribes," vol. i. p. 86.

NOTES—CHAPTER XXII.

2377

See, for instance, Desnoyer's "Recherches sur les Cavernes" in the "Dict. Univ. d'Hist. nat." Pengelly, *Geologist*, vol. v. p. 65. *Trans. Devon. Assoc.*, vol. i. pt. iii. p. 31. Lyell, "Princ. of Geol.," 10th edit., vol. ii. p. 514, &c.; and W. Boyd Dawkins, "Cave-hunting," 1874. Many British caverns have been well described by Mr. E. A. Martel in his "Irlande et Cavernes Anglaises," Paris, 1897.

2378

"Gutta cavat lapidem, consumitur annulus usu."—De Pont., lib. iv. El. x. v. 5. See also Lucretius, lib. i. v. 313:—

"Annulus in digito subtertenuatur habendo

Stillicidi casus lapidem cavat."

2379

See Prestwich, *Quar. Journ. Geol. Soc.*, vol. xi. p. 64.

2380

See Rev. H. Eley, F.G.S., in *Geol.*, vol. iv. p. 521. Pengelly, *Geol.*, vol. v. p. 65.

2381

Lyell, "Princ. of Geol.," 10th edit., vol. ii. p. 520.

2382

"Elements of Geol.," 6th edit., p. 122.

2383

Plin., "Nat. Hist.," lib. vii. cap. 56.

2384

Æschylus, "Prom. Vinct.," l. 452.

2385

"Laus Serenæ," v. 77.

2386

Described in the "Reliquiæ Aquitanicæ," London, 1875.

2387

"Recherches sur les Ossemens fossiles découverts dans les Cavernes de la Province de Liège," 2 vols., 1833.

2388

Ann. des Sc. Nat. (Zool.), 4th S., vol. xv. p. 231.

2389

"Les Temps Antéhistoriques en Belgique," 1871.

2390

Matériaux, vol. iv. p. 453; v. p. 172. *Cong. Préh. Bruxelles*, 1872, p. 432. *Rev. d'Anthrop.*, 1st S., vol. i. p. 432. "Musée Préhist." Tableau.

2391

Lartet and Christy in *Rev. Arch.*, vol. ix. p. 238. Le Hon, "L'homme foss.," 36, 62. Mortillet, *Matériaux*, vol. iii. p. 191.

2392

"Le Mâcon préh.," *Arch. du Mus. d'hist. nat. de Lyon*, 1872, vol. i.

2393

L'Anthropologie, vol. ii. p. 141; vol. vii., 1896, p. 385. *Nature*, vol. lv., 1897, p. 229.

2394

"Age de la Pierre," Alcan, Paris, 1891. *Bull. de la Soc. dauphinoise d'Ethn.*, 5 mars, 1894.

2395

Quar. Journ. G. S., vol. xxv., 1869, p. 192. "Cave-hunting," p. 359.

2396

Trans. Prehist. Cong., 1868, p. 278.

2397

Trans. Preh. Cong., 1868, p. 272.

2398

Beitr. zür Anth. Baierns, vol. ii. p. 210, pl. xii.

2399

Trans. Preh. Cong., 1868, p. 275. "Cave-hunting," p. 234.

2400

See "Rel. Aquit.," pp. 93, 94. *Trans. Dev. Assoc.*, vol. vi. p. 322. *Journ. Anth. Inst.*, vol. ii. p. 2.

2401

Wilson's "Preh. Ann. of Scot.," vol. i. p. 48.

2402

"Pal. Mem.," vol. ii. p. 522.

2403

Trans. Devonsh. Assoc., vol. ii. p. 469; iii. 191; iv. 467. To this paper I am largely indebted.

2404

L. c., vol. iii. p. 203.

2405

Trans. Dev. Assoc., vol. iii. p. 321.

2406

L. c., p. 327.

2407

Proc. G. S., vol. iii. p. 386. *Trans. G. S.*, 2nd S., vol. vi. p. 433.

2408

Vol. iii. p. 353.

2409

See *Reports of the Brit. Assoc. for the Advancement of Science*, 1865–71, inclusive. See also a lecture on "Kent's Cavern, Torquay," by W. Pengelly, Esq., F.R.S., F.G.S., in *Proc. R. I. Gt. Britain*, Feb. 23, 1866. Dawkins, "Early Man in Britain," p. 194. "Cave-hunting," p. 324.

2410

Vols. vi. to xviii. See also *Quar. Journ. of Science*, April, 1874.

2411

See *Report Brit. Assoc.* 1873, pp. 206, 209.

2412

Op. cit., p. 209.

2413

"Recherches Chimiques sur la Patine des Silex taillés." Montauban, 1866. See also Judd, in *Proc. Geol. Assoc.*, vol. x. p. 218, and Lobley, *op. cit.*, p. 226; as also *Comptes Rendus de l'Ac. des Sc.*, 1875, p. 979.

2414

Nature, vol. xlii. p. 7.

2415

Nilsson, "Stone Age," p. 44.

2416

Dupont, "L'Homme pend. les Ages de la Pierre," p. 71.

2417

See p. 325 *supra*.

2418

"Lapland" (1704), p. 223.

2419

Dawkins, "Cave-hunting," p. 112.

2420

P. 50.

2421

L'Anthropologie, vol. vi. 1895, p. 276, and Cartailhac, *op. cit.*, vii. p. 309.

2422

P. 127.

2423

P. 361.

2424

Trans. Dev. Assoc., vol. v. p. 179; vii. p. 247.

2425

L'Anthropologie, vol. v., 1894, p. 371.

2426

"Palæont. Mem.," vol. ii. p. 486.

2427

Quar. Journ. Geol. Soc., 1860, vol. xvi. p. 189. Lubbock, "Preh. Times," 4th ed., p. 321. *Geologist*, vol. i. p. 538; vol. iv. p. 153. *Brit. Assoc. Report*, 1858.

2428

P. 471.

2429

Proc. Dev. Assoc., vol. vi. p. 775.

2430

"Cave-hunting," p. 319.

2431

Lyell, "Ant. of Man," 3rd ed., p. 99. *Trans. Devon. Assoc.*, vol. i. pt. iii. 31.

2432

Lubbock, "Preh. Times," 4th ed., p. 296.

2433

Geologist, vol. iv. p. 154.

2434

Such as "Reliq. Aquit.," A., pl. v. fig. 2.

2435

See *Proc. Devon. Assoc.*, vol. vi. p. 835. *Phil. Trans.*, 1873, p. 551.

2436

Proc. Soc. Ant., 2nd S., vol. viii. p. 247.

2437

Op. cit., p. 462.

2438

Trans. Devon. Assoc., vol. xviii. p. 161.

2439

Op. cit., vol. xix. p. 419.

2440

Vol. xviii., 1862, p. 115; xix., 1863, 260. See also Dawkins on "The Habits and Conditions of the Two earliest-known Races of Men," *Quart. Journ. of Science*, 1866, *Macmillan's Magazine*, Oct. and Dec., 1870, "Cave-hunting," p. 295, and "Early Man in Brit.," p. 193, and Hamy, "Paléont. Humaine," p. 117.

2441

Vol. xviii. p. 118. For the use of this block I am indebted to the Council of the Geological Society.

2442

See Lubbock's "Preh. Times," 4th ed., p. 329.

2443

"Ant. of Man," 3rd ed., p. 171.

2444

Falconer, "Palæont. Mem.," vol. ii. p. 538. *Quar. Journ. Geol. Soc.*, vol. xvi., 1860, p. 487. *Geologist*, vol. iii. p. 413.

2445

"Pal. Mem.," vol. ii. p. 540.

2446

"Ant. of Man," 3rd ed., p. 173.

2447

Geologist, vol. vi. p. 47; v. 115.

2448

Geol. Mag., vol. ii. p. 471.

2449

Proc. Geol. Assoc., vol. ix. p. 9.

2450

Q. J. G. S., vol. xlii. p. 9; xliii. p. 9. *Proc. Geol. Assoc.*, vol. ix. p. 26.

2451

Q. J. G. S., vol. xliii. p. 112; xliv. 112. *Proc. Geol. Assoc.*, vol. x. p. 14. *Nature*, vol. ix. p. 14. *Brit. Assoc. Rep.*, 1886.

2452

Q. J. G. S., vol. xliv. p. 564.

2453

Q. J. G. S., vol. xliii. p. 116. *Journ. Anth. Inst.*, vol. iii. p. 387. *Q. J. G. S.*, vol. xxxii. p. 91. Dawkins, "Early Man in Brit.," p. 192.

2454

Geol. Mag., vol. viii. p. 433. *Brit. Assoc. Report*, 1871.

2455

Q. J. G. S., vol. xxxi. p. 679; xxxii. p. 240; xxxiii. p. 579; xxxv. p. 724.

2456

"Early Man in Brit.," p. 175. See also Pennington's "Barrows, and Bone Caves of Derbyshire," p. 99. *Journ. Derb. A. and N. H. Soc.*, vol. iv. (1882), p. 169.

2457

Jour. Anth. Inst., vol. iii. pp. 392, 516. *B. A. Rep.*, 1874–5. Miall's "Geol., &c., of Craven," 1878, p. 25. J. Geikie's "Preh. Europe," p. 97. Dawkin's "Cave-hunting," p. 81.

2458

Tr. Derb. A. and N. H. Soc., N. S., vol. i. p. 177.

NOTES—CHAPTER XXIII.

2459

See Prestwich, *Phil. Trans.*, 1860, p. 277—1864, 247; Evans, *Arch.*, vol. xxxviii. p. 280; vol. xxxix. p. 57. Sir J. Lubbock, "Preh. Times," p. 349. *Nat. Hist. Rev.* (1862), p. 244. Sir C. Lyell, "Ant. of Man," p. 93. Wilson, "Prehist. Man," vol. i. p. 105. Falconer, "Palæont. Mem.," vol. ii. p. 596. *London Review*, Jan., 1860; *Gentleman's Magazine*, March and April, 1861; *Blackwood's Magazine*, Oct., 1860; *Quarterly Review*, Oct., 1863; *Edinburgh Review*, July, 1863; *Proc. Royal Inst.*, Feb. 26, 1864, &c. It seems needless now (1897) to add to these references.

2460

"Mémoire sur des Instruments en Silex trouvés à St. Acheul, près Amiens."

2461

"Pal. Mem.," vol. ii. p. 597.

2462

P. Salmon, "Dict. Pal. du Dép. de l'Aube," 1882, p. 179.

2463

Matériaux, vol. xiii., 1878, p. 22; vol. xvi., 1881, p. 329, 410. E. Chouquet, "Les Silex taillés de Chelles," 4to, 1883.

2464

L'Anthropologie, vol. vi., 1895, p. 497.

2465

Cochet, "Seine Inéfrieure," p. 248.

2466

Op. cit., p. 503.

2467

G. Dumoutier, 1882.

2468

Gosselet, Lille, 1891.

2469

"Mus. Préh.," 44, 46. *Mat.*, vol. viii., 1873, pp. 163, 245.

2470

Rev. Arch. du Midi de la France, 1868. *Mat.*, vol. xiii., 1878, 40.

2471

Bull. Soc. Ant. de Brux., vol. xiii. 1894–5.

2472

Ann. Soc. Arch. de Brux., vol. v. p. 145. *Rev. des Quest. scient.*, July, 1891. See also *Cong. Préh. Bruxelles*, 1872, p. 250, and *Cong. Arch. de Brux.*, 1891, p. 538.

2473

Zeitsch. f. Ethn., vol. xxiv., 1892, p. 366. *Mitth. d'Ant. Ges. in Wien*, N. S., vol. xiii., 1893, p. 204. *L'Anthropologie*, vol. viii., 1897, p. 53.

2474

Cong. Préh. Buda-Pest, 1876, p. 33.

2475

Mitth. d'Anth. Ges. in Wien, N. S. vol. xiii. 1893, p. 77.

2476

L'Anthrop., vol. vi. 1895, p. 1. De Baye, "Rapport sur les découvertes de M. Savenkow dans la Sibérie Orient.," 1894.

2477

Nicolucci, *Rendiconte dell' Accad. di Napoli*, August, 1868. Rossi, *Rev. Arch.*, vol. xvi. p. 48. Ceselli, "Stromenti in Silice di Roma," 1866. *Macmillan's Magazine*, September, 1867.

2478

Concezio Rosa, "Ricerche di Arch. Preist." Firenze, 1871, pl. ii. 1.

2479

Arch. per l'Ant. e la Etn., vol. viii., 1878, p. 41.

2480

Gastaldi, "Iconografia," 1869, 4to, vol. ii.

2481

Bull. di Paletn. Ital., 1876, p. 122, pl. iv. 1.

2482

Bull. Soc. Géol. de France, 2 S., t. xx., 1863, p. 698.

2483

L'Anthrop., vol. vi., 1895, p. 616.

2484

"Ages préh. de l'Esp. et du Port.," 1886, p. 26.

2485

"Les premiers Ages du mét. en Espagne," 1887, p. 249.

2486

Cong. préh. Lisbonne, 1880, p. 237.

2487

"Ages préh. de l'Esp. et du Port.," 1886, p. 30.

2488

Rev. Arch., vol. xv. p. 18.

2489

"Rivers and their Catchment Basins."

2490

Athenæum, April 4, 1863, p. 459.

2491

Wyatt in *Quar. Journ. Geol. Soc.*, vol. xviii., p. 113; xx., p. 187. *Geologist*, vol. iv. p. 242. See also *Bedfordshire Archit. and Archæol. Soc. Trans.*, 1861 and 1862. Prestwich, *Phil. Trans.*, 1864, p. 253. *Quar. Journ. Geol. Soc.*, vol. xvii., p. 366. Evans, *Arch.*, vol. xxxix. p. 69. Lyell, "Ant. of Man," p. 163.

2492

Matt. Paris, "Vit. Offæ II.," p. 32.

2493

Walsingham, "Hist. Ang.," *s. a.* 1399.

2494

Phil. Trans., 1864, p. 254.

2495

Prestwich, *Quar. Journ. Geol. Soc.*, vol. xvii., p. 367.

2496

Quar. Journ. Geol. Soc., vol. xviii., p. 113; xx., p. 185.

2497

Prestwich, *Phil. Trans.*, 1864, p. 284. Wyatt, *ubi sup.*

2498

Vol. xxxix. pl. iii.

2499

Trans. Herts. Nat. Hist. Soc., vol. viii., 1896, pl. xi. 6.

2500

Trans. Herts. Nat. Hist. Soc., vol. viii., 1896, pl. xi. 2.

2501

Trans. Watford Nat. Hist. Soc., vol. i. p. lxi. *Trans. Herts. Nat. Hist. Soc.*, vol. viii., 1896, pl. xi. 7.

2502

Several are figured in *Trans. Herts. Nat. Hist. Soc.*, vol. viii., 1896, pl. xii.

2503

"Man the Prim. Savage," p. 261.

2504

Proc. Geol. Assoc., vol. xiv., 1896, p. 417.

2505

A detailed account of Mr. Reid's work is given in the *Proc. Roy. Soc.*, March 4th, 1897, vol. lxi. p. 40.

2506

Proc. Soc. Ant., 2nd S., vol. v. p. 35.

2507

Seeley, *Quar. Journ. Geol. Soc.* (1866), vol. xxii. p. 475.

2508

Antiquarian Comm., vol. ii. p. 201.

2509

Geol. Mag., 2nd Decade, vol. v. (1878), p. 400. See also *Camb. Ant. Comm.*, vol. iv. p. 177, where the specimens are figured.

2510

Nature, vol. xxx. (1884), p. 632.

2511

Quar. Journ. Geol. Soc. (1866), vol. xxii. p. 478.

2512

Nature, vol. xxxiv. (1886), p. 521.

2513

Quar. Journ. Geol. Soc. (1861), vol. xvii. p. 363.

2514

"Flint Chips," p. 43.

2515

Arch. Assoc. Journ., vol. xxxviii. p. 208.

2516

Journ. Anth. Inst., vol. xiv. p. 51, pl. iv.–vi. "Man the Primeval Savage," p. 280.

2517

Phil. Trans., 1864, p. 253. See also *Quar. Journ. Geol. Soc.* (1861), vol. xvii. p. 364. Evans, *Arch.*, vol. xxxviii. p. 302; vol. xxxix. p. 63. Lyell, "Ant. of Man," p. 169.

2518

"Rel. Aquit.," A. pl. v.

2519

"Rel. Aquit.," A. pl. xvii. 3, 4.

2520

Quar. Journ. Suff. Inst. of Arch. and N. H., vol. i. p. 4.

2521

Quar. Journ. Geol. Soc. (1866), vol. xxii. p. 567; (1867), vol. xxiii. p. 45.

2522

Quar. Journ. Geol. Soc. (1869), vol. xxv. pp. 272, 449.

2523

Mr. Trigg (*Quar. Journ. Suff. Inst.*, vol. i. p. 5) gives the following section:—

1. Surface soil	1 foot.
2. Yellow sand, slightly argillaceous, interspersed with ferruginous seams and layers of small flint shingle	5 to 7 feet.
3. Slightly rolled and sub-angular flints in an ochreous sandy matrix, with seams of silt and chalky detritus—variable	6 to 9 feet.
4. A similar matrix, with larger chalky patches, large masses of flint but slightly broken, and some sub-angular flints—variable	6 to 9 feet.

It is in No. 3 that the implements are usually met with.

2524

Mr. Flower is mistaken in saying that these are some feet above the gravel in which the implements occur. Implements are found both above and below such seams, though for the most part towards the base of the gravel.

2525

Proc. Soc. Ant., 2nd S., vol. iii. p. 431.

2526

Quar. Journ. Geol. Soc. (1867), vol. xxiii. p. 47.

2527

Arch., vol. xxxix. p. 77.

2528

Q. J. G. S. (1867), vol. xxiii. pp. 49, 52.

2529

Quar. Journ. Suff. Inst., vol. i. p. 4.

2530

Quar. Journ. Geol. Soc. (1869), vol. xxv. pl. xx.

2531

See an article, "On some Cavities in the Gravel of the Little Ouse," *Geol. Mag.*, vol. v. p. 443.

2532

Franks, *Proc. Soc. Ant.*, 2nd S., vol. iv. p. 124.

2533

Quar. Journ. Geol. Soc. (1869), vol. xxv. pp. 272, 449.

2534

Geol. Mag., vol. v. p. 445.

2535

Quar. Journ. Geol. Soc. (1869), vol. xxv. p. 449.

2536

Quar. Journ. Geol. Soc. (1869), vol. xxv. p. 449.

2537

Proc. Camb. Phil. Soc., vol. iii. p. 285.

2538

Geol. Survey Mem. "On the Manufacture of Gun-flints," 1879, p. 68. J. Geikie, "Preh. Europe," 1881, p. 263. Miller and Skertchly, "The Fenland," 1868, p. 546, *et seqq.*

2539

Quar. Journ. Suff. Inst., vol. i. p. 4.

2540

Quar. Journ. Geol. Soc. (1869), vol. xxv. p. 452.

2541

Essex Nat., vol. ii. p. 97.

2542

This discovery is mentioned in Miller and Skertchly, "The Fenland" (1878), p. 353.

2543

Natural Science, vol. x. (1897) p. 89.

2544

Arch. Journ., vol. xxxv. p. 265.

2545

Arch., vol. xiii. p. 204.

2546

4th ed., pp. 353, 354. See also *Geologist*, vol. iv. p. 19.

2547

1860, p. 277; 1864, p. 247. See also Lyell, "Ant. of Man," p. 166.

2548

Prestwich, *Phil. Trans.*, 1860, p. 307.

2549

Geologist, vol. iii. p. 347.

2550

Skelton's "Meyrick's Armour," pl. xlvi.

2551

Phil. Trans., 1860, pl. xiv. 6.

2552

Arch., vol. xiii. pl. xv.

2553

1876, p. 289.

2554

Report, 1888, p. 674.

2555

Report, 1895, p. 679.

2556

Report, 1895, p. lxxxvi.

2557

Report, 1896, p. 400. *Essex Nat.*, vol. ix., p. 245.

2558

Essex Nat., vol. ii. p. 187.

2559

Essex Nat., vol. vi. p. 78.

2560

Vol. i. p. lxiv.

2561

Vol. xxxviii. p. 301. See also Lyell, "Ant. of Man," p. 160. Lubbock, "Preh. Times," 4th ed., p. 352. "Horæ Ferales," p. 132, pl. i. 21. Dawkins, "Early Man in Brit.," 1880, p. 156.

2562

Nature, vol. xxviii. p. 564.

2563

Nature, vol. xxix. p. 15.

2564

Nature, vol. xxviii. p. 564.

2565

Stanford, 1894.

2566

Quar. Journ. Geol. Soc., vol. xi. p. 107.

2567

Geol. Mag., vol. v. p. 392.

2568

Geol. and Nat. Hist. Repert., vol. i. p. 373.

2569

"Ant. of Man," pp. 161, 124.

2570

Geol. Mag., vol. v. p. 391. See also *Quar. Journ. Geol. Soc.* (1869), vol. xxv. p. 95.

2571

Quar. Journ. Geol. Soc. (1869), vol. xxv. p. 99.

2572

"Man, the Prim. Savage," p. 214. *Nature*, vol. xxvii. p. 270.

2573

Journ. Anth. Inst., vol. xii. p. 176; xiii. p. 357. *Nature*, vol. xxv. p. 460; xxvi. p. 579. *Proc. Geol. Assoc.*, vol. viii. p. 126. *Essex Naturalist*, vol. i. p. 125.

2574

Proc. Geol. Assoc., vol. viii. p. 336.

2575

Op. cit., vol. viii., p. 344.

2576

Mem. Geol. Survey, "The Geology of London, &c.," vol. i., 1889.

2577

"Man the Prim. Sav.," p. 222, fig. 148.

2578

Op. cit., p. 225, fig. 151.

2579

Op. cit., p. 239, fig. 165.

2580

Op. cit., p. 224, fig. 150. See also *Trans. Herts Nat. Hist. Soc.*, vol. viii., 1896. pl. xiii., xiv.

2581

Brit. Assoc. Report, 1869, p. 130. He has also kindly furnished me with other particulars.

2582

Q. J. G. S., vol. xxviii. p. 449.

2583

J. A. Brown, "Palæolithic Man in N.W. Middlesex," p. 113.

2584

Quar. Journ. of Science, vol. viii., 1878, p. 316.

2585

Q. J. G. S., vol. xlii., 1886, p. 197. "Palæolithic Man in N.W. Middlesex," London, 1887. *Nature*, vol. xxxv., p. 555. *Proc. Geol. Assoc.*, June 18, 1887, vol. x., 1888, p. 172. *Trans. Middlesex Nat. Hist. Soc.*, Feb. 12, 1889, Whitaker, "Geol. of Lond.," p. 308.

2586

Proc. S. A., 2nd S., vol. xi. p. 211.

2587

Journ. Anth. Inst., vol. ix. p. 316; 1881, p. 1. *Proc. Geol. Assoc.*, vol. xiv., p. 153.

2588

Proc. Geol. Assoc., vol. x., 1888, p. 361.

2589

"Man the Prim. Savage," p. 241. *Nature*, vol. xxvi. p. 293; xxviii. p. 617.

2590

Tr. Berks. Archæol. and Archit. Soc., vol. ii., 1896, pp. 16, 39, 43.

2591

"Pal. Man in N.W. Middlesex," p. 31.

2592

Journ. Arch. Assoc., vol. xxxvii. pp. 1, 79. *Proc. Geol. Assoc., vol. viii. p. 348. Tr. Berks. A. and A. Soc.*, 1882.

2593

Q. J. G. S., vol. xxxvi. p. 296.

2594

Q. J. G. S., vol. xlvi., 1890, p. 582. See also Mr. H. W. Monckton, F.G.S., in *Q. J. G. S.*, vol. xlix., 1893, p. 310.

2595

Journ. Anth. Inst., vol. xxiv., 1895, p. 44, pl. iii.

2596

Q. J. G. S., vol. xlix., 1893, p. 321.

2597

Journ. Anth. Inst., vol. xiv., 1885, p. 192.

2598

See also Hedges' "Wallingford," 1881, vol. i. p. 29.

2599

Op. cit., p. 29.

2600

Antiquary, vol. xxx. pp. 148, 192. *Brit. Assoc. Rep.*, 1894 (Oxford), p. 663.

2601

Evans, *Arch.*, vol. xxxix. p. 72; Prestwich, *Quar. Journ. Geol. Soc.* (1861), vol. xvii. p. 367; Lyell, "Ant. of Man," p. 161; Lubbock, "Preh. Times," 4th ed., p. 353.

2602

Quar. Journ. Geol. Soc., vol. vii. p. 278.

2603

Surr. Arch. Coll., vol. xi.

2604

Proc. Geol. Assoc., vol. xiii. p. 77.

2605

Proc. Geol. Assoc., vol. xiii. p. 80.

2606

Arch., vol. xxxix. p. 73. Prestwich, *Quar. Journ. Geol. Soc.*, vol. xvii. p. 368. Lubbock, "Preh. Times," 4th ed., p. 355.

2607

Trans. Herts Nat. Hist. Soc., vol. viii. pl. xi. 8.

2608

Stanford, London, 8vo, 1894.

2609

"Man, the Prim. Savage," p. 179.

2610

Op. cit., p. 91.

2611

Op. cit., p. 170. *Nature*, vol. xliii. p. 345.

2612

Nature, vol. xl. p. 151.

2613

Nature, vol. xxiv. p. 582; vol. xxviii. p. 490.

2614

"Man the Prim. Savage," figs. 97, 98, 99, pp. 135, 136. See also *Essex Nat.*, vol. i.

2615

Figs. 58, 69, 70, and 71, in "Man the Prim. Savage."

2616

Vol. ii., 1888, p. 67.

2617

Op. cit., p. 101, fig. 65.

2618

Trans. Herts Nat. Hist. Soc., vol. viii., 1896, pl. xi. 4.

2619

Op. cit., p. 180, fig. 125. *Essex Nat.*, vol. i. p. 36.

2620

Op. cit. p. 184.

2621

Proc. Soc. Ant., 2nd S., vol. v. p. 165.

2622

Trans. Herts Nat. Hist. Soc., vol. viii., 1896, pl. xi. 3.

2623

Trans. Herts Nat. Hist. Soc., vol. viii., 1896, pl. xi. 5.

2624

Op. cit., p. 184. *Journ. Anth. Inst.*, vol. viii., 1879, p. 278. *Nature*, vol. xxiii. p. 604.

2625

Op. cit., p. 185.

2626

Op. cit., p. 214.

2627

Essex Nat., vol. iii. p. 235.

2628

Essex Nat., vol. iv. p. 17.

2629

Essex Nat., vol. ii. p. 262.

2630

Nature, vol. xxviii. p. 367.

2631

Q. J. G. S., vol. xxviii., 1872, p. 462.

2632

Journ. Anth. Inst., vol. xii. p. 230.

2633

"Note on the Disc. at Church Field, West Wickham," privately printed. *Arch. Cant.*, vol. xiv., 1883, p. 88. *Antiq.*, vol. ix. p. 213. Clinch, "Antiq. Jottings," 1889, pp. 180, 186.

2634

Proc. Soc. Ant., 2nd S., vol. xi. p. 164.

2635

Lubbock, "Preh. Times," 4th ed., p. 355.

2636

Q. J. G. S., vol. xlvii., 1891, p. 145.

2637

Q. J. G. S., vol. xxxvi., 1880, p. 547.

2638

Arch. Journ., vol. xxxvii. 1880, p. 294, pl. i.

2639

Geol. Mag., vol. ix., 1872, p. 268. *Q. J. G. S.*, vol. xxviii., 1872, p. 414. *Geol. Mag.*, 2nd Dec., vol. i., 1874, p. 479.

2640

Brit. Assoc. Rep., 1875, p. 175. *Nat.*, vol. xii. p. 202. *Proc. W. Lond. Sci. Assoc.*, 1876.

2641

Sep., 1875, p. 263.

2642

"Early Man in Brit.," 1880, p. 136.

2643

Op. cit., p. 135.

2644

Q. J. G. S., vol. xlvii., 1891, p. 129, pl. vi.

2645

Q. J. G. S., vol. li., 1895, p. 505.

2646

Op. cit., p. 505.

2647

Op. cit., p. 523.

2648

Arch., vol. xxxix. p. 74; Lubbock, "Preh. Times," 4th ed., p. 355.

2649

Journ. Anth. Inst., vol. xxi., 1892, p. 246.

2650

Q. J. G. S., vol. xlvii., 1891, p. 130.

2651

Journ. Anth. Inst., vol. xxi. p. 263.

2652

Brit. Assoc. Rep., 1891, pp. 353, 652.

2653

Q. J. G. S., vol. xlv., 1889, p. 270.

2654

Q. J. G. S., vol. xlvii., 1891, p. 126. See also *Journ. Anth. Inst.*, vol. xxi., 1892, p. 246; and Prestwich, "Controverted Questions in Geology," 1895.

2655

Proc. Geol. Assoc., vol. xi. p. lxxxii.

2656

"Geology of the Weald," pp. 193, 194, 297.

2657

Journ. Anth. Inst., vol. xxi., 1892, pl. 18.

2658

Archæologia, vol. xxxix. p. 63.

2659

Quar. Journ. Geol. Soc., vol. xvii. p. 365. Lyell, "Ant. of Man," p. 161. Lubbock, "Preh. Times," 4th ed., p. 355. *Geologist*, vol. vii. p. 118. *Once a Week*, June 19, 1869. *Geol. Mag.*, vol. iii. p. 335. *Proc. Soc. Ant.*, 2nd S., vol. iii. p. 465.

2660

Jour. Anth. Inst., vol. iv. p. 38.

2661

Vol. xxxix. pl. i. 1; pl. ii. 1.

2662

Vol. iii. p. 501.

2663

Geologist, vol. v. p. 333.

2664

Quar. Journ. Geol. Soc., vol. xvii. p. 364.

2665

Vol. xxxix. p. 66.

2666

Lyell, "Prin. of Geol.," 10th ed., vol. i. p. 523.

2667

Arch., vol. xxxix. pl. ii. 2.

2668

Phil. Trans., 1864, p. 254.

2669

Geologist, vol. iv. p. 391.

2670

This specimen is also figured in *Once a Week*, June 19, 1869, p. 501.

2671

"Man the Prim. Savage," fig. 144, p. 214.

2672

Quar. Journ. Geol. Soc., vol. xi. p. 110.

2673

"Flint Chips," p. 45.

2674

Codrington, *Quar. Journ. Geol. Soc.*, vol. xxvi. p. 537.

2675

Geologist, vol. vi. pp. 110–154.

2676

Quar. Journ. Geol. Soc., vol. xx. p. 188. See also Lyell, "Prin. of Geol.," 10th ed., vol. ii. p. 560.

2677

"Flint Chips," p. 45.

2678

Codrington, *Quar. Journ. Geol. Soc.* (1870), vol. xxvi. pl. xxxvi.

2679

Quar. Journ. Geol. Soc. (1870), vol. xxvi. pl. xxxvi. p. 541.

2680

Proc. Soc. Ant., 2nd S., vol. xv. p. 72.

2681

"Opening of the Blackmore Mus.," p. 29. "Flint Chips," p. 47.

2682

"Flint Chips," p. 47.

2683

Q. J. G. S. (1861), vol. xx. p. 188. See also Lyell, "Ant. of Man," 3rd ed., p. 519; and *Geologist*, vol. vi. p. 395.

2684

"Flint Chips," p. 47. *Quar. Journ. Geol. Soc.* (1865), vol. xxi. p. 252.

2685

Proc. Geol. Soc., vol. i. p. 25.

2686

Quar. Journ. Geol. Soc. (1865), vol. xi. p. 101.

2687

Phil. Trans. (1860), p. 302.

2688

Prestwich, *Quar. Journ. Geol. Soc.*, vol. xi. p. 103. Stevens, "Flint Chips," p. 12.

2689

Formerly described erroneously as *Bos longifrons*.

2690

Quar. Journ. Geol. Soc. (1865), vol. xxi. p. 250. *Arch. Journ.*, vol. xxi. pp. 243, 269.

2691

Wilts Arch. Mag., vol. xxii. p. 117.

2692

Quar. Journ. Geol. Soc. (1872), vol. xxviii. p. 39.

2693

"Flint Chips," p. 47.

2694

"Flint Chips," p. 28. Codrington, *Quar. Journ. Geol. Soc.* (1870), vol. xxvi. p. 537.

2695

"Flint Chips," p. 48. Lyell, "Prin. of Geol.," 10th ed., vol. ii. p. 562. Codrington, *Quar. Journ. Geol. Soc.* (1870), vol. xxvi. p. 537.

2696

Q. J. G. S., vol. xlix. (1893), p. 327.

2697

"Flint Chips," p. 28.

2698

Brit. Assoc. Rep., 1877, p. 116. *Journ. Anth. Inst.*, vol. vii., 1878, p. 499.

2699

Geol. Mag., Dec. 2, vol. v., 1878, p. 37. See also *Trans. Dev. Assoc.*, vol. xvi., 1884, p. 501.

2700

"Natural Science," vol. x. (1897), p. 224.

2701

Geol. Mag., 2nd Dec., vol. vi., 1879, p. 480. *Trans. Devon. Assoc.*, vol. xii., 1880, p. 445.

NOTES—CHAPTER XXIV.

2702

Archæol., xxxix. pl. iv.

2703

Phil. Trans., 1860, p. 310. *Arch.*, vol. xxxviii. p. 289.

2704

Arch., vol. xxxix., p. 57.

2705

"Flint Chips," p. 41.

2706

Nature, vol. xxv., 1881, p. 173.

2707

Watelet, 1866.

2708

"Flint Chips," p. 41.

2709

Arch., vol. xxxviii., 1860, p. 291.

2710

Arch., vol. xli. p. 401. pl. xviii. 9.

2711

Aarböger f. Nord. Oldk. og Hist., 1867. p. 283.

2712

Q. J. G. S. (1867), vol. xxiii. pp. 48, 52.

2713

Madras Journ. Lit. and Science, Oct., 1866. *Geol. Mag.*, vol ii. p. 503. *Q. J. G. S.*, 1868, vol. xxiv. p. 484. *Trans. of Inter. Cong. of Preh. Arch.*, 1868, p. 224. *Proc. As. Soc. Bengal*, Sept., 1867. *Aarbög. f. Nord. Oldk.*, 1869, p. 339. *Mem. Geol. Survey India*, vol. x., 1873, p. 43. *Essex Naturalist*, vol. ii. p. 97. *Geol. Mag.*, Dec. 2, vol. vii., 1880, p. 542.

2714

Q. J. G. S., 1868, vol. xxiv. p. 493.

2715

Mem. G. S. India, vol. xii. p. 241.

2716

Rec. G. S. India, Aug., 1873, p. 49. Dawkins, "Early Man in Brit.," p. 166.

2717

Journ. Anth. Inst., vol. xvii., 1888, p. 57.

2718

Journ. As. Soc. Bengal, vol. lvi., 1887, p. 249.

2719

Proc. Soc. Ant., 2nd S., vol. i. p. 66. "Horæ Ferales," p. 132, pl. i. 19.

2720

Trans. Preh. Cong. 1878, p. 278.

2721

Mat., vol. viii. 1873, p. 179.

2722

Journ. Anth. Inst., vol. x., 1881, p. 428.

2723

Brit. Assoc. Rep., 1880, p. 624.

2724

Mat., vol. x., 1875, p. 197.

2725

Mat., vol. xxii. 1888, p. 221.

2726

Journ. Anth. Inst., vol. x. 1881, p. 318, pl. xvi.

2727

L'Anthrop., vol. v., 1894, p. 530.

2728

Proc. Soc. Ant., 2nd S., vol. v. p. 331.

2729

Journ. Anth. Inst., vol. iv., 1875, p. 215, pl. xvi.

2730

Journ. Anth. Inst., vol. xi., 1882, p. 382.

2731

Brit. Assoc. Rep., 1880, p. 624.

2732

"Hawara," 1889, pl. xxvii., and subsequent expeditions.

2733

"Rech. sur les Origines de l'Egypte," 1896, *q.v.*

2734

Journ. Anth. Inst., vol. xxv. 1896, p. 272, pl. xix.–xxi. *Brit. Assoc. Rep.*, 1895, p. 824. *Proc. R. S.*, vol. lx., 1896, p. 19.

2735

Q. J. Ethn. Soc., vol. ii. p. 41, pl. i. 3.

2736

Journ. Anth. Inst., vol. xi., 1882, p. 124. *Brit. Assoc. Rep.*, 1880, p. 622.

2737

Journ. Anth. Inst., vol. xvi., 1887, p. 68.

2738

Camb. Ant. Comm., vol. v. p. 57, 6 plates.

2739

Proc. Roy. Soc., vol. lx., 1896, p. 19.

2740

C. C. Abbott, "Primitive Industry," 1881; Report, 1877, 1878. *Proc. U. S. Nat. Hist. Mus.*, 1888, Appendix; 1890, pp. 187, 371. *Proc. Bost. Nat. Hist. Soc.*, vol. xxi. pp. 124, 132. T. Wilson, "La Période paléol. dans l'Amér. du Nord.," Paris, 1892.

2741

W. H. Holmes, *Smithsonian Inst. Rep.*, 1894. *Nature*, vol. xlviii., 1893, p. 253; vol. lv. 1897, p. 459 v.; Mercer's "Res. upon the Ant. of Man in the Delaware Valley," 1897.

2742

"Flint Chips," p. 42.

2743

"Ant. Celt. et Antéd.," vol. iii. p. 76, *et seqq.*; 455, *et seqq.*

2744

Arch., vol. xxxviii. p. 291.

2745

Nat. Hist. Rev., 1862, p. 250.

2746

"Man the Prim. Savage," p. 268.

2747

P. 542 *supra*.

2748

P. 607 *supra*.

2749

Nature, vol. xxvii., 1883, pp. 8, 53, 54, 102.

2750

Nature, vol. xxix., 1884, p. 83. "Man the Prim. Savage," p. 272.

2751

Cong. Inter. d'Anthrop., &c., 1867, p. 70. Hamy, "Paléont. Hum.," p. 49.

2752

See F. C. J. Spurrell in *Arch. Journ.*, vol. xlviii., 1891, p. 315. *Journ. Anth. Inst.*, vol. xxiii. p. 260. *Brit. Assoc. Rep.*, 1892, p. 900. *Nat. Science*, vol. v., Oct., 1894.

2753

"Explication de l'apparence de taille, &c.," Dieppe, 1881.

2754

See Worthington Smith in *Journ. Anth. Inst.*, vol. xiii., 1884, p. 377, and "Man, the Prim. Savage," p. 294 *et seqq.*

2755

See also Prestwich, *Phil. Trans.*, 1860, p. 297.

2756

See *antea*, p. 565.

2757

C. R. *du Cong. Intern. des Sci. Anthrop.*, 1880, p. 234.

NOTES—CHAPTER XXV.

2758

See *Trans. Watford Nat. Hist. Soc.*, vol. i., 1878, p. 137.

2759

Lyell, "Principles of Geol.," 10th ed., vol. i. p. 354.

2760

Op. Cit., p. 350.

2761

Quar. Journ. Geol. Soc., vol. xix. (1863), p. 321.

2762

"Encyc. Brit."—Art. "Rivers." Lyell, "Princ. of Geol," 10th ed., vol. i. p. 348. Lubbock, "Prehistoric Times," 4th ed., p. 382.

2763

Quar. Journ. Geol. Soc., vol. ix. (1853), p. 48.

2764

Lyell's "Princ. of Geol.," vol. i. p. 458. Geikie, *Geol. Mag.*, vol. v. p. 250.

2765

Geol. Mag. (1868), vol. v. p. 250.

2766

Phil. Trans., 1864, p. 293. See also Lyell, "Princ. of Geol.," vol. i. p. 366.

2767

Annales de Chimie et de Physique, 1866. Trans. in *Smithsonian Report*, 1866, p. 425.

2768

Phil. Trans., 1864, p. 296.

2769

See p. 664.

2770

H. G. Seeley, *Q. J. G. S.*, vol. xxii. p. 472.

2771

Q. J. G. S., vol. xxv. p. 455.

2772

Quar. Journ. Geol. Soc., vol. xxv. p. 453.

2773

Phil. Trans., 1860, pl. xi.

2774

Prestwich, *Phil. Trans.*, 1860, pl. xi. See p. 577, *supra*.

2775

Brit. Assoc. Report, 1896, p. 400.

2776

Geol. Mag., vol. iii. p. 348.

2777

Q. J. Geol. Soc., vol. xxvi. p. 528.

2778

Q. J. Geol. Soc., vol. xv. p. 219.

2779

Q. J. Geol. Soc., vol. xx. p. 189.

2780

Geologist, vol. v. p. 452.

2781

"Rivers and their Catchment Basins."

2782

R. A. C. Godwin-Austen, *Q. J. G. S.*, vol. xiii. p. 50.

2783

There may be some decree of uncertainty whether the gravels at this spot are to be connected immediately with the main stream, or with an affluent running into it approximately by the same course as that of the present Bourne, but this is of little moment.

2784

Q. J. G. S., vol. xiii. p. 45.

2785

Q. J. G. S., vol. xxvi. p. 532.

2786

Phil. Trans., 1864, p. 266.

2787

Phil. Trans., 1864, p. 291.

2788

Q. J. G. S., vol. xxv. p. 209.

2789

P. 580 *supra*.

2790

Q. J. G. S., vol. vii. p. 31.

2791

Q. J. G. S., vol. xxii. p. 553.

2792

"Heat considered as a Mode of Motion," p. 182. Lubbock, "Preh. Times," 4th ed., p. 408.

2793

Q. J. G. S., vol. xxiv. p. 103; xxv. p. 57.

2794

Phil. Trans., 1864, p. 278, &c.

2795

"Flint Chips," p. 47.

2796

Ravin, *Mém. de la Soc. d'Emul. d' Abbeville*, 1838, p. 196. *Phil. Trans.*, 1860, p. 301.

2797

"Preh. Times," 4th ed., p. 365.

2798

Athenæum, 1863, July 4.

2799

Hamy, "Paléontologie humaine," p. 210, *et seqq*. *Bull. Soc. d'Anthrop. de Paris*, 2nd S., vol. iii. p. 331. Belgrand, "Bassin de la Seine," pl. xlviii. and xlix.

2800

Rec. Geol. Sur. of India, vol. xxvii., 1894, p. 101. *Geol. Mag.*, Dec. 4, vol. i., 1894, p. 525. *Nat. Science*, vol. v. p. 345, vol. x. p. 233.

2801

Trans. Herts. Nat. Hist. Soc., vol. i. p. 145. *Brit. Assoc. Rep.*, 1890, p. 963. *Nature*, vol. xlii. p. 50.

2802

Several writers have attempted to bridge over this gap, or to show that it does not exist. See *Journ. Anth. Inst.*, vol. xxii. p. 66. Cazalis de Fondouce, *Cong. Préh. Stockholm*, 1874, p. 112. Brown, "Early Man in Midd." Worthington Smith, "Man the Prim. Savage."

2803

Trans. Preh. Cong., 1868, p. 278. *Supra*, p. 485.

2804

"Princ. of Geol.," 10th ed., vol. i. p. 295.

2805

"Preh. Times," 4th ed. p. 423.

2806

Geol. Mag., vol. v. p. 249.

2807

Phil. Trans., 1864, p. 299. *Proc. R. S.*, xiii. p. 135.

2808

Lubbock, "Preh. Times," 4th ed., p. 430.